SKILLS For SUCCESS

with Microsoft®
Excel 2016 Comprehensive

CHANEY ADKINS | HAWKINS

PEARSON

Boston Columbus Indianapolis New York San Francisco
Amsterdam Cape Town Dubai London Madrid Milan Munich Paris Montréal Toronto
Delhi Mexico City São Paulo Sydney Hong Kong Seoul Singapore Taipei Tokyo

Library of Congress Cataloging-in-Publication Data

Names: Chaney Adkins, Margo, author. | Hawkins, Lisa, author.
Title: Skills for success with Excel 2016 comprehensive / Margo Chaney
  Adkins, Lisa Hawkins.
Description: Hoboken, New Jersey : Pearson Education, Inc., [2017]
Identifiers: LCCN 2016007723 | ISBN 9780134479507
Subjects: LCSH: Microsoft Excel (Computer file) | Business—Computer
  programs. | Electronic spreadsheets.
Classification: LCC HF5548.4.M523 A444 2017 | DDC 005.54—dc23
LC record available at http://lccn.loc.gov/2016007723

Editorial Director: *Andrew Gilfillan*	**Senior Operations Specialist:** *Maura Zaldivar Garcia*
Executive Editor: *Jenifer Niles*	**Senior Art Director:** *Diane Ernsberger*
Team Lead, Project Management: *Laura Burgess*	**Manager, Permissions:** *Karen Sanatar*
Project Manager: *Anne Garcia*	**Interior and Cover Design:** *Studio Montage*
Program Manager: *Emily Biberger*	**Cover Photo:** *Courtesy of Shutterstock® Images*
Development Editor: *Toni Ackley*	**Associate Director of Design:** *Blair Brown*
Editorial Assistant: *Michael Campbell*	**Product Strategy Manager:** *Eric Hakanson*
Director of Product Marketing: *Maggie Waples*	**Vice President, Product Strategy:** *Jason Fournier*
Director of Field Marketing: *Leigh Ann Sims*	**Digital Product Manager:** *Zachary Alexander*
Product Marketing Manager: *Kaylee Carlson*	**Media Project Manager, Production:** *John Cassar*
Field Marketing Managers: *Joanna Sabella & Molly Schmidt*	**Full-Service Project Management:** *Cenveo Publisher Services*
Marketing Assistant: *Kelli Fisher*	**Composition:** *Cenveo Publisher Services*
Efficacy Implementation: *Candice Madden*	

Credits and acknowledgments borrowed from other sources and reproduced, with permission, in this textbook appear on appropriate page within text.

2   16
ISBN-10: 0-13-4479505
ISBN-13: 978-0-13-4479507

Contents in Brief

Table of Contents

Series Reviewers

We'd like to thank the following people for their reviewing of Skills for Success series:

Focus Group Participants

Rose Volynskiy	*Howard Community College*	Lex Mulder	*College of Western Idaho*
Fernando Paniagua	*The Community College of Baltimore County*	Kristy McAuliffe	*San Jacinto College South*
Jeff Roth	*Heald College*	Jan Hime	*University of Nebraska, Lincoln*
William Bodine	*Mesa Community College*	Deb Fells	*Mesa Community College*

Reviewers

Barbara Anderson	*Lake Washington Institute of Technology*	Deb Fells	*Mesa Community College*
Janet Anderson	*Lake Washington Institute of Technology*	Tushnelda C Fernandez	*Miami Dade College*
Ralph Argiento	*Guilford Technical Community College*	Jean Finley	*Asheville-Buncombe Technical Community College*
Tanisha Arnett	*Pima County Community College*		
Greg Ballinger	*Miami Dade College*	Jim Flannery	*Central Carolina Community College*
Autumn Becker	*Allegany College of Maryland*	Alyssa Foskey	*Wiregrass Georgia Technical College*
Bob Benavides	*Collin College*	David Freer	*Miami Dade College*
Howard Blauser	*North GA Technical College*	Marvin Ganote	*University of Dayton*
William Bodine	*Mesa Community College*	David Grant	*Paradise Valley Community College*
Nancy Bogage	*The Community College of Baltimore County*	Clara Groeper	*Illinois Central College*
Maria Bright	*San Jacinto College*	Carol Heeter	*Ivy Tech Community College*
Adell Brooks	*Hinds Community College*	Jan Hime	*University of Nebraska*
Judy Brown	*Western Illinois University*	Marilyn Holden	*Gateway Technical College*
Maria Brownlow	*Chaminade*	Ralph Hunsberger	*Bucks County Community College*
Jennifer Buchholz	*UW Washington County*	Juan Iglesias	*University of Texas at Brownsville*
Kathea Buck	*Gateway Technical College*	Carl Eric Johnson	*Great Bay Community College*
LeAnn Cady	*Minnesota State College—Southeast Technical*	Joan Johnson	*Lake Sumter Community College*
John Cameron	*Rio Hondo College*	Mech Johnson	*UW Washington County*
Tammy Campbell	*Eastern Arizona College*	Deborah Jones	*Southwest Georgia Technical College*
Patricia Christian	*Southwest Georgia Technical College*	Hazel Kates	*Miami-Dade College, Kendall Campus*
Tina Cipriano	*Gateway Technical College*	Jane Klotzle	*Lake Sumter Community College*
Paulette Comet	*The Community College of Baltimore County*	Kurt Kominek	*Northeast State Community College*
Jean Condon	*Mid-Plains Community College*	Vivian Krenzke	*Gateway Technical College*
Joy DePover	*Minneapolis. Com. & Tech College*	Renuka Kumar	*Community College of Baltimore County*
Gina Donovan	*County College of Morris*	Lisa LaCaria	*Central Piedmont Community College*
Alina Dragne	*Flagler College*	Sue Lannen	*Brazosport College*
Russ Dulaney	*Rasmussen College*	Freda Leonard	*Delgado Community College*
Mimi Duncan	*University of Missouri St. Louis*	Susan Mahon	*Collin College*
Paula Jo Elson	*Sierra College*	Nicki Maines	*Mesa Community College*
Bernice Eng	*Brookdale Community College*	Pam Manning	*Gateway Technical College*
Jill Fall	*Gateway Technical College*	Juan Marquez	*Mesa Community College*

Alysia Martinez	*Gateway Technical College*	Jeff Roth	*Heald College*
Kristy McAuliffe	*San Jacinto College*	Diane Ruscito	*Brazosport College*
Robert McCloud	*Sacred Heart University*	June Scott	*County College of Morris*
Susan Miner	*Lehigh Carbon Community College*	Vicky Seehusen	*MSU Denver*
Namdar Mogharreban	*Southern Illinois University*	Emily Shepard	*Central Carolina Community College*
Daniel Moix	*College of the Ouachitas*	Pamela Silvers	*A-B Tech*
Lindsey Moore	*Wiregrass Georgia Technical College*	Martha Soderholm	*York College*
Lex Mulder	*College of Western Idaho*	Yaacov Sragovich	*Queensborough Community College*
Patricia Newman	*Cuyamaca College*	Jody Sterr	*Blackhawk Technical College*
Melinda Norris	*Coker College*	Julia Sweitzer	*Lake-Sumter Community College*
Karen Nunan	*Northeast State Community College*	Laree Thomas	*Okefenokee Technical College*
Fernando Paniagua	*The Community College of Baltimore County*	Joyce Thompson	*Lehigh Carbon Community College*
Christine Parrish	*Southwest Georgia Technical College*	Barbara Tietsort	*University of Cincinnati, Blue Ash College*
Linda Pennachio	*Mount Saint Mary College*	Rose Volynskiy	*Howard Community College*
Amy Pezzimenti	*Ocean County College*	Sandra Weber	*Gateway Technical College*
Leah Ramalingam	*Riversity City College*	Steven Weitz	*Lehigh Carbon Community College*
Mary Rasley	*Lehigh Carbon Community College*	Berthenia Williams	*Savannah Technical College*
Cheryl Reuss	*Estrella Mountain Community College*	David Wilson	*Parkland College*
Wendy Revolinski	*Gateway Technical College*	Allan Wood	*Great Bay Community College*
Kenneth Rogers	*Cecil College*	Roger Yaeger	*Estrella Mountain Community College*

Skills for Success Office 2016

With Microsoft Office 2016, productivity is truly possible anywhere, anytime! Understanding this and being able to think and adapt to new environments is critical for today's learners. The *Skills for Success* series focuses on teaching essential productivity skills by providing a highly visual, step-by-step approach for learning Microsoft Office. This concise approach is very effective and provides the depth of skill coverage needed to succeed at work, school, and for MOS certification preparation. Using this approach, students learn the skills they need, and then put their knowledge to work through a progression of review, problem-solving, critical thinking projects, and proficiency demonstration with the NEW *Collaborating with Google* projects. For Office 2016, MOS exam objectives are also woven into the lessons, so students can review and prepare as they learn. Combine the visual approach and real-world projects of the text with the matching, live-in-the-application grader projects and high fidelity Office simulation training and assessments in MyITLab, and you have a truly effective learning approach!

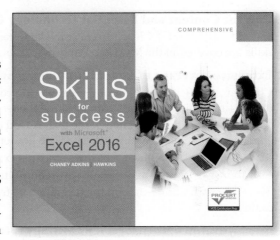

Series Hallmarks

- **Highly Visual Two-Page Landscape Layout** — Gives students the visual illustrations right with the steps—no flipping pages

- **Clearly Outlined Skills** — Each skill is presented in a single two-page spread so that students can easily follow along

- **Numbered Steps and Bulleted Text** — Students don't read long paragraphs or text, but they will read information presented concisely

- **Wide Coverage of Skills** — Gives students the knowledge needed to learn the core skills for work success

Skills for Success with Microsoft Office 2016

Personalized, engaging, effective learning with MyITLab 2016

Using the *Grader* projects and MyITLab *simulations*, students receive immediate feedback on their work to ensure understanding and help students progress.

(MyITLab® Grader) **Live-in-the-application Grader Projects**—provide hands-on, autograded options for practice and assessment with immediate feedback and detailed performance comments. Grader projects cover all the skills taught in the chapter, including a new grader covering all four *More Skills*.

(MyITLab® Simulation) **MyITLab Simulation Trainings and Assessment** provide an interactive, highly-realistic simulated environment to practice the Microsoft skills and projects taught in the book. Students receive immediate assistance with the learning aids, *Read, Watch, Practice,* and *detailed click stream data* reports provide effective review of their work. In the simulation assessments, students demonstrate their understanding through a new scenario exam without learning aids. Please note that for chapters 5 – 10, the simulations are topic-based; they cover the skills in chapter, but are not based on the same scenario.

Current Content and Essential Technology Coverage

Three Fundamental Chapters cover the latest technology concepts, key Windows 10 skills, and Internet Browsing with Edge and Chrome. Windows 10 skills are covered in the MyITLab Windows 10 simulations.

Extensive coverage of key skills students need for professional and personal success.

Chapters cover 10 Skills through real-world projects to meet the Learning Objectives and Outcomes. All 10 Skills are covered in the MyITLab grader projects and training and assessment simulations.

More Skills are now included in the text instead of online. These projects go beyond the main skills covered to provide additional training and to meet chapter learning objectives. NEW MyITLab grader project covers the skills from all four.

MOS Objective integration ensures students explore the MOS objectives as they are covered in the text for exam awareness and preparation.

Collaborating with Google projects—require students to apply their knowledge with another tool, replicating real-world work environments.

MOS appendix and icons in the text allow instructors to tailor preparation for Microsoft Office Specialist candidates by mapping MOS requirements to the text.

Clearly Defined, Measurable Learning Outcomes and Objectives

Learning *Outcomes* and Objectives have been clarified and expanded at the beginning of each chapter to define what students will learn, and are tied to the chapter assessments for clear measurement and efficacy.

Wide range of projects to ensure learning objectives and outcomes are achieved

Objective-based: Matching & Multiple choice, Discussion;

Review projects: Skills Review, Skills Assessments 1 & 2;

Problem-Solving: My Skills and Visual Skills Check;

Critical Thinking: Skills Challenges 1 & 2 and More Skills Assessment

Application Capstone Projects provided for each application help instructors ensure that students are ready to move on to the next application. Also delivered as grader projects in MyITLab.

Integrated Projects follow each application so that as students learn a new application, they also learn how to use it with other applications.

Office Online Projects provide hands-on experience with the web version of the Office applications to ensure students are familiar with the differences and become proficient with working between different versions of the tools.

Effective Learning Tools and Resources

Project Summary Chart—details the end of chapter projects from review, and problem-solving, to critical thinking, and demonstration of proficiency.

Skills Summary Chart lists all the Skills and Procedures and shortcut keys covered in the chapter making remembering what was covered easier!

Watch Skill Videos (formerly Student Training videos) are author-created training videos for each Skill in the chapter! Makes learning and remediation easier. Linked in ebook.

Wide screen images with clear callouts provide better viewing and usability.

Application Introductions provide a brief overview of the application and put the chapters in context for students.

Stay Current

IT Innovation Station keeps you up to date with Office and Windows updates, news, and trends with help from your Pearson authors! Look for the IT "Innovation Station," articles on the MyITLab Community site. These monthly articles from Pearson authors on all things Microsoft Office, include tips for understanding automatic updates, adjusting to and utilizing new capabilities, and optimizing your Office course.

A Microsoft® Office textbook that recognizes how students learn today

Skills for Success
with Microsoft® Excel 2016 Comprehensive

Application Introductions provide students with a concise overview of each application to put the chapters in context

Two Page Chapter Introduction — Briefs students on what is important and sets the stage for the project they will create

Learning Outcomes and Chapter Objectives clearly define what students will learn and achieve

Clock — Tells how much time students need to complete the chapter

File Summary — A quick summary of the files the students need to open and the names of the files they will turn in

Watch Skills videos (formerly Student Training) for each Skill in the chapter provide a personal, instructor-led walk through

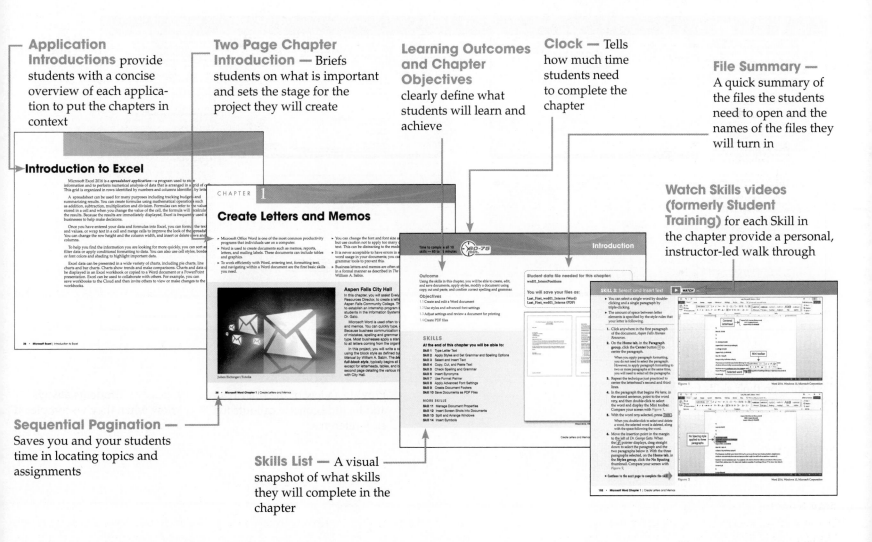

Sequential Pagination — Saves you and your students time in locating topics and assignments

Skills List — A visual snapshot of what skills they will complete in the chapter

Skills for Success

Written for Today's Students — Skills are taught with numbered steps and bulleted text so students are less likely to skip valuable information

Two-Page Spreads — Each skill is presented in a concise, two-page spread to give students the visual illustration right with the steps—no flipping pages

Colored Text — Clearly shows what a student types

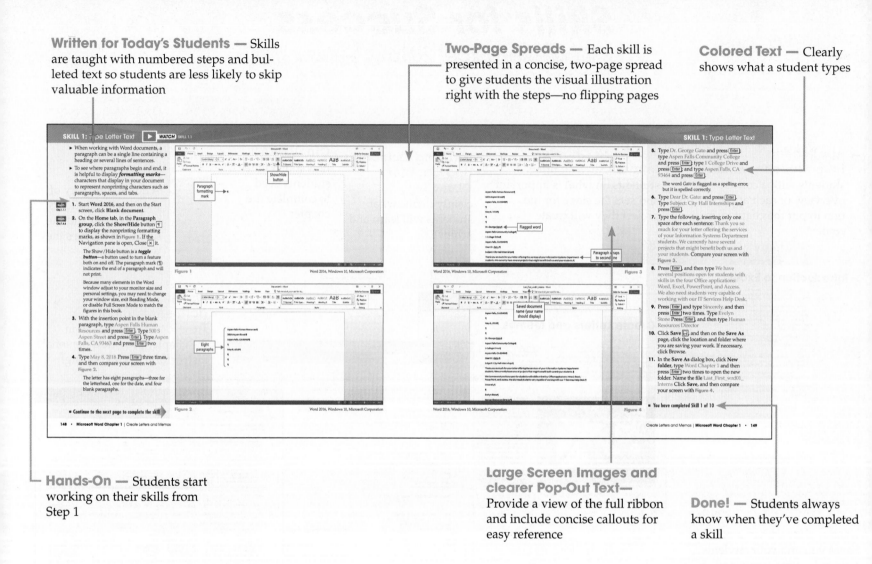

Hands-On — Students start working on their skills from Step 1

Large Screen Images and clearer Pop-Out Text— Provide a view of the full ribbon and include concise callouts for easy reference

Done! — Students always know when they've completed a skill

BizSkills Videos and Discussion Questions — Covering the important business skills students need to succeed: *Communication, Dress for Success, Interview Prep,* and more

More Skills — Additional skills previously provided online are now included in the chapter to ensure students learn these important skills.

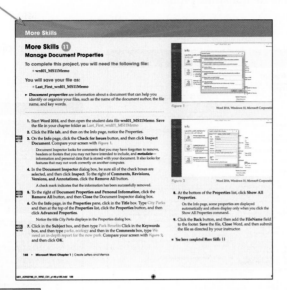

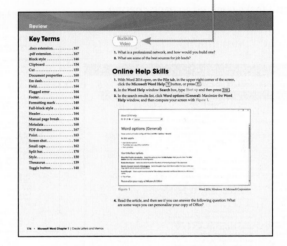

MOS Objectives — Integrated into the text for quick review and exam prep.

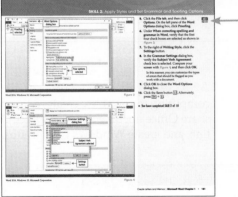

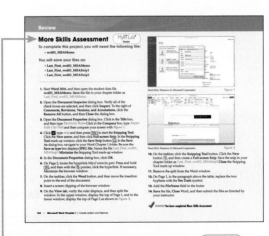

More Skills Assessment — MyITLab® Grader
Covers the core skills from the the four More Skills projects in a linear project that tells students what to do, but not necessarily how to do it.

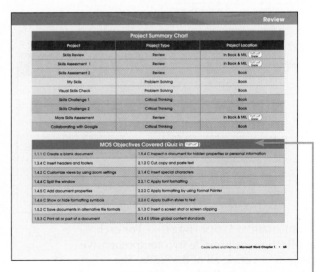

NEW MOS Summary table — Provides quick overview of objectives covered.

NEW Collaborating with Google — Hands-on projects that allow students to apply the skills they have learned in a Google project to demonstrate proficiency.

Skills and Procedures Summary Chart — Provides a quick review of the skills and tasks covered in each chapter

NEW Project Summary Chart — Provides an overview of project types and locations.

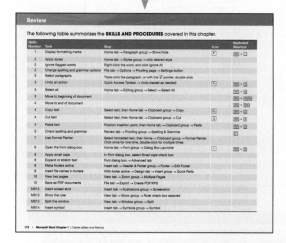

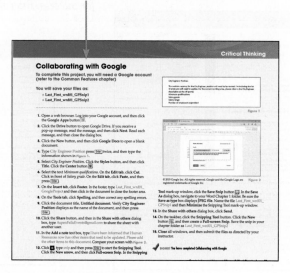

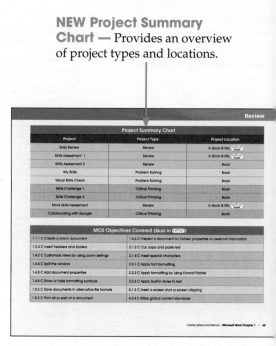

Application Capstones — For each application we provide two comprehensive projects covering all of the Skills. The capstones are available as a Homework and Assessment version, with the Assessment version earning a MIL Badge. Also available as a Grader project in MyITLab.

Office Online (formerly Web App) Projects — Students use Cloud computing to save files; create, edit, and share Office documents using Office Online; and create Windows Live groups.

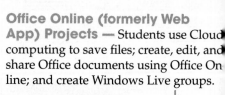

EXCEL ONLINE PROJECT

Using Excel Online to Create a Flyer

Skills for Success

MyITLab grader project
covering all 10 skills (homework
and assessment versions)

A stronger progression from point and click to
practice, and critical thinking.

From Point and Click to Critical Thinking

Skills 1–10 Guided learning	Annotated linear steps that tell 'where to click' and why.
Skills Review Guided practice	Linear steps that tell them 'where to click' one more time.
2 Skills Assessments Independent practice	Linear steps that tell them 'what to click' but not necessarily where.
My Skills Transfer of skills	Students transfer their skills to a different scenario—a personal document, instead of business document.
Visual Skills Check Non-linear problem-solving	Students determine their own steps to create the document shown in the figure and described in the directions.
Skills Challenge 1 Apply skills to fix problems	Typically a document that needs 'fixed' by apply the skills in the chapter. The problems are described in a way that the challenge is deciding how to fix the problems, not figuring out what the directions mean or how it will be graded.
Skills Challenge 2 Conduct research to solve a problem	Typically a project that requires some research to determine the content of the document. Directions are written in a way that the challenge is deciding what to say and how best to format the document, not figuring out what the directions mean or how it will be graded.
More Skills Assessment	A linear project that tells them "what" to do, but not necessarily "where" to do it. Covers the core skills from the the 4 More Skills projects

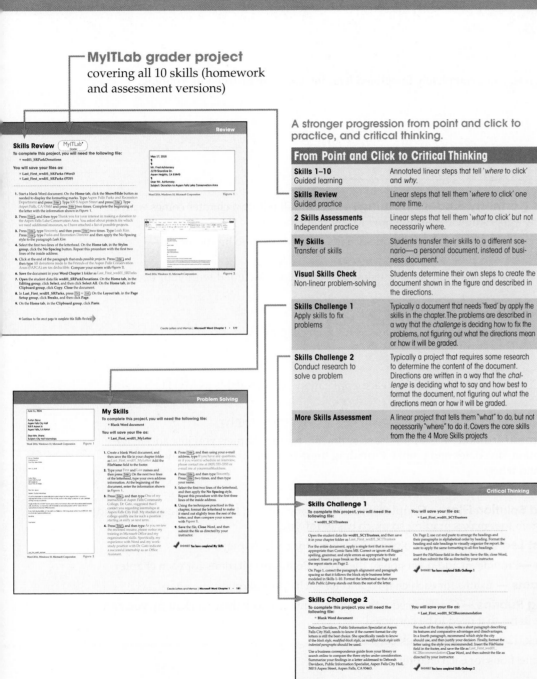

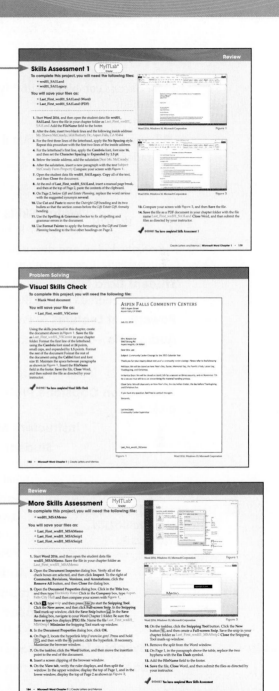

Skills for Success

MyITLab MyITLab®

Skills for Success combined with MyITLab gives you a completely integrated learning solution: Instruction, Training, & Assessment

- eText
- Training & Assessment Simulations
- Grader Projects

Student Resources and Videos!

 WATCH Watch Skills videos (formerly Student Training) — Each skill within a chapter comes with an instructor-led video that walks students through how to complete the skill.

BizSkills Video *BizSkills Videos* and discussion questions cover the important business skills students need to be successful— *Interviewing, Communication, Dressing for Success,* and more.

Student Data Files — are all available on the Companion Website using the access code included with your book. pearsonhighered.com/skills

PowerPoint Lectures — PowerPoint presentations for each chapter

Audio PPTs —Provide an audio version of the PowerPoint presentations for each chapter

Instructor Materials

Application Capstone Projects — Covering all of the Skills for each application. Also available as MyITLab grader projects

Instructor's Manual — Teaching tips and additional resources for each chapter

Student Assignment Tracker — Lists all the assignments for the chapter; you just add in the course information, due dates and points. Providing these to students ensures they will know what is due and when

All Student and Instructor Materials available in MyITLab.

Scripted Lectures — Classroom lectures prepared for you

Annotated Solution Files — Coupled with the scoring rubrics, these create a grading and scoring system that makes grading so much easier for you

PowerPoint Lectures — PowerPoint presentations for each chapter

Audio PPTs —Provide an audio version of the PowerPoint presentations for each chapter

Prepared Exams — Exams for each chapter and for each application

Detailed Scoring Rubrics — Can be used either by students to check their work or by you as a quick check-off for the items that need to be corrected

Syllabus Templates — For 8-week, 12-week, and 16-week courses

Test Bank — Includes a variety of test questions for each chapter

Margo Chaney Adkins is an Assistant Professor of Information Technology at Carroll Community College in Westminster, Maryland. She holds a bachelor's degree in Information Systems and master's degree in Post-Secondary Education from Salisbury University. She teaches computer application and office technology courses, both online and in the classroom. She enjoys athletic activities, gardening, and traveling with her husband.

Lisa Hawkins is a Professor of Computer and Information Sciences at Frederick Community College in Maryland. She earned a PhD in Information Technology from Capella University. Lisa has also worked as a database administrator, E-commerce manager, and systems administrator. She enjoys adventure sports, gardening, and making glass beads.

A Special Thank You Pearson Prentice Hall gratefully acknowledges the contribution made by Shelley Gaskin to the first edition publication of this series—*Skills for Success with Office 2007*. The series has truly benefited from her dedication toward developing a textbook that aims to help students and instructors. We thank her for her continued support of this series.

Common Features of Office 2016

- ▶ Microsoft Office is a suite of several programs—Word, PowerPoint, Excel, Access, and others.
- ▶ Each Office program is used to create different types of personal and business documents.
- ▶ The programs in Office 2016 share common tools that you use in a consistent, easy-to-learn manner.

- ▶ Some common tasks include opening and saving files, entering and formatting text, inserting pictures, and printing your work.
- ▶ Because of the consistent design and layout of the Office applications, when you learn to use one Microsoft Office application, you can apply many of the same techniques when working in the other Microsoft Office applications.

lculig/Fotolia

Aspen Falls City Hall

In this project, you will create documents for the Aspen Falls City Hall, which provides essential services for the citizens and visitors of Aspen Falls, California. You will assist Janet Neal, Finance Director, to prepare a presentation for the City Council. The presentation will explain retail sales trends in the city. The information will help the council to predict revenue from local sales taxes.

Microsoft Office is a suite of tools designed for specific tasks. In this project, the data was originally stored in an Access database. You will use Word to write a memo to update your supervisor about the project's status. Next, you will use Excel to create a chart from that data, and then use PowerPoint to display the chart to an audience. In this way, each application performs a different function and creates a different type of document.

In this project, you will create a Word document, and open existing files in Excel and PowerPoint. You will write a memo, format an Excel worksheet, and update chart data, and then place a copy of the chart into a PowerPoint presentation. You will also format a database report in Access. In all four applications, you will apply the same formatting to provide a consistent look and feel.

Outcome

Using the skills in this chapter, you will be able to open Office applications, save files, edit and format text and pictures, apply themes, use the Mini toolbar and Backstage view, format worksheets and reports, and paste objects into presentations.

Objectives

1 Explain the common features of Office 2016 applications

2 Modify documents

3 Prepare a presentation

4 Differentiate the uses of each Office 2016 application

5 Create Word, Excel, PowerPoint, and Access files for a presentation

Student data files needed for this chapter:

cf01_Memo (Word)
cf01_Parks (Word)
cf01_RetailChart (Excel)
cf01_RetailSlides (PowerPoint)
cf01_RetailData (Access)

You will save your files as:

Last_First_cf01_Parks (Word)
Last_First_cf01_Memo (Word)
Last_First_cf01_RetailMemo (Word)
Last_First_cf01_RetailChart (Excel)
Last_First_cf01_RetailSlides (PowerPoint)
Last_First_cf01_RetailData (Access)

SKILLS

At the end of this chapter, you will be able to:

Skill 1 Start Office Applications
Skill 2 Open and Save Student Data Files
Skill 3 Type and Edit Text
Skill 4 Format Text and Save Files
Skill 5 Apply Themes and Use the Mini Toolbar
Skill 6 Use Backstage View
Skill 7 Insert and Format Images
Skill 8 Format Worksheets
Skill 9 Copy and Paste Objects and Format Slides
Skill 10 Format Access Reports

MORE SKILLS

Skill 11 Store Files Online
Skill 12 Share Office Files
Skill 13 Install Office Add-ins
Skill 14 Customize the Ribbon and Options

Aspen Falls City Hall

Memo

To: Janet Neal
From: Maria Martinez
cc: First Last
Date: September 12, 2018
Re: Sales Revenue Slides

As per your request, the *Retail Sales* slides will be ready by the end of today. I will send them to you so you can insert them into your presentation. Let me know if you have any questions.

Office 2016, Windows 10, Microsoft Corporation

▶ The way that you start an Office application depends on what operating system you are using and how your computer is configured.

▶ Each application's start screen displays links to recently viewed documents and thumbnails of sample documents that you can open.

1. If necessary, turn on the computer, sign in, and navigate to the desktop. Take a few moments to familiarize yourself with the various methods for starting Office applications as summarized in **Figure 1**.

   One method that works in both Windows 8.1 and Windows 10 is to press ■ (the Windows key located between Ctrl and Alt) to display the Start menu or screen. With Start displayed, type the application name, verify that Word is selected, and then press Enter .

2. Use one of the methods described in the previous step to start **Word 2016**, and then take a few moments to familiarize yourself with the Word start screen as shown in **Figure 2**.

   Your list of recent documents will vary depending on what Word documents you have worked with previously. Below the list of recent documents, the *Open Other Documents* link is used to open Word files that are not listed.

Common Methods to Start Office 2016 Applications	
Location	**Description**
Start screen tile	Click the application's tile
Desktop	Double-click the application's desktop icon
Taskbar	Click the application's taskbar button
Windows 10 Start menu	Click Start and look in pinned or most used apps. Or click All apps and locate the Office application or the Microsoft Office 2016 folder.
All locations	Press ■, type the application's name, select the correct application, and then press Enter .
Search the web and Windows	Type the application's name, and then press Enter

Figure 1

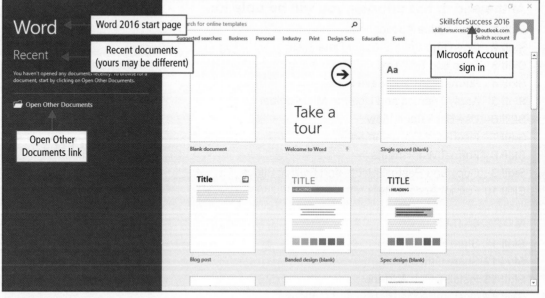

Figure 2

Word 2016, Windows 10, Microsoft Corporation

■ **Continue to the next page to complete the skill** ➤

Excel 2016, Windows 10, Microsoft Corporation

Figure 3

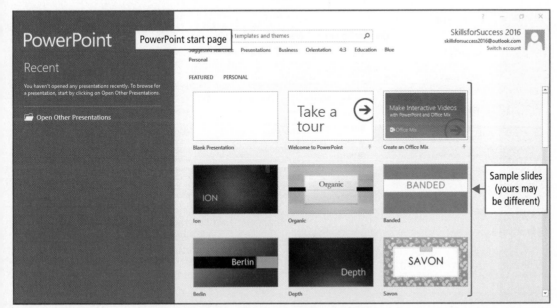

PowerPoint 2016, Windows 10, Microsoft Corporation

Figure 4

3. If desired, click **Sign in to get the most out of Office**, and then follow the onscreen directions to sign in using your Microsoft account.

Logging in enables you to access Microsoft Cloud services such as opening and saving files stored on your OneDrive. Unless otherwise directed, signing in to your Microsoft account is optional in this book. To protect your privacy, you should sign in only if you are already signed in to Windows using a unique username, not a shared account. For example, many public computers share an account for guests. When you are logged in to your Microsoft account, your name and picture will display in the upper right corner of the window.

4. Using the technique just practiced, start **Excel 2016**, and then compare your screen with **Figure 3**.

Worksheets are divided into *cells*—boxes formed by the intersection of a row and column into which text, objects, and data can be inserted. In Excel, cells can contain text, formulas, and functions. Worksheets can also display charts based on the values in the cells.

5. Start **PowerPoint 2016**, and then compare your screen with **Figure 4**.

PowerPoint presentations consist of *slides*—individual pages in a presentation that can contain text, pictures, or other objects. PowerPoint slides are designed to be projected as you talk in front of a group of people. The PowerPoint start screen has thumbnails of several slides formatted in different ways.

- **You have completed Skill 1 of 10**

▶ In this book, you will frequently open student data files.

1. Before beginning this skill, download the student data files for this chapter and unzip or copy them; use **Figure 1** as an example. Follow the instructions in the Getting Started with Windows 10 chapter or provided by your instructor.

2. On the taskbar, click the **Word** button . If necessary, start Word.

3. On the **Word** start page, click **Open Other Documents** to display the Open page. If you already had a blank document open, click the File tab instead.

4. On the **Open** page, click **This PC**, and then click the **Browse** button.

5. In the **Open** dialog box navigation pane, navigate to the student files for this chapter, and then compare your screen with **Figure 2**.

6. In the **Open** dialog box, select **cf01_Memo**, and then click the **Open** button.

7. If the **Protected View** message displays, click the **Enable Editing** button.

   Files downloaded from a website typically open in *Protected View*—a view applied to files downloaded from the Internet that allows you to decide if the content is safe before working with the file.

8. On the **File tab**, click **Save As**. Click **Browse**. Navigate to the location where you will be saving your files. In the **Save As** dialog box, click the **New folder** button, and then type Common Features Chapter

   Save As is used to select the location where you want to save your work. You can choose to save to your OneDrive or other locations on your computer.

■ **Continue to the next page to complete the skill** ▶

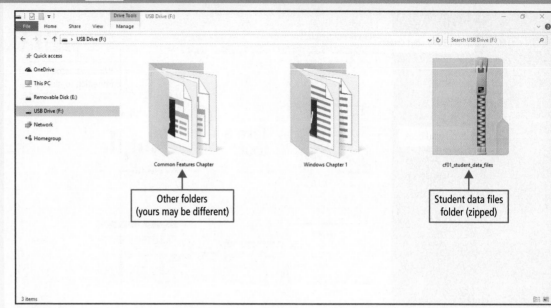

Figure 1   Word 2016, Windows 10, Microsoft Corporation

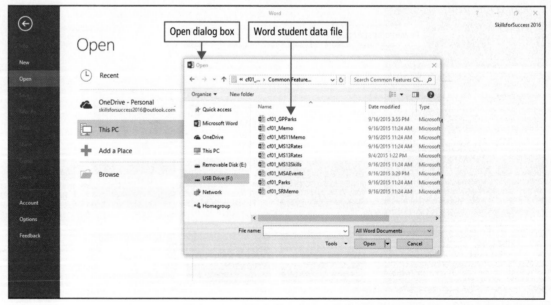

Figure 2   Word 2016, Windows 10, Microsoft Corporation

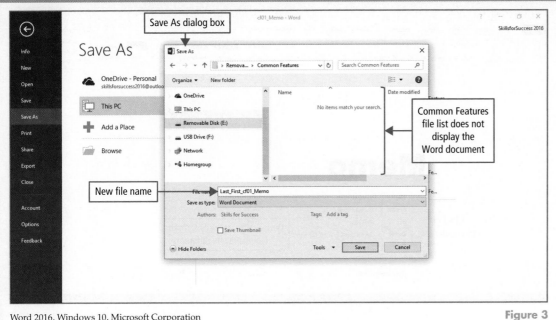

Word 2016, Windows 10, Microsoft Corporation

Figure 3

PowerPoint 2016, Windows 10, Microsoft Corporation

Figure 4

9. Press Enter twice. In the **File name** box, change the text to Last_First_cf01_Memo using your own name.

   In this book, you should substitute your first and last name whenever you see the text *Last_First* or *Your Name*.

10. Compare your screen with **Figure 3**, and then click the **Save** button.

    You can use Save As to create a copy of a file with a new name. The original student data file will remain unchanged.

    By default, the Save As dialog box displays only those files saved in the current application file format.

11. On the taskbar, click the **PowerPoint** button to return to the PowerPoint start screen. If necessary, start PowerPoint.

12. On the **PowerPoint 2016** start screen, click **Open Other Presentations** to display the Open page. If you already had a blank presentation open, click the File tab instead.

13. On the **Open** page, click **This PC**, and then click the **Browse** button. In the **Open** dialog box, navigate to the student files for this chapter, and then open **cf01_RetailSlides**. If necessary, enable the content.

14. On the **File tab**, click **Save As**, and then use the **Save As** page to navigate as needed to open your **Common Features Chapter** folder in the Save As dialog box.

    On most computers, your Word and Excel files will not display because the PowerPoint Save As dialog box is set to display only presentation files.

15. Type Last_First_cf01_RetailSlides and then click **Save**. Compare your screen with **Figure 4**.

■ **You have completed Skill 2 of 10**

▶ New documents are stored in **RAM**—the computer's temporary memory—until you save them to more permanent storage such as your hard drive, USB flash drive, or online storage.

▶ To **edit** is to insert, delete, or replace text in an Office document, workbook, or presentation.

▶ To edit text, position the **insertion point**—a flashing vertical line that indicates where text will be inserted when you start typing—at the desired location or select the text you want to replace.

1. On the taskbar, click the **Word** button to return to the *Last_First_cf01_Memo* document.

2. Click the **Date** placeholder—[*Click to select date*]—and then click the **date arrow** to open the calendar. In the calendar, click the current date.

   Placeholders—are reserved, formatted spaces into which you enter your own text or objects. If no text is entered, the placeholder text will not print.

3. In the **Subject** placeholder, type Sales Tax Revenues Compare your screen with **Figure 1**.

4. Press Ctrl + End to place the insertion point in the **Type memo here** placeholder—[*Type memo here*]—and then type the following: As per your request, the Retail Sales slides will be ready by the end of today. I will send them to you so you can insert them into your presentation. Let me know if you have any questions. Compare your screen with **Figure 2**.

   Word determines whether the word will fit within the established margin. If it does not fit, Word moves the entire word to the beginning of the next line. This feature is called **word wrap**.

■ **Continue to the next page to complete the skill**

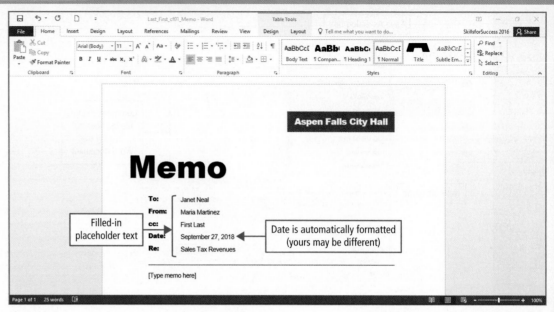

Figure 1

Word 2016, Windows 10, Microsoft Corporation

Figure 2

Word 2016, Windows 10, Microsoft Corporation

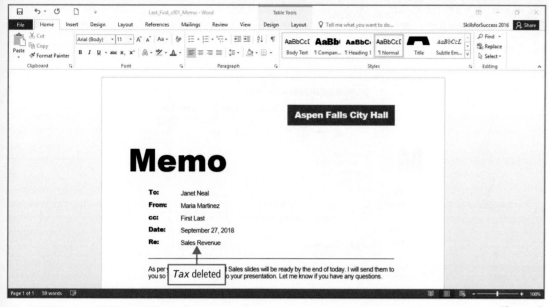

As per ___ Tax deleted ___ Sales slides will be ready by the end of today. I will send them to you so ___ to your presentation. Let me know if you have any questions.

Word 2016, Windows 10, Microsoft Corporation

Figure 3

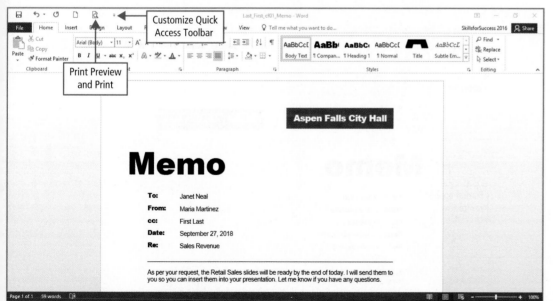

As per your request, the Retail Sales slides will be ready by the end of today. I will send them to you so you can insert them into your presentation. Let me know if you have any questions.

Word 2016, Windows 10, Microsoft Corporation

Figure 4

5. In the **Re:** line, click to the left of *Tax* to place the insertion point at the beginning of the word. Press Delete four times to delete the word *Tax* and the space following it.

   The Delete key deletes one letter at a time moving from left to right. The name on your keyboard may vary—for example, DEL, Del or Delete. Another option would be to **double-click**— is to click the left mouse button two times quickly without moving the mouse—or to **double-tap**—tap the screen in the same place two times quickly—the text to delete the word.

   After selecting text, the **Mini toolbar**—a toolbar with common formatting commands—displays near the selection.

6. Click to the right of *Revenues*. Press Backspace one time to delete the letter *s*, and then compare your screen with **Figure 3**.

   The Backspace key deletes one letter at a time moving from right to left. The name on your keyboard may vary—for example, BACK, Backspace, or simply a left-facing arrow.

7. Press Ctrl + End. Type Thank you On the Quick Access Toolbar, and then click **Undo Typing**.

8. Click the **Customize Quick Access Toolbar** button, and then from the menu, click **Print Preview and Print** Compare your screen with **Figure 4**.

9. Click the **Print Preview and Print** button to view how the memo will look in printed form. Click the **Back** button to return to the document. Keep the file open for the next skill.

■ **You have completed Skill 3 of 10**

▶ To **format** is to change the appearance of the text—for example, changing the text color to red.

▶ The **Format Painter** copies formatting from selected text and applies that formatting to other text.

1. Select the text *Janet Neal*. On the **Home tab**, in the **Font group**, click the **Font Dialog Box Launcher** 🔲 to open the Font dialog box. Compare your screen with **Figure 1**.

2. In the **Font dialog** box, under **Font**, scroll down until you can see the *Calibri* font. Click **Calibri**, and then under **Size**, click **12**. Click **OK**.

3. Verify that the text *Janet Neal* is selected. On the **Home tab**, in the **Clipboard group**, double-click the **Format Painter** button.

4. With the **Format Painter** selected, double-click the word **Maria** to apply the formatting from the text *Janet Neal*.

5. **Drag**—press and hold the left mouse button while moving the mouse—to select the text **Martinez** to apply the formatting from the text *Janet Neal*. Use the techniques just practiced to apply the formatting to **First** and **Last** name, the **date**, and **Sales Revenue**. Compare your screen with **Figure 2**.

   The Calibri font and font size of 12 are copied from the text *Janet Neal* and applied to the other text.

■ **Continue to the next page to complete the skill** ➤

Figure 1   Word 2016, Windows 10, Microsoft Corporation

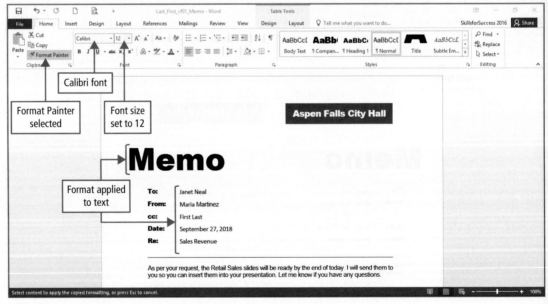

Figure 2   Word 2016, Windows 10, Microsoft Corporation

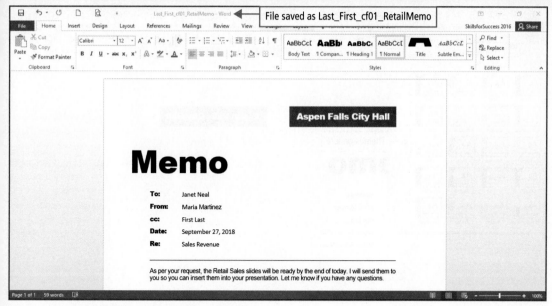

File saved as Last_First_cf01_RetailMemo

Word 2016, Windows 10, Microsoft Corporation

Figure 3

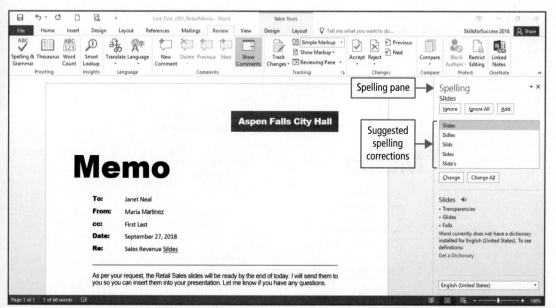

Spelling pane

Suggested spelling corrections

Word 2016, Windows 10, Microsoft Corporation

Figure 4

6. Click the **Format Painter** button to deselect it.

   When you single-click the format painter, you can apply the formatting to one other text selection. When you double-click the format painter, it will remain active until you click it again to deselect it.

7. In the **cc:** line, replace the text **First Last** with your first and last names. Click the **File tab**, and then click **Save As**.

8. Click **Browse** to navigate to your **Common Features Chapter** folder, and then in the **Save As** dialog box, change the **File name** to Last_First_cf01_RetailMemo

9. Click **Save**, and then compare your screen to **Figure 3**.

10. In the **Re:** line, click to the right of *Revenue* to place the insertion point at the end of the word. Type Sildes

11. Click the **Review tab**. In the **Proofing group**, click the **Spelling & Grammar** button. Compare your screen with **Figure 4**.

    The Spelling pane provides suggested spelling corrections.

12. In the **Spelling pane**, if necessary, click the first option **Slides**, and then click **Change** to correct the spelling of the word **Slides**. Read the dialog box message, and then click **OK**.

    After the document is saved, the name of the file displays on the title bar at the top of the window.

13. Leave the memo open for the next skill.

■ **You have completed Skill 4 of 10**

WATCH SKILL 1.5

► When formatting an Office document, it is a good idea to pick a *theme*—a prebuilt set of unified formatting choices including colors and fonts.

1. Click the **Design tab**. In the **Document Formatting group**, click the **Themes** button, and then compare your screen with **Figure 1**.

   Each theme displays as a thumbnail in a *gallery*—a visual display of selections from which you can choose.

2. In the **Themes** gallery, point to—but do not click—each thumbnail to preview its formatting with *Live Preview*—a feature that displays what the results of a formatting change will be if you select it.

3. In the **Themes** gallery, click the third theme in the second row—**Retrospect**.

   A *font* is a set of characters with the same design and shape. Each theme has two font categories—one for headings and one for body text.

4. Click anywhere in the text *Aspen Falls City Hall* to make it the active paragraph. With the insertion point in the paragraph, click the **Home tab**.

5. In the **Paragraph group**, click the **Shading arrow** ⬛▾. In the first row of the gallery under **Theme Colors**, click the sixth choice—**Orange, Accent 2**. Compare your screen with **Figure 2**.

   In all themes, the Accent 2 color is the sixth choice in the color gallery, but the color varies depending on the theme. Here, the Retrospect theme Accent 2 color is a shade of orange.

■ **Continue to the next page to complete the skill**

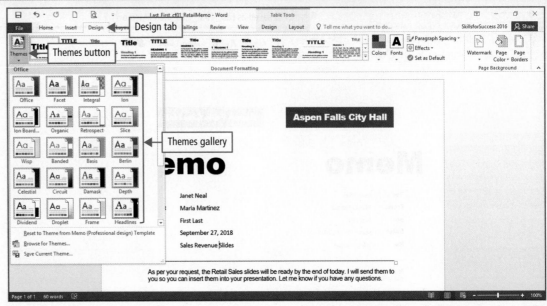

Figure 1

Word 2016, Windows 10, Microsoft Corporation

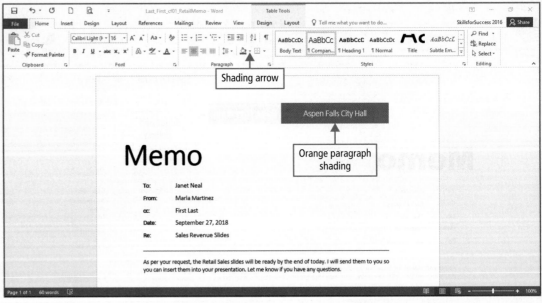

Figure 2

Word 2016, Windows 10, Microsoft Corporation

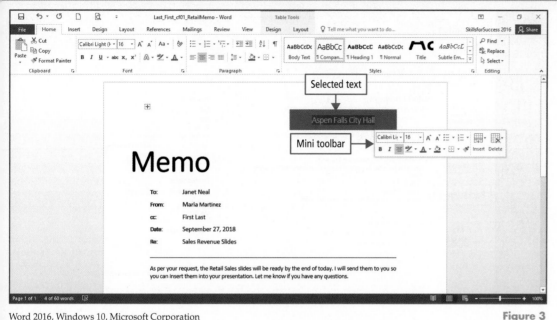

Word 2016, Windows 10, Microsoft Corporation

Figure 3

Word 2016, Windows 10, Microsoft Corporation

Figure 4

6. In the upper right corner, select the text *Aspen Falls City Hall*, and then compare your screen with Figure 3. To select by dragging with a touch display, tap in the text and then drag the selection handle.

> If the Mini toolbar does not display, you can right-click or tap the selected text.

7. On the Mini toolbar, click the **Font Size arrow** 11 , and then from the list, click **20** to increase the size of the selected text. On the Mini toolbar, click the **Bold** button B .

8. On the Mini toolbar, click the **Font Color arrow** A , and then under **Theme colors**, click the first color in the first row—**White, Background 1** Alternatively, on the Home tab, in the Font group, click the Font Color arrow.

9. In the paragraph that begins *As per your*, drag to select the text *Retail Sales*. From the Mini toolbar, click the **Italic** button I .

> Alternatively, you can use a *keyboard shortcut*—a combination of keys that performs a command. To apply italic, you could press Ctrl + I .

10. Click a blank area of the document, and then compare your screen with Figure 4. Carefully check the memo for spelling errors. If spelling errors are found, use the techniques previously practiced to correct them.

11. **Save** the file.

■ **You have completed Skill 5 of 10**

▶ **Backstage view** is a collection of options on the File tab used to open, save, print, and perform other file management tasks. In Backstage view, you can return to the open document by clicking the Back button.

1. Click the **File tab**, and then compare your screen with **Figure 1**.

2. On the **File tab**, click **Print** to display the Print page. In the lower right corner of the **Print** page, click the **Zoom In** button until the zoom level displays **100%**, and then compare your screen with **Figure 2**.

   The Printer list displays available printers for your computer along with their status. For example, a printer may be offline because it is not turned on. The **default printer** is automatically selected when you do not choose a different printer—indicated by a check mark.

   In a school lab or office, it is a good idea to check the list of available printers and verify that the correct printer is selected. It is also important that you know where the printer is located so that you can retrieve your printout.

   The size of the print preview depends on the size of your monitor. When previewed on smaller monitors, some documents may not display accurately. If this happens, you can zoom in to see a more accurate view.

3. If you are printing your work for this project, note the location of the selected printer, click the **Print** button, and then retrieve your printouts from the printer.

■ **Continue to the next page to complete the skill** ▶

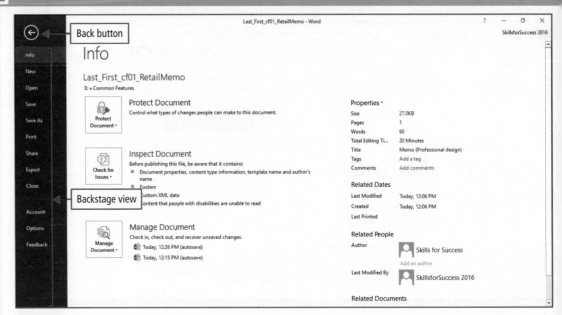

Figure 1

Word 2016, Windows 10, Microsoft Corporation

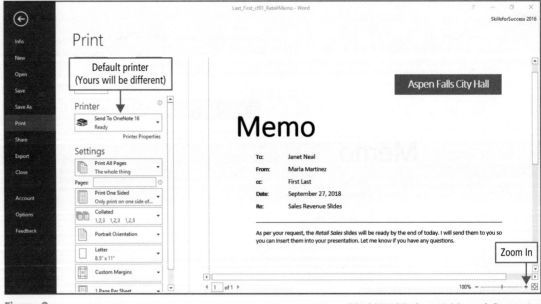

Figure 2

Word 2016, Windows 10, Microsoft Corporation

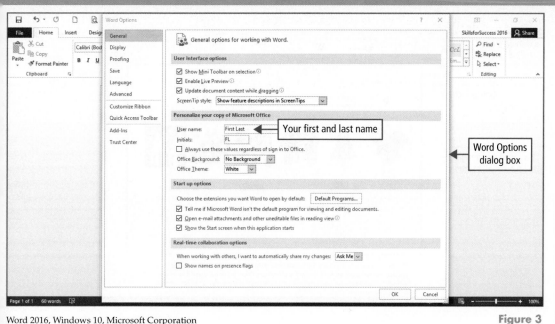

Your first and last name

Word Options dialog box

Word 2016, Windows 10, Microsoft Corporation

Figure 3

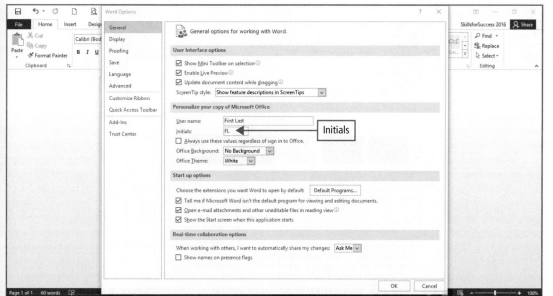

Initials

Word 2016, Windows 10, Microsoft Corporation

Figure 4

4. If necessary, click the **File tab**, and then click **Options**.

5. Under **Personalize your copy of Microsoft Office**, in the **User name** text box, replace the existing text with your First and Last name. Compare your screen with **Figure 3**.

6. Press Tab to select the text in the **Initials** text box, and then type your initials. Compare your screen to **Figure 4**, and then click **OK**.

7. Click the **Layout tab**. In the **Page Setup group**, click the **Margins** button.

8. Click the second option in the list—**Moderate**—to adjust the margins of the document.

   > When changing the margins of the document, you should verify that the document will still print properly.

9. Click the **File tab**, and then click **Print**.

10. Under the **Settings** options, click the **Portrait Orientation** button, and then click **Landscape Orientation**.

    > In Portrait Orientation, the page is taller than it is wide. In Landscape Orientation, the page is wider than it is tall.

11. Click the **Back** button ⊙, and then click **Save** 🔲. **Close** ✕ the file.

■ **You have completed Skill 6 of 10**

▶ You can insert images into documents from files or online resources.

▶ Images can be resized or rotated or the color of the picture can be changed. You can also add frames and artistic effects to images.

1. Start **Word 2016**, and then open the student data file **cf01_Parks**. On the **File tab**, click **Save As**. Click **Browse**, navigate to the folder for this chapter, and then save the file as Last_First_cf01_Parks

2. If the Security Warning message displays, enable the content.

3. If necessary, click the upper left portion of the document, to place the insertion point in the blank area above the *Park Events* title.

4. Click the **Insert tab**. In the **Illustrations group**, click the **Online Pictures** button.

5. In the **Insert Pictures** dialog box, in the **Bing Image Search** text box, type Forest and then press Enter . Compare your screen with **Figure 1**.

6. Scroll down to view the available images. Select an image of a forest. Compare your screen with **Figure 2**, and then click **Insert**. If you are unable to locate the image shown in the figure, choose a similar picture.

7. If necessary, scroll down so you can view the entire image. With the **Resize** pointer , drag the lower right corner of the image upward and to the left until the right edge of the image aligns with the space between the words *Park* and *Events* in the document title.

■ **Continue to the next page to complete the skill**

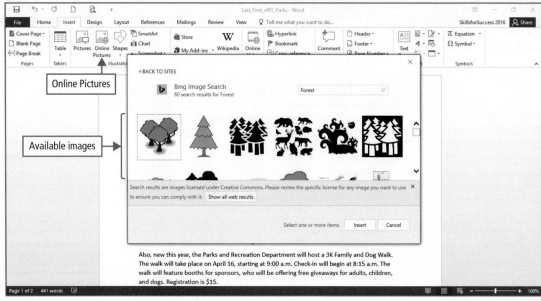

Figure 1

Word 2016, Windows 10, Microsoft Corporation

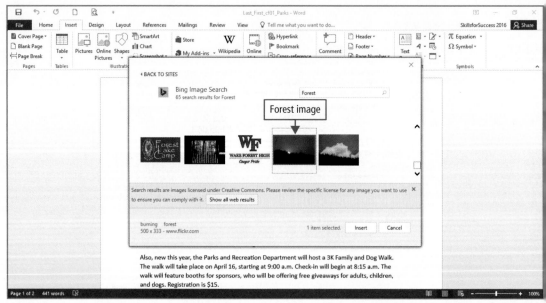

Figure 2

Word 2016, Windows 10, Microsoft Corporation

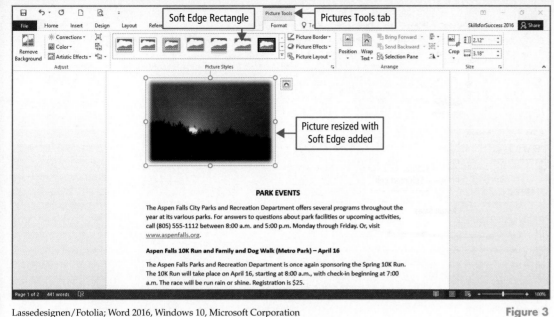

Lassedesignen/Fotolia; Word 2016, Windows 10, Microsoft Corporation

Figure 3

Lassedesignen/Fotolia; Word 2016, Windows 10, Microsoft Corporation

Figure 4

8. On the **Picture Tools Format tab**, in the **Picture Styles group**, click the sixth option—**Soft Edge Rectangle**. Compare your screen with **Figure 3**.

9. With the image still selected, press Ctrl + E to center the image on the page.

> Keyboard shortcuts can be used to edit text, change the position of images on a page, or navigate throughout the document.

10. Next to the **Format tab**, click **Tell me what you want to do...**, and then type Find and Replace Press Enter.

11. In the **Find and Replace dialog box**, in the **Find what** text box, type accessories In the **Replace with** text box, type tools and then compare your screen with **Figure 4**.

12. In the **Find and Replace dialog box**, click **Replace All**.

13. Read the message, and then click **Yes**. Read the next message, and then click **OK**.

14. In the **Find and Replace dialog box**, click **Close**.

15. Click **Save**, and then **Close** the file.

■ **You have completed Skill 7 of 10**

▶ To keep formatting consistent across all Office files, the same themes are available in Word, Excel, PowerPoint, and Access.

▶ To format text in Excel, you select the cell that holds the text, and then click the desired formatting command.

1. On the taskbar, click the **Excel** button . On the **Start** screen, click **Open Other Workbooks**. Click **Browse** to navigate to the student data files, and then double-click **cf01_RetailChart**.

2. Click the **File tab**, and then click **Save As**. Navigate to the folder for this chapter, and then save the file as Last_First_cf01_RetailChart

3. Click cell **B9**—the intersection of column B and row 9—to select the cell. Compare your screen with **Figure 1**.

   A selected cell is indicated by a thick, dark-green border.

4. With cell **B9** selected, type 4.37 and then press Enter to update the chart.

   The chart is based on the data in columns A and B. When the data is changed, the chart changes to reflect the new values.

5. On the **Page Layout tab**, in the **Themes group**, click the **Themes** button, and then click the **Retrospect** thumbnail. Compare your screen with **Figure 2**.

   The Retrospect theme applies the same colors, fonts, and effects as the Retrospect theme of other Office applications. Here, the font was changed to Calibri.

■ **Continue to the next page to complete the skill**

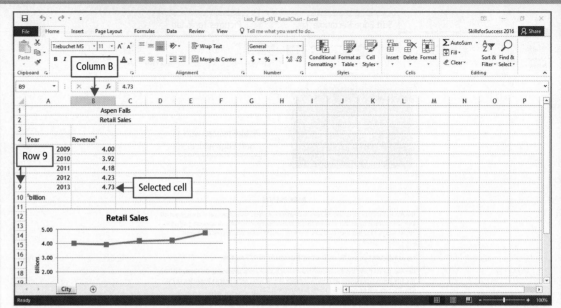

Figure 1

Excel 2016, Windows 10, Microsoft Corporation

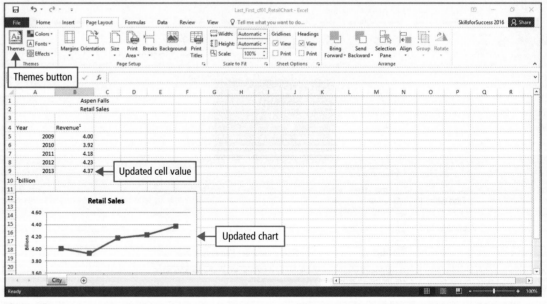

Figure 2

Excel 2016, Windows 10, Microsoft Corporation

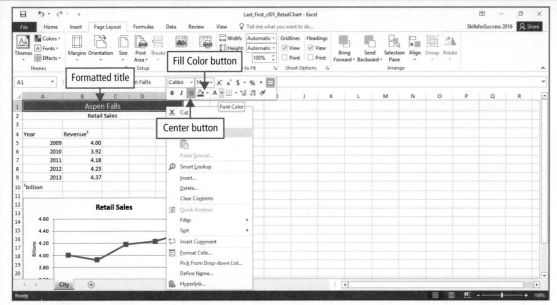

Excel 2016, Windows 10, Microsoft Corporation   **Figure 3**

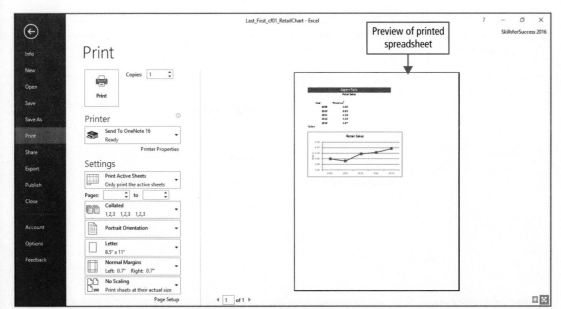

Excel 2016, Windows 10, Microsoft Corporation   **Figure 4**

6. Right-click cell **A1** containing the text *Aspen Falls* to display the Mini toolbar. Click the **Font Size arrow**, and then click **14** to increase the font size. Click the **Center** button ☰ to center the title.

7. With cell **A1** still selected, on the Mini toolbar, click the **Fill Color arrow** 🖌▾, and then under **Theme Colors**, click the sixth choice—**Orange, Accent 2**.

8. On the Mini toolbar, click the **Font Color arrow** 🅰▾, and then under **Theme Colors**, click the first choice—**White, Background 1**. Compare your screen with **Figure 3**.

9. Click cell **A4**. On the **Home tab**, in the **Alignment group**, click the **Center** button ☰ to center the text. In the **Clipboard group**, click the **Format Painter** button 🖌 one time, click cell **B4** to apply the center format, and then turn off the Format Painter.

10. Click cell **A10**, and then in the **Font group**, change the **Font Size** to **9**.

11. On the **File tab**, click **Print**, and then compare your screen with **Figure 4**.

    The Excel Print page is used in the same manner as the Word Print page. Here, you can preview the document, select your printer, and verify that the worksheet will print on a single page. By default, the gridlines do not print.

12. If you are printing your work for this project, print the worksheet. Otherwise, click the **Back** button ⬅ to return to Normal view.

13. Click **Save** 🖫.

■ **You have completed Skill 8 of 10**

▶ In Office, the *copy* command places a copy of the selected text or object in the **Office Clipboard**—a temporary storage area that holds text or an object that has been cut or copied.

▶ The *paste* command inserts a copy of the text or object from the Office Clipboard.

1. In the Excel window, click the border of the chart to select the chart. Compare your screen with **Figure 1**.

   In Office, certain graphics such as charts and SmartArt display a thick border when they are selected.

2. Right-click a blank area of the chart, and then click the **Copy** button 🗐 to place a copy of the chart into the Office Clipboard.

3. On the taskbar, click the **PowerPoint** button 📧 to return to the **Last_First_ cf01_RetailSlides** presentation.

4. With **Slide 1** as the active slide, on the **Home tab**, in the **Clipboard group**, click the **Paste** button to insert the copied Excel chart. If you accidentally clicked the Paste arrow to display the Paste Options, click the Paste button that is above it. Click a blank area of the slide, and then compare your screen with **Figure 2**.

5. Click the **Design tab**, and then in the **Themes group**, click the **More** button ▾ . Point to the thumbnails to preview their formatting, and then under Office, click the seventh choice—**Retrospect**.

   In PowerPoint, themes are sets of colors, fonts, and effects optimized for viewing in a large room with the presentation projected onto a screen in front of the audience.

■ **Continue to the next page to complete the skill** ➡

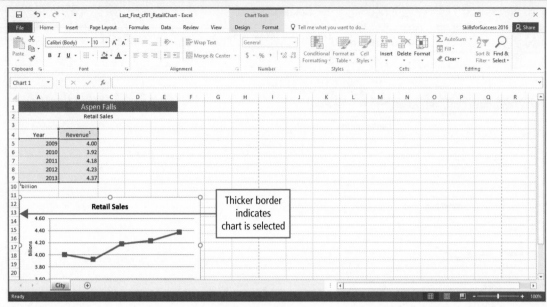

Figure 1

Excel 2016, Windows 10, Microsoft Corporation

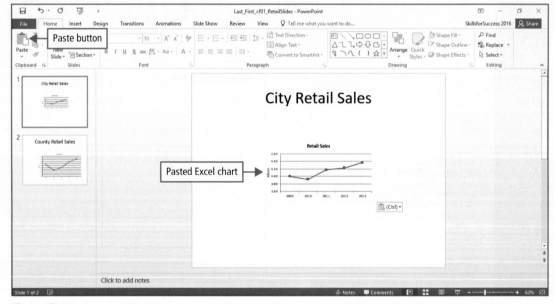

Figure 2

PowerPoint 2016, Windows 10, Microsoft Corporation

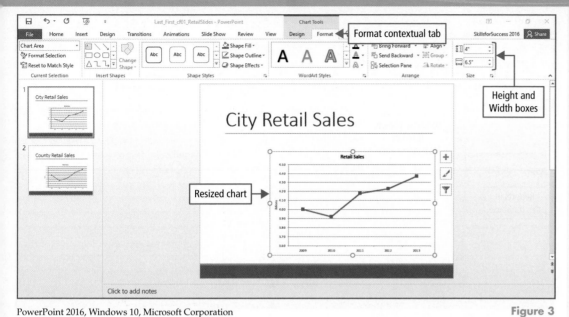

PowerPoint 2016, Windows 10, Microsoft Corporation

Figure 3

6. Drag to select the slide title text *City Retail Sales*. On the **Home tab**, in the **Font group**, click the **Font Size arrow**, and then click **60**. Alternatively, right-click the selected text, and then use the Mini toolbar to change the font size.

7. Click any area in the chart, and then click the border of the chart so that only the chart is selected.

8. Click the **Chart Tools Format tab**, and then in the **Size group**, click the **Shape Height arrow** until the value is **4"**. Repeat this technique to change the **Width** value to **6.5"**, and then compare your screen with **Figure 3**.

> The Format tab is a *contextual tab*—a tab that displays on the ribbon only when a related object such as a graphic or chart is selected.

9. On the **File tab**, click **Print**. On the **Print** page, under **Settings**, click the **Full Page Slides** button. In the gallery, under **Handouts**, click **2 Slides**. Compare your screen with **Figure 4**.

10. If you are printing your work, click **Print** to print the handout. Otherwise, click **Save** to return to Normal view. **Close** ☒ PowerPoint.

11. On the taskbar, click the **Excel** button 🗷, and then **Close** ☒ Excel. If a message displays asking you to save changes, click Save.

■ **You have completed Skill 9 of 10**

PowerPoint 2016, Windows 10, Microsoft Corporation

Figure 4

▶ Access *reports* are database objects that present tables or query results in a way that is optimized for onscreen viewing or printing.

1. Start **Access 2016** 🅰, and then on the Start screen, click **Open Other Files**. On the **Open** page, click **Browse**.

2. In the **Open** dialog box, navigate to the student data files for this chapter. In the **Open** dialog box, select **cf01_RetailData**, and then click the **Open** button. If necessary, enable the content.

3. Take a few moments to familiarize yourself with the Access objects in the Navigation Pane as shown in **Figure 1**.

   Database files contain several different types of objects such as tables, queries, forms, and reports. Each object has a special purpose summarized in the table in **Figure 2**.

4. On the **File tab**, click **Save As**. With **Save Database As** selected, click the **Save As** button.

5. In the **Save As** dialog box, navigate to your **Common Features Chapter** folder. In the **File name** box, name the file Last_First_cf01_RetailData and then click **Save**. If a security message displays, click the Enable Content button.

   Malicious persons sometimes place objects in database files that could harm your computer. For this reason, the security message may display when you open a database that you did not create. You should click the Enable Content button only when you know the file is from a trusted source.

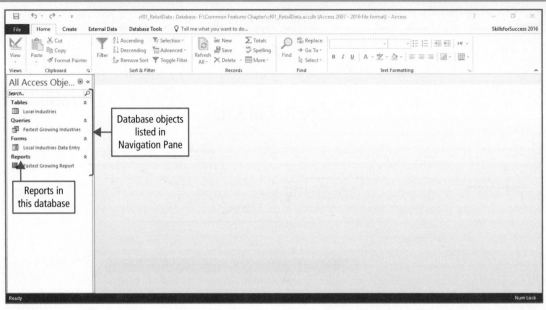

Figure 1

Access 2016, Windows 10, Microsoft Corporation

Common Database Objects	
Object	**Description**
Table	Stores the database data so that records are in rows and fields are in columns.
Query	Displays a subset of data in response to a question.
Form	Used to find, update, and add table records.
Report	Presents tables or query results optimized for onscreen viewing or printing.

Figure 2

■ **Continue to the next page to complete the skill** ▶

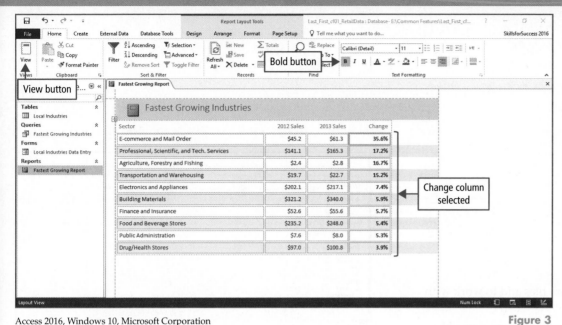

Access 2016, Windows 10, Microsoft Corporation

Figure 3

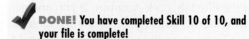

Access 2016, Windows 10, Microsoft Corporation

Figure 4

6. In the **Navigation Pane**, under **Reports**, double-click **Fastest Growing Report**.

7. On the **Home tab**, in the **Views group**, click the **View** button one time to switch to Layout view.

8. On the **Design tab**, in the **Themes group**, click **Themes**, and then click the seventh thumbnail—**Retrospect**.

9. Near the top of the **Change** column, click the first value—*35.6%*—to select all the values in the column.

10. Click the **Home tab**, and then in the **Text Formatting group**, click the **Bold** button. Compare your screen with **Figure 3**.

11. On the **Home tab**, click the **View arrow**, and then click **Print Preview**. Compare your screen with **Figure 4**. If necessary, in the Zoom group, click the One Page button to zoom to 100%.

12. If your instructor asked you to print your work, click the **Print** button, and then print the report.

13. **Save** 🖫 the formatting changes, and then **Close** ✕ the report.

> Objects such as reports are opened and closed without closing the Access application itself.

14. **Close** ✕ Access, and then submit your printouts or files for this chapter as directed by your instructor.

✔ **DONE! You have completed Skill 10 of 10, and your file is complete!**

More Skills 11

Store Files Online

To complete this project, you will need the following files:

- cf01_MS11Memo (Word)
- cf01_MS11Chart (Excel)
- cf01_MS11Slide (PowerPoint)

You will save your files as:

- Last_First_cf01_MS11Memo (Word)
- Last_First_cf01_MS11Chart (Excel)
- Last_First_cf01_MS11Slide (PowerPoint)
- Last_First_cf01_MS11Snip

▶ *The Cloud*—an Internet technology used to store files and to work with programs that are stored in a central location.

▶ *Microsoft account*—personal account that you use to access your files, settings, and online services from devices connected to the Internet.

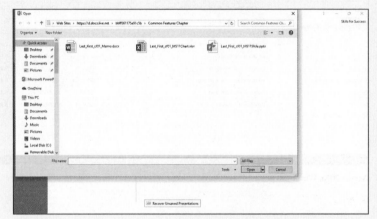

Figure 1   Office 2016, Windows 10, Microsoft Corporation

1. Start **Word 2016**. Open the student data file **cf01_MS11Memo**. In the upper right corner of the Word window, check to see if your Microsoft account name displays. If your account name displays, skip to step 3; otherwise, click **Sign In**.

2. In the dialog box, type your e-mail address. Click **Next**. In the **Sign in** screen, type your password. Click **Sign in**. If you don't have a Microsoft account, click **Sign up now**. Follow the onscreen directions to create an account.

3. On the **File tab**, click **Account**. If you are using an operating system other than Windows, this option is not available, skip to step 4. If your OneDrive is not listed as a connected service, click **Add a service**, point to **Storage**, and then click **OneDrive**.

4. Click **Save As**, and then double-click **OneDrive - Personal** connected to your Microsoft account. In the **Save As** dialog box, click **New folder**. Save the folder as Common Features Chapter Press [Enter] two times. Save the file as Last_First_cf01_MS11Memo

5. Replace the text *Your Name* with your First and Last names. **Save** 🖫 the file. Notice the green arrow on the save button. This indicates the file is syncing to OneDrive.

6. Start **Excel 2016**, and then open the student data file **cf01_MS11Chart**. Click the **File tab**, click **Save As**, and then double-click **OneDrive-Personal**. In the dialog box, double-click the **Common Features Chapter** folder. Save the file as Last_First_cf01_MS11Chart

7. Repeat the technique previously practiced to save the student data file **cf01_MS11Slides** to your OneDrive folder as Last_First_cf01_MS11Slide

8. On the **File tab**, click **Open**. Click **Browse**. In the dialog box, click the **File Type arrow**, and then click **All Files** to view the three files in the OneDrive folder. Compare your screen with **Figure 1**. Take a full-screen snip. Save the snip to your chapter folder as Last_First_cf01_MS11Snip

9. **Close** ✕ all open files. Submit the file as directed by your instructor.

■ **You have completed More Skills 11**

More Skills 12

Share Office Files

To complete this project, you will need the following file:

- cf01_MS12Rates

You will save your files as:

- Last_First_cf01_MS12Rates
- Last_First_cf01_MS12Share

▶ If you are working on a team project, you can share files, and provide others with editing or viewing privileges.

▶ You can share files instead of sending them as an e-mail attachment.

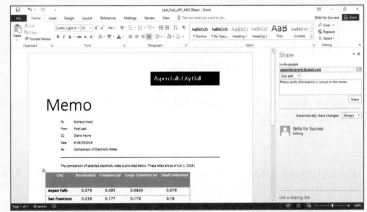

Word 2016, Windows 10, Microsoft Corporation

Figure 1

1. Start **Word 2016**. Open the student data file **cf01_MS12Rates**. Replace the *From:* placeholder text in the memo with your First and Last names.

2. In the upper right corner of the window, click the **Share** button. In the **Share** pane, click the **Save to Cloud** button.

3. If you are signed in to your Microsoft account, skip to step 4. If your computer does not show your Microsoft account, then click **Add a Place**. In the **Add a Place** page, click **OneDrive**. In the dialog box, type your e-mail address. Click **Next**. In the **Sign in** screen, type your password. Click **Sign in**. If you don't have a Microsoft account, click **Sign up now**. Follow the onscreen directions to create an account.

4. Click **OneDrive - Personal** connected to your Microsoft account. If you completed the More Skills 11 project, then skip to step 5; otherwise, double-click **OneDrive - Personal** to open your online folders. Click **New folder**, and then rename the folder as Common Features Chapter

5. Double-click the **Common Features Chapter** folder to open it. Save the file as Last_First_cf01_MS12Rates

6. In the **Share** pane, type the e-mail address as directed by your instructor in the **Invite people** box. Verify that *Can edit* is displayed, and then type the message Please verify information is correct in the memo. Click the **arrow** to **Automatically share changes**, and then click **Always**. Compare your screen with Figure 1.

An e-mail is sent to the owner of the e-mail address with a link. Saving files to the cloud ensures a link is created to the file and revisions are updated in one location. Sharing options allow shared files to be edited or viewed. If changes are allowed, options for sharing changes can be set.

7. Click the **Share** button below the message to share the file. Once the share is processed, the account associated with the e-mail address you shared the file with displays at the bottom of the Share pane.

8. Press ⊞, and type Snip Open the **Snipping Tool**, and then take a full-screen snip. Save the snip to your chapter folder as Last_First_cf01_MS12Share

9. **Save** 🖫 the file, and then **Close** ✕ Word. Submit the file as directed by your instructor.

■ **You have completed More Skills 12**

More Skills 13

Install Office Add-ins

To complete this project, you will need the following file:

- cf01_MS13Skills

You will save your files as:

- Last_First_cf01_MS13Skills
- Last_First_cf01_MS13Cloud

▶ *Office Add-ins* are plugins that add extra features or custom commands to Office programs.

---

1. Start **Word 2016**, and then open the student data file **cf01_MS13Skills**. Save the file in your chapter folder as Last_First_cf01_MS13Skills

2. Click the **File tab**, and then replace the *Author* with your First and Last names. Click the **Back arrow**, and then click the **Insert tab**. In the **Header & Footer group**, click the **Header arrow**, and then click **Edit Header**. On the **Header & Footer Tools Design tab**, in the **Insert group**, click the **Document Info** button. Click **Author** to insert the Author's name in the header.

   Word inserts the author's name found in the document properties. Since you revised this property in step 2, your name will display.

3. Click **Close Header and Footer**. Starting with the text *Desktop Applications*, drag to select both columns through the text *Clipboard*.

4. Click the **Insert tab**, and then in the **Add-ins group**, click the **Store** button. Compare your screen with **Figure 1**.

   The Office add-ins available for Word display in the window. When you open other Office applications, add-ins associated with those applications will display.

5. Use the scroll bar on the right side of the Office Add-ins window to review the Add-ins. Notice there are also categories on the left of the window that provide several additional choices. If you have clicked any of the categories, click the Back arrow until the *Finalize and Polish Your Documents* category displays.

6. Click **Pro Word Cloud**. In the **Office Add-ins** window, click **Trust It**.

7. In the **Pro Word Cloud** pane, click the **Font arrow**, scroll down, and then click **Silentina Movie**. Click the **Colors arrow**, and then click **Sun Set**. Click the **Layout arrow**, and then click **Half And Half**. Verify the **Remove common words** check box is selected, and then click the **Create Word Cloud** button.

Figure 1　　　　　Word 2016, Windows 10, Microsoft Corporation

8. The word *cloud* will display in the top of the pane. Right-click the word **cloud**, and then click **Save Picture As**. Navigate to the folder for this chapter, and then save the file as Last_First_cf01_MS13Cloud

9. Close the **Pro Word Cloud** pane. **Save** 🖫, and then **Close** ✕ the file. Submit the files as directed by your instructor.

■ **You have completed More Skills 13**

More Skills (14)

Customize the Ribbon and Options

To complete this project, you will need the following file:

- cf01_MS14Slide

You will save your file as:

- Last_First_cf01_MS14Ribbon

▶ The **Ribbon** contains commands placed in groups that are organized by tabs so that you can quickly find the tools you need.

1. Start **PowerPoint 2016**, and then open the student data file **cf01_MS14Slide**. Click the **Insert tab**. In the **Text group**, click the **Header & Footer** button. On the **Slide tab**, click the *Footer* check box. In the box, type your First and Last names, and then click **Apply**.

2. Click the **File tab**, and then click **Options**. Review the list, and then on the left, click **Save**. Under *Save presentations*, click the **arrow** to change **Save AutoRecover information every** to **5** minutes.

3. In the **PowerPoint Options** list, click **Customize Ribbon**. Compare your screen to **Figure 1**.

    Two panes display. In the left pane are the commands available to add to the ribbon. In the right pane are tabs and groups already added to the ribbon.

4. At the bottom of the right pane, click the **New Tab** button. Click **New Tab (Custom)**, and then click the **Rename** button. Type Common Features and then click **OK**. Click **New Group (Custom)**, click the **Rename** button, type Editing and then click **OK**.

5. In the left pane, click **Copy**, and then click the **Add** button. Notice the copy command appears in the *Editing (Custom)* group. Repeat this technique to add the commands **Cut**, **Font**, **Font Color**, **Font Size**, and **Format Painter**.

6. Click **Common Features (Custom),** and then click the **New Group** button. Click the **Rename** button, type Objects and click **OK**.

7. Repeat the technique previously practiced to add the commands **Add Table**, **Format Object**, **Insert Pictures**, and **Insert Text Box**. Click **OK** to close the Options window.

8. Review the tabs available, and then click the **Common Features tab** to view your new ribbon, groups, and commands.

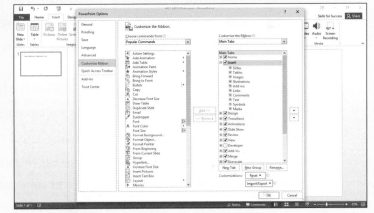

Access 2016, Windows 10, Microsoft Corporation

Figure 1

9. Press ⊞, and then type Snip Open the **Snipping Tool**, and then take a full-screen snip. Save the snip to your chapter folder as Last_First_cf01_MS14Ribbon

10. Click the **File tab**, click **Options**, and then click **Customize Ribbon**. At the bottom of the right pane, click the **Reset arrow**, click **Reset all customizations**, and then click **Yes** to delete the customizations. Click **OK** to close the Options window. Notice the tab is removed from the ribbon.

11. **Close** ☒ PowerPoint without saving the file. Submit the file as directed by your instructor.

■ **You have completed More Skills 14**

Review

The following table summarizes the **SKILLS AND PROCEDURES** covered in this chapter.

Skills Number	Task	Step	Icon	Keyboard Shortcut
1	Start Office applications	Display Start menu or screen, and then type application name	⊞	⊞
2	Create a new folder while saving	Save As dialog box toolbar → New folder		
2	Save	Quick Access Toolbar → Save		Ctrl + S
2	Open a file	File tab → Open		Ctrl + O
2	Save a file with new name and location	File tab → Save As		F12
3	Apply bold	Home tab → Text Formatting group → Bold	B	Ctrl + B
3	Preview the printed page	File tab → Print		Alt + Ctrl + I
4	Change a font	Home tab → Font group → Font arrow		Ctrl + Shift + F
4	Change font size	Home tab → Font group → Font Size arrow	11 ▾	Ctrl + < Ctrl + >
5	Apply italic	Select text → Mini toolbar → Italic	I	Ctrl + I
5	Change font color	Home tab → Font group → Font Color arrow	A ▾	
5	Apply a theme	Design tab → Themes		
6	Change document properties	File tab → Options		
7	Insert online picture	Insert tab → Illustrations group → Online Pictures → Bing Image Search		
8	Fill Color	Mini toolbar → Fill Color arrow	abc	
8	Center align text	Select text → Mini toolbar → Center	☰ ▾	Ctrl + E
9	Copy	Select text or object → Right-click → Copy	✂	Ctrl + C
9	Paste	Home tab → Clipboard group → Paste		Ctrl + V
9	Save	File tab → Save		
10	Change report view	Home tab → View arrow		
MS11	Save files to OneDrive	File tab → OneDrive - Personal → Save		
MS11	View files in OneDrive	File tab → Open → Browse → All Files		
MS12	Share Office files	Share button → Sign in → Share		
MS13	Install Office Add-ins	Insert tab → Add-ins group → Store		
MS14	Customize Ribbon	File tab → Customize Ribbon		

Project Summary Chart

Project	Project Type	Project Location
Skills Review	Review	In Book & MIL MyITLab® Grader
Skills Assessment 1	Review	In Book & MIL MyITLab® Grader
Skills Assessment 2	Review	Book
My Skills	Problem Solving	Book
Visual Skills Check	Problem Solving	Book
Skills Challenge 1	Critical Thinking	Book
Skills Challenge 2	Critical Thinking	Book
More Skills Assessment	Review	In Book & MIL MyITLab® Grader
Collaborating with Google	Critical Thinking	Book

Key Terms

Matching

Match each term in the second column with its correct definition in the first column by writing the letter of the term on the blank line in front of the correct definition.

____ **1.** An individual page in a presentation that can contain text, pictures, or other objects.

____ **2.** The tool used to copy formatting from selected text and apply it to other text in the document, worksheet, or slide.

____ **3.** A menu with options such as Copy or Paste, available after selected text is right-clicked.

____ **4.** To insert, delete, or replace text in an Office document, spreadsheet, or presentation.

____ **5.** A prebuilt set of unified formatting choices including colors, fonts, and effects.

____ **6.** To change the appearance of text.

____ **7.** A set of characters with the same design and shape.

____ **8.** A feature that displays the result of a formatting change if you select it.

____ **9.** A view applied to documents downloaded from the Internet that allows you to decide if the content is safe before working with the document.

____ **10.** A command that moves a copy of the selected text or object to the Office Clipboard.

A Format Painter

B Copy

C Edit

D Font

E Format

F Live Preview

G Protected

H Slide

I Shortcut Menu

J Theme

Multiple Choice

Choose the correct answer.

1. The flashing vertical line that indicates where text will be inserted when you start typing.
   A. Cell reference
   B. Insertion point
   C. KeyTip

2. A reserved, formatted space into which you enter your own text or object.
   A. Gallery
   B. Placeholder
   C. Title

3. Until you save a document, the document is stored here.
   A. Office Clipboard
   B. Live Preview
   C. RAM

4. A collection of options on the File tab used to open, save, print, and perform other file management tasks.
   A. Backstage view
   B. Page Layout view
   C. File gallery

5. A temporary storage area that holds text or an object that has been cut or copied.
   A. Office Clipboard
   B. Dialog box
   C. Live Preview

6. A toolbar with common formatting buttons that displays after you select text.
   A. Gallery toolbar
   B. Mini toolbar
   C. Taskbar toolbar

7. A command that inserts a copy of the text or object from the Office Clipboard.
   A. Copy
   B. Insert
   C. Paste

8. A visual display of choices—typically thumbnails—from which you can choose.
   A. Gallery
   B. Options menu
   C. Shortcut menu

9. A tab that displays on the ribbon only when a related object such as a graphic or chart is selected.
   A. Contextual tab
   B. File tab
   C. Page Layout tab

10. A database object that presents tables or query results in a way that is optimized for onscreen viewing or printing.
    A. Form
    B. Report
    C. Table

Topics for Discussion

1. You have briefly worked with four Microsoft Office programs: Word, Excel, PowerPoint, and Access. Based on your experience, describe the overall purpose of each program.

2. Many believe that computers enable offices to go paperless—that is, to share files electronically instead of printing and then distributing them. What are the advantages of sharing files electronically, and in what situations is it best to print documents?

Skills Review

MyITLab®
Grader

To complete this project, you will need the following files:

- cf01_SRData (Access)
- cf01_SRChart (Excel)
- cf01_SRSlide (PowerPoint)
- cf01_SRMemo (Word)

You will save your files as:

- Last_First_cf01_SRData (Access)
- Last_First_cf01_SRChart (Excel)
- Last_First_cf01_SRSlide (PowerPoint)
- Last_First_cf01_SRMemo (Word)

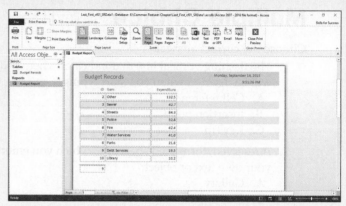

Figure 1 Access 2016, Windows 10, Microsoft Corporation

1. Start **Access 2016**, and then click **Open Other Files**. Click **Browse**. In the **Open** dialog box, navigate to the student data files for this chapter and open **cf01_SRData**.

2. On the **File tab**, click **Save As**, and then click the **Save As** button. In the **Save As** dialog box, navigate to your chapter folder, and then save the file as Last_First_cf01_SRData Click **Save**. If necessary, enable the content.

3. In the **Navigation Pane**, double-click **Budget Report**, and then click the **View** button to switch to Layout view. On the **Design tab**, click **Themes**, and then click **Retrospect**.

4 Click the **View arrow**, click **Print Preview**, and then compare your screen with **Figure 1**. If you are printing this project, print the report.

5. Click **Save**, **Close** the report, and then **Close** Access.

6. Start **Excel 2016**, and then click **Open Other Workbooks**. Use the **Open** page to locate and open the student data file **cf01_SRChart**.

7. Navigate to your chapter folder, and then save the file as Last_First_cf01_SRChart

8. With **A1** selected, on the **Home tab**, in the **Font group**, click the **Font Size arrow**, and then click **24**.

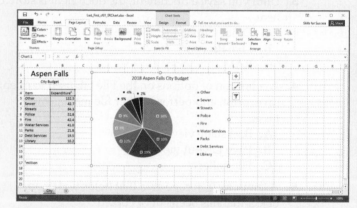

Figure 2 Excel 2016, Windows 10, Microsoft Corporation

9. On the **Page Layout tab**, click **Themes**, and then click **Retrospect**.

10. Click cell **B7**, and then type 84.3 Press Enter, and then click **Save**.

11. Click the border of the chart, and then compare your screen with **Figure 2**.

■ Continue to the next page to complete this Skills Review

12. On the **Home tab**, in the **Clipboard group**, click the **Copy** button.

13. Start **PowerPoint 2016**. Click **Open Other Presentations**, and then open the student data file **cf01_SRSlide**.

14. On the **File tab**, click **Save As**. Click **Browse**, and then save the file in your chapter folder as Last_First_cf01_SRSlide

15. On the **Home tab**, in the **Clipboard group**, click **Paste** to insert the chart.

16. On the **Design tab**, in the **Themes group**, click the **More** button, and then click the seventh choice—**Retrospect**. Compare your screen with Figure 3.

17. If you are printing this project, on the **File tab**, click **Print**, change the **Settings** to **Handouts**, **1 Slide**, and then print the handout.

18. Click **Save**, and then **Close** PowerPoint.

19. Click cell **A4**. In the **Clipboard group**, click the **Format Painter**, and then click cell **B4**.

20. Click **Save**, and then **Close** Excel.

21. Start **Word 2016**, and then click **Open Other Documents**. Use the **Open** page to locate and open the student data file **cf01_SRMemo**.

22. On the **File tab**, click **Save As**. Click **Browse**, and then save the file in your chapter folder as Last_First_cf01_SRMemo

23. Click *[RECIPIENT NAME]*, and then type Janet Neal

24. Change *[YOUR NAME]* to your own name, and then change *[SUBJECT]* to City Budget

25. Change *[CLICK TO SELECT DATE]* to the current date, and then change *[NAME]* to Maria Martinez

26. Change *[Type your memo text here]* to the following: I am pleased to tell you that the city budget items that you requested are ready. I will send you the Access report and PowerPoint slide today.

27. Click to the left of *INTEROFFICE*, and then press Delete as needed to delete the word and the space following it.

28. On the **Design tab**, click the **Themes** button, and then click **Retrospect**.

29. Double-click the word *MEMORANDUM* to select it. On the Mini toolbar, click the **Font Color arrow**, and then click the fifth color—**Orange, Accent 1**.

30. With *MEMORANDUM* still selected, on the Mini toolbar, click the **Bold** button one time to remove the bold formatting from the selection, and then change the **Font Size** to **24**.

31. Click **Save**, and then compare your screen with Figure 4.

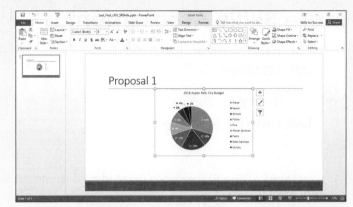

Access 2016, Windows 10, Microsoft Corporation — Figure 3

Word 2016, Windows 10, Microsoft Corporation — Figure 4

32. Click the **File tab**, and then click **Options**. Replace the User name with your First and Last names. Close the dialog box to save the change.

33. If you are printing your work, print the memo. Click **Save**, and then **Close** Word. Submit your printouts or files as directed by your instructor.

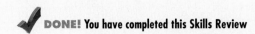 **DONE! You have completed this Skills Review**

More Skills Assessment

To complete this project, you will need the following file:

- cf01_MSAEvents

You will save your file as:

- Last_First_cf01_MSASnip

---

1. Start **Word 2016**, and then open the student data file **cf01_MSAEvents**.

2. Starting with the text *Park Events*, drag to select the text through *October 2*.

3. Using **My Add-ins**, insert the **Pro Word Cloud** add-in.

4. Create a word cloud using the **Steelfish** font and **Bluebell Glade** colors. Click **Create Word Cloud**.

5. Right-click the word cloud image, and then paste it to the top of the document. Close the **Pro Word Cloud** pane.

6. Open **Word Options**, and then replace the User name with your First and Last names.

7. Create a new tab, and then rename the tab Common Features and the group Tasks Add the *Popular Commands* **Copy**, **Cut**, **Delete**, and **Format Painter** to the *Tasks* group.

8. Open the new tab, and then view the commands in the group.

9. **Share** the file with the e-mail address as directed by your instructor, and then **Save** the file as Last_First_cf01_MSAEvents to **OneDrive - Personal** linked to your account in the **Common Features Chapter** folder.

10. Set the share options to **Can edit**, and then type the message I've created the word cloud for the events flyer.

11. Edit the **Author** property, and then insert your First and Last names. Insert the **Document Info** property **Author** as the header, and then **Close** the header. Compare your screen with **Figure 1**.

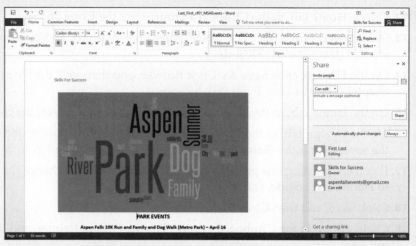

Figure 1   Word 2016, Windows 10, Microsoft Corporation

12. Click the **Common Features tab**, and then use the **Snipping Tool** to take a **Full-screen Snip** of your screen. **Save** the file as Last_First_cf01_MSASnip

13. **Close** the Snipping Tool window. **Save** the file, and then **Close** Word. Submit the file as directed by your instructor.

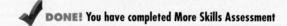 **DONE! You have completed More Skills Assessment**

Collaborating with Google

To complete this project, you will need a Google account (refer to the Common Features chapter) and the following files:

- cf01_GPParks
- cf01_GPImage

You will save your file as:

- Last_First_cf01_GPParks

Google; Word 2016, Windows 10, Microsoft Corporation

Figure 1

1. Open the **Google Chrome**  web browser. If you already have a Google account, skip to step 2. In the upper right corner, click **Gmail**. In the next window, click **Create an account**. Follow the onscreen directions to create an account.

2. Log into your Google account, and then click the **Apps** button ⊞. Click **Drive** 🛆 to open Google Drive.

3. Click **NEW**, and then click **File upload**. Navigate to the student data files, and then open **cf01_GPParks**.

4. Select the **cf01_GPParks** file in **Google Drive**. Click **More actions** More ▾ , point to **Open with**, and then click **Google Docs**.

5. Position the insertion point after the title in the document. Click **Insert** on the menu, and then click **Image**. In the **Insert image** window, ensure **Upload** is selected. Click **Choose an Image to upload**, and then navigate to the student data files, click **cf01_GPImage**, and then click **Open**. Click the image, and then drag the lower middle sizing handle up until the image height is resized about 1 inch.

6. Drag to select the title text above image. On the toolbar, click the **Font arrow**, and then click **Georgia**. Click the **Font size arrow**, and then click **18**. Click **Text color** 🇦 , and then click the third option in the second row—**orange**.

7. With the title text selected, click **Paint format** 🖌. Scroll down to the *Events* table. Drag to select the text *Parks and Recreation*, and then apply the **title format**.

8. In the first column, drag to select the text *Event*. Click the **Font size arrow**, and then click **10**. Double-click **Paint format** 🖌, and then copy the format to the other column titles. Drag to select all of the column titles, and then click **Center** ▤. Compare your screen with **Figure 1**.

9. Click the **File tab**, point to **Download as**, and then click **Microsoft Word (.docx)**. Open the downloaded file, click **Enable Editing**, and then save the file in the chapter folder as Last_First_cf01_GPParks

10. Close all windows, and then submit your file as directed by your instructor.

✔ **DONE! You have completed Collaborating with Google**

Introduction to Excel

Microsoft Excel 2016 is a *spreadsheet application*—a program used to store information and to perform numerical analysis of data that is arranged in a grid of cells. This grid is organized in rows identified by numbers and columns identified by letters.

A spreadsheet can be used for many purposes including tracking budgets and summarizing results. You can create formulas using mathematical operations such as addition, subtraction, multiplication and division. Formulas can refer to the value stored in a cell and when you change the value of the cell, the formula will recalculate the results. Because the results are immediately displayed, Excel is frequently used in businesses to help make decisions.

Once you have entered your data and formulas into Excel, you can format the text and values, or wrap text in a cell and merge cells to improve the look of the spreadsheet. You can change the row height and the column width, and insert or delete rows and columns.

To help you find the information you are looking for more quickly, you can sort and filter data or apply conditional formatting to data. You can also use cell styles, borders, or font colors and shading to highlight important data.

Excel data can be presented in a wide variety of charts, including pie charts, line charts and bar charts. Charts show trends and make comparisons. Charts and data can be displayed in an Excel workbook or copied to a Word document or a PowerPoint presentation. Excel can be used to collaborate with others. For example, you can save workbooks to the Cloud and then invite others to view or make changes to the workbooks.

Cell styles applied

Merged cells

Formatted values

Column chart

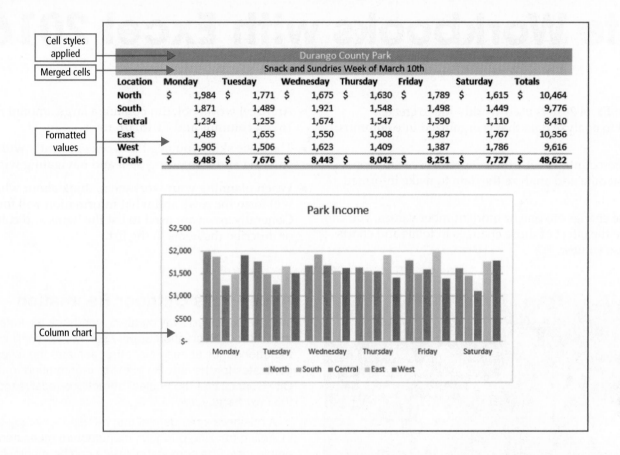

Location	Monday	Tuesday	Wednesday	Thursday	Friday	Saturday	Totals
Durango County Park							
Snack and Sundries Week of March 10th							
North	$ 1,984	$ 1,771	$ 1,675	$ 1,630	$ 1,789	$ 1,615	$ 10,464
South	1,871	1,489	1,921	1,548	1,498	1,449	9,776
Central	1,234	1,255	1,674	1,547	1,590	1,110	8,410
East	1,489	1,655	1,550	1,908	1,987	1,767	10,356
West	1,905	1,506	1,623	1,409	1,387	1,786	9,616
Totals	$ 8,483	$ 7,676	$ 8,443	$ 8,042	$ 8,251	$ 7,727	$ 48,622

Park Income

$2,500
$2,000
$1,500
$1,000
$500
$-

Monday   Tuesday   Wednesday   Thursday   Friday   Saturday

■ North ■ South ■ Central ■ East ■ West

CHAPTER 1

Create Workbooks with Excel 2016

- ▶ Microsoft Office Excel 2016 is used worldwide to create workbooks and to analyze data that is organized into columns and rows.

- ▶ After data is entered into Excel, you can perform calculations on the numerical data and analyze the data to make informed decisions.

- ▶ When you make changes to one or more number values, you can immediately see the effect of those changes in totals and charts that rely on those values.

- ▶ An Excel workbook can contain a large amount of data—up to 16,384 columns and 1,048,576 rows.

- ▶ The basic skills you need to work efficiently with Excel include entering and formatting data and navigating within Excel.

- ▶ When planning your worksheet, think about what information will form the rows and what information will form the columns. Generally, rows are used to list the items and columns to group or describe the items in the list.

Vlad_g/Fotolia

Aspen Falls Outdoor Recreation

In this chapter, you will create a workbook for Amado Pettinelli, the Outdoor Recreation Supervisor. Mr. Pettinelli wants to know the attendance at each city attraction and the revenue each venue generates for the city. He plans to recommend to the Aspen Falls City Council that the busiest attractions receive more city funding in the next fiscal year.

A business spreadsheet can be used for many purposes including tracking budgets, manufacture measurements, or employees. The spreadsheet data can be manipulated using arithmetic and mathematical formulas commonly used in the modern-day business world. If you are asked to create a spreadsheet, you need to know if the results of the data manipulation will be presented in numerical or graphical format.

In this project, you will create a new Excel workbook and enter data that displays the total number of visitors at the various city attractions in Aspen Falls. You will format the data, construct formulas, and insert functions. You will calculate the percentage of weekday visitors at each of the locations and insert a footer. Finally, you will check the spelling in the workbook.

Outcome

Using the skills in this chapter, you will be able to create, edit, and save workbooks; create addition, subtraction, multiplication, and division formulas and functions; modify cell and worksheet formats; and apply print settings.

Objectives:

1.1 Create and enter data into worksheets

1.2 Construct basic functions and formulas

1.3 Apply cell formatting

1.4 Adjust settings and review worksheets for printing

SKILLS MyITLab®

Skills 1–10 Training

At the end of this chapter you will be able to:

Skill 1 Create and Save Workbooks

Skill 2 Enter Data and Merge and Center Titles

Skill 3 Construct Addition and Subtraction Formulas

Skill 4 Construct Multiplication and Division Formulas

Skill 5 Adjust Column Widths and Apply Cell Styles

Skill 6 Insert the SUM Function

Skill 7 AutoFill Formulas and Data

Skill 8 Format, Edit, and Check Spelling

Skill 9 Insert Footers and Adjust Page Settings

Skill 10 Display Formulas and Print Worksheets

MORE SKILLS

Skill 11 Set Print Areas

Skill 12 Fill Data with Flash Fill

Skill 13 Create Templates and Workbooks from Templates

Skill 14 Manage Document Properties

Student data file needed for this chapter:

Blank Excel workbook

You will save your file as:

Last_First_exl01_Visitors

Aspen Falls Outdoor Recreation						
Visitors to City Attractions						
Location	Weekends	Weekdays	All Visitors	Difference	Entrance Fee	Total Fees
Zoo	3,169	1,739	4,908	1,430	$ 10	$ 49,080
Pool	5,338	3,352	8,690	1,986	10	86,900
Aquarium	9,027	3,868	12,895	5,159	12	154,740
Garden	4,738	2,788	7,526	1,950	4	30,104
Museum	3,876	913	4,789	2,963	11	52,679
Total	26,148	12,660	38,808			$ 373,503
Percent of Weekday Visitors						
Zoo	35.4%					
Pool	38.6%					
Aquarium	30.0%					
Garden	37.0%					
Museum	19.1%					

Excel 2016, Windows 10, Microsoft Corporation

▶ An Excel *workbook* is a file that you can use to organize various kinds of related information. A workbook contains *worksheets*, also called *spreadsheets*—the primary documents that you use in Excel to store and work with data.

▶ The worksheet forms a grid of vertical columns and horizontal rows. The small box where one column and one row meet is a cell.

 MOS
Obj 1.1.1 C

1. Start **Excel 2016**, and then click **Blank workbook**. In the lower right, notice the zoom level.

   Your zoom level should be 100%, but most figures in this chapter are zoomed to 120%.

2. Verify the cell in the upper left corner is the *active cell*—as shown in Figure 1.

   active cell—the cell outlined in green in which data is entered when you begin typing. In a worksheet, columns have alphabetical headings across the top, and rows have numerical headings down the left side. When a cell is active, the headings for the column and row in which the cell is located are shaded. The column letter and row number that identify a cell compose the **cell address**, also called the **cell reference**.

3. In cell **A1**, type Aspen Falls Outdoor Recreation and then press Enter to accept the entry.

4. In cell **A2**, type Visitors and then press Enter two times. Compare your screen with Figure 2.

5. In cell **A4**, type Location and press Tab to make the cell to the right—**B4**—active.

■ **Continue to the next page to complete the skill** ▶

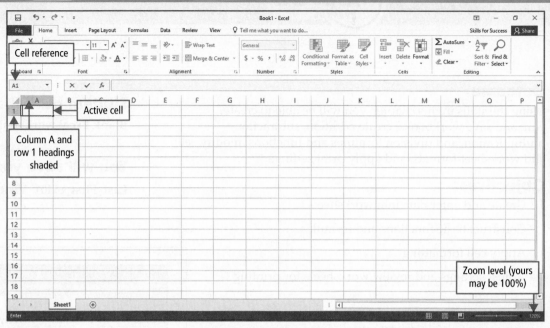

Figure 1

Excel 2016, Windows 10, Microsoft Corporation

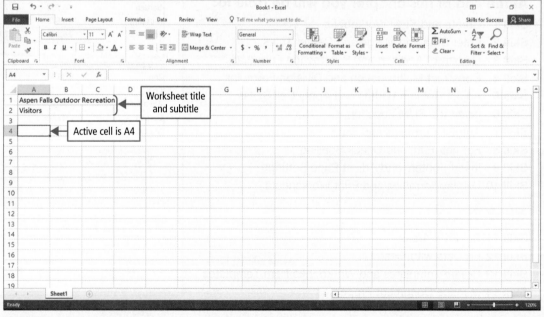

Figure 2

Excel 2016, Windows 10, Microsoft Corporation

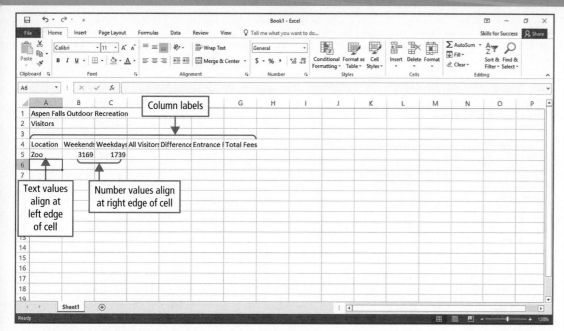

Excel 2016, Windows 10, Microsoft Corporation

Figure 3

Common Ways to Move or Scroll Through a Worksheet	
Key	**Description**
Enter	Move down one row.
Tab	Move one column to the right.
Shift + Tab	Move one column to the left.
↓ ↑ → ←	Move one cell in the direction of the arrow.
Ctrl + Home	Move to cell A1.
Ctrl + End	Move to the last row and last column farthest to the bottom right that contains data.

Figure 4

6. With cell **B4** the active cell, type the following labels, pressing Tab between each label:

Weekends

Weekdays

All Visitors

Difference

Entrance Fee

Total Fees

> Labels at the beginning of columns or rows help readers understand the data.

> To correct typing errors, click a cell and retype the data. The new typing will replace the existing data.

7. Click cell **A5**, type Zoo and then press Tab. Type 3169 and then press Tab. Type 1739 and then press Enter. Compare your screen with **Figure 3**.

> Data in a cell is called a *value*. You can have a *text value*—character data in a cell that usually labels number values, or a *number value*—numeric data in a cell. A text value is often used as a *label*. Text values align at the left cell edge, and number values align at the right cell edge.

8. Click **Save** 🖫, and then on the **Save As** page, click the **Browse** button. In the **Save As** dialog box, navigate to the location where you are saving your files. Click **New folder**, type Excel Chapter 1 and then press Enter two times. In the **File name** box, name the file Last_First_ exl01_Visitors and then press Enter.

9. Take a few moments to familiarize yourself with common methods to move between cells as summarized in the table in **Figure 4**.

■ **You have completed Skill 1 of 10**

▶ To create an effective worksheet, you enter titles and subtitles and add labels for each row and column of data. It is a good idea to have the worksheet title and subtitle span across all the columns containing data.

1. In cell **A6**, type Aquarium and then press Tab.

2. In cell **B6**, type 9027 and then press Tab. In cell **C6**, type 3868 and then press Enter.

3. In row 7 and row 8, type the following data:

   Garden | 5738 | 2877

   Museum | 3876 | 913

4. In cell **A9**, type Total and then press Enter. Compare your screen with **Figure 1**.

5. Click cell **B1**, type Worksheet and then press Enter. Click cell **A1**, and then compare your screen with **Figure 2**.

   When text is too long to fit in a cell and the cell to the right of it contains data, the text will be **truncated**—cut off. Here, the text in cell A1 is truncated.

   The **formula bar** is a bar below the ribbon that displays the value contained in the active cell and is used to enter or edit values or formulas.

   Data displayed in a cell is the **displayed value**. Data displayed in the formula bar is the **underlying value**. Displayed values often do not match their underlying values.

6. On the Quick Access Toolbar, click the **Undo** button ↺ to remove the text in cell B1.

   Long text in cells overlaps into other columns only when those cells are empty. Here, A1 text now overlaps B1 because that cell is empty.

■ **Continue to the next page to complete the skill**

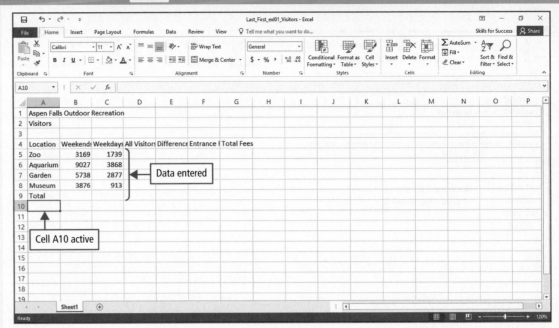

Figure 1

Excel 2016, Windows 10, Microsoft Corporation

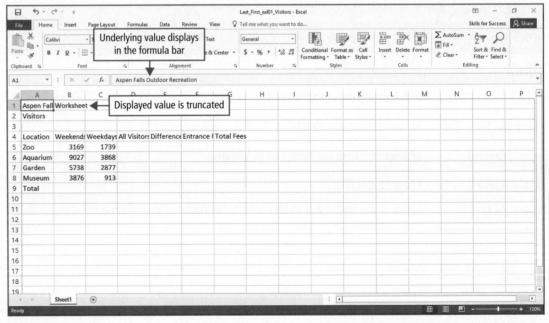

Figure 2

Excel 2016, Windows 10, Microsoft Corporation

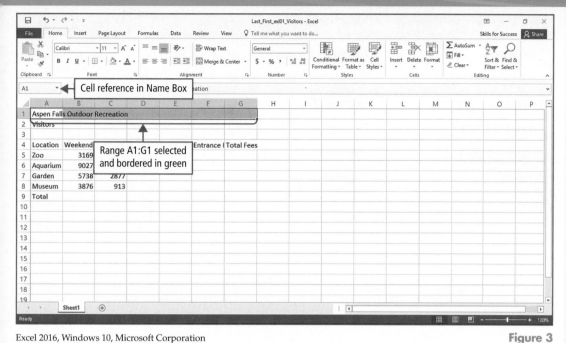

Excel 2016, Windows 10, Microsoft Corporation

Figure 3

Excel 2016, Windows 10, Microsoft Corporation

Figure 4

7. Point to the middle of cell **A1** to display the ⊕ pointer. Hold down the left mouse button, and then drag to the right to select cells **A1** through **G1**. Compare your screen with **Figure 3**. To select a range on a touch screen, tap the cell, and then drag the selection handle.

The selected range is referred to as *A1:G1* (A1 through G1). A ***range*** is two or more cells in a worksheet that are adjacent (next to each other). A colon (:) between two cell references indicates that the range includes the two cell references and all the cells between them. When you select a range, a thick green line surrounds the range, and all but the first cell in the range are shaded. The first cell reference will be displayed in the ***Name Box***—an area by the formula bar that displays the active cell reference.

8. On the **Home tab**, in the **Alignment group**, click the **Merge & Center** button ▦▾.

The selected range, A1:G1, merges into one larger cell, and the data is centered in the new cell. The cells in B1 through G1 can no longer be selected individually because they are merged into cell A1.

9. Using the technique just practiced, merge and center the range **A2:G2**.

10. Save 🖫 the file, and then compare your screen with **Figure 4**.

■ **You have completed Skill 2 of 10**

▶ A cell's underlying value can be a text value, a number value, or a *formula*—an equation that performs mathematical calculations on number values in the worksheet.

▶ Formulas begin with an equal sign and often include an ***arithmetic operator***—a symbol that specifies a mathematical operation such as addition or subtraction.

1. Study the symbols that Excel uses to perform mathematical operations, as summarized in the table in **Figure 1**.

2. In cell **D5**, type =B5+C5 and then press Enter.

   When you include cell references in formulas, the values in those cells are inserted. Here, the total number of visitors for the zoo location equals the sum of the values in cells B5 and C5 (3169 + 1739 = 4908).

   When you type a formula, you might see a brief display of function names that match the first letter you type. This Excel feature, called ***Formula AutoComplete***, suggests values as you type a function.

3. In cell **D6**, type the formula to add cells B6 and C6, =B6+C6 and then press Enter.

4. In cell **D7**, type = and then click cell **B7** to automatically insert *B7* into the formula. Compare your screen with **Figure 2**.

   Cell B7 is surrounded by a moving border indicating that it is part of an active formula.

5. Type + Click cell **C7**, and then press Enter to display the result *8615*.

   You can either type formulas or construct them by pointing and clicking in this manner.

■ **Continue to the next page to complete the skill**

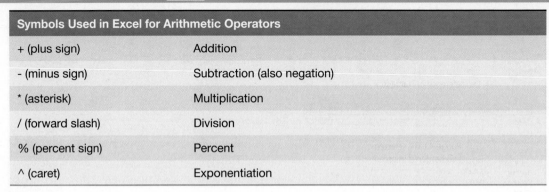

Symbols Used in Excel for Arithmetic Operators

+ (plus sign)	Addition
- (minus sign)	Subtraction (also negation)
* (asterisk)	Multiplication
/ (forward slash)	Division
% (percent sign)	Percent
^ (caret)	Exponentiation

Figure 1

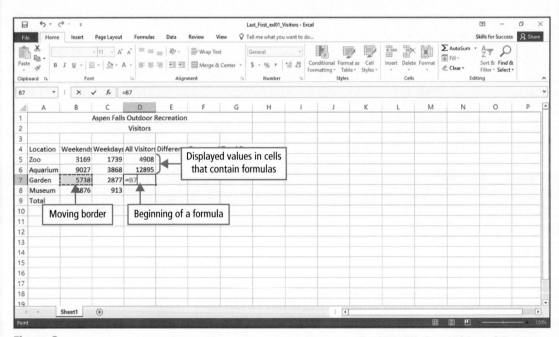

Figure 2

Excel 2016, Windows 10, Microsoft Corporation

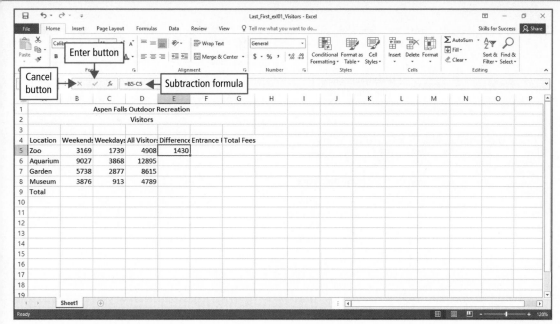

Excel 2016, Windows 10, Microsoft Corporation

Figure 3

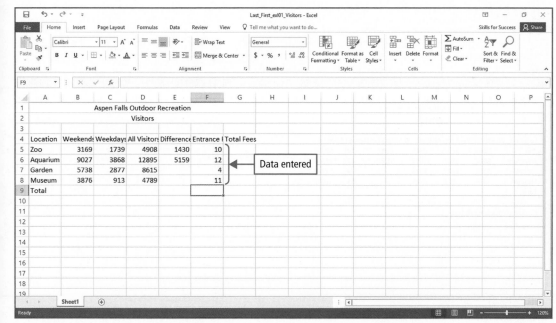

Excel 2016, Windows 10, Microsoft Corporation

Figure 4

6. In cell **D8**, use point and click to construct a formula that adds cells **B8** and **C8**. Press Enter when done.

7. In cell **E5**, type =B5-C5 On the formula bar, click the **Enter** button ☑ to confirm the entry while keeping cell **E5** the active cell, and then compare your screen with Figure 3.

> Here, the underlying value for cell E5 displays as a formula in the formula bar and displays as a value, *1430*, in the cell as a result of the formula.

> If you make an error entering a formula, you can click the Cancel button ☒ and then start over. Alternately, you can press the Esc key.

8. In cell **E6**, use point and click to enter the formula =B6-C6 to display the difference for the aquarium weekend and weekday visitors. (You will complete the column E formulas in Skill 7.)

9. In column **F**, type the following data as listed in the table below, and then compare your screen with Figure 4.

Cell	Value
F5	10
F6	12
F7	4
F8	11

10. **Save** 🖫 the file.

- **You have completed Skill 3 of 10**

▶ The four most common operators for addition (+), subtraction (−), multiplication (*), and division (/) can be found on the number keypad at the right side of a standard keyboard or on the number keys at the top of a keyboard.

1. In cell **G5**, type =D5*F5 This formula multiplies the total zoo visitors by its entrance fee. On the formula bar, click the **Enter** button ☑, and then compare your screen with **Figure 1**.

   The *underlying formula*—the formula as displayed in the formula bar—multiplies the value in cell D5 (*4908*) by the value in cell F5 (*10*) and displays the result in cell G5 (*49080*).

2. In the range **G6:G8**, enter the following formulas:

Cell	Formula
G6	=D6*F6
G7	=D7*F7
G8	=D8*F8

3. In cell **A11**, type Percent of Weekday Visitors and then press [Enter]. Compare your screen with **Figure 2**.

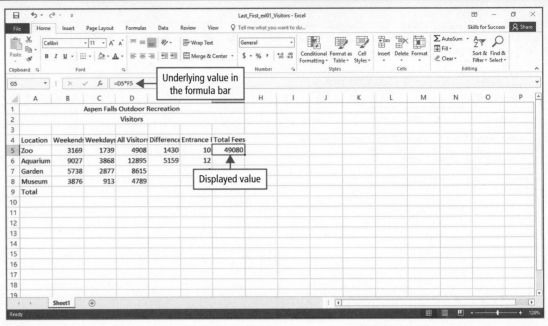

Figure 1

Excel 2016, Windows 10, Microsoft Corporation

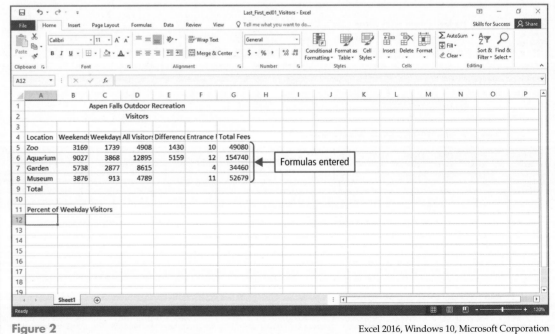

Figure 2

Excel 2016, Windows 10, Microsoft Corporation

■ Continue to the next page to complete the skill

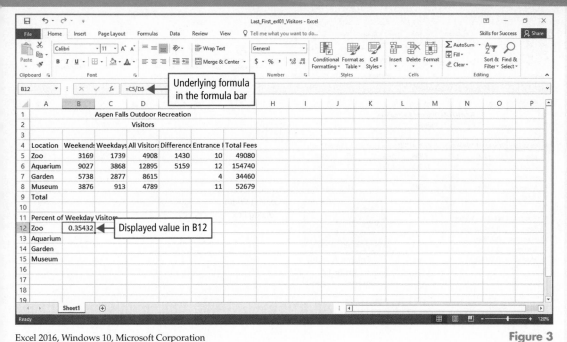

Excel 2016, Windows 10, Microsoft Corporation

Figure 3

4. Select the range **A5:A8**, and then on the **Home tab**, in the **Clipboard group**, click the **Copy** button. Click cell **A12**, and then in the **Clipboard group**, click the **Paste** button.

Obj 2.1.2 C

> The four location labels are copied to the range A12:A15.

5. Press [Esc] to remove the moving border around the copied cells.

6. In cell **B12**, construct the formula to divide the number of weekday zoo visitors by the total zoo visitors, $=C5/D5$ and then click the **Enter** button. Compare your screen with **Figure 3**.

> Percentages are calculated by taking the amount divided by the total and will be displayed in decimal format. Here, the underlying formula in B12 (=C5/D5) divides the weekday zoo visitors (*1739*) by the total zoo visitors (*4908*).

7. Construct the following formulas to calculate the percentage of weekday visitors for each location, and then compare your screen with **Figure 4**.

Cell	Formula
B13	$=C6/D6$
B14	$=C7/D7$
B15	$=C8/D8$

8. **Save** the file.

■ **You have completed Skill 4 of 10**

Excel 2016, Windows 10, Microsoft Corporation

Figure 4

► The **column heading** is the letter that displays at the top of a column. The number that displays at the left of a row is the **row heading**.

► **Formatting** is the process of specifying the appearance of cells or the overall layout of a worksheet.

Obj 1.3.7 C
1. Click cell **A4**. On the **Home tab**, in the **Cells group**, click the **Format** button, and then click **Column Width**. In the **Column Width** dialog box, type 13

2. Compare your screen with **Figure 1**, and then click **OK**.

   The default column width will display as 8.43 characters when formatted in the standard font. Here, the width is increased to display more characters.

3. Select the range **B4:G4**. In the **Cells group**, click the **Format** button, and then click **Column Width**. In the **Column Width** dialog box, type 12 and then click **OK**.

   As an alternate method, you can select the column range to format the column widths.

4. Select cells **A11:B11**. On the **Home tab**, in the **Alignment group**, click the **Merge & Center arrow**, and then on the displayed list, click **Merge Across**. Compare your screen with **Figure 2**.

   Merge Across merges the selected cells without centering them.

Obj 1.3.7 C
5. Click cell **A1** to select the merged and centered range A1:G1. In the **Cells group**, click the **Format** button, and then click **Row Height**. In the **Row Height** dialog box, type 22.5 and then click **OK**.

■ Continue to the next page to complete the skill ►

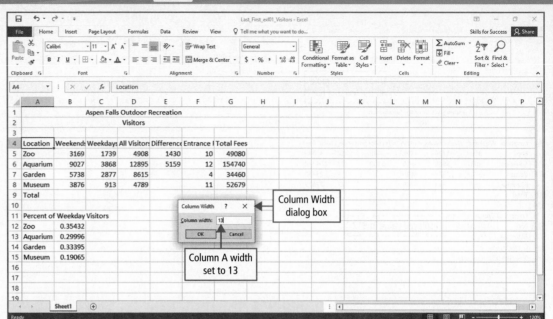

Figure 1   Excel 2016, Windows 10, Microsoft Corporation

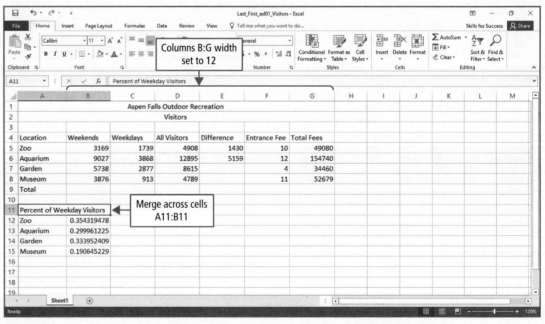

Figure 2   Excel 2016, Windows 10, Microsoft Corporation

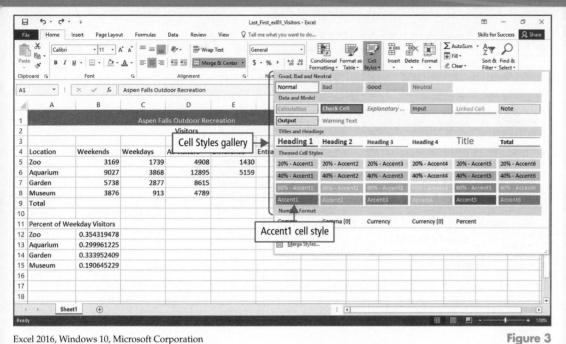

Excel 2016, Windows 10, Microsoft Corporation

Figure 3

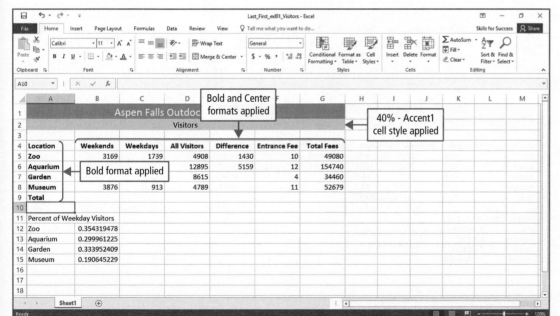

Excel 2016, Windows 10, Microsoft Corporation

Figure 4

6. With **A1:G1** still selected, in the **Styles group**, click the **Cell Styles** button. In the **Cell Styles** gallery, under **Titles and Headings**, use Live Preview to view the title as you point to **Heading 1** and then **Heading 2**.

   A *cell style* is a prebuilt set of formatting characteristics, such as font, font size, font color, cell borders, and cell shading.

7. Under **Themed Cell Styles**, point to the **Accent1** style. Compare your screen with **Figure 3**, and then click **Accent1**.

8. In the **Font group**, click the **Font Size arrow** 11 ▾, and then click **16**.

9. Click cell **A2**, and then using the technique you just practiced, apply the **40% - Accent1** cell style. In the **Font group**, click the **Increase Font Size** button A˄ one time to change the font size to **12**.

10. Select the range **B4:G4**. Right-click the selected range to display a shortcut menu and the Mini toolbar. On the Mini toolbar, click the **Bold** button B and then click the **Center** button ≡ to apply bold and to center the text within each of the selected cells.

11. Select the range **A4:A9**. Display the Mini toolbar, and then apply **Bold** to the selected range. Click cell **A10**, and then compare your screen with **Figure 4**.

12. **Save** 🖫 the file.

■ **You have completed Skill 5 of 10**

 **WATCH** SKILL 1.6

▶ You can create your own formulas, or you can use a *function*—a prewritten Excel formula that takes a value or values, performs an operation, and returns a value or values.

▶ The AutoSum button is used to insert common summary functions into a worksheet.

▶ When cell references are used in a formula or function, the results are automatically recalculated whenever those cells are edited.

1. Click cell **B9**. On the **Home tab**, in the **Editing group**, click the **AutoSum** button ∑ AutoSum ▾, and then compare your screen with **Figure 1**.

   SUM is an Excel function that adds all the numbers in a range of cells. The range in parentheses, *(B5:B8)*, indicates the range of cells on which the SUM function will be performed.

   When the AutoSum button is used, Excel first looks *above* the selected cell for a range of cells to sum. If there is no data detected in the range above the selected cell, Excel then looks to the *left* and proposes a range of cells to sum. Here, the range B5:B8 is surrounded by a moving border, and *=SUM(B5:B8)* displays in cell B9.

2. Press Enter to display the function result—*21810*.

3. Select the range **C9:D9**. In the **Editing group**, click the **AutoSum** button ∑ AutoSum ▾, and then compare your screen with **Figure 2**.

■ **Continue to the next page to complete the skill**

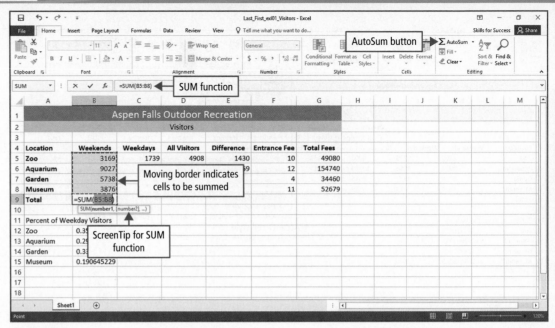

Figure 1 Excel 2016, Windows 10, Microsoft Corporation

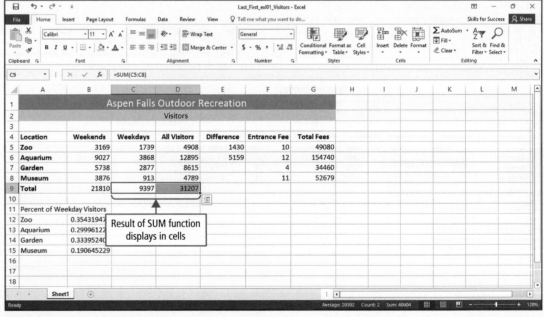

Figure 2 Excel 2016, Windows 10, Microsoft Corporation

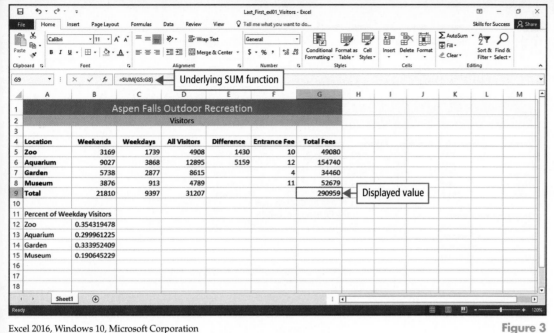

Excel 2016, Windows 10, Microsoft Corporation

Figure 3

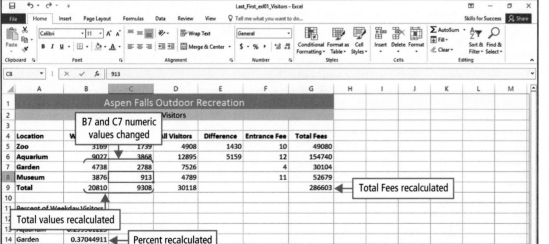

Excel 2016, Windows 10, Microsoft Corporation

Figure 4

4. Click cell **C9**, and then in the formula bar, verify that the SUM function adds the values in the range *C5:C8*.

5. Click cell **D9**, and then verify that the SUM function adds the values in the range *D5:D8*.

6. Using the technique just practiced, in cell **G9**, insert the SUM function to add the values in the range **G5:G8**. Select cell G9, and then compare your screen with **Figure 3**.

7. In cell **B7**, type 4738 Watch the total in cell **B9** update as you press `Tab`.

   In cell B9, the displayed value changed to 20810, but the underlying formula remained the same.

8. In cell **C7**, type 2788 and then press `Enter` to update the totals in cells C9, G7, and G9. Compare your screen with **Figure 4**.

   The amounts were recalculated when the data was changed because cell references were used in the functions.

9. **Save** 💾 the file.

■ **You have completed Skill 6 of 10**

WATCH SKILL 1.7

- Text, numbers, formulas, and functions can be copied down rows and across columns to insert formulas and functions quickly.

- When a formula is copied to another cell, Excel adjusts the cell references relative to the new location of the formula.

Obj 2.1.4 C

1. Click cell **E6**. With cell **E6** selected, point to the *fill handle*—the small green square in the lower right corner of the selection—until the ⊞ pointer displays, as shown in **Figure 1**.

   To use the fill handle, first select the cell that contains the content you want to copy—here the formula =B6-C6.

2. Drag the ⊞ pointer down to cell **E8**, and then release the mouse button.

Obj 4.1.1 C

3. Click cell **E7**, and verify on the formula bar that the formula copied from E6 changed to =B7-C7. Click cell **E8**, and then compare your screen with **Figure 2**.

   In each row, the cell references in the formula adjusted *relative to* the row number—B6 changed to B7 and then to B8. This adjustment is called a *relative cell reference* because it refers to cells based on their position *in relation to* (relative to) the cell that contains the formula.

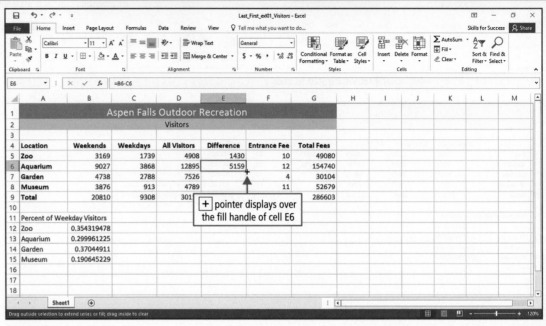

Figure 1

Excel 2016, Windows 10, Microsoft Corporation

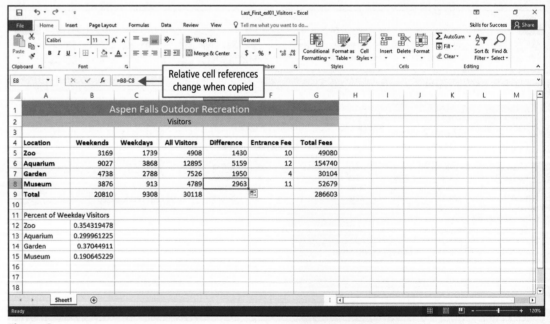

Figure 2

Excel 2016, Windows 10, Microsoft Corporation

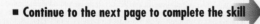
■ **Continue to the next page to complete the skill**

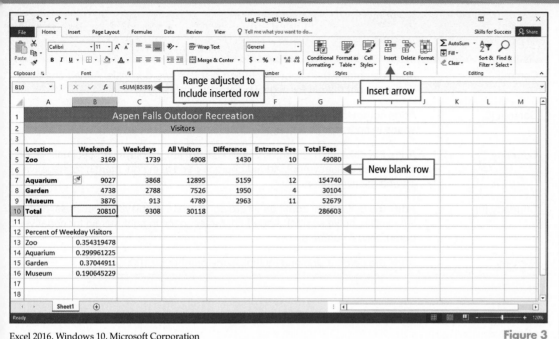

Excel 2016, Windows 10, Microsoft Corporation

Figure 3

Excel 2016, Windows 10, Microsoft Corporation

Figure 4

4. Click cell **A6**. In the **Cells group**, click the **Insert arrow**, and then click **Insert Sheet Rows**. Click cell **B10**, and then compare your screen with **Figure 3**.

    When you insert a new row or column, the cell references and the ranges in formulas or in functions adjust to include the new row or column. Here, in cell B10, the range in the function automatically updated to include the new row in the range.

5. In cell **A6**, type Pool and then press Tab.

    By default, formatting (bold) from the row above is applied to an inserted row.

6. In cell **B6**, type 5338 and then press Tab to enter the value and update the column total in cell B10 to *26148*.

7. In cell **C6**, type 3352 and then press Tab.

8. Select cells **D5:G5**. Point to the fill handle until the ⊞ pointer displays, and then drag the ⊞ pointer down one row. Release the mouse button, and then click the **Auto Fill Options** button 🖫. Compare your screen with **Figure 4**.

    Obj 2.1.4 C

    Three formulas and a number are copied. When you copy number values using the fill handle, the numbers automatically increment for each row or column. Here, the number value in cell F5 increased by one when it was copied to cell F6.

9. In the **Auto Fill Options** menu, click **Copy Cells**.

    With the Copy Cells option, number values are copied exactly and do not increment. Here, the number value in cell F6 changes to 10.

10. **Save** 🖫 the file.

■ **You have completed Skill 7 of 10**

▶ Always check spelling after you have completed formatting and editing worksheet data.

1. Click cell **A14**, and then repeat the technique used previously to insert a new row. In cell **A14**, type Pool and then press Enter.

2. Click cell **B13**, and then use the fill handle to copy the formula down to cell **B14**.

3. Double-click cell **A2** to edit the cell contents. Use the arrow keys to move to the right of the word *Visitors*. Add a space, type to City Attractions and then press Enter.

Obj 2.2.7 C

4. Select the range **F5:G5**. In the **Styles group**, click the **Cell Styles** button, and then under **Number Format**, click **Currency [0]**. Repeat this technique to apply the **Currency [0]** format to cell **G10**. Review Cell Style Number Formats as summarized in the table in **Figure 1**.

   When applying number formats, general practice is to apply the currency symbol to the top and bottom amounts.

5. Select the range **B5:E10**. Click the **Cell Styles** button, and then under **Number Format**, click **Comma [0]**. Repeat the technique to apply the **Comma [0]** format to the range **F6:G9**.

Obj 2.2.5 C

6. Select the range **B13:B17**. In the **Number group**, click the **Percent Style** button %, and then click the **Increase Decimal** button one time. Compare your screen with **Figure 2**.

   The Increase Decimal and Decrease Decimal buttons do not add or remove decimals; they change how the decimal values *display* in the cells.

■ Continue to the next page to complete the skill ▶

Number Formats	
Format	**Description**
Comma	Adds commas where appropriate and displays two decimals. Added character space in right margin for negative parenthetical numbers.
Comma [0]	Adds commas where appropriate and displays no decimals. Added character space in right margin for negative parenthetical numbers.
Currency	Adds the dollar sign, commas where appropriate, displays two decimals, and left justifies dollar symbol. Added character space in right margin for negative parenthetical numbers.
Currency [0]	Adds the dollar sign, commas where appropriate, displays no decimals, and left justifies dollar symbol. Added character space in right margin for negative parenthetical numbers.
Percent	Adds the percent sign and multiplies the number by 100.

Figure 1

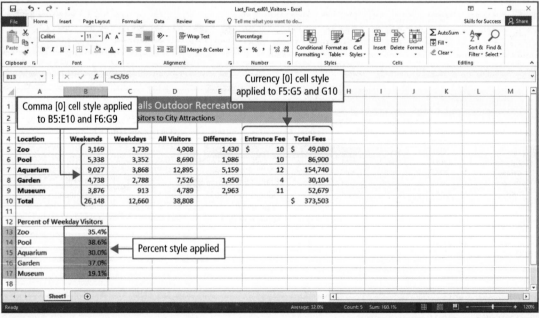

Figure 2

Excel 2016, Windows 10, Microsoft Corporation

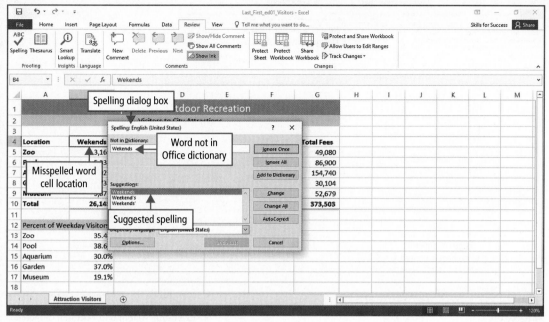

Excel 2016, Windows 10, Microsoft Corporation

Figure 3

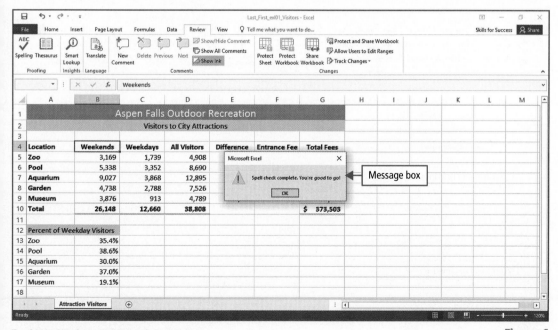

Excel 2016, Windows 10, Microsoft Corporation

Figure 4

7. Select the range **B10:D10**. Hold down Ctrl, and then click cell **G10**. Click the **Cell Styles** button. Under **Titles and Headings**, click the **Total** style.

8. Select cell **A12**, and then click the **Cell Styles** button. Under **Themed Cell Styles**, click **40% - Accent1**.

9. Press Ctrl + Home to make cell **A1** active. On the **Review tab**, in the **Proofing group**, click the **Spelling** button.

> The Spelling checker starts with the active cell and moves to the right and down. Making cell A1 the active cell verifies the spreadsheet is checked from the beginning.

> If the Spelling dialog box opens to reveal unrecognized words not in the Office dictionary, as shown in **Figure 3** (your screen may be different), the words not in the dictionary are not necessarily misspelled. Many proper nouns or less commonly used words are not in the Office dictionary.

> To correct a misspelled word and to move to the next word not in the Office dictionary, under Suggestions, verify that the correct spelling is selected, and then click the Change button.

10. Use the Spelling checker to correct any errors you may have made. When the **Spell check complete. You're good to go!** message box displays, as shown in **Figure 4**, click **OK**.

> When words you use often are not in the Office dictionary, you can click *Add to Dictionary* to add them.

11. Save 🖫 the file.

■ **You have completed Skill 8 of 10**

▶ In Excel, *Page Layout view* is used to adjust how a worksheet will look when it is printed.

 MOS Obj 1.4.6 C

1. Click the **Insert tab**, in the **Text group**, click the **Header & Footer** button to switch to **Page Layout view** and to display the **Header & Footer Tools Design** contextual tab.

 MOS Obj 1.3.8 C

2. On the **Design tab**, in the **Navigation group**, click the **Go to Footer** button to move to the Footer area. Click just above the word **Footer** to place the insertion point in the left section of the Footer area. Compare your screen with **Figure 1**.

3. In the **Header & Footer Elements group**, click the **File Name** button, and then click any cell in the workbook to view the file name, if necessary.

> Predefined headers and footers insert placeholders with instructions for printing. Here, the *&[File]* placeholder instructs Excel to insert the file name when the worksheet is printed.

 MOS Obj 1.3.2 C

4. At the bottom of your worksheet, right-click the **Sheet1** worksheet tab, and then from the shortcut menu, click **Rename**. Type Attraction Visitors and then press Enter to change the worksheet tab name. Compare your screen with **Figure 2**.

5. Click in the middle section of the Footer area, click the **Header & Footer Tools tab**, and then click the **Current Date** button. Click the right section of the Footer area, and then click the **Sheet Name** button. Click in a cell just above the footer to exit the Footer area, and then press Ctrl + Home.

■ **Continue to the next page to complete the skill**

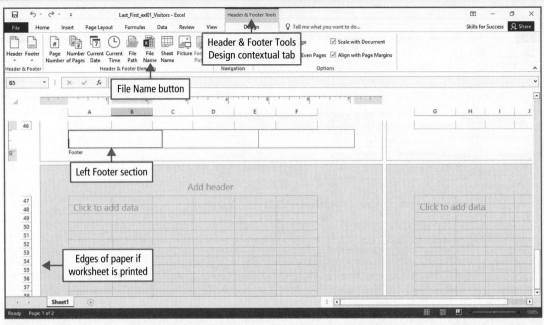

Figure 1

Excel 2016, Windows 10, Microsoft Corporation

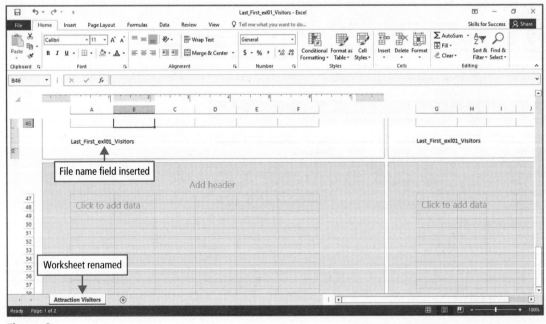

Figure 2

Excel 2016, Windows 10, Microsoft Corporation

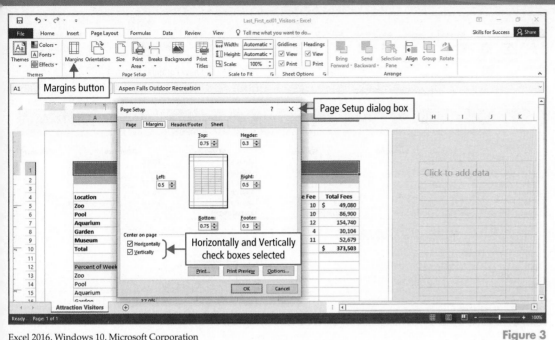

Excel 2016, Windows 10, Microsoft Corporation

Figure 3

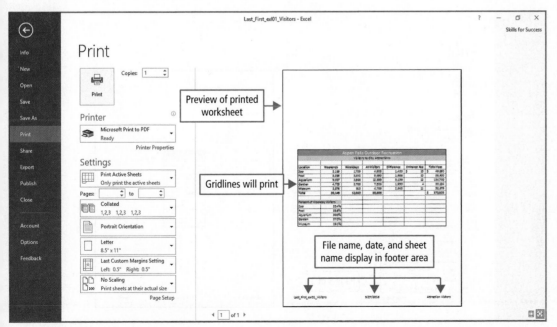

Excel 2016, Windows 10, Microsoft Corporation

Figure 4

6. Click the **Page Layout tab**. In the **Sheet Options group**, under **Gridlines**, select the **Print** check box.

7. In the **Page Setup group**, click the **Margins** button. Below the **Margins** gallery, click **Custom Margin**, and then type 0.5 in the **Left** and **Right** margins.

8. In the **Page Setup** dialog box, under **Center on page**, click to select the **Horizontally** and **Vertically** check boxes, and then compare your screen with **Figure 3**.

9. In the **Page Setup** dialog box, click **Print Preview**, and then compare your screen with **Figure 4**.

10. Click the **Back** button. On the lower right side of the status bar, click the **Normal** button to return to Normal view.

> **Normal view** maximizes the number of cells visible on the screen. The page break—the dotted line between columns G and H—indicates where one page ends and a new page begins.

11. **Save** the file.

■ **You have completed Skill 9 of 10**

▶ Underlying formulas and functions can be displayed and printed.

▶ When formulas are displayed in cells, the orientation and worksheet scale may need to be changed so that the worksheet prints on a single page.

1. Click the **Formulas tab**. In the **Formula Auditing group**, click the **Show Formulas** button [⊞] to display the underlying formulas in the cells. Compare your screen with **Figure 1**.

Columns often become wider when formulas are displayed. Here, the printed worksheet extends to a third page.

2. Click the **File tab**, and then click **Print**.

Below the preview of the printed page, *1 of 3* indicates that the worksheet will print on three pages.

3. In **Backstage** view, on the bottom of the **Print** page, click the **Next Page** button [▶] two times to view the second and third pages, and then compare your screen with **Figure 2**.

4. Click the **Back** button [←]. On the **Page Layout tab**, in the **Page Setup group**, click the **Orientation** button, and then click **Landscape** so that the page orientation will be wider than it is tall.

Figure 1   Excel 2016, Windows 10, Microsoft Corporation

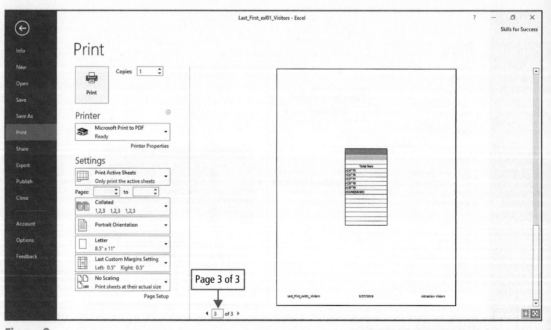

Figure 2   Excel 2016, Windows 10, Microsoft Corporation

■ **Continue to the next page to complete the skill** ▶

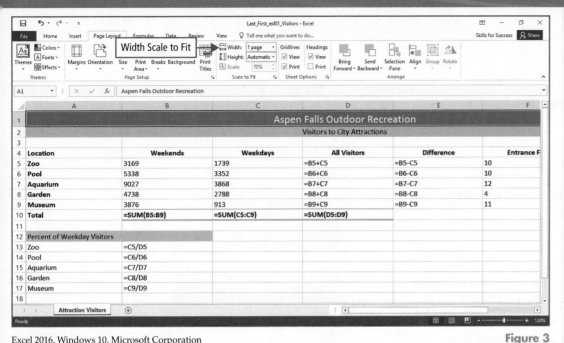

Excel 2016, Windows 10, Microsoft Corporation

Figure 3

5. In the **Scale to Fit group**, click the **Width arrow**, and then click **1 page**. Compare your screen with Figure 3. [MOS] Obj 1.5.4 C

Scaling adjusts the size of the printed worksheet to fit on the number of pages that you specify.

6. Click the **File tab**, and then click **Print**. Compare your screen with Figure 4.

1 of 1 displays at the bottom of the Print page to notify you that the worksheet will now print on one page.

7. If you are directed by your instructor to submit a printout with your formulas displayed, click the Print button.

8. Click the **Back** button 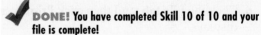. On the **Formulas tab**, in the **Formula Auditing group**, click the **Show Formulas** button to hide the formulas.

9. If you are printing your work, print the worksheet with the values displayed and formulas hidden. [MOS] Obj 1.4.4 C

10. Save  the file, and then **Close** X Excel. Submit the file as directed by your instructor.

DONE! You have completed Skill 10 of 10 and your file is complete!

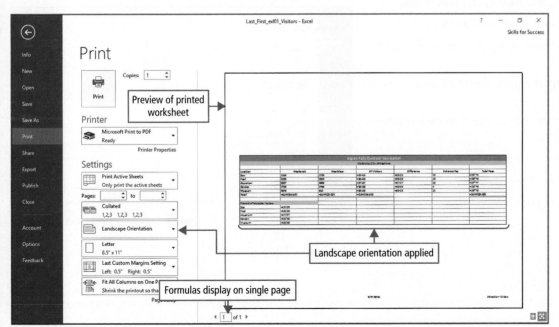

Excel 2016, Windows 10, Microsoft Corporation

Figure 4

More Skills 11

Set Print Areas

To complete this project, you will need the following file:

- exl01_MS11Business

You will save your file as:

- Last_First_exl01_MS11Business

▶ If the same portion of a worksheet needs to be printed repeatedly, you can save time by setting a print area.

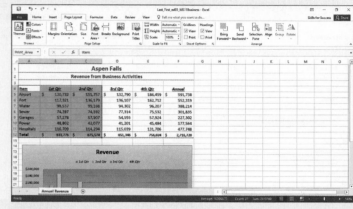

1. Start **Excel 2016**, open the student data file **exl01_MS11Business**, and then save the file in your chapter folder as Last_First_exl01_MS11Business

MOS
Obj 1.5.1 C

2. Select the range **A4:C12**. On the **Page Layout tab**, in the **Page Setup group**, click the **Print Area** button, and then click **Set Print Area**.

3. Click cell **A1**, and notice that a border surrounds the print area.

Figure 1   Excel 2016, Windows 10, Microsoft Corporation

MOS
Obj 1.2.2 C

4. Click the **Name Box arrow** above column A, and then click **Print_Area.**

When a print area is set, the range of selected cells is named Print_Area.

5. Verify that the range **A4:C12** is selected, and then compare your screen with Figure 1.

6. Click the **File tab**, and then click **Print**. Verify that only the print area displays.

To print a worksheet portion only once, select the cells, and then on the File tab, click Print. Under Settings, select Print Selection.

7. Compare your screen with **Figure 2**, and then click **Save** 🖫.

The print area setting is saved when the workbook is saved.

8. **Close** ☒ Excel. Submit the file as directed by your instructor.

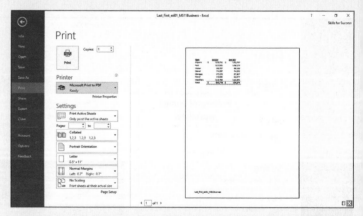

Figure 2   Excel 2016, Windows 10, Microsoft Corporation

- **You have completed More Skills 11**

More Skills 12
Fill Data with Flash Fill

To complete this project, you will need the following file:

- exl01_MS12Employees

You will save your file as:

- Last_First_exl01_MS12Employees

▶ *Flash Fill* recognizes a pattern in data and automatically enters the rest of the data.

---

1. Start **Excel 2016**, open the student data file **exl01_MS12Employees**, and then save the file in your chapter folder as Last_First_exl01_MS12Employees

2. Add the file name in the worksheet's left footer, and then return to **Normal** view. Press ⌃Ctrl + ⌂Home.

   Often, data imported from a database will place spaces between data instead of placing each field in a separate column.

3. Click cell **B4**, type Ron and then press ⏎Enter. In cell **B5**, type Re and then pause to preview all the employee first names in column B.

   Flash Fill recognizes the first name pattern in your data.

4. Press ⏎Enter to automatically fill all employee first names.

5. Using the technique just practiced, use Flash Fill to enter the last names into column **C** and the e-mail addresses into column **D**. Compare your screen with **Figure 1**.

6. **Save** 🖫 the file, and then **Close** ✕ Excel. Submit the file as directed by your instructor.

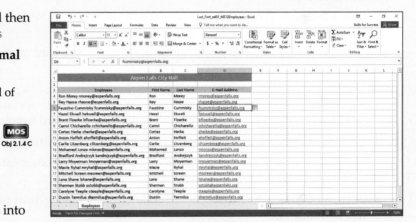

Excel 2016, Windows 10, Microsoft Corporation

Figure 1

■ **You have completed More Skills 12**

More Skills 13

Create Templates and Workbooks from Templates

To complete this project, you will need the following file:

- Blank Excel workbook

You will save your files as:

- Last_First_exl01_MS13Timecard
- Last_First_exl01_MS13Template

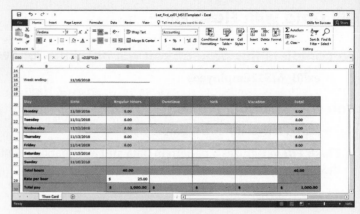

► A *template*—a prebuilt workbook used as a pattern for creating new workbooks—is used to build workbooks without having to start from a blank workbook.

► When a template is opened, a copy of the file is created to keep the original template.

► A workbook submitted on a regular basis, such as a time card or an expense report, can be saved as a template.

---

1. Start **Excel 2016**. At the top of the window, in the search box, type time card and then press Enter. If necessary, scroll to find the **Time card** template.

2. Click the **Time card** template, and then click the **Create** button.

   If you are not able to locate this template, navigate to your student data files and open exl01_MS13Timecard.

3. With cell **C7** the active cell, type the following data using your name where indicated.

Title	Cell	Data
Employee	C7	Your First Last Name
[Street Address]	C9	500 S Aspen Street
[City, ST ZIP Code]	C13	Aspen Falls, CA 93463
Manager	G7	Maria Martinez
Employee phone	G9	(805) 555-9080

MOS
Obj 1.5.2 C

4. On the **File tab**, click **Save As**, and then in **Backstage** view, click the **Browse** button. In the **Save As** dialog box, click the **Save as type arrow**, and then click **Excel Template**. Save the file in your chapter folder as Last_First_exl01_MS13Template

   By default, Excel saves templates in the Templates folder.

5. Click **Save** 🖫, and then **Close** ✕ Excel.

6. Navigate to your chapter folder, and then open the file **Last_First_exl01_MS13Template** to create a new workbook.

7. In cell **C16**, type 11/16/2018 and then press Enter. Scroll down to display row **30**.

   When a date is entered in cell C16, functions in C21:C27 automatically display the corresponding dates.

MOS
Obj 2.1.4 C

8. In cell **D21**, type 8 and then, on the formula bar, click the **Enter** button ✓. Fill the number 8 down through the cells **D22:D25**. Click the **Auto Fill Options** button , and then click **Fill Without Formatting**. In cell **D29**, type 25 and then press Enter. Compare your screen with **Figure 1**.

   When the regular hours are entered in cells D21:D25, the total hours in cell D28 are automatically calculated.

   Formatting symbols, such as the dollar sign in cell D29, are already formatted in a template.

9. Save the file as Last_First_exl01_MS13Timecard and then **Close** ✕ Excel. Submit the files as directed by your instructor.

- **You have completed More Skills 13**

More Skills (14)

Manage Document Properties

To complete this project, you will need the following file:

- exl01_MS14Revenue

You will save your files as:

- Last_First_exl01_MS14Revenue
- Last_First_exl01_MS14Snip

▶ **Document properties** are details about a file that describe or identify the file, such as title, author, and keywords.

▶ The document properties are stored as part of the Excel file.

---

1. Start **Excel 2016**, open the student data file **exl01_MS14Revenue**, and then save the file in your chapter folder as Last_First_exl01_MS14Revenue

2. Click the **File tab**. In **Backstage** view, on the right side of the **Info** page, click the **Title** box, and then type Park Revenue

3. In the **Tags** box, type first half, park, revenue, chart

4. In the **Author** box, replace the existing text with your First and Last names.

5. Select the **Show All Properties** link.

6. In the **Status** box, type Draft

7. At the top of the right panel, click **Properties**, click **Advanced Properties**, [MOS] Obj 1.4.6 C and then ensure the **Summary tab** is selected.

8. In the **Company** box, type Aspen Falls In the **Comments** box, type Need to increase marketing effort

9. In the **Properties** dialog box, click **OK**.

10. Start the **Snipping Tool**, click the **New arrow**, and then click **Full-screen Snip**.

11. Click the **Save Snip** button . In the **Save As** dialog box, navigate to your chapter folder. **Save** the file as Last_First_exl01_MS14Snip and then **Close** the Snipping Tool window. Compare your screen with **Figure 1**.

Excel 2016, Windows 10, Microsoft Corporation

Figure 1

12. **Close** the Document Information Panel. **Save** the file, and then **Close** Excel. Submit the files as directed by your instructor.

■ **You have completed More Skills 14**

The following table summarizes the **SKILLS AND PROCEDURES** covered in this chapter.

Skills Number	Task	Step	Icon	Keyboard Shortcut
2	Merge cells	Home tab → Alignment group → Merge & Center	🔲▾	
3	Accept a cell entry	Formula bar → Enter	✓	Enter
5	Adjust column width	Home tab → Cells group → Format → Column Width		
5	Adjust row height	Home tab → Cells group → Format → Row Height		
5	Apply Cell Styles	Home tab → Styles group → Cell Styles		
6	Insert SUM function	Home tab → Editing group → AutoSum	Σ AutoSum ▾	Alt + =
7	Insert a row	Home tab → Cells group → Insert → Insert Sheet Rows		
8	Check spelling	Review tab → Proofing group → Spelling		F7
8	Edit inside cells	Double-click		F2
8	Increase decimals	Home tab → Number group → Increase Decimal		
8	Decrease decimals	Home tab → Number group → Decrease Decimal		
9	Display workbook in Normal View	Status bar → Normal	⊞	
9	Move to cell A1			Ctrl + Home
9	Insert text and fields into footers	Insert tab → Text group → Header & Footer		
9	Rename a worksheet tab	Right-click worksheet tab → Rename		
10	Display formulas	Formulas tab → Formula Auditing group → Show Formulas		Ctrl + [']
10	Scale to print on one page	Page Layout tab → Scale to Fit group → Width / Height		
10	Change page orientation	Page Layout tab → Page Setup group → Orientation		
MS 11	Set print area	Page Layout tab → Page Setup group → Print Area		
MS 12	Flash Fill	Type Text → Home tab → Editing group → Fill		
MS 13	Create template	Excel Start Screen → Search box → Create		
MS 14	Document properties	File tab → Backstage view → Info		

Project Summary Chart

Project	Project Type	Project Location
Skills Review	Review	In Book & MIL MyITLab® Grader
Skills Assessment 1	Review	In Book & MIL MyITLab® Grader
Skills Assessment 2	Review	Book
My Skills	Problem Solving	Book
Visual Skills Check	Problem Solving	Book
Skills Challenge 1	Critical Thinking	Book
Skills Challenge 2	Critical Thinking	Book
More Skills Assessment	Review	In Book & MIL MyITLab® Grader
Collaborating with Google	Critical Thinking	Book

MOS Objectives Covered (Quiz in MyITLab®)

1.1.1 C Create a workbook	1.5.1 C Set a print area
1.2.2 C Navigate to a named cell, range, or workbook element	1.5.2 C Save workbooks in alternative file formats
1.3.2 C Rename a worksheet	1.5.4 C Set print scaling
1.3.4 C Modify page setup	2.1.2 C Copy and paste data
1.3.7 C Adjust column width	2.1.4 C Fill cells by using AutoFill
1.3.7 C Adjust row height	2.2.1 C Merge cells
1.3.8 C Insert headers and footers	2.2.5 C Apply number formats
1.4.4 C Change workbook views	2.2.7 C Apply cell styles
1.4.6 C Modify document properties	4.1.1 C Insert references
1.4.8 C Display formulas	4.1.2 C Perform calculations by using the SUM function

Review

Key Terms

BizSkills Video

1. What are the best ways to network online?

2. What are some of the biggest pitfalls in using social media to communicate a personal brand?

Online Help Skills

1. Start **Excel 2016**, and then in the upper right corner of the start page, click the **Help** button ? .

2. In the **Excel Help** window **Search help** box, type broken formula and then press Enter .

3. In the search result list, click **How to avoid broken formulas**, **Maximize** the Help window, and then compare your screen with **Figure 1**.

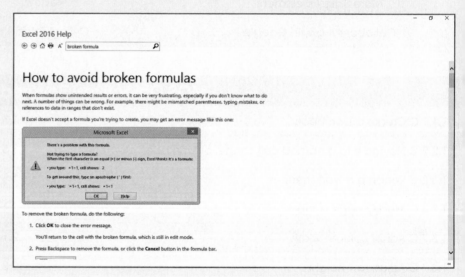

Figure 1   Excel 2016, Windows 10, Microsoft Corporation

4. Read the article to answer the following questions: How do you remove a broken formula? What sign does every function start with?

Matching

Match each term in the second column with its correct definition in the first column by writing the letter of the term on the blank line in front of the correct definition.

____ **1.** An Excel file that contains one or more worksheets.

____ **2.** The primary document that you use in Excel to store and work with data.

____ **3.** The cell, surrounded by a green border, ready to receive data or be affected by the next Excel command.

____ **4.** The identification of a specific cell by its intersecting column letter and row number.

____ **5.** Data in a cell—text or numbers.

____ **6.** Data in a cell made up of text only.

____ **7.** Data in a cell made up of numbers only.

____ **8.** Two or more cells on a worksheet.

____ **9.** The Excel window area that displays the address of a selected cell.

____ **10.** An Excel feature that suggests values as you type a function.

A Active cell

B Cell reference

C Formula AutoComplete

D Name Box

E Number value

F Range

G Text value

H Value

I Workbook

J Worksheet

Multiple Choice MyITLab®

Choose the correct answer.

1. An Excel window area that displays the value contained in the active cell.
   - A. Formula bar
   - B. Workbook
   - C. Name Box

2. The column letter and row number that identify a cell.
   - A. Cell window
   - B. Cell address
   - C. Cell file name

3. The data displayed in a cell.
   - A. Viewed value
   - B. Inspected value
   - C. Displayed value

4. An equation that performs mathematical calculations on number values.
   - A. Method
   - B. Formula
   - C. System

5. Page headers and footers can be changed in this view.
   - A. Print preview
   - B. Page Layout view
   - C. Normal view

6. Symbols that specify mathematical operations such as addition or subtraction.
   - A. Hyperlinks
   - B. Bookmarks
   - C. Arithmetic operators

7. The number that displays at the left of a row.
   - A. Row heading
   - B. Row name
   - C. Row border

8. A prewritten Excel formula.
   - A. Method
   - B. Function
   - C. Exponent

9. The small green square in the lower right corner of the active cell.
   - A. Border
   - B. Fill handle
   - C. Edge

10. A view that maximizes the number of cells visible on the screen.
    - A. Page Layout view
    - B. Standard view
    - C. Normal view

Topics for Discussion

1. What is the advantage of using cell references instead of actual number values in formulas and functions?

2. What are some things you can do to make your worksheet easier for others to read and understand?

3. According to the introduction to this chapter, how do you decide which information to put in columns and which to put in rows?

Skills Review

To complete this project, you will need the following file:

- **Blank Excel document**

You will save your file as:

- **Last_First_exl01_SRFitness**

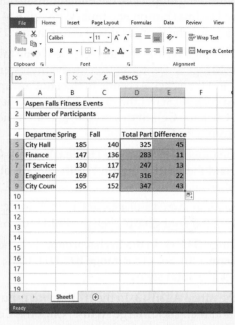

Excel 2016, Windows 10, Microsoft Corporation

Figure 1

1. Start **Excel 2016**. In cell **A1**, type Aspen Falls Fitness Events and then in cell **A2**, type Number of Participants In cell **A4**, type Department and then pressing ⎯Tab⎯ after each label, type Spring | Fall | Total Participants | Difference

2. In rows **5** through **9**, enter the following data starting in cell **A5**:

City Hall	185	140
Finance	147	136
IT Services	130	117
Engineering	169	147
City Council	195	152

3. In cell **D5**, type =B5+C5 and then in cell **E5**, type =B5-C5 Select the range **D5:E5**. Point to the fill handle, and then drag down through row **9**. Compare your screen with **Figure 1**.

4. **Save** the file in your chapter folder with the name Last_First_exl01_SRFitness

5. On the **Insert tab**, in the **Text group**, click the **Header & Footer** button. In the **Navigation group**, click the **Go to Footer** button, and then click in the left footer. In the **Header & Footer Elements group**, click the **File Name** button. Click in a cell just above the footer. On the lower right side of the status bar, click the **Normal** button, and then press ⎯Ctrl⎯ + ⎯Home⎯.

6. In cell **A10**, type Total and then select the range **B10:D10**. On the **Home tab**, in the **Editing group**, click the **AutoSum** button.

7. Click cell **A7**. In the **Cells group**, click the **Insert arrow**, and then click **Insert Sheet Rows**. In the new row 7, type the following data in columns **A:C**: Public Works | 95 | 87

8. Select the range **D6:E6**, and then use the fill handle to copy the formulas down one row.

9. In cell **A13**, type Fall Participants as Percent of Total

10. Select the range **A5:A10**, and then on the **Home tab**, in the **Clipboard group**, click the **Copy** button. Click cell **A14**, and then in the **Clipboard group**, click the **Paste** button. Press ⎯Esc⎯, and then compare your screen with **Figure 2**.

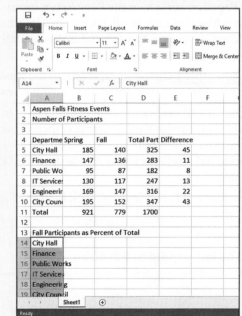

Excel 2016, Windows 10, Microsoft Corporation

Figure 2

■ Continue to the next page to complete this Skills Review

11. In cell **B14**, type =C5/D5 and then on the formula bar, click the **Enter** button. In the **Number group**, click the **Percent Style** button, and then click the **Increase Decimal** button one time. With cell **B14** still the active cell, use the fill handle to copy the formula down through row **19**.

12. Select the range **A1:E1**, and then on the **Home tab**, in the **Alignment group**, click the **Merge & Center** button. In the **Styles group**, click the **Cell Styles** button, and then click **Accent6**. In the **Font group**, click the **Font Size arrow**, and then click **16**. Select the range **A2:E2**, and then click the **Merge & Center** button. Click the **Cell Styles** button, and then click **60% - Accent6**. Compare your screen with **Figure 3**.

13. Select the range **A4:E4**. On the **Home tab**, in the **Cells group**, click the **Format** button, and then click **Column Width**. In the **Column Width** dialog box, type 16 and then click **OK**.

14. With the range **A4:E4** still selected, hold down Ctrl, and then select the range **A5:A11**. In the **Font group**, click the **Bold** button.

15. Select range **B5:E11**. In the **Styles group**, click the **Cell Styles** button, and then click **Comma [0]**. Select the range **B11:D11**. Click the **Cell Styles** button, and then click the **Total** style.

16. Select the range **A13:B13**. In the **Alignment group**, click the **Merge & Center arrow**, and then click **Merge Across**. Click the **Cell Styles** button, and then click **40% - Accent6**.

17. On the **Page Layout tab**, in the **Page Setup group**, click the **Margins** button. Below the **Margins** gallery, click **Custom Margins**. In the **Page Setup** dialog box, under **Center on page**, select the **Horizontally** check box, and then click **OK**.

18. Press Ctrl + Home. On the **Review tab**, in the **Proofing group**, click the **Spelling** button, and then correct any spelling errors.

19. Right-click the **Sheet1 worksheet tab**, and then from the shortcut menu, click **Rename**. Type Fitness Participants and then press Enter. Press Ctrl + Home. Compare your screen with **Figure 4**. If directed by your instructor, display and format the worksheet formulas as described in Skill 10, and then print the worksheet.

20. **Save** the file, and then **Close** Excel. Submit the file as directed by your instructor.

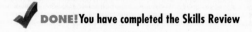

DONE! You have completed the Skills Review

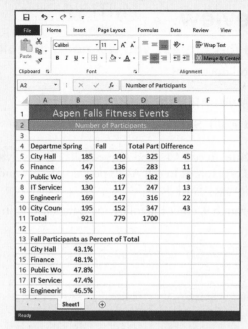

Figure 3

Excel 2016, Windows 10, Microsoft Corporation

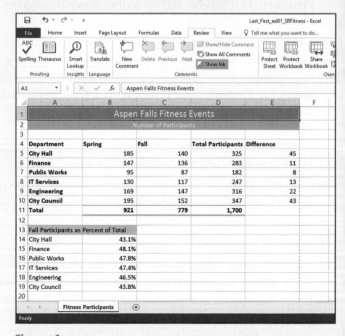

Figure 4

Excel 2016, Windows 10, Microsoft Corporation

Skills Assessment 1

To complete this project, you will need the following file:

- exl01_SA1Path

You will save your file as:

- Last_First_exl01_SA1Path

Aspen Falls				
Bike Path Construction Costs				
Location	Brush Clearing	Paving	Landscaping	Total Cost
Cornish Forest	$ 5,883	$ 15,580	$ 3,271	$ 24,734
Haack Center	6,234	18,916	1,697	26,847
Aspen Lakes	4,763	18,846	1,498	25,107
Hamilton Hills Park	4,981	17,169	1,805	23,955
Hansen Hills	4,209	14,062	2,437	20,708
Plasek Park	3,247	12,691	3,971	19,909
Price Lakes	3,648	19,387	2,927	25,962
Rodman Creek	4,515	13,120	1,934	19,569
Schroder Brook	3,862	19,166	2,036	25,064
Terry Park	2,569	17,506	1,756	21,831
Total	$ 43,911	$ 166,443	$ 23,332	$ 233,686
Location	Increase	Cost Increase		
Cornish Forest	3%	$ 742.02		
Haack Center	3%	805.41		
Aspen Lakes	5%	1,255.35		
Hamilton Hills Park	5%	1,197.75		
Hansen Hills	6%	1,242.48		
Plasek Park	6%	1,194.54		
Price Lakes	6%	1,557.72		
Rodman Creek	6%	1,174.14		
Schroder Brook	6%	1,503.84		
Terry Park	6%	1,309.86		
Total		$ 11,983.11		

Figure 1

1. Start **Excel 2016**. From your student data files, open **exl01_SA1Path**. Save the file in your chapter folder as Last_First_exl01_SA1Path Rename the **Sheet1** worksheet tab as Path Costs

2. Add the file name to the worksheet's left footer, add the current date to the center footer, and then in the right footer, insert the sheet name. Return to **Normal** view.

3. For the range **A1:E1**, merge and center and apply the **Accent5** cell style. Increase the font size to **18** points. For the range **A2:E2**, merge and center and apply the **40% - Accent5** cell style. Increase the width of column **A** to **20**. For all column and row labels **A4:E4**, **A5:A14**, and **A17:C17**, apply **Bold**.

4. For the range **E5:E13**, insert the **SUM** function to add the three costs for each row. In the range **B14:E14**, insert the **SUM** function to provide totals for each column.

5. Select the nonadjacent ranges **B5:E5** and **B14:E14**. Apply the **Currency [0]** cell style.

6. Select the range **B6:E13**, and then apply the **Comma [0]** cell style. Select the range **B14:E14**, and then apply the **Total** cell style.

7. Insert a new row above row 7. In cell **A7**, type Aspen Lakes and as the costs for the new location, type 4763 | 18846 | 1498 Use the fill handle to copy the formula in cell **E6** to cell **E7**.

8. **Copy** the location names from the range **A5:A14** to the range **A19:A28**. In cell **A29**, type Total

9. In cells **B19** and **B20**, type .03 In cells **B21** and **B22**, type .05 In cell **B23**, type .06 Use the fill handle to copy the value in cell **B23** down through cell **B28**. Select the range **B19:B28**, and then apply the **Percent Style** cell style.

10. In cell **C19**, enter a formula that calculates the cost increase by multiplying cell **E5** by cell **B19**. Fill the formula in cell **C19** down through cell **C28**.

11. In cell **C29**, insert the **SUM** function to add the total cost increase, and then apply the **Total** cell style.

12. Select the range **C20:C28**, apply the **Comma [0]** cell style, and then increase the decimal two times.

13. Use **Page Setup** to center the worksheet **Horizontally**. Set the **Gridlines** to print.

14. Review and correct any spelling errors, ignoring proper names. Press [Ctrl] + [Home].

15. **Save** the file, and then compare your screen with **Figure 1**.

16. **Close** the file, and then submit the file as directed by your instructor.

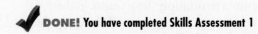 **DONE! You have completed Skills Assessment 1**

Skills Assessment 2

To complete this project, you will need the following file:

- exl01_SA2Guests

You will save your file as:

- Last_First_exl01_SA2Guests

---

1. Start **Excel 2016**. From the student data files, open **exl01_SA2Guests**. Save the file in your chapter folder as Last_First_exl01_SA2Guests

2. Rename the worksheet tab Aspen Lake Guests Add the file name to the worksheet's left footer, and then add the current date to the right footer. Return to **Normal** view.

3. In cell **D5**, construct a formula to add the *1st Qtr.* and *2nd Qtr.* guests who are *Over 70*. In cell **E5**, construct a formula to calculate the increase of guests from the *1st Qtr.* to the *2nd Qtr.* who are *Over 70*.

4. In cell **F5** for the *Over 70* row, construct a formula to divide *2nd Qtr.* guests by the *1st Half Total Guests*. Fill the formulas in **D5:F5** down through row **17**.

5. In cell **A18**, type Total and then in row **18**, insert the function to total columns **B:D**.

6. Insert a new row above row **15**, and then using the other rows as an example, enter the following data: 20 to 25 | 17196 | 19133

7. For the range **B5:E19**, apply the **Comma [0]** cell style, and then for the range **F5:F18**, apply the **Percent** cell style and display one decimal.

8. Merge and center the range **A1:F1**, and then apply the **Accent6** cell style. Increase the font size to **18**. Merge and center the range **A2:F2**, and then apply the **40% - Accent6** cell style. Increase the font size to **14**.

9. Increase the column widths of **A:C** to **11.00**, and then increase the column widths of **D:F** to **14.00**.

10. For the column and row labels, apply **Bold**. In the range **B19:D19**, apply the **Total** cell style.

11. For the range **A21:C21**, apply the **Merge Across** alignment and the **40% - Accent6** cell style.

12. In cell **C23**, construct a formula to multiply *Total Guests* in the *Over 70* row by the *Projected Percent Increase* in cell **B23**. Apply the **Comma [0]** cell style. Fill the formula down through row **36**.

13. Review and correct any spelling errors.

14. Use **Page Setup** to center the page **Horizontally**, and then set the **Gridlines** to print.

15. If you are instructed to do so, display the worksheet formulas, scale the worksheet to print on one page, and then print with the formulas displayed.

16. Compare your screen with **Figure 1**. Save the file, and then **Close** Excel. Submit the file as directed by your instructor.

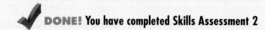 **DONE! You have completed Skills Assessment 2**

Aspen Lake Recreation Area					
Number of Guests					
Ages	1st Quarter	2nd Quarter	Total Guests	2nd Quarter Increase	2nd Quarter as Percent of Total
Over 70	14,102	15,216	29,318	1,114	51.9%
65 to 70	15,125	17,854	32,979	2,729	54.1%
60 to 65	11,175	18,273	29,448	7,098	62.1%
55 to 60	15,110	16,572	31,682	1,462	52.3%
50 to 55	19,114	19,841	38,955	727	50.9%
45 to 50	18,475	21,418	39,893	2,943	53.7%
40 to 45	12,064	13,242	25,306	1,178	52.3%
35 to 40	14,628	16,232	30,860	1,604	52.6%
30 to 35	14,543	19,975	34,518	5,432	57.9%
25 to 30	17,933	19,724	37,657	1,791	52.4%
20 to 25	17,196	19,133	36,329	1,937	52.7%
15 to 20	30,516	32,597	63,113	2,081	51.6%
10 to 15	13,469	17,439	30,908	3,970	56.4%
Under 10	17,876	19,599	37,475	1,723	52.3%
Total	231,326	267,115	498,441		

Projected 2nd Half Guests		
Ages	Projected Percentage Increase	Projected Increase in Guests
Over 70	2%	586
65 to 70	8%	2,638
60 to 65	4%	1,178
55 to 60	1%	317
50 to 55	5%	1,948
45 to 50	6%	2,394
40 to 45	9%	2,278
35 to 40	3%	926
30 to 35	6%	2,071
25 to 30	15%	5,649
20 to 25	14%	5,086
15 to 20	18%	11,360
10 to 15	21%	6,491
Under 10	23%	8,619

Figure 1

My College Enrollment

Course Name	Fall	Spring	Summer	Course Total
Algebra	1,173	938	415	2,526
Intro to Computers	1,043	857	497	2,397
Biology	578	311	253	1,142
World History	688	549	372	1,609
American History	824	598	397	1,819
Management	367	228	103	698
English	1,292	1,125	573	2,990
Semester Total	5,965	4,606	2,610	13,181

Summer as a Percent of Total	
Algebra	16.4%
Intro to Computers	20.7%
Biology	22.2%
World History	23.1%
American History	21.8%
Management	14.8%
English	19.2%

Figure 1

My Skills

To complete this project, you will need the following file:

- exl01_MYCollege

You will save your file as:

- Last_First_exl01_MYCollege

---

1. Start **Excel 2016**. From the student data files, open **exl01_MYCollege**. Save the file in your chapter folder as Last_First_exl01_MYCollege Rename the **Sheet1** worksheet tab as Enrollment

2. Add the file name to the worksheet's left footer, insert the sheet name in the right footer, and then return to **Normal** view.

3. For the range **A1:E1**, merge and center and apply the **Accent3** cell style, and then change the font size to 16

4. Increase the width of column **A** to 20 and then increase the width of columns **B:E** to 12

5. For the range **B3:E3**, center the labels. For all column and row labels, apply **Bold**.

6. For cell **E4**, insert the **SUM** function to provide the total for the row. Fill the formula in cell **E4** down through cell **E9**.

7. Insert the **SUM** function for the range **B10:E10** to provide totals for each column. With the range **B10:E10** still selected, apply the **Total** cell style.

8. For the range **B4:E10**, apply the **Comma [0]** cell style.

9. Insert a new row above row **7**. In cell **A7**, type World History and then as the

enrollment for the new course, type 688 | 549 | 372 Fill the formula in cell **E6** to cell **E7**.

10. **Copy** the course names from the range **A4:A10** to the range **A15:A21**.

11. In cell **B15**, create a formula that calculates the summer semester as a percentage of the total course enrollment by dividing cell **D4** by cell **E4**. Apply the **Percent Style** cell style, and then display one decimal. Fill the formula in cell **B15** down through cell **B21**.

12. For the range **A14:B14**, merge across and apply the **40% - Accent3** cell style.

13. Use **Page Setup** to center the worksheet **Horizontally**.

14. Check and correct any spelling errors.

15. Compare your screen with **Figure 1**. If you are instructed to do so, display the worksheet formulas, and scale the worksheet to print on one page.

16. **Save** the file, and **then Close** Excel. Submit the file as directed by your instructor.

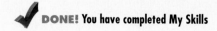 **DONE! You have completed My Skills**

Visual Skills Check

To complete this project, you will need the following file:

- Blank Excel workbook

You will save your file as:

- Last_First_exl01_VSWorkers

Start **Excel 2016.** Open a blank workbook, and then **Save** the file in your chapter folder as Last_First_exl01_VSWorkers Create the worksheet shown in **Figure 1.** The width of column **A** is **20** and the width of columns **B:F** is **13.** Construct formulas that display the results shown in columns **D** and **F,** row **13,** and the range **B16:B23.** The title uses the **Accent4** cell style, and the font size is **20.** The subtitle uses the **40% - Accent4** cell style, and the font size is **16.** The title and subtitle should be merged and centered. Using **Figure 1** as your guide, apply the **Currency [0]** cell style, the **Comma [0]** cell style, the **Total** cell style, the **Percent** cell style with one decimal place, and the **Bold** format. On the range **A15:C15,** use **Merge Across** and apply the **20% - Accent4** cell style. Rename the Sheet1 worksheet tab as Park Workers Check and correct any spelling errors. Add the file name to the left footer. **Save** the file, **Close** Excel, and then submit the file as directed by your instructor.

Aspen Falls					
Park Workers					
	Price Park	Silkwood Park	Total Workers	Wage	Total Wages
Ticket Sellers	75	52	127	$ 15	$ 1,905
Security	92	79	171	25	4,275
Landscapers	19	11	30	20	600
Life Guards	23	23	46	15	690
Cashiers	73	58	131	15	1,965
Parking Attendants	15	11	26	15	390
Maintenance	21	28	49	20	980
Cleaning	29	17	46	18	828
Total	347	279	626		$ 11,633
Price Park as Percent of Total Workers					
Ticket Sellers	59.1%				
Security	53.8%				
Landscapers	63.3%				
Life Guards	50.0%				
Cashiers	55.7%				
Parking Attendants	57.7%				
Maintenance	42.9%				
Cleaning	63.0%				

Figure 1

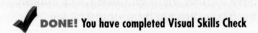

DONE! You have completed Visual Skills Check

Skills Challenge 1

To complete this project, you will need the following file:

- exl01_SC1Employees

You will save your file as:

- Last_First_exl01_SC1Employees

Start **Excel 2016**, and then from the student data files, open **exl01_SC1Employees**. Save the file in your chapter folder as Last_First_exl01_SC1Employees Duncan Chueng, the Park Operations Manager for Aspen Falls, wants to total and compare the number of employees at the city recreation areas. Using the skills you practiced in this chapter, correct the SUM function for each row and column. Format the worksheet using cell styles as practiced in this chapter. Merge and center the title across the correct columns. Correct the number formats. No decimals should display in rows 5:11. Adjust column widths as necessary to display all data. Set the

gridlines to print, and center the data horizontally on the page. Add the file name in the worksheet's left footer, and check for spelling errors. Save the file, and then close Excel. Submit the file as directed by your instructor.

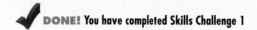 **DONE!** You have completed Skills Challenge 1

Skills Challenge 2

To complete this project, you will need the following file:

- exl01_SC2Painting

You will save your file as:

- Last_First_exl01_SC2Painting

Start **Excel 2016**, and then from the student data files, open **exl01_SC2Painting**. Save the file in your chapter folder as Last_First_exl01_SC2Painting The Art Center wants to total and compare the number of students enrolled in the painting classes in the different neighborhoods. Using the skills you practiced in this chapter, insert appropriate formulas and functions. Adjust column widths and row heights as necessary

to display all data. Format the worksheet as appropriate. Add the file name in the worksheet's left footer, and check for spelling errors. Save the file, and then close Excel. Submit the file as directed by your instructor.

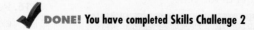 **DONE!** You have completed Skills Challenge 2

More Skills Assessment

MyITLab®
Grader

To complete this project, you will need the following files:

- Blank Excel workbook
- exl01_MSAAnalysis

You will save your files as:

- Last_First_exl01_MSATemplate
- Last_First_exl01_MSACalendar
- Last_First_exl01_MSAAnalysis

1. Start **Excel 2016**. At the top of the screen, in the search box, type Academic calendar

2. Select the template, and then Create the template file. If necessary, scroll through and find the Academic calendar template. If you do not have an Internet connection, navigate to your student data files and open exl01_MSAAssessment.

3. Save your workbook as an Excel template in your chapter folder as Last_First_exl01_MSATemplate Create a new workbook using the template, and then save your workbook in your chapter folder as Last_First_exl01_MSACalendar

4. In cell **B1**, click the **spinner arrow** to change the start year to **2018**.

5. Click the merged cell **C1**, and then click the **arrow** in the lower right corner to display the months.

6. From the displayed list, click **September**. In the worksheet, scroll down to view the months that follow.

7. Select the four sample calendar entries in the nonadjacent range **E7:F7** and cells **B9** and **F13**. Delete the four entries.

8. Click cell **G5**, the cell for September 1. Enter your name, Last First

9. Enter or replace the following data in the cells.

Date	Cell	Data
September 4	C7	New Student Orientation
September 7	F7	Review Biology Lab Procedures
September 12	D9	Access data analysis due
September 14	F9	Draft of English paper due

![September 2018 academic calendar template]

Figure 1

10. Set the print area for the range **A1:H15**, and then **Save** the workbook. Preview the document, and then compare your screen with **Figure 1**.

11. On the right side of the **Info** page, revise the **Title** to Calendar 2018

12. Enter calendar, academic, 2018 as **Tags**.

13. In the **Author** box, replace the existing text with your First and Last names, and then **Save** the workbook.

14. Open the student data file **exl01_MSAAnalysis**, and then save the file in your chapter folder as Last_First_exl01_MSAAnalysis

15. In cell **B4**, enter Anten In cell **B5**, enter Boy and then flash fill the list of first names in column B.

16. Repeat this technique to enter the last names into column **C** and the e-mail addresses into column **D**.

17. **Save** the file. Close all open windows, and then submit the files as directed by your instructor.

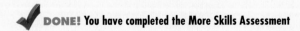 **DONE! You have completed the More Skills Assessment**

Collaborating with Google

To complete this project, you will need a Google account (refer to the Common Features chapter) and the following file:

- exl01_GPCityFees

You will save your file as:

- Last_First_exl01_GPSnip

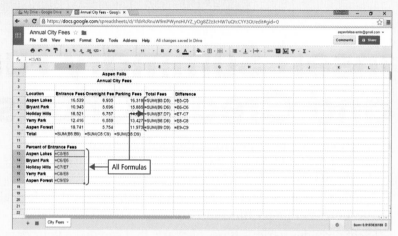

Figure 1

1. Open the Google Chrome web browser. Log into your Google account, and then click **Google Apps** .

2. Click **Drive** to open Google Drive. If you receive a pop-up message, read the message, and then click **Next**. Read each message, and then close the dialog box.

3. Click **New**, and then click **Google Sheets** to open a blank spreadsheet.

4. Open the workbook from the student data file **exl01_GPCityFees**. Copy the range **A1:F17** from the *City Fees* worksheet, and then paste it in cell **A1** of the blank Google worksheet.

5. Click the spreadsheet title, **Untitled spreadsheet**. Type Annual City Fees as the name of the spreadsheet, and then click **OK**. Rename the *Sheet1* worksheet tab as City Fees

6. Select the range **A1:F1**, click **Merge** , and then click **Center** . Repeat this process to apply the same formatting to the range **A2:F2**.

7. Select the range **B10:D10**, and then insert the **SUM** function to calculate total fees. Repeat this technique to apply the **SUM** function to the range **E5:E9** to calculate the total for each location.

8. In the range **F5:F9**, enter a formula to calculate the difference, subtracting Overnight Fees from Total Fees.

9. Select the range **B5:F10**. Click **Format**. Point to **Number**, click the **Financial** number format, and then select **Decrease decimal places** two times.

10. Apply **Bold** format to all worksheet headings and row and column headings.

11. In the range **B13:B17**, enter a formula to calculate Overnight Fees divided by Total Fees for each location. With the range **B13:B17** still selected, point to **Format**, point to **Number**, and then click **Percent**.

12. Click **View**, select **All Formulas**, and then compare your screen with **Figure 1**.

13. Click **Share** , and then in the **Share with others** dialog box, type AspenFallsEvents@gmail.com

14. In the **Add a note** text box, type Please review and contact me with any questions.

15. Click **Send**. Press , type snip and then press to start the **Snipping Tool**. Click the **New arrow**, and then click **Window Snip**. Point to the Windows Explorer window, and then when a red border displays around the window, click one time.

16. In the **Snipping Tool** mark-up window, click the **Save Snip** button . In the **Save As** dialog box, navigate to your Excel Chapter 1 folder. Be sure the **Save as type** box displays **JPEG file**. Name the file Last_First_exl01_GPSnip and then press .

17. Close all windows, and then submit the file as directed by your instructor.

DONE! You have completed Collaborating with Google

Insert Summary Functions and Create Charts

- Functions are prewritten formulas that have two parts—the name of the function and the arguments that specify the values or cells to be used by the function.

- Functions analyze data to answer financial, statistical, or logical questions. Summary functions are used to recap information.

- Excel provides various types of charts that can make your data easier to understand.

- Column charts show data changes over a period of time or illustrate comparisons among items.

- Pie charts illustrate how each part relates to the whole. Pie charts display the relative sizes of items in a single data series.

- Charts can be enhanced with effects such as 3-D and soft shadows to create compelling graphical summaries.

Djile/Fotolia

Aspen Falls City Hall

In this chapter, you will finish a workbook for Thelma Perkins, a Risk Management Specialist in the Finance Department. The workbook displays the department expenditures for Aspen Falls. The City Council requires that the Finance Department present the departmental information annually for review and approval.

Companies use formulas and statistical functions to manipulate and summarize data to make better decisions. Summary results can include the data totals or averages. Results can be displayed graphically as charts, providing a visual representation of data. Commonly used chart types include line charts to illustrate trends over time or bar charts to illustrate comparisons among individual items. Based on the type of data selected, the Quick Analysis tools provide chart type options.

In this project, you will open an existing workbook, construct formulas containing absolute cell references, and AutoFill the formulas to other cells. You will insert the statistical functions AVERAGE, MAX, and MIN. You will create and format column charts and pie charts and insert WordArt. Finally, you will prepare the chart sheet and the worksheet to meet printing requirements.

Time to complete all 10 skills — 60 to 90 minutes

Outcome

Using the skills in this chapter, you will be able to modify cell and number formats; create formulas using absolute cell references and average, minimum, and maximum functions; create, edit, and format pie and column charts; and update print settings for multiple worksheets.

Objectives

2.1 Construct statistical functions

2.2 Generate formulas using absolute cell references

2.3 Apply cell and number formatting

2.4 Create, edit, and format basic charts

2.5 Modify workbook print settings

Student data file needed for this chapter:

exl02_Expenditures

You will save your file as:

Last_First_exl02_Expenditures

SKILLS

Skills 1-10 Training

At the end of this chapter you will be able to:

Skill 1 Align and Wrap Text
Skill 2 Apply Absolute Cell References
Skill 3 Format Numbers
Skill 4 Insert the AVERAGE Function
Skill 5 Insert the MIN and MAX Functions
Skill 6 Create Column Charts
Skill 7 Format Column Charts
Skill 8 Create and Format Pie Charts
Skill 9 Update Charts and Insert WordArt
Skill 10 Preview and Print Multiple Worksheets

MORE SKILLS

Skill 11 Validate Workbooks for Accessibility
Skill 12 Change Chart Types
Skill 13 Copy Excel Data to Word Documents
Skill 14 Create Line Charts

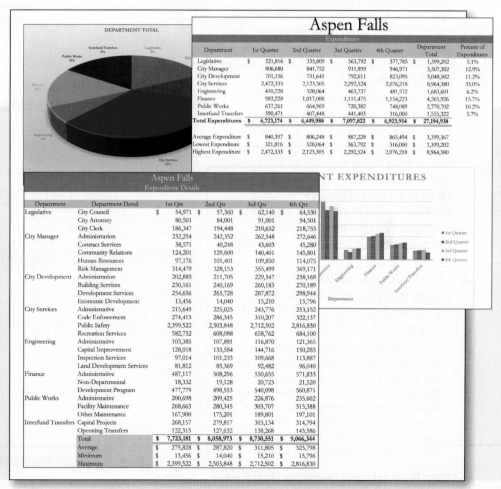

 **WATCH** SKILL 2.1

▶ The ***Text wrap*** format displays text on multiple lines within a cell.

1. Start **Excel 2016**, open the student data file **exl02_Expenditures**, and then compare your screen with **Figure 1**.

   When columns in a worksheet are not wide enough, the labels in the cells will be truncated and values will display as # characters.

2. On the **File tab**, click **Save As**. On the **Save As** page, click the **Browse** button. Navigate to the location where you are saving your files. Click **New folder**, type Excel Chapter 2 and then press [Enter] two times. In the **File name** box, name the workbook Last_First_exl02_Expenditures and then press [Enter].

3. Verify **Expenditures** is the active worksheet. Click the **Insert tab**, and then in the **Text group**, click the **Header & Footer** button. In the **Navigation group**, click the **Go to Footer** button. Click just above the word **Footer**, and then in the **Header & Footer Elements group**, click the **File Name** button. Click a cell above the footer. On the status bar, click the **Normal** button ▦, and then press [Ctrl] + [Home].

4. Click cell **B2**. Point at the fill handle to display the ✚ pointer, and then drag right through cell **E2** to AutoFill the labels. Compare your screen with **Figure 2**.

   Excel's AutoFill feature can generate a series of values into adjacent cells. A ***series*** is a group of numbers, text, dates, or time periods that come one after another in succession. For example, the months *January, February, March* are a series. Likewise, *1st Quarter, 2nd Quarter, 3rd Quarter*, and *4th Quarter* form a series.

■ **Continue to the next page to complete the skill** ▶

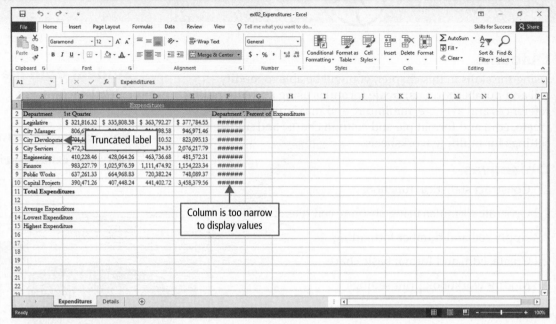

Figure 1

Excel 2016, Windows 10, Microsoft Corporation

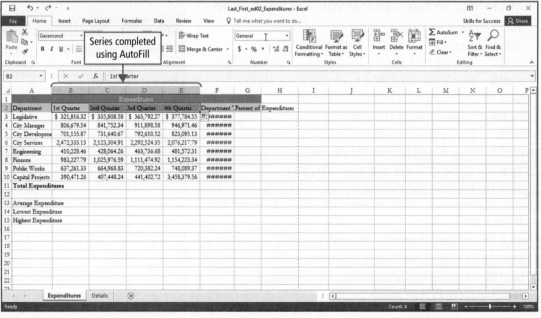

Figure 2

Excel 2016, Windows 10, Microsoft Corporation

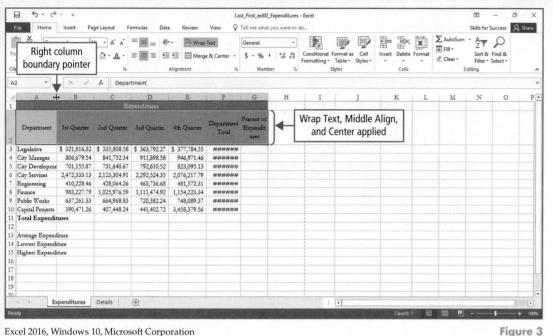

Excel 2016, Windows 10, Microsoft Corporation

Figure 3

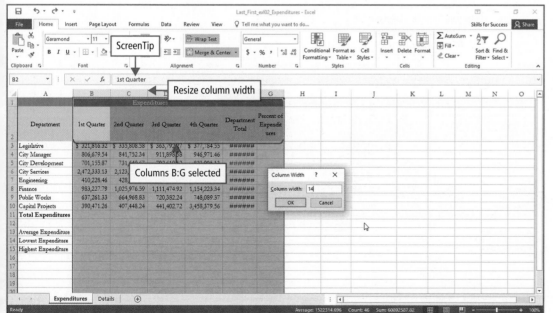

Excel 2016, Windows 10, Microsoft Corporation

Figure 4

5. Select the range **A2:G2**. On the **Home tab**, in the **Alignment group**, click the **Wrap Text** button, the **Middle Align** button, and the **Center** button.

6. In the column heading area, point to the right boundary of column **A** to display the pointer, as shown in **Figure 3**.

7. With the pointer displayed, double-click to **AutoFit** the column.

   AutoFit—automatically change the column width to accommodate the longest entry.

8. In the column heading area, click the column **B** heading, and then drag right through column **G** to select columns **B:G**. Right-click the boundary of column G to display the Column Width box, type 14 in the box, and then compare your screen with **Figure 4**. Click OK to change the width.

9. Select the range **A3:A10**, and then in the **Alignment group**, click the **Increase Indent** button.

10. **Save** the file.

■ **You have completed Skill 1 of 10**

▶ The Quick Analysis button is used to apply conditional formatting or to insert charts and totals.

▶ Excel uses rules to check for formula errors. When a formula breaks a rule, the cell displays an *error indicator*—a green triangle that indicates a possible error in a formula.

▶ An *absolute cell reference* is a cell reference address that remains the same when it is copied or filled to other cells. To make a cell reference absolute, insert a dollar sign ($) before the row and column references.

Obj 5.1.4 C

1. Select **B3:F10**, click the **Quick Analysis** button, and then compare your screen with **Figure 1**.

2. In the **Quick Analysis** gallery, click **Totals**, and then click the first option—**SUM**—to insert column totals.

3. Click cell **G3**, and then type =F3/F11 On the formula bar, click the **Enter** button. Double-click cell **G3** to display the range finder, and then compare your screen with **Figure 2**.

   The *range finder* outlines all of the cells referenced in a formula. It is useful for verifying which cells are used in a formula and for editing formulas.

4. Press Esc to close the range finder. Point to the **G3** fill handle, and then AutoFill the formula down through **G10** to display error values.

   Error values—messages that display whenever a formula or function cannot perform its calculations. The #DIV/0! error value displays in a cell whenever the underlying formula attempts to divide by zero.

■ **Continue to the next page to complete the skill**

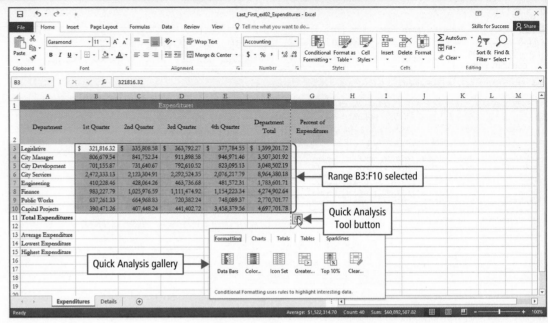

Figure 1

Excel 2016, Windows 10, Microsoft Corporation

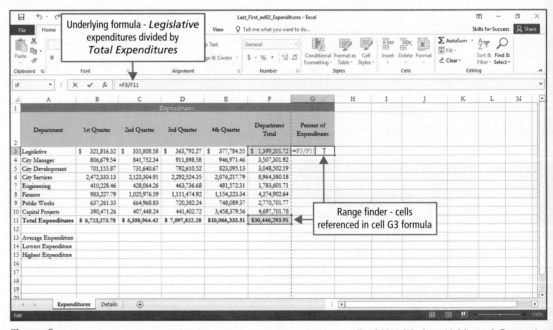

Figure 2

Excel 2016, Windows 10, Microsoft Corporation

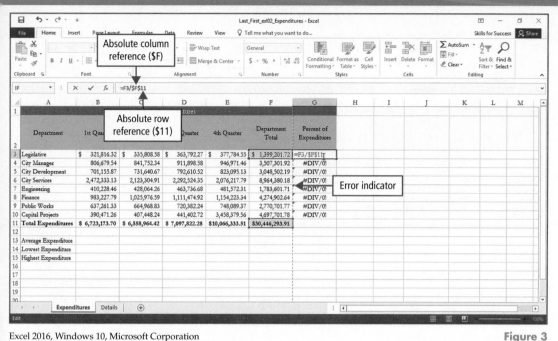

Excel 2016, Windows 10, Microsoft Corporation

Figure 3

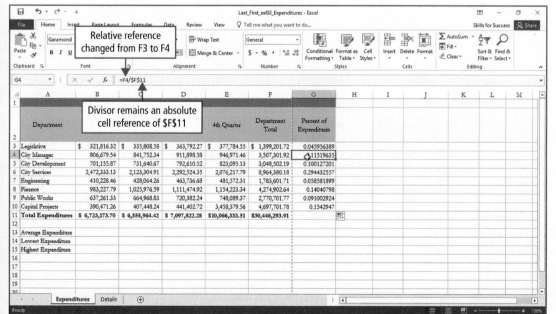

Excel 2016, Windows 10, Microsoft Corporation

Figure 4

5. Click cell **G4**. To the left of the cell, point to the **Error Message** button to display the ScreenTip—*The formula or function used is dividing by zero or empty cells.*

6. Double-click cell **G4** to display the range finder.

The formula was copied with a relative cell reference. In the copied formula, the cell reference to cell F4 is correct, but the formula is dividing by the value in cell F12, an empty cell. In this calculation, the divisor must be cell F11.

7. Press Esc , and then double-click cell **G3**. In the formula, click after the reference to cell F11, and then press F4 to insert a dollar sign ($) before the column reference *F* and the row reference *11*, as shown in **Figure 3**.

MOS
Obj 4.1.1 C

The dollar signs are used to indicate an absolute cell reference.

8. On the formula bar, click the **Enter** button ✔, and then AutoFill the formula in cell **G3** down through cell **G10**.

9. Click cell **G4**, and verify that the divisor refers to cell *$F$11*, as shown in **Figure 4**.

The cell reference for the row *City Manager Department Total* changed relative to its row; however, the value used as the divisor—*Total Expenditures* in cell F11—remains absolute.

10. Press the ↓ two times and verify the contents of each cell. Notice that the divisor remains constant—$F$11—while the dividend changes relative to the row.

11. Save 💾 the file.

■ **You have completed Skill 2 of 10**

▶ A **number format** is a specific way that Excel displays numbers; for example, the number of decimals or whether commas and special symbols, such as dollar signs, display.

▶ By default, Excel displays the **General format**—a number format that does not display commas or trailing zeros to the right of a decimal point.

1. Click cell **B2**, and then on the **Home tab**, in the **Number group**, notice that *General* displays. Compare your screen with **Figure 1**.

2. Select the range **B3:F3**, press Ctrl, and then select the range **B11:F11**. In the **Number group**, click the **Decrease Decimal** button ⬚ two times to round the number and hide the decimals. Select the range **B4:F10**. In the **Number group**, click the **Decrease Decimal** button ⬚ two times. Click cell **B6**, and then compare your screen with **Figure 2**.

   The Decrease Decimal button hides the displayed value decimals. The underlying value shows the decimals.

3. Select the range **G3:G10**. In the **Number group**, click the **Percent Style** button %, and then click the **Increase Decimal** button ⬚ one time to add one decimal to the applied Percent Style. In the **Alignment group**, click the **Center** button ≡.

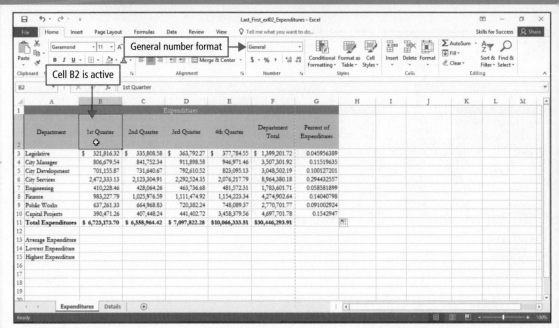

Figure 1

Excel 2016, Windows 10, Microsoft Corporation

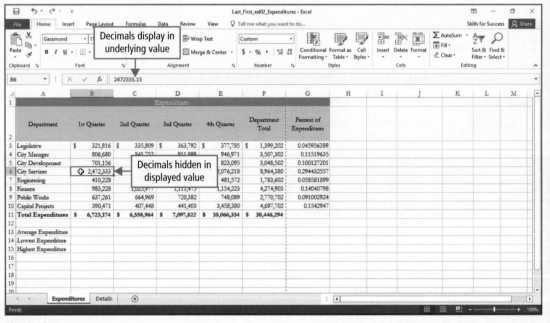

Figure 2

Excel 2016, Windows 10, Microsoft Corporation

■ **Continue to the next page to complete the skill**

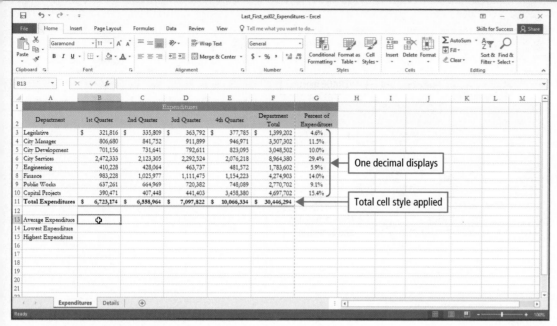

Excel 2016, Windows 10, Microsoft Corporation

Figure 3

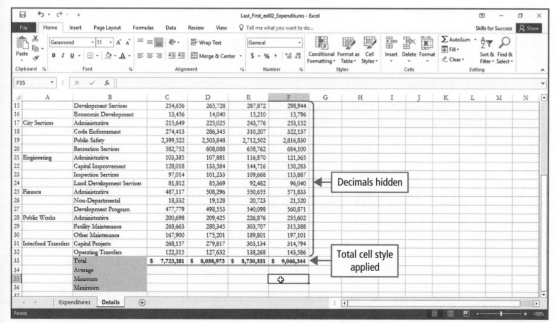

Excel 2016, Windows 10, Microsoft Corporation

Figure 4

4. Select the range **B11:F11**. In the **Styles group**, click the **Cell Styles** button, and then under **Titles and Headings**, click **Total**. Click cell **B13**, and then compare your screen with Figure 3.

5. Along the bottom of the Excel window, notice the worksheet tabs. Click the **Details** worksheet tab to make it the active worksheet.

    Worksheet tabs, the labels along the lower border of the workbook window that identify each worksheet.

6. Click cell **C5**. Hold down the Ctrl + Shift keys. With both keys held down, press the ↓ one time and the → one time to select the range C5:F32.

7. With the range **C5:F32** selected, click the **Quick Analysis** button. In the **Quick Analysis** gallery, click **Totals**, and then click the first option—**SUM**.

8. Select the range **C5:F5**, press Ctrl, and then select the range **C33:F33**. In the **Number group**, click the **Decrease Decimal** button two times. Select the range **C6:F32**. In the **Number group**, click the **Decrease Decimal** button two times.

9. Select the range **C33:F33**, and then apply the **Total** cell style. Click cell **F35**, and then compare your screen with Figure 4.

    MOS Obj 2.2.7 C

10. **Save** the file.

- **You have completed Skill 3 of 10**

▶ **Statistical functions** are predefined formulas that describe a collection of data—for example, averages, maximums, and minimums.

▶ The **AVERAGE function** adds a group of values and then divides the result by the number of values in the group.

1. Click the **Expenditures** worksheet tab, and then click cell **B13**. On the **Home tab**, in the **Editing group**, click the **AutoSum arrow**, and then in the list of functions, click **Average**. Look in the formula bar and in cell B13 to verify that the range *B3:B12* is the suggested range of cells that will be averaged, as shown in **Figure 1**.

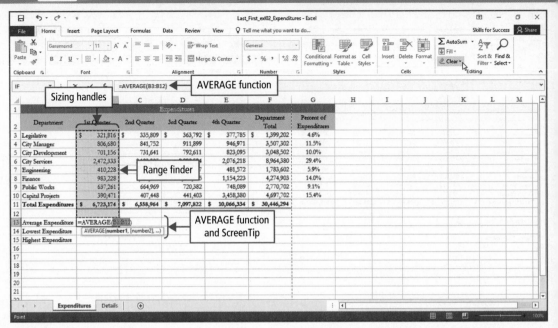

Figure 1   Excel 2016, Windows 10, Microsoft Corporation

   The range in parentheses is the function **argument**—the values that a function uses to perform operations or calculations. The arguments each function uses are specific to that function. Common arguments include numbers, text, cell references, and range names.

   When data is above or to the left of a selected cell, the function argument will automatically be entered. Often, you will need to edit the argument range.

2. With the function argument still active in cell B13, click cell **B3**. On the range finder, click a bottom corner sizing handle, and then drag down to select the argument range **B3:B10**, to exclude the *Total Expenditures* value in cell B11. On the formula bar, click the **Enter** button ☑ to display the result *$840,397*. Compare your screen with **Figure 2**.

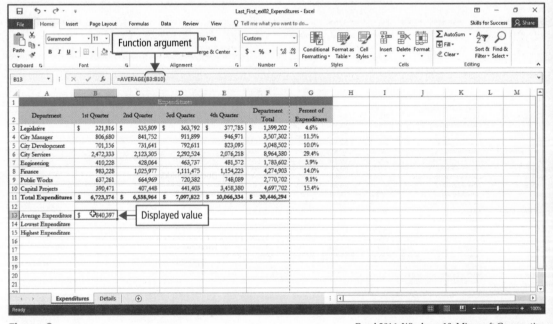

Figure 2   Excel 2016, Windows 10, Microsoft Corporation

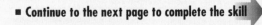

■ **Continue to the next page to complete the skill**

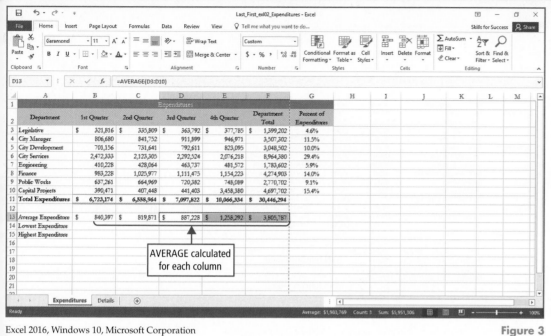

AVERAGE calculated for each column

Excel 2016, Windows 10, Microsoft Corporation

Figure 3

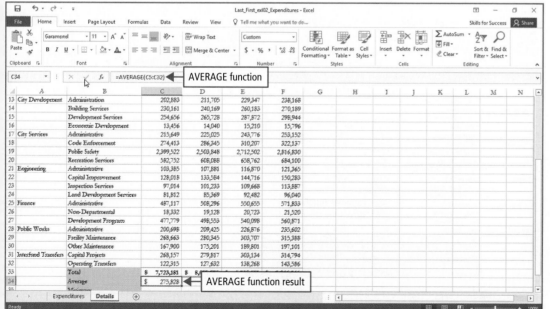

AVERAGE function

AVERAGE function result

Excel 2016, Windows 10, Microsoft Corporation

Figure 4

3. Click cell **C13**. In the **Editing group**, click the **AutoSum arrow**, and then in the list of functions, click **Average**. In the formula bar and in the cell, notice that Excel proposes to average the value in cell *B13*, not the values in column C.

4. With cell reference **B13** highlighted in the function argument, click cell **C3**, and then use the range finder sizing handle to select the range **C3:C10**. On the formula bar, click the **Enter** button ☑ to display the result *$819,871*.

5. Click cell **D13**. Using the techniques just practiced, enter the **AVERAGE** function using the argument range **D3:D10**, and then on the formula bar, click the **Enter** button ☑.

6. Verify that cell *D13* is the active cell, and then AutoFill the function to the right through cell **F13**. Compare your sheet to **Figure 3**.

7. Click the **Details** worksheet tab, and then click cell **C34**. Enter the **AVERAGE** function using the argument range **C5:C32**. Do not include the *Total* value in cell *C33* in the function argument. Compare your sheet to **Figure 4**.

8. Display the worksheet footers, click in the left footer, and then click the **File Name** button. Click in the right footer, and then click the **Sheet Name** button. Click in a cell above the footer, and then press Ctrl + Home . Return to **Normal** view.

9. **Save** ☐ the file.

■ **You have completed Skill 4 of 10**

▶ The **MIN function** returns the smallest value in a range of cells.

▶ The **MAX function** returns the largest value in a range of cells.

1. On the **Details** worksheet, click cell **C35**. Type =Mi and then in the **Formula AutoComplete** list, double-click **MIN**. With the insertion point blinking in the function argument, click cell **C32**, and then use the range finder top corner sizing handles to drag up and select the range **C5:C32**. Press Enter to display the result *$13,456*.

> The MIN function evaluates the range provided in the function argument—C5:C32—and then returns the lowest value—*$13,456*. Here, the *Total* and *Average* values in cells *C33* and *C34* should not be included in the argument range.

2. Verify that **C36** is the active cell. Type =Ma and then in the **Formula AutoComplete** list, double-click **MAX**. Using the technique just practiced, select the range **C5:C32**, and then on the formula bar, click the **Enter** button ✓ to display the result *$2,399,522*. Compare your screen with **Figure 1**.

> The MAX function evaluates all of the values in the range C5:C32 and then returns the highest value found in the range.

3. Select the range **C34:C36**. AutoFill the formulas to the right through column **F**, and then compare your screen with **Figure 2**.

> In this manner, you can AutoFill several different functions or formulas at the same time. Here, the different functions at the beginning of each row are filled across the columns.

■ **Continue to the next page to complete the skill**

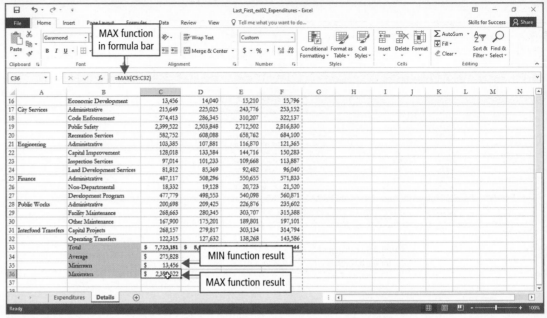

Figure 1

Excel 2016, Windows 10, Microsoft Corporation

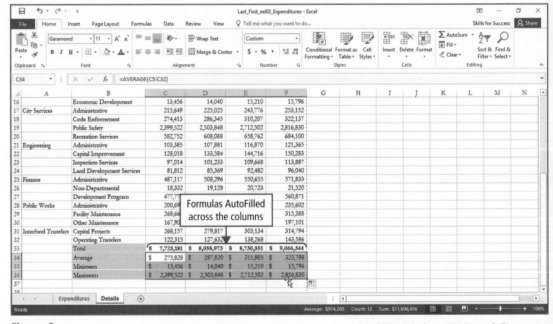

Figure 2

Excel 2016, Windows 10, Microsoft Corporation

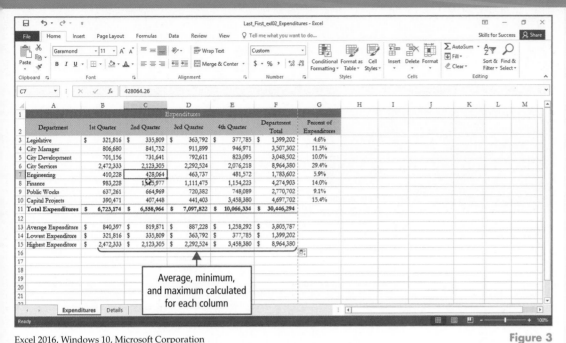

Excel 2016, Windows 10, Microsoft Corporation

Figure 3

Excel 2016, Windows 10, Microsoft Corporation

Figure 4

4. Click the **Expenditures** worksheet tab. In cell **B14**, repeat the technique just practiced to insert the **MIN** function using the range **B3:B10** as the function argument in the parentheses. Verify that the result is *$321,816*.

5. In cell **B15**, insert the **MAX** function using the range **B3:B10** as the function argument. Verify that the result is *$2,472,333*. Take care that the argument range does not include the cells with the total expenditures or average expenditures.

6. AutoFill the formulas in **B14:B15** to the right through column **F**. Review the functions, and verify that the lowest and highest values in each column were selected from each of the ranges for the MIN and MAX functions. Click cell **C7**, and then compare your screen with Figure 3.

7. With cell **C7** as the active cell, type 328064 and then press Enter . In cell **C8**, type 4025977 and then press Enter . Verify that the MIN and MAX values in cells **C14** and **C15** and the SUM and AVERAGE functions were automatically updated. Compare your screen with Figure 4.

8. Save the file.

■ **You have completed Skill 5 of 10**

▶ **WATCH** SKILL 2.6

▶ A *chart* is a graphical representation of data used to show comparisons, patterns, and trends.

▶ A *column chart* is useful for illustrating comparisons among related numbers.

MOS
Obj 5.1.4 C

1. On the **Expenditures** worksheet, select the range **A2:E10**—do *not* include the *Department Total* column or the *Total Expenditures* row in your selection. Click the **Quick Analysis** button 📊, and then in the **Quick Analysis** gallery, click **Charts**. Compare your screen with **Figure 1**.

MOS
Obj 5.1.1 C

2. In the **Quick Analysis** gallery, click the third chart—**Clustered Column**—to insert the chart and display the *Chart Tools* contextual tabs. Compare your screen with **Figure 2**.

When you insert a chart in this manner, an *embedded chart*—a chart that is placed on the worksheet containing the data—is created. Embedded charts are beneficial when you want to view or print a chart with its source data.

An *axis* is a line bordering the chart plot area that is used as a frame of reference for measurement. The *category axis* is the axis that displays the category labels. A *category label* is nonnumeric text that identifies the categories of data. Here, the worksheet's row labels—the department names in A3:A10—are used for the category labels.

The *value axis* is the axis that displays the worksheet's numeric data.

The *y-axis* is the vertical axis of a chart, and the *x-axis* is the horizontal axis of a chart.

■ **Continue to the next page to complete the skill**

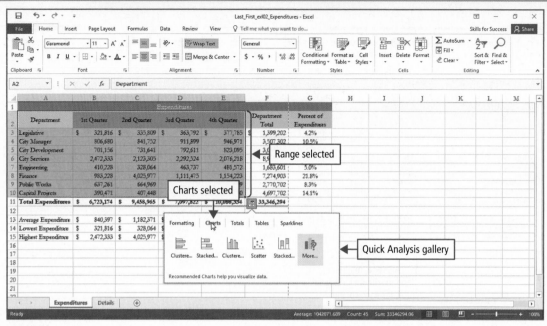

Figure 1

Excel 2016, Windows 10, Microsoft Corporation

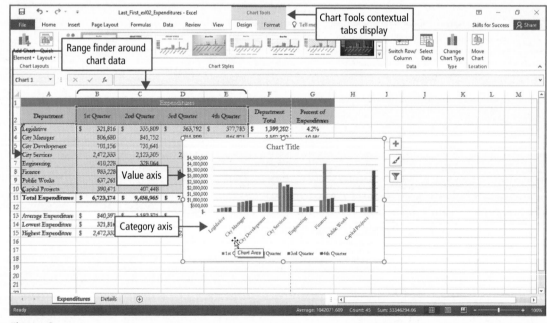

Figure 2

Excel 2016, Windows 10, Microsoft Corporation

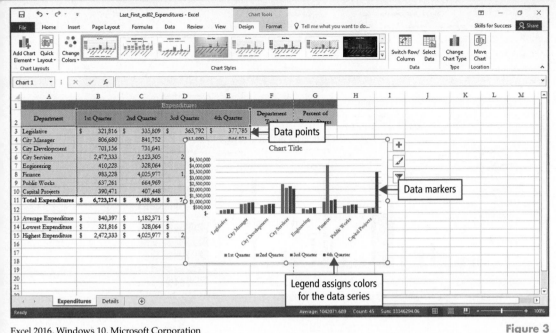

Excel 2016, Windows 10, Microsoft Corporation

Figure 3

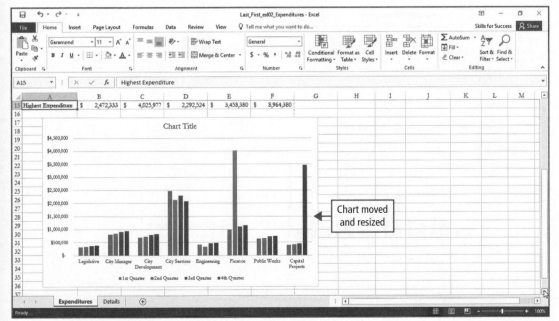

Excel 2016, Windows 10, Microsoft Corporation

Figure 4

3. On the left side of the chart, locate the numerical scale, and then on the bottom, locate the quarters displayed in the legend. Compare your screen with **Figure 3**.

In the worksheet, each cell in the blue range finder is referred to as a *data point*—a chart value that originates in a worksheet cell. Each data point is represented in a chart by a *data marker*—a column, a bar, an area, a dot, a pie slice, or another symbol that represents a single data point.

Data points that are related to one another form a *data series*, and each data series has a unique color or pattern represented in the chart *legend*—a box that identifies the patterns or colors that are assigned to the data series or categories in the chart. Here, each quarter is a different data series, and the legend shows the color assigned to each quarter.

4. With the chart selected, point to the upper border of the chart to display the [⬚] pointer, and then move the chart to position its upper left corner in the middle of cell **A17**. If you are working with a touch screen, you can touch the chart and slide it to the correct position.

5. Scroll down to display row **36**. Point to the lower right corner of the chart to display the [⬚] pointer, and then drag to resize the chart until the lower right chart corner is in the middle of cell **G36**. Click cell **G15**, and then compare your screen with **Figure 4**.

Obj 5.2.1 C

6. **Save** [💾] the file.

▪ **You have completed Skill 6 of 10**

▶ You can modify the overall look of a chart by applying a ***chart layout***—a prebuilt set of chart elements that can include a title, a legend, or labels.

▶ You can modify the overall look of a chart by applying a ***chart style***—a prebuilt chart format that applies an overall visual look to a chart by modifying its graphic effects, colors, and backgrounds.

1. Click the border of the chart to select the chart and display the chart buttons.

2. To the right of the chart, click the **Chart Styles** button 🖌, and then click **Style 3**. At the top of the **Chart Styles** gallery, click the **Color tab**, and then under **Colorful**, click **Color 3**. Compare your screen with **Figure 1**.

3. Click the **Chart Styles** button 🖌 to close the gallery.

4. On the **Design tab**, in the **Chart Layouts group**, click the **Quick Layout** button. Point at the different layouts to preview the layouts on the chart. Point at **Layout 9**, and then compare your screen with **Figure 2**.

5. In the **Quick Layout** gallery, click **Layout 9** to add the axes titles and to move the legend to the right side of the chart.

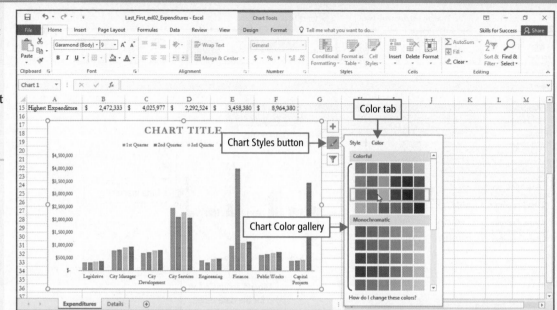

Figure 1   Excel 2016, Windows 10, Microsoft Corporation

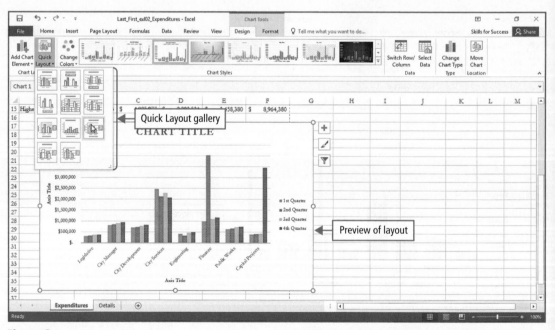

Figure 2   Excel 2016, Windows 10, Microsoft Corporation

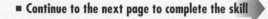
■ **Continue to the next page to complete the skill**

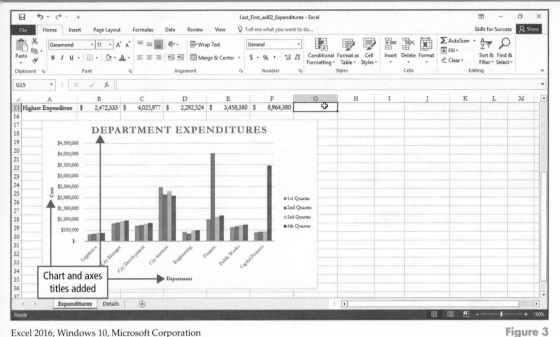

Excel 2016, Windows 10, Microsoft Corporation

Figure 3

Chart and axes titles added

6. At the top of the chart, click the text *Chart Title*, and then type Department Expenditures to insert the text into the formula bar. Press Enter to accept the text. Verify that your text replaced any text in the chart title.

7. Below the horizontal axis, click the text *Axis Title*, type Department and then press Enter.

8. To the left of the vertical axis, click the text *Axis Title*, type Cost and then press Enter.

9. Click cell **G15** to deselect the chart. **Save** the file, and then compare your screen with **Figure 3**.

10. Take a moment to examine the various types of charts available in Excel, as summarized in **Figure 4**.

■ **You have completed Skill 7 of 10**

Chart Types Commonly Used in Excel	
Chart type	**Used to**
Column	Illustrate data changes over a period of time or illustrate comparisons among items.
Line	Illustrate trends over time, with time displayed along the horizontal axis and the data point values connected by a line.
Pie	Illustrate the relationship of parts to a whole.
Bar	Illustrate comparisons among individual items.
Area	Emphasize the magnitude of change over time.

Figure 4

▶ A *pie chart* displays the relationship of parts to a whole.

▶ A *chart sheet* is a workbook sheet that contains only a chart and is useful when you want to view a chart separately from the worksheet data.

1. Verify that *Expenditures* is the active sheet. Select the range **A2:A10**. Hold down Ctrl, and then select the nonadjacent range **F2:F10**.

2. On the **Insert tab**, in the **Charts group**, click the **Recommended Charts** button, and then compare your screen with **Figure 1**.

3. In the **Insert Chart** dialog box, click the **Pie** thumbnail, and then click **OK**.

   Here, the row labels identify the slices of the pie chart, and the department totals are the data series that determine the size of each pie slice.

4. On the **Design tab**, in the **Location group**, click the **Move Chart** button. In the **Move Chart** dialog box, select the **New sheet** option button. In the **New sheet** box, replace the highlighted text *Chart1* with Expenditure Chart as shown in **Figure 2**.

5. In the **Move Chart** dialog box, click **OK** to move the pie chart to a chart sheet.

6. On the **Design tab**, in the **Type group**, click the **Change Chart Type** button. In the **Change Chart Type** dialog box, click the **3-D Pie** thumbnail, and then click **OK**.

   The chart is changed from a two-dimensional chart to a three-dimensional chart. **3-D**, which is short for *three-dimensional*, refers to an image that appears to have all three spatial dimensions—length, width, and depth.

■ **Continue to the next page to complete the skill**

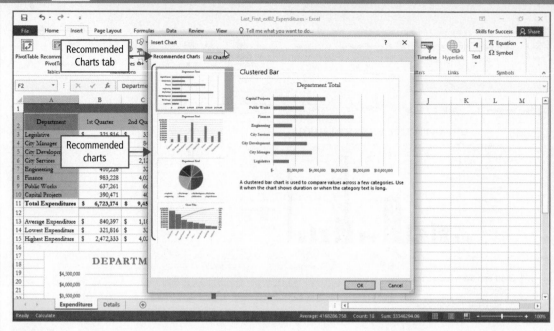

Figure 1

Excel 2016, Windows 10, Microsoft Corporation

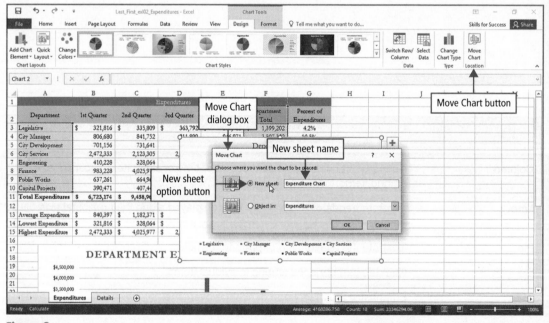

Figure 2

Excel 2016, Windows 10, Microsoft Corporation

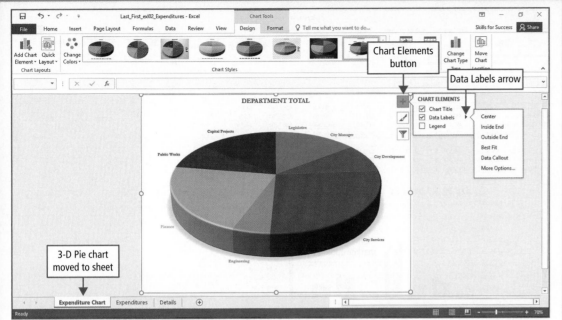

7. To the right of the chart, click the **Chart Styles** button. In the **Chart Styles** gallery, scroll down, and then click **Style 8**.

8. To the right of the chart, click the **Chart Elements** button. Under **Chart Elements**, point at **Data Labels**, and then click the **Data Labels arrow**. Compare your screen with Figure 3.

9. In the **Data Labels** list, click **More Options** to open the Format Data Labels pane.

10. In the **Format Data Labels** pane, under **Label Contains**, select the **Percentage** check box. Verify that the **Category Name** check box is selected, and then clear any other check boxes.

11. At the top of the pane, click the **Label Options arrow**, and then click **Chart Area** to open the Format Chart Area pane. In the **Format Chart Area** pane, click the **Fill & Line** button, and then click **Fill**. Click the **Gradient fill** option button, and verify that the Type is Linear. Compare your screen with Figure 4.

12. **Close** the **Format Chart Area** pane.

13. On the **Insert tab**, in the **Text group**, click the **Header & Footer** button. In the **Page Setup** dialog box, click the **Custom Footer** button. Verify that the insertion point is in the **Left section** box, and then click the **Insert File Name** button. Click in the **Right section** box, and then click the **Insert Sheet Name** button. Click **OK** two times.

14. **Save** the file.

■ **You have completed Skill 8 of 10**

Excel 2016, Windows 10, Microsoft Corporation

Figure 3

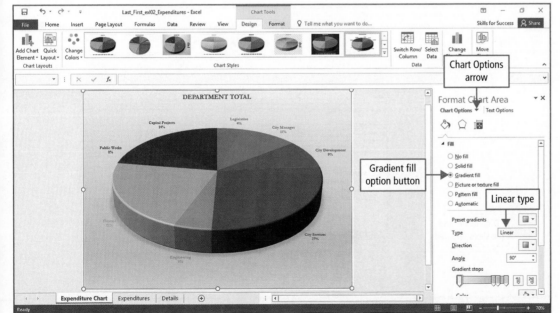

Excel 2016, Windows 10, Microsoft Corporation

Figure 4

▶ A chart's data series and labels are linked to the source data in the worksheet. When worksheet values are changed, the chart is automatically updated.

1. Click the **Expenditures** worksheet tab to display the worksheet. Scroll as necessary to display row **8** at the top of the window and the chart at the bottom of the window. In the column chart, note the height of the *Finance* data marker for the 2nd Quarter and the *Capital Projects* data marker for the 4th Quarter.

2. Click cell **C8**. Type 1017000 and then press Enter to accept the new value. Notice the animation in the chart when changes are made to its source data. Compare your screen with **Figure 1**.

3. Click cell **E10**, type 316000 and then press Enter. In cell G10, the *Capital Projects* expenditure now represents 5.7% of the projected total.

4. Click the **Expenditure Chart** worksheet tab to display the pie chart. Verify that in the pie chart, the slice for *Capital Projects* displays 6%.

   When underlying data is changed, the pie chart percentages and pie slices are automatically recalculated and resized. On the chart, 5.7% is rounded up to 6%.

5. Right-click the *Capital Projects* data label to select all of the data labels, and then in the shortcut menu, click **Font**. In the **Size** box, type 11 Compare your screen with **Figure 2**, and then click **OK**.

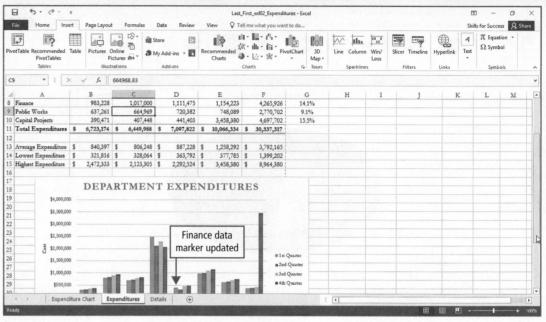

Figure 1

Excel 2016, Windows 10, Microsoft Corporation

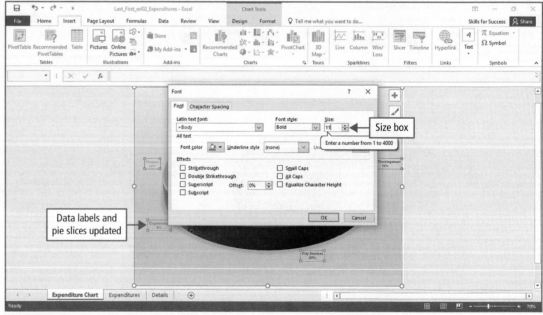

Figure 2

Excel 2016, Windows 10, Microsoft Corporation

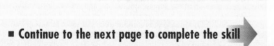

■ **Continue to the next page to complete the skill**

Excel 2016, Windows 10, Microsoft Corporation

Figure 3

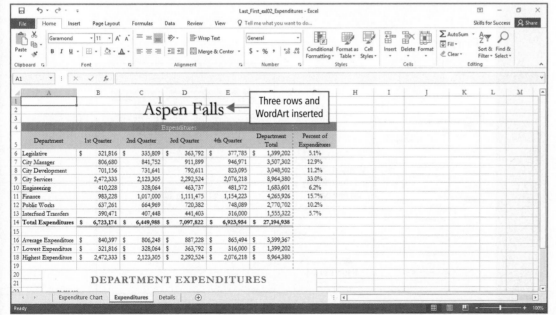

Excel 2016, Windows 10, Microsoft Corporation

Figure 4

6. Click the **Expenditures** worksheet tab, and then in cell **A10**, change *Capital Projects* to Interfund Transfers Press Enter , and then scroll down to verify that the column chart category label changed. Compare your screen with **Figure 3**.

7. Click the **Expenditure Chart** worksheet tab, and verify that the data label on the pie chart displays as *Interfund Transfers*.

8. Click the **Expenditures** worksheet tab. Scroll up, and then select the range **A1:G3**. On the **Home tab**, in the **Cells group**, click the **Insert arrow**, and then click **Insert Sheet Rows** to insert three blank rows.

Obj 1.3.4 C

9. On the **Insert tab**, in the **Text group**, click the **Insert WordArt** button 4▾. In the **WordArt** gallery, click the first style in the first row—**Fill - Black, Text 1, Shadow**. Immediately type Aspen Falls

10. Select the WordArt text. On the Mini toolbar, click the **Font Size** button 11 ▾, and then click **32**.

11. Point to the bottom border of the WordArt box, and then with the pointer, drag to position the WordArt object to approximately the range **C1:E3**. Click cell **A1** to deselect the WordArt, and then compare your screen with **Figure 4**.

12. Save 🖫 the file.

■ **You have completed Skill 9 of 10**

▶ Before you print an Excel worksheet, you can use Page Layout view to preview and adjust the printed document.

1. Verify that *Expenditures* is the active worksheet. Scroll down, and then click the column chart to select the chart. Click the **File tab**, and then click **Print**. Compare your screen with **Figure 1**.

    When an embedded chart is selected, only the chart will print.

2. Click the **Back** button ⊙. Click cell **A19** to deselect the chart.

3. Click the **View tab**, and then in the **Workbook Views group**, click the **Page Layout** button. On the left side of the status bar, notice that *Page: 1 of 2* displays, informing you that the data and the column chart would print on two pages.

MOS
Obj 1.5.4 C

4. Click the **Page Layout tab**, and then in the **Scale to Fit group**, click the **Width arrow**. Click **1 page**. Click the **File tab**, and then click **Print**. Compare your screen with **Figure 2**.

    1 of 1 displays at the bottom of the screen, indicating that the WordArt, the data, and the column chart will all print on one page.

5. Click the **Back** button ⊙. On the status bar, click the **Normal** button ▦, and then press `Ctrl` + `Home` to make cell **A1** the active cell.

■ **Continue to the next page to complete the skill** ➤

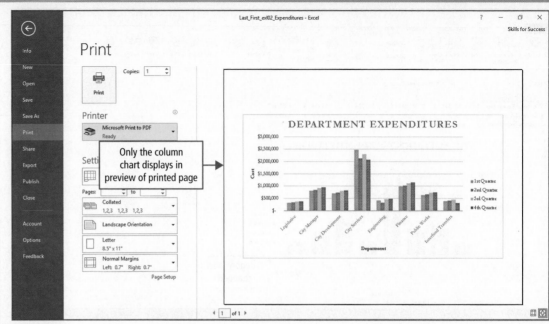

Only the column chart displays in preview of printed page

Figure 1   Excel 2016, Windows 10, Microsoft Corporation

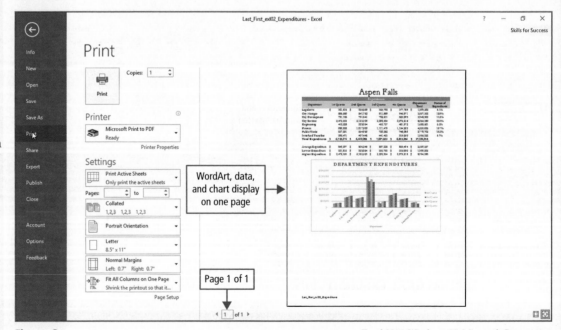

WordArt, data, and chart display on one page

Page 1 of 1

Figure 2   Excel 2016, Windows 10, Microsoft Corporation

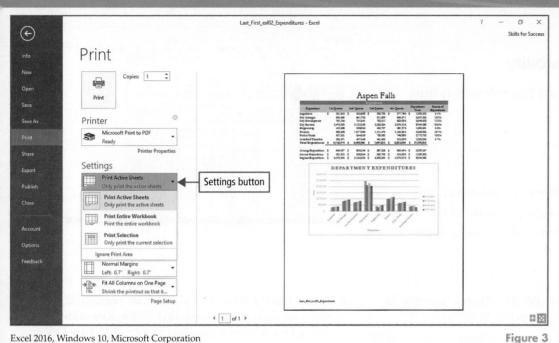

Excel 2016, Windows 10, Microsoft Corporation

Figure 3

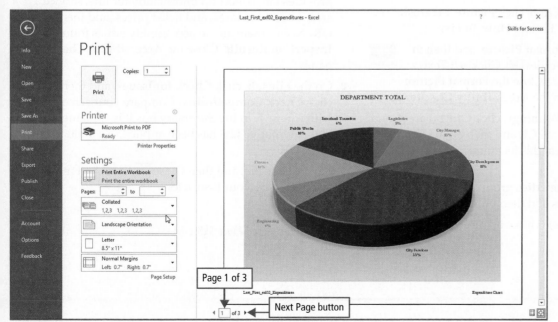

Excel 2016, Windows 10, Microsoft Corporation

Figure 4

6. Click the **Review tab**, and then in the **Proofing group**, click the **Spelling** button. Check the spelling of the worksheet. Click **Ignore All** for Interfund suggestion. When the message *Spell check complete. You're good to go!* displays, click **OK**.

7. **Save** 💾 the file.

8. Click the **File tab**, and then click **Print**. Under **Settings**, click the first button. Compare your screen with Figure 3.

9. On the displayed list, click **Print Entire Workbook**. Notice at the bottom of the screen that *1 of 3* displays and the chart sheet with the pie chart is the first page. Compare your screen with Figure 4.

Obj 1.5.3 C

10. At the bottom of the screen, click the **Next Page** button ▶ to preview the worksheet containing your **WordArt**, the data, and the column chart. **Save** the workbook. Submit the file as directed by your instructor. Otherwise, click the **Back** button ⬅.

11. If instructed, print the formulas. Display the worksheet formulas, AutoFit the column widths, and then print the formulas.

12. **Close** ✕ Excel. Submit the file as directed by your instructor.

✔ **DONE! You have completed Skill 10 of 10, and your file is complete!**

More Skills 11

Validate Workbooks for Accessibility

To complete this project, you will need the following file:

- exl02_MS11Fares

You will save your file as:

- Last_First_exl02_MS11Fares

▶ *Accessibility*—technologies that adapt the display for nonvisual users.

▶ *Accessibility Checker*—finds potential accessibility issues and creates a report.

▶ *Alternative (Alt) text*—text used in documents and web pages to provide a text description of an object.

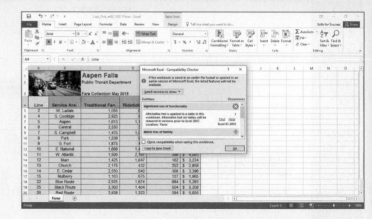

Figure 1 Excel 2016, Windows 10, Microsoft Corporation

1. **Start** Excel 2016. Open the student data file **exl02_MS11Fares**. Save the file in your chapter folder with the name Last_First_exl02_MS11Fares

2. On the **File tab**, click **Check for Issues**, and then click **Check Accessibility**. Obj 1.5.7 C

3. In the **Accessibility Checker** pane, under **Errors** click **Picture 1 (Fares)**. Under **Additional Information**, read **Why Fix** and **How To Fix**.

4. Right-click the image in cell **A1:B3**. Click **Format Picture**, and then in the **Format Picture** pane, click **Size & Properties** 🔳. Click **Alt Text**, and then in the **Title** box type Transit Picture Close the **Format Picture** pane. Notice the error no longer displays in the **Accessibility Checker** pane. Obj 5.3.4 C

5. In the **Accessibility Checker** pane, under **Warnings**, click **C1:F1 (Fares)**, and then read **Why Fix** and **How To Fix**. Click cell **C1**, and then on the **Home tab**, click the **Merge & Center** button. Repeat this technique to unmerge the remaining cells to remove the warnings.

6. Click cell **A4**. On the **Design tab**, in the **Properties group**, click in the **Table Name** box. Replace the text with TableFares and then press Enter.

   Defining table names can assist in the navigation of a worksheet for people with disabilities.

7. Right-click the table. In the short-cut menu click **Table**, and then click **Alternative Text**. In the **Alternative Text** dialog box, with the insertion point in the **Title** box, type Fares Table In the **Description** box type The table provides fare collection information for line, service area, traditional fares, and ticket prices. and then click **OK**. Notice there are no accessibility issues found in the **Inspection Results**. Close the **Accessibility Checker** pane.

8. On the **File tab**, click **Check for Issues**, and then click **Check Compatibility**. Compare your screen with **Figure 1**. In the **Summary** box it is explained that Alternative text has been applied to a table. Click **OK**. 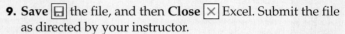 Obj 1.5.8 C

9. **Save** 🔳 the file, and then **Close** ✕ Excel. Submit the file as directed by your instructor.

▪ **You have completed More Skills 11**

More Skills 12

Change Chart Types

To complete this project, you will need the following file:

- exl02_MS12Specials

You will save your files as:

- Last_First_exl02_MS12Specials

▶ *Chart type* is a specific design of how data is displayed or compared in a chart.

▶ In a *bar chart*, the categories are displayed on the vertical axis, and the values are displayed on the horizontal axis. A bar chart illustrates comparisons among individual items.

▶ In a column chart, the values are displayed on the vertical axis, and the categories are displayed on the horizontal axis.

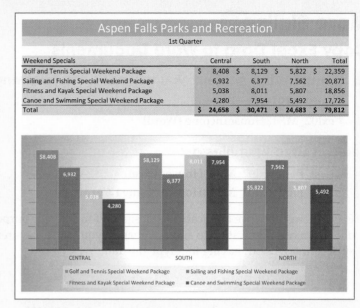

Weekend Specials	Central	South	North	Total
Golf and Tennis Special Weekend Package	$ 8,408	$ 8,129	$ 5,822	$ 22,359
Sailing and Fishing Special Weekend Package	6,932	6,377	7,562	20,871
Fitness and Kayak Special Weekend Package	5,038	8,011	5,807	18,856
Canoe and Swimming Special Weekend Package	4,280	7,954	5,492	17,726
Total	$ 24,658	$ 30,471	$ 24,683	$ 79,812

Aspen Falls Parks and Recreation — 1st Quarter

Excel 2016, Windows 10, Microsoft Corporation   Figure 1

1. Start **Excel 2016**. Open the student data file **exl02_MS12Specials**, and then save the file in your chapter folder as Last_First_exl02_MS12Specials

2. Add the file name in the worksheet's left footer, and then return to Normal view.

3. Select the range **A4:D8**. Click the **Insert tab**, and then in the **Charts group**, click the **Recommended Charts** button. In the **Insert Chart** dialog box, verify that the **Clustered Bar** thumbnail is selected, and then click **OK**.

   Recall that each of the cells bordered in blue is referred to as a data point—a value that originates in a worksheet cell.

   Related data points form a data series; for example, there is a data series for *Central*, a data series for *South*, and a data series for *North*.

4. On the **Design tab**, in the **Type group**, click the **Change Chart Type** button. In the **Change Chart Type** dialog box, on the **All Charts tab**, click **Line** to preview the data in a line chart.

5. In the left pane of the **Change Chart Type** dialog box, click **Column**, and then under **Clustered Column**, click the second thumbnail, and then click **OK** to change the chart type.

6. Move the chart so that the upper left corner is inside the upper left corner of cell **A12**. Use the lower right sizing handle to resize the chart so that the chart covers the range **A12:E27**.

7. At the top right corner of the chart, click the **Chart Elements** button, and then clear the **Chart Title** check box.

8. At the top right corner of the chart, click the **Chart Styles** button. Scroll down, and then click the fourth thumbnail—**Style 4**. At the top of the **Chart Styles** gallery, click **Color**, and then click the fourth color in the **Colorful** section—**Color 4**.

9. Click cell **A10** to deselect the chart. Click the **File tab**, and then click **Print** to preview the printed page as shown in Figure 1.

10. **Save** the file, and then **Close** Excel. Submit the file as directed by your instructor.

- **You have completed More Skills 12**

More Skills 13

Copy Excel Data to Word Documents

To complete this project, you will need the following files:

- exl02_MS13House (Excel)
- exl02_MS13HouseIncome (Word)

You will save your files as:

- Last_First_exl02_MS13House (Excel)
- Last_First_exl02_MS13HouseIncome (Word)

▶ Each Microsoft Office application is designed for different purposes. Copying data from one application to another enables you to use the strengths of each application without having to retype the data.

1. Start **Excel 2016**. Open the student data file **exl02_MS13House**, and then save the file in your chapter folder as Last_First_exl02_MS13House

2. Start **Word 2016**. Open the student data file **exl02_MS13HouseIncome**, and then save the file in your chapter folder as Last_First_exl02_MS13HouseIncome

3. In the Word document, click the **Insert tab**. In the **Header & Footer group**, click the **Footer** button, and then click **Edit Footer**. On the **Header & Footer Tools Design tab**, in the **Insert group**, click the **Quick Parts** button, and then click **Field**. In the **Field** dialog box, under **Field names**, scroll down and then click **File Name**. Click the **OK** button. In the **Close group**, click the **Close Header and Footer** button.

4. At the bottom of the screen, on the taskbar, click the **Microsoft Excel** icon to display the Excel window. Select the range **A3:C6**, and then on the **Home tab**, in the **Clipboard group**, click the **Copy** button.

5. On the taskbar, click the **Microsoft Word** window. Press Ctrl + End to move to the end of the document. On the **Home tab**, in the **Clipboard group**, click the **Paste** button.

6. At the bottom of the screen, on the taskbar, click the **Microsoft Excel** icon to open the Excel window, and then press Esc to cancel the copy command.

7. Click the border of the chart to select the entire chart, and then on the **Home tab**, in the **Clipboard group**, click the **Copy** button.

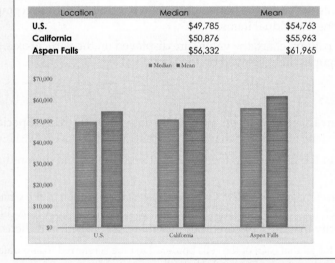

MEMORANDUM

TO: Richard Mack, Assistant City Manager

FROM: Cyril Shore, Planning Council Director

DATE: November 25, 2018

RE: Aspen Falls Annual Household Income

Aspen Falls' mid-point (or median) household income was $56,332, about 17 percent higher than the United States and 11 percent higher than California as a whole. The average (or mean) household income for Aspen Falls was $63,965 or 21 percent higher than the nation and 15 percent higher than California as a whole. It is expected that Aspen Falls' income figures would be higher, reflecting a higher concentration of well-educated individuals. Following is the data and chart that reflect these numbers.

Location	Median	Mean
U.S.	$49,785	$54,763
California	$50,876	$55,963
Aspen Falls	$56,332	$61,965

Figure 1   Excel 2016, Windows 10, Microsoft Corporation

8. Display the **Microsoft Word** window. Verify the insertion point is at the end of the document. On the **Home tab**, in the **Clipboard group**, click the **Paste** button.

9. Click the **File tab**, and then click **Print**. Compare your screen with **Figure 1**.

10. **Save** the file, and then **Close** ⊠ Word and Excel. Submit the files as directed by your instructor.

- **You have completed More Skills 13**

More Skills 14
Create Line Charts

To complete this project, you will need the following file:

- exl02_MS14Growth

You will save your file as:

- Last_First_exl02_MS14Growth

▶ A *line chart*, allows you to compare more than one set of values, each group of values is connected by a different line.

1. Start **Excel 2016**. Open the student data file **exl02_MS14Growth**, and then save the file in your chapter folder as Last_First_exl02_MS14Growth

2. Select the range **A4:F7**. Click the **Insert tab**, and then in the **Charts group**, click the **Recommended Charts** button. In the **Insert Chart** dialog box, click the **All Charts tab**. Click **Line**, and then click the fourth chart—**Line with Markers**. Click **OK**. 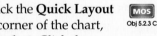 Obj 5.1.1 C

3. On the **Design tab**, in the **Location group**, click the **Move Chart** button. In the displayed **Move Chart** dialog box, select the **New sheet** option button, replace the text with Growth Chart and then click **OK**. Obj 5.2.4 C

4. On the **Design tab**, in the **Chart Layouts group**, click the **Quick Layout** button, and then click **Layout 6**. At the top right corner of the chart, click the **Chart Styles** button , and then click **Style 8**. Click the **Chart Styles** button to close the gallery. Obj 5.2.3 C

   The years display at the bottom of the chart, and the population growth is represented by the lines in the chart.

5. Click the **Format tab**. In the **Current Selection group**, click the **Chart Elements arrow**, and then click **Vertical (Value) Axis**. In the **Current Selection group**, click the **Format Selection** button to open the Format Axis pane.

6. In the **Format Axis** pane, under **Axis Options**, in the **Minimum** box, replace the number with 250000 Press Enter, and then watch the chart as the vertical axis minimum changes from 0 to 250,000. Obj 5.2.2 C

7. In the **Format Axis** pane, scroll down and click **Tick Marks**. Scroll down and click the **Major type arrow**.

8. In the **Tick Marks** list, click **Cross** to display marks on the vertical axis.

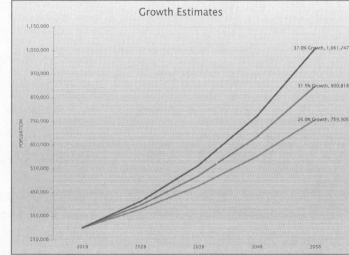

Growth Estimates

Excel 2016, Windows 10, Microsoft Corporation

Figure 1

9. In the **Format Axis** pane, click the **Axis Options arrow**, and then click **Chart Area** to display the Format Chart Area pane. Click the **Fill & Line** button, and then click **Fill**. Select the **Gradient fill** option button. **Close** the Format Chart Area pane.

10. At the top of the chart, click the **Chart Title**, type Growth Estimates and then press Enter.

11. At the left side of the chart, click the vertical **Axis Title**, type Population and then press Enter. Compare your screen with **Figure 1**. Obj 5.2.2 C

12. **Save** the file, and then **Close** Excel. Submit the file as directed by your instructor.

- **You have completed More Skills 14**

Review

The following table summarizes the **SKILLS AND PROCEDURES** covered in this chapter.

Skills Number	Task	Step	Icon	Keyboard Shortcut
1	Wrap text	Home tab → Alignment group → Wrap Text		
1	Middle align text	Home tab → Alignment group → Middle Align		
1	Center text	Home tab → Alignment group → Center		
1	Increase indent	Home tab → Alignment group → Increase Indent		
2	Insert the SUM function	Quick Analysis button → Totals → SUM		
2	Create an absolute cell reference	Select cell reference → Type $		F4
3	Apply the Percent style	Home tab → Number group → Percent Style	%	
3	Increase the number of display decimals	Home tab → Number group → Increase Decimal		
4	Calculate an average	Home tab → Editing group → AutoSum arrow → Average		
5	Calculate a minimum	Home tab → Editing group → AutoSum arrow → Min		
5	Calculate a maximum	Home tab → Editing group → AutoSum arrow → Max		
6	Insert a chart using Quick Analysis	Quick Analysis button → Charts → select chart		
7	Apply a chart style	Chart Style → Style		
7	Apply a chart layout	Design tab → Chart Layouts group → Quick Layout → Layout		
8	Insert a recommended chart	Insert tab → Charts group → Recommended Charts → select desired chart		
8	Move a chart to its own worksheet	Design tab → Locations group → Move Chart → New sheet		
8	Change the chart type	Design tab → Type group → Change Chart Type → Type		
8	Change chart data labels	Design tab → Locations group → Move Chart → New sheet		
9	Insert WordArt	Insert tab → Text group → WordArt		
10	Adjust scale page width	Page Layout tab → Scale to Fit group → Width arrow → Page		
10	Print an entire workbook	File tab → Print → Settings → Print Entire Workbook		
MS 11	Check accessibility	File tab → Check for Issues → Check Accessibility		
MS 11	Insert Alt Text picture	Format picture → Size & Properties → Alt Text		
MS 11	Insert Alt Text table	Table → Alternative Text		
MS 11	Check compatibility	File tab → Check for Issues → Check Compatibility		
MS 13	Copy Excel data to documents	Home tab → Clipboard Group → Copy		
MS 14	Create line charts	Insert tab → Chart Group → Line Chart		

Project Summary Chart

Project	Project Type	Project Location
Skills Review	Review	In Book & MIL MyITLab° Grader
Skills Assessment 1	Review	In Book & MIL MyITLab° Grader
Skills Assessment 2	Review	Book
My Skills	Problem Solving	Book
Visual Skills Check	Problem Solving	Book
Skills Challenge 1	Critical Thinking	Book
Skills Challenge 2	Critical Thinking	Book
More Skills Assessment	Review	In Book & MIL MyITLab° Grader
Collaborating with Google	Critical Thinking	Book

MOS Objectives Covered (Quiz in MyITLab°)

1.3.4 C Insert and deleting columns and rows	4.1.3 C Perform calculations by using the MIN and MAX functions
1.5.3 C Print individual worksheets	4.1.5 C Perform calculations by using the AVERAGE function
1.5.4 C Set print scaling	5.1.1 C Create a new chart
1.5.7 C Check accessibility	5.1.4 C Use Quick Analysis
1.5.8 C Inspect a workbook for compatibility issues	5.2.1 C Resize charts
2.2.2 C Modify cell alignment and indentation	5.2.2 C Add and modify chart elements
2.2.4 C Wrap text within cells	5.2.3 C Apply chart layouts and styles
2.2.5 C Apply number formats	5.2.4 C Move charts to a chart sheet
2.2.7 C Apply cell styles	5.3.4 C Add alternative text to objects for accessibility
4.1.1 C Insert references (relative, mixed, absolute, across worksheets)	

Key Terms

BizSkills Video

1. What are the best ways to network online?
2. What are some of the biggest pitfalls in using social media to communicate a personal brand?

Online Help Skills

1. Start **Excel 2016**, and then in the upper right corner of the start page, click the **Help** button ⃞ ? .
2. In the **Excel Help** window **Search help** box, type Keyboard shortcuts and then press ⃞ Enter .
3. In the search result list, click **Keyboard shortcuts in Excel**. **Maximize** the Help window, and then compare your screen with **Figure 1**.

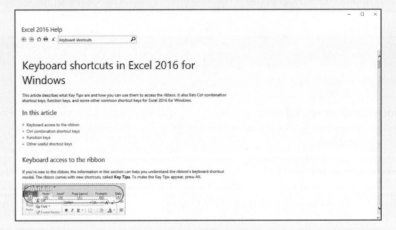

Figure 1   Excel 2016, Windows 10, Microsoft Corporation

4. Read the article to answer the following question: How can you use Key Tips to access the Ribbon?

Matching

Match each term in the second column with its correct definition in the first column by writing the letter of the term on the blank line in front of the correct definition.

___ **1.** A command with which you can display text on multiple lines within a cell.

___ **2.** A cell reference that refers to a cell by its fixed position in a worksheet and does not change when the formula is copied.

___ **3.** Rules that specify the way numbers should display.

___ **4.** The default format applied to numbers.

___ **5.** The value(s) that determine(s) how a function should be used.

___ **6.** A graphical representation of data in a worksheet that shows comparisons, patterns, and trends.

___ **7.** A chart line that contains words as labels.

___ **8.** A chart line that contains numeric data.

___ **9.** The function that adds a group of values and then divides the result by the number of values in the group.

___ **10.** The Excel feature that outlines all of the cells referenced in a formula.

A Absolute cell reference

B Argument

C AVERAGE function

D Category axis

E Chart

F General format

G Number format

H Range finder

I Text wrap

J Value axis

Multiple Choice

Choose the correct answer.

1. Automatically changing the column width to accommodate the longest column entry.
   A. Drag and drop
   B. AutoFit
   C. Auto adjust

2. A green triangle that indicates a possible error in a formula.
   A. Error indicator
   B. Message
   C. Dialog Box Launcher

3. A chart type useful for illustrating comparisons among related numbers.
   A. Pie chart
   B. Area chart
   C. Column chart

4. A chart placed on a worksheet with the source data.
   A. Chart sheet
   B. Column chart
   C. Embedded chart

5. The related data points in a chart.
   A. Column
   B. Data series
   C. Chart point

6. The box that identifies the patterns or colors assigned to the data series.
   A. Legend
   B. Dialog box
   C. Message box

7. A predesigned combination of chart elements.
   A. 3-D chart
   B. Chart layout
   C. Chart

8. A prebuilt chart format that applies an overall visual look to a chart.
   A. Data marker
   B. Chart finder
   C. Chart style

9. The chart type that best displays the relationship of parts to a whole.
   A. Pie chart
   B. Area chart
   C. Column chart

10. A worksheet that contains only a chart.
    A. Worksheet
    B. Chart area
    C. Chart sheet

Topics for Discussion

1. Search current newspapers and magazines for examples of charts. Which charts catch your eye, and why? Do the charts appeal to you because of their color or format? Is something intriguing revealed to you in the chart that you have never considered before? What are some formatting changes that you think make a chart interesting and valuable to a reader?

2. Do you think 3-D pie charts distort the data in a way that is misleading? Why or why not?

Skills Review

To complete this project, you will need the following file:

- exl02_SRRevenue

You will save your file as:

- Last_First_exl02_SRRevenue

1. Start **Excel 2016**, and open the file **exl02_SRRevenue**. **Save** the file in your chapter folder as Last_First_exl02_SRRevenue Add the file name in the worksheet's left footer and the sheet name in the right footer. Return to **Normal** view.

2. In the column heading area, point to the right boundary of column **A**, and then double-click to AutoFit the column width. Click the column **B** heading, and then drag right to select columns **B:F**. Click the right boundary of column B, and then drag to the right until the ScreenTip indicates *Width:13:00 (96 pixels)*.

3. Select the range **A1:F1**. On the **Home tab**, in the **Alignment group**, click the **Wrap Text**, **Middle Align**, and **Center** buttons.

4. Select the range **B2:E13**. Click the **Quick Analysis** button, click **Totals**, and then click the first option—**SUM**.

5. Select the nonadjacent ranges **B2:E2** and **B14:E14**. In the **Number group**, click the **Decrease Decimal** button two times. Select the range **B3:E13**. In the **Number group**, click the **Decrease Decimal** button two times. Select the range **B14:E14**. In the **Styles group**, click the **Cell Styles** button, and then click **Total**.

6. In cell **F2**, type=E2/$E$14 and then on the formula bar, click the **Enter** button. With cell F2 as the active cell, in the **Number group**, click the **Percent Style** button, and then click the **Increase Decimal** button once. In the **Alignment group**, click the **Center** button. AutoFill the formula in cell **F2** down through cell **F13**. Click cell **A15**, and then compare your screen with Figure 1.

7. Click cell **B16**. Type =Av and then in the **Formula AutoComplete** list, double-click **AVERAGE**. For the function argument, select the range **B2:B13**, and then press Enter. Using the same function argument range, in cell **B17**, enter the **MAX** function. Select the range **B16:B17**, and then AutoFill the formulas to the right through column **D**. Compare your screen with Figure 2.

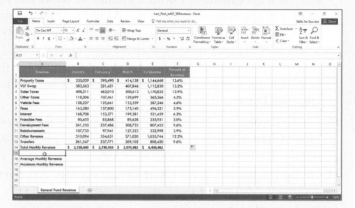

Figure 1   Excel 2016, Windows 10, Microsoft Corporation

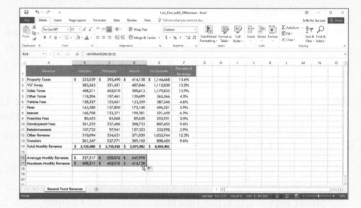

Figure 2   Excel 2016, Windows 10, Microsoft Corporation

■ **Continue to the next page to complete this Skills Review**

8. Select the range **A1:D13**. Click the **Quick Analysis** button, click **Charts**, and then click the **Clustered Column** thumbnail. Move and resize the chart to display in approximately the range **A19:F35**. At the top right corner of the chart, click the **Chart Styles** button, and then click the **Style 9** thumbnail. Select **Chart Title**, type General Fund Revenue and then press [Enter].

9. Select the nonadjacent ranges **A1:A13** and **E1:E13**. Click the **Insert tab**, and then in the **Charts group**, click the **Recommended Charts** button. On the **All Charts tab**, click **Pie**, and then click **OK**.

10. On the **Design tab**, in the **Location group**, click the **Move Chart** button. In the **Move Chart** dialog box, select the **New sheet** option button, type the sheet name Revenue Chart and then click **OK**.

11. On the **Design tab**, in the **Chart Layouts group**, click the **Quick Layout** button, and then click **Layout 1**.

12. Click the **Chart Elements** button, click the **Data Labels arrow**, and then click **More Options**. In the **Format Data Labels** pane, under **Label Position**, click **Outside End**.

13. Click the **Label Options arrow**, and then click **Chart Area**. In the **Format Chart Area** pane, click the **Fill & Line** button, and then click **Fill**. Select the **Gradient fill** option button, and then **Close** the Format Chart Area pane. Compare your screen with **Figure 3**.

14. Click the **Insert tab**, and then in the **Text group**, click the **Header & Footer** button. In the **Page Setup** dialog box, click the **Custom Footer** button. Insert the **File Name** in the left section, and then insert the **Sheet Name** in the right section. Click **OK** twice.

15. Click the **General Fund Revenue worksheet tab**. Select the range **A1:A3**. On the **Home tab**, in the **Cells group**, click the **Insert arrow**, and then click **Insert Sheet Rows**. Click the **Insert tab**. In the **Text group**, click the **Insert WordArt** button, and then in the first row, click the second thumbnail—**Fill - Blue, Accent 1, Shadow**. Immediately type Aspen Falls Revenue Select the text in the WordArt. On the Mini toolbar, change the **Font Size** to **36**. Point to the bottom border of the WordArt, and then move the WordArt to center approximately within the range **A1:E3**.

16. Click cell **A1**. Click the **Page Layout tab**. In the **Scale to Fit group**, click the **Width arrow**, and then click the **1 page** button.

17. Click the **File tab**, and then click **Print**. Compare your screen with **Figure 4**.

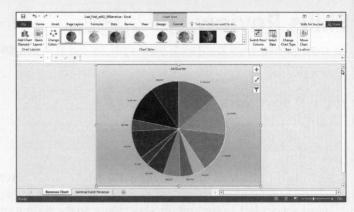

Excel 2016, Windows 10, Microsoft Corporation · Figure 3

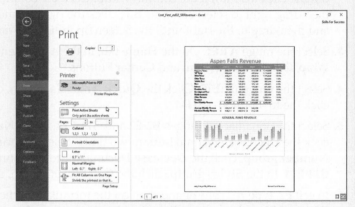

Excel 2016, Windows 10, Microsoft Corporation · Figure 4

18. Save the file, and then **Close** Excel. Submit the file as directed by your instructor.

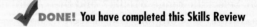
DONE! You have completed this Skills Review

Skills Assessment 1

To complete this project, you will need the following file:

- exl02_SA1Debt

You will save your file as:

- Last_First_exl02_SA1Debt

1. Start **Excel 2016**, and open the file **exl02_SA1Debt**. **Save** the workbook in your chapter folder as Last_First_exl02_SA1Debt Add the file name in the worksheet's left footer and the sheet name in the right footer. Return to **Normal** view.

2. Select the range **A2:I2**, and then apply the alignment **Wrap Text** and **Middle Align**.

3. Select the column headings **B:I**, and then AutoFit the column widths.

4. In the range **B8:H8**, insert the column totals, and then apply the **Total** cell style.

5. Select the nonadjacent ranges **B3:H3** and **B8:H8**, and then display no decimals. Select the range **B4:H7**, and then display no decimals.

6. In cell **I3**, calculate the *Percent of Total Debt*. In the formula, use an absolute cell reference when referring to cell **H8**. AutoFill the formula down through cell **I7**, and then format the results as percentages with one decimal place.

7. In the range **B10:G10**, insert a function to calculate the highest monthly debt. In the range **B11:G11**, insert a function to calculate the lowest monthly debt. In the range **B12:G12**, insert a function to calculate the average monthly debt.

8. Insert a **Pie** chart based on the nonadjacent ranges **A2:A7** and **H2:H7**. Move the pie chart to a chart sheet with the sheet name Debt Chart

9. For the pie chart, apply **Layout 6**, and then apply the **Chart Style 3**. Change the data label **Font Size** to **12**, and then position to **Center**. Add the file name in the chart sheet's left footer and the sheet name in the right footer.

10. On the **Debt** worksheet, insert a **Clustered Column** chart based on the range **A2:G7**. Move the chart below the data, and then resize the chart to approximately the range **A14:I28**. Apply the chart **Style 5**. Change the chart title to City Debt

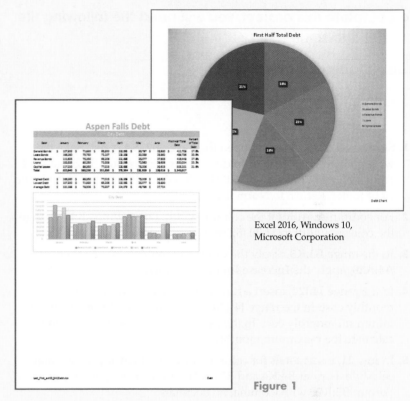

Excel 2016, Windows 10, Microsoft Corporation

Figure 1

11. Insert three sheet rows at the top of the worksheet. Insert **WordArt**, using the style **Fill - Gold, Accent 4, Soft Bevel**. Change the WordArt text to Aspen Falls Debt and then change the **Font Size** to **36**. Move the WordArt to the top of the worksheet, centering it above the data.

12. Adjust the **Scale to Fit** to fit the WordArt, data, and column chart on one page.

13. Revise the Print Settings to **Print Entire Workbook**, and then compare your screen with **Figure 1**.

14. **Save** the file, and then **Close** Excel. Submit the file as directed by your instructor.

 **DONE! You have completed Skills Assessment 1**

Skills Assessment 2

To complete this project, you will need the following file:

- exl02_SA2Cost

You will save your file as:

- Last_First_exl02_SA2Cost

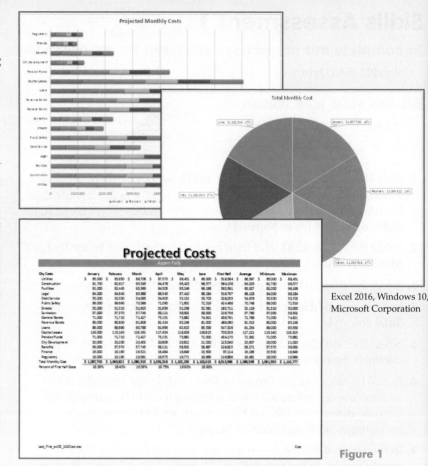

Excel 2016, Windows 10, Microsoft Corporation

Figure 1

1. Start **Excel 2016**, and then open the file **exl02_SA2Cost**. **Save** the workbook in your chapter folder as Last_First_exl02_SA2Cost Add the file name in the worksheet's left footer and the sheet name in the right footer. Return to **Normal** view.

2. For column **A**, AutoFit the column width. For columns **B:K**, change the column width to **11.00 (82 pixels)**.

3. In the range **B3:K3**, apply the **Center** alignment. In the range **A4:A20**, apply the **Increase Indent** alignment.

4. In the range **I4:I20**, insert a function to calculate the average monthly cost. In the range **J4:J20**, insert a function to calculate the minimum monthly cost. In the range **K4:K20**, insert a function to calculate the maximum monthly cost.

5. In row **21**, insert totals for columns **B:K**, and then apply the **Total** cell style. Format **B4:K4** and **B21:K21** with Currency, no decimals. Format **B5:K20** with Comma, no decimals.

6. In cell **B22**, calculate the *Percent of First Half Costs*. In the formula, use an absolute cell reference when referring to cell **H21**. Format the result as a percentage and display two decimals. AutoFill the formula to the right through column **G**.

7. Insert a **Stacked Bar** chart based on the range **A3:G20**. Move the stacked bar chart to a chart sheet named Projected Costs Apply the chart **Style 11**. Change the chart title to Projected Monthly Costs Add the file name in the chart sheet's left footer and the sheet name in the right footer.

8. Click the **Cost worksheet tab**. Insert a **Pie** chart based on the nonadjacent ranges **A3:G3** and **A21:G21**. Move the pie chart to a chart sheet named Total Monthly Costs Apply the chart **Layout 1**. Change the data label position to **Data Callout**, and then change the data label **Font Size** to **12**.

9. On the **Cost** worksheet, insert four blank lines at the top of the worksheet. Insert a WordArt with the **Fill - Black, Text 1, Outline - Background 1, Hard Shadow - Background 1** style. In the WordArt, type the text Projected Costs and then change the **Font Size** to **44**. Move the WordArt to the top of the worksheet, centering it above the data.

10. Scale the **Cost** worksheet to print on **1 page**.

11. **Print Preview** the workbook, and then compare your screen with Figure 1.

12. **Save** the file, and then **Close** Excel. Submit the file as directed by your instructor.

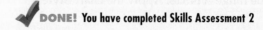 **DONE! You have completed Skills Assessment 2**

My Skills

To complete this project, you will need the following file:

- exl02_MYPersonalBudget

You will save your file as:

- Last_First_exl02_MYPersonalBudget

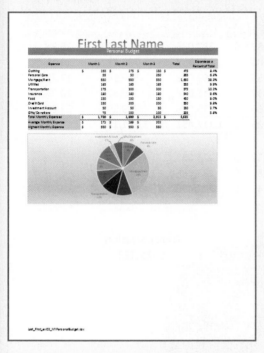

Excel 2016, Windows 10, Microsoft Corporation   **Figure 1**

1. Start **Excel 2016**, and then open the file **exl02_MYPersonalBudget**. **Save** the file in your chapter folder as Last_First_exl02_MYPersonalBudget Add the file name in the worksheet's left footer, and then return to **Normal** view.

2. Change the alignments of the row **3** labels, and then indent the column **A** expense labels. In the range **B14:E14**, insert the column totals.

3. In the range **B15:D15**, insert a function to calculate the average monthly expense. In the range **B16:D16**, insert a function to calculate the maximum monthly expense.

4. In cell **F4**, calculate the *Expense as a Percent of Total*. In the formula, use an absolute cell reference when referring to the total. Format the results as percentages with one decimal, and then AutoFill the formula down through cell **F13**.

5. Apply the **Total** cell style where appropriate.

6. Insert a **Pie** chart based on the nonadjacent ranges **A3:A13** and **E3:E13**.

7. Move the pie chart to an appropriate location below your data, and then resize the chart.

8. Format the pie chart with any of the chart options of your choice including layout, style, or color.

9. At the top of the worksheet, insert three blank rows. Insert a WordArt using your first and last names as the WordArt text. Move the WordArt above the data, and then resize to fit in the blank rows.

10. Adjust the scaling to fit the data and the pie chart on one page when printed. **Print Preview** the workbook, and then compare your screen with **Figure 1**.

11. **Save** the file, and then **Close** Excel. Submit the file as directed by your instructor.

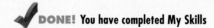 **DONE!** You have completed My Skills

Visual Skills Check

To complete this project, you will need the following file:

- exl02_VSNetAssets

You will save your file as:

- Last_First_exl02_VSNetAssets

Start **Excel 2016**, and then open the student data file **exl02_VSNetAssets**. **Save** the file in your chapter folder as Last_First_exl02_VSNetAssets Create the worksheet as shown in **Figure 1**. Calculate the *Percent of Total Net Assets* using an absolute cell reference. In rows **13:15**, insert the statistical functions that correspond with the row labels. Format the values and text as shown. Create the pie chart, and then move and resize the chart as shown in the figure. The chart uses the **Layout 4** chart layout, and **Color 8**, with data label font size **12** and **Bold**. Insert the file name in the worksheet's left footer. **Save** the file, and then **Close** Excel. Submit the file as directed by your instructor.

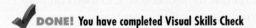 **DONE!** You have completed Visual Skills Check

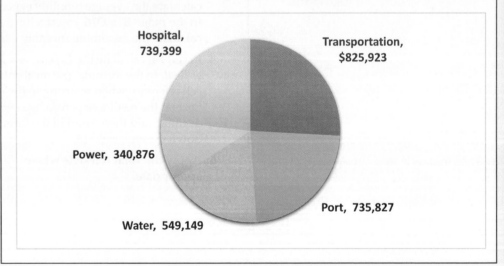

Aspen Falls Net Assets Business-type Activities					
Asset	July	August	September	Total	Percent of Total Net Assets
Transportation	$ 268,755	$ 275,082	$ 282,086	$ 825,923	25.9%
Port	242,886	245,688	247,253	735,827	23.1%
Water	175,885	180,256	193,008	549,149	17.2%
Power	117,006	108,832	115,038	340,876	10.7%
Hospital	213,468	250,865	275,066	739,399	23.2%
Total Net Assets	$ 1,018,000	$ 1,060,723	$ 1,112,451	$ 3,191,174	
Minimum Asset	$ 117,006	$ 108,832	$ 115,038		
Maximum Asset	$ 268,755	$ 275,082	$ 282,086		
Average Asset	$ 203,600	$ 212,145	$ 222,490		

Figure 1

Excel 2016, Windows 10, Microsoft Corporation

Skills Challenge 1

To complete this project, you will need the following file:

- exl02_SC1Budget

You will save your file as:

- Last_First_exl02_SC1Budget

Start **Excel 2016**. Open the file **exl02_SC1Budget**, and then save the file in your chapter folder as Last_First_exl02_SC1Budget During the fourth quarter of this year, the Accounting Department developed a summary of the proposed Aspen Falls budget. Correct the errors in the statistical functions—you may want to display the formulas. Use an absolute cell reference when correcting the percentage. Correct the number formats, and format the labels appropriately. Modify the WordArt and the column chart. Verify that the WordArt, data, and column chart will print on one page. Add the file name in the worksheet's left footer. Save the file, and Close Excel. Submit the file as directed by your instructor.

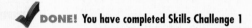 **DONE!** You have completed Skills Challenge 1

Skills Challenge 2

To complete this project, you will need the following file:

- exl02_SC2Classes

You will save your file as:

- Last_First_exl02_SC2Classes

Start **Excel 2016**, and then open the workbook **exl02_SC2Classes**. Save the file in your chapter folder as Last_First_exl02_SC2Classes Carter Horikoshi, the Art Center Supervisor, created a workbook to track how many students attended the Community Center classes last summer. He wants to determine if he should offer more classes this summer based on the number of students from last summer. He wants to know the total enrollment and the average enrollment for each month and for each class. He would like to view a chart that summarizes the enrollment data. Using the skills you learned in this chapter, provide Mr. Horikoshi a workbook to assist him in his decision. Add the file name in the worksheet's left footer. Save the file and Close Excel. Submit the file as directed by your instructor.

DONE! You have completed Skills Challenge 2

More Skills Assessment

To complete this project, you will need the following files:

- exl02_MSARecycling (Excel)
- exl02_MSARecycling (Word)

You will save your files as:

- Last_First_exl02_MSARecycling (Excel)
- Last_First_exl02_MSARecycling (Word)
- Last_First_exl02_MSARecycling (JPG)

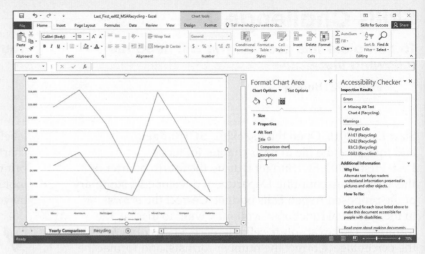

Figure 1   Excel 2016, Windows 10, Microsoft Corporation

1. Start **Excel 2016**. Open the workbook **exl02_MSARecycling**, and then save the file in your chapter folder as Last_First_exl02_MSARecycling

2. Select the **Clustered Bar Chart**. Use the **Chart Tools** to change the **Chart Type** to a **Clustered Column** chart. Apply **Chart Style 7** to the chart.

3. Start **Word 2016**. Open the student data file **exl02_MSARecycling**, and then save the file in your chapter folder as Last_First_exl02_MSARecycling

4. At the bottom of the screen, on the taskbar, click the **Microsoft Excel** icon to display the Excel window. Copy the *Recycling Revenue* chart.

5. Display the **Microsoft Word** window. Move to the end of the document, and then paste the chart from Excel. Resize the chart so that the right edge is at the right margin.

6. Select the chart, and apply **Alt Text** using the title Recycling Chart Close the Format Chart pane. **Save** the file, and then **Close** the Word document.

7. At the bottom of the screen, on the taskbar, click the **Microsoft Excel** icon to open the Excel window, and then deselect the copied cells.

8. Using data in the range **A5:C12**, create a **Stacked Line** chart. Move the Stacked Line chart to a chart sheet named Yearly Comparison and then clear the **Chart Title**. Click the **Recycling** sheet, and then **Save** the file.

9. Check Accessibility for the workbook. Format **Chart 1 (Yearly Comparison)** using Alt Text and apply Comparison Chart as the Title. Compare your screen with **Figure 1**.

10. Format **Chart 4 (Recycling)** using Alt Text and apply Recycling Revenue Chart as the Title.

11. Clear any warnings by unmerging cells as needed. Close all open panes.

12. **Save** the file, and then **Close** all open windows. Submit the files as directed by your instructor.

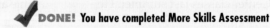 **DONE! You have completed More Skills Assessment**

Collaborating with Google

To complete this project, you will need a Google account (refer to the Common Features chapter) and the following file:

- exl02_GPRentalRevenue

You will save your file as:

- Last_First_exl02_GPRentalRevenue

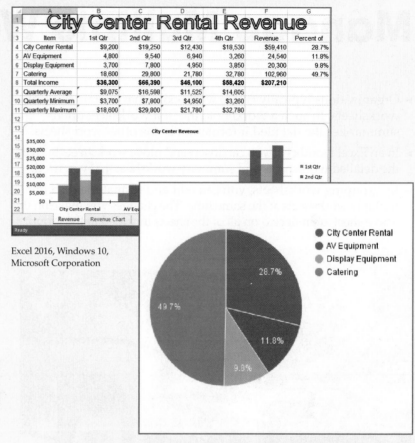

Excel 2016, Windows 10,
Microsoft Corporation

Figure 1

1. Log into your Google account, click **Google Apps** ⬚, and then click **Drive** ☁. Create a new Google Sheet, and then replace the title with Rental Revenue

2. From the student data files, open **exl02_GPRentalRevenue**. Copy the range **A1:G9** from the *Revenue* worksheet, and then paste it in cell **A1** of the blank Google worksheet. Rename the sheet Revenue

3. Select the range **A1:G1**. Click **Center** ≣ align. Click **Format**, point to **Text wrapping**, and then click **Wrap**.

4. In cell **B7**, enter the **AVERAGE** function for the *1st Quarter*. Use AutoFill to copy the formula through **E7**.

5. In cell **B8**, enter the **MIN** function for the *1st Quarter*. Use AutoFill to copy the formula through **E8**.

6. In cell **B9**, enter the **MAX** function for the *1st Quarter*. Use AutoFill to copy the formula through **E9**.

7. In cell **G2**, calculate *Revenue as a Percent of Total Income* using absolute cell reference for **F6**. Format the result as a percentage with one decimal. AutoFill the formula down through **G5**.

8. Select rows **1** and **2**. Click **Insert**, and then click **2 Rows above**. Click **Insert**, click **Drawing**, click **Actions**, and then click **WordArt**. Type City Center Rental Revenue press ⏎ Enter, and then click **Save & Close**. Move the WordArt to rows **1** and **2**. On the Insert tab, click Chart the data and resize.

9. Select the range **A3:E7**. Click **Insert**, and then click **Chart**. Verify the first thumbnail is selected, and then click **Insert**. Resize the chart to fit in cells **A13:G24**. Select the title, and then replace the current text with City Center Revenue

10. Select the nonadjacent ranges **A3:A7** and **F3:F7**. Click **Insert**, and then click **Chart**. Scroll down, select the **Pie Chart**, and then click **Insert**. In the upper right corner of the chart, click the arrow, and then select **Move to own sheet . . . .** Rename the sheet Revenue Chart Right click the chart title, and then click **Clear title**.

11. Click **File**, point to **Download as**, and then click **Microsoft Excel (.xlsx)**. Open the downloaded file, and then save the file in your chapter folder as Last_First_exl02_GPRentalRevenue Compare your screen with **Figure 1**.

12. Close all windows, and then submit your file as directed by your instructor.

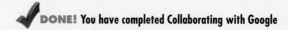

DONE! You have completed Collaborating with Google

CHAPTER 3

Manage Multiple Worksheets

- ▶ Organizations typically create workbooks that contain multiple worksheets. In such a workbook, the first worksheet often summarizes the detailed information in the other worksheets.

- ▶ In an Excel workbook, you can insert and move worksheets to create the detailed worksheets and summary worksheet that you need.

- ▶ By grouping worksheets, you can edit and format the data in multiple worksheets at the same time. The changes you make on the active sheet are reflected on all of the sheets included in the group.

- ▶ You can create multiple worksheets quickly by copying and pasting information from one worksheet to other worksheets.

- ▶ You can color code each worksheet tab so that detailed information can be quickly located.

- ▶ When you use multiple math operators in a single formula, you must take care to ensure the operations are carried out in the intended order.

- ▶ When building a summary worksheet, you will typically use formulas that refer to cells in the other worksheets.

Franco Nadalin/Fotolia

Aspen Falls City Hall

In this chapter, you will work with a spreadsheet for Diane Payne, the Public Works Director in Aspen Falls. She wants to know the revenue generated from parking meters and parking tickets in different locations throughout the city. Understanding how much revenue is generated from the meters and tickets and the costs associated with park maintenance and upgrades will help Diane decide if more meters should be added and if more personnel should be hired to enforce parking regulations. She is also considering the removal of the parking meters in parts of the city and would like to know how much revenue would be lost.

A workbook, composed of multiple worksheets, allows Diane to collect data from different worksheets but analyze those worksheets grouped together as a whole. When you have a large amount of data to organize in a workbook, dividing the data into logical elements, such as locations or time periods, and then placing each element in a separate worksheet often makes sense. In other words, it is often better to design a system of worksheets instead of trying to fit all of the information on a single worksheet. You can then collect and input the data on an individual basis and see the summarized results with minimal effort.

In this project, you will work with grouped worksheets to enter formulas and apply formatting on all selected worksheets at the same time. You will create formulas that use multiple math operators, construct formulas that refer to cells in other worksheets, and create and format a clustered bar chart.

Time to complete all 10 skills—60 to 90 minutes

60-90 min.

Outcome

Using the skills in this chapter, you will be able to move and clear cell contents using paste options, edit grouped worksheets, create summary sheets, create bar charts, and rename, delete, and organize worksheet tabs.

Objectives

3.1 Revise cell contents

3.2 Reorganize and edit worksheet tabs

3.3 Combine and edit data in grouped worksheets

3.4 Construct multiple operator and summary formulas

3.5 Design clustered bar charts

Student data file needed for this chapter:

exl03_Parking

You will save your file as:

Last_First_exl03_Parking

SKILLS  MyITLab® Skills 1-10 Training

At the end of this chapter you will be able to:

Skill 1 Organize Worksheet Tabs

Skill 2 Enter and Format Dates

Skill 3 Clear Cell Contents and Formats

Skill 4 Move Cell Contents and Use Paste Options

Skill 5 Enter Data in Grouped Worksheets

Skill 6 Insert Multiple Math Operators in Formulas

Skill 7 Format Grouped Worksheets

Skill 8 Insert, Hide, Delete, and Move Worksheets

Skill 9 Create Summary Worksheets

Skill 10 Create Clustered Bar Charts

MORE SKILLS

Skill 11 Create SmartArt Organization Charts

Skill 12 Create and Insert Screen Shots

Skill 13 Modify the Quick Access Toolbar

Skill 14 Create and Edit Hyperlinks

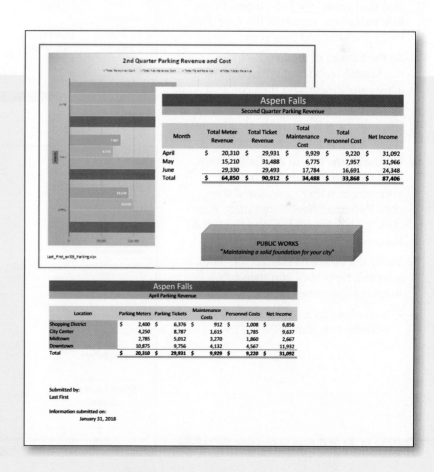

▶ **WATCH** SKILL 3.1

▶ When a file contains more than one worksheet, you can move among worksheets by clicking the worksheet tabs.

▶ **Tab scrolling buttons** are buttons to the left of worksheet tabs used to display worksheet tabs that are not in view.

1. Start **Excel 2016**, and then open the student data file **exl03_Parking**. Click the **File tab**, and then click **Save As**. Click the **Browse** button, and then navigate to the location where you are saving your files. Click **New folder**, type Excel Chapter 3 and then press Enter two times. In the **File name** box, name the file Last_First_exl03_Parking and then press Enter.

2. At the bottom of the Excel window, click the **Sheet2** worksheet tab to make it the active worksheet, and then compare your screen with **Figure 1**.

3. Click the **Sheet1** worksheet tab to make it the active worksheet.

4. On the **Home tab**, in the **Cells group**, click the **Format** button. Compare your screen with **Figure 2**, and then click **Rename Sheet**. Alternately, right-click the worksheet tab, and then click Rename.

MOS
Obj 1.3.2 C

5. Verify the *Sheet1* worksheet tab name is selected, type April and then press Enter to accept the name change.

> You can use up to 31 characters in a worksheet tab name.

■ **Continue to the next page to complete the skill**

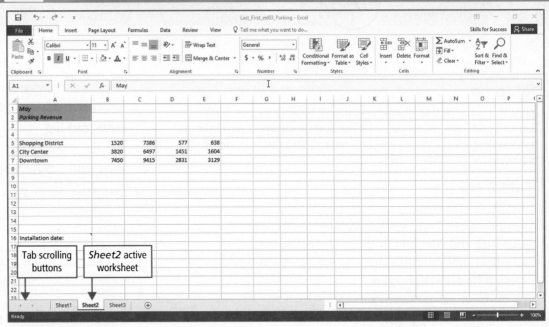

Tab scrolling buttons

Sheet2 active worksheet

Figure 1

Excel 2016, Windows 10, Microsoft Corporation

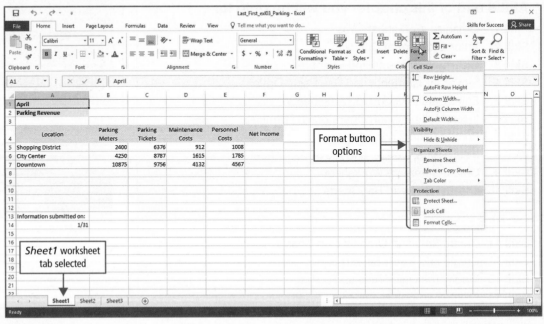

Format button options

Sheet1 worksheet tab selected

Figure 2

Excel 2016, Windows 10, Microsoft Corporation

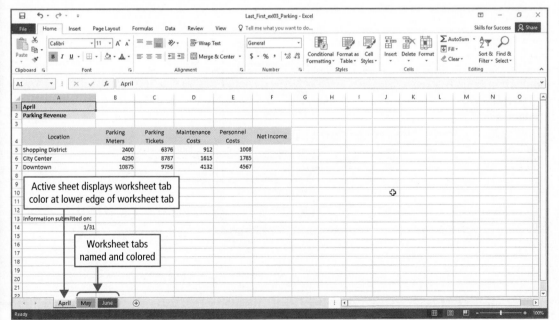

Excel 2016, Windows 10, Microsoft Corporation

Figure 3

6. Double-click the **Sheet2** worksheet tab to make it the active sheet and to select the sheet name. Compare your screen with Figure 3.

7. With the *Sheet2* worksheet tab name selected, type May and then press Enter.

8. Using either of the two methods just practiced, rename the **Sheet3** worksheet tab as June and then press Enter.

9. Verify that the *June* sheet is the active worksheet. Click the **Page Layout tab**, and then in the **Themes group**, click the **Colors** button. Scroll down, and then click **Slipstream** to change the theme colors for this workbook.

Obj 1.3.6 C

10. Click the **Home tab**. In the **Cells group**, click the **Format** button, and then point to **Tab Color** to display the colors associated with the *Slipstream* theme colors. Click the fifth color in the first row—**Blue, Accent 1**. Alternately, right-click the worksheet tab, and then click Tab Color.

Obj 1.3.1 C

    The gradient color on a worksheet tab indicates that the worksheet is active. When a worksheet is not active, the entire worksheet tab is filled with the selected color.

11. Use the technique just practiced to change the worksheet tab color of the **May** worksheet tab to the sixth color in the first row—**Turquoise, Accent 2**.

12. Change the worksheet tab color of the **April** worksheet tab to the seventh color in the first row—**Green, Accent 3**. Compare your screen with Figure 4.

13. **Save** the file.

■ **You have completed Skill 1 of 10**

Excel 2016, Windows 10, Microsoft Corporation

Figure 4

▶ When you enter a date, it is assigned a *serial number*—a sequential number.

▶ Dates are stored as sequential serial numbers so they can be used in calculations. By default, January 1, 1900, is serial number 1. January 1, 2018, is serial number 43100 because it is 43,100 days after January 1, 1900. Serial numbers make it possible to perform calculations on dates, for example, to find the number of days between two dates by subtracting the older date from the more recent date.

▶ When you type any of the following values into cells, Excel interprets them as dates: 7/4/18, 4-Jul, 4-Jul-18, Jul-18. When typing in these dates formats, the $\boxed{-}$ (hyphen) key and the $\boxed{/}$ (forward slash) key function identically.

▶ You can enter months using the entire name or the first three characters. Years can be entered as two or four digits. When the year is left off, the current year will be inserted.

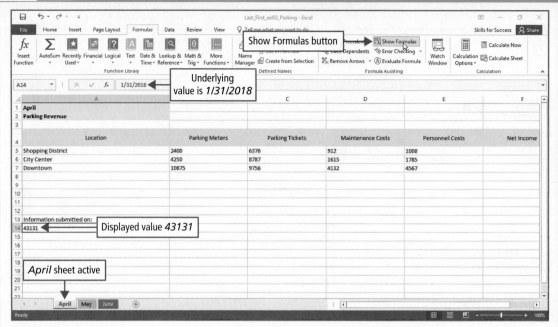

Figure 1   Excel 2016, Windows 10, Microsoft Corporation

Obj 1.4.8 C

1. On the **April** sheet, click cell **A14** to display the underlying value *1/31/2018* in the formula bar. Click the **Formulas tab**, and then in the **Formula Auditing group**, click the **Show Formulas** button. Compare your screen with **Figure 1**.

   The date, *January 31, 2018*, displays as 43131—the number of days since the reference date of January 1, 1900.

2. On the **Formulas tab**, in the **Formula Auditing group**, click the **Show Formulas** button to display the date.

3. Click the **Home tab**, and in the **Number group**, click the **Number Format arrow** (**Figure 2**).

   In the Number Format list, you can select common date, time, and number formats, or click *More Number Formats* to display additional built-in number formats.

■ **Continue to the next page to complete the skill** ▶

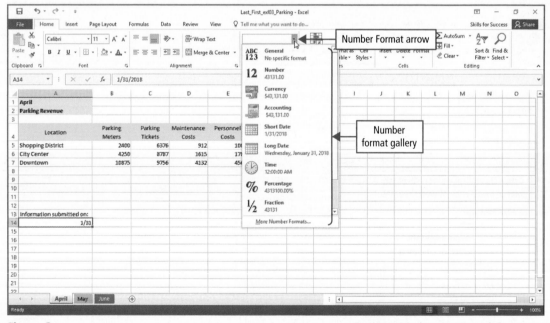

Figure 2   Excel 2016, Windows 10, Microsoft Corporation

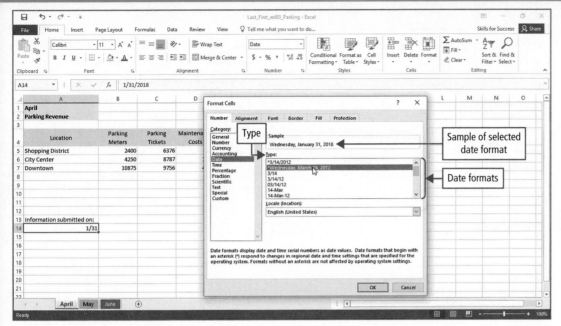

Excel 2016, Windows 10, Microsoft Corporation

Figure 3

4. At the bottom of the **Number Format** list, click **More Number Formats**. On the **Number tab** of the **Format Cells** dialog box, notice Date is selected at the left. Under **Type**, click ***Wednesday, March 14, 2012** to show a sample of the selected date format. Compare your screen with **Figure 3**.

 The date *Wednesday, March 14, 2012* will not display in your worksheet. This is a sample of a format that can be applied to your current date.

5. Under **Type**, scroll down, click **March 14, 2012**, and then click **OK** to display the date in cell A14 as *January 31, 2018*.

6. Click the **May** worksheet tab to make it the active worksheet, and then click cell **A17**. Type 8/11/98 and then on the formula bar, click the **Enter** button ✓ to accept the entry and change the year from *98* to *1998*.

 When a two-digit year between 30 and 99 is entered, a twentieth-century date is applied to the date format—*8/11/1998*.

7. Click the **June** worksheet tab, and then click cell **A17**. Hold down Ctrl and press ;—the semicolon key—to enter the current date. Press Enter to confirm the entry.

 The Ctrl + ; shortcut enters the current date, obtained from your computer, into the selected cell using the default date format. The table in **Figure 4** summarizes how Excel interprets various date entries.

8. **Save** 🖫 the file.

■ **You have completed Skill 2 of 10**

Date Format AutoComplete	
Date Typed As	**Completed by Excel As**
7/4/18	7/4/2018
7-4-98	7/4/1998
7/4 or 7-4	4-Jul (current year assumed)
July 4 or Jul 4	4-Jul (current year assumed)
Jul/4 or Jul-4	4-Jul (current year assumed)
July 4, 1998	4-Jul-98
July 2018	Jul-18 (the first day of the month is assumed)
July 1998	Jul-98 (the first day of the month is assumed)

Figure 4

► Cells can contain formatting, comments, hyperlinks, and *content*—underlying formulas and data in a cell.

► You can clear the formatting, comments, hyperlinks, or contents of a cell.

1. Click the **April** worksheet tab, and then click cell **A1**. On the **Home tab**, in the **Editing group**, click the **Clear** button, and then compare your screen with Figure 1.

2. On the menu, click **Clear Contents**. Look at cell **A1**, and verify that the text has been cleared but that the fill color applied to the cell still displays.

   Alternately, to delete the contents of a cell, you can press Delete .

3. In cell **A1**, type Parking Revenue and then on the formula bar, click the **Enter** button ✔.

4. With cell **A1** still selected, in the **Editing group**, click the **Clear** button, and then click **Clear Formats** to clear the formatting from the cell. Compare your screen with Figure 2.

5. Click cell **A2**. On the **Home tab**, in the **Editing group**, click the **Clear** button, and then click **Clear All** to clear both the cell contents and the cell formatting.

   Alternately, tap a cell on a touchscreen, and then on the Mini toolbar, click Clear.

■ **Continue to the next page to complete the skill** ➡

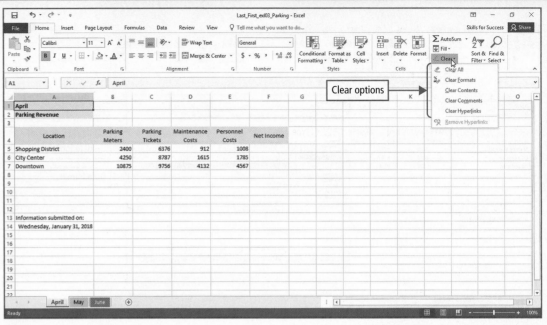

Figure 1

Excel 2016, Windows 10, Microsoft Corporation

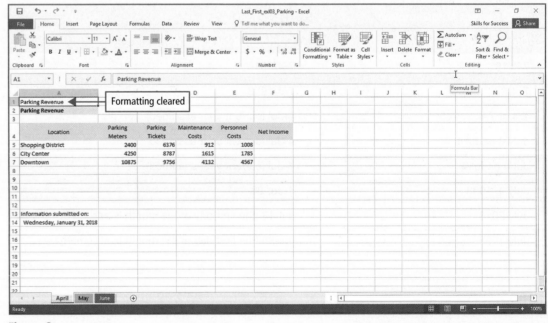

Figure 2

Excel 2016, Windows 10, Microsoft Corporation

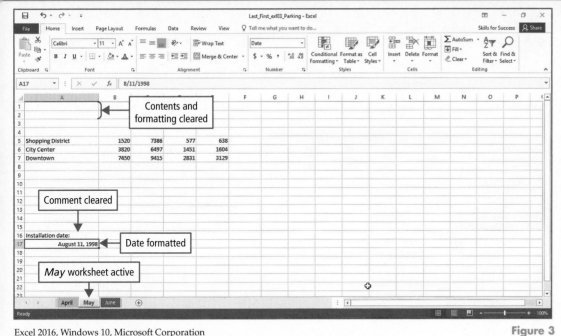

Excel 2016, Windows 10, Microsoft Corporation

Figure 3

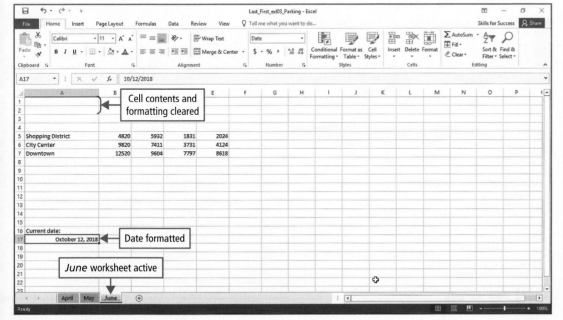

Excel 2016, Windows 10, Microsoft Corporation

Figure 4

6. Display the **May** worksheet, and then select the range **A1:A2**. In the **Editing group**, click the **Clear** button, and then click **Clear All**.

7. Click cell **A16** to display the comment. On the **Home tab**, in the **Editing group**, click the **Clear** button, and then click **Clear Comments** to clear the comment from the cell.

8. Click cell **A17**. On the **Home tab**, in the **Number group**, click the **Number Format arrow**. At the bottom of the **Number Format** list, click **More Number Formats**. In the **Format Cells** dialog box, under **Type**, scroll down, click **March 14, 2012**, and then click **OK** to display the date in cell A17 as *August 11, 1998*. Compare your screen with **Figure 3**.

9. Display the **June** worksheet. Select the range **A1:A2**, and then use the technique just practiced to clear the contents and formatting from the selected range.

10. Click cell **A17**, and then use the technique just practiced to apply the date format *March 14, 2012*, to the current date. Compare your screen with **Figure 4**.

11. Make **April** the active worksheet, and then **Save** 🖫 the file.

■ **You have completed Skill 3 of 10**

▶ Data from cells and ranges can be copied and then pasted to other cells in the same worksheet, to other worksheets, or to worksheets in another workbook.

▶ The ***Clipboard*** is a temporary storage area for text and graphics. When you use either the Copy command or the Cut command, the selected data is placed in the Clipboard, from which the data is available to paste.

1. On the **April** sheet, select the range **A13:A14**. Point to the lower edge of the green border surrounding the selected range until the pointer displays. Drag downward until the ScreenTip displays *A16:A17*, as shown in **Figure 1**, and then release the left mouse button to complete the move.

    Drag and drop is a method of moving objects in which you point to the selection and then drag it to a new location.

2. Select the range **A4:F4**. In the **Clipboard group**, click the **Copy** button 📋

    A moving border surrounds the selected range, and a message on the status bar indicates *Select destination and press ENTER or choose Paste*, confirming that your selected range has been copied to the Clipboard.

3. Display the **May** sheet, and then click cell **A4**. In the **Clipboard group**, click the **Paste arrow** to display the **Paste Options** gallery. Point at the second option in the second row—**Keep Source Column Width** and then compare your screen with **Figure 2**.

■ **Continue to the next page to complete the skill**

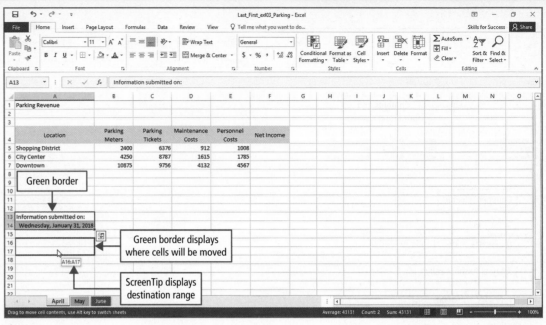

Figure 1

Excel 2016, Windows 10, Microsoft Corporation

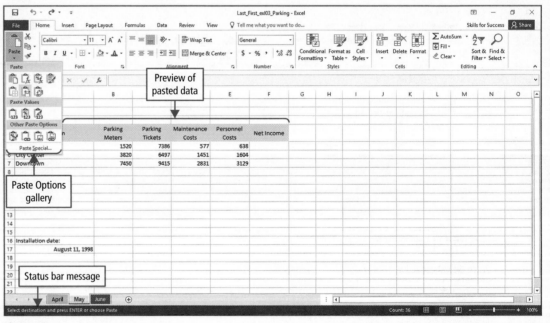

Figure 2

Excel 2016, Windows 10, Microsoft Corporation

Paste Options

Option	Icon	Content and format pasted
Paste		Both the contents and cell formatting
Formulas		Only the formula
Formulas & Number Formatting		Both the formula and the number formatting
Keep Source Formatting		All content and cell formatting from original cells
No Borders		All content and cell formatting except borders
Keep Source Column Widths		All content and formatting including the column width format
Transpose		Orientation of pasted entries changes—data in rows are pasted as columns
Formatting		Only the formatting

Figure 3

4. In the **Paste Options** gallery, click the option **Keep Source Column Widths** to paste the column labels and to retain the column widths from the source worksheet. The table in Figure 3 summarizes the Paste Options.

   When pasting a range of cells, you need to select only the cell in the upper left corner of the *paste area*—the target destination for data that has been cut or copied. When an item is pasted, it is not removed from the Clipboard, as indicated by the status bar message.

5. Display the **June** sheet, and then click cell **A4**. Using the technique just practiced, paste the column labels using the Paste Option **Keep Source Column Widths**.

6. Click cell **A17**, and then point to the upper green border surrounding the cell to display the pointer. Drag up to move the cell contents to cell **A16**. In the message box *There's already data here. Do you want to replace it?* click **OK** to replace the contents. Compare your screen with Figure 4.

7. Click the **April** worksheet tab. **Save** the file.

■ **You have completed Skill 4 of 10**

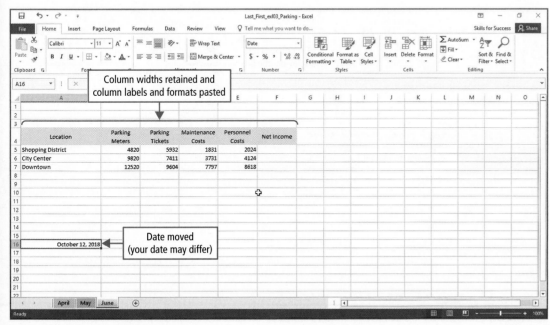

Column widths retained and column labels and formats pasted

Date moved (your date may differ)

Excel 2016, Windows 10, Microsoft Corporation

Figure 4

▶ You can group any number of worksheets in a workbook. After the worksheets are grouped, you can edit data in all of the grouped worksheets at the same time.

▶ Grouping worksheets is useful when you are creating or modifying a set of worksheets that are similar in purpose and structure.

1. Right-click the **April** worksheet tab, and then from the shortcut menu, click **Select All Sheets**.

2. At the top of the screen, on the title bar, verify that *[Group]* displays as shown in **Figure 1**.

   Here, all three worksheet tabs are shaded with a gradient color and *[Group]* displays on the title bar to indicate that the three worksheets are active as a group.

3. Select the range **A5:A7**, and then apply the **40% - Accent1** cell style.

4. Display the **May** worksheet to ungroup the sheets and to verify that the cell style you selected in the previous step displays as shown in **Figure 2**.

   In the worksheet tab area, both the *April* worksheet tab and the *June* worksheet tab display a solid color, indicating that they are no longer active in the group. At the top of your screen, *[Group]* no longer displays on the title bar.

   Selecting a single worksheet cancels a grouping. Because the worksheets were grouped, formatting was applied to all of the selected worksheets. In this manner, you can make the same changes to all selected worksheets at the same time.

■ **Continue to the next page to complete the skill**

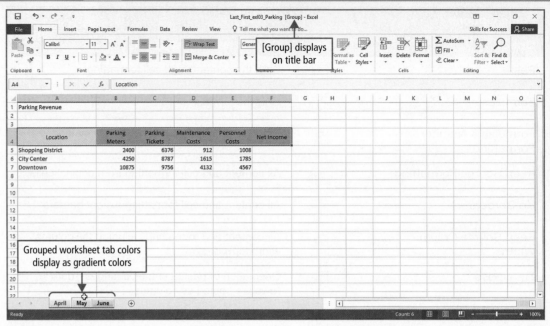

Figure 1

Excel 2016, Windows 10, Microsoft Corporation

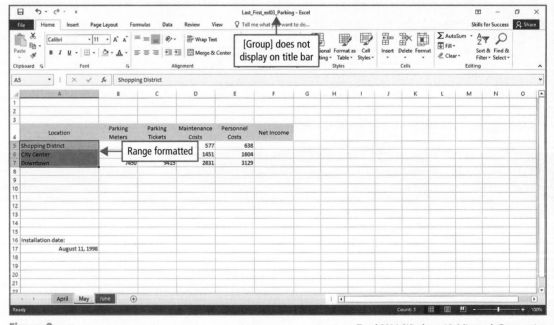

Figure 2

Excel 2016, Windows 10, Microsoft Corporation

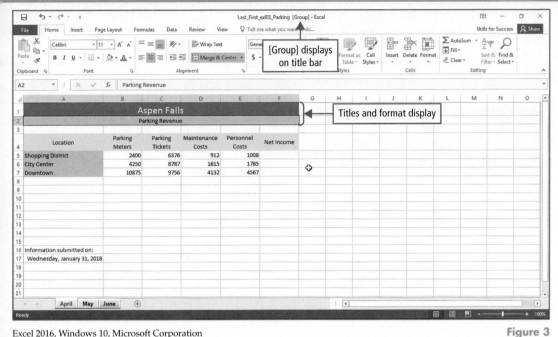

Excel 2016, Windows 10, Microsoft Corporation

Figure 3

Excel 2016, Windows 10, Microsoft Corporation

Figure 4

5. Right-click the **April** worksheet tab, and then from the shortcut menu, click **Select All Sheets**.

6. Click cell **A1**, type Aspen Falls to replace the current text, and then press Enter . Select the range **A1:F1**, and then in the **Alignment group**, click the **Merge & Center** button . Apply the **Accent1** cell style. Click the **Font Size** button , and then click **18**.

7. In cell **A2**, type Parking Revenue and then press Enter . Select the range **A2:F2**, and then click the **Merge & Center** button . Apply the **40% - Accent1** cell style, and then compare your screen with **Figure 3**.

8. Right-click the **April** worksheet tab, and then from the shortcut menu, click **Ungroup Sheets**. Verify that [Group] no longer displays on the title bar.

9. Double-click cell **A2** to edit the cell contents. Use the arrow keys to move to the left of the word *Parking*. Type April and add a space, and then press Enter . Display the **May** worksheet. Using the same technique, edit cell **A2** to May Parking Revenue Display the **June** worksheet, and then edit cell **A2** to June Parking Revenue Compare your screen with **Figure 4**.

10. **Save** the file.

■ **You have completed Skill 5 of 10**

▶ When you combine several math operators in a single formula, ***operator precedence***—a set of mathematical rules for performing calculations within a formula—is followed. Expressions within parentheses are calculated first. Exponentials are calculated second. Then multiplication and division are performed before addition and subtraction.

▶ When a formula contains operators with the same precedence level, Excel evaluates the operators from left to right. Multiplication and division are considered to be on the same level of precedence. Addition and subtraction are considered to be on the same level of precedence.

1. Right-click the **June** worksheet tab, and then click **Select All Sheets**. Verify that *[Group]* displays on the title bar.

2. Click cell **F5**, enter the formula =(B5+C5)-(D5+E5) and then compare your screen with **Figure 1**.

   The formula *Net Income = Total Revenue – Total Cost* is represented by (*Parking Meters + Parking Tickets*) – (*Maintenance Cost + Personnel Cost*). By placing parentheses in the formula, the revenue is first added together, the costs are added together, and then the total costs are subtracted from the total revenues. Without the parentheses, the formula would give an incorrect result.

3. On the formula bar, click the **Enter** button ✓. AutoFill the formula down through cell **F7**. Compare your screen with **Figure 2**.

■ Continue to the next page to complete the skill

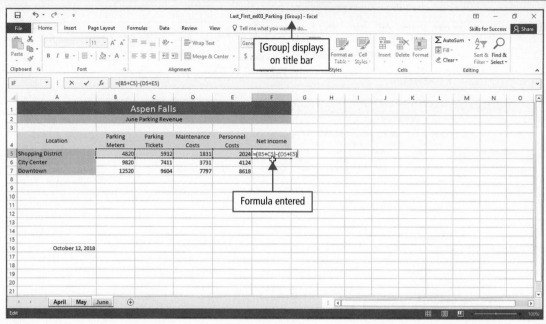

Figure 1

Excel 2016, Windows 10, Microsoft Corporation

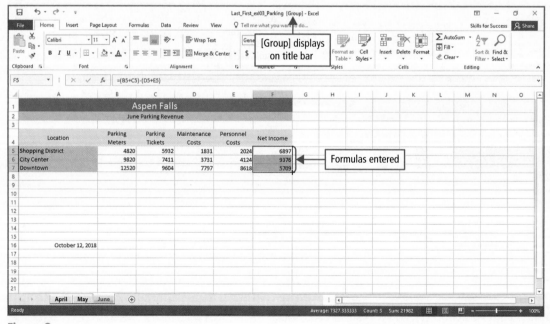

Figure 2

Excel 2016, Windows 10, Microsoft Corporation

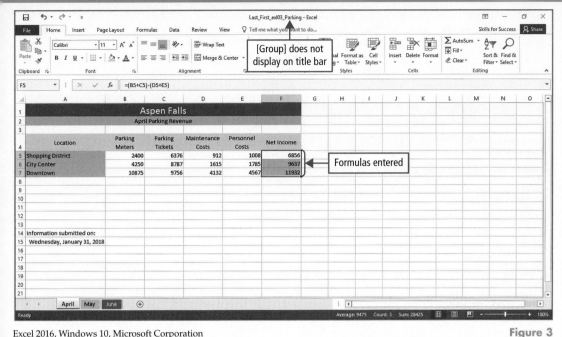

Excel 2016, Windows 10, Microsoft Corporation

Figure 3

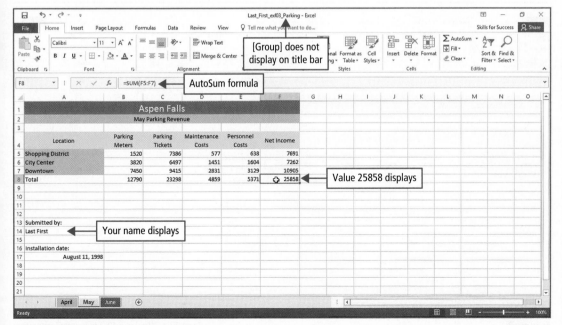

Excel 2016, Windows 10, Microsoft Corporation

Figure 4

4. Display the **April** worksheet to ungroup the sheets and to verify that the formula results display in the worksheet. Compare your screen with Figure 3.

Because the worksheets were grouped, the formulas have been entered on all selected worksheets.

5. Right-click the **April** worksheet tab, and then click **Select All Sheets**. Verify that *[Group]* displays on the title bar.

6. In cell **A8**, type Total and then press Enter. Select the range **B8:F8**, and then on the **Home tab**, in the **Editing group**, click the **AutoSum** button to insert the column totals.

7. Click cell **A13**, type Submitted by: and then press Enter. In cell **A14**, using your name, type Last First and then press Enter.

8. Click the **May** worksheet tab. Click cell **F8**, and then compare your screen with Figure 4.

On the *May* worksheet, the formula in cell F8 displays as the value *25858*.

9. Save 💾 the file.

■ **You have completed Skill 6 of 10**

▶ When worksheets are grouped, any formatting applied to a single worksheet is made to each worksheet in the group. For example, if you change the width of a column or add a row, all the worksheets in the group are changed in the same manner.

1. Right-click the **May** worksheet tab, and then click **Select All Sheets**.

2. In the row heading area, point to row **7** to display the ⊕ pointer. Right-click, and then compare your screen with **Figure 1**.

3. From the shortcut menu, click **Insert** to insert a new blank row above the *Downtown* row in all of the grouped worksheets. In cell **A7**, type Midtown and then press Tab .

4. Click the **April** worksheet tab to make it the active worksheet and to ungroup the worksheets. Beginning in cell **B7**, enter the following *Midtown* data for April:

   2785 | 5012 | 3270 | 1860

5. Click the **May** worksheet tab, and then beginning in cell **B7**, enter the following *Midtown* data for May:

   2420 | 8190 | 1916 | 2586

6. Click the **June** worksheet tab, and then beginning in cell **B7**, enter the following *Midtown* data for June:

   2170 | 6546 | 4425 | 1925

7. Click each of the worksheet tabs, and then verify that you entered the values correctly. Click the **June** worksheet tab, and then compare your screen with **Figure 2**.

■ **Continue to the next page to complete the skill**

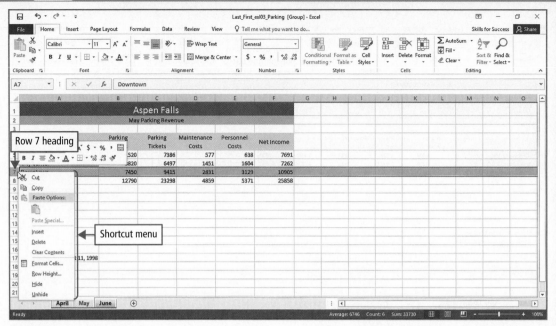

Figure 1

Excel 2016, Windows 10, Microsoft Corporation

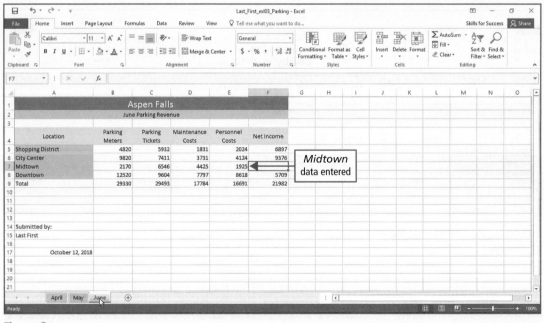

Figure 2

Excel 2016, Windows 10, Microsoft Corporation

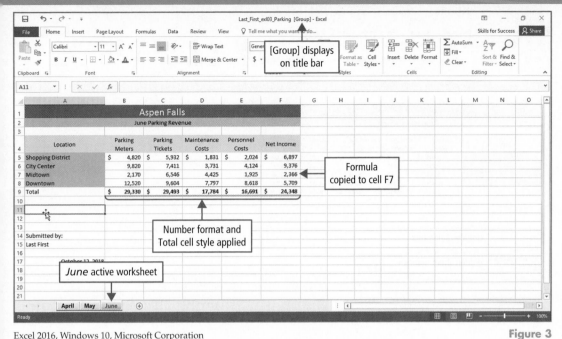

Excel 2016, Windows 10, Microsoft Corporation

Figure 3

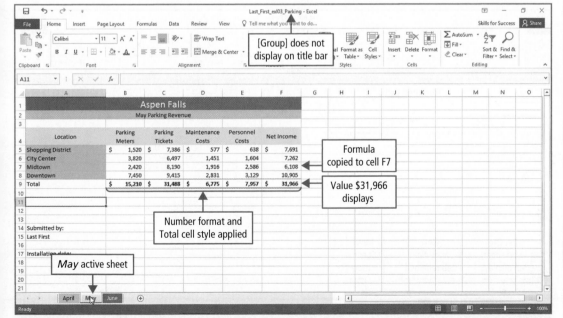

Excel 2016, Windows 10, Microsoft Corporation

Figure 4

8. Right-click the **June** worksheet tab, and then click **Select All Sheets**. Click cell **F6**, and then AutoFill the formula down to cell **F7**.

On the *June* worksheet, the formula in cell *F9* displays as the value *24348*.

9. Select the range **B5:F5**, hold down Ctrl, and then select the range **B9:F9**. With the nonadjacent ranges selected, in the **Styles group**, click the **Cell Styles** button, and then click **Currency [0]**.

10. Select the range **B6:F8**, and then apply the **Comma [0]** cell style.

11. Select the range **B9:F9**, and then apply the **Total** cell style. Click cell **A11**, and then compare your screen with **Figure 3**.

12. Display the **April** sheet, and then verify that the same formatting was applied.

13. Click the **May** worksheet tab to make it the active worksheet, and then verify that the formulas and formatting changes were made. Compare your screen with **Figure 4**.

On the *May* sheet, the formula in cell *F9* displays as the value *$31,966*.

14. Save 🖫 the file.

■ **You have completed Skill 7 of 10**

▶ To organize a workbook, you can position worksheet tabs in any order.

▶ You can add new worksheets to accommodate new information.

1. Right-click the **April** worksheet tab, and then from the shortcut menu, click **Unhide**. Compare your screen with **Figure 1**.

2. In the **Unhide** dialog box, verify *1st Qtr* is selected, and then click **OK**. Use the same technique to **Unhide** the **2015** and the **2016** worksheets.

3. Right-click the **2015** worksheet tab, and then click **Delete**. Read the message that displays, and then click **Delete**. Use the same technique to **Delete** the **2016** worksheet.

   Because you can't undo a worksheet deletion, it is a good idea to verify that you selected the correct worksheet before you click Delete.

4. To the right of the **June** worksheet tab, click the **New Sheet** button ⊕ to create a new worksheet. Rename the new worksheet tab as Summary

5. In cell **A2**, type Second Quarter Parking Revenue and then press Enter. In cell **A4**, type Month and then press Tab. Type the following labels in row **4**, pressing Tab after each label: Total Meter Revenue | Total Ticket Revenue | Total Maintenance Cost | Total Personnel Cost | Net Income

6. In cell **A5**, type April and then AutoFill the months down through cell **A7**.

7. Change the **Column Width** of **columns A:F** to 12 Click cell **A9**, and then compare your screen with **Figure 2**.

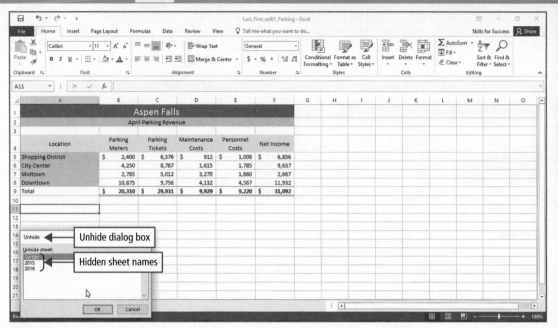

Figure 1

Excel 2016, Windows 10, Microsoft Corporation

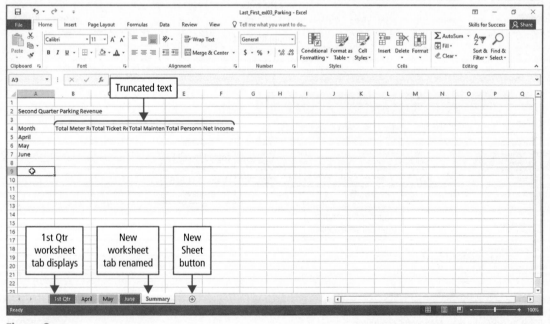

Figure 2

Excel 2016, Windows 10, Microsoft Corporation

■ **Continue to the next page to complete the skill**

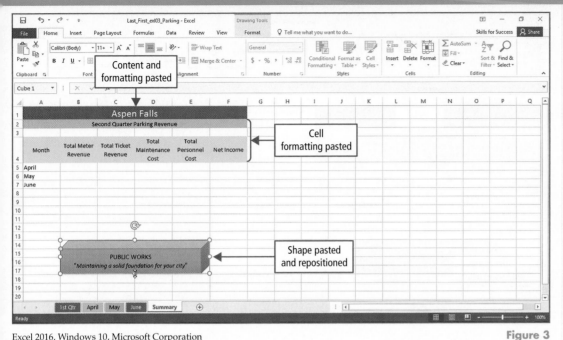

Content and formatting pasted

Cell formatting pasted

Shape pasted and repositioned

Excel 2016, Windows 10, Microsoft Corporation

Figure 3

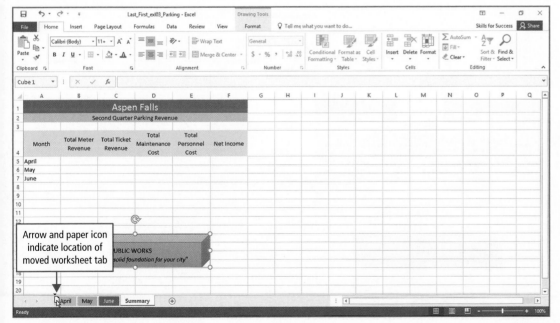

Arrow and paper icon indicate location of moved worksheet tab

Excel 2016, Windows 10, Microsoft Corporation

Figure 4

8. Display the **June** sheet. Click cell **A1**, and then in the **Clipboard group**, click the **Copy** button. Display the **Summary** sheet. Click cell **A1**, and then click the **Paste** button to paste the cell content and format. Obj 2.1.2 C

9. Display the **June** sheet, and then press Esc to remove the moving border. Select the range **A2:F4**, and then click the **Copy** button. Display the **Summary** sheet, and then click the cell **A2**. In the **Clipboard group**, click the **Paste arrow**. In the **Paste Options** gallery, under **Other Paste Options**, click the first option—**Formatting**—to paste only the format.

10. Display the **1st Qtr** sheet. Click the shape, and then click the **Copy** button. Display the **Summary** sheet. In the **Clipboard group**, click the **Paste** button. Move and resize the shape to approximately the range **B14:E17**. Compare your screen with **Figure 3**.

11. Right-click the **1st Qtr** worksheet tab, and then click **Hide**. Obj 1.4.1 C

12. Click the **Summary** worksheet tab. Hold down the left mouse button and drag to the left to display an arrow and the pointer. Drag to the left until the arrow is to the left of the **April** worksheet tab, as shown in **Figure 4**. Obj 1.3.3 C

13. Release the left mouse button to complete the worksheet move. **Save** the file.

■ **You have completed Skill 8 of 10**

 **WATCH** SKILL 3.9

▶ A *summary sheet* is a worksheet that displays and summarizes totals from other worksheets. A *detail sheet* is a worksheet with cells referred to by summary sheet formulas.

▶ Changes made to the detail sheets that affect totals will automatically recalculate and display on the summary sheet.

1. On the **Summary** sheet, click cell **B5**. Type = and then click the **April** worksheet tab. On the **April** sheet, click cell **B9**, and then press Enter to display the April sheet B9 value in the Summary sheet B5 cell.

2. On the **Summary** sheet, click cell **B5**. In the formula bar, notice that the cell reference in the underlying formula includes both a worksheet reference and a cell reference, as shown in **Figure 1**.

    By using a formula that refers to another worksheet, changes made to the Total in cell *B9* of the *April* sheet will be automatically updated in this *Summary* sheet.

3. Click cell **B6**, type = and then click the **May** worksheet tab. On the **May** sheet, click cell **B9**, and then press Enter.

4. On the **Summary** sheet, repeat the technique just practiced to display the **June** sheet **B9** value in the **Summary** sheet **B7** cell.

5. On the **Summary** sheet, select the range **B5:B7**, and then AutoFill to the right through column **F**. Click cell **F7**, and then compare your screen with **Figure 2**.

■ Continue to the next page to complete the skill

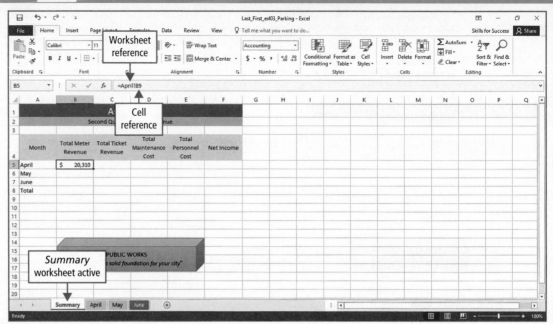

Figure 1

Excel 2016, Windows 10, Microsoft Corporation

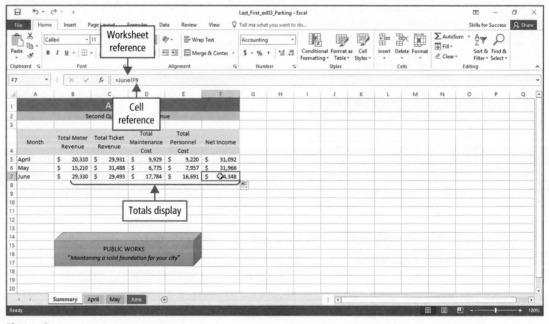

Figure 2

Excel 2016, Windows 10, Microsoft Corporation

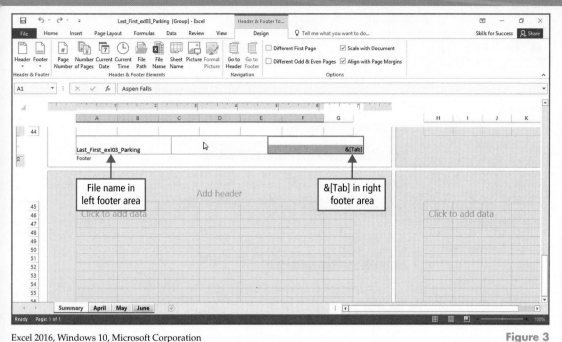

Excel 2016, Windows 10, Microsoft Corporation

Figure 3

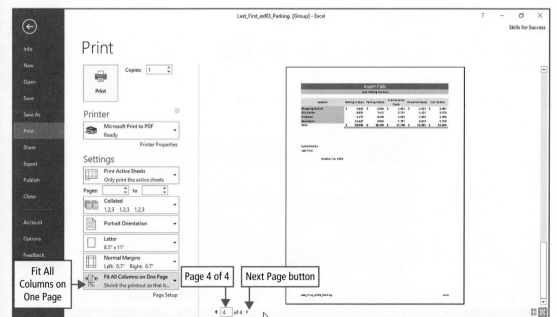

Excel 2016, Windows 10, Microsoft Corporation

Figure 4

6. On the **Summary** sheet, click cell **A8**, type Total and then select the range **B8:F8**. In the **Editing group**, click the **AutoSum** button ∑ AutoSum ·, and then apply the **Total** cell style. Select the range **B6:F7** and then apply the **Comma [0]** cell style.

7. Right-click the **Summary** worksheet tab, and then click **Select All Sheets**.

8. Insert the File Name in the worksheet's left footer, and then insert the Sheet Name in the right footer. Compare your screen with **Figure 3**.

   By grouping worksheets, you can insert headers and footers into each worksheet quickly and consistently.

9. Click in a cell just above the footer to exit the **Footer** area. On the lower right side of the status bar, click the **Normal** button ▦. Hold down Ctrl, and then press Home to make cell **A1** the active cell on all selected worksheets.

10. With the sheets still grouped, click the **File tab**, and then click **Print**. Under **Settings**, click the last option arrow, and then click **Fit All Columns on One Page**. At the bottom of the screen, click the **Next Page** button ▶ three times to view each of the four worksheets, and then compare your screen with **Figure 4**.

    Because the worksheets are grouped, all four worksheets are included in the preview.

11. **Save** the file.

■ **You have completed Skill 9 of 10**

 **WATCH** SKILL 3.10

▸ A *clustered bar chart* is useful when you want to compare values across categories; bar charts organize categories along the vertical axis and values along the horizontal axis.

1. Right-click the **Summary** worksheet tab, and then click **Ungroup Sheets**. On the **Summary** sheet, select the range **A4:E7**. Click the **Insert tab**, and then in the **Charts group**, click the **Recommended Charts** button. In the **Insert Chart** dialog box, verify the first choice is selected— **Clustered Bar**, and then click **OK**.

2. On the **Design tab**, in the **Location group**, click the **Move Chart** button. In the **Move Chart** dialog box, select the **New sheet** option button, type 2nd Qtr Chart and then click **OK**.

3. On the **Design tab**, in the **Data group**, click the **Switch Row/Column** button to display the months on the vertical axis. Compare your screen with **Figure 1**.

Because you want to look at revenue and costs by month, displaying the months on the vertical axis is useful.

4. In the **Chart Layouts group**, click the **Quick Layout** button, and then click **Layout 3**.

5. To the right of the chart, click the **Chart Styles** button , and then click **Style 3**.

6. Edit the **Chart Title** to 2nd Quarter Parking Revenue and Cost and then compare your screen with **Figure 2**.

■ **Continue to the next page to complete the skill**

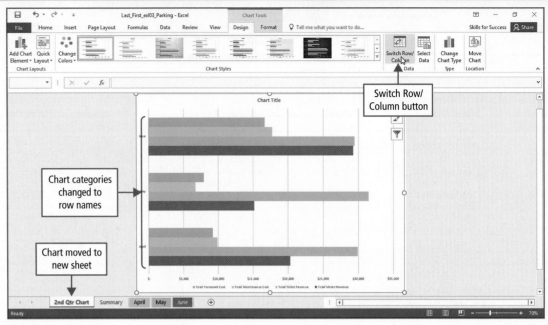

Figure 1

Excel 2016, Windows 10, Microsoft Corporation

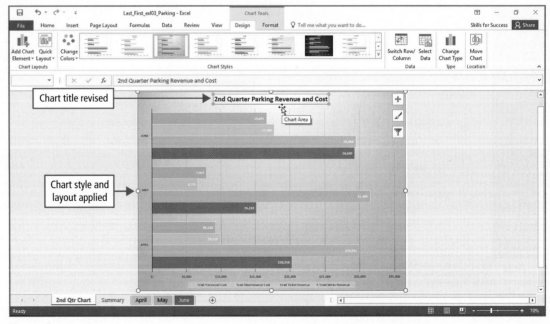

Figure 2

Excel 2016, Windows 10, Microsoft Corporation

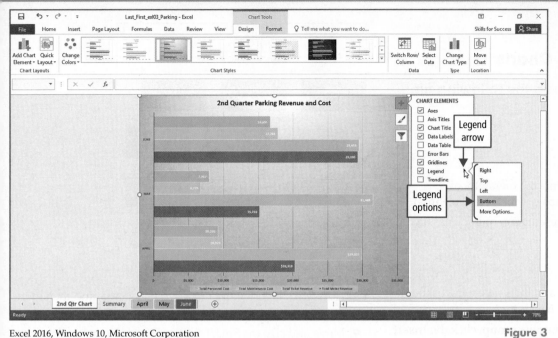

Excel 2016, Windows 10, Microsoft Corporation

Figure 3

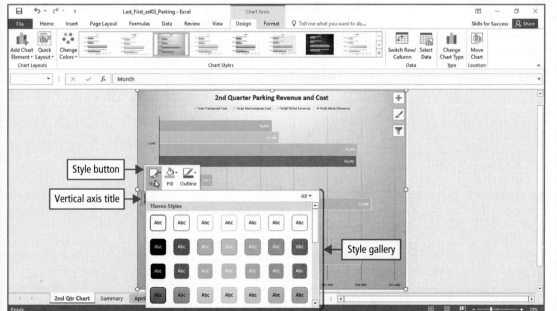

Excel 2016, Windows 10, Microsoft Corporation

Figure 4

7. At the top right corner of the chart, click the **Chart Elements** button ⊞. Point to **Legend**, and then click the **Legend arrow**. Compare your screen with **Figure 3**.

8. In the list, click **Top** to move the legend to the top of the chart sheet.

9. In the **Chart Elements** gallery, point to **Axis Titles**, and then click the **Axis Titles arrow**. Select the **Primary Vertical** check box to add the vertical axis title. Click the **Chart Elements** button ⊞ to close the gallery.

10. On the left side of the chart, change the vertical **Axis Title** text to Month Right-click the *Month* title, and then on the Mini toolbar, click the **Style** button. Compare your screen with **Figure 4**.

11. In the **Style** gallery, click the second thumbnail in the fourth row—**Subtle Effect - Blue, Accent 1**.

12. Click the **Insert tab**, and then in the **Text group**, click the **Header & Footer** button. In the **Page Setup** dialog box, click the **Custom Footer** button. In the **Footer** dialog box, verify the insertion point is in the **Left section**, and then click the **Insert File Name** button. Click the **Right section** of the footer, and then click the **Insert Sheet Name** button. Click **OK** two times.

13. **Save** 🖫 the file, and then **Close** ☒ Excel. Submit the file as directed by your instructor.

✔ **DONE!** You have completed Skill 10 of 10, and your file is complete!

More Skills 11

Create SmartArt Organization Charts

To complete this project, you will need the following file:

- Blank Excel workbook

You will save your file as:

- Last_First_exl03_MS11Organization

▶ An *organization chart* graphically represents the hierarchy of relationships between individuals and groups within an organization.

▶ A *SmartArt graphic* provides a visual representation of information used to effectively communicate ideas.

Figure 1

---

1. Start **Excel 2016**. Open a blank workbook, and then save the workbook in your chapter folder as Last_First_exl03_MS11Organization

2. Click the **Insert tab**, and then in the **Illustrations group**, click the **Insert a SmartArt Graphic** button 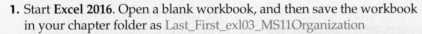. In the **Choose a SmartArt Graphic** dialog box, click **Hierarchy**. In the **SmartArt Layout** gallery, click **Organization Chart**, and then click **OK**.

3. At the top of the SmartArt graphic, click the first shape that displays *Text*. Type Maria Martinez press Enter , and then type City Manager

4. Click the border of the second shape, and then press Delete to delete the text box.

5. Click the first shape in the second row, and then replace *Text* by typing Park Operations Repeat this process and type Park Development in the middle shape and Recreation in the last shape.

6. Click the *Park Operations* shape. On the **Design tab**, in the **Create Graphic group**, click the **Add Shape** button. With the new shape selected, type Grounds and then click the **Add Shape button arrow** and **Add Shape After**. In the new shape, type Buildings Alternatively, you can use the **Text Pane** button to enter text in the shapes.

7. Using the technique just practiced, add two shapes below the *Park Development* shape, and then in the two shapes, type the following text: Planning and Capital Development

8. Add two shapes below the *Recreation* shape, and then in the two shapes, type Sports and Aquatics

9. Move and size the SmartArt graphic to display in the range **A1:I22**.

10. In the **SmartArt Styles group**, click the **More arrow**, and then under **3-D**, click **Polished**.

11. In the **SmartArt Styles group**, click the **Change Colors** button. Under **Colorful**, click **Colorful Range – Accent Colors 5 to 6**.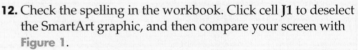

12. Check the spelling in the workbook. Click cell **J1** to deselect the SmartArt graphic, and then compare your screen with **Figure 1**.

13. **Save** 🖫 the file, and then **Close** ☒ Excel. Submit the file as directed by your instructor.

- **You have completed More Skills 11**

More Skills 12

Create and Insert Screen Shots

To complete this project, you will need the following file:

- **exl03_MS12Labor**

You will save your file as:

- **Last_First_exl03_MS12Labor**

▸ A ***screen shot*** is an image of the computer screen.

---

1. Close all open windows on your computer, and then open a web browser—for example, **Edge**. In the address bar, type aspenfalls.org and then press Enter to display the *City of Aspen Falls* web site. Click the link **Aspen Falls Labor Statistics**.
2. Start **Excel 2016**, and then open the file **exl03_MS12Labor**. Save the file in your chapter folder as Last_First_exl03_MS12Labor
3. Select cell **A1**. On the **Insert tab**, in the **Illustrations group**, click the **Take a Screenshot** button.

   A ***screen clipping*** is a picture of a portion of the computer screen that can be inserted into a worksheet. It can be very small or as large as the entire screen.

4. In the **Available Windows** gallery, click the text **Screen Clipping**. The web page opens for *Aspen Falls Labor Statistics*, and then after a moment, the screen is dimmed.
5. Place the **Precision** select pointer at the top left of the BLS logo, and then drag to trace the logo outline. Release the mouse button.

   The image that was captured is placed into cell A1, and is treated as a picture.

   MOS Obj 5.3.2 C

6. Select the image, and then on the **Picture Tools Format tab**, in the **Size group**, adjust the width to **1"**. The height will adjust to approximately 1.06" automatically.
7. In the **Picture Styles group**, apply the **Reflected Rounded Rectangle** style, which is the fifth option in row 1. Select an empty cell. Compare your screen with **Figure 1**.
8. **Save** the file, and then **Close** Excel. Submit the file as directed by your instructor.

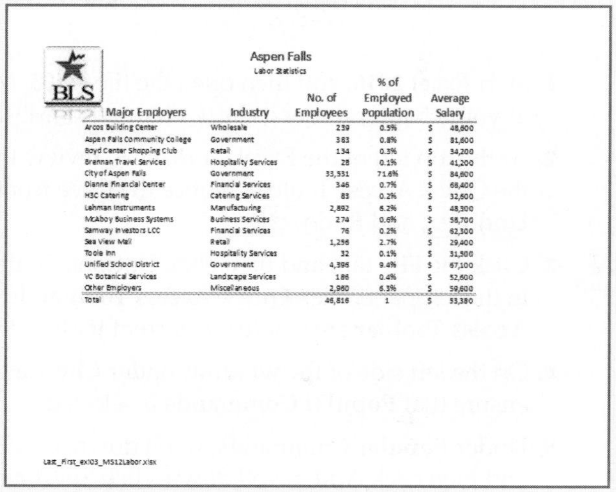

Aspen Falls
Labor Statistics

Major Employers	Industry	No. of Employees	% of Employed Population	Average Salary
Arcos Building Center	Wholesale	239	0.5%	$ 48,600
Aspen Falls Community College	Government	383	0.8%	$ 81,600
Boyd Center Shopping Club	Retail	134	0.3%	$ 34,200
Brennan Travel Services	Hospitality Services	28	0.1%	$ 41,200
City of Aspen Falls	Government	33,531	71.6%	$ 84,600
Dianne Financial Center	Financial Services	346	0.7%	$ 68,400
H3C Catering	Catering Services	83	0.2%	$ 32,600
Lehman Instruments	Manufacturing	2,892	6.2%	$ 48,300
McAboy Business Systems	Business Services	274	0.6%	$ 58,700
Samway Investors LCC	Financial Services	76	0.2%	$ 62,300
Sea View Mall	Retail	1,256	2.7%	$ 29,400
Toole Inn	Hospitality Services	32	0.1%	$ 31,500
Unified School District	Government	4,396	9.4%	$ 67,100
VC Botanical Services	Landscape Services	186	0.4%	$ 52,600
Other Employers	Miscellaneous	2,960	6.3%	$ 59,600
Total		46,816	1	$ 53,380

Last_First_exl03_MS12Labor.xlsx

Figure 1

■ **You have completed More Skills 12**

More Skills 13

Modify the Quick Access Toolbar

To complete this project, you will need the following file:

- exl03_MS13Members

You will save your files as:

- Last_First_exl03_MS13Members
- Last_First_exl03_MS13Snip

▶ The *Quick Access Toolbar* is a small toolbar that contains buttons for commonly used commands such as Save and Undo.

1. Start **Excel 2016**, and then open the file **exl03_MS13Members**. **Save** the file in your chapter folder as Last_First_exl03_MS13Members

2. At the top left of the Excel worksheet, review the current tools assigned to the Quick Access Toolbar. Notice the three icons on the toolbar, **Save** 🖫, **Undo** � , and **Redo** ↻.

MOS
Obj 1.4.3 C

3. Click the **File tab**, and then click **Options**. In the **Excel Options** dialog box, in the left pane, click **Quick Access Toolbar**. In the **Customize the Quick Access Toolbar** area, note the current tools in the pane.

4. On the left side of the window, under **Choose commands from arrow**, ensure that **Popular Commands** is selected.

5. Under **Popular Commands**, scroll down, click **Print Preview and Print**, and then click **Add**. Scroll down, click **Spelling**, and then click **Add**.

6. At the bottom of the **Excel Options** dialog box, click **OK**.

7. Review the Quick Access Toolbar located at the top left of the Excel window. Print Preview and Print 🖶 and Spelling icons have been added to the ribbon. Compare your screen with **Figure 1**.

8. Using the **Snipping Tool**, take a **Full-screen Snip** of your screen. Save the file as Last_First_exl03_MS13Snip

9. **Save** 🖫 the file, and then **Close** ✕ Excel. Submit the files as directed by your instructor.

- **You have completed More Skills 13**

Figure 1

Excel 2016, Windows 10, Microsoft Corporation

More Skills 14

Create and Edit Hyperlinks

To complete this project, you will need the following file:

- exl03_MS14Weekends

You will save your file as:

- Last_First_exl03_MS14Weekends

▶ **Hyperlinks** are text or graphics that you click to go to a file, a location in a file, a web page on the World Wide Web, or a web page on an organization's intranet.

---

1. Start **Excel 2016**, open the student data file **exl03_MS14Weekends**, and then **Save** the file in your chapter folder as Last_First_exl03_MS14Weekends If a security warning appears, enable the content.

2. Verify that the **Summary** worksheet is the active worksheet. Click cell **A1**. Click the **Insert tab**, and then in the **Links group**, click the **Hyperlink** button.

MOS
Obj 1.2.3 C

3. At the left of the displayed **Insert Hyperlink** dialog box, under **Link to**, verify that **Existing File or Web Page** is selected.

4. At the bottom of the **Insert Hyperlink** dialog box, click in the **Address** box, and then if necessary, delete any text. Type www.aspenfalls.org

   As you type, Excel will try to assist you by inserting the name of websites you have previously visited.

5. In the dialog box, click **OK**, and then verify that *Aspen Falls* displays in a different color and is underlined.

   The different color and underline indicate that the word is a hyperlink.

6. Point to the hyperlink *Aspen Falls* to display the 👆 pointer and the ScreenTip with the URL. Click the hyperlink *Aspen Falls*.

   Your web browser opens to the home page of the City of Aspen Falls website.

7. **Close** ☒ the web browser. Notice that after you have clicked a hyperlink, the color of the hyperlink changes to indicate that you have visited the site.

8. Right-click cell **A1**, and then click **Edit Hyperlink**. In the **Edit Hyperlink** dialog box, click the **ScreenTip** button, and then enter the ScreenTip City of Aspen Falls Click **OK** two times.

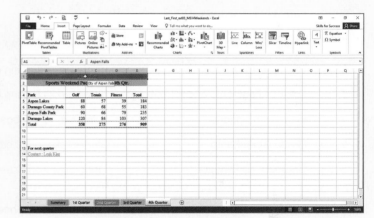

Excel 2016, Windows 10, Microsoft Corporation   **Figure 1**

9. Point to the hyperlink *Aspen Falls* to display the ScreenTip, and notice there is no URL. Compare your screen with **Figure 1**.

10. **Save** 🖫 the file, and then **Close** ☒ Excel. Submit the file as directed by your instructor.

- **You have completed More Skills 14**

Review

The following table summarizes the **SKILLS AND PROCEDURES** covered in this chapter.

Skills Number	Task	Step	Icon	Keyboard Shortcut
1	Rename worksheet tab	Home tab → Cells group → Format → Rename Sheet → Type new name → Enter		
1	Rename worksheet tab	Double-click worksheet tab → Type new name → Enter		
1	Format worksheet tab	Home tab → Cells group → Format → Tab Color		
1	Format worksheet tab	Right-click worksheet tab → Tab Color		
2	Format dates	Home tab → Number group → Number Format arrow → More Number Formats		
2	Enter the current date			Ctrl + :
3	Clear cell contents	Home tab → Editing group → Clear → Clear Contents		Delete
3	Clear cell formatting	Home tab → Editing group → Clear → Clear Formats		
3	Clear cell contents and formatting	Home tab → Editing group→ Clear → Clear All		
4	Paste with options	Home tab → Clipboard group → Paste arrow → Select desired option		
5	Group worksheets	Right-click worksheet tab → Select All Sheets		
5	Ungroup worksheets	Right-click worksheet tab → Ungroup Sheets or click a single worksheet tab		
8	Insert worksheet	Taskbar → New Sheet button	⊕	
8	Delete worksheet	Right-click worksheet tab → Delete		
8	Hide worksheet	Right-click worksheet tab → Hide		
8	Unhide worksheet	Right-click worksheet tab → Unhide → Worksheet name		
8	Move worksheet tab	Drag worksheet tab to new location		
MS11	Insert SmartArt	Insert tab → Illustrations group → Insert a SmartArt Graphic	▣	
MS12	Create and insert screen shot	Insert tab → Illustrations group → Take a Screenshot	▣+	
MS13	Modify Quick Access Toolbar	File tab → Options → Quick Access Toolbar		
MS14	Insert hyperlink	Insert tab → Links group → Hyperlink		
MS14	Edit hyperlink	Right-click hyperlink → Edit Hyperlink		

Project Summary Chart

Project	Project Type	Project Location
Skills Review	Review	In Book & MIL MyITLab® Grader
Skills Assessment 1	Review	In Book & MIL MyITLab® Grader
Skills Assessment 2	Review	Book
My Skills	Problem Solving	Book
Visual Skills Check	Problem Solving	Book
Skills Challenge 1	Critical Thinking	Book
Skills Challenge 2	Critical Thinking	Book
More Skills Assessment	Review	In Book & MIL MyITLab® Grader
Collaborating with Google	Critical Thinking	Book

MOS Objectives Covered (Quiz in MyITLab®)

1.1.3 C Add a worksheet to an existing workbook	2.1.2 C Cut, copy, or paste data
1.2.3 C Insert hyperlinks	2.1.3 C Paste data by using special paste options
1.3.1 C Change worksheet tab color	4.1.1 C Insert references
1.3.2 C Rename a worksheet	5.1.1 C Create a new chart
1.3.3 C Change worksheet order	5.1.3 C Switch between rows and columns in source data
1.3.6 C Change workbook themes	5.2.2 C Add and modify chart elements
1.3.8 C Insert headers and footers	5.2.3 C Apply chart layouts and styles
1.4.1 C Hide or unhide worksheets	5.2.4 C Move charts to a chart sheet
1.4.3 C Customize the Quick Access toolbar	5.3.2 C Insert images
1.4.8 C Display formulas	5.3.3 C Modify object properties
1.5.4 C Set print scaling	

Key Terms

> BizSkills
> Video

1. Why should you arrive early for an interview?

2. What should you do at the end of an interview?

Online Help Skills

1. Start **Excel 2016**, and then in the upper right corner of the start page, click the **Help** button ? .

2. In the **Excel Help** window **Search help** box, type date function and then press Enter .

3. In the search result list, click **DATE function**. **Maximize** the Help window, and then compare your screen with **Figure 1**.

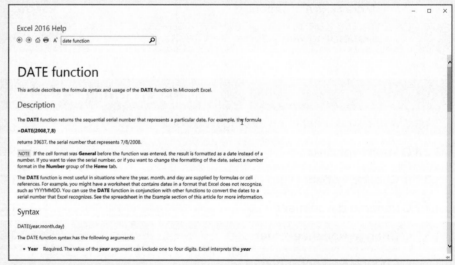

Figure 1   Excel 2016, Windows 10, Microsoft Corporation

4. Read the article to see if you can answer the following question: What cell format can be applied to stop changing numbers into dates?

Matching

Match each term in the second column with its correct definition in the first column by writing the letter of the term on the blank line in front of the correct definition.

____ **1.** The labels along the lower edge of the workbook window that identify each worksheet.

____ **2.** Buttons to the left of the worksheet tabs used to display worksheet tabs that are not in view.

____ **3.** A sequential number assigned to a date.

____ **4.** A temporary storage area for text and graphics.

____ **5.** A method of moving or copying the content of selected cells in which you point to the selection and then drag it to a new location.

____ **6.** The target destination for data that has been cut or copied using the Clipboard.

____ **7.** The mathematical rules that specify the order that calculations are performed.

____ **8.** A worksheet that displays and summarizes totals from other worksheets.

____ **9.** A worksheet that contains the detailed information in a workbook.

____ **10.** A chart type that is useful when you want to compare values across categories.

A Clipboard

B Clustered bar chart

C Detail sheet

D Drag and drop

E Operator precedence

F Paste area

G Serial number

H Summary sheet

I Tab scrolling buttons

J Worksheet tabs

Multiple Choice

Choose the correct answer.

1. An active tab color displays this way in the worksheet.
   A. With a solid tab color
   B. With a gradient tab color
   C. Always as the first worksheet

2. The method used to group worksheets in a workbook.
   A. Right-clicking a worksheet tab and then clicking Select All Sheets
   B. Double-clicking a worksheet tab
   C. Clicking the New Sheet button

3. This will be deleted when clearing the contents of a cell.
   A. Only the contents
   B. Only the formatting
   C. Both contents and formatting

4. When pasting a range of cells, this cell needs to be selected in the paste area.
   A. Bottom right cell
   B. Center cell
   C. Top left cell

5. The method used to hide worksheets.
   A. Move the worksheet as the last sheet
   B. Right-click a worksheet tab and then click Hide
   C. Double-click a worksheet tab

6. If a workbook contains grouped worksheets, this word will display on the title bar.
   A. [Collection]
   B. [Set]
   C. [Group]

7. When a formula contains operators with the same precedence level, the operators are evaluated in this order.
   A. Left to right
   B. Right to left
   C. From the center out

8. Addition and this mathematical operator are considered to be on the same precedence level.
   A. Multiplication
   B. Division
   C. Subtraction

9. Changes made in a detail worksheet will automatically recalculate and display on this sheet.
   A. Summary
   B. Final
   C. Outline

10. This will be pasted when the paste option Keep Source Column Widths is selected.
    A. The cell formatting
    B. Only the column width formatting
    C. All content and cell formatting including the column width format

Topics for Discussion

1. Some people in an organization will only view the summary worksheet without examining the detail worksheets. When might this practice be acceptable and when might it cause mistakes?

2. Illustrate some examples of how a formula's results will be incorrect if parentheses are not used to group calculations in the order they should be performed. Think of a class where you have three exam grades and a final exam grade. If the three tests together count as 50 percent of your course grade, and the final exam counts as 50 percent of your course grade, how would you write the formula to get the correct result?

Skills Review

To complete this project, you will need the following file:

- exl03_SRPayroll

You will save your file as:

- Last_First_exl03_SRPayroll

1. Start **Excel 2016**, and then open the file **exl03_SRPayroll**. Save the file in your chapter folder as Last_First_exl03_SRPayroll

2. Right-click the **Community Center** worksheet tab, and then click **Select All Sheets**. Click cell **A19**. On the **Home tab**, in the **Editing group**, click the **Clear** button, and then click **Clear All**. Select the range **A4:F4**, and then apply the **40% - Accent3** cell style. In the **Alignment group**, click the **Wrap Text** and the **Center** buttons.

3. In cell **F5**, type =B5-(C5+D5+E5) and then press $\boxed{\text{Enter}}$ to compute Net Pay as *Total Gross Pay – (Income Tax + Social Security (FICA) Tax + Health Insurance)*. AutoFill the formula in cell **F5** down through cell **F12**, and then compare your screen with **Figure 1**.

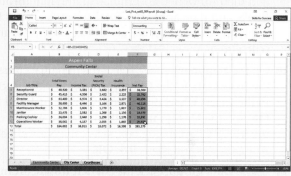

Excel 2016, Windows 10, Microsoft Corporation   **Figure 1**

4. Verify that the worksheets are still grouped. Select the range **B6:F12**, and then apply the **Comma [0]** cell style. Select the range **B13:F13**, and then apply the **Total** cell style.

5. To the right of the **Courthouse** worksheet tab, click the **New Sheet** button. Rename the new worksheet tab Summary and then change the **Tab Color** to **Orange** under **Standard Colors**. Click the **Summary** worksheet tab, and then drag it to the left of the **Community Center** worksheet tab.

6. Right-click the **Summary** worksheet tab, and then click **Select All Sheets**. Add the file name to the worksheet's left footer. Click the **right footer section**, and then in the **Header & Footer Elements** group, click the **Sheet Name** button. Return to **Normal** view, and then press $\boxed{\text{Ctrl}}$ + $\boxed{\text{Home}}$.

7. Display the **Community Center** sheet, select the range **A1:F4**, and then click **Copy**. Display the **Summary** sheet, and then click cell **A1**. Click the **Paste arrow**, and then click **Keep Source Column Widths**. In cell **A2**, replace the text with City Payroll In cell **A4**, replace the text with Location and then press $\boxed{\text{Enter}}$. Type the following labels in column A, pressing $\boxed{\text{Enter}}$ after each label: Community Center | City Center | Courthouse | Total Compare your screen with **Figure 2**.

Excel 2016, Windows 10, Microsoft Corporation   **Figure 2**

■ Continue to the next page to complete this Skills Review

8. On the **Summary** sheet, click cell **B5**, type = and then click the **Community Center** worksheet tab. On the **Community Center** sheet, click cell **B13**, and then press Enter. Use the same technique in cells **B6** and **B7** to place the *Total Gross Pay* amounts from the *City Center* and the *Courthouse* sheets on the *Summary* sheet.

9. On the **Summary** sheet, select the range **B5:B7**. Click the **Quick Analysis** button, click **Totals**, and then click the first option **Sum**. Select the range **B5:B8**, and then AutoFill the formulas to the right through column **F**. Select the range **B8:F8**, and then apply the **Total** cell style. Select the range **B6:F7**, and then apply the **Comma [0]** cell style. Click cell **A10**, and then compare your screen with Figure 3.

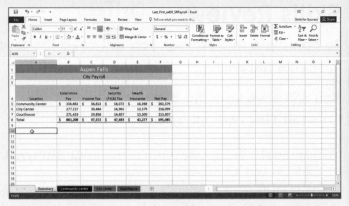

10. On the **Summary** sheet, select the nonadjacent ranges **A4:A7** and **C4:E7**. On the **Insert tab**, in the **Charts group**, click the **Recommended Charts** button. In the **Insert Chart** dialog box, verify **Clustered Bar** is selected, and then click **OK**. On the **Design tab**, in the **Location group**, click the **Move Chart** button. In the **Move Chart** dialog box, select the **New sheet** option button, type Payroll Adjustments and then click **OK**.

Figure 3   Excel 2016, Windows 10, Microsoft Corporation

11. In the **Data group**, click the **Switch Row/Column** button. Click the **Chart Styles** button, and then click **Style 2**. Change the **Chart Title** to Payroll Adjustments by Location Click the **Chart Elements** button, click **Axis Title**, and then click the **Axis Title arrow**. Click the **Primary Horizontal** option box, and then type Deduction

12. On the **Summary** sheet, click cell **A12**, type Date Created and then click Enter. In cell **A13**, press Ctrl + ; (the semicolon), and then press Enter.

13. Right-click the **Summary** worksheet tab, and then click **Unhide**. In the **Unhide** dialog box, click **OK**. Right-click the **Art Center** worksheet tab, and then click **Delete**. In the message box, click **Delete**.

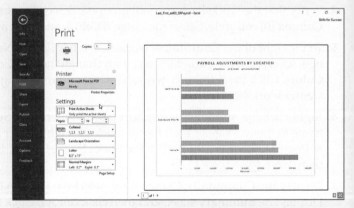

14. Group the worksheets, and then check the spelling. Ungroup the worksheets, and then click the **Payroll Adjustments tab**.

15. Click the **File tab**, click **Print**, and then compare your screen with Figure 4.

16. **Save** the file, **Close** Excel, and then submit the file as directed by your instructor.

Figure 4   Excel 2016, Windows 10, Microsoft Corporation

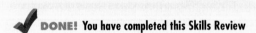

DONE! You have completed this Skills Review

Skills Assessment 1

To complete this project, you will need the following file:

- exl03_SA1Center

You will save your file as:

- Last_First_exl03_SA1Center

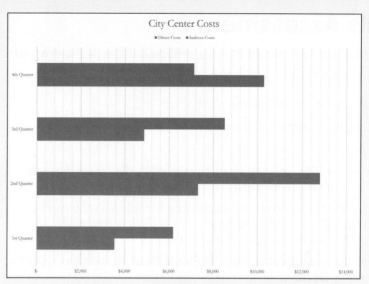

1. Start **Excel 2016**, and then open the file **exl03_SA1Center**. **Save** the file in your chapter folder as Last_First_exl03_SA1Center

2. Group the worksheets. In cell **E5**, construct a formula to compute *Net Income = Income – (Indirect Costs + Direct Costs)*. AutoFill the formula down through cell **E7**.

3. In the nonadjacent ranges **B5:E5** and **B8:E8**, apply the **Currency [0]** cell style.

4. Insert a new worksheet, and then rename the tab as Summary Apply the worksheet tab color **Gold, Accent 6**. Move the *Summary* sheet tab to make it the first worksheet in the workbook.

5. Copy the range **A1:E4** from any of the detail worksheets. On the **Summary** sheet, click cell **A1**, and then paste the range using the **Keep Source Column Widths** paste option. Change the subtitle of cell **A2** to City Center Annual Revenue and then change the label in cell **A4** to Quarter

6. In cell **A5**, type 1st Quarter and then AutoFill the labels through the range **A6:A8**. In cell **A9**, type Total

7. On the **Summary** worksheet, enter a formula in cell **B5** setting the cell to equal cell **B8** in the *1st Quarter* worksheet. On the **Summary** worksheet, enter the *Income* total from the *2nd Quarter*, the *3rd Quarter*, and the *4th Quarter* worksheets in the range **B6:B8**.

8. Select the range **B5:B8**, and then use the **Quick Analysis** button to insert the column total.

9. AutoFill the range **B5:B9** to the right through column **E**. In row **9**, apply the **Total** cell style to the range **B9:E9**. In the range **B6:E8**, apply the **Comma [0]** cell style.

10. Insert a **Clustered Bar** chart using the nonadjacent ranges **A4:A8** and **C4:D8** as the source data. Move the chart to a chart sheet with the sheet name City Center

11. Apply the **Style 10** chart style. Change the **Chart Title** to City Center Costs

12. Group the worksheets using the *Summary* tab. Add the file name in the left footer and the sheet name in the right footer. Return to **Normal** view, and then press Ctrl + Home.

13. Check the spelling of the workbook, and then ungroup the sheets.

14. **Save** the file, and then compare your screen with **Figure 1**. **Close** Excel, and then submit the file as directed by your instructor.

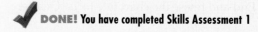 **DONE! You have completed Skills Assessment 1**

Figure 1

Skills Assessment 2

To complete this project, you will need the following file:

- exl03_SA2Taxes

You will save your file as:

- Last_First_exl03_SA2Taxes

---

1. Start **Excel 2016**, and then open the file **exl03_SA2Taxes**. **Save** the file in your chapter folder as Last_First_exl03_SA2Taxes

2. Group the sheets. In cell **F5**, construct a formula to compute *Net Revenue = (Taxes Paid + Late Fees) – (Office Costs + Personnel Costs)*. AutoFill the formula down through **F10**.

3. Select the nonadjacent ranges **B5:F5** and **B11:F11**, and then apply the **Currency [0]** cell style.

4. Ungroup the worksheets, and then hide the April worksheet. Compare the *January* worksheet with **Figure 1**.

5. Insert a new sheet, rename the worksheet tab 1st Qtr Summary and then change the worksheet tab color to **Orange, Accent 1**. Move the worksheet to the first position in the workbook. Copy the range **A1:F4** from another worksheet, and then paste the range at the top of the *1st Qtr Summary* sheet using the **Keep Source Column Widths** paste option.

6. On the **1st Qtr Summary** sheet, change the subtitle in cell **A2** to 1st Quarter Tax Revenue and then change the label in cell **A4** to Month In the range **A5:A7**, enter the months January | February | March and in cell **A8**, type Total

7. In cell **B5**, enter a formula setting the cell to equal the total *Taxes Paid* in the *January* worksheet. In cells **B6** and **B7** of the *1st Qtr Summary* sheet, enter the total *Taxes Paid* from the *February* and the *March* worksheets.

8. Total column **B**, and then AutoFill the range **B5:B8** to the right through column **F**. In the range **B8:F8**, apply the **Total** cell style. In the range **B6:F7**, apply the **Comma [0]** cell style.

9. Select the range **A4:C7**, and then insert a **Clustered Bar** chart. Move and resize the chart to the range **A10:F24**. Switch the rows and columns in the chart.

10. Apply the **Layout 2** chart layout and the **Style 8** chart style. Change the data labels to **Inside End** and revise the chart title to 1st Quarter

11. Group the worksheets, and then check the spelling of the workbook. Add the file name in the left footer and the sheet name in the right footer. Return to **Normal** view, and then press Ctrl + Home.

12. **Save** the file, and then compare your *1st Qtr Summary* sheet with **Figure 2**. **Close** Excel, and then submit the file as directed by your instructor.

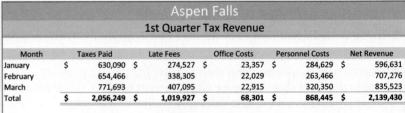

| | Aspen Falls | | | | |
| | January Tax Revenue | | | | |
Tax	Taxes Paid	Late Fees	Office Costs	Personnel Costs	Net Revenue
Motor Vehicle	$ 82,831	$ 58,255	$ 2,879	$ 49,255	$ 88,952
Sales	154,520	47,280	3,796	51,529	146,475
Franchise	72,956	46,998	4,915	60,061	54,978
Utilities	98,750	35,107	5,688	38,378	89,791
Property	120,000	40,762	3,200	24,320	133,242
Other	101,033	46,125	2,879	61,086	83,193
Totals	$ 630,090	$ 274,527	$ 23,357	$ 284,629	$ 596,631

Figure 1

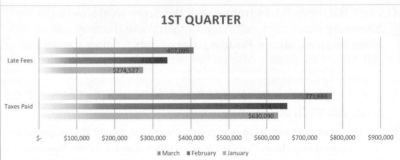

| | Aspen Falls | | | | |
| | 1st Quarter Tax Revenue | | | | |
Month	Taxes Paid	Late Fees	Office Costs	Personnel Costs	Net Revenue
January	$ 630,090	$ 274,527	$ 23,357	$ 284,629	$ 596,631
February	654,466	338,305	22,029	263,466	707,276
March	771,693	407,095	22,915	320,350	835,523
Total	$ 2,056,249	$ 1,019,927	$ 68,301	$ 868,445	$ 2,139,430

Figure 2

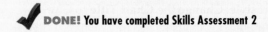

DONE! You have completed Skills Assessment 2

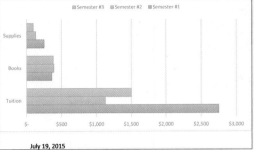

July 19, 2015

Semester Expenses				
Semester #1				
Class	Tuition	Books	Supplies	Class Total
Class 1	$ 500 $	125 $	50 $	675
Class 2	250	50	55	355
Class 3	500	50	50	600
Class 4	750	75	45	870
Class 5	750	60	50	860
Total	$ 2,750 $	360 $	250 $	3,360

Figure 1

My Skills

To complete this project, you will need the following file:

- exl03_MYClasses

You will save your file as:

- Last_First_exl03_MYClasses

1. Start **Excel 2016**, and then open the file **exl03_MYClasses**. **Save** the file in your chapter folder as Last_First_exl03_MYClasses

2. Group the worksheets. In cell **E5**, use the SUM function to total the row, and then AutoFill the formula down through cell **E9**. In row **10**, use the SUM function to total the columns. Apply the **Comma [0]** cell style to **E6:E9**.

3. Select cell **A2**, and then apply the **60% - Accent3** cell style.

4. Insert a new worksheet. Rename the new worksheet tab Semester Costs and then apply the worksheet tab color **Blue-Gray, Accent 6**. Move the new worksheet tab to make it the first worksheet in the workbook.

5. Copy the range **A1:E4** from any of the detail worksheets, and then on the **Semester Costs** worksheet, click cell **A1**. Paste the range using the **Keep Source Column Widths** paste option. Change the subtitle of cell **A2** to Combined Semesters and then change the label in cell **A4** to Semester and change the label in cell **E4** to Semester Total

6. In cell **A5**, type Semester #1 and then AutoFill the label down through **A7**. In cell **A8**, type Total

7. In cell **B5**, insert a formula to equal the value in cell **B10** in the *Semester #1* worksheet. In cells **B6** and **B7**, insert

formulas that equal the *Tuition* total from the *Semester #2* and *Semester #3* worksheets.

8. Use **Quick Analysis** to insert the column **B** total, and then AutoFill the formulas in column **B** to the right through column **E**. Select the range **B8:E8**, and then apply the **Total** cell style. Apply the **Comma [0]** cell style to **B6:E7**.

9. Insert a **Clustered Bar** chart using the range **A4:D7** as the source data. Move and resize the chart to display below the data in approximately the range **A10:E24**.

10. Apply the **Style 4** chart style, and then delete the **Chart Title**. Move the legend to the top of the chart.

11. On the **Semester Costs** sheet, in cell **A26**, enter the current date, and then apply the **March 14, 2012** date format.

12. Group the worksheets. Add the file name in the left footer and the sheet name in the right footer. Return to **Normal** view, and then press Ctrl + Home.

13. Check the spelling of the workbook, and then ungroup the sheets. Compare your completed file with **Figure 1**.

14. **Save** the file, and then **Close** Excel. Submit the file as directed by your instructor.

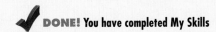

✔ **DONE! You have completed My Skills**

Visual Skills Check

To complete this project, you will need the following file:

■ exl03_VSWater

You will save your file as:

■ Last_First_exl03_VSWater

Start **Excel 2016**, and then open the file **exl03_VSWater**. **Save** the file in your chapter folder as Last_First_exl03_VSWater Create a summary sheet as shown in Figure 1 for the 4th Quarter with the totals from each month and the titles as shown in the figure. Name the worksheet tab 4th Qtr Summary and then apply the worksheet tab color **Teal, Accent 5**. Move the Summary sheet to be the first worksheet. Insert a **Clustered Bar** chart based on the range **A4:D7**, and then move the chart below the data. Apply **Layout 3** and **Chart Style 12**. Delete the chart title, and then move the legend to the **Top**. On all sheets, add a footer with the file name in the left section and the sheet name in the right section. **Save** the file, **Close** Excel, and then submit the file as directed by your instructor.

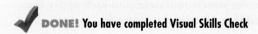 **DONE!** You have completed Visual Skills Check

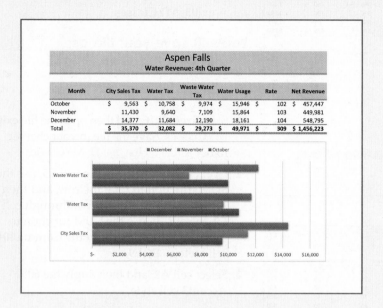

Month	City Sales Tax	Water Tax	Waste Water Tax	Water Usage	Rate	Net Revenue
October	$ 9,563	$ 10,758	$ 9,974	$ 15,946	$ 102	$ 457,447
November	11,430	9,640	7,109	15,864	103	449,981
December	14,377	11,684	12,190	18,161	104	548,795
Total	$ 35,370	$ 32,082	$ 29,273	$ 49,971	$ 309	$ 1,456,223

Aspen Falls
Water Revenue: October

Building Type	City Sales Tax	Water Tax	Waste Water Tax	Water Usage	Rate	Net Revenue
Residential	$ 1,575	$ 1,890	$ 1,507	3,181	$ 19	$ 65,411
Commercial	4,233	5,762	5,671	5,440	27	162,546
Industrial	3,170	2,404	2,191	6,118	31	197,423
Apartments	585	702	605	1,207	25	32,067
Total	$ 9,563	$ 10,758	$ 9,974	15,946	$ 102	457,447

Figure 1

Skills Challenge 1

To complete this project, you will need the following file:

- exl03_SC1Visitors

You will save your file as:

- Last_First_exl03_SC1Visitors

During each quarter, Carter Horikoshi, the Art Center Supervisor, tracked the revenue and costs at the Art Center. Open the file **exl03_SC1Visitors**, and then save the file in your chapter folder as Last_First_exl03_SC1Visitors Hide the Convention Center worksheet, and then move the remaining worksheets into the correct order. Assign a tab color to each worksheet tab. Group the worksheets, and then adjust the column widths to display all values. Format the labels in rows 1 through 4 consistently across all the worksheets. In cell F5, insert parentheses so that the sum of *Marketing Costs* and *Operating Costs* is subtracted from the sum of *Entrance Fees* and *Food Revenue*. Copy the corrected formula down. Format the numbers appropriately. Unhide the Annual Summary worksheet, and then move it as the first worksheet. Move and

resize the bar chart to display below the data. On the Annual Summary sheet, format the values and the chart appropriately using the clustered bar chart and switching rows and columns. Move the Chart Legend to the top, and then delete the Chart Title. Verify that the formulas on the Summary sheet are correct. On all sheets, insert the file name in the left footer and the sheet name in the right footer. Check the spelling of the workbook, and then verify that all columns for each sheet will print on one page. Save the file, close Excel, and then submit the file as directed by your instructor.

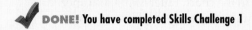 **DONE!** You have completed Skills Challenge 1

Skills Challenge 2

To complete this project, you will need the following file:

- exl03_SC2Durango

You will save your file as:

- Last_First_exl03_SC2Durango

During each month of the summer season, Duncan Chueng, the Park Operations Manager, tracked the revenue and costs at the various locations in the Durango County Recreation Area. Open the file **exl03_SC2Durango**, and then save the file in your chapter folder as Last_First_exl03_SC2Durango Using the skills you learned in the chapter, create a new summary worksheet for the 3rd Quarter with an appropriate sheet name. Hide the worksheet tabs not included as part of the 3rd Quarter. Insert a clustered bar chart that displays the ticket revenue for each month, and then move it to a new sheet

with an appropriate sheet name. Move the chart to the second position in the workbook. Format the chart appropriately. Move the summary sheet to the first position in the workbook. On all sheets, insert the file name in the left footer and the sheet name in the right footer. Adjust the page settings to print each worksheet on one page. Save the file, close Excel, and then submit the file as directed by your instructor.

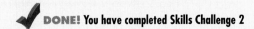 **DONE!** You have completed Skills Challenge 2

More Skills Assessment

MyITLab®
Grader

To complete this project, you will need the following file:

- exl03_MSAHierarchy

You will save your files as:

- Last_First_exl03_MSAHierarchy
- Last_First_exl03_MSASnip

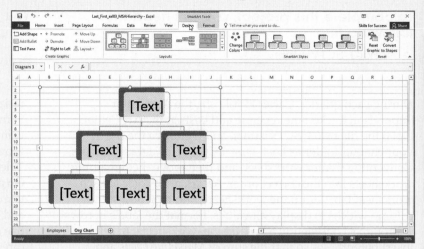

1. Start **Excel 2016**. Open the file **exl03_MSAHierarchy**, and then save the file in your chapter folder as Last_First_exl03_MSAHierarchy

2. On the **Org Chart** sheet, insert a SmartArt graphic, and then select the **Hierarchy** format. Move and resize the chart so the borders touch **B2:J20**. Compare your screen with **Figure 1**.

Figure 1   Excel 2016, Windows 10, Microsoft Corporation

3. Using the employee names from the *Employees* sheet, insert the employees' first and last names in the chart. Enter Maria Martinez in the top shape, and then enter the remaining employees in the shapes using their level to guide you.

4. Format the SmartArt color as **Colorful - Accent Colors** and the style as **3-D Inset**.

5. On the **Employees** sheet, **hyperlink** the text in cell **A1** to www .aspenfalls.org and then set a **ScreenTip** to display as Aspen Falls City Hall

6. Select the link to open the website, and then click on the **Employee** link. In cell **B12**, insert a screen clipping of the organization chart graphic. Apply the **Simple Frame, White** style to the object. Adjust the height to 2".

7. Open **Excel Options**, and then under *Popular Commands*, add **QuickPrint** and **Save As** to the Quick Access Toolbar.

8. View the new icons on the toolbar, and then compare your screen with **Figure 2**.

9. Using the **Snipping Tool**, take a **Full-Screen** snip of your screen. **Save** the file as Last_First_exl03_MSASnip

10. **Save** the file. **Close** all open windows, and then submit the files as directed by your instructor.

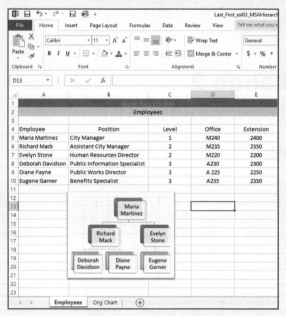

Figure 2   Excel 2016, Windows 10, Microsoft Corporation

DONE! You have completed More Skills Assessment

Collaborating with Google

To complete this project, you will need a Google account (refer to the Common Features chapter) and the following file:

- exl03_GPGarage

You will save your file as:

- Last_First_exl03_GPSnip

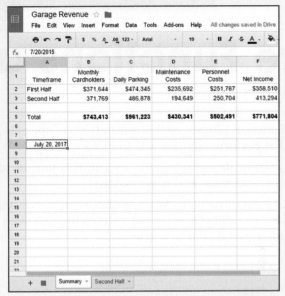

Excel 2016, Windows 10, Microsoft Corporation   **Figure 1**

1. Open the Google Chrome web browser. Log into your Google account, and then click **Google Apps** ⊞.

2. Click **Drive** ⊿ to open Google Drive.

3. Click the **New** button, and then click **Google Sheets** to open a blank spreadsheet.

4. Select the sheet title. In the dialog box, type Garage Revenue and then click **OK**. Rename the *Sheet1* worksheet tab as Summary Insert two tabs by clicking the **Add Sheet** button ⊕, and then rename the tabs First Half | Second Half

5. Open the student data file **exl03_GPGarage**.

6. On the **Summary** sheet, copy the range **A4:F8**, and then paste it to cell **A1** in the **Summary** sheet in the **Garage Revenue** workbook. Use the technique just practiced to copy the **A4:F8** range from the **First Half** and **Second Half** sheets to the workbook. When finished, close the student data file **exl03_GPGarage** without saving changes if prompted.

7. Click the **Summary** sheet, and then select the range **A1:F1**. Click the **Format tab**, point to **Text wrapping**, and then click **Wrap**.

8. Click the **First Half** sheet, and then in cell **F2**, enter the formula =(B2+C2)-(D2+E2) Click cell **F2**, click the **Edit tab**, and then click **Copy**. Select the range **F3:F5**. Click the **Edit tab**, point to **Paste special**, and then click **Paste formula only**. Select the range **F2:F5**, and then using the technique just practiced, paste it to the range **F2:F5** in the **Second Half** worksheet.

9. Click the **Summary** worksheet, and then click cell **B2**. Type = click the **First Half** sheet, click cell **B5**, and then press Enter.

10. On the **Summary** sheet, repeat the technique just practiced to display the **Second Half** sheet **B5** value in the **Summary** sheet **B3** cell. In cell **B5**, enter the SUM function for **B2:B3**.

11. On the **Summary** sheet, select the range **B2:B5**, and then AutoFill to the right through column **F**.

12. Click cell **A8**, and then enter today's date. With cell **A8** active, click the **Format tab**. Point to **Number, More Formats**, and then click **More date and time formats**. Scroll down the list, select the format **August 5, 1930**, and then click **Apply**.

13. On the **Summary** tab, click the **arrow**, and then select **Move Right**

14. Click the **First Half tab**, and then click **Hide sheet**. Compare your screen with **Figure 1**.

15. Using the **Snipping Tool**, take a **Full-Screen** snip of your screen. **Save** the file in your chapter folder as Last_First_exl03_GPSnip

16. **Close** all windows, and then submit your file as directed by your instructor.

 **DONE! You have completed Collaborating with Google**

CHAPTER 4

More Functions and Excel Tables

▶ The Excel Function Library contains hundreds of special functions that perform complex calculations quickly.

▶ Function Library categories include statistical, financial, logical, date and time, and math and trigonometry.

▶ Conditional formatting helps you see important trends and exceptions in your data by applying various formats such as colored gradients, data bars, or icons.

▶ You can convert data that is organized in rows and columns into an Excel table that adds formatting, filtering, and AutoComplete features.

▶ An Excel table helps you manage information by providing ways to sort and filter the data and to analyze the data using summary rows and calculated columns.

Marcuspon/Fotolia

Aspen Falls City Hall

In this chapter, you will revise a spreadsheet for Jack Ruiz, the Aspen Falls Community Services Director. He has received permission from the City Council to create community gardens in open space areas in Aspen Falls. In order to promote the gardens, the city will provide materials to community members. He has a workbook with a list of materials and wants to know if any items need to be reordered and if new suppliers should be contacted for quotes when replacing the items. He is also tracking the donations received from local retail stores.

Using workbooks to track information is a primary function of a spreadsheet application. Because spreadsheets can be set up to globally update when underlying data is changed, managers often use Excel to help them make decisions in real time. An effective workbook uses functions, conditional formatting, summary statistics, and charts in ways that describe past trends and help decision makers accurately forecast future needs.

In this project, you will use the functions TODAY, NOW, COUNT, and IF to generate useful information for the director. You will apply conditional formatting to highlight outlying data and create sparklines to display trends. To update the underlying data, you will use the Find and Replace tool. Finally, you will create and format Excel tables, and then search the tables for data.

Time to complete all 10 skills — 60 to 90 minutes

Outcome

Using the skills in this chapter, you will be able to insert and move date and time functions, apply logical functions, format worksheets with borders, rotate text, lock panes, and apply conditional formatting. Also, you will insert sparkline charts, create, sort, and filter data in tables, and adjust print settings for large worksheets.

Objectives

4.1 Construct date and time functions
4.2 Apply logical conditions and formats to data
4.3 Modify worksheet formatting
4.4 Distinguish data using cell charts and filters
4.5 Understand large worksheet print options

SKILLS

MyITLab®
Skills 1–10 Training

Skill 1 Insert the TODAY, NOW, and COUNT Functions
Skill 2 Insert the IF Function
Skill 3 Move Functions, Add Borders, and Rotate Text
Skill 4 Apply Conditional Formatting
Skill 5 Insert Sparklines
Skill 6 Use Find and Replace
Skill 7 Freeze and Unfreeze Panes
Skill 8 Create and Sort Excel Tables
Skill 9 Filter Excel Tables
Skill 10 Convert Tables to Ranges and Adjust Worksheet Print Settings

MORE SKILLS

Skill 11 Add and Remove Table Columns and Rows
Skill 12 Insert the Payment (PMT) Function
Skill 13 Customize Workbook Views
Skill 14 Use Text and Lookup Functions

Student data file needed for this chapter:

exl04_Garden

You will save your file as:

Last_First_exl04_Garden

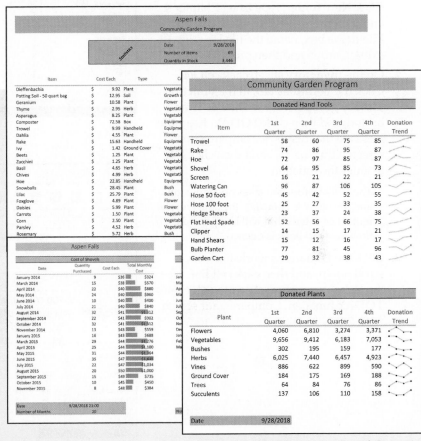

Excel 2016, Windows 10, Microsoft Corporation

▶ The ***TODAY function*** returns the serial number of the current date.

▶ The ***NOW function*** returns the serial number of the current date and time.

▶ The ***COUNT function*** counts the number of cells that contain numbers.

1. Start **Excel 2016**, and then open the student data file **exl04_Garden**. Click the **File tab**, and then click **Save As**. Click the **Browse** button, and then navigate to the location where you are saving your files. Click **New folder**, type Excel Chapter 4 and then press ⌜Enter⌟ two times. In the **File name** box, name the file Last_First_exl04_Garden and then press ⌜Enter⌟.

2. On the **Inventory** sheet, click cell **E4**. Click the **Formulas tab**, in the **Function Library group**, click the **Date & Time** button, and then click **TODAY**. Read the message that displays, compare your screen with **Figure 1**, and then click **OK** to enter the function.

    The TODAY function takes no arguments, and the result is *volatile*—the date will not remain as entered but will be updated each time the workbook is opened.

3. Click the **Donations** worksheet tab, scroll down, and then click cell **B36**. Use the technique just practiced to enter the **TODAY** function. Compare your screen with **Figure 2**.

■ Continue to the next page to complete the skill ▶

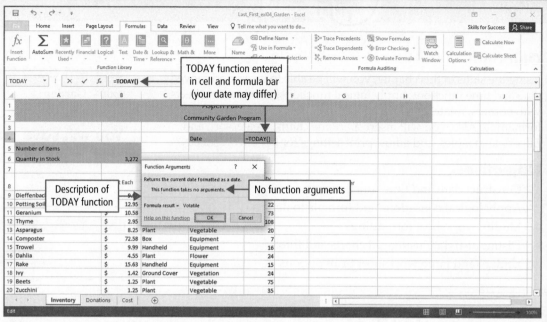

Figure 1

Excel 2016, Windows 10, Microsoft Corporation

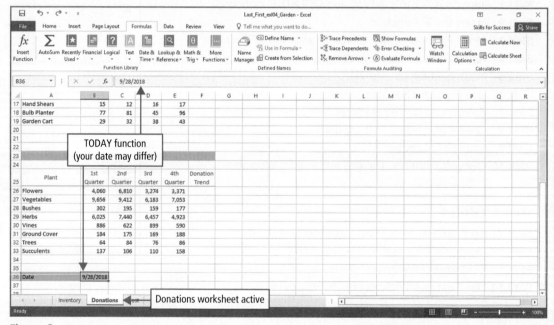

Figure 2

Excel 2016, Windows 10, Microsoft Corporation

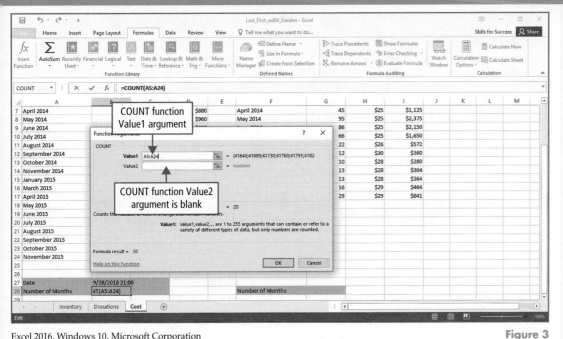

COUNT function Value1 argument

COUNT function Value2 argument is blank

Excel 2016, Windows 10, Microsoft Corporation

Figure 3

4. Click the **Cost** worksheet tab, scroll down, and then click the merged cell **B27**. In the **Function Library group**, click the **Date & Time** button, and then click **NOW**. Read the message that displays, and then click **OK** to insert the function.

5. Click cell **B28**. In the **Function Library group**, click the **More Functions** button. Point to **Statistical**, and then click **COUNT**.

6. In the **Function Arguments** dialog box, in the **Value1** box, type A5:A24 and then compare your screen with **Figure 3**.

7. In the **Function Arguments** dialog box, click **OK**.

   The number of cells in the range A5:A24 that contain values is *20*.

8. Click cell **G28**. Use the technique just practiced to enter a **COUNT** function with the range F5:F17 as the **Value1** argument.

   The result should be 13.

9. Click the **Inventory** worksheet tab, and then click cell **B5**. In the **Function Library group**, click the **More Functions** button, point to **Statistical**, and then click **COUNT**. If necessary, move the Function Arguments dialog box to the right to view column B. In the **Function Arguments** dialog box, with the insertion point in the **Value1** box, click cell **B9**. Press `Ctrl` + `Shift` + `↓` to select the range **B9:B77**. Click **OK** to display the result *69*. Compare your screen with **Figure 4**.

10. Save 🖫 the file.

- **You have completed Skill 1 of 10**

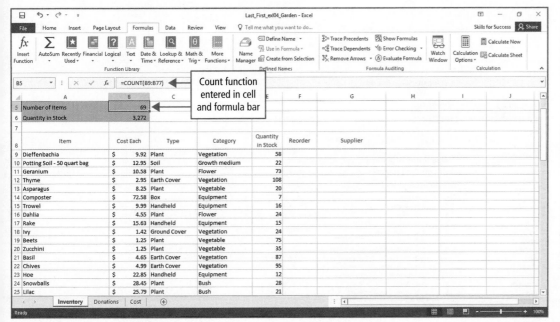

Count function entered in cell and formula bar

Excel 2016, Windows 10, Microsoft Corporation

Figure 4

- A **logical function** applies a logical test to determine whether a specific condition is met.

- A **logical test** is any value or expression that can be evaluated as TRUE or FALSE.

- **Criteria** are the conditions specified in the logical test.

- The **IF function** is a logical function that checks whether criteria are met, and then returns one value when the condition is TRUE and another value when the condition is FALSE.

1. On the **Inventory** worksheet, click cell **F9**. In the **Function Library group**, click the **Logical** button, and then on the list, click **IF**.

MOS
Obj 4.2.1 C

2. In the **Function Arguments** dialog box, with the insertion point in the **Logical_ test** box, type E9<10

   A **comparison operator** compares two values and returns either TRUE or FALSE. Here, the logical test *E9<10* uses the less than comparison operator, and will return TRUE only when the value in E9 is less than 10. The table in **Figure 1** lists commonly used comparison operators.

3. Press Tab to move the insertion point to the **Value_if_true** box, and then type Order

4. Press Tab to move the insertion point to the **Value_if_false** box, type Level OK and then compare your screen with **Figure 2**.

   In function arguments, text values are surrounded by quotation marks. Here, quotation marks display around *Order* and will automatically be inserted around *Level OK* after you click OK.

■ **Continue to the next page to complete the skill** ▶

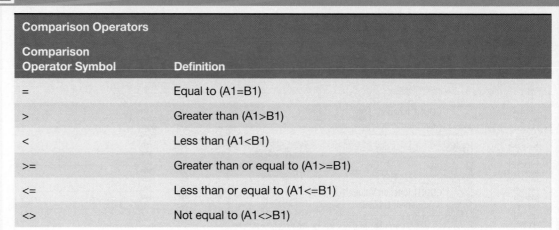

Comparison Operators

Comparison Operator Symbol	Definition
=	Equal to (A1=B1)
>	Greater than (A1>B1)
<	Less than (A1<B1)
>=	Greater than or equal to (A1>=B1)
<=	Less than or equal to (A1<=B1)
<>	Not equal to (A1<>B1)

Figure 1   Excel 2016, Windows 10, Microsoft Corporation

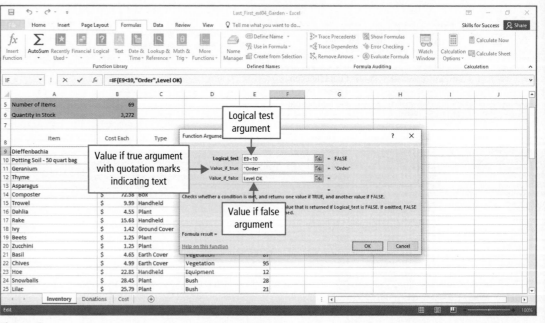

Figure 2   Excel 2016, Windows 10, Microsoft Corporation

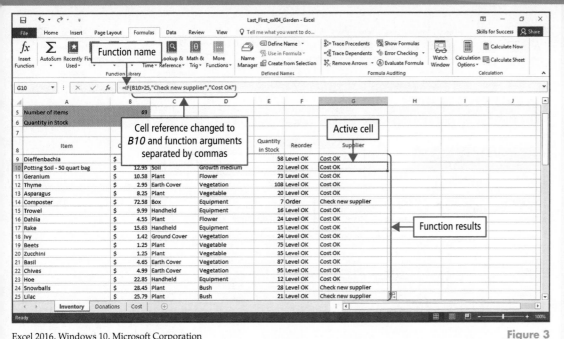

Excel 2016, Windows 10, Microsoft Corporation

Figure 3

Excel 2016, Windows 10, Microsoft Corporation

Figure 4

5. Click **OK** to display the result *Level OK*.

The IF function tests whether E9 is less than 10. When this condition is TRUE, *Order* will display. Because E9 contains the value *58*, the condition is FALSE, and *Level OK* displays.

6. Click cell **G9**. In the **Function Library group**, click the **Logical** button, and then click **IF**. In the **Logical_test** box, type B9>25 and then in the **Value_if_true** box, type Check new supplier In the **Value_if_false** box, type Cost OK and then click the **OK** button to display *Cost OK*.

7. Select the range **F9:G9**. Point to the fill handle to display the ⊞ pointer, and then double-click to AutoFill the functions down through row **77**. Click **G10**, and then compare your screen with **Figure 3**.

In each row of column G, the function evaluates the value in column B. When the value in column B is greater than $25, the text *Check new supplier* displays. Otherwise, the text *Cost OK* displays.

When a function has multiple arguments, each argument is separated by a comma.

When the function was copied down to G10, the cell reference changed from B9 to B10.

8. Scroll down and verify that nine items meet the condition and display the text *Check new supplier*. Click cell **G9**. In the formula bar, change the number *25* to *30* and then click the **Enter** button ✓. AutoFill the function down through cell **G77**. Scroll down to verify that five items meet the changed condition. Click cell **G56**, and then compare your screen with **Figure 4**.

9. Save 🖫 the file.

■ **You have completed Skill 2 of 10**

▶ When you move cells containing formulas or functions by dragging them, the cell references in the formulas or functions do not change.

▶ Borders and shading emphasize a cell or a range of cells, and rotated or angled text draws attention to text on a worksheet.

Obj 2.1.1 C

1. On the **Inventory** worksheet, press Ctrl + Home . Select the range **A5:B6**. Point to the top edge of the selected range to display the 🔀 pointer. Drag the selected range to the right until the ScreenTip displays the range *D5:E6*, as shown in **Figure 1**, and then release the mouse button to complete the move.

2. Click cell **E5**. Notice that the cell references in the function did not change.

3. Click the **Donations** worksheet tab. Select the merged cell **A3**. Click the **Home tab**, and then in the **Font group**, click the **Border arrow** ⊞ ▾. In the center of the list, click **Top and Bottom Border**.

4. Click the merged cell **A23**. In the **Font group**, click the **Top and Bottom Border** button ⊞ ▾ to apply a top and bottom border. Click cell **A5**, and then compare your screen with **Figure 2**.

   Once the border has been changed, the button on the ribbon will now show the new border format.

5. Click the **Cost** worksheet tab. Click the merged cell **A3**. Hold down Ctrl , and then click the merged cell **F3**. Release Ctrl , and then use the technique just practiced to apply a top and bottom border.

■ **Continue to the next page to complete the skill**

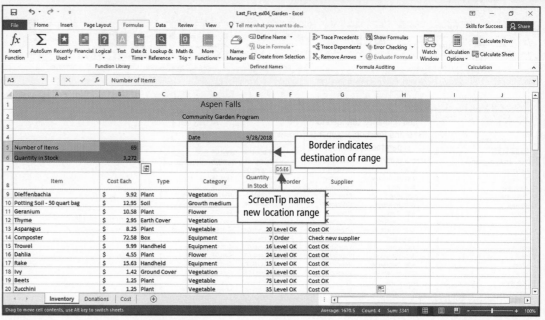

Figure 1

Excel 2016, Windows 10, Microsoft Corporation

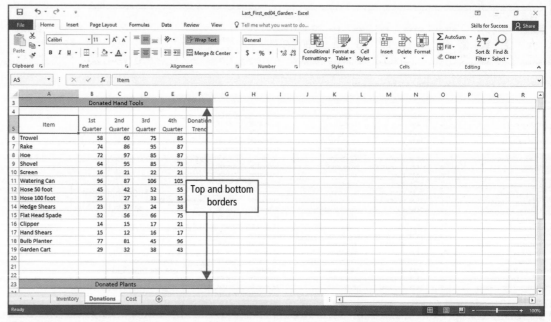

Figure 2

Excel 2016, Windows 10, Microsoft Corporation

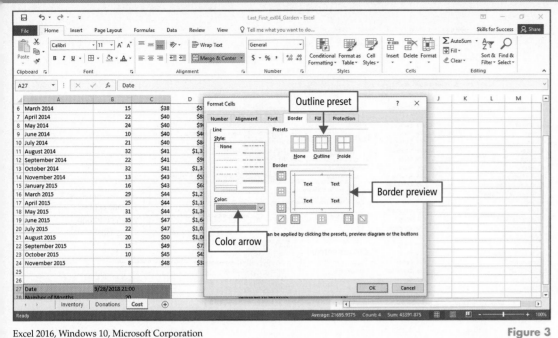

Excel 2016, Windows 10, Microsoft Corporation

Figure 3

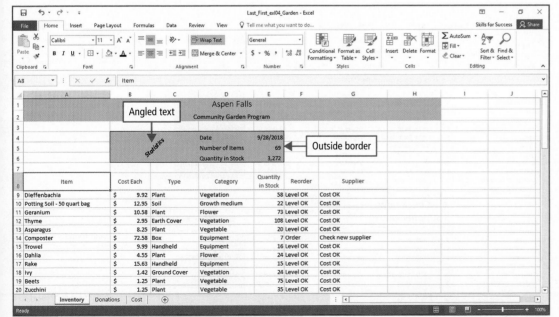

Excel 2016, Windows 10, Microsoft Corporation

Figure 4

6. Scroll down, and then select the range **A27:C28**. In the **Font group**, click the **Top and Bottom Border arrow**. At the bottom of the **Borders** gallery, click **More Borders**.

7. In the **Format Cells** dialog box, click the **Color arrow**, and then click the sixth color in the first row—**Orange, Accent 2**. Under **Presets**, click **Outline**. Compare your screen with Figure 3, and then click **OK**.

8. Select the range **F28:G28**. Press F4 to repeat the last command, and then click cell **F30**.

    Pressing F4 will repeat the last command. In this instance, it will apply an orange border to the selected range.

9. Click the **Inventory** worksheet tab. Click cell **B4**, type Statistics and then press Enter.

10. Select the range **B4:C6**. On the **Home tab**, in the **Alignment group**, click the **Merge & Center** button. Apply the **60% - Accent6** cell style, and then click **Middle Align**, **Bold**, and **Italic**. Click the **Font Color arrow**, and then click **Automatic**.

11. With the merged cell still selected, in the **Alignment group**, click the **Orientation** button, and then click **Angle Counterclockwise**.

12. Select the range **B4:E6**. In the **Font group**, click the **Border arrow**, and then click **Outside Borders**. Click cell **A8**, and then compare your screen with Figure 4.

13. **Save** the file.

▪ **You have completed Skill 3 of 10**

► **Conditional formatting** is a format, such as cell shading or font color that is applied to cells when a specified condition is true.

► Conditional formatting makes analyzing data easier by emphasizing differences in cell values.

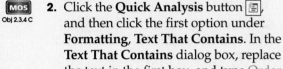

1. On the **Inventory** worksheet, click cell **F9**. Press [Ctrl] + [Shift] + [↓] to select the range **F9:F77**.

2. Click the **Quick Analysis** button, and then click the first option under **Formatting**, **Text That Contains**. In the **Text That Contains** dialog box, replace the text in the first box, and type Order Compare your screen with **Figure 1**, and then click **OK**.

   Within the range F9:F77, cells that contain the text *Order* display with light red fill and dark red text formatting.

3. Using the technique just practiced, select the range **G9:G77**, and then open the **Text That Contains** dialog box. In the first box, type Check new supplier To the right of the format box, click the **arrow**, and then compare your screen with **Figure 2**.

   You can use the Text That Contains dialog box to specify the formatting that should be applied when a condition is true. If the formatting choice you need is not listed, you can open the Format Cells dialog box by clicking the Custom Format command.

■ **Continue to the next page to complete the skill**

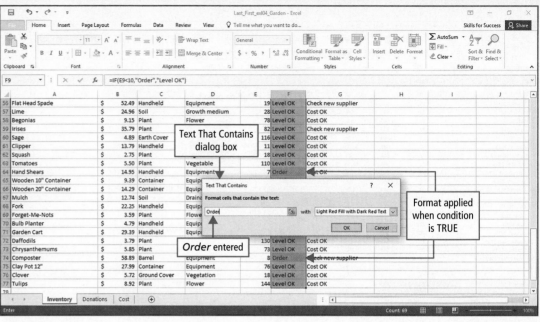

Figure 1

Excel 2016, Windows 10, Microsoft Corporation

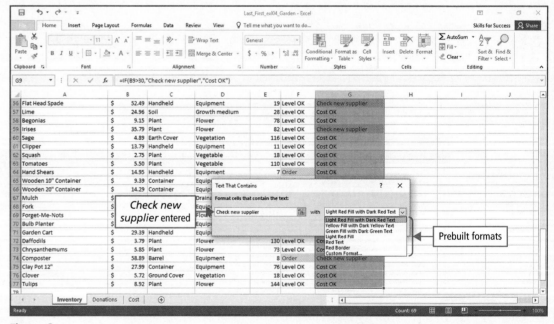

Figure 2

Excel 2016, Windows 10, Microsoft Corporation

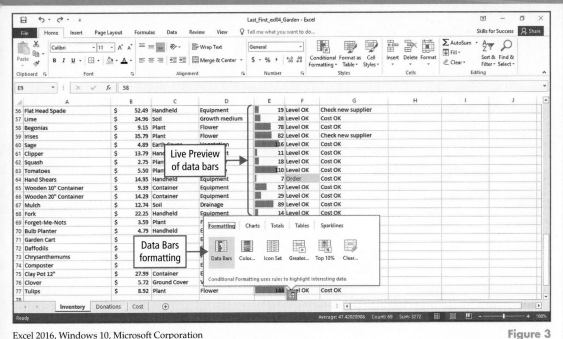

Excel 2016, Windows 10, Microsoft Corporation

Figure 3

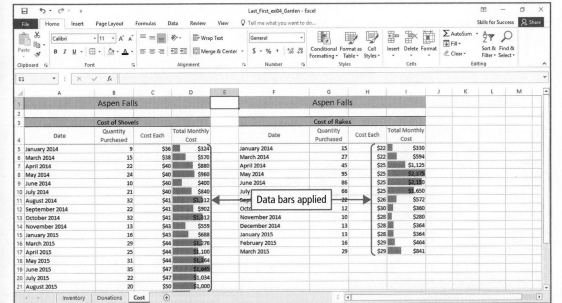

Excel 2016, Windows 10, Microsoft Corporation

Figure 4

4. In the list of conditional formats, click **Green Fill with Dark Green Text**, and then click **OK**.

5. Select the range **E9:E77**. Press `Ctrl` + `Q`, and then point to **Data Bars**. Compare your screen with **Figure 3**.

> A *data bar* is a format that provides a visual cue about the value of a cell relative to other cells in a range. Data bars are useful to quickly identify higher and lower numbers within a large group of data, such as very high or very low levels of inventory.

6. In the **Quick Analysis** gallery, click **Data Bars** to apply the conditional formatting.

7. Scroll up, and then click cell **E15**. Type 190 and then press `Enter` to adjust all data bars to the new value.

> Data bars are sized relative to the maximum value within a range. Here, when a new maximum value of 190 was entered, all the data bars adjusted.

8. Click the **Cost** worksheet tab. Select the range **D5:D24**, and then use the technique just practiced to apply the default data bar conditional format.

9. Select the range **I5:I17**, and then apply the default data bar conditional format. Click cell **E1**, and then compare your screen with **Figure 4**.

10. Save 💾 the file.

■ **You have completed Skill 4 of 10**

▶ A ***sparkline*** is a chart contained in a single cell that is used to show data trends.

1. Click the **Donations** worksheet tab to make it the active sheet, and then select the range **B6:E19**.

2. Click the **Quick Analysis** button 📧, and then click **Sparklines**. In the **Sparklines** gallery, point to **Line** to display sparklines in column F. Compare your screen with **Figure 1**, and then click **Line**.

3. With the range **F6:F19** selected, on the **Design tab**, in the **Show group**, click the **High Point** check box to mark the highest point of data on each sparkline.

4. In the **Style group**, click the **Sparkline Color** button, and then click the fifth color in the first row—**Orange-Accent 2**. Click cell **E20**, and then compare your screen with **Figure 2**.

The sparklines in column F show that the donation levels of hand tools are generally increasing over time.

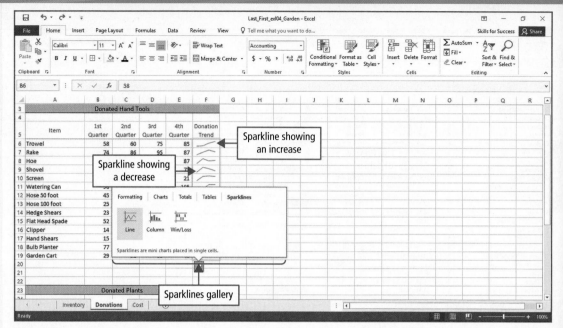

Figure 1

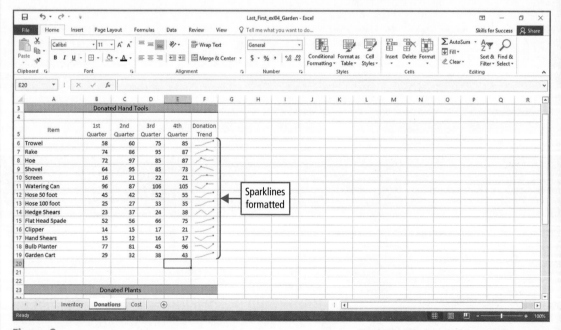

Figure 2

■ **Continue to the next page to complete the skill** ▶

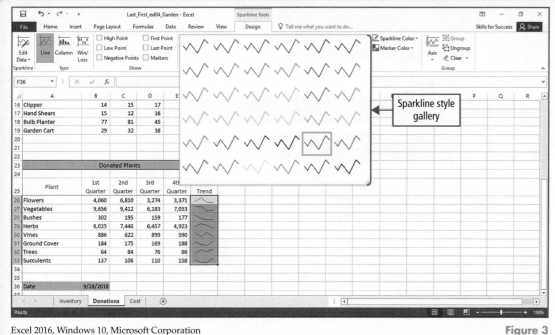

Excel 2016, Windows 10, Microsoft Corporation

Figure 3

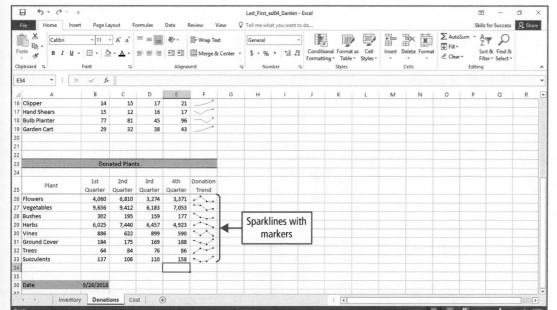

Excel 2016, Windows 10, Microsoft Corporation

Figure 4

5. Scroll down, and then select the range **B26:E33**. Use the technique just practiced to insert the default **Line** sparklines.

6. With the range **F26:F33** selected, on the **Design tab**, in the **Style group**, click the **More** button, and then compare your screen with Figure 3.

7. In the **Style** gallery, click the second color in the third row—**Sparkline Style Accent 2, (no dark or light)**.

8. In the **Style group**, click the **Marker Color** button. In the displayed list, point to **Markers**, and then click the second color in the first row—**Black, Text 1**—to mark each data point on the sparklines. Click cell **E34**, and then compare your screen with Figure 4.

9. Right-click the **Donations** worksheet tab, and then click **Select All Sheets**. Add the file name to the worksheet's left footer and the sheet name to the right footer. Return to **Normal** view, and then press Ctrl + Home to make cell **A1** the active cell on each of the grouped worksheets.

10. Right-click the **Donations** worksheet tab, and then click **Ungroup Sheets**.

11. **Save** the file.

■ **You have completed Skill 5 of 10**

 **WATCH** SKILL 4.6

▶ The ***Replace*** feature finds and then replaces a character or string of characters in a worksheet or in a selected range.

1. Click the **Inventory** worksheet tab, and then verify that cell **A1** is the active cell. On the **Home tab**, in the **Editing group**, click the **Find & Select** button, and then click **Replace**.

2. In the **Find and Replace** dialog box, in the **Find what** box, type Earth Cover and then press Tab. In the **Replace with** box, type Herb and then compare your screen with **Figure 1**.

3. Click the **Find Next** button, and then verify that cell **C12** is the active cell. In the **Find and Replace** dialog box, click the **Replace** button to replace the value in cell *C12* with *Herb* and to select the next occurrence of *Earth Cover* in cell *C21*.

4. In the **Find and Replace** dialog box, click the **Replace All** button. Read the message that displays. Compare your screen with **Figure 2**, and then click **OK**.

The Replace All option replaces all matches of an occurrence of a character or string of characters with the replacement value. Here, six values were replaced. Only use the Replace All option when the search string is unique.

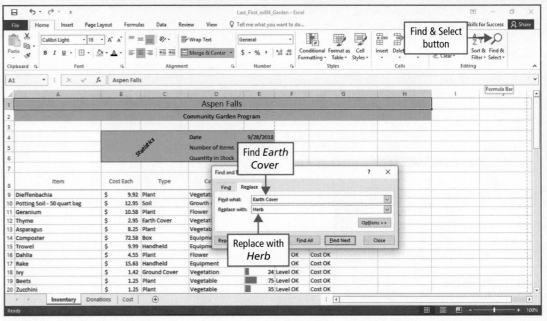

Figure 1   Excel 2016, Windows 10, Microsoft Corporation

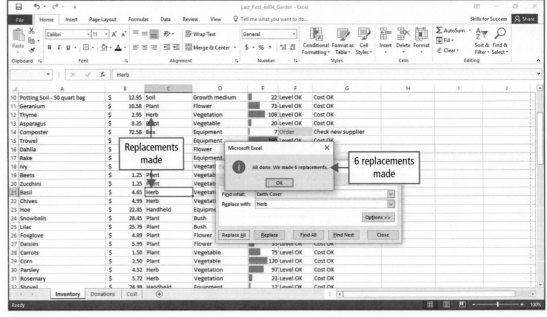

Figure 2   Excel 2016, Windows 10, Microsoft Corporation

 **Continue to the next page to complete the skill**

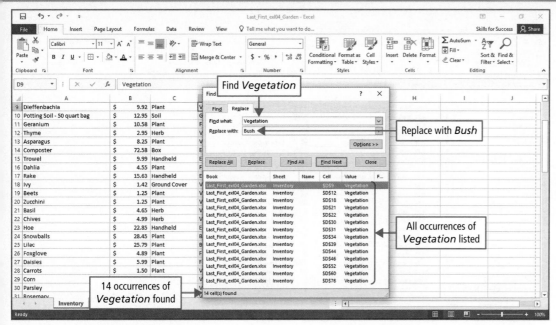

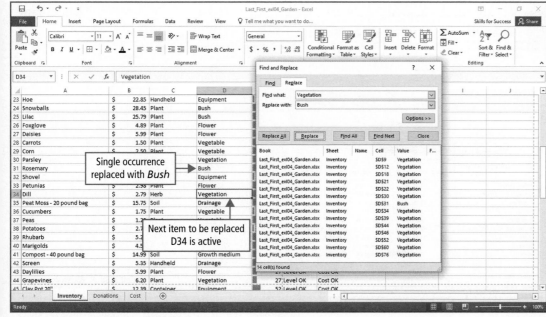

Excel 2016, Windows 10, Microsoft Corporation

Figure 3

Excel 2016, Windows 10, Microsoft Corporation

Figure 4

5. In the **Find and Replace** dialog box, in the **Find what** box, replace the text *Earth Cover* with Vegetation and then press Tab. In the **Replace with** box, replace the text *Herb* with Bush and then click the **Find All** button.

6. In the **Find and Replace** dialog box, point to the bottom border, and then with the ↕ pointer, drag down to resize the dialog box until each listed occurrence displays as shown in **Figure 3**. If necessary, move the dialog box to display all occurrences.

   The Find All option finds all occurrences of the search criteria.

7. In the lower portion of the **Find and Replace** dialog box, in the **Cell** column, click **$D$31** to make cell *D31* the active cell, and then click the **Replace** button. Compare your screen with **Figure 4**.

   In this manner, you can find all occurrences of cell text and use the list to replace only the occurrences you desire.

8. Use the technique just practiced to replace the two occurrences of the word Clay with the word Terracotta and then close all message and dialog boxes.

9. **Save** 💾 the file.

■ **You have completed Skill 6 of 10**

▶ The **Freeze Panes** command keeps rows or columns visible when scrolling in a worksheet. The frozen rows and columns become separate panes so that you can always identify rows and columns when working with large worksheets.

1. On the **Inventory** sheet, scroll until row **50** displays at the bottom of your window and the column labels are out of view. Compare your screen with **Figure 1**.

   When you scroll in large worksheets, the column and row labels may not be visible, which can make identifying the purpose of each row or column difficult.

2. Press Ctrl + Home, and then click cell **C15**. Click the **View tab**, and then in the **Window group**, click the **Freeze Panes** button. Click the first option **Freeze Panes** to freeze the rows above and the columns to the left of **C15**—the active cell.

   A line displays along the upper border of row 15 and on the left border of column C to show where the panes are frozen.

3. Click the **Scroll Down** ▾ and **Scroll Right** ▸ **arrows** to display cell **M80**, and then notice that the top and left panes remain frozen. Compare your screen with **Figure 2**.

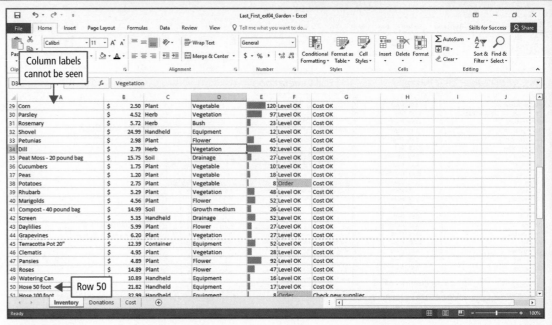

Figure 1   Excel 2016, Windows 10, Microsoft Corporation

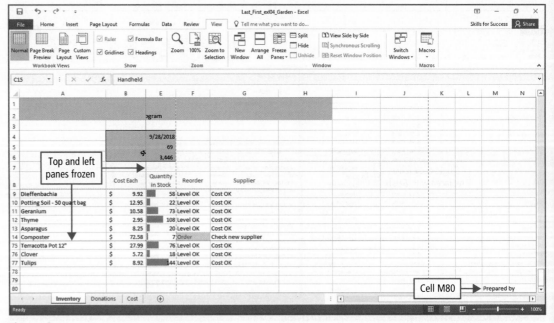

Figure 2   Excel 2016, Windows 10, Microsoft Corporation

■ Continue to the next page to complete the skill

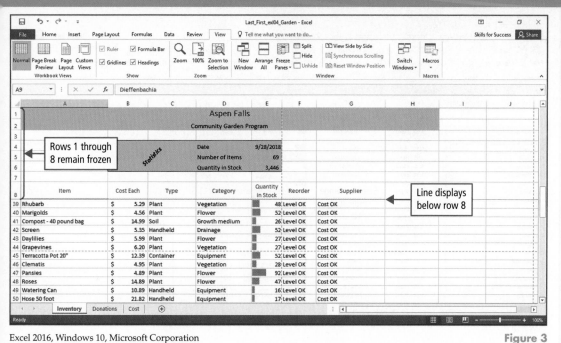

Excel 2016, Windows 10, Microsoft Corporation

Figure 3

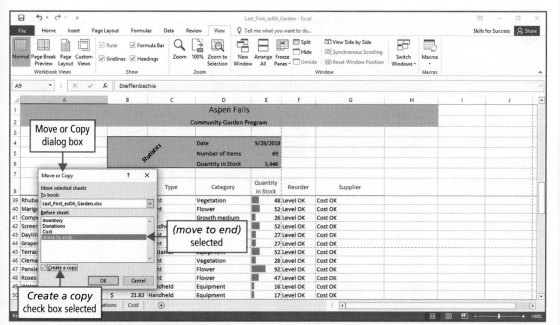

Excel 2016, Windows 10, Microsoft Corporation

Figure 4

4. Click cell **M80**, and then press Delete.

5. In the **Window group**, click the **Freeze Panes** button, and then click **Unfreeze Panes**.

> The rows and columns are no longer frozen, and the border no longer displays on row 15 and on column C.

6. Click cell **A9**. In the **Window group**, click the **Freeze Panes** button, and then click **Freeze Panes** to freeze the rows above **row 9**.

7. Watch the row numbers below **row 8** as you scroll down to **row 50**. Compare your screen with Figure 3.

> The labels in row 1 through row 8 stay frozen while the remaining rows of data continue to scroll.

8. Right-click the **Inventory** worksheet tab, and then from the list, click **Move or Copy**. In the **Move or Copy** dialog box, click (**move to end**), and then click the **Create a copy** check box. Compare your screen with Figure 4.

Obj 1.1.4 C

9. In the **Move or Copy** dialog box, click **OK** to create a copy of the worksheet named *Inventory (2)*.

> A (2) displays in the name because two sheets in a workbook cannot have the same name.

10. Right-click the **Inventory (2)** worksheet tab, click **Rename**, type Sort by Cost and then press Enter.

11. In the **Window group**, click the **Freeze Panes** button, and then click **Unfreeze Panes** to unfreeze the panes.

12. Click the **Inventory** worksheet tab, and then verify the panes are still frozen on this worksheet.

13. Save the file.

■ **You have completed Skill 7 of 10**

▶ To analyze a group of related data, you can convert a range into an *Excel table*—a series of rows and columns that contain related data that have been formatted as a table. Data in an Excel table are managed independently from the data in other rows and columns in the worksheet.

▶ Data in Excel tables can be sorted in a variety of ways—for example, in ascending order or by color.

1. Click the **Sort by Cost** worksheet tab, and then click cell **A11**. On the **Home tab**, in the **Styles group**, click the **Format as Table** button. In the gallery, under **Light**, click the seventh choice in the first row—**Table Style Light 7**.

2. In the **Format as Table** dialog box, under **Where is the data for your table?**, verify that the range **=$A$8:$G$77** displays. Verify that the **My table has headers** check box is selected. Compare your screen with **Figure 1**, and then click **OK** to convert the range to an Excel table.

   When creating an Excel table, you only need to click in the data. The layout of column and row headings determines the default range provided in the Format As Table dialog box. If needed, the data range can also be edited in the dialog box, or alternatively, the user can click to drag and select the correct range.

3. Click cell **H8**, type Total Cost and then press [Enter] to automatically add the formatted column to the Excel table.

4. In cell **H9**, type =B9*E9 and then press [Enter]. Compare your screen with **Figure 2**.

   The new column is a *calculated column*—a column in an Excel table that uses a single formula that adjusts for each row.

■ Continue to the next page to complete the skill ▶

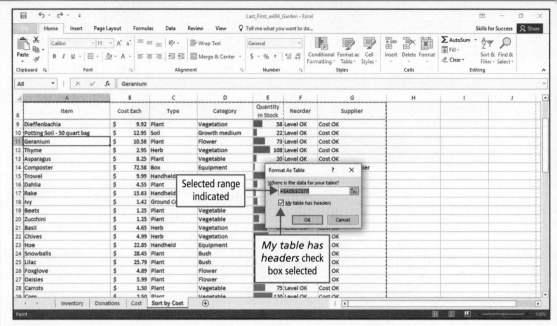

Figure 1

Excel 2016, Windows 10, Microsoft Corporation

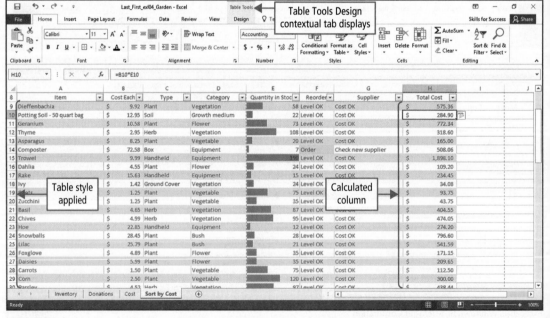

Figure 2

Excel 2016, Windows 10, Microsoft Corporation

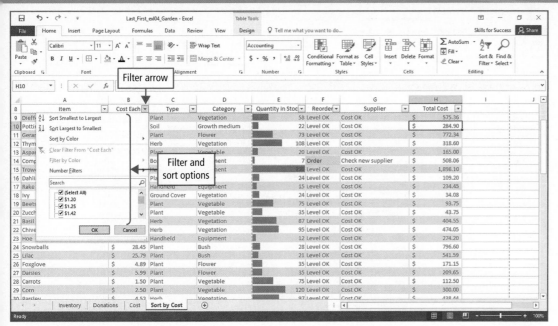

5. In the header row of the Excel table, click the **Cost Each filter arrow**, and then compare your screen with **Figure 3**.

6. In the **Filter** gallery, click **Sort Smallest to Largest**.

> The rows in the table are sorted by the *Cost Each* values, from the lowest to the highest, as indicated by the up arrow on the column's filter button.

7. In the header row, click the **Total Cost filter arrow**, and then click **Sort Largest to Smallest**.

> The rows in the table are now sorted from the highest to lowest *Total Cost* value, and the small arrow in the Total Cost filter arrow points down, indicating a descending sort. The previous sort on the *Cost Each* column no longer displays.

8. Right-click the **Sort by Cost** worksheet tab, and then click **Move or Copy**. In the **Move or Copy** dialog box, click **(move to end)**, select the **Create a copy** check box, and then click **OK**.

Excel 2016, Windows 10, Microsoft Corporation

Figure 3

9. Rename the **Sort by Cost (2)** worksheet tab as Items to Reorder

10. On the **Items to Reorder** worksheet, click the **Reorder filter arrow**, and then point to **Sort by Color**. Notice that the color formats in column **F** display in the list. Compare your screen with **Figure 4**.

> If you have applied manual or conditional formatting to a range of cells, you can sort by these colors.

11. In the list, under **Sort by Cell Color**, click the **Light Red** color to place the six items that need to be ordered at the top of the Excel table.

12. Save the file.

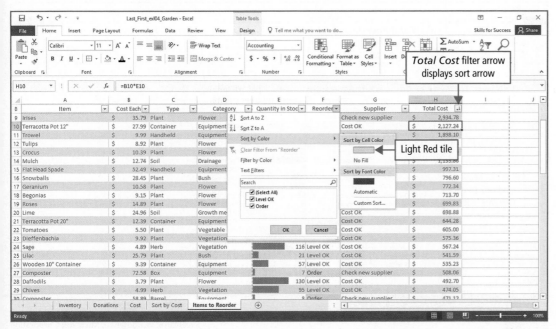

Excel 2016, Windows 10, Microsoft Corporation

Figure 4

■ **You have completed Skill 8 of 10**

▶ You can *filter* data to display only the rows of a table that meet specified criteria. Filtering temporarily hides rows that do not meet the criteria.

1. On the **Items to Reorder** worksheet, click the **Category filter arrow**. From the menu, clear the **(Select All)** check box to clear all the check boxes. Click the **Equipment** check box, as shown in **Figure 1**, and then click **OK** to display only the rows containing *Equipment*.

   The rows not meeting this criteria are hidden from view.

2. Click the **Design tab**, and then in the **Table Style Options group**, click the **Total Row** check box to display the column total in cell **H78**. Select the range **H10:H72**. Click the **Home tab**, and then in the **Number group**, click the **Comma Style** button .

   The *Total row* displays as the last row in an Excel table and provides summary functions in drop-down lists for each column. Here, *Total* displays in cell A78. In cell H78, the number *$10,400.26* indicates the SUM of the Total Cost column for the filtered *Equipment* rows.

3. In the **Total** row, click cell **D78**, and then click the **arrow** that displays to the right of the selected cell. Compare your screen with **Figure 2**.

4. In the list of summary functions, click **Count** to count only the visible rows in column D—*20*.

5. In the header row, click the **Type filter arrow**. From the menu, scroll down and clear the **Handheld** check box, and then click **OK**.

   Filters can be applied to more than one column. Here, both the Type and Category columns are filtered.

■ **Continue to the next page to complete the skill** ▶

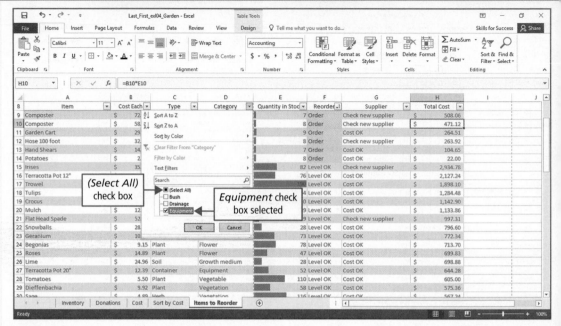

Figure 1

Excel 2016, Windows 10, Microsoft Corporation

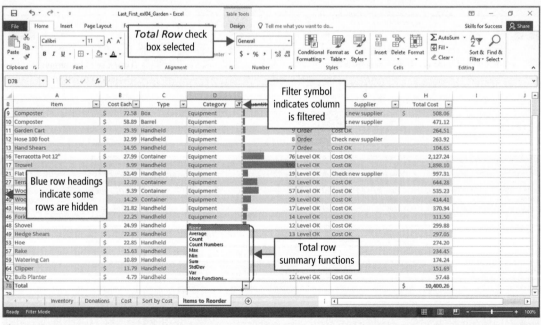

Figure 2

Excel 2016, Windows 10, Microsoft Corporation

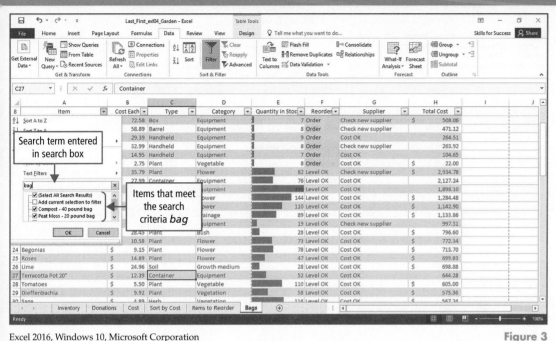

Excel 2016, Windows 10, Microsoft Corporation

Figure 3

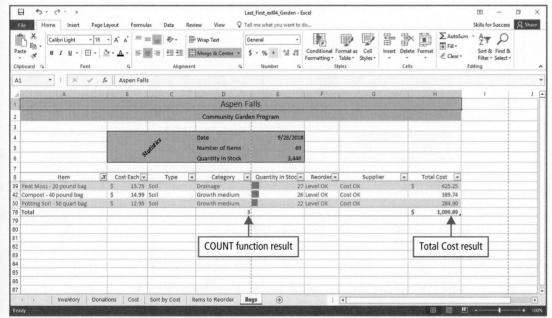

Excel 2016, Windows 10, Microsoft Corporation

Figure 4

6. Right-click the **Items to Reorder** worksheet tab, and then using the techniques previously practiced, create a copy of the worksheet, and move the sheet to the end. Rename the **Items to Reorder (2)** worksheet tab as Bags

7. With the **Bags** worksheet active, click any cell in the Excel table to make the Excel table active. Click the **Data tab**, and then in the **Sort & Filter group**, click the **Clear** button to clear all the filters and to display all the rows in the Excel table.

> The cells in column H show a mixture of Comma and Accounting Style format because cells were hidden when this column was formatted in step 2.

8. In the header row, click the **Item filter arrow**. In the **Filter** list, click in the **Search** box, type bag and then compare your screen with **Figure 3**.

9. Click **OK** to display the three rows containing the text *bag* in the Item column. Click the range **H42:H50**. Click the **Home tab**, and then in the **Number group**, click the **Comma Style** button. Press Ctrl + Home , and then compare your screen with **Figure 4**.

> In the Total row, the Category count is in cell D78, and the Total Cost in cell H78 displays the results of the filtered rows.

10. **Save** 💾 the file.

■ **You have completed Skill 9 of 10**

▶ An Excel table can be converted into a range retaining the table format.

▶ When a worksheet is too wide or too long to print on a single page, row and column headings can be printed on each page.

1. Right-click the **Bags** worksheet tab, create a copy of the sheet, and then move it to the end of the workbook. Rename the **Bags (2)** worksheet tab as All Items

2. In the **All Items** sheet, click cell **A8**. On the **Design tab**, in the **Tools group**, click the **Convert to Range** button. Read the message box, as shown in **Figure 1**, and then click **Yes**.

Obj 3.1.2 C

> When converting a table into a range, all filters are removed and the heading row no longer displays filter buttons. Any existing sorts and formatting remain.

3. Click the **File tab**, and then click **Print**. Click the **Next Page** button ▶ three times to view the four pages.

4. Click the **Back** button ⬅. On the **Page Layout tab**, in the **Scale to Fit group**, click the **Width arrow**, and then click **1 page**. Click the **Height arrow**, and then click **1 page**.

5. Click the **Inventory** worksheet tab. In the **Scale to Fit group**, click the **Width arrow**, and then click **1 page**.

Obj 1.5.4 C

6. In the **Page Setup group**, click the **Print Titles** button, and then in the **Page Setup** dialog box, under **Print titles**, click in the **Rows to repeat at top** box. In the worksheet, click **row 8**, and then compare your screen with **Figure 2**.

Obj 1.5.5 C

■ **Continue to the next page to complete the skill**

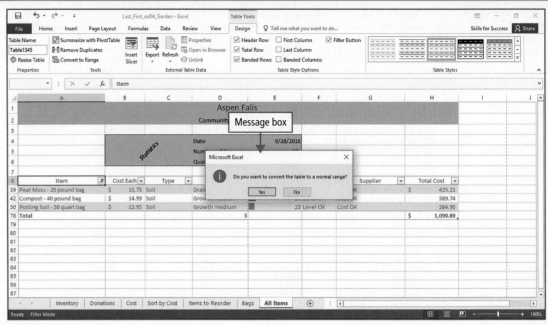

Figure 1

Excel 2016, Windows 10, Microsoft Corporation

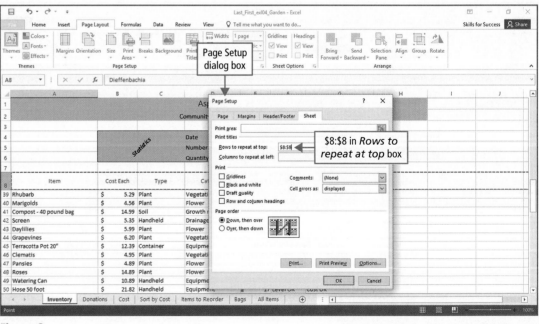

Figure 2

Excel 2016, Windows 10, Microsoft Corporation

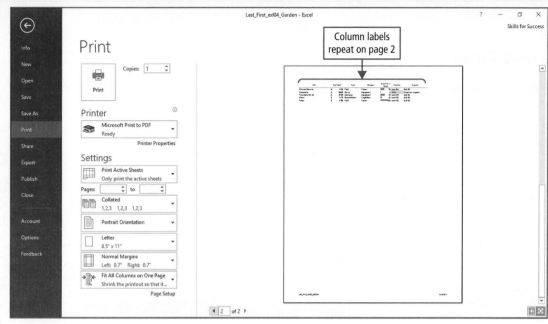

Excel 2016, Windows 10, Microsoft Corporation

Figure 3

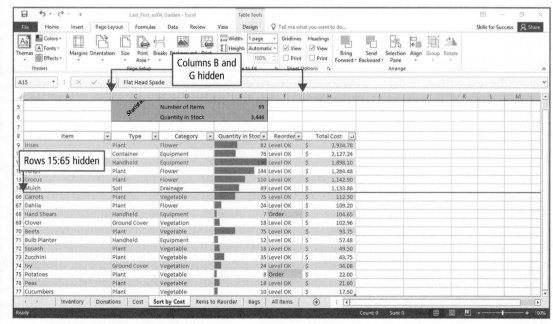

Excel 2016, Windows 10, Microsoft Corporation

Figure 4

7. In the **Page Setup** dialog box, click the **Print Preview** button. Click the **Next Page** button ▶ to verify that the column labels from **row 8** display at the top of Page 2. Compare your screen with **Figure 3**.

8. Click the **Back** button .

9. Click the **Cost** worksheet tab. Hold down Ctrl, and then click the **Items to Reorder** and the **Bags** worksheet tabs to group the three worksheets. In the **Page Setup group**, click the **Orientation** button, and then click **Landscape**. In the **Scale to Fit group**, click the **Width arrow**, and then click **1 page**.

   With the worksheets grouped, the orientation and scaling are applied to all three worksheets.

10. Click the **Sort by Cost** worksheet tab to select the worksheet and ungroup the three worksheets. Click cell **B13**. On the **Home tab**, in the **Cells group**, click the **Format** button. In the list, point to **Hide & Unhide**, and then click **Hide Columns**. Use the technique just practiced to hide **column G**.

11. Select rows **15:65**. In the **Cells group**, click the **Format** button, point to **Hide & Unhide**, and then click **Hide Rows**.

12. On the **Page Layout tab**, in the **Page Setup group**, click the **Orientation** button, and then click **Landscape**. Compare your screen with **Figure 4**.

13. **Save** 🖫 the file, and then **Close** ☒ Excel. Submit the file as directed by your instructor.

DONE! You have completed Skill 10 of 10, and your file is complete!

More Skills 11

Add and Remove Table Columns and Rows

To complete this project, you will need the following file:

- exl04_MS11Orders

You will save your file as:

- Last_First_exl04_MS11Orders

▶ Various methods can be used to add and remove columns and rows in tables.

1. Start **Excel 2016**, and then open the student data file **exl04_MS11Orders**. Save the file in your chapter folder as Last_First_exl04_MS11Orders

2. On the **Sort by Cost** sheet, click row **9**, and then drag down to select through row **71**. On the **Home tab**, in the **Cells group**, click the **Delete arrow**, and then click **Delete Sheet Rows**.

3. On the **Sort by Cost** sheet, select the range **A11:A12**. Right-click to open the shortcut menu, point to **Delete**, and then click **Table Rows**.

   Only the Order items remain in the table.

4. On the **Sort by Cost** sheet, click column **G**. On the **Home tab**, in the **Cells group**, click the **Insert arrow**, and then click **Insert Sheet Columns**.

5. Double-click the text *Column1* in cell **G8**, and replace the text with Supplier

6. Click cell **G9**, type Check new supplier and then press [Ctrl] + [Enter]. Point to the fill handle in **G9**, and then drag down through **G12**. Point to the line between columns **G** and **H,** and then double-click to AutoFit the column size.

7. Click the **Items to Reorder** sheet, and then click column **D**. On the **Home tab**, in the **Cells group**, click the **Delete arrow**, and then click **Delete Sheet Columns**.

8. Select the rows **16:40** as previously practiced. Right-click to open the shortcut menu, and then click **Delete Row**.

9. Click the **All Items** sheet. Select the rows **15:77**, and then press [Ctrl] + [–]. Select cell **A1**, and then compare your screen to **Figure 1**.

10. Save 🖫 the file, and then **Close** ✕ Excel. Submit the file as directed by your instructor.

- **You have completed More Skills 11**

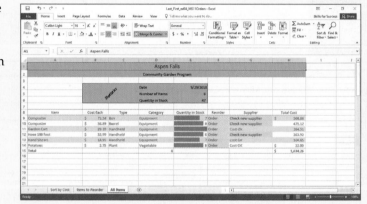

Figure 1   Excel 2016, Windows 10, Microsoft Corporation

More Skills 12

Insert the Payment (PMT) Function

To complete this project, you will need the following file:

- exl04_MS12Loans

You will save your file as:

- Last_First_exl04_MS12Loans

▶ The **PMT function** calculates the payment for a loan based on constant payments and a constant interest rate.

▶ The **interest** is the charge you pay for borrowing the money; it is generally a percentage of the amount borrowed. The **rate** is the percentage that is paid for the use of the borrowed money.

▶ The **principal** or **Present value (Pv)** of a loan is the initial amount of the loan—the total amount that a series of future payments is worth today.

▶ In the PMT function, the number of time periods, **Nper**, is the total number of payments for the loan. The value at the end of the time periods is the **Future value (Fv)**—the cash balance you want to attain after the last payment is made. The future value for a loan is usually zero.

---

1. Start **Excel 2016**, open the student data file **exl04_MS12Loans**, and then save the file in your chapter folder as Last_First_exl04_MS12Loans

2. Click cell **B8**. On the **Formulas tab**, in the **Function Library group**, click the **Financial** button. Scroll down, and then click **PMT**.

   The Function Arguments dialog box displays the arguments for the PMT function. When the insertion point is in an argument box, a description of that argument is provided in the Function Arguments dialog box.

3. If necessary, move the Function Arguments dialog box so you can view the data in columns A and B. Click in the **Rate** argument box, type B7/12 Press Tab .

   The payments on a loan are usually made monthly; however, when borrowing money, the interest rate and the number of periods are generally quoted in years. Here, the annual interest rate of 6 percent located in cell B7 is divided by 12—the number of months in a year—which results in a monthly interest rate.

4. In the **Nper** argument box, type B6*12 to calculate the number of monthly payments in the loan—60. Press Tab .

5. In the **Pv** argument box, type B5

Aspen Falls
Construction Loans

Garage Construction Loan

Amount of Loan	$ 500,000.00
Period (years)	5
Interest rate (per year)	6%
Payment (per month)	$ 9,666.40

Hospital Construction Loan

Amount of Loan	$ 8,500,000.00
Period (years)	20
Interest rate (per year)	5%
Payment (per month)	$ 56,096.24

Water Plant Construction Loan

Amount of Loan	$ 2,500,000.00
Period (years)	15
Interest rate (per year)	10%
Payment (per month)	$ 26,865.13

Figure 1

6. In the **Function Arguments** dialog box, click **OK** to display the monthly payment amount, *($9,666.40)*.

7. On the formula bar, click in the function arguments to position the insertion point in front of *B5*. Type – (minus sign), and then press Enter . Compare your screen with **Figure 1**.

   By placing a minus sign in the function, the monthly payment amount displays as a positive number.

8. **Save** 🖫 the file, and then **Close** ☒ Excel. Submit the file as directed by your instructor.

■ **You have completed More Skills 12**

More Skills 13

Customize Workbook Views

To complete this project, you will need the following files:

- exl04_MS13Plants
- exl04_MS13Inventory

You will save your files as:

- Last_First_exl04_MS13Plants
- Last_First_exl04_MS13Snip

▶ The *split window* is a command that divides the window into separate panes so that each pane can be scrolled separately.

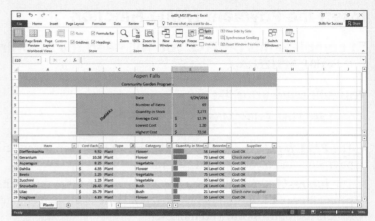

Figure 1   Excel 2016, Windows 10, Microsoft Corporation

1. Start **Excel 2016**, and then open the file **exl04_MS13Plants**. Save the file in your chapter folder as Last_First_exl04_MS13Plants

2. Use the scroll bar on the right side of the windows to scroll down to view all of the rows in this worksheet, scroll up, and then click cell **E10**.

3. Click the **View tab**, and then in the **Window group**, click the **Split** button. **MOS** Notice the spreadsheet is now split into four sections, and then compare Obj 1.4.5 C your screen with **Figure 1**.

   Horizontal and vertical bars split the window. Vertical scrollbars display for the upper and lower panes, and horizontal scrollbars display for the left and right panes.

4. Drag the lower vertical scrollbar up to view **row 1**, and then drag the right horizontal scrollbar to the left to view the statistics in **B4:E9**.

5. Drag the upper vertical scrollbar down to view **row 80**.

   Statistics for the plant costs can be compared with the costs for plants to check for a new supplier.

6. **Save** 💾 the file, and then open **exl04_MS13Inventory**.

7. On the **View tab**, and then in the **Window group**, click the **View Side** **MOS** **by Side** button. Obj 1.4.5 C

8. In the top pane, in the **Window group**, click the **Synchronous Scrolling** button to turn it off.

9. In the bottom pane, in the **Window group**, click the **Synchronous Scrolling** button to turn it off. Compare your screen with **Figure 2**.

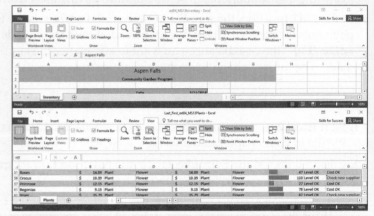

Figure 2   Excel 2016, Windows 10, Microsoft Corporation

Both open workbooks display in the window. The workbooks can be compared side by side.

10. Using the Windows **Snipping Tool**, take a **Full-Screen** snip, and then **Save** the file to your chapter folder as Last_First_exl04_MS13Snip

11. **Close** ☒ all open windows, and then submit the files as directed by your instructor.

■ **You have completed More Skills 13**

More Skills (14)

Use Text and Lookup Functions

To complete this project, you will need the following file:

- exl04_MS14Revenue

You will save your file as:

- Last_First_exl04_MS14Revenue

▶ The **LOWER** *function* is a text function used to convert a text string to all lowercase letters.

▶ The **UPPER** *function* is a text function used to convert a text string to all uppercase letters.

▶ The **TRANSPOSE** *function* is a lookup function used to convert a vertical range of cells to a horizontal range, or vice versa.

---

1. Start **Excel 2016**, and then open the student data file **exl04_MS14Revenue**. Save the file in your chapter folder as Last_First_exl04_MS14Revenue

2. On the **Home tab**, in the **Editing group**, click the **Find & Select** button. In the list, click **Go To**. In the **Go To** dialog box, click in the **Reference** box, and then type Location!A1 Click **OK**. 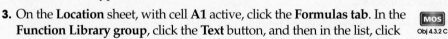 Obj 1.2.2 C

3. On the **Location** sheet, with cell **A1** active, click the **Formulas tab**. In the **Function Library group**, click the **Text** button, and then in the list, click **UPPER**. 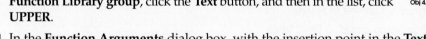 Obj 4.3.2 C

4. In the **Function Arguments** dialog box, with the insertion point in the **Text** box, type Quarter!A1 and then click **OK**.

   The text *Aspen Falls* from the Quarter worksheet is entered into cell A1 in all capital letters.

5. Click cell **A2**. In the **Function Library group**, click the **Text** button, and then in the list, click **LOWER**. **MOS** obj 4.3.2C

6. In the **Function Arguments** dialog box, with the insertion point in the **Text** box, type Quarter!A2 and then click **OK**.

   The text *Quarterly Revenue* from the Quarter worksheet is entered into cell A2 in all lowercase letters.

7. On the **Location** worksheet, select the range **A4:A8**. In the **Function Library group**, click the **Lookup & Reference** button, and then in the list, click **TRANSPOSE**.

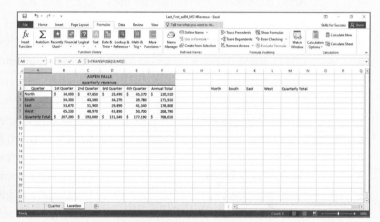

Excel 2016, Windows 10, Microsoft Corporation

Figure 1

8. With the insertion point in the **Array** box, drag to select the range **I3:M3**. Press and hold Ctrl and Shift, and then press Enter.

9. The data from I3:M3 appears in **A4:A8**, and the array function {=TRANSPOSE(I3:M3)} appears in the formula bar. Compare your screen to **Figure 1**.

10. **Save** 🔲 the file, and then **Close** ☒ Excel. Submit the file as directed by your instructor.

■ **You have completed More Skills 14**

The following table summarizes the **SKILLS AND PROCEDURES** covered in this chapter.

Skills Number	Task	Step	Icon	Keyboard Shortcut
1	Insert TODAY functions	Formula tab → Function Library group → Date & Time → TODAY		
1	Insert NOW functions	Formula tab → Function Library group → Date & Time → NOW		
1	Insert COUNT functions	Formula tab → Function Library group → More Functions → Statistical → COUNT		
2	Insert IF functions	Formula tab → Function Library group → Logical → IF		
3	Add borders	Home tab → Font group → Border arrow → Border	⊞ ▾	
3	Angle text	Home tab → Alignment group → Orientation		
4	Apply conditional formatting to text	Quick Analysis → Text Contains		Ctrl + Q
4	Apply conditional formatting data bars	Quick Analysis → Data Bars		Ctrl + Q
5	Insert sparklines	Quick Analysis → Sparklines		Ctrl + Q
5	Add sparkline high points	Design tab → Show group → High Point		
6	Use Find and Replace	Home tab → Editing group → Find & Select → Replace		Ctrl + H
7	Freeze panes	View tab → Window group → Freeze Panes		
7	Unfreeze panes	View tab → Window group → Unfreeze Panes		
8	Create Excel tables	Home tab → Styles group → Format as Table		
8	Filter Excel tables	Click the column filter arrow		
8	Sort Excel tables	Column filter arrow		
9	Search Excel tables	Column filter arrow → Search criteria		
9	Insert total rows	Design tab → Table Style Options group → Total Row		
10	Convert Excel tables to ranges	Design tab → Tools group → Convert to Range		
10	Repeat rows at the top of each printed page	Page Layout tab → Page Setup group → Print Titles		
10	Hide columns	Home tab → Cells group → Format → Hide & Unhide → Hide Columns		Ctrl + 0
10	Hide rows	Home tab → Cells group → Format → Hide & Unhide → Hide Rows		Ctrl + 9
MS11	Insert row/column	Home tab → Cells group → Insert		Ctrl + +
MS11	Delete row/column	Home tab → Cells group → Delete		Ctrl + −
MS12	Using financial functions	Formulas tab → Function Library group → Financial → PMT		
MS13	Split worksheet window	View tab → Window group → Split		
MS14	Use Go To	Home tab → Editing group → Find & Select → Go To		
MS14	Insert UPPER function	Formulas tab → Function Library group →Text → UPPER		
MS14	Insert LOWER function	Formulas tab → Function Library group →Text → LOWER		
MS14	Insert TRANSPOSE function	Formulas tab → Function Library group → Lookup & Reference → TRANSPOSE		

Project Summary Chart

Project	Project Type	Project Location
Skills Review	Review	In Book & MIL MyITLab® Grader
Skills Assessment 1	Review	In Book & MIL MyITLab® Grader
Skills Assessment 2	Review	Book
My Skills	Problem Solving	Book
Visual Skills Check	Problem Solving	Book
Skills Challenge 1	Critical Thinking	Book
Skills Challenge 2	Critical Thinking	Book
More Skills Assessment	Review	In Book & MIL MyITLab® Grader
Collaborating with Google	Critical Thinking	Book

MOS Objectives Covered (Quiz in MyITLab®)

1.1.4 C Copy and move a worksheet	3.1.1 C Create an Excel table from a cell range
1.2.1 C Search for data within a workbook	3.1.2 C Convert a table to a cell range
1.2.2 C Navigate to a named cell, range, or workbook element	3.1.3 C Add and remove table rows and columns
1.4.2 C Hide or unhide columns and rows	3.2.1 C Apply styles to tables
1.4.5 C Change window views	3.2.3 C Insert total rows
1.5.4 C Set print scaling	3.3.1 C Filter records
1.5.5 C Display repeating row and column titles on multipage worksheets	3.3.2 C Sort data by multiple columns
2.1.1 C Replace data	3.3.3 C Change sort order
2.2.2 C Modify cell alignment and indention	4.1.4 C Perform calculations by using the COUNT function
2.2.6 C Apply cell formats	4.2.1 C Perform logical operations by using the IF function
2.3.1 C Insert sparklines	4.3.2C Format text by using UPPER, LOWER, and PROPER functions
2.3.4 C Apply conditional formatting	

Key Terms

BizSkills
Video

1. What are some of the positive behaviors of the second applicant?

2. If you were the interviewer, which applicant would you hire, and why would you hire that person?

Online Help Skills

1. Start **Excel 2016**, and then in the upper right corner of the start page, click the **Help** button ? .

2. In the **Excel Help** window **Search** box, type formulas in Excel tables and then press Enter .

3. In the search result list, click **Define and use names in formulas**, and then in **Learn more about using names**, scroll down and click the link under *Table name*—**Using structured references with Excel tables**. **Maximize** the **Excel Help** window, and then compare your screen with **Figure 1**.

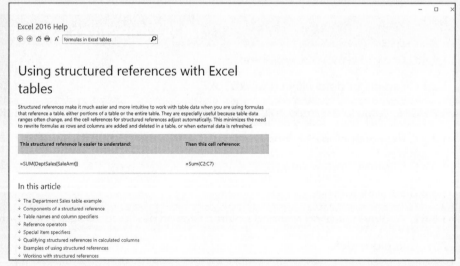

Figure 1   Excel 2016, Windows 10, Microsoft Corporation

4. Read the article to see if you can answer the following questions: What are structured references, and why would you use them?

Matching

Match each term in the second column with its correct definition in the first column by writing the letter of the term on the blank line in front of the correct definition.

___ **1.** An Excel function that returns the serial number of the current date.

___ **2.** The result of a function that will be updated each time the workbook is opened.

___ **3.** The type of function that tests for specific conditions and typically uses conditional tests to determine whether specified conditions are TRUE or FALSE.

___ **4.** Conditions that determine how conditional formatting is applied or what values are returned in logical functions.

___ **5.** The cell shading or font color that is applied to cells when a specified circumstance is met.

___ **6.** A chart inside a single cell used to show data trends.

___ **7.** A series of rows and columns that are formatted together.

___ **8.** The column in an Excel table that uses a single formula that adjusts for each row.

___ **9.** A command to display only the rows of a table that meet specified criteria.

___ **10.** The row that provides summary functions in an Excel table.

A Calculated column

B Conditional formatting

C Criteria

D Excel table

E Filter

F Logical function

G Sparkline

H TODAY function

I Total row

J Volatile

Multiple Choice

Choose the correct answer.

1. The logical function that checks whether criteria are met and returns one value if TRUE and another value if FALSE.
   - A. IF
   - B. UNKNOWN
   - C. NEW

2. These symbols are inserted into logical functions to determine whether a condition is true or false—(<) and (=), for example.
   - A. Comparison operators
   - B. Mathematical operators
   - C. Logical symbols

3. Applying this format to text draws attention to the text on a worksheet.
   - A. Angle
   - B. Slope
   - C. Slant

4. A format, such as cell shading, that is applied to cells when a specified condition is true.
   - A. Filtered
   - B. Conditional
   - C. Calculated

5. The format that provides a visual cue about the value of a cell relative to other cells.
   - A. Cell style
   - B. Quick style
   - C. Data bar

6. This command ensures that header rows and columns remain visible when a worksheet is scrolled.
   - A. Total Panes
   - B. Excel Panes
   - C. Freeze Panes

7. Data in an Excel table can be sorted in this way.
   - A. Large to largest
   - B. Smallest to largest
   - C. Small to smallest

8. A command to display only the rows of a table that meet specified criteria.
   - A. Filter
   - B. Standard
   - C. Chart

9. The row that displays as the last row in an Excel table and provides summary statistics.
   - A. Total
   - B. Sorted
   - C. Changeable

10. This word describes the result of a function that is updated each time the workbook is opened.
    - A. Volatile
    - B. Changeable
    - C. Unstable

Topics for Discussion

1. Think about current news stories, including sports stories, and identify statistical data that is presented by the media. What are the advantages of using conditional formatting with this type of data?

2. Sorting and filtering are two of the most valuable ways to analyze data. If you were presented with an Excel table containing names and addresses, what are some of the ways you might sort or filter the data? If you were presented with an Excel table of a day's cash transactions at your college's cafeteria, what are some ways you could sort, filter, and total?

Skills Review

To complete this project, you will need the following file:

- exl04_SRAuction

You will save your file as:

- Last_First_exl04_SRAuction

1. Start **Excel 2016**, and then open the file **exl04_SRAuction**. Save the file in your chapter folder as Last_First_exl04_SRAuction

2. On the **Materials** sheet, click cell **B4**. On the **Formulas tab**, in the **Function Library group**, click the **Date & Time** button, and then click **TODAY**. In the message box, click **OK**. Click cell **B5**. In the **Function Library group**, click the **More Functions** button. Point to **Statistical**, and then click **COUNT**. In the **Value1** box, enter the range **B9:B48** and then press Enter. Compare your screen with **Figure 1**.

3. Select the range **A4:B6**. Point to the right border of the selected range, and then move the data to the range **D4:E6**.

4. In cell **B4**, type Surplus and then merge and center the title in the range **B4:C6**. On the **Home tab**, in the **Alignment group**, click the **Middle Align** button. Click the **Orientation** button, and then click **Angle Counterclockwise**. Select the range **B4:E6**. In the **Font group**, click the **Border arrow**, and then click **Outside Borders**.

5. Click cell **A1**. In the **Editing group**, click the **Find & Select** button, and then click **Replace**. In the **Find what** box, type Sedan In the **Replace with** box, type Car and then click **Replace All**. Click **OK** for the message of 5 replacements, and then **Close** the dialog box.

6. Click cell **G9**. On the **Formulas tab**, in the **Function Library group**, click **Logical**. In the list, click **IF**, and then in the **Logical_test** box, type E9="Yes" In the **Value_if_true** box, type B9*F9 In the **Value_if_false** box, type 0 and then click **OK**. AutoFill the function down through **G48**, and then compare your screen with **Figure 2**.

Excel 2016, Windows 10, Microsoft Corporation

Figure 1

Excel 2016, Windows 10, Microsoft Corporation

Figure 2

- Continue to the next page to complete this Skills Review

7. Click cell **A9**. On the **View tab**, in the **Window group**, click the **Freeze Panes** button. Click **Freeze Panes**.

8. Right-click the **Materials** worksheet tab, and then click **Move or Copy**. In the **Move or Copy** dialog box, click **(move to end)**, select the **Create a copy** check box, and then click **OK**. Rename the new worksheet tab as Price by Car

9. On the **Price by Car** sheet, in the **Window group**, click the **Freeze Panes** button, and then click **Unfreeze Panes**. On the **Home tab**, in the **Styles group**, click the **Format as Table** button. Click **Table Style Light 17**. In the **Format As Table** dialog box, verify that the **My table has headers** check box is selected, and then click **OK**.

10. In the **Type** column, click the **filter arrow**, and then clear the **(Select All)** check box. Select the **Car** check box, and then click **OK**. Click the **Total Price filter arrow**, and then click **Sort Largest to Smallest**. On the **Design tab**, in the **Table Style Options group**, select the **Total Row** check box.

11. Select the range **F12:G48**, and then apply the **Comma [0]** cell style. Select the range **F9:F48**. Click the **Quick Analysis** button, and then click **Data Bars**. Click cell **A9**, and then compare your screen with **Figure 3**.

12. Create a copy of the *Price by Car* sheet, move to the end, and then rename the worksheet tab to Pickups On the **Data tab**, in the **Sort & Filter group**, click the **Clear** button. Click the **Item filter arrow**. In the **Search** box, type Pickup and then click **OK**.

13. Click the **Annual Sales** worksheet tab, and then select the range **B4:F9**. Click the **Quick Analysis** button, click **Sparklines**, and then click the **Column** button.

14. Right-click the **Annual Sales** worksheet, and then click **Select All Sheets**. On the **Page Layout tab**, in the **Page Setup group**, click the **Orientation** button, and then click **Landscape**. In the **Scale to Fit group**, change the **Width** to **1 page**. Ungroup the worksheets.

15. Click the **Materials** worksheet. On the **Page Layout tab**, in the **Page Setup group**, click the **Print Titles** button. In the **Page Setup** dialog box, click in the **Rows to repeat at top** box, click row **8** in the worksheet, and then click **OK**.

16. **Save** the file. Click the **File tab**, and then click **Print**. Compare your screen with **Figure 4**. **Close** Excel, and then submit the file as directed by your instructor.

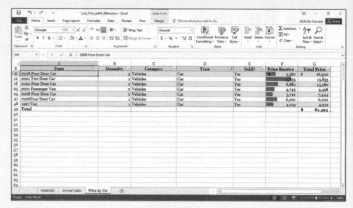

Figure 3   Excel 2016, Windows 10, Microsoft Corporation

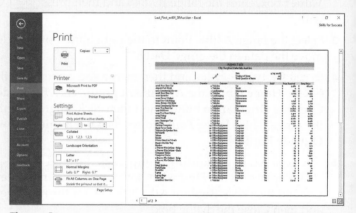

Figure 4   Excel 2016, Windows 10, Microsoft Corporation

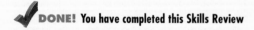

DONE! You have completed this Skills Review

Skills Assessment 1  MyITLab®
Grader

To complete this project, you will need the following file:

- exl04_SA1Recycling

You will save your file as:

- Last_First_exl04_SA1Recycling

---

1. Start **Excel 2016**, and then open the file **exl04_SA1Recycling**. Save the file in your chapter folder as Last_First_exl04_SA1Recycling

2. In cell **E3**, insert the **NOW** function. Select **A5:G5**, and then apply a **Bottom Border**.

3. In range **F6:F27**, insert **Line Sparklines** using the data in columns **B:E**. Show the **Low Point**.

4. In cell **G6**, insert the **IF** function. For the logical test, check whether the **FY 2017** result is greater than the **FY 2016** value in the same row. If the logical test is TRUE, Yes should display, and if it is FALSE, Needs Work should display. **Center** the results, and then AutoFill **G6** down through **G27**.

5. In the **Improved from previous year** column, apply a **Text Contains** conditional format that will display any cells that contain *Needs Work* formatted with **Light Red Fill**.

6. Create a copy of the sheet, and then move the copy to the end of the workbook. Rename the new worksheet tab Improvements

7. On the **Improvements** sheet, format **A5:G27** as an Excel table using the **Table Style Light 16**. Filter column **G** to display only the rows that improved from the previous year.

8. Display the **Total** row, and then display the four **FY** sums. Apply **Currency [0]** to the totals. In **G28**, select **None**.

9. Sort the **FY 2017** column from the smallest to the largest value, and then hide column **B**.

10. On the **Improvements** sheet, click cell **A1**, and then change the **Height** scale to fit on 1 page. On the **Recycling** sheet, change the **Page Setup** to repeat the titles in row **5**.

11. Group the worksheets. Change the page orientation to **Landscape**. Add the file name in the left footer and the sheet name in the right footer. Return to **Normal** view.

Recycling Volumes
Aspen Falls (in tons)
8/15/2017 10:18

Type	FY 2014	FY 2015	FY 2016	FY 2017	Trend	Improved from previous year?
Glass	10,820	8,857	10,928	11,036		Yes
Tin Cans	825	650	833	842		Yes
White goods	11,010	12,250	11,120	11,230		Yes
Other ferrous	61,150	63,000	61,762	62,373		Yes
Aluminum cans	1,150	1,320	1,262	1,173		Needs Work
Non-ferrous	13,160	13,270	13,292	13,423		Yes
High Grade Paper	1,830	2,490	1,848	1,867		Yes
Newsprint	14,790	13,370	14,938	15,086		Yes
Cardboard	19,640	16,350	21,836	20,033		Needs Work
Other paper	4,340	5,900	4,383	4,427		Yes
PETE	703	960	710	717		Yes
HDPE	417	710	421	425		Yes
Other plastics	588	920	594	600		Yes
Yard waste	57,200	55,829	59,772	58,344		Needs Work
Wood waste	10,630	11,825	11,736	10,843		Needs Work
Batteries	2,900	3,030	2,929	2,958		Yes
Oil	8,840	6,360	8,928	9,017		Yes
Tires	1,010	806	1,020	1,030		Yes
Textiles	6,410	6,208	6,474	6,538		Yes
Gypsum	225	180	227	230		Yes
Electronics	1,850	1,050	1,869	1,887		Yes
Other	1,990	2,500	2,010	2,030		Yes

Figure 1

Recycling Volumes
Aspen Falls (in tons)
8/15/2017 10:18

Type	FY 2015	FY 2016	FY 2017	Trend	Improved from previous year?
Gypsum	180	227	230		Yes
HDPE	710	421	425		Yes
Other plastics	920	594	600		Yes
PETE	960	710	717		Yes
Tin Cans	650	833	842		Yes
Tires	806	1,020	1,030		Yes
High Grade Paper	2,490	1,848	1,867		Yes
Electronics	1,050	1,869	1,887		Yes
Other	2,500	2,010	2,030		Yes
Batteries	3,030	2,929	2,958		Yes
Other paper	5,900	4,383	4,427		Yes
Textiles	6,208	6,474	6,538		Yes
Oil	6,360	8,928	9,017		Yes
Glass	8,857	10,928	11,036		Yes
White goods	12,250	11,120	11,230		Yes
Non-ferrous	13,270	13,292	13,423		Yes
Newsprint	13,370	14,938	15,086		Yes
Other ferrous	63,000	61,762	62,373		Yes
Total	$ 142,511	$ 144,287	$ 145,715		

Figure 2

12. **Print Preview** the workbook, and then compare your screen with Figure 1 and Figure 2. **Save** the file, and then **Close** Excel. Submit the file as directed by your instructor.

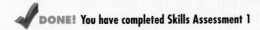 **DONE!** You have completed Skills Assessment 1

Skills Assessment 2

To complete this project, you will need the following file:

- exl04_SA2Equipment

You will save your file as:

- Last_First_exl04_SA2Equipment

1. Start **Excel 2016**, and then open the file **exl04_SA2Equipment**. Save the file in your chapter folder as Last_First_exl04_SA2Equipment

2. In cell **A2**, insert the **TODAY** function.

3. Apply **Thick Outside Borders** to the range **A4:G4**.

4. In the **Stock Level** column, insert the **IF** function. For the logical test, check whether the **Quantity in Stock** is less than **10**. If the logical test is TRUE, Order should display. If the logical test is FALSE, Level OK should display.

5. In the **Stock Level** column, apply a **Text Contains** conditional format that will display any cells that indicate *Order* formatted with **Red Text**.

6. In the worksheet, find all occurrences of Removal and replace with Extrication and then find all occurrences of Stick and replace with Baton

7. Format the range **A4:G63** as an Excel table using the **Table Style Medium 23** table style.

8. Create a copy of the worksheet, and then move the sheet to the end of the workbook. Rename the new sheet tab Safety On the **Safety** worksheet, **Sort** the table in alphabetical order by **Category**. **Filter** the Excel table to display the **Safety** type.

9. Display the **Total** row, and then in cell **B64**, display the count for column **B**, and apply **Currency [0]** cell style to **G64**. Hide column **D**.

10. On the **Equipment** sheet, convert the table to a normal range. Freeze the rows above **row 5**, and then set the titles in row **4** to repeat on each printed page.

11. Group the worksheets. Add a custom footer with the file name in the left footer and the sheet name in the right footer. Change the page orientation to **Landscape**.

Figure 1

Quantity in Stock	Item	Cost Each	Type	Category	Stock Level	Total Cost
53	Coil Headphones	$30	Radio	Communication	Order	1,589
40	Radio Strap/Holder	$45	Radio	Communication	Order	1,800
3	Retractable Mic Keeper	$20	Radio	Communication	Level OK	60
41	Leather Radio Holder	$25	Radio	Communication	Order	1,025
20	10" Zipper Boots	$320	Boots	Footwear	Order	6,400
21	Leather Fire Boots	$340	Boots	Footwear	Order	7,140
26	Rubber Lug Boot	$109	Boots	Footwear	Order	2,834
27	Rubber Fire Boots	$169	Boots	Footwear	Order	4,563
28	Rubber Bunker Boots	$129	Boots	Footwear	Order	3,612
10	Hazmat Boot	$149	Boots	Footwear	Level OK	1,490
25	Fire Gloves	$89	Gloves	Outerwear	Order	2,225
27	Proximity Gear Gloves	$124	Gloves	Outerwear	Order	3,348
9	Extrication Gloves	$77	Gloves	Extrication Gear	Level OK	693
34	Rescue Glove Liners	$39	Gloves	Outerwear	Order	1,326
17	Extrication Coat	$223	Coat	Extrication Gear	Order	3,791
14	Extrication Pants	$189	Pants	Extrication Gear	Order	2,646
11	Extrication Coveralls	$359	Coveralls	Extrication Gear	Order	3,949
9	Gas Mask	$259	Safety	Safety Equipment	Level OK	2,331
9	Gas Mask Pouch	$35	Safety	Safety Equipment	Level OK	315
13	Respirator	$369	Safety	Safety Equipment	Order	4,797
19	Coverall with Hood	$159	Coveralls	Outerwear	Order	3,021
45	Disaster Safe Bag	$13	Safety	Safety Equipment	Order	585
10	Chemical Overboot	$52	Boots	Footwear	Level OK	520
10	Haz-Mat Boots	$89	Boots	Footwear	Level OK	890
57	Disaster Kit	$99	Safety	Safety Equipment	Order	5,643
10	Helmet	$229	Helmet	Outerwear	Level OK	2,290
51	Structural Fire Helmet	$179	Helmet	Outerwear	Order	9,129
25	Helmet with Eye Shield	$339	Shield	Safety Equipment	Order	8,475
8	Megaphone	$79	Megaphone	Communication	Level OK	632
53	Barrier Tape	$12	Tape	Traffic	Order	636
18	Fire Pants	$649	Pants	Outerwear	Order	11,682
19	Fire Coat	$989	Coat	Outerwear	Order	18,791
25	Proximity Coat	$1,299	Coat	Outerwear	Order	32,475
17	Proximity Pants	$1,059	Pants	Outerwear	Order	18,003
11	Radio Chest Harness	$35	Safety	Safety Equipment	Order	385
87	Rope Gloves	$32	Gloves	Outerwear	Order	2,784
28	Safety Harness	$199	Safety	Safety Equipment	Order	5,572
29	Chest Harness	$99	Safety	Safety Equipment	Order	2,871
35	EMS Jacket	$399	Coat	Outerwear	Order	13,965
47	EMS Pants	$289	Pants	Outerwear	Order	13,583
89	Breakaway Vest	$29	Vest	Outerwear	Order	2,581
15	Mesh Vest	$17	Vest	Outerwear	Order	255
25	Mesh Traffic Vest	$29	Vest	Outerwear	Order	725
89	Reflective Nylon Vest	$11	Vest	Outerwear	Order	979
16	Handheld Remote Siren	$289	Siren	Traffic	Order	4,624
19	Siren	$189	Siren	Traffic	Order	3,591
27	Traffic Baton	$19	Baton	Traffic	Order	513
37	Flare Beacon Kit	$305	Light	Traffic	Order	11,285
90	Flares with Stands	$99	Light	Traffic	Order	8,910
26	Traffic Flashlight	$18	Light	Traffic	Order	468
56	Night Barrier Tape	$15	Tape	Traffic	Order	840
17	Water Rescue Kit	$119	Safety	Water Rescue	Order	2,023
38	Water Rescue Vest	$99	Safety	Water Rescue	Order	3,762
4	Water Tether System	$59	Safety	Water Rescue	Level OK	236
18	Wildfire Helmet	$59	Helmet	Outerwear	Order	1,062
17	Full-Brim Helmet	$59	Helmet	Outerwear	Order	1,003
58	Firefighting Goggles	$49	Safety	Safety Equipment	Order	2,842
31	Water Throw Bag	$59	Safety	Water Rescue	Order	1,829
32	Dry Bag	$18	Safety	Water Rescue	Order	576

Figure 1

12. **Print Preview** the workbook, and then compare your screen with **Figure 1** and **Figure 2**. **Save** the file, and then **Close** Excel. Submit the file as directed by your instructor.

Figure 2

Quantity in Stock	Item	Cost Each	Category	Stock Level	Total Cost
9	Gas Mask	$259	Safety Equipment	Level OK	2,331
9	Gas Mask Pouch	$35	Safety Equipment	Level OK	315
13	Respirator	$369	Safety Equipment	Order	4,797
45	Disaster Safe Bag	$13	Safety Equipment	Order	585
57	Disaster Kit	$99	Safety Equipment	Order	5,643
11	Radio Chest Harness	$35	Safety Equipment	Order	385
28	Safety Harness	$199	Safety Equipment	Order	5,572
29	Chest Harness	$99	Safety Equipment	Order	2,871
17	Water Rescue Kit	$119	Water Rescue	Order	2,023
38	Water Rescue Vest	$99	Water Rescue	Order	3,762
4	Water Tether System	$59	Water Rescue	Level OK	236
31	Water Throw Bag	$59	Water Rescue	Order	1,829
32	Dry Bag	$18	Water Rescue	Order	576
Total	13				$ 30,925

Figure 2

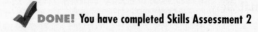

DONE! You have completed Skills Assessment 2

My Skills

To complete this project, you will need the following file:

- exl04_MYExpenses

You will save your file as:

- Last_First_exl04_MYExpenses

My Expenses

			Current Date:	8/15/2018 12:33	
Spending Category	**Spending Type**	**February**	**March**	**April**	**Trend**
Clothing	Work Uniform	85.00	90.00	92.00	
Clothing	Leisure Clothing	45.00	47.00	43.00	
Entertainment	Eating out	50.00	60.00	70.00	
Entertainment	Health Club	55.00	55.00	55.00	
Food	Groceries	155.00	145.00	147.00	
Housing	Rent	475.00	475.00	475.00	
Housing	Telephone	95.00	100.00	105.00	
Housing	Internet	85.00	90.00	90.00	
Housing	Electricity	75.00	80.00	90.00	
Housing	Renters Insurance	55.00	55.00	60.00	
Loans	Student Loan	65.00	65.00	65.00	
Loans	Credit Card	55.00	50.00	70.00	
Personal Care	Hair cut	50.00	-	55.00	
Pets	Pet Food	25.00	27.00	29.00	
Pets	Veterinarian	50.00	-	55.00	
Pets	Pet Toys	20.00	22.00	25.00	
Transportation	Car Payment	135.00	135.00	135.00	
Transportation	Fuel	50.00	60.00	70.00	
Transportation	Car Insurance	85.00	85.00	95.00	
Total		$ 1,710.00	$ 1,641.00	$ 1,826.00	

Figure 1

My Expenses

			Current Date:	8/15/2018 12:33	
Spending Category	**Spending Type**	**February**	**March**	**April**	**Trend**
Housing	Rent	475.00	475.00	475.00	
Food	Groceries	155.00	145.00	147.00	
Transportation	Car Payment	135.00	135.00	135.00	
Housing	Telephone	95.00	100.00	105.00	
Transportation	Car Insurance	85.00	85.00	95.00	
Clothing	Work Uniform	85.00	90.00	92.00	
Housing	Internet	85.00	90.00	90.00	
Housing	Electricity	75.00	80.00	90.00	
Entertainment	Eating out	50.00	60.00	70.00	
Loans	Credit Card	55.00	50.00	70.00	
Transportation	Fuel	50.00	60.00	70.00	
Loans	Student Loan	65.00	65.00	65.00	
Housing	Renters Insurance	55.00	55.00	60.00	
Entertainment	Health Club	55.00	55.00	55.00	
Total		$ 1,520.00	$ 1,545.00	$ 1,619.00	

Figure 2

1. Start **Excel 2016**, and then open the file **exl04_MYExpenses**. Save the file in your chapter folder as Last_First_exl04_MYExpenses

2. Click the merged cell **E2**, and then insert the **NOW** function.

3. Apply the **Outside Borders** to the range **D2:F2**.

4. Insert **Data Bars** to the data in the range **C5:E23**.

5. In the range **F5:F23**, insert **Line Sparklines** using the data in the columns **C:E**. On the sparklines, show the **High Point**.

6. Format the range **A4:F23** as an Excel table using **Table Style Light 19**. Sort the **Spending Category** column in alphabetical order.

7. Apply the **Total** row. Display the sums for **C24:E24**, and then apply the **Accounting** number format. In the **Trend** column total row, select **None**.

8. Select cell **A1**. Change the **Width** scale to fit on one page.

9. Create a copy of the worksheet, and then move the sheet to the end of the workbook. Rename the new tab High Expenses

10. On the **High Expenses** worksheet, sort the **April** column from largest to smallest. Hide **rows 19:23**.

11. Group the sheets, and then add the file name in the left footer and the sheet name in the right footer. Return to **Normal** view. Select cell **A1** in the **High Expenses** worksheet.

12. **Print Preview** the workbook, and then compare your screen with **Figure 1** and **Figure 2**. **Save** the file, and then **Close** Excel. Submit the file as directed by your instructor.

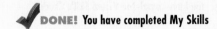

DONE! You have completed My Skills

Visual Skills Check

To complete this project, you will need the following file:

- exl04_VSArt

You will save your file as:

- Last_First_exl04_VSArt

Start **Excel 2016**, and then open the file **exl04_VSArt**. Save the file in your chapter folder as Last_First_exl04_VSArt Add the file name in the worksheet's left footer. Set the **Width** to scale to **1 page**. Insert the current date using a date function. Your date may be different than shown. Apply **Counterclockwise** orientation to the text **Artwork**. In the **Insurance** column, use a logical function indicating *Insure* for art with a value greater than $50,000; otherwise indicate *No*. The **conditional formatting** in the **Insurance column** for values to be Insured is **Light Red Fill with Dark Red Text**. Display **Data Bars** in the **Value** column. Format the data as an Excel table using the **Table Style Light 14** table style. Filter and sort the Excel table, and then display the functions on the **Total** row as shown in **Figure 1**. **Save** the file, and then **Close** Excel. Submit the file as directed by your instructor.

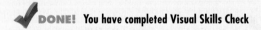 **DONE!** You have completed Visual Skills Check

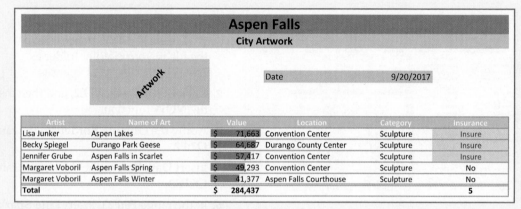

Aspen Falls					
City Artwork					

Date   9/20/2017

Artist	Name of Art	Value	Location	Category	Insurance
Lisa Junker	Aspen Lakes	$ 71,663	Convention Center	Sculpture	Insure
Becky Spiegel	Durango Park Geese	$ 64,687	Durango County Center	Sculpture	Insure
Jennifer Grube	Aspen Falls in Scarlet	$ 57,417	Convention Center	Sculpture	Insure
Margaret Voboril	Aspen Falls Spring	$ 49,293	Convention Center	Sculpture	No
Margaret Voboril	Aspen Falls Winter	$ 41,377	Aspen Falls Courthouse	Sculpture	No
Total		$ 284,437			5

Figure 1

Skills Challenge 1

To complete this project, you will need the following file:

- exl04_SC1Classes

You will save your file as:

- Last_First_exl04_SC1Classes

Start **Excel 2016**, and then open the file **exl04_SC1Classes**. Save the file in your chapter folder as Last_First_exl04_SC1Classes Carter Horikoshi, the Art Center Supervisor, has started a workbook to track the art classes offered at different locations. He is concerned about large class sizes and wonders if he should hire an assistant for the instructors. Using the skills practiced in this chapter, on the Classes worksheet, correct the date function. The panes no longer need to be frozen. In the Excel table, display all rows. Data bars should be applied to all data in column D. In column E, the logical function should calculate whether a class needs a class assistant—a class needs a class assistant if the class size is greater than 30. Filter the worksheet to show the Computer Basics, Drawing, Painting, and Woodworking classes, and sorted from the largest to smallest class size. Repeat the titles in row 6 on each page, and the columns should fit on one page. For the Enrollment sheet, format the sparklines to emphasize the high and low values only in each row. The Enrollment sheet should print on one page. On both worksheets, add the file name in the left footer and the sheet name in the right footer. Save the file, and then Close Excel. Submit the file as directed by your instructor.

 **DONE!** You have completed Skills Challenge 1

Skills Challenge 2

To complete this project, you will need the following file:

- exl04_SC2Water

You will save your file as:

- Last_First_exl04_SC2Water

Start **Excel 2016**, and then open the file **exl04_SC2Water**. Save the file in your chapter folder as Last_First_exl04_SC2Water Diane Payne, the Public Works Director, is responsible for testing the city water supply. She has started a workbook to track the water test results. Using the skills practiced in this chapter, insert functions in the Water worksheet that provide the current date and count the number of samples. Format the statistics shaded area with a border, and format the orientation and alignment of the text in the merged cells. Insert a logical function to determine if the High Test amount is greater than the Farm Water Limit for each quarter. Display Yes if TRUE and No if FALSE. Format the data as an Excel table using the table style of your choice, and then filter the table to display violations. On the Results worksheet, insert sparklines to display trends. On both worksheets, add the file name in the left footer and the sheet name in the right footer. Each worksheet should print on one page. Save the file, and then Close Excel. Submit the file as directed by your instructor.

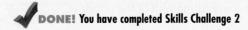 **DONE!** You have completed Skills Challenge 2

More Skills Assessment

To complete this project, you will need the following files:

- exl04_MSAPayments
- exl04_MSAValues

You will save your files as:

- Last_First_exl04_MSAPayments
- Last_First_exl04_MSASnip

1. Start **Excel 2016**. Open the file **exl04_MSAPayments**, and then save the file in your chapter folder as Last_First_exl04_MSAPayments

2. On the **Loans** worksheet, enter a function in cell **B8** to calculate the monthly payment for the utility van. The **Rate** is the **Interest rate** divided by 12 The **Nper** is the **Period** multiplied by 12 The **Pv** is the current amount of the loan, entered as a negative value.

3. Enter a function in cell **B16** to calculate the monthly payment for the fire truck using the previous method and arguments provided.

4. On the **Utility Van** worksheet, in cell **A1**, use a function to enter the text from cell **A2** on the **Loans** sheet as all uppercase letters.

5. In cell **A2**, use a function to enter the text from cell **A4** on the **Loans** worksheet as all lowercase letters.

6. On the **Fire Truck** worksheet, use the previous method to enter uppercase text in cell **A1** from cell **A2** on the **Loans** sheet, and lowercase text in cell **A2** for the fire truck loan from the **Loans** sheet.

7. In the range **C7:F7**, use an array function to enter the labels from **A3:A6**, and then center and wrap the text.

8. On the **Utility Van** worksheet, repeat the previous method to enter the array function in the range **C7:F7**, and then format the text.

9. **Save** the file, and then open the file **exl04_MSAValues**.

10. Sort the **Values** worksheet, **Year Paid Off** column, smallest to largest, and then delete the loans for **2018**. Delete column **B**.

11. View the worksheets **Side by Side**, and then turn off **Synchronous Scrolling**. If necessary, resize both worksheets so that they are both viewable horizontally and evenly filling half of the window. Compare your screen with **Figure 1**.

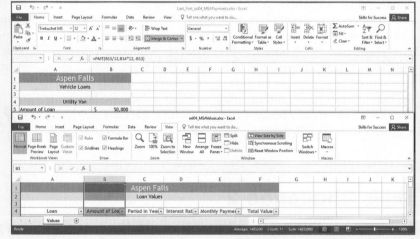

Figure 1

Excel 2016, Windows 10, Microsoft Corporation

12. Use the **Snipping Tool** to take a **Full-Screen** snip of your screen, and then save the file as Last_First_exl04_MSASnip

13. Close all of the windows without saving, except for **Last_First_exl04_MSAPayment**.

14. On the **Utility Van** worksheet, select cell **B7**, and then **Split** the window.

15. **Save** the file, and then **Close** Excel. Submit the files as directed by your instructor.

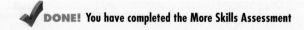 **DONE!** You have completed the More Skills Assessment

Collaborating with Google

To complete this project, you will need a Google account (refer to the **Common Features chapter**) and the following file:

- exl04_GPRentals

You will save your file as:

- Last_First_exl04_GPRentals

1. Open the Google Chrome web browser. Log into your Google account, and then click **Google Apps** .

2. Click **Drive** to open Google Drive.

3. Click **New**, and then click **File upload**. Navigate to the student data files and open exl04_GPRentals

4. Double-click the **exl04_GPRentals** file in **Google Drive**, and then click Open to view the workbook in **Google Sheets**.

5. On the **Rentals** worksheet, click cell **A203**. Type =TODAY to enter the current date.

6. Click cell **F2**, and then type =IF(E2>4, "Discount", "None") Autofill the formula down through **F201**.

7. Click **Format**, and then click **Conditional Formatting**. In the **Apply to range** box, verify F2:F201 is entered. Click the **Format cells if arrow**, and then click **Text is exactly**. Replace the text *Value or formula* with Discount Click the **Formatting style arrow**, click **Red background**, and then click the **Bold** button. Click **Done**. Close the **Conditional Format rules** pane.

8. Click the **Rooms** worksheet. Click **Edit**, and then click **Find and replace**. In the **Find** box, type Gymnasium and in the **Replace with** box, type Athletic Center Click **Replace all**, and then click **Done**.

9. Click **Data**, and then click **Filter**.

10. Click the **Center** column **filter arrow**, clear the **Central, Northeast**, and **Northwest** checks, and then click **OK**.

11. Click the **Type** column **filter arrow**, and then click **Sort A → Z**. Compare your screen with **Figure 1**.

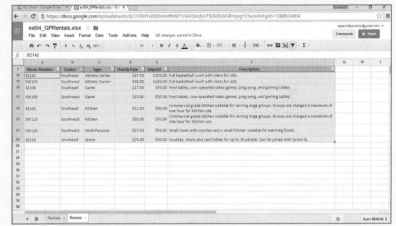

Figure 1

12. Click the **Rentals** worksheet, and then click cell **A2**. On the **View tab**, point to **Freeze,** and then click **1 row**.

13. Click **File**, point to **Download as**, and then click **Microsoft Excel (.xlsx)**.

14. Save the file in your chapter folder as Last_First_exl04_GPRentals

15. Close all windows, and then submit the file as directed by your instructor.

✓ **DONE!** You have completed Collaborating with Google

CAPSTONE PROJECT

To complete this project, you will need the following file:
exl_CAPBudget

MyITLab®
Grader

You will save your file as:
Last_First_exl_CAPBudget

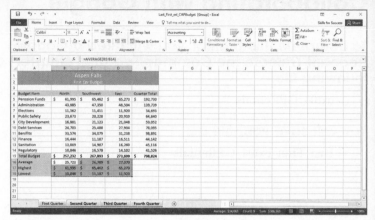

Figure 1   Excel 2016, Windows 10, Microsoft Corporation

1. Start **Excel 2016**, and then open the student data file **exl_CAPBudget**. Create a new folder named Excel Capstone Projects and then save the file in your chapter folder as Last_First_exl_CAPBudget

2. Group the worksheets. Widen columns **B:E** to *13.00*. Change the height of row **4** to *15.00*. In cell **E5**, insert a function to total the row, and then AutoFill **E5** down through **E14**. In the range **E6:E14**, apply the **Comma [0]** cell style. In the range **B15:E15**, insert a function to total the columns, and then apply the **Total** cell style.

3. With the worksheets still grouped, in cell **B16**, insert a function to calculate the average *North* budget item. In cell **B17**, insert a function to calculate the highest *North* budget item.

4. In cell **B18**, insert a function to calculate the lowest *North* budget item.

5. AutoFill the range **B16:B18** to the right through column **D**, and then compare your screen with **Figure 1**.

6. Ungroup the worksheets. Insert a new worksheet. Rename the new worksheet tab Summary and then apply the worksheet tab color **Orange, Accent 2**. Move the new worksheet tab to make it the first worksheet in the workbook.

7. Copy the range **A1:E4** from any of the quarter worksheets, and then on the **Summary** worksheet, paste the range into **A1:E4** using the **Keep Source Column Widths** paste option.

8. On the **Summary** worksheet, change the subtitle of cell **A2** to Annual Budget and then change the label in cell **A4** to Quarter

9. On the **Summary** worksheet, in cell **A5**, type 1st Quarter and then AutoFill **A5** down through cell **A8**. In cell **A9**, type Annual Total

10. On the **Summary** worksheet, enter a formula in cell **B5** setting the cell equal to cell **B15** in the *First Quarter* worksheet.

11. On the **Summary** worksheet, enter a formula for the *North* total from the *Second Quarter*, the *Third Quarter*, and the *Fourth Quarter* worksheets in the range **B6:B8**. AutoFill the range **B5:B8** to the right through column **E**. **Save** the file, and then compare your screen with **Figure 2**.

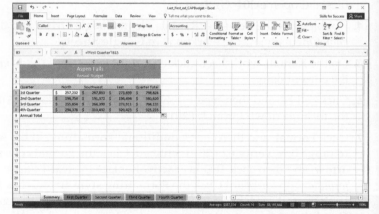

Figure 2   Excel 2016, Windows 10, Microsoft Corporation

12. On the **Summary** worksheet, in the range **B9:E9**, insert a function to calculate the column totals. Apply the **Comma [0]** cell style to **B6:E8**, and then apply the **Total** cell style to **B9:E9**.

■ **Continue to the next page to complete the skill**

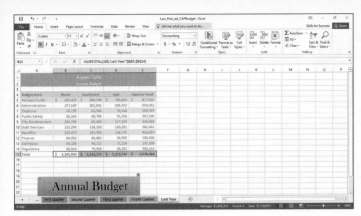

Excel 2016, Windows 10, Microsoft Corporation   **Figure 3**

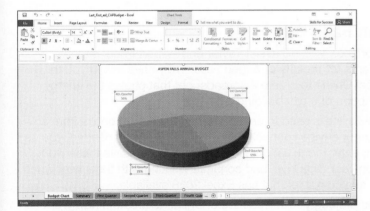

Excel 2016, Windows 10, Microsoft Corporation   **Figure 4**

13. In cell **A11**, type Bonus if less than and then in cell **A12**, type 1100000 and apply the **Accounting Number Format** with zero decimal places. Select the range **A11:A12**, and then apply **Outside Borders**.

14. In cell **B11**, insert the **IF** function. For the logical test, check whether the **North** total is less than the value in cell **A12**. If the logical test is true, 500 should display, and if the logical test is false, 50 should display. In the function, use an absolute cell reference when referring to cell **A12**.

15. In cell **B11**, apply the **Currency [0]** cell style, and then AutoFill cell **B11** to the right through cell **D11**.

16. Select the range **B5:D8**, and then insert the default **Data Bars** conditional format.

17. In cell **A17**, insert the **TODAY** function. Format the date with the **March 14, 2012** date format.

18. Unhide the **Last Year** worksheet. **Copy** the *Annual Budget* shape, and then paste the shape in the **Summary** worksheet. Move and resize the shape to approximately the range **A19:E23**.

19. On the **Last Year** worksheet, format the range **A4:E14** as a table, and then apply **Table Style Light 2**. Add a **Total row**, and then apply **Sum** to **B15:D15**. Convert the table to a normal range, and then apply the **Currency [0]** cell style to **B15:E15**. Compare your screen with **Figure 3**.

20. Hide the **Last Year** worksheet.

21. Group the worksheets, and then press Ctrl + Home. Find and replace the four occurrences of Qtr with Quarter

22. With the worksheets still grouped, check and correct any spelling errors. Add the file name to the left footer and the sheet name to the right footer. Return to **Normal** view, and then make cell **A1** the active cell. Ungroup the worksheets.

23. Make the **Summary** worksheet the active worksheet. Insert a **3-D Pie** chart based on the nonadjacent ranges **A4:A8** and **E4:E8**. Move the pie chart to a chart sheet with the sheet name Budget Chart

24. Format the chart. Apply **Layout 1**, and then apply **Chart Style 8**. Change the chart title to Aspen Falls Annual Budget and then change the data labels to a font size of **14**. Compare your screen with **Figure 4**.

25. **Save**, and then **Close** Excel. Submit the file as directed by your instructor.

 **DONE! You have completed the Excel Capstone Project**

Create Workbooks Using Excel Online

▶ **_Excel Online_** is a cloud-based application used to complete basic spreadsheet formulas using a web browser.

▶ Excel Online can be used to create or edit workbooks using a web browser instead of the Excel program—Excel 2016 does not need to be installed on your computer.

▶ When you create a document using Excel Online, it is saved on your OneDrive so that you can work with it from any computer connected to the Internet.

▶ You can use Excel Online to insert a chart and perform basic chart formatting tasks.

▶ If you need a feature not available in Excel Online, you can edit the workbook in Microsoft Excel and save it on your OneDrive.

Maxim Kazmin/Fotolia

Aspen Falls City Hall

In this project, you will assist Taylor and Robert Price, energy consultants for the city of Aspen Falls. They have asked you to use Excel Online to create a spreadsheet that shows the energy consumption of a city building.

Excel Online is used to create or open Excel workbooks from any computer or device connected to the Internet. When needed, you can edit text, enter formulas, or insert charts. You can save these workbooks on your OneDrive, and continue working with them later when you are at a computer that has Excel 2016 available.

In this project, you will use Excel Online to create a new workbook. You will enter data and then apply formats and number styles. You will insert formulas, functions, and a chart. Finally, you will open the workbook in Excel 2016 to format the chart and check the spelling of the worksheet.

Time to complete this project—30 to 60 minutes

Outcome

Using the skills in this chapter, you will be able to build and edit Excel workbooks using Excel Online, and edit the workbooks using Excel 2016.

Objectives

1 Generate workbooks in Excel Online

2 Format workbooks in Excel Online

3 Analyze data using pie charts

4 Modify online workbooks

Student data file needed for this project:

New blank Excel Online workbook

You will save your file as:

Last_First_exl_OPEnergy

SKILLS

At the end of this project, you will be able to:

► Create new Excel workbooks using OneDrive

► Enter data in editing view

► Apply number styles

► Enter summary functions

► Enter formulas using absolute cell references

► Insert and format pie charts

► Edit workbooks created by Excel Online in Excel 2016

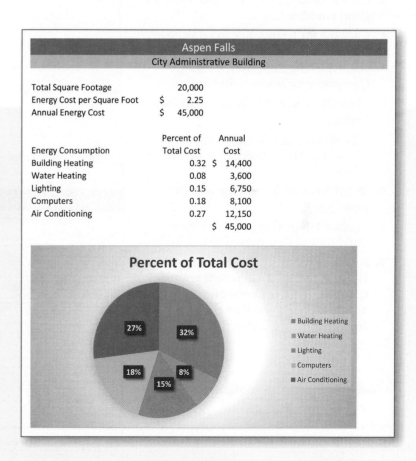

1. Start **Edge**, navigate to live.com and then log on to your Microsoft account. If you do not have an account, follow the links and directions on the page to create one.

2. After logging in, navigate as needed to display the OneDrive page.

   OneDrive and Office Online technologies are accessed through Web pages that can change often, and the formatting and layout of some pages may often be different than the figures in this book. When this happens, you may need to adapt the steps to complete the actions they describe.

3. On the toolbar, click **New**, and then click **Excel workbook**.

4. Click the **FILE tab**. Click **Save As**, then click the **Rename** button. In the **Rename** box, type Last_First_exl_OPEnergy Compare your screen with **Figure 1**.

5. Click **OK** to save the file and start Excel Online.

   Excel Online displays six tabs in Editing view: File, Home, Insert, Data, Review, and View.

6. In cell **A1**, type Aspen Falls and then press Enter.

7. In cell **A2**, type City Administrative Building and then press Enter.

8. Select the range **A1:F1**, and then on the **HOME tab**, in the **Alignment group**, click the **Merge & Center** button. Select the range **A2:F2**, and then click the **Merge & Center** button. Compare your screen with **Figure 2**.

■ **Continue to the next page to complete the project**

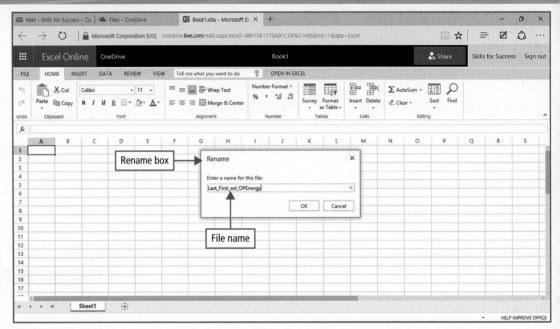

Figure 1

Excel 2016, Windows 10, Microsoft Corporation

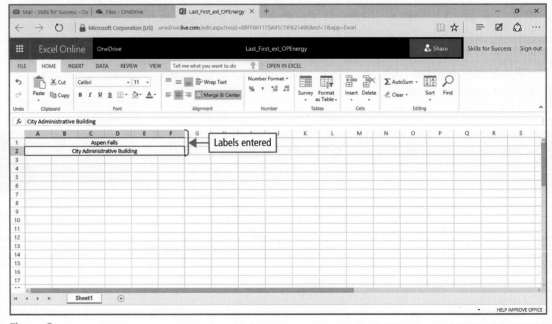

Figure 2

Excel 2016, Windows 10, Microsoft Corporation

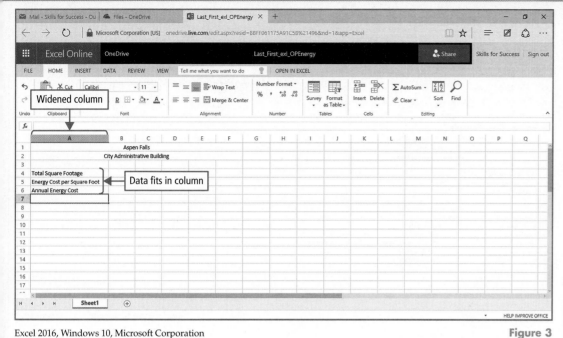

Excel 2016, Windows 10, Microsoft Corporation

Figure 3

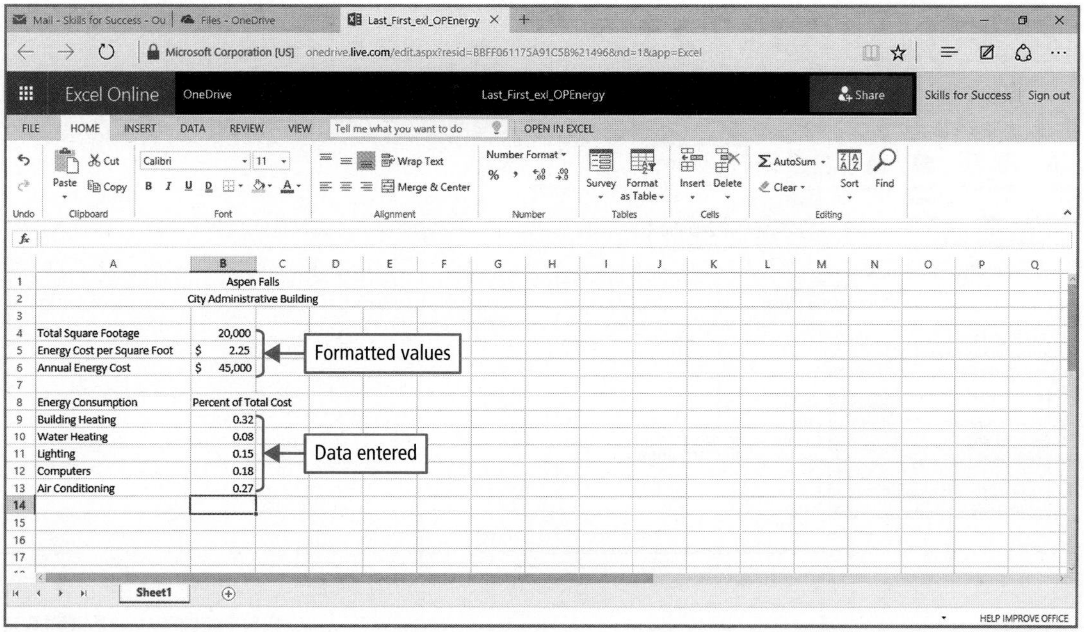

Excel 2016, Windows 10, Microsoft Corporation

Figure 4

9. In cell **A4**, type Total Square Footage and then press Enter.

10. In cell **A5**, type Energy Cost per Square Foot and then press Enter.

11. In cell **A6**, type Annual Energy Cost and then press Enter.

12. In the column heading area, point to the right boundary of column A to display the ⊹ pointer. Double-click the line between columns **A** and **B** to display all of the contents of cell **A5** in the column. Compare your screen with **Figure 3**.

13. Make cell **B4** the active cell. Type 20000 and then press Enter. Click cell **B4**, and then on the **HOME tab**, in the **Number group**, click the **Comma Style** button ❚. Click the **Decrease Decimal** button ⫶ two times.

14. In cell **B5**, type 2.25 and then press Enter.

15. In cell **B6**, type =B4*B5 and then press Enter.

16. Click cell **B5**. On the **HOME tab**, in the **Number group**, click the **Number Format** button, and then click **Accounting**.

17. Click cell **B6**, and then apply the **Accounting** number format. Click the **Decrease Decimal** button ⫶ two times.

18. Click cell **A8**, type Energy Consumption and then press Enter.

19. In the range **A9:A13**, pressing Enter after each entry, type Building Heating | Water Heating | Lighting | Computers | Air Conditioning

20. Click cell **B8**, type Percent of Total Cost and then press Enter.

21. In the range **B9:B13**, making sure you type the decimal in front of each number and pressing Enter after each entry, type the following values: .32 | .08 | .15 | .18 | .27 Compare your screen with **Figure 4**.

■ **Continue to the next page to complete the project**

22. Select the range **B9:B13**. In the **Number group**, click the **Number Format** arrow, and then click **Percentage**. Click the **Decrease Decimal** button two times.

23. Click cell **C8**, type Annual Cost and then press Enter.

24. Select the range **B8:C8**. In the **Alignment group**, click the **Wrap Text** button, click the **Middle Align** button, and then click the **Center** button.

25. Click cell **C9**, type =B9*$B$6 and then press Enter.

26. Click cell **C9**, point to the **fill handle**, and then drag the fill handle to copy the formula down through cell **C13**. Compare your screen with **Figure 5**.

> The absolute cell reference to $B$6 is copied to each of the other formulas.

27. Click cell **C14**. In the **Editing group**, click the **AutoSum** button, and then press Enter. Select the range **C10:C13**, and then in the **Number group**, click the **Comma Style** button. Click the **Decrease Decimal** button two times.

28. Select the range **A8:B13**. On the **INSERT tab**, in the **Charts group**, click the **Pie** button, and then point to the first chart—**2-D Pie**. Compare your screen with **Figure 6**, and then click the first chart.

> A contextual tab—the Chart Tools tab—displays on the ribbon.

29. Move the chart to approximately the range **A16:F30**.

30. To the right of the **Tell me what you want to do** box, click **OPEN IN EXCEL**. If prompted, click **OK** for the security warning, and then enter your ID and password.

31. If necessary, at the top of the screen, on the **Protected View** bar, click **Enable Editing**.

- **Continue to the next page to complete the project**

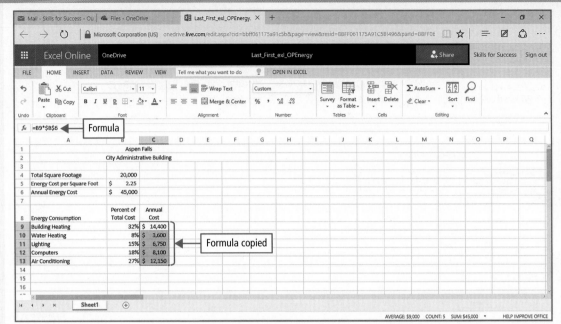

Figure 5

Excel 2016, Windows 10, Microsoft Corporation

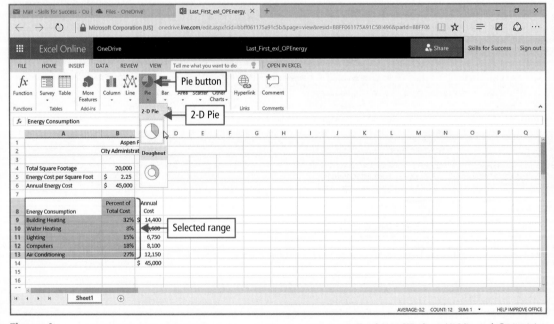

Figure 6

Excel 2016, Windows 10, Microsoft Corporation

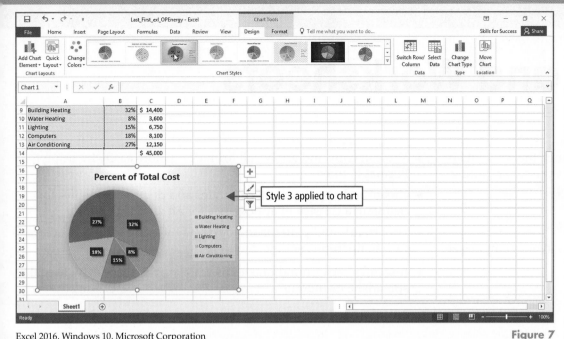

Excel 2016, Windows 10, Microsoft Corporation

Figure 7

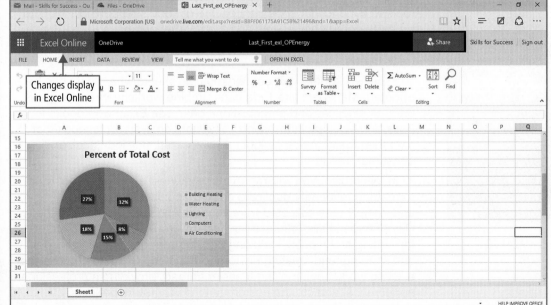

Excel 2016, Windows 10, Microsoft Corporation

Figure 8

32. Click cell **A1**. On the **HOME tab**, in the **Styles group**, click the **Cell Styles** button, and then click **Accent5**. In the **Font group**, click the **Font Size** button 11 ▾, and then click **14**. In the **Cells group**, click the **Format** button, and then click **Row Height**. In the **Row Height** dialog box, type 20 and then click **OK**.

33. Click cell **A2**. In the **Styles group**, click the **Cell Styles** button, and then click **40% - Accent5**. In the **Font group**, click the **Font Size** button 11 ▾, and then click **12**.

34. If necessary, scroll to view the chart. Click the chart, and then on the **Chart Tools Design tab**, in the **Chart Styles group**, click the third style—**Style 3**. Compare your screen with **Figure 7**.

35. Click the **REVIEW tab**. In the **Proofing group**, click the **Spelling** button to check and correct any spelling errors. **Save** 🖫 the file, and then **Close** ✕ Excel.

36. On the **OneDrive** page, open the file in Excel Online. Scroll as necessary to compare your screen with **Figure 8**.

> The cell styles and the chart style 3 have been applied. Features not supported by Excel Online, such as styles, cannot be changed in the online application, but they can be viewed.

37. **Download** the file, and then **Save** 🖫 the file to your chapter folder as Last_First_exl_ OPEnergy or **Share** the file as directed by your instructor.

38. **Sign out** of your Microsoft account, and then **Close** ✕ the browser.

✔ **DONE! You have completed Excel Online Project**

CHAPTER 5

Format Cells and Worksheets

▶ In a worksheet, cells can be formatted to change the way data is displayed without changing the underlying values. Formatting the background and border of a cell often improves the appearance of the worksheet.

▶ Symbols are inserted to identify and format text.

▶ Cells can be formatted to provide a comparison or to emphasize cell values.

▶ You can copy and apply cell formatting more easily by using the Format Painter.

▶ Create and apply custom cell styles and document themes to maintain a consistent appearance for all worksheets.

▶ Spot trends and patterns in your data by using icons and colors to visually represent the data.

▶ Inserting background images as watermarks allows you to make spreadsheets unique.

Kwest / Fotolia

Aspen Falls City Hall

In this chapter, you will support Todd Austin, the Aspen Falls Tourism Director, by editing an existing workbook and using Excel formatting tools to enhance its appearance. One of Todd's responsibilities is to promote community events and then gather and analyze the Bureau of Tourism sales data. This data helps Todd plan future events and track trends.

Excel workbooks can contain multiple sheets where data can be updated. Managers like Todd can combine worksheets to compare data. Businesses and organizations often use Excel workbooks to track and evaluate information using data analysis techniques that help them gain greater insight into organizational, industrial, and consumer trends.

In this project you will improve a worksheet's format by applying formatting to identify duplicate data, recognize data patterns, and identify fees collected from vendors and ticket sales from the City of Aspen Falls Annual Wine Festival. You will also use Excel formatting techniques, including copying formats, applying borders and shading, and creating custom formats and fonts, to improve the existing worksheet, making it easier to read, providing a professional appearance, and storing custom settings for future projects.

Time to complete all 10 skills — 60 to 90 minutes

Outcome

Using the skills in this chapter, you will be able to create and apply custom themes, number formats, and cell styles, and customize cell backgrounds and conditional formatting rules.

Objectives

5.1 Understand how to insert symbols and number formats

5.2 Modify worksheet cells, backgrounds, and borders

5.3 Apply conditional formatting using formulas

5.4 Change worksheet columns and rows

Student data files needed for this chapter:

exl05_Festival (Excel)
exl05_FestivalLogo (JPG)

You will save your file as:

Last_First_exl05_Festival

SKILLS

Skills 1-10 Training

Skill 1   Insert Symbols and Create Custom Number Formats
Skill 2   Format Cells Using Format Painter
Skill 3   Apply Icon Sets as Conditional Formatting
Skill 4   Insert Formulas into Conditional Formatting Rules
Skill 5   Insert and Delete Rows, Columns, and Cells
Skill 6   Modify Cell Backgrounds and Borders
Skill 7   Create and Apply Custom Cell Styles
Skill 8   Customize, Save, and Apply Themes
Skill 9   Add Watermarks and Modify Background Colors
Skill 10 Hide Gridlines and Column and Row Headings

MORE SKILLS

Skill 11 Convert Comma-Separated Text into Columns
Skill 12 Inspect Document Properties to Remove Personal Information
Skill 13 Remove Duplicate Records
Skill 14 Insert Shapes and Text Boxes

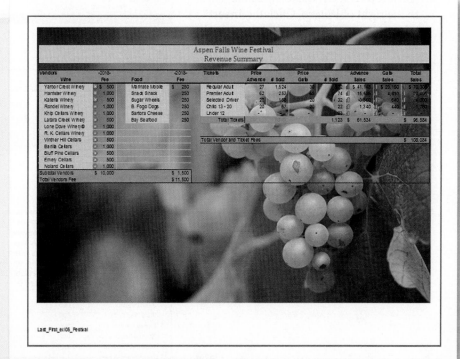

Excel 2016, Windows 10, Microsoft Corporation

▶ A *symbol* is a character such as a font symbol or a bullet character that is not found on common keyboards.

▶ Symbols are inserted to identify and format text.

▶ Once a symbol is inserted into a cell, the cell contents can be formatted as text.

1. Start **Excel 2016**, and then open the student data file **exl05_Festival**. Click the **File tab**, and then click **Save As**. Click the **Browse** button, and then navigate to the location where you are saving your files. Click **New folder**, type Excel Chapter 5 and then press Enter two times. In the **File name** box, save the file as Last_First_exl05_Festival and then press Enter.

2. Click cell **A11**. On the formula bar, click to the right of *Winery*. Click the **Insert tab**, and then in the **Symbols group**, click the **Symbol** button.

3. In the **Symbol** dialog box, click the **Special Characters tab**. Compare your screen with **Figure 1**.

   Special characters are characters such as the degree symbol and trademark symbol that are not found on the standard keyboard, but are included on a shorter list of frequently used symbols on the Special Characters tab.

4. Under **Character**, click the **Registered** (®) character. Click **Insert** to insert the character in cell **A11**, and then in the **Symbol** dialog box, click **Close**. Press Enter, and then compare your screen with **Figure 2**.

■ Continue to the next page to complete the skill

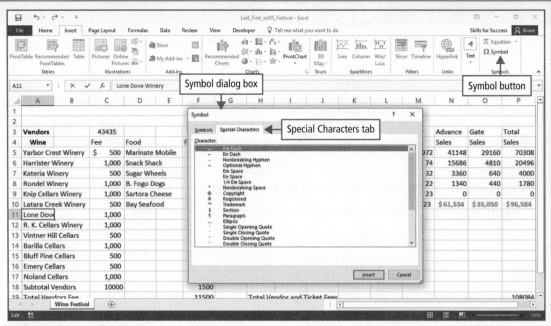

Figure 1

Excel 2016, Windows 10, Microsoft Corporation

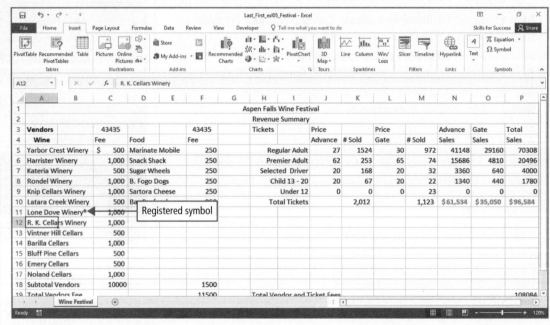

Figure 2

Excel 2016, Windows 10, Microsoft Corporation

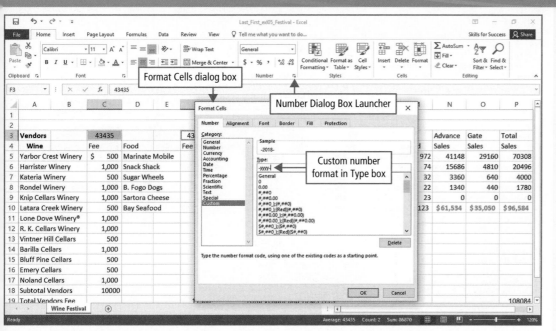

Excel 2016, Windows 10, Microsoft Corporation

Figure 3

5. Click cell **C3**. Press and hold Ctrl, click cell **F3**, and then release Ctrl.

6. With cells **C3** and **F3** selected, click the **Home tab**. In the **Number group**, click the **Number Format Dialog Box Launcher** .

7. In the **Format Cells** dialog box, on the **Number tab**, under **Category**, click **Custom**. In the **Type** box, replace the existing value by typing -yyyy- Be sure to include the hyphen characters (-), as shown in Figure 3.

   Obj 2.1.1 E

   In this manner, you can create your own custom number formats. Here, the four characters indicate the numbers used to create a four-digit year, and the hyphens will be inserted before and after the number. Common formatting characters are summarized in the table shown in Figure 4.

8. Click **OK**. Notice the custom number format is applied to the two cells.

9. Save the file.

■ **You have completed Skill 1 of 10**

Common Custom Formatting Characters	
Character	**Description**
#	Specifies a placeholder for a digit.
0	Specifies a placeholder for any digit. When the value is less than zero, a 0 will be displayed.
.	Specifies the location of a decimal point.
,	Specifies the location where a comma will be displayed.
[color]	Specifies the color used to display negative numbers.
Mm	Displays the month with a leading zero.
Dd	Displays the day with a leading zero.
yyyy	Displays the year with four digits.

Figure 4

▶ In Excel, the *Format Painter* is a tool used to copy formatting from one place to another.

MOS
Obj 2.2.3 C

1. Click cell **A4**. On the **Home tab**, in the **Clipboard group**, click **Format Painter** 🖌. With the 🔲 pointer, drag across the range **C4:F4**, and then release the left mouse button.

2. With the range **C4:F4** still selected, click **Format Painter** 🖌, drag across the range **H3:P4**, and then release the left mouse button.

3. Notice the format is applied, and the **Format Painter** is no longer active, as shown in **Figure 1**.

   When Format Painter is clicked once, the formatting can be applied one time to a cell or a range of cells.

4. Drag to select the range **C6:C17**. On the **Home tab**, in the **Clipboard group**, click **Format Painter** 🖌, and then drag across the range **J5:P9**.

5. Click **Format Painter** 🖌, and then use the skills previously practiced to apply the format to **F6:F10**. Compare your screen with **Figure 2**.

■ **Continue to the next page to complete the skill** ▶

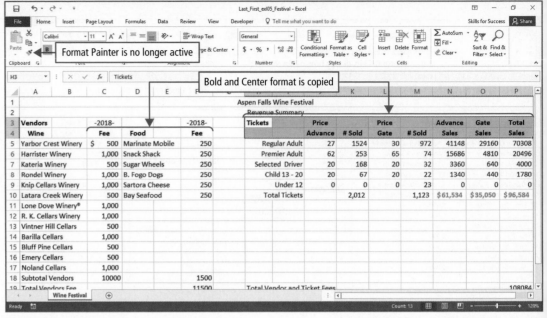

Figure 1

Excel 2016, Windows 10, Microsoft Corporation

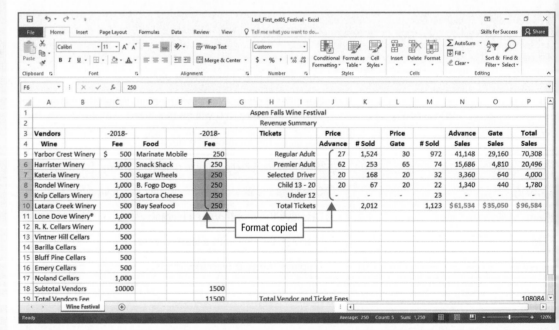

Figure 2

Excel 2016, Windows 10, Microsoft Corporation

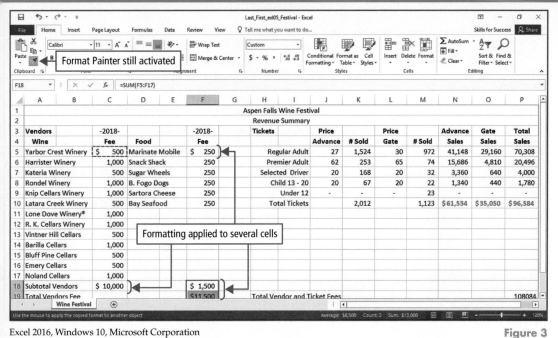

Excel 2016, Windows 10, Microsoft Corporation

Figure 3

6. Click cell **C5**. Double-click **Format Painter** 🖌. With the ⊕🖌 pointer, select cells **F5** and **C18**, and then drag down the range **F18:F19**. Notice the **Format Painter** is still activated, and then compare your screen with **Figure 3**.

When Format Painter is double-clicked, the formatting can be applied to multiple cells.

7. With **Format Painter** still activated, drag to select the range **N5:P5** and cell **P19**.

8. Click the **Format Painter** 🖌 to deactivate it. If necessary, AutoFit column **P**. Compare your screen with **Figure 4**.

9. **Save** 💾 the file.

■ **You have completed Skill 2 of 10**

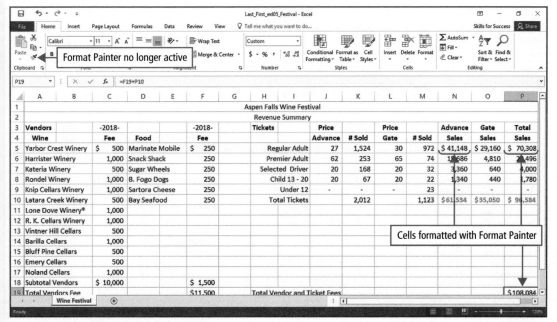

Excel 2016, Windows 10, Microsoft Corporation

Figure 4

▶ Recall that conditional formatting changes the appearance of a cell or range when a specified condition is true.

▶ **Icon sets** classify a range of data into three to five categories and display small graphics in each cell depending on that cell's value.

▶ In an icon set, styles or colors represent relative values of the cells in the range.

Obj 2.3.4 C

1. Select the range **C5:C17**. On the **Home tab**, in the **Styles group**, click the **Conditional Formatting** button. In the list, point to **Icon Sets**, and then compare your screen with **Figure 1**. Under **Indicators**, click the first choice—**3 Symbols (Circled)**.

   In this manner, you can add conditional formatting quickly by selecting a predefined icon set.

Obj 2.2.1 E

2. Select the range **N5:N9**, click the **Conditional Formatting** button, and then click **New Rule**. Compare your screen with **Figure 2**.

3. In the **New Formatting Rule** dialog box, under **Edit the Rule Description**, click the **Format Style arrow**, and then click **Icon Sets**.

   There are a number of predefined icon sets available.

4. Click the **Icon Style arrow**, scroll down the gallery, and then click the third from last option—**5 Ratings**.

■ **Continue to the next page to complete the skill** ▶

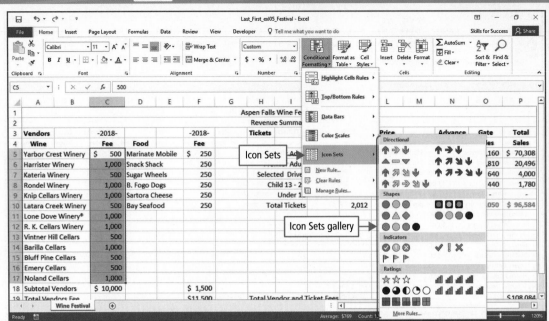

Figure 1

Excel 2016, Windows 10, Microsoft Corporation

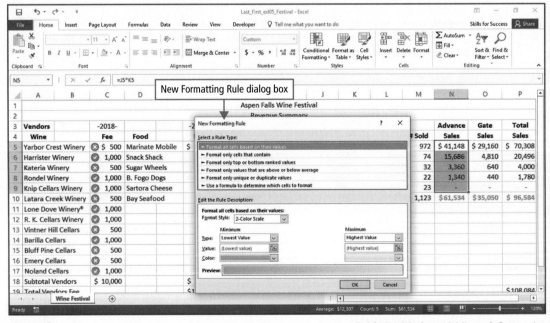

Figure 2

Excel 2016, Windows 10, Microsoft Corporation

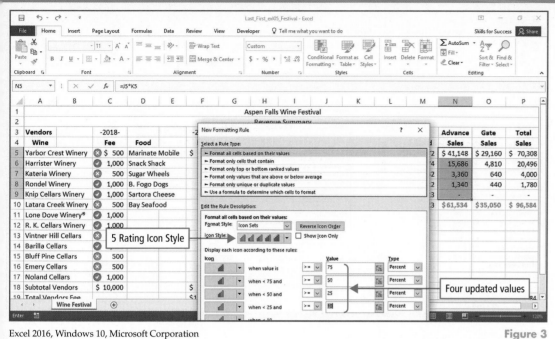

Excel 2016, Windows 10, Microsoft Corporation

Figure 3

5. Under **Value**, change the *first* >= value from *80* to *75* the second value to *50* the third value to *25* and the fourth value to *10* Compare your screen with **Figure 3**, and then click **OK** to close the **New Formatting Rule** dialog box.

You can use the New Formatting Rule dialog box to create custom conditional formatting rules.

6. With the range still selected, click **Format Painter**, and then apply the formatting to **O5:P9**. Click the **View tab**, and then in the **Zoom group**, click the **100%** button. Select columns **N:P**. Click the **Home tab**, and in the **Cells group**, click the **Format arrow**. In the list select **AutoFit Column Width**. Compare your screen with **Figure 4**.

In this manner, you can create custom icon sets. Here, cells N5 and P5 reflect sales at 75 percent or higher; O5, N6, and P6 reflect sales at 25 percent but less than 50 percent; and the remaining cells reflect sales at 10 percent or less.

7. Save 💾 the file.

■ **You have completed Skill 3 of 10**

Excel 2016, Windows 10, Microsoft Corporation

Figure 4

▶ WATCH SKILL 5.4

► Formulas can be inserted into conditional formatting rules so that cells display formatting based on the results of those rules.

MOS
Obj 2.2.2 E

1. Click cell **K10**. On the **Home tab**, in the **Styles group**, click **Conditional Formatting**, and then click **New Rule**.

2. In the **New Formatting Rule** dialog box, under **Select a Rule Type**, click **Use a formula to determine which cells to format**. Compare your screen with **Figure 1**.

3. Under **Edit the Rule Description**, in the **Format values where this formula is true** box, type =K10>2000

4. Click the **Format** button. In the **Format Cells** dialog box, on the **Font tab**, under **Font style**, click **Bold**.

5. Click the **Color arrow**, and then under **Standard Colors**, click the sixth color— **Green**. Click **OK**, and then compare your screen with **Figure 2**.

This rule applies the desired formatting only when the value in cell K10 is greater than 2,000—the desired number of advance tickets sold. If true, the cell will be green and bold.

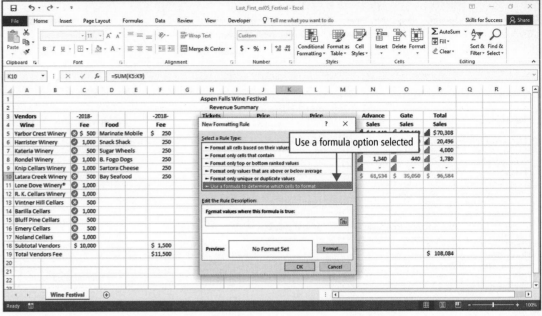

Figure 1

Excel 2016, Windows 10, Microsoft Corporation

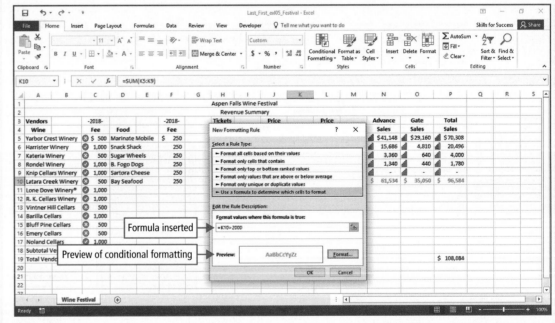

Figure 2

Excel 2016, Windows 10, Microsoft Corporation

■ **Continue to the next page to complete the skill** ▷

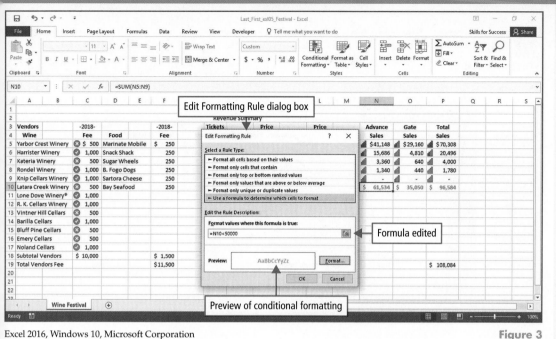

Edit Formatting Rule dialog box

Formula edited

Preview of conditional formatting

Excel 2016, Windows 10, Microsoft Corporation

Figure 3

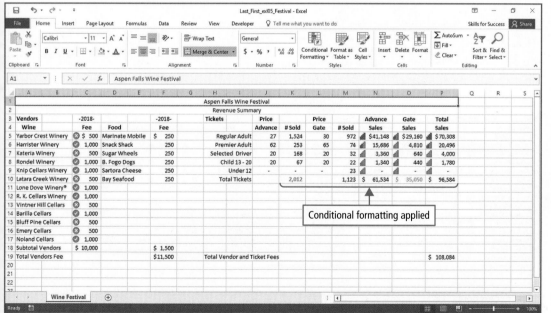

Conditional formatting applied

Excel 2016, Windows 10, Microsoft Corporation

Figure 4

6. Click **OK** to close the **New Formatting Rule** dialog box and apply the formatting.

7. Click cell **N10**. Click **Conditional Formatting**, and then click **Manage Rules**. In the **Conditional Formatting Rules Manager** dialog box, click the **Edit Rule** button.

8. In the **Edit Formatting Rule** dialog box, under **Select a Rule Type**, verify **Use a formula to determine which cells to format** is selected. Edit the formula to =N10<50000

9. Click the **Format** button. In the **Format Cells** dialog box, click the **Color arrow**, and then in the first row, click the sixth color—**Orange, Accent 2**. Click **OK**, and then compare your screen with **Figure 3**.

> The preview box displays how the cell will be formatted when its value is less than $50,000.

10. Click **OK** two times. View the formatting change in the range **O10:P10**. Click cell **A1**, and then compare your screen with **Figure 4**.

> The estimated ticket sales were $50,000; values less than $50,000 appear in orange.

11. **Save** 💾 the file.

■ **You have completed Skill 4 of 10**

▶ Cells can be deleted or inserted without affecting an entire column or row—but you need to specify in which direction the remaining cells will move.

▶ Column widths and cell ranges can be adjusted to fit text as needed.

MOS
Obj 1.3.5 C

1. AutoFit column **A**. Select column **B**. On the **Home tab**, in the **Cells group**, click the **Delete arrow**, and then click **Delete Sheet Columns**. Compare your screen with **Figure 1**.

   Alternatively, right-click the column, and then, from the shortcut menu, click Delete.

2. Click cell **A3**. In the **Cells group**, click the **Insert arrow**, and then click **Insert Sheet Rows**.

   A row is inserted above and the text in row 3 is moved to row 4. Rows and columns can be deleted or inserted by selecting a cell, row, or column.

3. Select the range **G14:O19**. In the **Cells group**, click the **Delete arrow**, and then click **Delete Cells**. In the **Delete** dialog box, verify the **Shift cells up** option is selected. Compare your screen with **Figure 2**, and then click **OK**.

   The range of cells is deleted, and the cells that contain text are moved up.

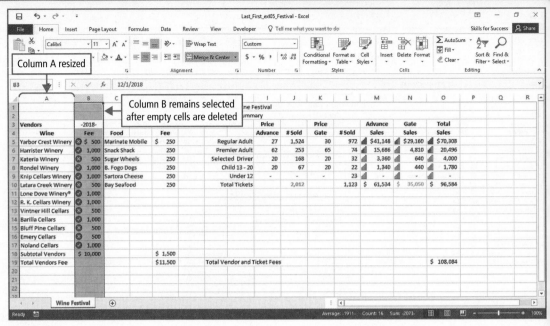
Figure 1

Excel 2016, Windows 10, Microsoft Corporation

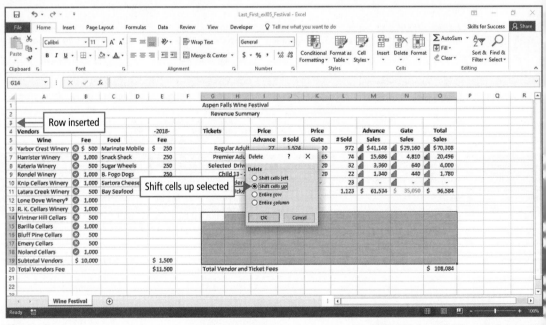
Figure 2

Excel 2016, Windows 10, Microsoft Corporation

▪ **Continue to the next page to complete the skill**

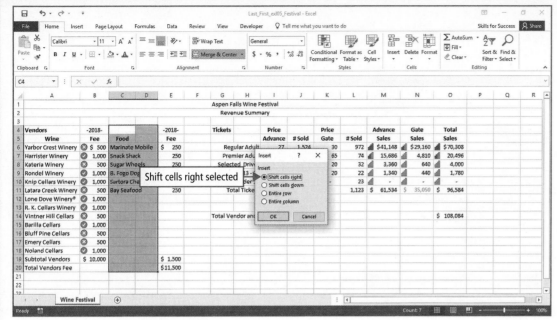

Excel 2016, Windows 10, Microsoft Corporation

Figure 3

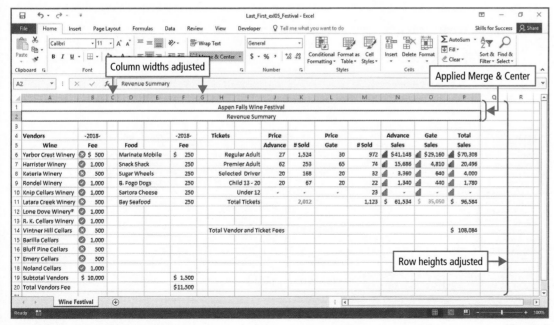

Excel 2016, Windows 10, Microsoft Corporation

Figure 4

4. Select the range **C4:D20**. In the **Cells group**, click the **Insert arrow**, and then click **Insert Cells**. In the **Insert** dialog box, verify the **Shift cells right** option is selected. Compare your screen with **Figure 3**, and then click **OK**.

   Cells are inserted, and the cells that contain text are moved to the right.

5. Select column **C**. In the **Cells group**, click the **Delete arrow**, and then click **Delete Sheet Columns**. With column **C** selected, press and hold Ctrl, and then select column **G**. Release Ctrl.

6. In the **Cells group**, click the **Format arrow**, and then under **Cell Size**, click **Column Width**. In the **Column Width** dialog box, type 3 and then click **OK**. AutoFit columns **F**, **O**, and **P**.

7. Click the **Select All** button ⬜. In the **Cells group**, click the **Format arrow**, and then under **Cell Size**, click **Row Height**. In the **Row Height** dialog box, type 16.5 and then click **OK**.

8. Select the range **A1:P1**. In the **Alignment group**, click **Merge & Center** two times. Repeat this technique to **Merge & Center** the range **A2:P2**. Compare your screen with **Figure 4**.

9. **Save** 🖫 the file.

■ **You have completed Skill 5 of 10**

▶ A *cell fill color*—also known as a *background color*—is the shading assigned to a cell.

▶ A *cell border*—decorative lines that can be applied to worksheet cells—is added to differentiate, emphasize, or group cells.

1. Select the range **A4:A5**, press and hold Ctrl, click the range **H4:I5**, and then release Ctrl.

2. On the **Home tab**, in the **Font group**, click the **Fill Color arrow** 🖌▾, and then in the fourth row, click the first color—**White, Background 1, Darker 25%**. Click cell **A1**, and then compare your screen with **Figure 1**.

3. Select the range **A19:F20**. In the **Font group**, click the **Fill Color** button 🖌▾. Click cell **A1**, and then compare your screen with **Figure 2**.

> The color calls attention to the vendor fees totals. The last cell fill color applied is now the default fill color and can be applied from the Fill Color button with a single click until a new color is needed.

4. Select the range **H11:P11**, and then click the **Fill Color** button 🖌▾. Repeat this technique to apply the formatting to **H14:P14**.

> The color calls attention to the Total Tickets sold, and the Total Vendor and Ticket Fees.

■ **Continue to the next page to complete the skill**

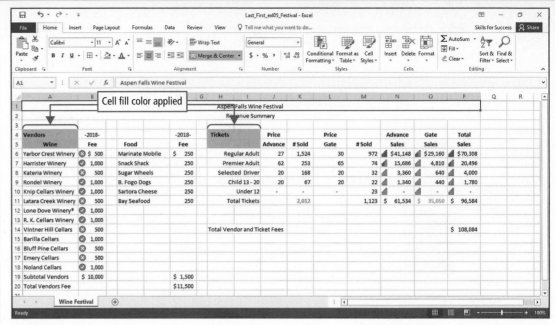

Figure 1

Excel 2016, Windows 10, Microsoft Corporation

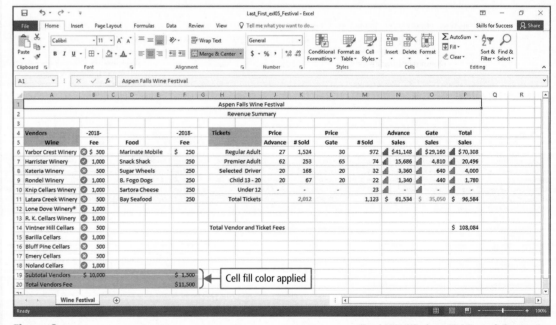

Figure 2

Excel 2016, Windows 10, Microsoft Corporation

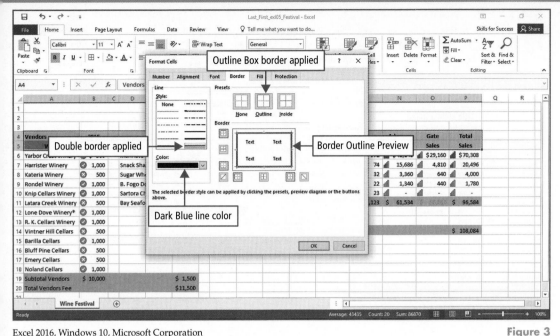

Excel 2016, Windows 10, Microsoft Corporation

Figure 3

5. Select the range **A4:P5**. Click the **Bottom Border arrow** ⊞ ▾, and then click **More Borders** to open the **Format Cells** dialog box.

6. On the **Border tab**, under **Line Style**, click the last option in the second column—double line. Click the **Color arrow**, and then under **Standard Colors**, click the ninth option—**Dark Blue**.

7. Under **Presets**, click **Outline**. Compare your screen with **Figure 3**, and then click **OK**.

8. In the **Font group**, click the **More Borders arrow** ⊞ ▾. Under **Draw Borders**, point to **Line Color**, and then under **Standard Colors**, click the ninth option—**Dark Blue**.

   The mouse pointer now appears as a pencil, which is the Draw Borders pointer.

9. With the **Draw Borders pointer** ✎ , drag to select the ranges **A19:F20**, **H11:P11**, and then **H14:P14**. Click Esc to turn the **Line Color** off.

10. Select the range **A1:P20**. In the **Font group**, click the **More Borders arrow** ⊞ ▾. Under **Borders**, select the eighth option—**Thick Outside Borders**. Click cell **A1**, and then compare your screen with **Figure 4**.

11. **Save** 🖫 the file.

■ **You have completed Skill 6 of 10**

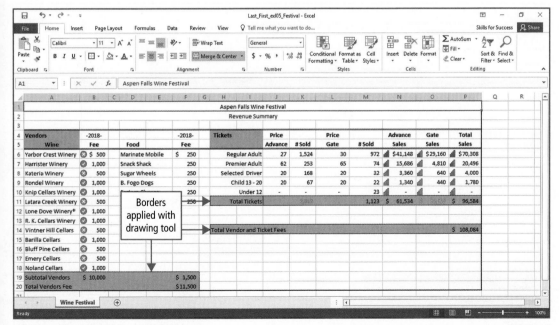

Excel 2016, Windows 10, Microsoft Corporation

Figure 4

- A *style* is a group of formatting choices that can be applied in a single step.
- Some cell styles already exist as part of the Cell Styles gallery.
- Styles can be created and saved as part of the workbook file.

MOS
Obj 2.2.7 C

1. Select the range **A1:P2**. On the **Home tab**, in the **Styles group**, click the **Cell Styles** button. Under **Titles and Headings**, click the **Title** style. AutoFit rows **1:2**, and then click cell **A3**.

MOS
Obj 2.3.2 E

2. In the **Styles group**, click the **Cell Styles** button, and then below the **Cell Styles** gallery, click **New Cell Style**.

3. In the **Style** dialog box, click in the **Style name** field. Replace the existing text with Wine Style and then compare your screen with **Figure 1**.

4. Click the **Format** button. In the **Format Cells** dialog box, click the **Number tab**, and then under **Category**, click **Text**.

   The *Text format* treats the cell value as text even when the cell contains numbers.

5. Click the **Alignment tab**. Under **Text Alignment**, click the **Horizontal arrow**, and then click **Left (Indent)**. Under **Indent**, click the spin up arrow to **1** and then compare your screen with **Figure 2**.

6. Click the **Font tab**. Under **Font**, scroll down, click **Arial**, and verify **Size 11** is selected. Click the **Color arrow**, and then click **Automatic**. Click **OK** two times.

▪ **Continue to the next page to complete the skill**

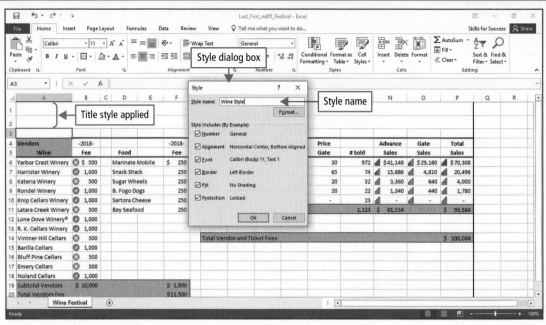

Figure 1

Excel 2016, Windows 10, Microsoft Corporation

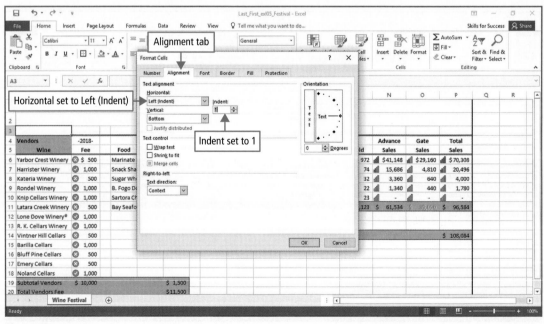

Figure 2

Excel 2016, Windows 10, Microsoft Corporation

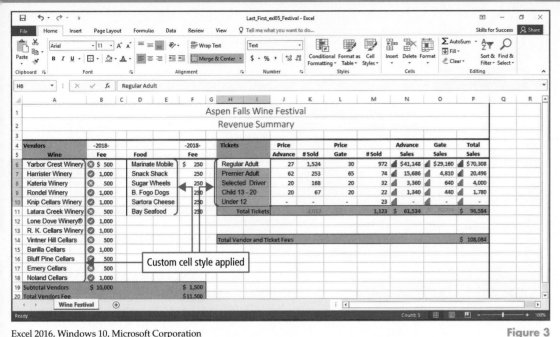

Excel 2016, Windows 10, Microsoft Corporation

Figure 3

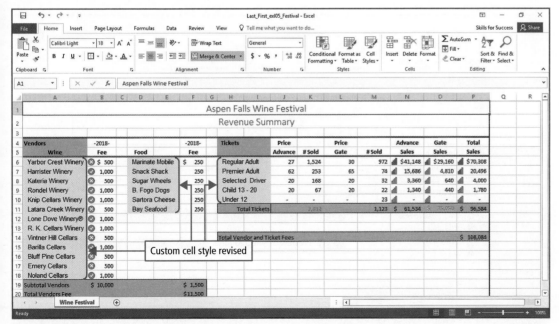

Excel 2016, Windows 10, Microsoft Corporation

Figure 4

7. Select the range **A6:A18**. In the **Styles group**, click **Cell Styles**, and then under **Custom**, click **Wine Style**. AutoFit column **A**.

   The custom cell style formatting is applied to the range.

8. Repeat this technique to apply the custom cell style to ranges **D6:E11** and **H6:I10**. Compare your screen with Figure 3.

9. In the **Styles group**, click the **Cell Styles** button. Under **Custom**, right-click **Wine Style**, and then click **Modify**. Click **Format**, and then click the **Fill tab**. Under **Background Color**, in the gallery, in the second row, click the fifth color—**Blue, Accent 1, Lighter 80%**. Click the **Border tab**, and then in the **Border preview**, click the left border to deselect it. Click **OK** two times, and then click cell **A1**. Compare your screen with Figure 4.

   The custom cell style is saved with the workbook and can be applied as often as needed within the workbook.

10. Save 💾 the file.

■ **You have completed Skill 7 of 10**

▶ Recall that a theme is a set of colors, fonts, lines, and fill effects that can be applied to entire worksheets or to individual cells.

▶ Themes can be customized by changing the colors, fonts, and effects assigned to them. Care should be taken to choose color combinations that look professional.

1. Click cell **A3**. Click the **Page Layout tab**, and then in the **Themes group**, click the **Theme Fonts** button. Compare your screen with **Figure 1**.

   A font theme consists of two fonts, one for titles and one for text. In Excel, most styles assign the same font to both.

2. Below the **Fonts** gallery, click **Customize Fonts**.

3. In the **Create New Theme Fonts** dialog box, click the **Heading font arrow**, scroll down the displayed list, and then click **Cambria**.

   When the new theme is applied, all heading cell styles will display in the Cambria font.

4. Click the **Body font arrow**, scroll up the displayed list, and then click **Arial**.

   The default font face and size for Excel 2016 is Calibri, size 11. When you change the body font, you change the default font for the workbook. Here, the default font has been changed to Arial.

   Under Sample, a sample of the selected font choices displays for the heading and body font styles.

5. In the **Name** field, replace the existing text with Festival Theme Compare your screen with **Figure 2**.

■ **Continue to the next page to complete the skill**

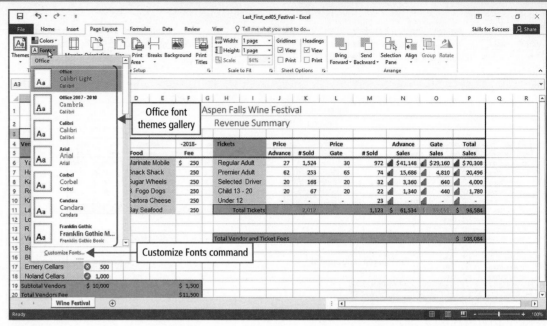

Figure 1

Excel 2016, Windows 10, Microsoft Corporation

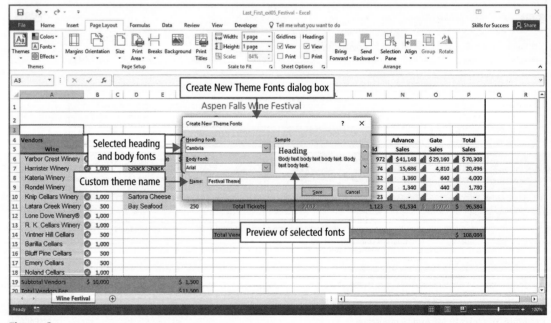

Figure 2

Excel 2016, Windows 10, Microsoft Corporation

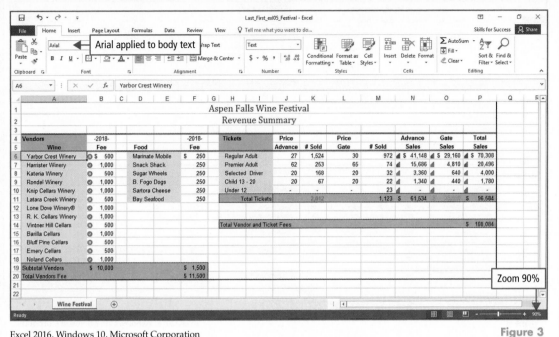

Excel 2016, Windows 10, Microsoft Corporation

Figure 3

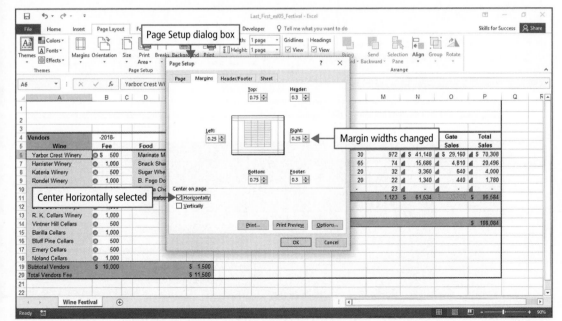

Excel 2016, Windows 10, Microsoft Corporation

Figure 4

6. Click **Save** to save the custom font theme. If necessary, adjust column widths. Click the **Home tab**, and then click cell **A6**. In the taskbar, click **Zoom Out** to decrease the **Zoom** to **90%**. Compare your screen with **Figure 3**.

> In the worksheet, the body fonts are formatted as Arial.

7. Click the **Page Layout tab**. In the **Themes group**, click the **Theme Fonts** button. Verify that the *Festival Theme* displays at the top of the displayed gallery, and then click the **Theme Fonts** button again to close the gallery.

8. In the **Page Setup group**, click the **Margins** button, and then below the gallery, click **Custom Margins**.

9. In the **Page Setup** dialog box, on the **Margins tab**, replace the **Left** value with 0.25 and the **Right** value with 0.25

> Reducing margins is a way to include all of the data on the printed page without having to decrease the size of the worksheet.

10. Under **Center on page**, click the **Horizontally** check box, and then compare your screen with **Figure 4**.

> This setting will center the spreadsheet on the printed page horizontally.

11. Click **OK**, and then **Save** 🖫 the file.

■ **You have completed Skill 8 of 10**

▶ A *watermark* is a graphic inserted into a workbook background. Watermarks are typically inserted into the header.

▶ Background colors can be applied to ranges of cells to add interest to a worksheet.

1. Click the **Insert tab**. In the **Text group**, click the **Header & Footer** button. Click cell **A1**. In the taskbar, click **Zoom Out** to decrease the **Zoom** to **80%**. Click *Add Header* in the center header, as shown in **Figure 1**.

2. Click the **Design tab**, and in the **Header & Footer Elements group**, click the **Picture** button.

3. In the **Insert Pictures** dialog box, click **Browse**, and then navigate to the student data files for this chapter. Select **exl05_FestivalLogo**, and then click **Insert**.

Recall that when objects are inserted into headers or footers, they are represented by fields. Here, &[Picture] represents the picture that was just inserted.

4. Click in the area above the header to deactivate the **Header & Footer** area and to display the watermark, as shown in **Figure 2**.

Any picture can be used as a watermark. By adding an image to the header, it is displayed behind the data on the spreadsheet instead of on top of the data.

5. Click the **View tab**, and then in the **Workbook Views group**, click **Normal**.

Recall that header and footer elements do not display in Normal view.

■ **Continue to the next page to complete the skill**

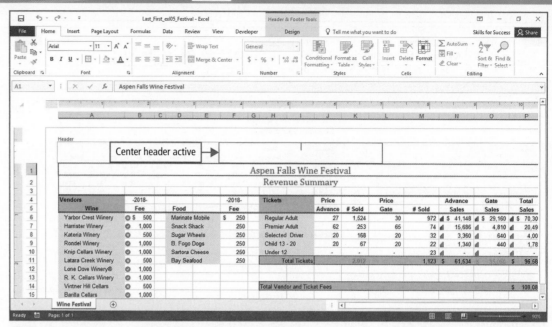

Figure 1

Excel 2016, Windows 10, Microsoft Corporation

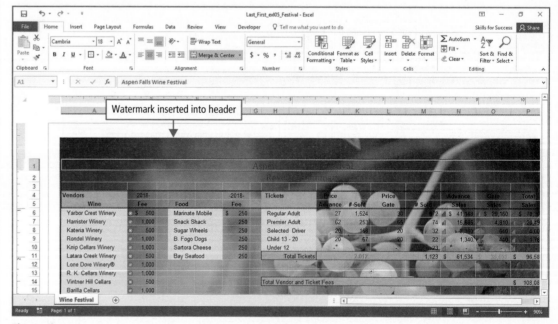

Figure 2

Excel 2016, Windows 10, Microsoft Corporation

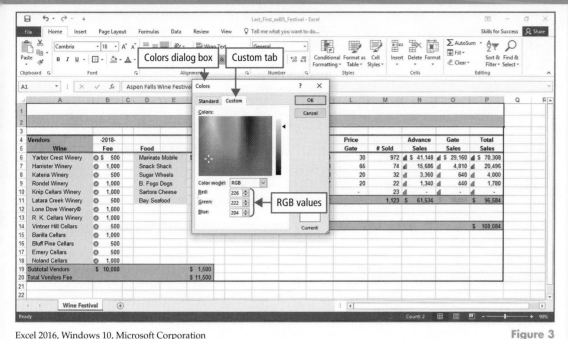

Excel 2016, Windows 10, Microsoft Corporation

Figure 3

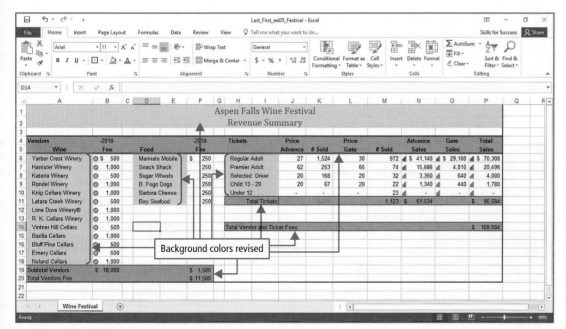

Excel 2016, Windows 10, Microsoft Corporation

Figure 4

6. Select the range **A1:P2**. Click the **Home tab**. In the **Font group**, click the **Fill Color arrow**, and then below the colors, click **More Colors**. In the **Colors** dialog box, click the **Custom tab**. Replace the **Red** value with 226 the **Green** value with 222 and the **Blue** value with 204

> In this manner, colors can be created that are not available in the gallery. *RGB values* are colors constructed from combinations of red, green, and blue.

7. Compare your screen with Figure 3, and then click **OK**.

8. Select the range **A6:A18**. In the **Font group**, click the **Fill Color** button. Repeat the technique just practiced to revise the fill color for **D6:E11** and **H6:I10**.

9. Select the range **A19:F20**. Click the **Fill Color arrow**. In the gallery, under **Theme Colors**, in the third row, click the third color—**Gray-25%, Background 2, Darker 25%**. Repeat the technique just practiced to revise the fill color for the ranges **H11:P11**, **H14:P14**, and **A4:P5**. Click any empty cell, and then compare your screen with Figure 4.

10. **Save** the file.

■ **You have completed Skill 9 of 10**

▶ **Gridlines** are lines that run horizontally and vertically across a worksheet and intersect to create cells.

▶ Gridlines are useful when working with a spreadsheet, but they can be hidden after the worksheet is completed.

1. Click the **Page Layout tab**. In the **Sheet Options group**, clear the **Gridlines View** check box. Compare your screen with **Figure 1**.

2. Select the range **A6:F18**, press and hold Ctrl, and then select the range **H6:P10**. Release Ctrl.

3. Click the **Home tab**. In the **Font group**, click the **Font Settings Dialog Box Launcher** 🔲. In the **Format Cells** dialog box, click the **Border tab**.

4. On the **Border tab**, under **Style**, select the last line style in the left column. Click the **Color arrow**. Under **Theme Colors**, in the third row, click the first color—**White, Background 1, Darker 15%**.

5. Under **Presets**, click the **Inside** button, and then compare your screen with **Figure 2**. Click **OK** to close the **Format Cells** dialog box.

   By selecting an inside border, the color is applied only to the inside borders.

■ **Continue to the next page to complete the skill**

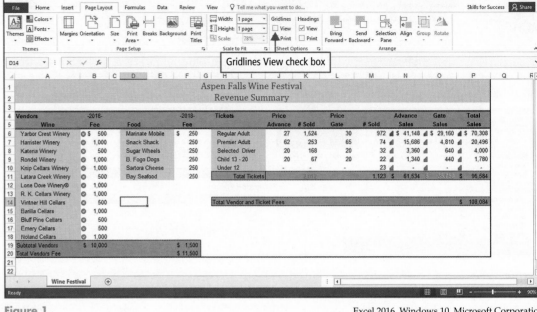

Figure 1

Excel 2016, Windows 10, Microsoft Corporation

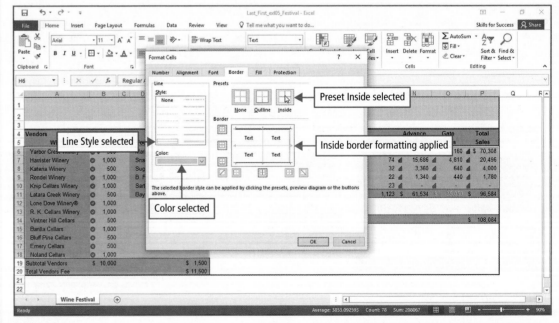

Figure 2

Excel 2016, Windows 10, Microsoft Corporation

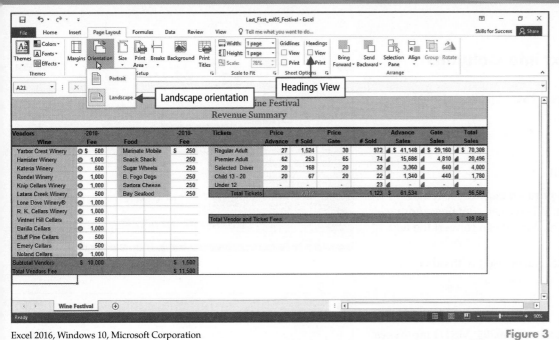

Excel 2016, Windows 10, Microsoft Corporation

Figure 3

6. Select the range **A1:P20**. On the **Home tab**, in the **Font group**, click the **Thick Outside Border arrow** . Click the seventh option, **Outside Borders**.

7. Click cell **A21**. Click the **Page Layout tab**, and then in the **Sheet Options group**, click to clear the **Headings View** check box.

8. In the **Page Setup group**, click the **Orientation button**, and verify that **Landscape** is selected. Compare your screen with **Figure 3**.

9. Click the **File tab**, and then click **Print**. Compare your screen with **Figure 4**.

10. **Save** the file, and then **Close** ☒ Excel. Submit the file as directed by your instructor.

✔ **DONE!** You have completed Skill 10 of 10, and your workbook is complete!

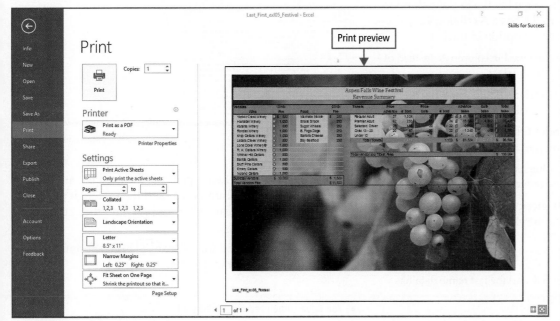

Excel 2016, Windows 10, Microsoft Corporation

Figure 4

More Skills 11

Convert Comma-Separated Text into Columns

To complete this project, you will need the following file:

- exl05_MS11Employees (CSV)

You will save your file as:

- Last_First_exl05_MS11Employees (Excel)

▶ Tabular data is often formatted as **comma-separated values**—text that uses commas to separate each column of text. When a cell contains comma-separated values, the Convert Text to Columns Wizard can convert the text into separate columns.

▶ Files that have been converted into this format can be used with other spreadsheet programs.

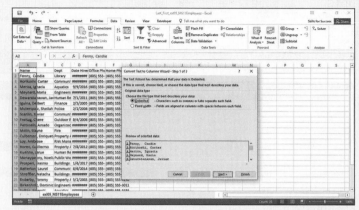

Figure 1   Excel 2016, Windows 10, Microsoft Corporation

1. Start **Excel 2016**, and then open the student data file **exl05_MS11Employees**. Since this is a .csv file, in the **Open** dialog box, click the **All Excel Files arrow**, and then select **All Files** to see the file. Save the file in your chapter folder as Last_First_exl05_MS11Employees In the **Save As** dialog box, change **Save as type** to **Excel Workbook**, the first option in the list.

In this worksheet, the first and last names are combined in column A. Instead of using columns, each row uses commas to separate the data.

2. Select column **B**, right-click, and then click **Insert**. Select the range **A2:A27**. Click the **Data tab**, and then in the **Data Tools group**, click **Text to Columns**.

3. In the **Convert Text to Columns Wizard**, under **Original data type**, verify that the **Delimited** option is selected, as shown in **Figure 1**.

A **delimiter** is the character used to separate columns of text in a data table. Common delimiters include commas, tabs, and semicolons.

4. Click **Next**. Under **Delimiters**, clear the **Tab** check box, and then click the **Comma** and **Space** check boxes. Under **Data preview**, notice that the data is arranged in two columns.

5. Click **Next**, and then click **Finish**.

The first name data is now inserted into column B, and the last name data has stayed in column A.

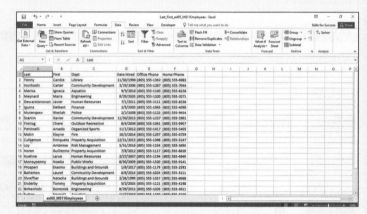

Figure 2   Excel 2016, Windows 10, Microsoft Corporation

6. Click cell **A1**, and then type Last Click cell **B1**, and then type First Select columns **A:F**, and then AutoFit the columns to fit the data. Click cell **A1**, and then compare your screen with **Figure 2**.

7. Save 🖫 the file, and then **Close** ☒ Excel. Submit the file as directed by your instructor.

■ **You have completed More Skills 11**

More Skills 12

Inspect Document Properties to Remove Personal Information

To complete this project, you will need the following file:

- exl05_MS12Costs

You will save your file as:

- Last_First_exl05_MS12Costs

▶ Recall that *document properties* are details about a file that describe or identify the file, such as the title, author name, and keywords.

▶ Before sharing a workbook, you should search for and remove any personal information that may be stored in the file.

1. Start **Excel 2016**, open the student data file **exl05_MS12Costs**, and then save the file in your chapter folder as Last_First_exl05_MS12Costs

2. Click the **File tab**, and then compare your screen with Figure 1.

   The Document Information Panel displays the file's *metadata*—information that describes the data in an Excel file. Here, the metadata has personally identifiable information, such as a name in the Author property.

3. In **Info** view, click **Check for Issues**, and then click **Inspect Document**. If necessary, read the message, and then click **Yes**.

4. In the **Document Inspector** dialog box, clear the **Comments and Annotations** check box.

   The Document Inspector is used to search for comments, metadata, headers, footers, and other elements that may be hidden from view.

5. In the **Document Inspector** dialog box, click **Inspect**.

   If an item is found in the Document Inspector, the Remove All button displays. In this workbook, Document properties, Author, and Absolute path to the workbook were found.

6. To the right of **Document Properties and Personal Information**, click **Remove All**, and then click **Reinspect**.

   MOS
   Obj 1.5.6 C

7. In the **Document Inspector** dialog box, click **Inspect**. Note the **Document Properties and Personal Information** section does not show any results. Click **Close**, and then compare your screen with Figure 2.

Excel 2016, Windows 10, Microsoft Corporation   **Figure 1**

Excel 2016, Windows 10, Microsoft Corporation   **Figure 2**

8. **Save** the file, and then **Close** Excel. Submit the file as directed by your instructor.

- **You have completed More Skills 12**

More Skills 13

Remove Duplicate Records

To complete this project, you will need the following file:

- exl05_MS13Departments

You will save your file as:

- Last_First_exl05_MS13Departments

▶ Duplicate records might appear in a table or worksheet when a record is accidently entered multiple times. For example, a person's name might be listed in more than one row.

▶ Duplicate records are removed using the Remove Duplicates tool.

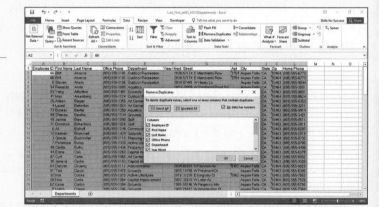

---

1. Start **Excel 2016**, and then open the file **exl05_MS13Departments**. Save the file in your chapter folder as Last_First_exl05_MS13Departments

2. Click cell **C1**. On the **Home tab**, in the **Editing group**, click the **Sort & Filter arrow**, and then click **Sort A to Z**. Notice that Employee ID 66—*Britt Abarca*—appears twice.

Obj 3.3.4 C

3. Click cell **A1**. Click the **Data tab**, and then in the **Data Tools group**, click **Remove Duplicates**. Compare your screen with Figure 1.

   In the Remove Duplicates box, you select the columns that might contain duplicate values so that you can later delete the duplicate entries.

4. In the **Remove Duplicates** dialog box, click **Unselect All**, and then verify that the **My data has headers** check box is selected.

5. Under **Columns**, select the **Employee ID** check box.

6. Click **OK**, and then read the displayed message. Compare your screen with Figure 2. Notice that five duplicate values were found and removed. Also, 104 unique values remain.

7. Click **OK**, and then, if necessary, click cell **A1**.

8. In the **Sort & Filter group**, click **Sort A to Z**. Scroll down and verify that there are no duplicate Employee ID numbers.

9. **Save** the file, and then **Close** Excel. Submit the file as directed by your instructor.

Figure 1   Excel 2016, Windows 10, Microsoft Corporation

Figure 2   Excel 2016, Windows 10, Microsoft Corporation

■ **You have completed More Skills 13**

More Skills 14

Insert Shapes and Text Boxes

To complete this project, you will need the following file:

- exl05_MS14Fundraiser

You will save your file as:

- Last_First_exl05_MS14Fundraiser

▶ A **Text Box** is a rectangular object on a worksheet or chart in which you type text.

▶ A **shape** is an object such as a line, arrow, rectangle, circle, square, or callout.

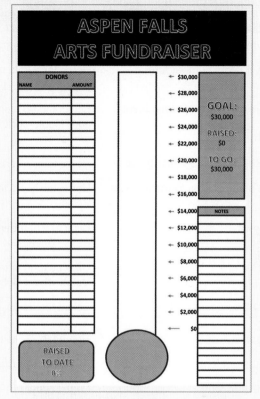

Figure 1

1. Start **Excel 2016**, and then open the student data file **exl05_MS14Fundraiser**. Save the file in your chapter folder as Last_First_exl05_MS14Fundraiser

2. Click the **Insert tab**. In the **Illustrations group**, click the **Shapes** button. Under **Basic Shapes**, click **Text Box**. Click the top left corner of cell **G10**, drag the cursor to the right edge of column **H**, and then drag down to the bottom of row **24**.

   MOS Obj 5.3.1 C

3. Click the **Drawing Tools Format tab**. In the **Shape Styles group**, click the **Shape Fill arrow**, and then apply the color in the ninth column, fourth row—**Blue, Accent 5, Lighter 40%**. Click the **Shape Outline arrow**, and then apply the color in the ninth column, sixth row—**Blue, Accent 5, Darker 50%**. Click the **Shape Outline arrow**, point to **Weight**, and then click **3 pt**.

4. In the text box, type GOAL: $30,000 | RAISED: $0 | TO GO: $30,000 Press Enter after each amount, as shown in **Figure 1**.

5. Select **GOAL:**, press and hold Ctrl, select **RAISED:**, and then select **TO GO:**. Release Ctrl. In the **WordArt Styles group**, click the **More** button, and then click the second option in the third row—**Fill - Black, Text 1, Outline - Background 1, Hard Shadow - Accent 5**. Apply **Font Size 25** to **GOAL:**, and then **Font Size 20** to **RAISED:** and **TO GO:**. Apply **Font Size 15** to the dollar amounts. Select all of the text, and then in the **Alignment group**, click **Middle Align** and **Center**.

6. Click the **Drawing Tools Format tab**. In the **Insert Shapes group**, click the **More** button, and then under **Rectangles**, click the second option—**Rounded Rectangle**.

7. Click cell **A42**. In the **Size group**, change the **Shape Height** to 1.30 and the **Shape Width** to 2.15 Move the shape to **A42:B47**. Using techniques previously practiced, apply the **Shape Fill** in the ninth column,

fourth row—**Blue, Accent 5, Lighter 40%**. Apply the **Shape Outline** in the ninth column, sixth row—**Blue, Accent 5, Darker 50%**, and then apply a **Weight** of 3 pt.

8. In the shape, using the techniques previously practiced, type RAISED | TO DATE | 0% Press Enter after RAISED and DATE. Select the text, and apply the **WordArt Style** in the second column, third row—**Fill - Black, Text 1, Outline - Background 1, Hard Shadow - Accent 5**. Apply a **Font Size** of 20, and **Center** the text. Click the **File tab**, click **Print**, and then compare your screen to **Figure 1**.

9. **Save** the file, and then **Close** Excel. Submit the file as directed by your instructor.

■ **You have completed More Skills 14**

Review

Skills Number	Task	Step	Icon	Keyboard Shortcut
1	Insert symbols	Insert tab → Symbols group → Symbol		
1	Create a custom number format	Home tab → Number group → Number Format Dialog Box Launcher → Number tab	⬓	
2	Copy formatting with Format Painter	Select the text format to copy → click Format Painter to copy once and double-click to copy more than once → select the text to be formatted	🖌	
3	Write a conditional formatting rule	Home tab → Styles group → Conditional Formatting → New Rule		
4	Manage a conditional formatting rule	Home tab → Styles group → Conditional Formatting → Manage Rules		
5	Delete rows	Click row number → Home tab → Cells group → Delete arrow → Delete Sheet Rows		Ctrl + Minus (−)
5	Delete columns	Click column letter → Home tab → Cells group → Delete arrow → Delete Sheet Columns		Ctrl + Shift + Minus (−)
6	Create cell borders	Select the range → Home tab → Font group → Border button	⊞ ▾	
7	Create cell styles	Home tab → Styles group → Cell Styles → New Cell Style		
8	Create custom fonts	Page Layout tab → Themes group → Fonts → Customize Fonts		
8	Apply custom fonts	Page Layout tab → Themes group → Fonts → click customized font name		
9	Insert a watermark	Insert tab → Text group → Header & Footer → Design tab → Header & Footer Elements group → click Picture		
10	View/hide gridlines	Page Layout tab → Sheet Options group → Gridlines → View check box		
10	View/hide row and column headings	Page Layout tab → Sheet Options group → Headings → View check box		
MS11	Convert comma-separated text	Data tab → Data Tools group → Text to Columns		
MS12	Remove document properties and personal information	Backstage view → Check for Issues → Inspect Document → Inspect → Remove All		
MS13	Remove duplicate records	Data tab → Data Tools group → Remove Duplicates		
MS14	Insert shapes and text boxes	Insert tab → Illustrations group → Shapes button		

Project Summary Chart

Project	Project Type	Project Location
Skills Review	Review	In Book & MIL MyITLab® Grader
Skills Assessment 1	Review	In Book & MIL MyITLab® Grader
Skills Assessment 2	Review	Book
My Skills	Problem Solving	Book
Visual Skills Check	Problem Solving	Book
Skills Challenge 1	Critical Thinking	Book
Skills Challenge 2	Critical Thinking	Book
More Skills Assessment	Review	In Book & MIL MyITLab® Grader
Collaborating with Google	Critical Thinking	Book

MOS Objectives Covered (Quiz in MyITLab®)

1.1.2 C Import data from a delimited text file	3.3.4 C Remove duplicate records
1.3.4 C Modify page setup	5.3.1 C Insert text boxes and shapes
1.3.5 C Insert and delete columns or rows	5.3.2 C Insert images
1.4.4 C Change workbook views	2.1.1 E Create custom number formats
1.4.7 C Change magnification by using zoom tools	2.2.1 E Create custom conditional formatting rules
1.5.6 C Inspect a workbook for hidden properties or personal information	2.2.2 E Create conditional formatting rules that use formulas
2.1.5 C Insert and delete cells	2.2.3 E Manage conditional formatting rules
2.2.3 C Format cells by using Format Painter	2.3.1 E Create custom color formats
2.2.7 C Apply cell styles	2.3.2 E Create and modify cell styles
2.3.4 C Apply conditional formatting	2.3.3 E Create and modify custom themes

Key Terms

Online Help Skills

1. Start **Excel 2016**, and then in the upper right corner of the start page, click the **Help** button ⟨?⟩.

2. In the **Excel 2016 Help** window **Search** box, type conditional formatting and then press ⟨Enter⟩.

3. In the search result list, click **Use a formula to apply conditional formatting**. **Maximize** the Excel Help window, and then compare your screen with **Figure 1**.

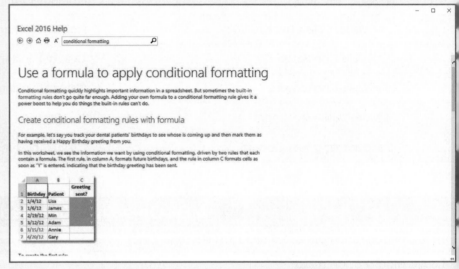

Figure 1   Excel 2016, Windows 10, Microsoft Corporation

4. Read the section to answer the following questions: What type of formula can be used to specify conditional formatting criteria? What types of cell references are automatically inserted when using conditional formatting?

Matching  MyITLab®

Match each term in the second column with its correct definition in the first column by writing the letter of the term on the blank line in front of the correct definition.

___ **1.** Decorative lines that can be applied to worksheet cells.

___ **2.** A set of design elements, including backgrounds, colors, and fonts, that are applied to a spreadsheet.

___ **3.** This treats a cell value as text even when the cell contains numbers.

___ **4.** Small graphics that visually represent a cell's value in relation to other cells.

___ **5.** A group of formatting choices that can be applied in a single step.

___ **6.** A tool that copies formatting from one cell to another.

___ **7.** Characters that are inserted and are not available on the keyboard.

___ **8.** The shading assigned to a cell.

___ **9.** By default, lines that run horizontally and vertically across a worksheet and intersect to create cells.

___ **10.** Formatting that changes the appearance of a cell or range when one or more conditions are true.

A Gridlines

B Format Painter

C Cell borders

D Fill color

E Icon set

F Conditional formatting

G Text format

H Symbol

I Theme

J Style

Multiple Choice (MyITLab®)

Choose the correct answer.

1. Which of the following is a character, such as the degree symbol or trademark symbol, that is a frequently used symbol located on a short list and not found on the keyboard?
   A. Wingding
   B. Insert
   C. Special character

2. Which of the following specifies the year with four digits?
   A. dd
   B. yyyy
   C. mm

3. Which of the following specifies a placeholder for a digit?
   A. #
   B. 0
   C. mm

4. Once a symbol is inserted into a cell, it can be formatted like this workbook element.
   A. Text
   B. Image
   C. Style

5. You must specify in which direction to move the surrounding cells whenever you perform this operation on a worksheet.
   A. Format
   B. Insert
   C. Copy

6. Which is the location where custom styles are saved?
   A. Application
   B. Workbook
   C. Desktop

7. Header and footer elements do not display in this view.
   A. Page Setup
   B. Print Preview
   C. Normal

8. A graphic that is inserted into a document background is called which of the following?
   A. Watermark
   B. Logo
   C. Cell Style

9. A watermark is typically inserted into this area of the page.
   A. Header
   B. Column
   C. Cell

10. Colors constructed from a combination of red, green, and blue are called which of the following?
    A. RGB values
    B. Colorscale
    C. HEX

Topics for Discussion

1. You have added conditional formatting that displays icon sets. Do you think these special formats add to or detract from the data's meaning? Why?

2. In this chapter, you placed borders and shading in cells and then hid the gridlines and column and row headings. Compare this format with one that displays only gridlines and headings but does not display borders and shading. Which format do you think is easiest for others to read? Why?

Skills Review

To complete this project, you will need the following files:

- exl05_SRTourism (Excel)
- exl05_SRLogo (JPG)

You will save your file as:

- Last_First_exl05_SRTourism

---

1. Start **Excel 2016**, and then open the student data file **exl05_SRTourism**. Save the file in your chapter folder as Last_First_exl05_SRTourism

2. Select the range **B5:D5**. On the **Home tab**, in the **Number group**, click the **Number Dialog Box Launcher**, and then under **Category**, click **Custom**. In the **Type** box, replace the existing value with -yyyy- and then click **OK**. In the **Clipboard group**, click the **Format Painter**, and then select the range **G5:I5**. Compare your screen with Figure 1.

3. Select the range **B6:D6**. In the **Clipboard group**, double-click the **Format Painter**. As previously practiced, apply the format to the ranges **G6:I6** and **G10:I10**, and then click **Format Painter**.

4. Click the cell **B7**. Click the **Format Painter**, and then as previously practiced, apply the format to **G7:I8**.

5. Select the range **A6:D14**. Press and hold [Ctrl], and then select the range **F6:I8**. Release [Ctrl]. In the **Font group**, click the **Fill Color arrow**. Under **Theme Colors**, in the second row, click the ninth color—**Blue, Accent 5, Lighter 80%**. In the **Font group**, click the **More Borders arrow**, and then click **Thick Outside Borders**. Click the **More Borders arrow**, and then click **More Borders**. Click the **Color arrow**. Under **Theme Colors**, in the sixth row, click the ninth color—**Blue, Accent 5, Darker 50%**, click **Outline**, and then click **OK**. Click any empty cell, and then compare your screen with Figure 2.

6. Select the range **G11:I11**. In the **Styles group**, click the **Conditional Formatting arrow**, point to **Icon Sets**, and then click **More Rules**. In the **New Formatting Rule** dialog box, under **Edit the Rule Description**, click the **Icon Style arrow**, and then click **3 Symbols (Uncircled)**. Click **Reverse Icon Order**, and then click **OK**.

7. Select the range **B16:D16**. In the **Styles group**, click the **Conditional Formatting arrow**, and then click **Manage Rules**. Click **Edit Rule**, and then in the **Format values where this formula is true** box, replace the text with =B16>185000

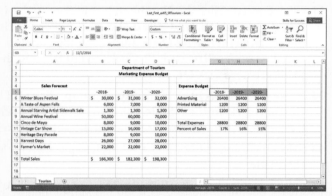

Excel 2016, Windows 10, Microsoft Corporation   Figure 1

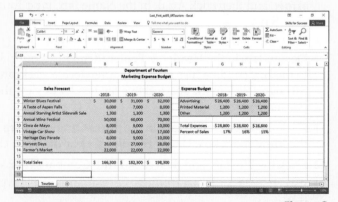

Excel 2016, Windows 10, Microsoft Corporation   Figure 2

■ Continue to the next page to complete this Skills Review

8. Click **Format**. On the **Font tab**, under **Font style**, click **Bold**. Click the **Color arrow**, and then in the gallery, under **Standard Colors**, click the sixth color—**Green**. Click **OK** three times.

9. Select the range **A16:D16**. Press and hold Ctrl, and then select the range **F10:I11**. In the **Font group**, click the **Fill Color arrow**. Under **Theme Colors**, click the second row, ninth color—**Blue, Accent 5, Lighter 80%**. Click the **More Borders arrow**, and then click **Thick Outside Borders**. Click cell **A1**, and then compare your screen with Figure 3.

10. In the **Styles group**, click **Cell Styles**, and then click **New Cell Style**. In the **Style name** box, type Tourism Style

11. Click **Format**. Click the **Number tab**, and then under **Category**, click **Text**. Click the **Alignment tab**. Under **Text alignment**, click the **Horizontal arrow**, and then click **Center Across Selection**. Click the **Font tab**. Under **Font**, click **Arial**, and then under **Size**, click **12**. Click the **Fill tab**, and then in the sixth row, click the first color. Click **OK** two times.

12. Select the range **A4:D4**. In the **Styles group**, click **Cell Styles**, and then under **Custom**, click **Tourism Style**. Select the range **F4:I4**, and then using the technique previously practiced, apply the **Tourism Style**.

13. Select the range **A1:I2**. Click **Cell Styles**, and then under **Titles and Headings**, click **Title**.

14. Click the **Page Layout tab**. In the **Themes group**, click **Theme Fonts**, and then click **Customize Fonts**.

15. Click the **Heading font arrow**, and then click **Cambria**. Click the **Body font arrow**, and then click **Arial**. In the **Name** box, type Tourism Fonts and then click **Save**.

16. Click the **Insert tab**, and then in the **Text group**, click **Header & Footer**. On the **Design tab**, in the **Header & Footer Elements group**, click **Picture**. Navigate to the student data files for this chapter, locate, click, and then insert **exl05_SRLogo**. Click in the space above the header to view the watermark. Return to Normal view.

17. Click the **Page Layout tab**. In the **Sheet Options group**, under **Gridlines**, clear the **View** check box. Under **Headings**, clear the **View** check box.

18. Click the **File tab**, and then click **Print**. Compare your screen with Figure 4.

19. **Save** the file, and then **Close** Excel. Submit the file as directed by your instructor.

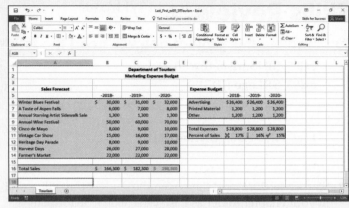

Figure 3   Excel 2016, Windows 10, Microsoft Corporation

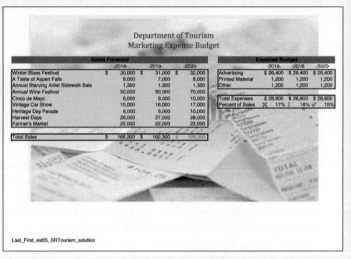

Figure 4   Excel 2016, Windows 10, Microsoft Corporation

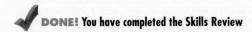

DONE! You have completed the Skills Review

Skill Assessment 1

MyITLab®
Grader

To complete this project, you will need the following files:

- exl05_SA1Travel (Excel)
- exl05_SA1Logo (JPG)

You will save your file as:

- Last_First_exl05_SA1Travel

1. Start **Excel 2016**, and then open the student data file **exl05_SA1Travel**. Save the file in your chapter folder as Last_First_exl05_SA1Travel

2. For the range **A3:D16**, apply an **Orange, Accent 2, Lighter 80%** fill color. Insert a new column **A**, and then resize the **A** column width to 3.5

3. Use **Format Painter** to copy the format in cell **C4** to the range **C16:E16**. Click cell **C5**, and then copy the format to the range **D5:D15**.

4. In cell **E4**, create a new conditional formatting rule with the following condition: =E4<0 When the condition is true, display the cell text as **Bold** and **Red**. Use **Format Painter** to apply the formatting in cell **E4** to the range **E5:E16**. Select **E5:E15**, and then apply **Comma [0]** cell style.

5. In the range **E4:E15**, apply the **3 Arrows (Colored)** icon set.

6. Create a new **Cell Style** named Travel Style Set the **Horizontal** alignment to **Center Across Selection**. Set the **Font** to **Arial**, size **18**, and **Font Color** to **Dark Blue**. Change the **Fill** color **Background** to **No Color**. Apply the **Travel Style** to the range **B1:E1**.

7. Select the range **B3:E16**. Apply **Thick Outside Borders** with **Green, Accent 6, Darker 50%** color. Apply a **thin** line **inside** border, **Green, Accent 6, Darker 50%**.

8. Create a new **Theme font**. Name the new font Travel Font Apply **Cambria** for the **Heading font**, and then **Arial** for the **Body font**.

9. Apply the **Heading 4** cell style to the range **C3:E3**, and then to cell **B16**. Apply **Travel Style** to **B2:E2**, and then set the font to size **12**. AutoFit columns **B:E**.

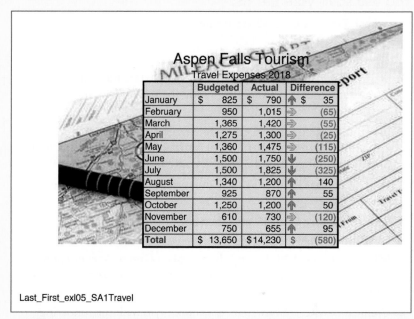

Last_First_exl05_SA1Travel

Excel 2016, Windows 10, Microsoft Corporation

Figure 1

10. Display the header and footer, and then in the middle header, insert a watermark using the file **exl05_SA1Logo**. Switch to **Normal** view, and then click cell **A1**. Click **File**, then **Print**, and then compare your screen with **Figure 1**.

11. **Save** the file, and then **Close** Excel. Submit the file as directed by your instructor.

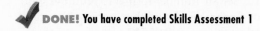
DONE! You have completed Skills Assessment 1

Skills Assessment 2

To complete this project, you will need the following file:

- exl05_SA2Attendance

You will save your file as:

- Last_First_exl05_SA2Attendance

1. Start **Excel 2016**, and then open the student data file **exl05_SA2Attendance**. Save the file in your chapter folder as Last_First_exl05_SA2Attendance

2. In cell **A4**, create a new **Cell Style** named Event Style For the style, apply the custom number format mmmm-yyyy Apply the **Event Style** to the range **A4:A15**. Set the width of column **A** to 15.50

3. Use the **Format Painter** to copy the format from cell **B4** to the range **B5:D16**.

4. Select the range **D4:D15**, and then apply the **3 Signs** icon set conditional formatting.

5. Select the range **A3:D16**, and then apply a **Green, Accent 6, Lighter 60%** fill color. Insert a new column **A**, and then resize columns **A** and **F** to **6**.

6. Create a new **Cell Style** named Event2 Style with the following formatting: horizontally **Center Across Selection**; **Cambria** font, size **14**; and font color **Blue-Gray, Text 2, Darker 25%**. Apply a thick, **Red** border along the **bottom** edge of the cell only. Apply the **Event2 Style** to the range **B2:E2**.

7. Insert a new row **1**, and then resize the row height to 20

8. Create a new **Cell Style** named Total Style Format the style with a double border, **Blue, Accent 5, Darker 50%** to the bottom of the cell only. Format the two sides with a thin line, **Blue, Accent 5, Darker 50%** border, and the top with a thick line, **Blue, Accent 5, Darker 50%** border. Set the fill color to the first row, sixth color in the gallery—**Orange, Accent 2**. Set the number format to **Number** with **0** decimal places. **Use 1000 Separator (,)**, and then verify **Alignment** to **Horizontal General**. Select the range **B17:E17**, and then apply the **Total Style**.

Aspen Falls Tourism			
Event Attendance 2018			
	Estimated	Actual	Variance
January-2018	2,000	1,755	(245)
February-2018	6,500	6,875	375
March-2018	1,500	1,365	(135)
April-2018	2,600	2,900	300
May-2018	1,300	1,200	(100)
June-2018	1,550	1,350	(200)
July-2018	1,800	2,100	300
August-2018	425	645	220
September-2018	600	475	(125)
October-2018	2,200	2,675	475
November-2018	2,800	2,665	(135)
December-2018	4,400	4,150	(250)
Total	27,675	28,155	480

Last_First_exl05_SA2Attendance

Figure 1

9. Select the range **A1:F18**, and then apply **Thick Outside Borders**. Select the range **B2:E17**, and then apply a **Dark Red, Thick Outline**. Select the range **B4:E16**, and then apply a **Dark Red, thin, inside border**.

10. Apply the **Title** style to the range **B2:E2**. Create a new **Theme font** named Event Fonts and then set the **Heading** to **Cambria** and the **Body** to **Arial**. Click cell **A1**.

11. **Print Preview** the worksheet, and then compare your screen with Figure 1.

12. **Save** the file, and then **Close** Excel. Submit the file as directed by your instructor.

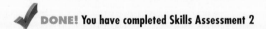 **DONE!** You have completed Skills Assessment 2

	A	B	C	D	E	F	G	H
1		First Last						
2		My Grades						
3								
4		Courses	Semester	Grades				
5		CIS-101	Fall 2018	90				
6		ENG-101	Fall 2018	80				
7		ACCT-101	Fall 2018	70				
8		BUAD-101	Fall 2018	80				
9		SOC-101	Fall 2018	90				
10		ACCT-102	Spring 20	80				
11		MKTG-201	Spring 20	70				
12		MGMT-201	Spring 20	80				
13		ENG-102	Spring 20	90				
14		HIST-101	Spring 20	80				
15		Average		81				
16								
17								
18								
19								
20								

Excel 2016, Windows 10, Microsoft Corporation   **Figure 1**

	First Last		
	My Grades		
Courses	**Semester**		**Grades**
CIS-101	Fall 2018	✓	90
ENG-101	Fall 2018	◔	80
ACCT-101	Fall 2018	✗	70
BUAD-101	Fall 2018	◔	80
SOC-101	Fall 2018	✓	90
ACCT-102	Spring 2019	◔	80
MKTG-201	Spring 2019	✗	70
MGMT-201	Spring 2019	◔	80
ENG-102	Spring 2019	✓	90
HIST-101	Spring 2019	◔	80
Average			81

Last_First_exl05_MYGrades

Excel 2016, Windows 10, Microsoft Corporation   **Figure 2**

My Skills

To complete this project, you will need the following file:

- exl05_MYGrades

You will save your file as:

- Last_First_exl05_MYGrades

---

1. Start **Excel 2106**, and then open the student data file **exl05_MYGrades**. Save the file in your chapter folder as Last_First_exl05_MYGrades

2. In the first cell, replace *Student Name* with your First and Last names.

3. Create a new **Cell Style** named Grades Style with the following formatting: horizontally **Center Across Selection**; **Arial** font, size **16**; and **Green, Accent 6** font color. Select the range **A1:E2**, and then apply the **Grades Style**.

4. Insert cells in **A3:A15**, as shown in Figure 1.

5. Apply the **Conditional Formatting 3 Symbols (Circled)** icon set to show whether each semester's grades in **D5:D14** exceed, meet, or are below the grade intended for each course.

6. Use the **Format Painter** to copy the formatting from **Courses**, and then apply it to **Semester**, **Grades**, and **Average**.

7. Create a new **Custom Font** named Grades Font Select **Arial** for the heading and body fonts. AutoFit columns **B:C**.

8. Select the range **A1:E15**. Apply **Thick Outside Borders**, and then apply the fill color **Blue-Gray**, **Text 2**, **Lighter 80%**.

9. Hide the worksheet **Gridlines** and **Headings**. **Print Preview** the worksheet, and then compare your screen with Figure 2.

10. **Save** the file, and then **Close** Excel. Submit the file as directed by your instructor.

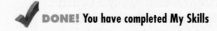 **DONE!** You have completed My Skills

Visual Skills Check

To complete this project, you will need the following file:

- exl05_VSCount

You will save your file as:

- Last_First_exl05_VSCount

Start **Excel 2016**, and then open the student data file **exl05_VSCount**. Save the file in your chapter folder as Last_First_exl05_VSCount Format the worksheet as shown in **Figure 1**. Create a new cell style named Count Style using the following formatting: **Center Across Selection**, **Century Schoolbook**, size **16**, **Bold**, and **Green, Accent 3, Darker 50%**. Apply the **Count Style** to the worksheet titles. Copy the number formatting in cell **B5**, and apply it to **C5:E9**. For the range **A1:E9**, apply **Tan, Accent 2, Lighter 40%** fill color. Apply **Green, Accent 3, Darker 50%**, **Thick Outside Borders** to the range **A1:E9**. Apply a thick top and bottom **Green, Accent 3, Darker 50%** border to **A3:E3**, and a **Green, Accent 3, Lighter 80%** fill color. Apply a thin **Green, Accent 3, Darker 50%** bottom border to **A4:E4**. Apply a **Green, Accent 3, Lighter 60%** thin inside border to the range **A5:E9**. Apply the **3 Triangles** icon set conditional formatting to the ranges **C5:C8** and **E5:E8**. Create a new conditional formatting rule in **D5:D8** using the **3 Traffic Lights (Unrimmed)** icon set. In **A9:E9**, apply a **Green, Accent 3, Lighter 80%** fill color. Adjust the **columns C:E** to **10.25**. **Print Preview** the worksheet. **Save** the file, and then **Close** Excel. Submit the file as directed by your instructor.

Aspen Falls Tourism Count

Quarter	Total Arrivals	Year 1		Year 2
	Count		Change	
1st Quarter	28,850 ▼	15,640 ●	(2,430) ▼	13,210
2nd Quarter	32,010 ▭	16,580 ○	(1,150) ▭	15,430
3rd Quarter	32,227 ▼	15,687 ●	853 ▲	16,540
4th Quarter	33,790 ▲	17,320 ○	(850) ▲	16,470
Total Count	126,877	65,227	(3,577)	61,650

Figure 1   Excel 2016, Windows 10, Microsoft Corporation

✔ **DONE! You have completed Visual Skills Check**

Skills Challenge 1

To complete this project, you will need the following file:

- exl05_SC1Spending

You will save your file as:

- Last_First_exl05_SC1Spending

The Aspen Falls Bureau of Tourism is trying to analyze tourism spending. Start **Excel 2016**, and then open the student data file **exl05_SC1Spending**. Save the file in your chapter folder as Last_First_exl05_SC1Spending Edit the custom style Spending Style applied to the worksheet headings. Apply formatting using more professional fonts, font color, and fill color. Edit the custom font Tourism Fonts, selecting fonts that are more appropriate for a business document. Edit the Labels cell style so that the borders, cell shading, and alignments

are consistent with the formatting practiced in the chapter. For the Variance column, apply conditional formatting so that the busiest years can be identified more easily. AutoFit columns, and delete columns and rows as necessary. Save the file, and then close Excel. Submit the file as directed by your instructor.

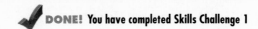 **DONE!** You have completed Skills Challenge 1

Skills Challenge 2

To complete this project, you will need the following file:

- exl05_SC2Growth

You will save your file as:

- Last_First_exl05_SC2Growth

Tourism Director Todd Austin would like to compare Aspen Falls's growth with growth data for your city. Go to http://quickfacts.census.gov/qfd/index.html and search for the state, then city in which you live. To find data for 10 years, you will also need to click the Browse Data Sets for (city) at the upper right corner of the table. Then select Historical population counts. If no data exists for your city, choose another nearby location. Start **Excel 2016**, open the student data file **exl05_SC2Growth**, and then save the file in your chapter folder as Last_First_exl05_SC2Growth Enter the

data provided from the website. Utilizing techniques practiced in this chapter, apply conditional formatting that visually represents the population changes in your area. Apply cell styles, background colors, and borders to the spreadsheet in a manner consistent with the techniques used in this chapter. Save the file, and then close Excel. Submit the file as directed by your instructor.

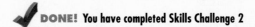 **DONE!** You have completed Skills Challenge 2

More Skills Assessment

MyITLab®
Grader

To complete this project, you will need the following files:

- exl05_MSADonations (Excel)
- exl05_MSADonors (CSV)

You will save your file as:

- Last_First_exl05_MSADonations

1. Start **Excel 2016**. Open the file **exl05_MSADonations**, and then save the file in your chapter folder as Last_First_exl05_MSADonations

2. Insert an **Oval** shape in the range **E16:H21**. Change the **Height** of the shape to 1.16 and the **Width** to 1.34

3. In the shape, type the text Goal $800,000 Format the font as size **14**, **Bold**, and **Center**. Click any cell. Compare your screen with **Figure 1**.

4. Inspect the workbook, and then remove all personal information.

5. Open the student data file **exl05_MSADonors**.

6. Using the **Data Tools**, remove the five duplicate name records from the workbook. Sort the Donor ID column from A to Z. AutoFit cells as necessary.

7. Move the **Donors** worksheet to the end of the **Last_First_exl05_MSADonations** workbook. Rename the worksheet tab Donors Compare your screen with **Figure 2**.

8. **Save** the file, and then **Close** Excel. Close any other open windows without saving.

9. Submit the file as directed by your instructor.

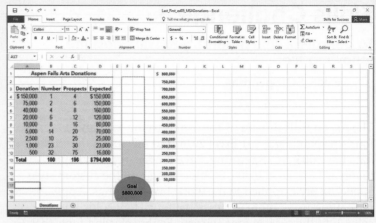

Figure 1 Excel 2016, Windows 10, Microsoft Corporation

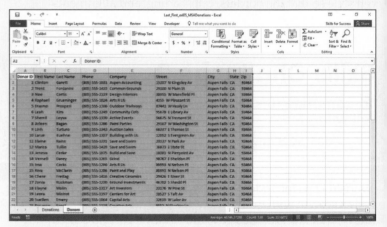

Figure 2 Excel 2016, Windows 10, Microsoft Corporation

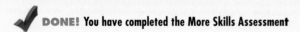
DONE! You have completed the More Skills Assessment

Collaborating with Google

To complete this project, you will need a Google account (refer to the Common Features chapter) and the following file:

- exl05_GPTime

You will save your file as:

- Last_First_exl05_GPTime

Figure 1

1. Open the **Google Chrome** web browser. Log into your Google account, and then click the **Apps** ⚏.

2. Click **Drive** ☁ to open Google Drive.

3. Click the **New** button, and then click **File upload**. Navigate to the student data files, and then open **exl05_GPTime**.

4. Double-click the **exl05_GPTime** file in **Google Drive**. Click **Open** to view the workbook in **Google Sheets**.

5. Click **Add-ons**, click **Get add-ons**, and then compare your screen with Figure 1. Click **Styles**. Your screen may be different, and you may need to scroll down. Click the **FREE** button in the upper right corner, and then click **Allow**.

6. With cell **A1** selected, in the **Styles** pane, under **Titles and Headings**, click **Title**. Select **A20:E20**, and then under **Titles and Headings**, click **Total**.

7. Select the range **A3:E3**, and then under **Themed Cell Styles**, click **40% A1**. Select the range **A4:E19**, and then under **Themed Cell Styles**, click **20% A1**. Close the **Styles** pane.

8. Click cell **A2**. Click the **Format tab**, point to **Number**, point to **More Formats**, and then click **Custom number format**. In the box, replace the current text with yyyy and then click **Apply**.

9. Select the range **C4:C19**. Click the **Format tab**, click **Conditional Formatting**, click **Color Scale**, and then at the bottom of the pane, click **Add another rule**. Click the **Midpoint arrow**, click **Number**, and then type 20 Click the **Maxpoint arrow**, click **Number**, and then type 40 Click **Done**.

10. Click the **View tab**, and then click **Gridlines**. Compare your screen with Figure 2.

11. Click the **File tab**, point to **Download as**, and then click **Microsoft Excel (.xlsx)**.

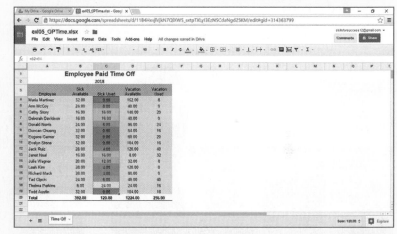

Figure 2

12. Save the file in your chapter folder as Last_First_exl05_GPTime

13. Close all windows, and then submit the file as directed by your instructor.

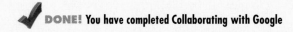 **DONE! You have completed Collaborating with Google**

CHAPTER 6

Insert Advanced Functions and Create Scenarios

- ► Functions are used to perform complex operations easily—for example, you can manipulate text to calculate the future value of assets.
- ► Analysis tools are used to perform what-if analyses and to determine which variables need to be changed in order to meet certain criteria.
- ► Future value can be calculated by using the FV function, when the interest rate is constant.
- ► Cell ranges can be calculated, using only the cells that meet specified criteria.

- ► Text functions are used to capitalize the beginning of proper nouns and to join text into one cell.
- ► Values can be retrieved by using lookup tables to determine a specific value.
- ► Logical functions are used to determine if values meet certain criteria.
- ► Array formulas can be used to calculate multiple ranges into one cell or a range of cells.

Picture-Factory / Fotolia

Aspen Falls City Hall

In this chapter, you will support Janet Neal, the Aspen Falls finance director, by editing an existing workbook and using Excel functions and formulas to calculate and analyze payroll-related expenses. Janet's responsibilities include planning, organizing, and controlling financial resources, and this workbook will assist her with predicting the present and future value of liabilities.

Excel workbooks can contain multiple sheets, and data can be copied and pasted between worksheets. Businesses and organizations often use Excel workbooks to create analyses for strategic planning and to predict future financial decisions. Functions can be used to insert values from tables, and a lookup function can be used to return the correct rate from a table.

In this project you will incorporate functions and formulas to calculate wages based on one or multiple criteria. You will also use text functions to join text, convert text, and paste values. You will practice using logical functions to determine certain criteria and use lookup functions to determine rates needed to calculate taxes and retirement deductions. You will also calculate the future value of assets and perform what-if analyses based on scenarios to help Janet and other stakeholders make financial planning decisions. Finally, you will use array formulas to perform calculations using multiple cell ranges.

Outcome

Using the skills in this chapter, you will be able to use paste options; construct lookup, logical, text, statistical, and financial functions; create arrays; and use the Scenario Manager.

Objectives

6.1 Construct text, logical, and lookup functions

6.2 Apply logical conditions and formats to data

6.3 Compute future values and conditional sums and averages

6.4 Analyze data using scenarios

6.5 Understand array formulas

Student data file needed for this chapter:

exl06_Payroll

You will save your file as:

Last_First_exl06_Payroll

SKILLS

Skills 1–10 Training

Skill 1	Modify Text Using Text Functions
Skill 2	Use Paste Options to Change Underlying Values
Skill 3	Look Up Data Using Lookup Functions
Skill 4	Edit Conditions in Logical Functions
Skill 5	Use COUNTA and COUNTIF Functions
Skill 6	Perform What-If Analyses Using Scenario Manager
Skill 7	Estimate Future Value
Skill 8	Insert Array Formulas
Skill 9	Calculate Conditional Sums
Skill 10	Calculate Conditional Averages

MORE SKILLS

Skill 11	Use Lookup and Nested Functions
Skill 12	Use Solver
Skill 13	Update Calculations Manually
Skill 14	Create Amortization Tables

Aspen Falls City Hall
Council Members Compensation

Name	Terms	Monthly Salary	Stipends	Stipends	Auto Allowance	Total Allowances	Gross Wages	Fed Tax	Health Insurance	Retirement	Net Wages
Candie Fenny	3	125.00	RA	600.00	500.00	1,100.00	1,100.00	242.00	251.70	143.00	463.30
Dexter Madise	2	125.00	HA	350.00	500.00	850.00	850.00	153.00	251.70	93.50	351.80
Ignacia Merica	2	125.00	HA	350.00	500.00	850.00	850.00	153.00	251.70	93.50	351.80
Maria Meynard	4	125.00	RA	600.00	500.00	1,100.00	1,100.00	242.00	503.40	165.00	189.60
Arleen Bagan	3	125.00	RA	600.00	500.00	1,100.00	1,100.00	242.00	503.40	143.00	211.60
Monthly Compensation		625.00		2,500.00	2,500.00	5,000.00	5,000.00	1,032.00	1,761.90	638.00	1,568.10
Total Employees	5										
Average High Allowances						1,000.00					

Retirement Future Value

Gross Wage	Fed Tax Rate	Terms	Retire Rate	Terms Served		Current Value	Value in 20 Years	High Benefits	High Value
500	0.18	1	0.08	0	Candie Fenny	28,440	131,574.08	FALSE	FALSE
1,000	0.22	2	0.11	2	Dexter Madise	16,560	80,723.57	FALSE	FALSE
1,500	0.25	3	0.13	2	Ignacia Merica	7,680	57,576.07	FALSE	FALSE
2,000	0.28	4	0.15	1	Maria Meynard	39,840	170,127.31	TRUE	TRUE
					Arleen Bagan	32,560	142,313.69	TRUE	TRUE

Stipends	Total	Total Allowances	Total Deductions			
Redevelopment Agency	1,800	5,000	3,432		*Total High FV*	312,441
Housing Authority	700				*Average High FV*	156,220

Last_First_exl06_Payroll

► The **CONCATENATE** function is a text function used to join the text from two or more cells into one cell.

► The **PROPER** function converts text to title case—the first letter of each word is capitalized.

1. Start **Excel 2016**, and then open the student data file **exl06_Payroll**. Click the **File tab**, and then click **Save As**. Click the **Browse** button, and then navigate to the location where you are saving your files. Click **New folder**, type Excel Chapter 6 and then press Enter two times. In the **File name** box, type Last_First_exl06_Payroll and then press Enter.

2. Click the **Employees** worksheet tab, and then click cell **M2**.

3. Click the **Formulas tab**. In the **Function Library group**, click the **Text** button, and then click **CONCATENATE**. Compare your screen with Figure 1.

4. In the **Function Arguments** dialog box, click in the **Text1** box, and then click cell **B2**. If necessary, move the dialog box. Press Tab to move the insertion point to the **Text2** box.

5. In the **Text2** box, press the Spacebar, and then press Tab to move to the **Text3** box. Notice the quotation marks inserted around the blank space in the **Text2** box.

   In function arguments, text must be enclosed in quotation marks. If they are not inserted, they will be added automatically. A **string** is any sequence of letters and numbers. It is designated by quotation marks.

6. With the insertion point in the **Text3** box, click cell **C2**. Compare your screen with Figure 2.

■ **Continue to the next page to complete the skill**

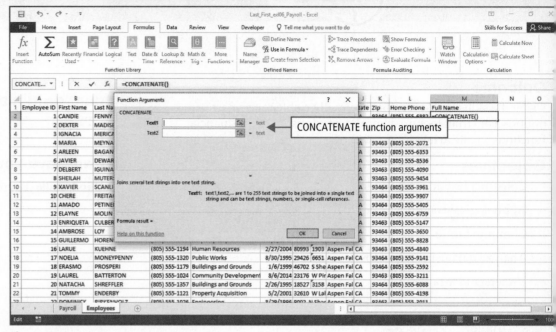

Figure 1

Excel 2016, Windows 10, Microsoft Corporation

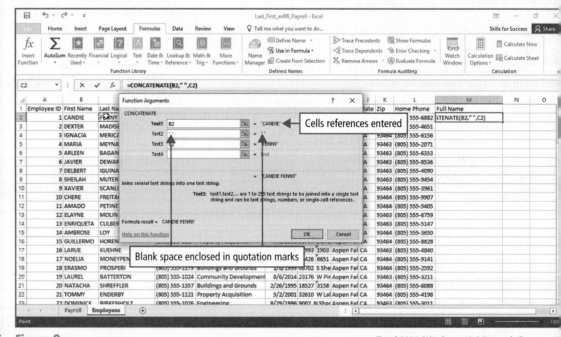

Figure 2

Excel 2016, Windows 10, Microsoft Corporation

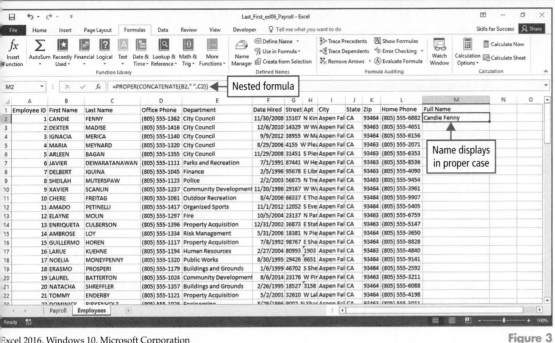

Excel 2016, Windows 10, Microsoft Corporation

Figure 3

7. Click **OK** to close the dialog box. Notice the displayed value in cell **M2**. Notice the full name displays in all capital letters.

> The CONCATENATE function combined the First Name and Last Name values into a single string. For readability, a blank space was inserted between the two fields.

8. With cell **M2** selected, click in the formula bar, and then position the insertion point between the (=) sign and the word *CONCATENATE*.

9. Type PROPER(Make sure to include the left open parenthesis after *PROPER*, and then press [End] to move the insertion point to the end of the expression in the formula bar. Add a closing parenthesis character) and then press [Enter]. Click cell **M2**, and then compare your screen with Figure 3.

> A *nested function* is a function placed inside another function. Here, the CONCATENATE function is nested within the PROPER function. The text is first concatenated, and then the PROPER function converts the result to title case.

10. With cell **M2** still selected, point to the **Fill Handle**, and then with the [+] pointer, drag down to cell **M103**. Press [Ctrl] + [Home], and then compare your screen with **Figure 4**.

11. Save [💾] the file.

■ **You have completed Skill 1 of 10**

Excel 2016, Windows 10, Microsoft Corporation

Figure 4

▶ When a cell or a group of cells is copied and then pasted into a new location, the formatting and underlying values of the original cell are pasted.

▶ You can use Paste Special to modify the formatting or underlying values of the contents being pasted.

1. On the **Employees** worksheet, select the range **M2:M6**. Click the **Home tab**, and in the **Clipboard group**, click **Copy** 📋.

2. Click the **Payroll** worksheet tab, and then click cell **A5**.

3. In the **Clipboard group**, click the **Paste** button. Point to the error message button ⚠ but do not click, and then read the message that displays, as shown in **Figure 1**.

The error indicator, error value (*#REF!*), and error message all indicate a problem with the function in the pasted cells. Here, the underlying values of the copied and pasted cells contain functions that concatenate text and convert it to title case. In the new location, these functions now refer to the wrong cells. Common error values are summarized in **Figure 2**.

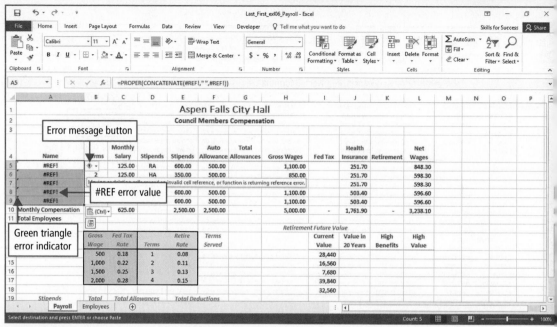

Figure 1

Excel 2016, Windows 10, Microsoft Corporation

Common Excel Error Values

Error Message	Error
#DIV/0!	Indicates that a number is being divided by zero
#N/A	When using a Lookup function, this displays if there is no match
#NAME?	Refers to formula text that Excel does not recognize in a formula
#REF?	Indicates that the referenced cells do not contain any data
#VALUE	Indicates that a formula contains the wrong type of data—for example, text instead of numbers

Figure 2

■ Continue to the next page to complete the skill

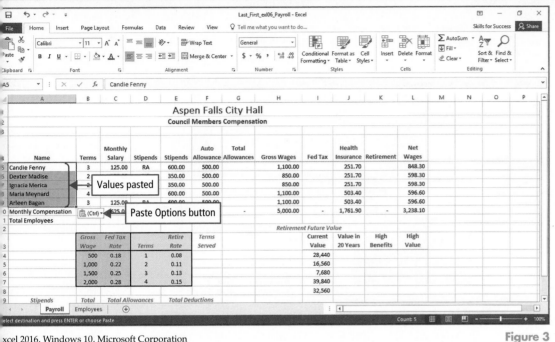

Figure 3

xcel 2016, Windows 10, Microsoft Corporation

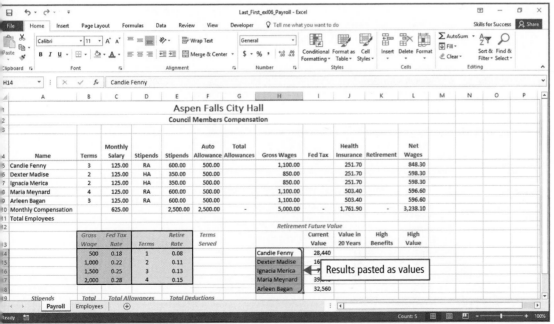

Figure 4

xcel 2016, Windows 10, Microsoft Corporation

4. Below and to the right of the range just pasted, click the **Paste Options** button. In the **Paste Options** gallery, under **Paste Values**, click the first button—**Values (V)**—and then compare your screen with Figure 3.

  The Values paste option pastes the displayed values of the copied cells instead of their underlying formulas. In this manner, the Paste Options button can change the underlying values when pasting cells.

5. Click cell **H14**. In the **Clipboard group**, click the **Paste arrow**, and then at the bottom of the **Paste gallery**, click **Paste Special**.

6. In the displayed **Paste Special** dialog box, under **Paste**, click **Values**, and then click **OK**. Press Esc, and then compare your screen with **Figure 4**.

  In this manner, you can choose a Paste Special option before pasting the contents.

7. **Save** the file.

■ **You have completed Skill 2 of 10**

▶ **Lookup functions** are used to find values that are stored in **lookup tables**—data organized into rows and columns in such a way that values can be easily retrieved.

▶ The **VLOOKUP** function finds values in a lookup table. The function searches down the table's first column.

MOS
Obj 3.2.1 E

1. Click cell **I5**. Click the **Formulas tab**. In the **Function Library group**, click the **Lookup & Reference** button, and then click **VLOOKUP**.

2. In the **Function Arguments** dialog box, with the insertion point in the **Lookup_value** box, type **H5** Press ⎄ Tab to move the insertion point to the **Table_array** box, and then compare your screen with **Figure 1**.

    The VLOOKUP function will search the lookup table for the Gross Wage value in cell H5.

3. In the **Table_array** box, click the **Collapse Dialog box** button 🔳, drag through the range **B14:C17**, and then press F4. Click the **Expand Dialog box** button 🔲, and then compare your screen with **Figure 2**.

    Recall that when you press F4, you create an absolute cell reference. Here, the lookup table is the range B14:C17. Referring to the lookup table using absolute cell references enables you to copy the cell reference to other cells without altering the cell references to the lookup table.

▪ **Continue to the next page to complete the skill** ➤

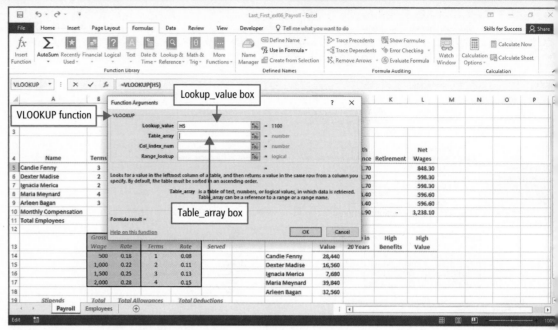

Figure 1

Excel 2016, Windows 10, Microsoft Corporation

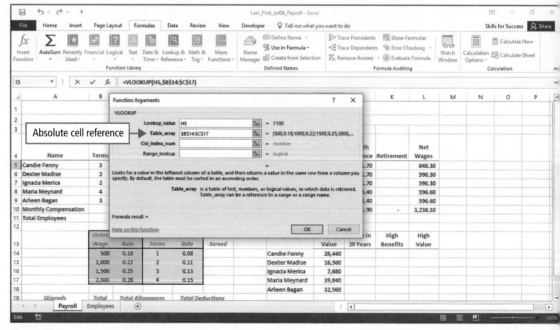

Figure 2

Excel 2016, Windows 10, Microsoft Corporation

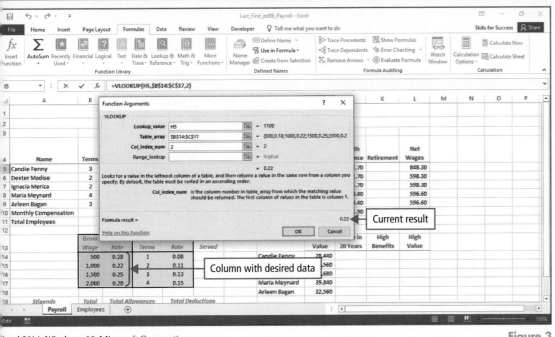

Excel 2016, Windows 10, Microsoft Corporation

Figure 3

4. Press [Tab] to move the insertion point to the **Col_index_num** box, and then type 2 Compare your screen with **Figure 3**.

   The VLOOKUP function searches the data table (B14:C17) for the value in cell H5. When it finds the value, it returns the value in the data table's second column (Col_index_num). The values in the first column of the table must be sorted in ascending order if an approximate match is desired.

5. Click **OK** to close the **Function Arguments** dialog box. In the formula bar, place the insertion point at the end of the formula, type *H5 and then click **Enter** ✓. Verify the value displayed is *242.00*—the result of gross wages times the tax rate for gross wages between 1,000 and 1,500. AutoFill the formula to the range **I6:I9**.

6. Click cell **K5**. In the **Function Library group**, click the **Lookup & Reference** button, and then click **VLOOKUP**. With the insertion point in the **Lookup_value** box, type B5 and then press [Tab].

7. Click the **Table_array Collapse Dialog** button 🔲, and then drag to select the range **D14:E17**. Press [F4], and then click the **Expand Dialog box** button 🔲. Press [Tab]. In the **Col_index_num** box, type 2 and then click **OK**.

8. Verify cell **K5** is selected. In the formula bar, type *H5 at the end of the formula, and then click **Enter** ✓. AutoFill the formula to the range **K6:K9**, and then compare your screen with **Figure 4**.

9. **Save** 🔲 the file.

■ **You have completed Skill 3 of 10**

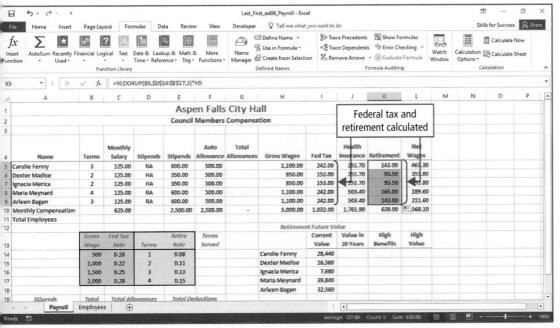

Excel 2016, Windows 10, Microsoft Corporation

Figure 4

▶ *Logical functions* are used to create formulas that test whether a condition is true or false.

1. Click cell **K14**, and then on the **Formulas tab**, in the **Function Library group**, click the **Logical** button. In the displayed list, click **AND**, and then compare your screen with **Figure 1**.

    The *AND* function evaluates two or more conditions. When all conditions are true, the displayed value is TRUE.

2. In the **Function Arguments** dialog box, with the cursor in the **Logical1** box, type J5>=255 Notice that this condition is *FALSE*.

3. Press Tab, and then in the **Logical2** box, type K5>125 Notice this condition is *TRUE*. Compare your screen with **Figure 2**.

4. Click **OK**. In cell **K14**, notice the displayed value is FALSE, indicating that Candie Fenny does not pay high benefits.

    Candie Fenny's health benefits deductions are less than $255, and her retirement benefits deductions are greater than $125. The benefits are being evaluated to see whether they meet both of the criteria. In this instance, only one condition meets the criteria.

■ **Continue to the next page to complete the skill** ▶

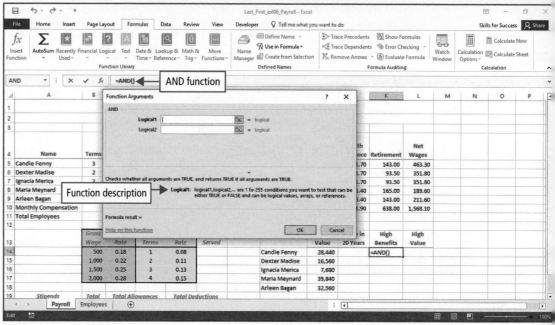

Figure 1

Excel 2016, Windows 10, Microsoft Corporation

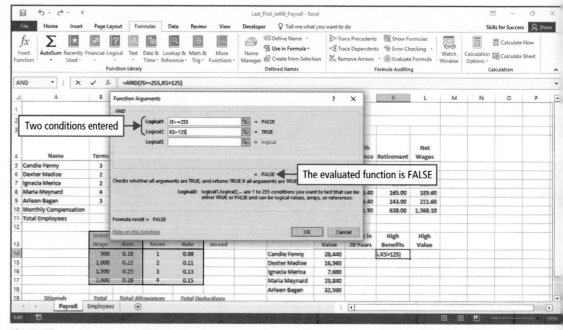

Figure 2

Excel 2016, Windows 10, Microsoft Corporation

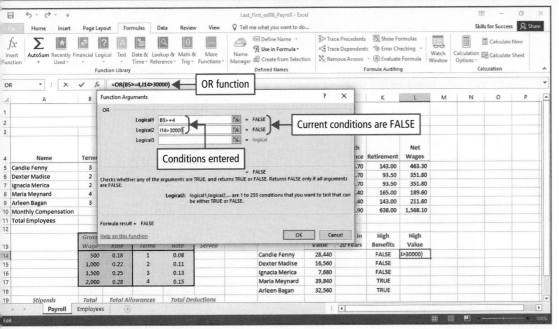

Excel 2016, Windows 10, Microsoft Corporation

Figure 3

Common Excel Logical Functions	
Function	**Description**
AND	Displays TRUE when all of the conditions are true
IF	Performs a test to determine when one of the specified conditions is true
IFERROR	Displays a message of your choice when there is an error in the formula; when there is not an error, it displays the result of the formula
NOT	Evaluates the opposite of a condition; for example, NOT<5 returns TRUE when the condition is not less than five
OR	Displays TRUE if any one of the conditions is TRUE

Figure 4

5. AutoFill the function in **K14** down through **K18**.

The values in K15:K16 are also FALSE because Dexter Madise and Ignacia Merica have low retirement and health insurance deductions. Maria Meynard and Arleen Bagan both have retirement deductions greater than $125 and health insurance deductions greater than $255, so the values returned are TRUE.

6. Click cell **L14**, and then in the **Function Library group**, click the **Logical** button. In the displayed list, click **OR**.
Obj 3.1.1 E

The **OR** function evaluates two or more conditions. If one condition is true, the displayed value is TRUE.

7. In the **Function Arguments** dialog box, with the cursor in the **Logical1** box, type B5>=4 Notice that this condition returns *FALSE*.

8. Press Tab, and then in the **Logical2** box, type I14>30000 Notice that this condition also returns *FALSE*. Compare your screen with **Figure 3**.

9. Click **OK**. AutoFill the function in **L14** down through **L18**.

The values in L14:L16 are FALSE because they don't meet either of the criteria; however, the values in L17:L18 are TRUE, even though the terms for Arleen Bagan do not meet those specified. Logical functions can be combined with each other or with many other functions to create a formula that is carefully designed to display the required information. Logical functions are summarized in **Figure 4**.

10. **Save** 💾 the file.

■ **You have completed Skill 4 of 10**

▶ The **COUNTA** function is used to count the number of cells containing specified values. When no values are specified, the number of cells in a range that are not blank is counted.

▶ The **COUNTIF** function is used to count the number of cells in a range that meet a specified condition. The condition might be a number, an expression, or text. When using COUNTIF, you need to specify the criterion that determines which cells in a range should be counted.

1. Click cell **B11**. On the **Formulas tab**, in the **Function Library group**, click the **More Functions** button. In the list, point to **Statistical**, and then click **COUNTA**. Compare your screen with Figure 1.

   COUNTA is a *statistical function*—used to describe a collection of data such as totals, counts, and averages.

2. In the **Function Arguments** dialog box, place the insertion point in the **Value1** box, and replace the existing text with A5:A9 Compare your screen with Figure 2, and then click **OK**.

3. Click cell **F14**. In the **Function Library group**, click the **More Functions** button, point to **Statistical**, and then click **COUNTIF**.

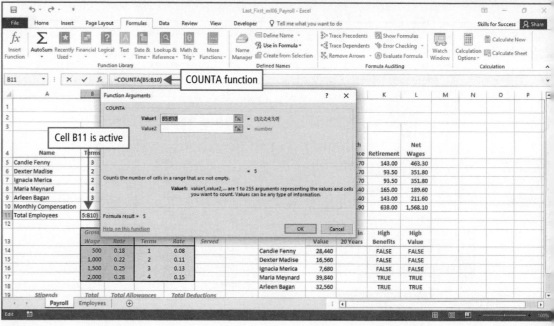

Figure 1   Excel 2016, Windows 10, Microsoft Corporation

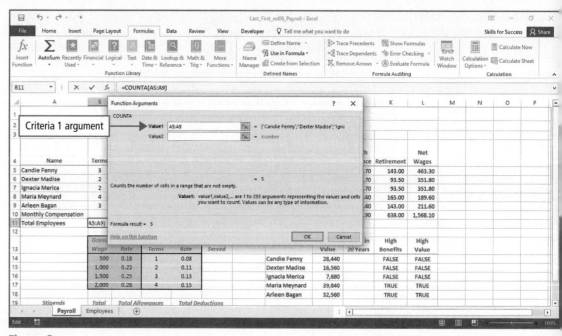

Figure 2   Excel 2016, Windows 10, Microsoft Corporation

■ Continue to the next page to complete the skill

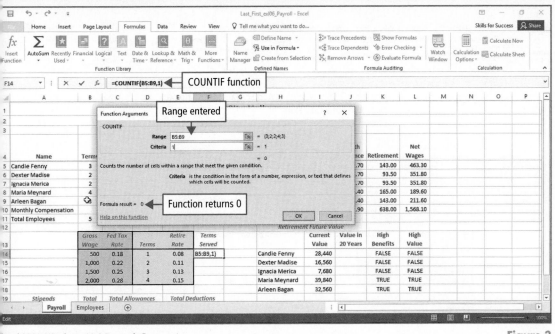

Excel 2016, Windows 10, Microsoft Corporation

Figure 3

4. In the **Function Arguments** dialog box, with the insertion point in the **Range** box, drag to select the range **B5:B9**, and then press [Tab].

5. In the **Criteria** box, type 1 Compare your screen with **Figure 3**, and then click **OK**.

Here, the COUNTIF function is used to count the number of cells with the value 1 in the range B5:B9. It returns the result of zero (0), which is displayed in the Function Arguments dialog box as a preview.

6. Click cell **F15**. In the **Function Library** group, click the **Recently Used** button, and then click **COUNTIF**. With the insertion point in the **Range** box, drag to select the range **B5:B9**, and then press [Tab]. In the **Criteria** box, type 2 and then click **OK**.

7. Click cell **F16**, and then repeat the technique previously practiced to insert a function that counts the number of times the value 3 is in the range **B5:B9**.

8. Click cell **F17**, and then repeat the technique previously practiced to insert a function that counts the number of times the value 4 is in the range **B5:B9**. Compare your screen with **Figure 4**.

9. Save 🖫 the file.

■ **You have completed Skill 5 of 10**

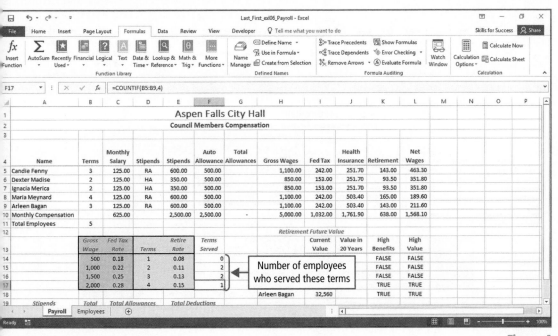

Excel 2016, Windows 10, Microsoft Corporation

Figure 4

▶ A ***what-if analysis*** is a set of tools that changes the values in cells to show how those changes affect the outcome of other formulas on the worksheet.

▶ In a what-if analysis, each set of assumptions is called a ***scenario***, which is a set of values that Excel can save and automatically substitute in cells.

▶ You can use Scenario Manager to save different groups of assumptions, and then switch to those scenarios to view the results.

1. Select the range **E14:E17**. Click the **Data tab**. In the **Forecast group**, click the **What-If Analysis** button, and then click **Scenario Manager**. If necessary, move the **Add Scenario** dialog box to the right to see the data in **E14:E17**.

   Before creating a scenario, you should select the cells that will change. Here, the Retire Rate values will be amended to show how the changes will affect the payroll.

2. In the **Scenario Manager** dialog box, click **Add**, and then compare your screen with Figure 1.

3. In the **Add Scenario** dialog box, with the insertion point in the **Scenario name** box, type Reduced Contributions and then press [Tab].

4. In the **Changing cells** box, verify that **E14:E17** is displayed, and then press [Tab]. Compare your screen with Figure 2.

   Because the range E14:E17 was selected when Scenario Manager was opened, the Changing cells box displays the selected range.

■ **Continue to the next page to complete the skill**

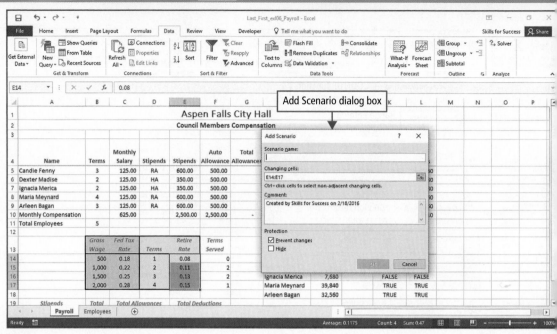

Figure 1

Excel 2016, Windows 10, Microsoft Corporation

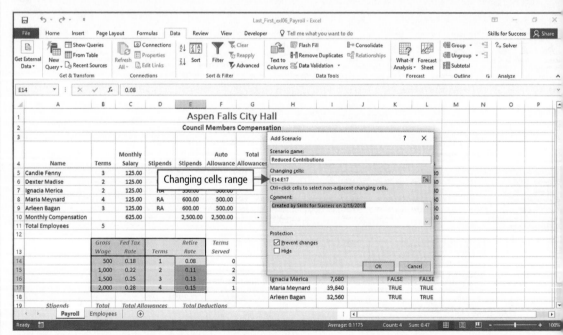

Figure 2

Excel 2016, Windows 10, Microsoft Corporation

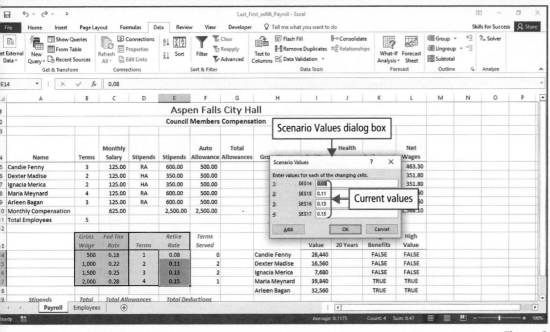

xcel 2016, Windows 10, Microsoft Corporation

Figure 3

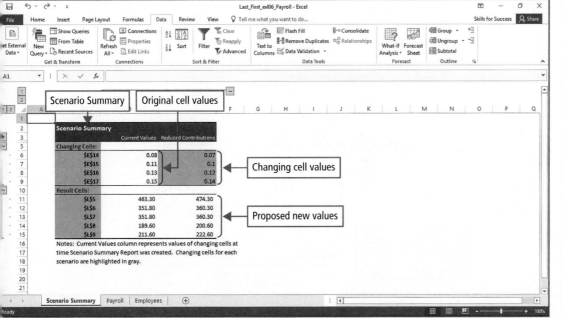

xcel 2016, Windows 10, Microsoft Corporation

Figure 4

5. In the **Comment** box, replace the existing text with Analyzes retirement rate reductions for council members

> A comment helps to recall the scenario assumptions and purpose.

6. Click **OK** to open the **Scenario Values** dialog box, and then compare your screen with **Figure 3**.

> The Scenario Values dialog box displays the current values in the range E14:E17. These values will be replaced with scenario values.

7. In the **Scenario Values** dialog box, with the insertion point in the box for **$E$14**, change the value to .07 Press Tab , and then change the value for **$E$15** to .10 Press Tab , and then change the value for **$E$16** to .12 In the **$E$17** box, change the value to .14 Click **OK**.

> Assuming these new values, final wages for each week can be calculated and presented as a proposal.

8. In the **Scenario Manager** dialog box, click **Summary**. In the **Scenario Summary** dialog box, in the **Result cells** box, type L5:L9 Click **OK**.

9. If necessary, display the **Scenario Summary** worksheet tab, and then compare your screen with **Figure 4**.

> The Scenario Summary worksheet displays the original and the Reduced Contributions scenario values. In this scenario, net wages increased.

10. Click the **Payroll** worksheet. Notice that none of the values in the range **E14:E17** changed on the original worksheet.

11. Save 🔚 the file.

■ **You have completed Skill 6 of 10**

▶ The *future value (FV)* of an asset, such as an investment or a home, is its value at the end of a period of time.

▶ The future value of an asset can be calculated when constant payments are made over time and the interest rate remains fixed.

1. On the **Payroll** worksheet tab, click cell **J14**.

2. Click the **Formulas tab**, and then in the **Function Library group**, click the **Financial** button. If necessary, scroll down the displayed list, and click **FV**. Compare your screen with **Figure 1**.

   The FV function requires three arguments: the interest rate for each payment, the total number of payments, and the payment amount. When calculating the future value of an investment, the present value of the investment can also be entered here. The Type argument also is optional. It is either 0 or 1; if omitted, it is assumed to be 0. This indicates payments are made at the end of the period.

3. In the **Function Arguments** dialog box, with the insertion point in the **Rate** box, type 4.8%/12 and then press Tab. Compare your screen with **Figure 2**.

   Here, the annual interest rate of 4.8% is divided by 12 to calculate the interest rate for each monthly payment.

4. In the **Nper** box, type 12*20 and then press Tab to move to the **Pmt** box.

   The monthly payments to the council members' retirement account will be made for 20 years. The total number of payments—Nper—equals 12 multiplied by 20.

▪ **Continue to the next page to complete the skill**

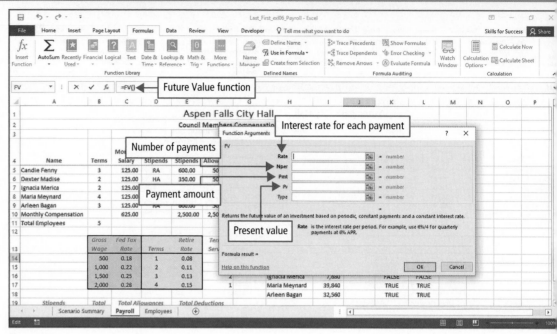

Figure 1

Excel 2016, Windows 10, Microsoft Corporation

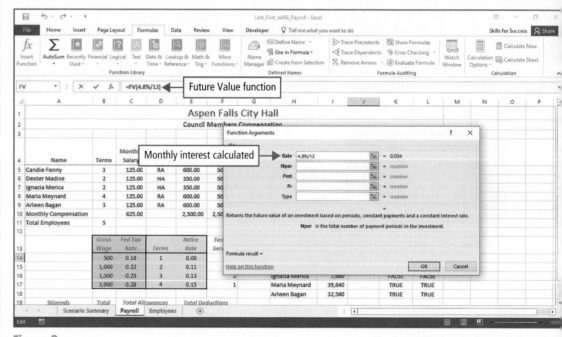

Figure 2

Excel 2016, Windows 10, Microsoft Corporation

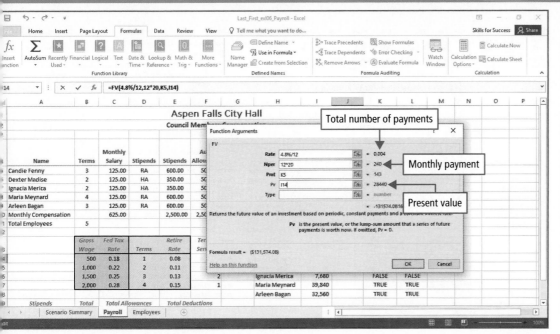

Total number of payments

Monthly payment

Present value

Figure 3

Excel 2016, Windows 10, Microsoft Corporation

Common Financial Functions

Function	Description
FV	The value of an investment or asset at some point in the future
NPER	The total number of payments made over the term of a loan or the total number of contributions made to an investment
PV	The value of an investment or loan at the beginning of its term
PMT	The amount of money being paid to reduce a loan value or increase the value of an asset
RATE	The interest earned by an investment or the interest paid for a loan

Figure 4

5. In the **Pmt** box, type K5 and then press [Tab] to move to the **Pv** box.

6. In the **Pv** box, type I14 and then compare your screen with Figure 3.

   The present value of this investment is the current value that is in cell I14—Candie Fenny's retirement account.

7. Click **OK** to close the dialog box. AutoFit column J.

8. With cell **J14** selected, place the insertion point in the **formula bar** between the (=) symbol and **FV**. Type - (minus sign), and then press [Enter].

   In financial formulas, payments are typically represented as negative numbers. Placing a negative sign before the formula converts the payment and future value into positive numbers.

9. AutoFill the function in **J14** down through **J18**.

   Common financial functions are summarized in Figure 4.

10. Save 🖫 the file.

■ **You have completed Skill 7 of 10**

▶ An *array* is a collection of data typically arranged in multiple columns and rows. Most workbooks arrange data in arrays.

▶ An *array formula* can perform calculations across multiple items in an array. For example, you can use an array formula to calculate the sum of the values in one column multiplied by the sum of the values in another column.

1. On the **Payroll** worksheet, select the range **G5:G9**.

    Because array formulas are applied to a range of cells, you should first select the range in which the array formula will be inserted.

2. Type = to begin the formula. Type E5:E9 type + and then type F5:F9 Press and hold [Ctrl] and [Shift], and then press [Enter]. Compare your screen with **Figure 1**.

    When you enter a formula using the [Ctrl] + [Shift] + [Enter] keyboard shortcut, the formula is enclosed with braces ({ and }) to signify that it is an array formula. Here, the results of the array formula are the same as adding the values in E5:E9 and F5:F9. However, with an array formula, the formula is the same in every row. In this manner, array formulas provide greater consistency than using AutoFill to write separate formulas.

3. Click cell **D20**. Type = to begin the sum function, and then type sum followed by a left parenthesis: (Compare your screen with **Figure 2**.

▪ **Continue to the next page to complete the skill** ▶

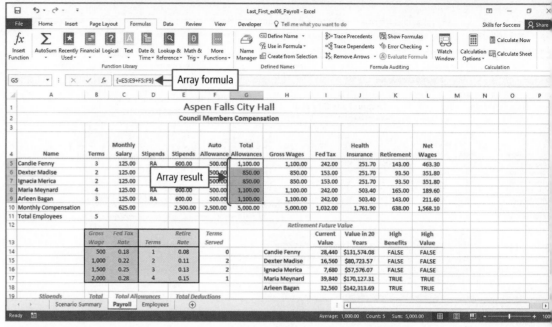

Figure 1

Excel 2016, Windows 10, Microsoft Corporation

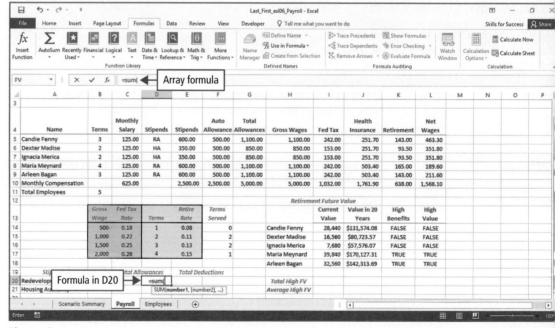

Figure 2

Excel 2016, Windows 10, Microsoft Corporation

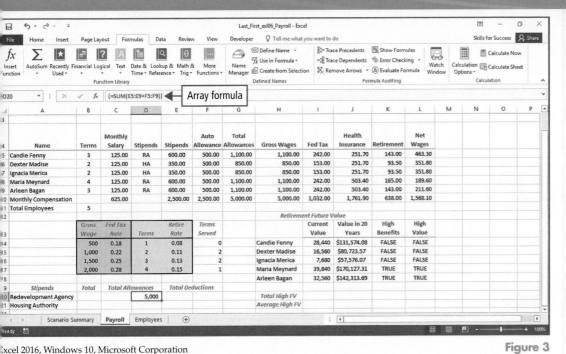

Figure 3

Excel 2016, Windows 10, Microsoft Corporation

4. Select the range **E5:E9**, and then type +
   Select the range **F5:F9**, and then type the
   right parenthesis:)

5. Press and hold Ctrl and Shift keys, and
   then press Enter . Compare your screen
   with **Figure 3**.

   In D20, the formula {=SUM(E5:E9+F5:F9)}
   appears in the formula bar, and represents
   the total number of allowances for the
   month.

6. Click cell **F20**. Type = to begin the sum
   function, and then type sum followed by
   a left parenthesis: (

7. Select the range **I5:I9**, and then type +
   Select the range **J5:J9**, and then type +

8. Select the range **K5:K9**, and then type the
   right parenthesis:)

9. Press and hold Ctrl and Shift keys, and
   then press Enter . Compare your screen
   with **Figure 4**.

   In F20, the formula {=SUM(I5:I9+J5:J9
   +K5:K9)} appears in the formula bar, and
   represents the total number of deductions
   for the month.

10. Save 🖫 the file.

■ **You have completed Skill 8 of 10**

Figure 4

Excel 2016, Windows 10, Microsoft Corporation

▶ The **SUMIF** function adds the cells in a range that meet a specified criterion.

▶ The **SUMIFS** function adds the cells in a range that meet multiple criteria.

---

1. On the **Payroll** worksheet, click cell **B20**.

MOS
Obj 4.2.2 C
2. Click the **Formulas tab**, and then in the **Function Library group**, click the **Math & Trig** button. Scroll down the displayed list, and then click **SUMIF**. Compare your screen with **Figure 1**.

3. In the **Function Arguments** dialog box, with the insertion point in the **Range** box, type D5:D9 and then press Tab.

   In the SUMIF function, the Range argument defines the range to be tested by the criteria. Here, the Range lists the stipends to be evaluated.

4. In the **Criteria** box, type RA and then press Tab.

   Here, only the cells where the job category equals RA will be added.

5. In the **Sum_range** box, type E5:E9 and then compare your screen with **Figure 2**. Click **OK**.

6. Click cell **B21**. Repeat the techniques previously practiced to create a **SUMIF** function applying the same **Range** and **Sum_Range**, but replacing the **Criteria** with HA

MOS
Obj 3.1.3 E
7. Click cell **I20**. On the **Formulas tab**, in the **Function Library group**, click the **Math & Trig** button. Scroll down the displayed list, and then click **SUMIFS**.

■ **Continue to the next page to complete the skill**

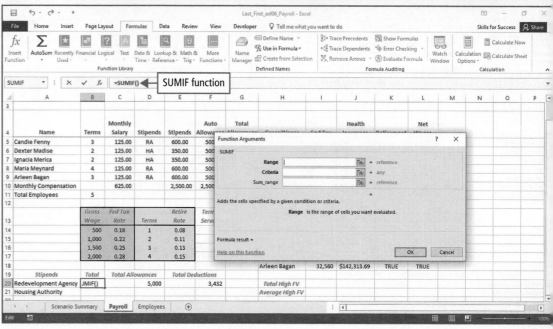

Figure 1

Excel 2016, Windows 10, Microsoft Corporation

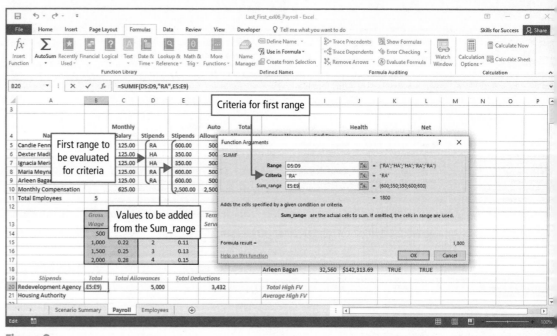

Figure 2

Excel 2016, Windows 10, Microsoft Corporation

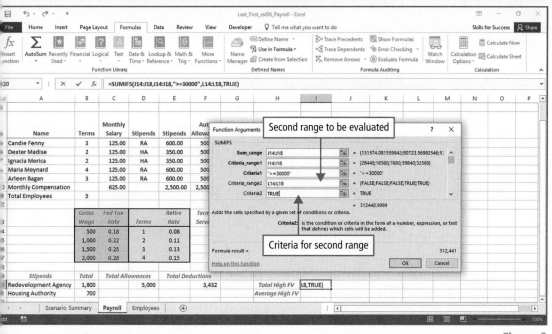

xcel 2016, Windows 10, Microsoft Corporation

Figure 3

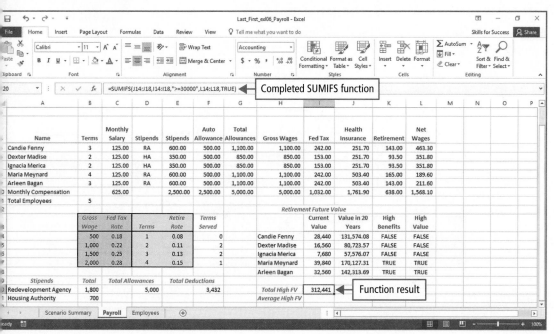

xcel 2016, Windows 10, Microsoft Corporation

Figure 4

8. In the **Function Arguments** dialog box, with the insertion point in the **Sum_range** box, type J14:J18 and then press Tab .

In the SUMIFS function, the Sum_range argument contains the values to be added. In this exercise, the Sum_range argument lists Future Retirement Value.

9. In the **Criteria_range1** box, type I14:I18 and then press Tab .

Criteria_range1 is the range that will be evaluated for the specified condition.

10. In the **Criteria1** box, type >=30000 and then press Tab .

Criteria1 is a condition or criterion in the form of a number, an expression, or text that defines which cells will be added.

11. In the **Criteria_range2** box, type L14:L18 and then press Tab .

Criteria_range2 is the range that will be evaluated for the second criterion.

12. In the **Criteria2** box, type TRUE Compare your screen with **Figure 3**.

Criteria2 is a condition or criterion in the form of a number, an expression, or text that defines which cells will be added for the second criterion.

13. Click **OK**, and then notice the value of cell **I20** is *312,441*, which is the sum of **J17:J18**. Compare your screen with **Figure 4**.

14. Save 🖫 the file.

■ **You have completed Skill 9 of 10**

▶ The **AVERAGEIF** function is used to calculate the average for cells that meet specified criteria.

▶ The **AVERAGEIFS** function is used to calculate the average for cells that meet multiple criteria.

1. On the **Payroll** worksheet, click cell **A12**. Type Average High Allowances AutoFit column **A**, and then click cell **G12**.

2. On the **Formulas tab**, in the **Function Library group**, click **More Functions**. Point to **Statistical**, and then click **AVERAGEIF**. Compare your screen with **Figure 1**.

3. In the **Function Arguments** dialog box, with the insertion point in the **Range** box, type E5:F9 and then press [Tab].

   In the AVERAGEIF function, the Range argument defines the range to be tested by the criteria. Here, the Range lists the allowances to be evaluated.

4. In the **Criteria** box, type >0 and then press [Tab].

   Here, only the cells where the stipend or auto allowance is greater than 0 will be averaged.

5. In the **Average_range** box, type G5:G9 and then compare your screen with **Figure 2**. Click **OK**.

   In the AVERAGEIF function, the Average_range argument contains the values to be averaged.

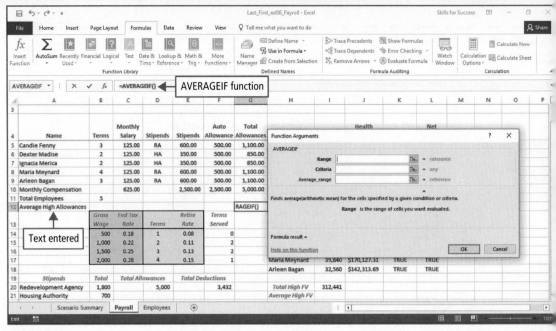

Figure 1

Excel 2016, Windows 10, Microsoft Corporatio

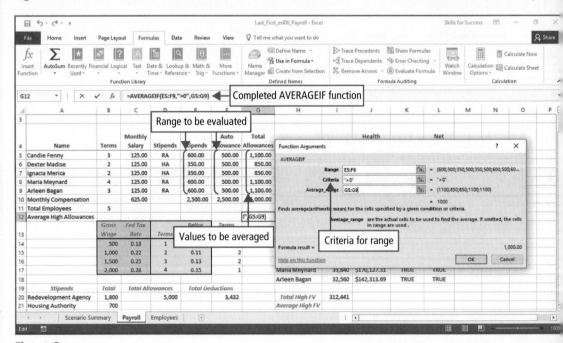

Figure 2

Excel 2016, Windows 10, Microsoft Corporatio

■ **Continue to the next page to complete the skill**

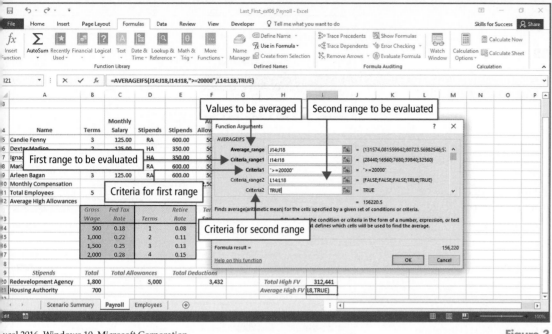

Excel 2016, Windows 10, Microsoft Corporation

Figure 3

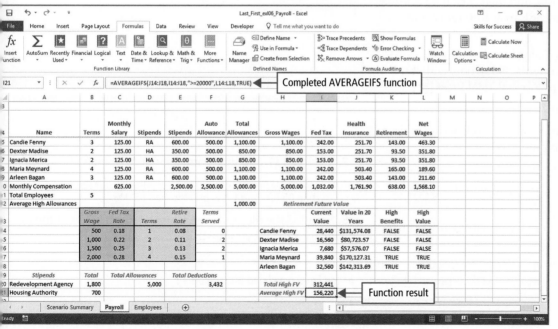

xcel 2016, Windows 10, Microsoft Corporation

Figure 4

6. Click cell **I21**. In the **Function Library** group, click **More Functions**, point to **Statistical**, and then click **AVERAGEIFS**.

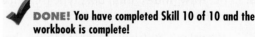

7. In the **Function Arguments** dialog box, with the insertion point in the **Average_range** box, type J14:J18 and then press Tab.

   In the AVERAGEIFS function, the Average_range argument contains the values to be averaged.

8. In the **Criteria_range1** box, type I14:I18 and then press Tab.

   Criteria_range1 is the range that will be evaluated for the first criterion.

9. In the **Criteria1** box, type >=20000 and then press Tab.

   Criteria1 defines which cell will be averaged.

10. In the **Criteria_range2** box, type L14:L18 and then press Tab.

    Criteria_range2 is the range that will be evaluated for the second criterion.

11. In the **Criteria2** box, type TRUE. Compare your screen with **Figure 3**.

    Criteria2 defines which cell will be averaged for the second criterion.

12. Click **OK**, and then notice that the value of cell **I21** is *156,220*, which is the average of **J17:J18**. Compare your screen with **Figure 4**.

13. **Save** the file, and then submit the file as directed by your instructor.

✔ **DONE! You have completed Skill 10 of 10 and the workbook is complete!**

More Skills 11

Use Lookup and Nested Functions

To complete this project, you will need the following file:

- exl06_MS11Revenue

You will save your file as:

- Last_First_exl06_MS11Revenue

▶ The **HLOOKUP** function looks for a value in the top row of a table or array of values and returns the value in the same column from a row you specify.

▶ When combining the logical functions IF, AND, and OR, the formula is more flexible and conditions can be added or removed without rewriting the entire formula.

Figure 1 Excel 2016, Windows 10, Microsoft Corporation

1. Start **Excel 2016**, and then open the student data file **exl06_MS11Revenue**. Save the file in your chapter folder as Last_First_exl06_MS11Revenue

2. Click the **Location** worksheet tab. Click cell **M4**, and then click the **Formulas tab**. In the **Function Library group**, click the **Lookup & Reference** button, and then click **HLOOKUP**.

3. If necessary, move the **Function Arguments** dialog box down to row **7** so you can see cell **M4**. In the **Function Arguments** dialog box, with the insertion point in the **Lookup_value** box, type Annual Total Press `Tab`.

   Here, *Annual Total* is the lookup value in the row.

4. With the insertion point in the **Table_array** box, click cell **A3**, and then drag to select the range **A3:F8**. Press `F4`, and then press `Tab`.

   This is the table_array where the data is looked up.

5. In the **Row_index_num** box, type 6 Compare your screen with **Figure 1**. Click **OK**.

   The value *708010* will appear in M4. It is the value located in the sixth row of the table_array under *Annual Total*.

6. Click cell **I4**. Type the formula =IF(OR(AND(A4="North",B4<35000),AND(B3="2nd Quarter",C4>35000)),"Increase","Decrease") and then press `Enter`.

Obj 3.1.2 E
Obj 3.1.1 E
Obj 4.2.1 C

Figure 2 Excel 2016, Windows 10, Microsoft Corporation

7. Click cell **I4**, and then compare your screen with **Figure 2**.

   Increase is the result in I4. A4 has the text North and B4 is less than 35,000 and C4 is greater than 35,000.

8. **Save** the file, and then **Close** Excel. Submit the file as directed by your instructor.

■ **You have completed More Skills 11**

More Skills 12

Use Solver

To complete this project, you will need the following file:

- exl06_MS12Funds

You will save your file as:

- Last_First_exl06_MS12Funds

▶ **Solver** is a what-if analysis tool used to find solutions to complex problems.
▶ Solver looks for solutions to achieve a desired goal.

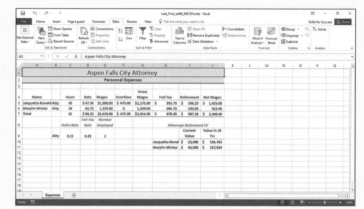

Excel 2016, Windows 10, Microsoft Corporation   Figure 1

1. Start **Excel 2016**, and then open the student data file **exl06_MS12Funds**. Save the file in your chapter folder as Last_First_exl06_MS12Funds

2. Click the **Data tab**, and then verify that the **Analyze group** and **Solver** button display as shown in Figure 1.

    Solver is an **Excel add-in**—a tool that adds features and commands to Excel, extending Excel's capabilities as if the tool were part of Excel. Add-ins must be installed before they can be used.

3. If the **Solver** button is displayed, then skip to Step 4. If not, click the **File tab**, and then click **Options**. In **Excel Options**, click **Add-ins**. If necessary, click the **Manage box arrow**, click **Excel Add-ins**, and then click **Go**. In the **Add-ins** dialog box, click the **Solver Add-in** check box, and then click **OK**. Verify that the **Solver** button has been installed.

4. Notice the values in **C9** and **J10:J11**. In the **Analyze group**, click **Solver**. In the **Solver Parameters** dialog box, with the insertion point in the **Set Objective** box, type $J$10   *(MOS)*   Obj 3.4.3 E

5. Click the **Value of** option button, and then in the box, type 250000

    The goal is to have $250,000 in retirement savings for Jacquetta Ronald by changing the retirement rate or the pay rate.

6. In the **By Changing Variable Cells** box, type D5, C9 and then click **Add**.

7. In the **Add Constraint** dialog box, in the **Cell Reference** box, type D5 In the **Constraint** box, type 55.00 and then click **Add**.

8. In the **Cell Reference** box, type C9 In the **Constraint** box, type 55.00 and then click **OK**.

9. Click **Solve**, and then read the **Solver Results** message box. Verify that the **Keep Solver Solution** option is selected, and then click **Save Scenario**. Save the **Scenario** as Maximize Retirement and then click **OK** two times. Notice the *Retire Rate* changed in **C9** and the *Value in 20 Yrs* changed in **J10:J11**.

10. If the Solver add-in was previously installed on your computer, skip to Step 11. Click the **File tab**, click **Options**, and then in **Excel Options**, click **Add-ins**. In the **Manage** box, click **Go**. In the **Add-ins** dialog box, clear the **Solver Add-in** check box, and then click **OK**.

11. **Save** ⊟ the file, and then **Close** ✕ Excel. Submit the file as directed by your instructor.

- **You have completed More Skills 12**

More Skills 13

Update Calculations Manually

To complete this project, you will need the following file:

- exl06_MS13Golf

You will save your files as:

- Last_First_exl06_MS13Golf
- Last_First_exl06_MS13Snip

▶ *Calculation* is the process that Excel uses to compute formulas and functions and display the results.

▶ The default calculation setting is automatic, which results in the calculations being updated each time a cell is changed.

▶ You can set calculations to update manually when you open the file or click the Calculate Now button.

---

1. Start **Excel 2016**, and then open the student data file **exl06_MS13Golf**. Save the file in your chapter folder as Last_First_exl06_MS13Golf As you complete the next step, watch the values in the range **L9:L12**.

2. Click cell **H9**, type 5 and then press Enter. In cell **H10**, type 6 and then press Enter. In cell **H11**, type 4 and then press Enter. In cell **H12**, type 4 and then click cell **A1**.

   The values in the range L9:L12 are calculated using a SUM function. Excel automatically recalculated the totals in column L as the figures were entered in column H.

3. Click the **Formulas tab**, and then in the **Calculation group**, click the **Calculation Options** button. Compare your screen with Figure 1.

   You can use Calculation Options to set the calculation method for a workbook. In workbooks with thousands of rows, you may want to perform calculations manually instead of each time a precedent cell value is changed.

4. In the **Calculation Options** list, click **Manual**.

5. Click cell **I9**, type 4 and then press Enter. In cell **I10**, type 5 and then press Enter. In cell **I11**, type 3 and then press Enter. In cell **I12**, type 4 and then press Enter. In **L9:L12**, notice that the values did not update to reflect the new values.

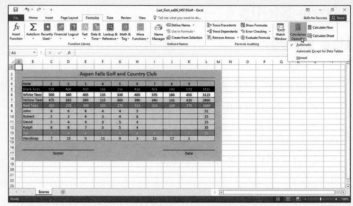

Figure 1 Excel 2016, Windows 10, Microsoft Corporation

6. On the **Formulas tab**, in the **Calculation group**, click the **Calculate Now** button to manually update the calculations.

7. Using the table below, enter the values in columns **J** and **K**. As you type, notice that the values in column **L** do not change:

Row	Column J	Column K
9	3	8
10	3	7
11	5	4
12	4	6

8. Use the **Snipping Tool** to take a full-screen snip of the window, and then save the file in your chapter folder as Last_First_exl06_MS13Snip **Close** ☒ the Snipping Tool window.

9. In the **Calculation group**, click **Calculation Options**, and then click **Automatic**.

   Here, the values in column L are updated.

10. **Save** 🖫 the file, and then **Close** ☒ Excel. Submit the files as directed by your instructor.

■ **You have completed More Skills 13**

More Skills 14

Create Amortization Tables

To complete this project, you will need the following file:

- exl06_MS14Loan

You will save your file as:

- Last_First_exl06_MS14Loan

▶ *Amortization tables* track loan payments over the life of a loan.

▶ Each row in an amortization table tracks how much of a payment is applied to the principal—the amount owed—and how much is applied to the interest—the cost of the loan.

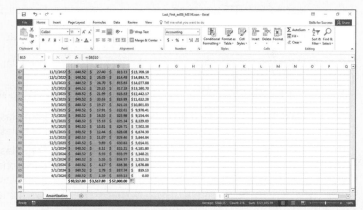

Excel 2016, Windows 10, Microsoft Corporation

Figure 1

1. Start **Excel 2016**, and then open the student data file **exl06_MS14Loan**. Save the file in your chapter folder as Last_First_exl06_MS14Loan

2. Click cell **B10**. Click the **Formulas tab**. In the **Function Library group**, click **Financial**, scroll down, and then click **PMT**.

   Obj 3.4.5 E

   Recall that the PMT function calculates the payment amount required to pay off a loan for a given amount, a given number and frequency of payments, and a given interest rate.

3. In the **Function Arguments** dialog box, with the insertion point in the **Rate** box, type B7/12 Press [Tab]. With the insertion point in the **Nper** box, click cell **B9**, and then press [Tab]. With the insertion point in the **Pv** box, click cell **B6**, and then click **OK**.

   The payment amount is displayed in red, indicating that the value is negative—an outflow of cash. Because payments are made each month, the interest rate is divided by 12 to convert the annual rate to a monthly rate.

4. Click cell **B15**, type =-$B$10 and then press [Tab].

   The amount will be converted to a positive number and the monthly payment will refer to the value in cell B15 for every row of the table. The reference needs to be an absolute cell reference so that it does not change when the formula is copied to the other rows.

5. In cell **C15**, type =E14*$B$7/12 and then press [Tab].

   The interest payment is equal to the current balance multiplied by the monthly interest rate. The interest rate is an absolute cell reference so that the formula refers to the value in cell B7 when the formula is copied.

6. In cell **D15**, type =B15-C15 and then press [Tab].

   The new balance is equal to the previous balance minus the payment amount applied to the loan principal.

7. Select the range **B15:D15**, and then drag the fill handle down to row **86**. Compare your screen to **Figure 1**.

   Row 86 shows that for the last payment, the interest charge is $1.39, $839.13 is applied to the principal, and the remaining balance is $0.00.

8. **Save** 🖫 the file, and then **Close** ☒ Excel. Submit the file as directed by your instructor.

- **You have completed More Skills 14**

Skills Number	Task	Step
1	Join text	Formulas tab → Function Library group → Text → CONCATENATE
1	Convert text to title case	Formulas tab → Function Library group → Text → PROPER
3	Calculate totals based on criteria	Formulas tab → Function Library group → Math & Trig → SUMIFS
4	Use lookup functions	Formulas tab → Function Library group → Lookup & Reference → VLOOKUP
4	Use logical function AND	Formulas tab → Function Library group → Logical → AND
4	Use logical function OR	Formulas tab → Function Library group → Logical → OR
5	Insert COUNTIF functions	Formulas tab → Function Library group → More Functions → Statistical → COUNTIF
6	Create and save scenarios	Data tab → Forecast group → What-If Analysis → Scenario Manager → Add → Enter Name
7	Calculate future value	Formulas tab → Function Library group → Financial → FV → Enter Rate, Nper, Pmt, and PV
8	Create array formulas	Press Ctrl + Shift + Enter after writing the desired formula
9	Calculate totals based on criteria	Formulas tab → Function Library group → Math & Trig → SUMIF Formulas tab → Function Library group → Math & Trig → SUMIFS
10	Calculate averages based on criteria	Formulas tab → Function Library group → More Functions → Statistical → AVERAGEIF Formulas tab → Function Library group → More Functions → Statistical → AVERAGEIFS
MS11	Use lookup function HLOOKUP	Formulas tab → Function Library group → Lookup & Reference button → HLOOKUP
MS12	Use Solver	Data tab → Analyze group → Solver
MS12	Install Excel add-ins	File tab → Options → Add-ins → Excel Add-ins
MS13	Update Calculations Manually	Formulas tab → Calculation group → Calculate Now
MS13	Change Calculation Settings	Formulas tab → Calculation group → Calculation Options
MS14	Use financial function PMT	Formulas tab → Function Library group → Financial → PMT

Project Summary Chart

Project	Project Type	Project Location
Skills Review	Review	In Book & MIL MyITLab® Grader
Skills Assessment 1	Review	In Book & MIL MyITLab® Grader
Skills Assessment 2	Review	Book
My Skills	Problem Solving	Book
Visual Skills Check	Problem Solving	Book
Skills Challenge 1	Critical Thinking	Book
Skills Challenge 2	Critical Thinking	Book
More Skills Assessment	Review	In Book & MIL MyITLab® Grader
Collaborating with Google	Critical Thinking	Book

MOS Objectives Covered (Quiz in MyITLab®)

2.1.3 C Paste data by using special paste options	3.1.1 E Perform logical operations by using AND, OR, and NOT functions
4.1.4 C Perform calculations by using the COUNT function	3.1.2 E Perform logical operations by using nested functions (other than IF)
4.2.1 C Perform logical functions by using the IF function	3.1.3 E Perform statistical operations by using AVERAGEIFS function
4.2.2 C Perform logical operations by using the SUMIF function	3.1.3 E Perform statistical operations by using SUMIFS function
4.2.3 C Perform logical operations by using the AVERAGEIF function	3.2.1 E Look up data by using the VLOOKUP function
4.2.4 C Perform statistical operations by using the COUNTIF function	3.2.2 E Utilize HLOOKUP function
4.3.2 C Format text by using PROPER functions	3.4.3 E Perform what-if analysis by using Goal Seek and Scenario Manager
4.3.3 C Format text by using the CONCATENATE function	3.4.5 E Calculate data by using financial functions
1.2.3 E Configure formula calculation options	3.5.3 E Validate formulas by using error checking rules

Key Terms

Online Help Skills

1. **Start Excel 2016**, and then in the upper right corner of the start page, click the **Help** button ⸢?⸣.

2. In the **Excel 2016 Help** window **Search** box, type what-if analysis and then press ⸢Enter⸣.

3. In the search result list, click **Calculate multiple results by using a data table**, and then click **What next?**. **Maximize** the Excel Help window, and then compare your screen with **Figure 1**.

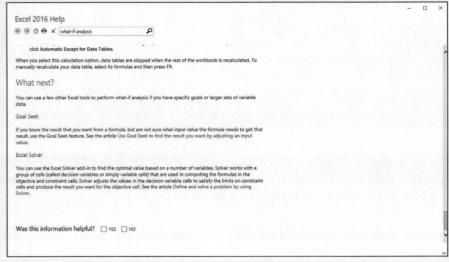

Figure 1   Excel 2016, Windows 10, Microsoft Corporation

4. Read the section to see if you can answer the following: When should you use the Goal Seek tool, and when should you use the Solver add-in?

Matching

Match each term in the second column with its correct definition in the first column by writing the letter of the term on the blank line in front of the correct definition.

___ **1.** A function that returns TRUE if *any* argument is true and returns FALSE if *both* arguments are false.

___ **2.** A function that counts the number of specified cells in a range.

___ **3.** A function placed inside another function.

___ **4.** A function that is used to find values that are stored in a table in a spreadsheet.

___ **5.** A function that displays TRUE only when all of the conditions are true.

___ **6.** A function that averages values based on multiple conditions.

___ **7.** A function that describes a collection of data; for example, COUNTA and COUNTIF.

___ **8.** A function that returns and displays either TRUE or FALSE.

___ **9.** A set of saved assumptions that can be used to view the results if those assumed values were accepted.

___ **10.** The function used to calculate the value of an investment or asset at some point in the future.

A AND

B AVERAGEIFS

C COUNTA

D FV

E Logical function

F Lookup function

G Nested function

H OR

I Scenario

J Statistical function

Multiple Choice (MyITLab®)

Choose the correct answer.

1. Use this option to change the formatting or underlying values of cells as they are pasted.
   - A. Paste
   - B. Paste Special
   - C. Copy

2. This function is used to convert text to title case.
   - A. CONCATENATE
   - B. PROPER
   - C. SUBSTITUTE

3. This function is used to count the number of cells in a range that meet a certain criterion.
   - A. COUNTA
   - B. SUM
   - C. COUNTIF

4. Use this tool to change cells to see how those changes affect a desired outcome.
   - A. Goal Seek analysis
   - B. What-if analysis
   - C. Data table

5. This is the correct format to calculate the annual interest rate.
   - A. rate/12
   - B. rate/6
   - C. rate/18

6. In Future Value functions, enter 0 or 1 in this box to indicate if payments are due at the beginning or end of the period.
   - A. Type
   - B. Pv
   - C. Rate

7. This function is used to join text from separate cells and columns.
   - A. LINK
   - B. CONCATENATE
   - C. JOIN

8. The amount of money being paid to reduce a loan value or increase the value of an asset.
   - A. Pv
   - B. PMT
   - C. NPER

9. This error indicates that the referenced cell does not contain any data.
   - A. #VALUE
   - B. #N/A
   - C. #REF

10. This type of formula performs calculations across multiple ranges.
    - A. COUNTIF
    - B. Array
    - C. Scenario

Topics for Discussion

1. When inputting assumed values in what-if analyses, you can copy and paste the results into separate worksheets or save them as scenarios using Scenario Manager. Which method do you think would be most effective, and why?

2. In Skill 8, you used an array formula. The same results could have been obtained by entering a regular formula and filling it down the column. Compare the two methods, and then discuss the advantages and disadvantages of each method.

Skills Review

MyITLab®
Grader

To complete this project, you will need the following file:

- exl06_SRTaxes

You will save your file as:

- Last_First_exl06_SRTaxes

---

1. Start **Excel 2016**, and then open the student data file **exl06_SRTaxes**. Save the file in your chapter folder as Last_First_exl06_SRTaxes

2. Display the **Properties** worksheet. Click cell **C2**. Click the **Formulas tab**. In the **Function Library group**, click the **Text** button, and then click **PROPER**. In the **Text** box, type aspen falls and then click **OK**. Copy the formula in **C2** down through **C38**.

3. Click cell **J2**. On the **Formulas tab**, in the **Function Library group**, click the **Text button**, and then click **CONCATENATE**. In the **Text1** box, type C2 In the **Text2** box, add a comma, and then a space. In the **Text3** box, type D2 and then click **OK**. AutoFit column **J**, and then copy the formula down through cell **J38**. Compare with Figure 1.

4. Copy the range **J2:J15**. Display the **Region 1** worksheet, and then click cell **D3**. Display the **Home tab**. In the **Clipboard group**, click the **Paste arrow**, and then under **Paste Values**, click the first option, **Values (V)**.

5. On the **Region 1** worksheet, click cell **F3**. Click the **Formulas tab**. In the **Function Library group**, click **Lookup & Reference**, and then click **VLOOKUP**. In the **Lookup_value** box, type E3 In the **Table_array** box, type $C$19:$D$24 In the **Col_index_num** box, type 2 and then click **OK**. Click in the **formula bar**, and then at the end of the formula, type *E3 Press Enter, and then copy the formula down through **F16**. Compare your screen with Figure 2.

6. Click cell **H3**. Using techniques previously practiced, insert a **VLOOKUP** function. In the **Lookup_value** box, type G3 In the **Table_array** box, type $C$19:$D$24 In the **Col_index_num** box, type 2 and then click **OK**. In the **formula bar**, at the end of the formula, type *G3 Press Enter, and then copy the formula down through **H16**.

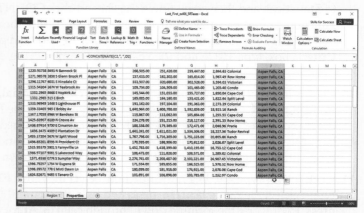

Excel 2016, Windows 10, Microsoft Corporation   Figure 1

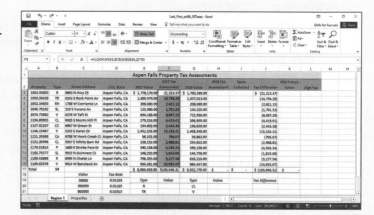

Excel 2016, Windows 10, Microsoft Corporation   Figure 2

■ **Continue to the next page to complete this Skills Review**

7. Click cell **L3**. In the **Function Library group**, click **Logical**, and then click **AND**. In the **Logical1** box, type F3>10000 In the **Logical2** box, type H3>10000 Click **OK**. Copy the formula down through cell **L16**.

8. Click cell **B17**. In the **Function Library group**, click **More Functions**, point to **Statistical**, and then click **COUNTA**. Verify that column **B** is visible. With the insertion point in the **Value1** box, drag to select the range **B3:B16**, and then click **OK**.

9. Click cell **L17**. In the **Function Library group**, click **More Functions**, point to **Statistical**, and then scroll down the list and click **COUNTIF**. Move the Function Arguments dialog box to view column **L**. With the insertion point in the **Range** box, drag to select the range **L3:L16**, and then press [Tab]. In the **Criteria** box, type TRUE and then click **OK**. Compare your screen with Figure 3.

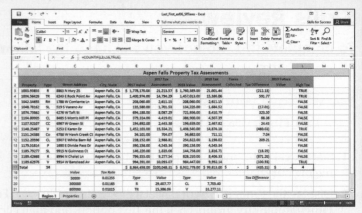

Figure 3   Excel 2016, Windows 10, Microsoft Corporation

10. Click cell **K3**. In the **Function Library group**, click **Financial**, and then click **FV**. In the **Rate** box, type .015 In the **Nper** box, type 12*.5 In the **Pmt** box, type 0 In the **Pv** box, type H3 and then click **OK**. With cell **K3** selected, in the formula bar, place the insertion point between the equals sign (=) and **FV**, and then type - (minus sign) and press [Enter]. Copy the formula down through **K16**.

11. Click cell **I3**. Type = to begin the function. Select the range **F3:F16**, and then type + Select the range **H3:H16**, press and hold the [Ctrl] and [Shift] keys, and then press [Enter]. Copy the formula down through cell **I16**. AutoFit the column.

12. Select **F3**, hold down [Ctrl] and select the range **H3:J3**, and then apply the **Accounting** number format with a dollar sign.

13. Click cell **J20**. Type =sum followed by a left parenthesis: (Select the range **J3:J16**, followed by a right parenthesis:) Press and hold the [Ctrl] and [Shift] keys, and then press [Enter].

14. Click cell **J23**. Click the **Formulas tab**, and then in the **Function Library group**, click **More Functions**. In the list, point to **Statistical**, and then click **AVERAGEIFS**.

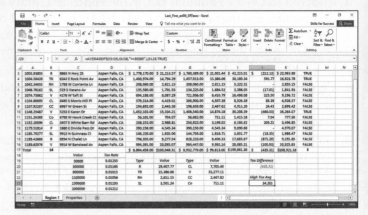

Figure 4   Excel 2016, Windows 10, Microsoft Corporation

15. With the insertion point in the **Average_range** box, select the range **I3:I16**. If necessary, move the dialog box to view the cells. In the **Criteria_range1** box, select the range **I3:I16** In the **Criteria1** box, type >=30000 In the **Criteria_range2** box, select the range **L3:L16** In the **Criteria2** box, type TRUE and then click **OK**. Compare your screen with Figure 4.

16. **Save** the file, and then **Close** Excel. Submit the file as directed by the instructor.

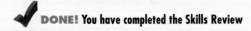

DONE! You have completed the Skills Review

Skills Assessment 1

MyITLab® Grader

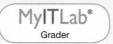

To complete this project, you will need the following file:

- exl06_SA1Bonds

You will save your file as:

- Last_First_exl06_SA1Bonds

1. Start **Excel 2016**, and then open the student data file **exl06_SA1Bonds**. Save the file in your chapter folder as Last_First_exl06_SA1Bonds
2. In cell **E6**, enter a **Future Value (FV)** function with the following arguments: For the **Rate**, enter C6 For **Nper**, enter D6 The **Pmt** should be left blank, and for the **Pv**, enter -B6 Copy the function down through cell **E10**. Apply **Comma [0]** cell style to **E7:E10**.
3. In cell **I14**, insert the **CONCATENATE** function to combine the following: **G14**, a space character, and then **H14**. In the function, nest the **PROPER** function so that title case is applied to the text. Copy the function down through cell **I17**, and then AutoFit column **I**.
4. In cell **H6**, insert the **VLOOKUP** function using G6 for the **Lookup_value**, $F$14:$I$17 for the **Table_array**, and 4 for the **Col_index_num**. Copy the function down through cell **H10**. AutoFit column **H**.
5. In cell **B14**, insert a function that counts the number of times the word *Roads* displays in **F6:F10**. Use the same function in **B15:B16**, substituting the appropriate **Criteria**.
6. In cell **C14**, insert the **SUMIF** function using $F$6:$F$10 as the **Range**, Roads as the **Criteria**, and $E$6:$E$10 as the **Sum_range**. Use the same function in the range **C15:C16**, substituting the appropriate **Criteria**.
7. In cell **C17**, insert an **Array** formula using the **FV** and the **Invested Amount** to calculate the **Value After Investment**.
8. In cell **F11**, insert the **COUNTA** function to count the number of bond investments.
9. From the **Data tab**, start the **What-If Analysis Scenario Manager**. Add a scenario named Investments Set **Changing cells** as **C6:C10**, and then click **OK**. In the **Scenario Values** dialog boxes, replace the current value in box 1 with .04 box 2 with .045 box 3 with .047 box 4 with .03 and box 5 with .038 Click **OK**. Click **Summary**. The **Result cells** should be E11. Click **OK**, and then compare your screen with **Figure 1**.

Scenario Summary		
	Current Values:	Investments
Changing Cells:		
$C$6	3.25%	4.00%
$C$7	4.00%	4.50%
$C$8	4.35%	4.70%
$C$9	2.80%	3.00%
$C$10	3.65%	3.80%
Result Cells:		
$E$11	$ 26,600,783	$ 27,661,782

Notes: Current Values column represents values of changing cells at time Scenario Summary Report was created. Changing cells for each scenario are highlighted in gray.

Figure 1

Aspen Falls Finance Department

Bond Investments Report

Bonds Sold

Year		Invested Amount	Interest Rate	Term		FV	Purpose	Investor ID	Investor Name	Lucrative
Year 1	$	2,150,000	3.25%	12	$	3,155,871	Sewer	3	Millon Financial	TRUE
Year 2		3,200,000	4.00%	10		4,736,782	Roads	8	Cita Bank	TRUE
Year 3		1,450,000	4.35%	15		2,746,343	Airport	16	Walls Savings	FALSE
Year 4		5,300,000	2.80%	12		7,382,326	Roads	8	Cita Bank	TRUE
Year 5		4,500,000	3.65%	18		8,579,461	Sewer	11	Feni Investments	FALSE
Total	$	16,600,000			$	26,600,783	5			

	Number	Value
Total Road Bonds	2	$ 12,119,108
Total Sewer Bonds	2	$ 11,735,332
Total Airport Bonds	1	$ 2,746,343
Value After Investment		$ 10,000,783
Average FV of Bonds		$ 5,320,157

Investors			
3	millon	financial	Millon Financial
8	cita	bank	Cita Bank
11	feni	investments	Feni Investments
16	walls	savings	Walls Savings

Figure 2

10. On the **Bonds** worksheet, in cell **I6**, insert the **Logical** function **AND** using C6<=0.04 as **Logical1** and D6<=15 as **Logical2**. Copy the function down through cell **I10**.
11. In cell **C19**, insert the **AVERAGEIFS** function using $E$6:$E$10 as the **Average_range**, $E$6:$E$10 as the **Criteria_range1**, and then >=2000000 as the **Criteria1**. Use $D$6:$D$10 as the **Criteria_range2**, and then >=10 as the **Criteria2**. Compare your screen with **Figure 2**.
12. **Save** the file, and then **Close** Excel. Submit the file as directed by the instructor.

DONE! You have completed Skills Assessment 1

Skills Assessment 2

To complete this project, you will need the following file:

- exl06_SA2Disputes

You will save your file as:

- Last_First_exl06_SA2Disputes

1. Start **Excel 2016**, and then open the student data file **exl06_SA2Disputes**. Save the file in your chapter folder as Last_First_exl06_SA2Disputes

2. Display the **Customers** worksheet. In cell **F2**, insert the **CONCATENATE** function. For **Text1**, use D2 for **Text2**, add a space, and then for **Text3**, use E2 Add the **PROPER** function to the result so that only the first letter of the month is capitalized. Copy the function down through cell **F12**. Compare your screen with **Figure 1**.

3. Copy the range **F2:F12**. Display the **Report** worksheet, and then paste the copied range to cell **D4** using the **Paste Values** option **Values (V)**.

4. In cell **E4**, insert a **VLOOKUP** function. For the arguments, use C4 for the **Lookup_value**, $J$4:$K$6 for the **Table_array**, and 2 for the **Col_index_num**. In the formula bar, at the end of the formula, type *C4 Copy the function down through cell **E14**. Apply the **Comma** number format to **E5:E14**.

5. In cell **E17**, insert the **SUMIFS** function. Use G4:G14 as the **Sum_range**, C4:C14 as **Criteria_range1**, >10000 as **Criteria1**, F4:F14 as **Criteria_range2**, and >300 as **Criteria2**.

6. In cell **E18**, insert the **SUMIF** function. Use Customers!E2:E12 as the **Range**, **Criteria** >=2017 and then G4:G14 as the **Sum_range**.

7. In cell **H17**, insert the **AVERAGEIF** function. Use F4:F14 as the **Range**, **Criteria** >0 and then F4:F14 as the **Average_range**.

8. In cell **H18**, insert the **AVERAGEIFS** function. Use G4:G14 as the **Average_range**, G4:G14 as **Criteria_range1**, >0 as **Criteria1**, Customers!E2:E12 as **Criteria_range2**, and >=2017 as **Criteria2**.

9. In cell **B15**, insert the **COUNTA** function to calculate the number of disputed water bills.

Customer ID	Type	Customer	Month	Year	Bill Date
C-1436	R	Grace Miller	MARCH	2018	March, 2018
C-1598	R	Lauren Batterdan	APRIL	2019	April, 2019
D-6983	C	Sohn Hern	DECEMBER	2017	December, 2017
F-7690	R	Alice Hoff	FEBRUARY	2019	February, 2019
V-3491	C	Penny Mubet	MAY	2018	May, 2018
H-3491	R	Cramer Niam	AUGUST	2018	August, 2018
G-4509	C	Canice Dessario	JULY	2017	July, 2017
V-1106	C	Natalie Sheffler	JUNE	2019	June, 2019
G-5609	R	Wally Serano	SEPTEMBER	2018	September, 2018
W-9087	R	Tristan Lemell	AUGUST	2017	August, 2017
Z-9723	R	Tyler Gregg	APRIL	2017	April, 2017

Figure 1

Aspen Falls Public Works Department										
Disputed Water Bills Report										
Customer	Type	Usage	Bill Date	Cost	Late Fees	Total Bill	Above Average	Average Usage	Usage in Gallons	Rate
Grace Miller	R	1,580	March, 2018	$ 67.15	$ 25.18	$ 92.33	TRUE	1050	0	0.0475
Lauren Batterdan	R	1,075	April, 2019	45.69	2.28	47.97	TRUE	980	1000	0.0425
Sohn Hern	C	155,640	December, 2017	6,147.78	2,766.50	8,914.28	TRUE	15250	10000	0.0395
Alice Hoff	R	2,370	February, 2019	100.73	10.07	110.80	TRUE	1106		
Penny Mubet	C	8,965	May, 2018	381.01	123.83	504.84	FALSE	9855		
Cramer Niam	R	680	August, 2018	32.30	89.63	121.93	TRUE	560		
Canice Dessario	C	14,500	July, 2017	572.75	343.65	916.40	TRUE	12000		
Natalie Sheffler	C	21,650	June, 2019	855.18	21.38	876.55	TRUE	10000		
Wally Serano	R	4,390	September, 2018	186.58	46.64	233.22	TRUE	1250		
Tristan Lemell	R	1,985	August, 2017	84.36	46.40	130.76	TRUE	900		
Tyler Gregg	R	12,570	April, 2017	496.52	322.73	819.25	TRUE	10255		
Total	11			$ 8,970.03	$ 3,798.31	$ 12,768.34		10	5746	

Residential Usage	24,650
Commercial Usage	200,755

High Usage and Late Fees	$ 10,650
Bills	$ 12,768

Average Late Fees	$ 345
Average Bills	$ 1,161

Figure 2

10. In cell **H15**, insert the **COUNTIF** function to calculate the number of above average water bills. Compare your screen with **Figure 2**.

11. **Save** the file, and then **Close** Excel. Submit the file as directed by the instructor.

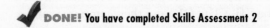
DONE! You have completed Skills Assessment 2

My Skills

To complete this project, you will need the following file:

- exl06_MYSavings

You will save your file as:

- Last_First_exl06_MYSavings

Scenario Summary

Scenario Summary		Current Values:	Scenario $100	Scenario $200
Changing Cells:				
$B$5	$	500.00	$ 1,000.00	$ 500.00
$B$11	$	500.00	$ 500.00	$ 1,000.00
Result Cells:				
$F$7	$	6,045.40	$ 6,655.89	$ 6,045.40
$F$13	$	11,293.69	$ 11,293.69	$ 11,889.17

Notes: Current Values column represents values of changing cells at time Scenario Summary Report was created. Changing cells for each scenario are highlighted in gray.

Figure 1

First Last
Savings Account Future Value

Year	1	2	3	4	5	6
Principal	$ 500.00	$1,742.62	$3,035.86	$4,381.79	$5,782.56	$7,240.40
Interest	$42.62	$93.24	$145.93	$200.77	$257.84	
Total	$ 543.62	$ 1,837.86	$ 3,184.79	$ 4,586.56	$ 6,045.40	

Year	1	2	3	4	5	6
Principal	$ 500.00	$2,956.66	$5,500.70	$8,135.22	$10,863.44	$13,688.69
Interest	$56.66	$144.04	$234.52	$328.22	$425.26	
Total	$ 557.66	$ 3,102.70	$ 5,738.22	$ 8,467.44	$ 11,293.69	

Last_First_exl06_MYSavings

Figure 2

1. Start **Excel 2016**, and then open the student data file **exl06_MYSavings**. Save the file in your chapter folder as Last_First_exl06_MYSavings

2. In the first cell, replace *Student Name* with your First and Last names.

3. In cell **C5**, create the future value of the savings account using a **Rate** of 4%/12 the number of payments of 12 and a monthly payment of 100 Use the cell reference as the present value of the account included in the worksheet. Edit the formula and enter a - (minus sign) between = and **FV**.

4. Copy the formula across for each year through year 6. In **B6**, determine the amount of interest earned each year through year 5, taking into account that you are depositing $100 each month. Create the total ending balance of the account through year 5 (using the **SUM** function).

5. Create a scenario named Scenario $100 using the **What-If Analysis** tool that will analyze the future value if the present value is $1000 and whose result is based on the total at the end of five years.

6. On the **Savings FV** worksheet, in cell **C11**, create the future value of the savings account using a **Rate** of 3.5%/12 number of payments of 12 and a monthly payment of 200 Use the cell reference as the present value of the account included in the worksheet. Edit the formula and enter a - (minus sign) between = and **FV**.

7. Copy the formula for each year through year 6. In **B12**, determine the amount of interest earned each year through year 5, taking into account that you are depositing $200 each month. Create the total ending balance of the account for each year (using the **SUM** function).

8. Create a scenario named Scenario $200 using the **What-If Analysis** tool that will analyze the future value if the present value is $1000 and whose result is based on the total at the end of five years. Compare your completed summary worksheets with Figure 1.

9. Display the **Savings FV** worksheet, and then compare your completed worksheet with Figure 2.

10. **Save** the file, and then **Close** Excel. Submit the file as directed by your instructor.

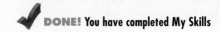 DONE! You have completed My Skills

Visual Skills Check

To complete this project, you will need the following file:

- **exl06_VSPermits**

You will save your file as:

- **Last_First_exl06_VSPermits**

Start **Excel 2016**, and then open the student data file **exl06_VSPermits**. Save the file in your chapter folder as Last_First_exl06_VSPermits

In the range **B4:B12**, use the appropriate statistical function to determine the number of permits sold using the **Permit Data** worksheet, based on each project. In the range **C4:C12**, use the appropriate **Math & Trig** function to add the fees by type of project using the **Permit Data** worksheet. In the range **D4:D12**, use a logical function to calculate if the **3rd Quarter** met or exceeded the projected **Total Number of Permits** of **10** and projected **Fees per Permit** of **$2,000**. In **G4:I4**, insert a **Math & Trig** function to add the fee by month from the **Permit Data** worksheet. In **G5:I21**, use **SUMIFS** and the **Permit Data** worksheet to calculate the total fees collected each day of the month based on the criteria of **Month** and **Day**. To copy the function for each month, the ranges should be formatted as absolute cell references, and the criteria for each day will change. In **J22**, use an **Array** formula to calculate the total fees collected for the **3rd Quarter** using the day data by month. Compare your screen with **Figure 1**. Save the file, and then close Excel. Submit the file as directed by the instructor.

Aspen Falls City Hall

Permits 3rd Quarter

Permit Type	Total Number of Permits	Fees per Permit	Projected	Projects by Month/Day	July	August	September	
Addition	14	$ 3,276.46	TRUE	Total	$ 5,376.42	$ 2,899.12	$ 4,664.66	
Carport	3	948.32	FALSE	1	1,144.76	296.01	-	
Fence	15	742.50	FALSE	2	-	-	1,045.48	
Deck	3	866.64	FALSE	6	1,049.67	346.50	648.61	
Garage	3	907.90	FALSE	8	-	-	526.21	
Remodel	22	2,732.20	TRUE	10	491.54	-	1,012.83	
Roof	7	1,539.85	FALSE	12	900.45	-	-	
Sprinkler System	2	372.00	FALSE	13	-	99.00	1,148.99	
Windows	6	1,554.33	FALSE	15	-	99.00	-	
Total	75	$ 12,940.20		17	369.99	99.00	282.54	
				19	408.67	302.00	-	
				21	518.25	-	-	
				23	-	550.52	-	
				24	362.79	-	-	
				26	-	116.00	-	
				28	-	58.00	-	
				29	130.30	-	-	
				30	-	933.09	-	
				Total				$ 12,940.20

Figure 1

DONE! You have completed Visual Skills Check

Skills Challenge 1

To complete this project, you will need the following file:

- exl06_SC1Retirement

You will save your file as:

- Last_First_exl06_SC1Retirement

Start **Excel 2016**, and then open the student data file **exl06_SC1Retirement**. Save the file in your chapter folder as Last_First_exl06_SC1Retirement On the Symbols worksheet, use a function in the range D2:D11 that combines the text in the Symbol1 and Symbol2 columns to display a four-character symbol. Copy the range D2:D11, and paste only the values into the range F5:F14 of the Projections worksheet. On the Projections worksheet, in the range E5:E14, calculate the positive future value of the

investments in 20 years, assuming monthly payments are made every month and the return is fixed as specified in the worksheet. Save the file, and then Close Excel. Submit the file as directed by your instructor.

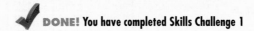 **DONE! You have completed Skills Challenge 1**

Skills Challenge 2

To complete this project, you will need the following file:

- exl06_SC2Services

You will save your file as:

- Last_First_exl06_SC2Services

Start **Excel 2016**, and then open the student data file **exl06_SC2Services**. Save the file in your chapter folder as Last_First_exl06_SC2Services Using skills learned from this chapter, insert an array formula in the range D4:D15 that calculates the increase/decrease in spending from Year 1 to Year 2. Use a formula practiced in the chapter to enter the Total Spending for Year 1 in B17 and Year 2 in C17. In D17, insert a formula that calculates the total increase/decrease using Year 1 and Year 2

actual data. Insert a statistical function in A16 to count the number of services. Save the file, and then close Excel. Submit the file as directed by your instructor.

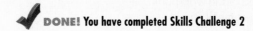 **DONE! You have completed Skills Challenge 2**

More Skills Assessment

MyITLab®
Grader

To complete this project, you will need the following file:

- exl06_MSAMortgage

You will save your file as:

- Last_First_exl06_MSAMortgage

---

1. Start **Excel 2016**. Open the file **exl06_MSAMortgage**, and then save the file in your chapter folder as Last_First_exl06_MSAMortgage

2. Verify the **Calculation Options** are set to **Manual**.

3. Enter a function in cell **B7** to look up the interest **Rate** value associated with the **Amount Financed** using these arguments: **Lookup_value** Rate **Table array** D4:E8 and **Row_index_num** 3

4. In cell **B10**, insert the **PMT** function to calculate the monthly payment. Use these arguments for the function: **Rate** B7/12 **Nper** B9 and **Pv** B6

5. Use **Calculation Options** to update the calculations.

6. Copy the range **B15:D15** down through row **134**, and update the calculations. Compare your screen with **Figure 1**.

7. Copy the worksheet to the end of the workbook, and then rename the worksheet tab Scenario

8. If necessary, install the **Solver** add-in.

9. On the **Scenario** worksheet, use **Solver** to create a what-if analysis using the following parameters: **Set Objective** $B$135 **Value Of** 215000 **Changing Variable Cells** $B$7 **Add** the constraints **Cell Reference** B15 **Constraint** 2000 Solve using **Keep Solver Solution**, and then save the scenario as Mortgage Compare your screen with **Figure 2**.

10. **Save** the file, and then **Close** Excel. Submit the file as directed by your instructor.

Figure 1

Aspen Falls City Hall
Mortgage Amortization

Property Description	Community Center		Amount	Rate
Cost	$	215,000	100,000	1.09%
Amount Financed	$	200,000	200,000	2.06%
Interest Rate		2.06%	300,000	2.30%
Payment Frequency	monthly		400,000	2.89%
Number of Payments		120		
Payment Amount		($1,845.65)		

Month	Payment	Interest	Principal	Balance
				$ 200,000.00
7/1/2018	$ 1,845.65	$ 343.33	$ 1,502.31	$ 198,497.69
8/1/2018	$ 1,845.65	$ 340.75	$ 1,504.89	$ 196,992.79
9/1/2018	$ 1,845.65	$ 338.17	$ 1,507.48	$ 195,485.31
10/1/2018	$ 1,845.65	$ 335.58	$ 1,510.07	$ 193,975.25
11/1/2018	$ 1,845.65	$ 332.99	$ 1,512.66	$ 192,462.59
12/1/2018	$ 1,845.65	$ 330.39	$ 1,515.25	$ 190,947.34
1/1/2019	$ 1,845.65	$ 327.79	$ 1,517.86	$ 189,429.48
2/1/2019	$ 1,845.65	$ 325.19	$ 1,520.46	$ 187,909.02
3/1/2019	$ 1,845.65	$ 322.58	$ 1,523.07	$ 186,385.95
4/1/2019	$ 1,845.65	$ 319.96	$ 1,525.69	$ 184,860.27
5/1/2019	$ 1,845.65	$ 317.34	$ 1,528.30	$ 183,331.96
6/1/2019	$ 1,845.65	$ 314.72	$ 1,530.93	$ 181,801.03
7/1/2019	$ 1,845.65	$ 312.09	$ 1,533.56	$ 180,267.48
8/1/2019	$ 1,845.65	$ 309.46	$ 1,536.19	$ 178,731.29
9/1/2019	$ 1,845.65	$ 306.82	$ 1,538.83	$ 177,192.46
10/1/2019	$ 1,845.65	$ 304.18	$ 1,541.47	$ 175,650.99
11/1/2019	$ 1,845.65	$ 301.53	$ 1,544.11	$ 174,106.88
12/1/2019	$ 1,845.65	$ 298.88	$ 1,546.76	$ 172,560.11
1/1/2020	$ 1,845.65	$ 296.23	$ 1,549.42	$ 171,010.69
2/1/2020	$ 1,845.65	$ 293.57	$ 1,552.08	$ 169,458.61
3/1/2020	$ 1,845.65	$ 290.90	$ 1,554.74	$ 167,903.87
4/1/2020	$ 1,845.65	$ 288.23	$ 1,557.41	$ 166,346.46
5/1/2020	$ 1,845.65	$ 285.56	$ 1,560.09	$ 164,786.37
6/1/2020	$ 1,845.65	$ 282.88	$ 1,562.76	$ 163,223.61
7/1/2020	$ 1,845.65	$ 280.20	$ 1,565.45	$ 161,658.16
8/1/2020	$ 1,845.65	$ 277.51	$ 1,568.13	$ 160,090.02
9/1/2020	$ 1,845.65	$ 274.82	$ 1,570.83	$ 158,519.20
10/1/2020	$ 1,845.65	$ 272.12	$ 1,573.52	$ 156,945.67
11/1/2020	$ 1,845.65	$ 269.42	$ 1,576.22	$ 155,369.45
12/1/2020	$ 1,845.65	$ 266.72	$ 1,578.93	$ 153,790.52
1/1/2021	$ 1,845.65	$ 264.01	$ 1,581.64	$ 152,208.88
2/1/2021	$ 1,845.65	$ 261.29	$ 1,584.36	$ 150,624.52
3/1/2021	$ 1,845.65	$ 258.57	$ 1,587.08	$ 149,037.44
4/1/2021	$ 1,845.65	$ 255.85	$ 1,589.80	$ 147,447.64
5/1/2021	$ 1,845.65	$ 253.12	$ 1,592.53	$ 145,855.11

6/1/2021	$ 1,845.65	$ 250.38	$ 1,595.26	$ 144,259.85
7/1/2021	$ 1,845.65	$ 247.65	$ 1,598.00	$ 142,661.85
8/1/2021	$ 1,845.65	$ 244.90	$ 1,600.75	$ 141,061.10
9/1/2021	$ 1,845.65	$ 242.15	$ 1,603.49	$ 139,457.61
10/1/2021	$ 1,845.65	$ 239.40	$ 1,606.25	$ 137,851.36
11/1/2021	$ 1,845.65	$ 236.64	$ 1,609.00	$ 136,242.36
12/1/2021	$ 1,845.65	$ 233.88	$ 1,611.77	$ 134,630.59
1/1/2022	$ 1,845.65	$ 231.12	$ 1,614.53	$ 133,016.06
2/1/2022	$ 1,845.65	$ 228.34	$ 1,617.30	$ 131,398.76
3/1/2022	$ 1,845.65	$ 225.57	$ 1,620.08	$ 129,778.68
4/1/2022	$ 1,845.65	$ 222.79	$ 1,622.86	$ 128,155.82
5/1/2022	$ 1,845.65	$ 220.00	$ 1,625.65	$ 126,530.17
6/1/2022	$ 1,845.65	$ 217.21	$ 1,628.44	$ 124,901.73
7/1/2022	$ 1,845.65	$ 214.41	$ 1,631.23	$ 123,270.50
8/1/2022	$ 1,845.65	$ 211.61	$ 1,634.03	$ 121,636.46
9/1/2022	$ 1,845.65	$ 208.81	$ 1,636.84	$ 119,999.62
10/1/2022	$ 1,845.65	$ 206.00	$ 1,639.65	$ 118,359.98
11/1/2022	$ 1,845.65	$ 203.18	$ 1,642.46	$ 116,717.51
12/1/2022	$ 1,845.65	$ 200.37	$ 1,645.28	$ 115,072.23
1/1/2023	$ 1,845.65	$ 197.54	$ 1,648.11	$ 113,424.12
2/1/2023	$ 1,845.65	$ 194.71	$ 1,650.94	$ 111,773.18
3/1/2023	$ 1,845.65	$ 191.88	$ 1,653.77	$ 110,119.41
4/1/2023	$ 1,845.65	$ 189.04	$ 1,656.61	$ 108,462.80
5/1/2023	$ 1,845.65	$ 186.19	$ 1,659.45	$ 106,803.35
6/1/2023	$ 1,845.65	$ 183.35	$ 1,662.30	$ 105,141.05
7/1/2023	$ 1,845.65	$ 180.49	$ 1,665.16	$ 103,475.89
8/1/2023	$ 1,845.65	$ 177.63	$ 1,668.01	$ 101,807.88
9/1/2023	$ 1,845.65	$ 174.77	$ 1,670.88	$ 100,137.00
10/1/2023	$ 1,845.65	$ 171.90	$ 1,673.75	$ 98,463.25
11/1/2023				

12/1/2023				
1/1/2024				
2/1/2024				
3/1/2024				
4/1/2024				
5/1/2024				
6/1/2024				
7/1/2024				
8/1/2024				
9/1/2024				
10/1/2024				
11/1/2024				
12/1/2024				
1/1/2025				
2/1/2025				
3/1/2025				
4/1/2025				
5/1/2025				
6/1/2025				
7/1/2025				

8/1/2025	$ 1,845.65	$ 107.54	$ 1,738.11	$ 60,905.09
9/1/2025	$ 1,845.65	$ 104.55	$ 1,741.09	$ 59,163.99
10/1/2025	$ 1,845.65	$ 101.56	$ 1,744.08	$ 57,419.91
11/1/2025	$ 1,845.65	$ 98.57	$ 1,747.08	$ 55,672.83
12/1/2025	$ 1,845.65	$ 95.57	$ 1,750.08	$ 53,922.76
1/1/2026	$ 1,845.65	$ 92.57	$ 1,753.08	$ 52,169.68
2/1/2026	$ 1,845.65	$ 89.56	$ 1,756.09	$ 50,413.59
3/1/2026	$ 1,845.65	$ 86.54	$ 1,759.10	$ 48,654.48
4/1/2026	$ 1,845.65	$ 83.52	$ 1,762.12	$ 46,892.36
5/1/2026	$ 1,845.65	$ 80.50	$ 1,765.15	$ 45,127.21
6/1/2026	$ 1,845.65	$ 77.47	$ 1,768.18	$ 43,359.03
7/1/2026	$ 1,845.65	$ 74.43	$ 1,771.22	$ 41,587.81
8/1/2026	$ 1,845.65	$ 71.39	$ 1,774.26	$ 39,813.56
9/1/2026	$ 1,845.65	$ 68.35	$ 1,777.30	$ 38,036.25
10/1/2026	$ 1,845.65	$ 65.30	$ 1,780.35	$ 36,255.90
11/1/2026	$ 1,845.65	$ 62.24	$ 1,783.41	$ 34,472.49
12/1/2026	$ 1,845.65	$ 59.18	$ 1,786.47	$ 32,686.02
1/1/2027	$ 1,845.65	$ 56.11	$ 1,789.54	$ 30,896.48
2/1/2027	$ 1,845.65	$ 53.04	$ 1,792.61	$ 29,103.88
3/1/2027	$ 1,845.65	$ 49.96	$ 1,795.69	$ 27,308.19
4/1/2027	$ 1,845.65	$ 46.88	$ 1,798.77	$ 25,509.42
5/1/2027	$ 1,845.65	$ 43.79	$ 1,801.86	$ 23,707.56
6/1/2027	$ 1,845.65	$ 40.70	$ 1,804.95	$ 21,902.61
7/1/2027	$ 1,845.65	$ 37.60	$ 1,808.05	$ 20,094.56
8/1/2027	$ 1,845.65	$ 34.50	$ 1,811.15	$ 18,283.41
9/1/2027	$ 1,845.65	$ 31.39	$ 1,814.26	$ 16,469.15
10/1/2027	$ 1,845.65	$ 28.27	$ 1,817.38	$ 14,651.77
11/1/2027	$ 1,845.65	$ 25.15	$ 1,820.50	$ 12,831.28
12/1/2027	$ 1,845.65	$ 22.03	$ 1,823.62	$ 11,007.66
1/1/2028	$ 1,845.65	$ 18.90	$ 1,826.75	$ 9,180.91
2/1/2028	$ 1,845.65	$ 15.76	$ 1,829.89	$ 7,351.02
3/1/2028	$ 1,845.65	$ 12.62	$ 1,833.03	$ 5,517.99
4/1/2028	$ 1,845.65	$ 9.47	$ 1,836.18	$ 3,681.81
5/1/2028	$ 1,845.65	$ 6.32	$ 1,839.33	$ 1,842.49
6/1/2028	$ 1,845.65	$ 3.16	$ 1,842.49	$ (0.00)
	$ 221,477.78	$ 21,477.78	$ 200,000.00	

Figure 2

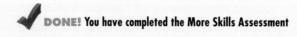
✓ **DONE!** You have completed the More Skills Assessment

Collaborating with Google

To complete this project, you will need a Google account (refer to the Common Features chapter) and the following file:

- exl06_GPAssessments

You will save your file as:

- Last_First_exl06_GPAssessments

---

1. Open the **Google Chrome** web browser. Log into your Google account, and then click the **Apps** button 田.

2. Click **Drive** 📁 to open Google Drive.

3. Click the **New** button, and then click **File upload**. Navigate to the student data files, and then open **exl06_GPAssessments**.

4. Double-click the **exl06_GPAssessments** in **Google Drive**, and then click **Open** to view the workbook in **Google Sheets**.

5. On the **Properties** sheet, click cell **J2**. Type =CONCATENATE (C2,", ",D2) Press Enter, and then copy cell **J2** down to cell **J38**. Select the range **J2:J15**, and then copy the range. Display the **Region 2** sheet, right-click cell **D3**, point to **Paste Special**, and then click **Paste values only**.

6. Click cell **B17**, and then type =COUNTA(B3:B16) Press Enter.

7. Click cell **H3**, and then type =VLOOKUP(G3,$C$19:$D$24,2)*G3 Press Enter. Copy cell **H3** down to cell **H16**.

8. Click cell **I3**, and then type =F3:F16+H3:H16 Press and hold the Ctrl and Shift keys, and then press Enter. Copy the formula down through cell **I16**. Select the range **E4:I16**, click **Format**, point to **Number**, and then click **Financial**.

9. Click cell **L3**, and then type =AND(F3>10000, H3>10000) Press Enter. Copy cell **L3** down to cell **L16**.

10. Click cell **L17**, and then type =COUNTIF(L3:L16,TRUE) Press Enter.

11. Click cell **H20**, and then type =SUMIF(B3:B16,"C",H3:H16) Press Enter. Scroll up and click an empty cell. Compare your screen with **Figure 1**.

12. Click the **File tab**, point to **Download as**, and then click **Microsoft Excel (.xlsx)**.

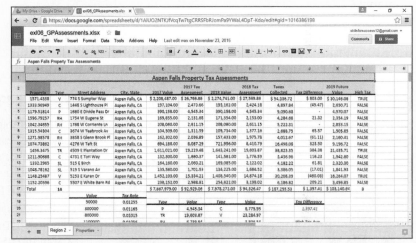

Figure 1

13. **Enable Editing**, and then select columns **A:L** and AutoFit the columns.

14. Save the file in your chapter folder as Last_First_exl06_GPAssessments

15. Close all windows, and then submit the file as directed by your instructor.

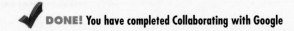 **DONE! You have completed Collaborating with Google**

CHAPTER 7

Work with Data and Audit Formulas

- ▶ You can import data into Excel from a variety of file formats and then analyze and manipulate that data.
- ▶ When errors occur in a formula, Excel provides tools to locate and fix the source of the error.
- ▶ You can sort and filter data to make it easier to manipulate and analyze.

- ▶ Subtotals can easily be added to worksheets.
- ▶ You can use sorting and conditional formatting to customize data as a table.

Apops/Fotolia

Aspen Falls City Hall

In this chapter, you will support Leah Kim, Parks and Recreation Director. You will assist her with editing an existing workbook and using Excel functions and data analysis tools to calculate and analyze financial loss for personal enrichment classes offered through the Recreation Division. This workbook will assist Leah in evaluating class participation, as well as break even points for classes and future profits.

Businesses and organizations often use Excel workbooks for data analysis. Two different types of tables used to analyze data are Excel tables and data tables. Excel tables are created to more easily manage and analyze a range of data using formatting, sorting, filtering, totals, and formulas. Data tables analyze a range of cells and show how changing one or two variables in formulas can affect the formula results. Using a subtotal as part of a table provides a calculation of filtered and summarized data. Custom filtering is used to filter data in a column based on more than one condition.

In this project, you will import data from a text file and use the data to incorporate functions and data analysis tools to analyze class profits and losses. You will sort data based on conditions and summarize data using subtotals. You will use Excel tools to evaluate formulas and determine if there are formula errors. Using analysis tools, you will revise values in existing formulas. You will evaluate data using cell ranges to determine possible scenarios based on changes in values and convert the ranges to allow filtering based on multiple conditions. Finally, you will create custom table formatting to enhance the readability of the data.

Time to complete all 10 skills — 60 to 90 minutes

60-90 min.

Outcome

Using the skills in this chapter, you will be able to import, sort, filter, and subtotal data; audit and trace formulas; create data tables; and name and edit tables.

Objectives

7.1 Analyze data using filter, sort, and conditional formatting

7.2 Evaluate formulas to understand errors

7.3 Construct data tables to evaluate future values

7.4 Apply custom styles to tables

7.5 Apply names to tables

Student data files needed for this chapter:

exl07_Classes (Excel)

exl07_Text (Text)

You will save your files as:

Last_First_exl07_Classes

Last_First_exl07_Snip1

Last_First_exl07_Snip2

SKILLS

MyITLab®
Skills 1–10 Training

Skill 1 Import Data from Text Files

Skill 2 Apply Advanced AutoFilters

Skill 3 Sort Data Using Conditional Formatting

Skill 4 Sort Data and Use the Subtotal Tool to Summarize Data

Skill 5 Trace and Evaluate Formulas

Skill 6 Audit Formulas Using Cell Watch

Skill 7 Create One-Variable Data Tables

Skill 8 Create Two-Variable Data Tables

Skill 9 Generate Custom Table Styles

Skill 10 Name Tables and Convert Tables to a Range

MORE SKILLS

Skill 11 Insert Names into Formulas

Skill 12 Use Goal Seek

Skill 13 Use MATCH and INDEX Functions: Part 1

Skill 14 Use MATCH and INDEX Functions: Part 2

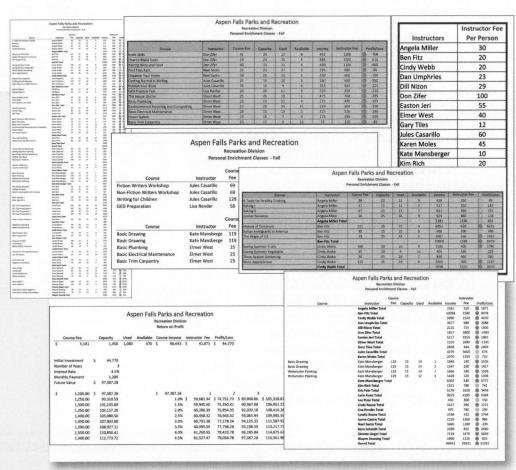

Excel 2016, Windows 10, Microsoft Corporation

▶ Data can be imported into a workbook from a ***delimited text file***—a file in which the data in each column is separated by an identifying character such as a comma, a space, or a tab stop.

1. Take a few moments to familiarize yourself with the text file shown in **Figure 1**.

   The data in the text file, which can be opened in Microsoft Word, is organized into rows and columns by using tab stops. A tab stop, indicated by an arrow, has been inserted to indicate each new column. The paragraph character at the end of each row indicates where a new row begins. In this manner, tabular data can be represented in a ***text file***—a file that stores only the text characters, not formatting or tables.

2. Start **Excel 2016**, and then open the student data file **exl07_Classes**. Click the **File tab**, and then click **Save As**. Click the **Browse** button, and then navigate to the location where you are saving your files. Click **New folder**, type Excel Chapter 7 and then press Enter two times. Name the file Last_First_exl07_Classes and then press Enter. If necessary, enable the content.

3. On the **Classes** worksheet, click cell **A6**, and then click the **Data tab**. Click the **Get External Data** button, and then click **From Text**. In the **Import Text File** dialog box, navigate to the student data files for this chapter. If necessary, move the Import Text File dialog box to view the ribbon. Compare your screen with **Figure 2**.

4. Select **exl07_Text**, and then click **Import**.

■ Continue to the next page to complete the skill

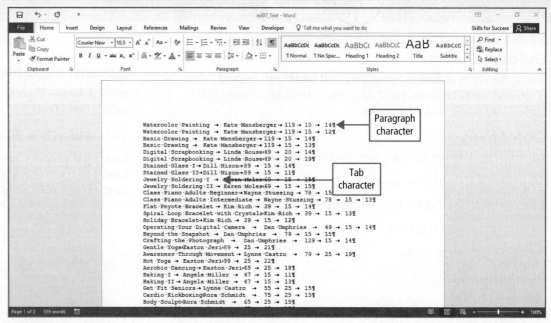

Figure 1

Word 2016, Windows 10, Microsoft Corporation

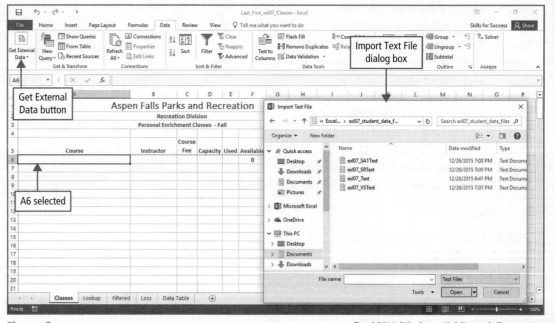

Figure 2

Excel 2016, Windows 10, Microsoft Corporation

MOS
Obj 1.1.2 C

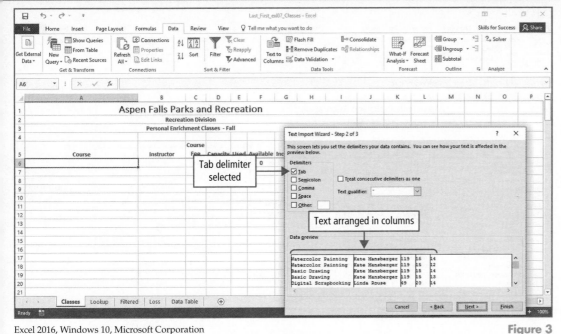

Excel 2016, Windows 10, Microsoft Corporation

Figure 3

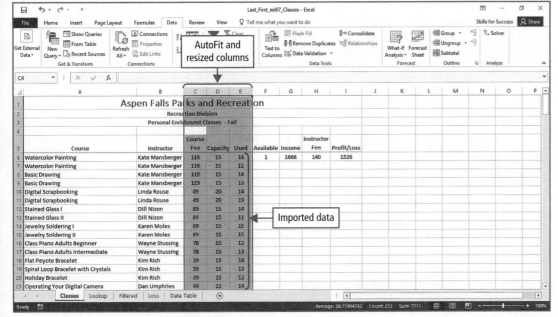

Excel 2016, Windows 10, Microsoft Corporation

Figure 4

5. In the **Text Import Wizard - Step 1 of 3**, under **Original data type**, verify that the **Delimited** option button is selected, and then click **Next**.

   Recall that a delimiter is the character used to separate columns of text in a data table.

6. In the **Text Import Wizard - Step 2 of 3**, under **Delimiters**, verify that the **Tab** check box is selected. Compare your screen with **Figure 3**.

   Under Data preview, the data is arranged into columns. The wizard uses the tab delimiter to determine in which column to place each value in the text file.

7. Click **Next**. In the **Text Import Wizard - Step 3 of 3**, under **Column data format**, verify that **General** is selected.

   This step allows you to select each column and then set the data format. The General format converts numeric values to numbers, date values to dates, and all remaining values to text.

8. Click **Finish**. In the **Import Data** dialog box, verify that the **Existing worksheet** option button is selected and that the box displays the text =$A$6, and then click **OK** to insert the text file into the worksheet starting in cell A6. AutoFit and resize columns as needed, and then compare your screen with **Figure 4**.

   The data was inserted into the worksheet. Each tab resulted in a new column, and each paragraph mark resulted in a new row.

9. **Save** 💾 the file.

■ **You have completed Skill 1 of 10**

▶ You can sort data by text, numbers, or dates, or by a custom list that includes colors and icon sets.

▶ Custom filters can be written using your own criteria, and then combined with other filters to apply multiple criteria.

1. Click cell **A6**. On the **Data tab**, in the **Sort & Filter group**, click **Filter**.

2. In cell **B5**, click the **Filter arrow** ⊡ . Point to **Text Filters**, and then click **Custom Filter**.

3. In the **Custom AutoFilter** dialog box, click the **arrow** in the box to the right of *equals*. Type j and then select **Jules Casarillo**.

4. Click the **Or** option button. In the box below *equals*, click the **arrow**, and then select **equals**. Click the **arrow** in the box next to *equals*, type li and then scroll to select **Lisa Render**. Compare your screen with **Figure 1**, and then click **OK**.

> *Or* is a logical operator that evaluates two conditions. The custom filter will display only the rows where either *Jules Casarillo* or *Lisa Render* is the instructor.

5. In cell **C5**, click the **Filter arrow** ⊡ . Point to **Number Filters**, and then click **Greater Than Or Equal To**. In the box next to *is greater than or equal to*, type 50 Click **OK**, and then compare your screen with **Figure 2**.

> When you apply filters to multiple columns, only the records that meet the criteria for both filters display. Here, only the Course Fees greater than or equal to 50 for Jules Casarillo and Lisa Render display.

■ **Continue to the next page to complete the skill**

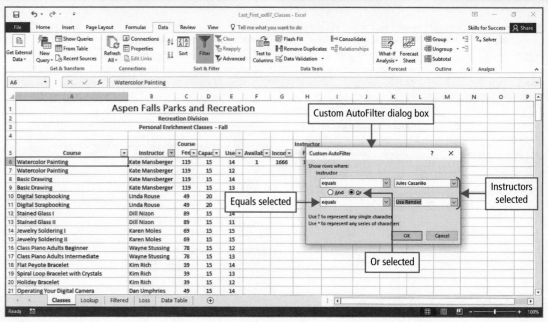

Figure 1

Excel 2016, Windows 10, Microsoft Corporation

Figure 2

Excel 2016, Windows 10, Microsoft Corporation

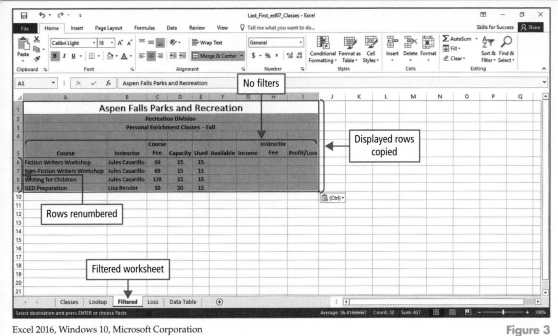

Excel 2016, Windows 10, Microsoft Corporation

Figure 3

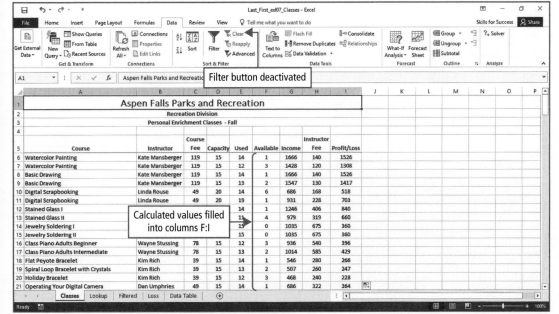

Excel 2016, Windows 10, Microsoft Corporation

Figure 4

6. Select the range **A1:I60**. Click the **Home tab**, and then in the **Clipboard group**, click **Copy**.

   When copying filtered records, only the displayed rows are copied. Here, only the four filtered rows were copied to the clipboard.

7. Click the **Filtered** worksheet tab. With cell **A1** selected, in the **Clipboard group**, click **Paste**. Compare your screen with **Figure 3**.

   The pasted rows are renumbered and are no longer filtered.

8. Click the **Classes** worksheet tab, and then press Esc. Click the **Data tab**, and then in the **Sort & Filter group**, click the **Filter** button to remove the custom filter.

9. Click cell **A6**, and then click the **Filter** button again. In cell **A5**, click the **Filter arrow**. Point to **Text Filters**, and then click **Begins With**.

10. In the dialog box, in the box to the right of *begins with*, type Basic and then click **OK**.

11. In cell **E5**, click the **Filter arrow**. Point to **Number Filters**, and then click **Less Than Or Equal To**. In the box to the right of *is less than or equal to*, type 15 and then click **OK**.

12. Select and copy the range **A5:I71**.

13. Click the **Filtered** worksheet tab, click cell **A11**, and then paste the data.

14. Click the **Classes** worksheet tab, and press Esc. On the **Data tab**, in the **Sort & Filter group**, click the **Filter** button to remove the custom filter.

15. Select the range **F6:I6**. **AutoFill** the functions in **F6:I6** down through **I75**. Click cell **A1**, and then compare your screen with **Figure 4**.

16. **Save** the file.

▪ **You have completed Skill 2 of 10**

 **WATCH** SKILL 7.3

▶ Data can be sorted based on the conditional formatting applied to each cell in a column. For example, when icon sets are applied to a column, you can sort the column by the icon set applied to each cell instead of the underlying numeric values in those cells.

1. On the **Classes** worksheet tab, select the range **I6:I75**.

2. Click the **Home tab**, and then in the **Styles group**, click **Conditional Formatting**. Point to **Icon Sets**, and then click **More Rules**.

3. In the **New Formatting Rule** dialog box, under **Edit the Rule Description**, click the first **arrow** below **Type**, and then click **Number**. In the first box below **Value**, replace the existing value with *750*

4. Click the second **arrow** below **Type**, and then click **Number**. In the second box below **Value**, verify *0* displays. Compare your screen with **Figure 1**, and then click **OK**.

   There is no option to change the third icon because all of the possible options are taken into consideration by changing the first two values.

5. Verify the range **I6:I75** is still selected, and then click the **Data tab**. In the **Sort & Filter group**, click the **Sort** button. Read the **Sort Warning** message box. Verify that the **Expand the selection** option button is selected, and then click **Sort**. Compare your screen with **Figure 2**.

   Expanding the selection will ensure that the row data does not become separated. If the selection is not expanded, only the selected column is sorted.

■ **Continue to the next page to complete the skill** ➤

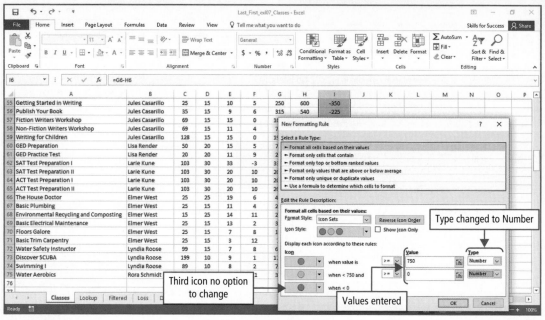

Figure 1

Excel 2016, Windows 10, Microsoft Corporation

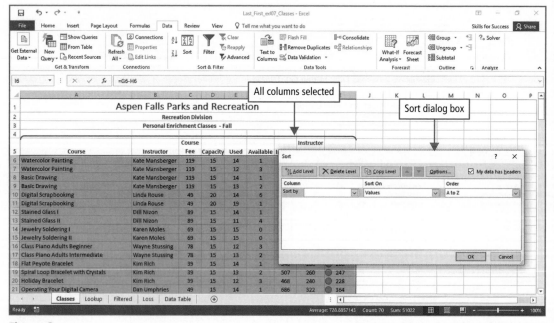

Figure 2

Excel 2016, Windows 10, Microsoft Corporation

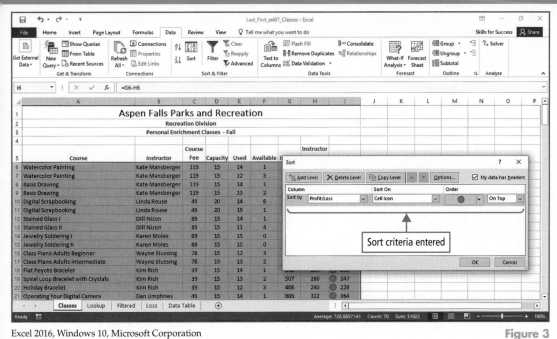

Excel 2016, Windows 10, Microsoft Corporation

Figure 3

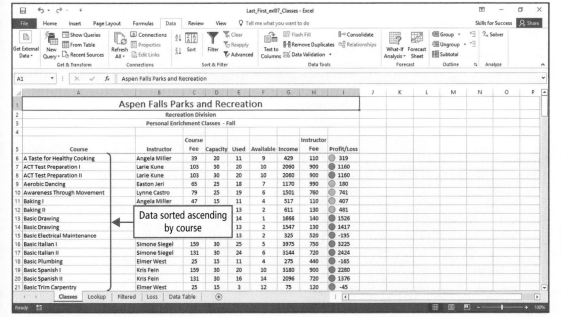

Excel 2016, Windows 10, Microsoft Corporation

Figure 4

6. In the **Sort** dialog box, under **Column**, click the **Sort by arrow**, and then click **Profit/Loss** to sort the rows by that column.

7. Click the **Sort On arrow**, and then in the list, click **Cell Icon**. Click the **Order arrow**, and then click the **Red Circle With Border**. In the last box, verify that *On Top* is displayed. Compare your screen with Figure 3, and then click **OK**.

MOS
Obj 3.3.2 C

The cells with the Red Circle With Border are now at the top of the list. These cells indicate classes that have lost money.

8. Select and copy the range **A1:I19**.

The worksheet titles and the first 14 rows of data are copied to the clipboard.

9. Display the **Loss** worksheet. Verify that cell **A1** is selected, and then paste the data.

10. Display the **Classes** worksheet, press [Esc], and then select the range **A6:I75**. Click the **Data tab**, and then in the **Sort & Filter group**, click the **Sort** button. In the **Sort** dialog box, click the **Sort by arrow**, and then click **Course**.

11. Click the **Sort On arrow**, and then in the list, click **Values**. In the **Order** box, verify that *A to Z* is displayed, and then click **OK** to sort the *Course* column in ascending order. Click cell **A1**, and then compare your screen with Figure 4.

When a sort order is not specified, the rows are sorted in ascending order. Here, the rows were sorted alphabetically (A-Z) by course.

12. **Save** 🖫 the file.

■ **You have completed Skill 3 of 10**

▶ When data is grouped, you can use the Excel Subtotal tool to display summary statistics—sums and counts, for example—for each group.

▶ Before adding subtotals to tabular data, the rows need to be sorted by the column being subtotaled.

1. On the **Classes** worksheet, click cell **B6**. On the **Data tab**, in the **Sort & Filter group**, click the **Sort A to Z** button ⫯. Compare your screen with **Figure 1**.

   The rows are now sorted by instructor. When sorted in this manner, the Subtotal tool can provide subtotals for each instructor.

 2. Click cell **A6**. In the **Outline group**, click **Subtotal**.

Obj 2.3.3 C

3. In the **Subtotal** dialog box, click the **At each change in arrow**, and then click **Instructor**. Verify that the **Use function** box displays *Sum*. Under **Add subtotal to**, click as necessary to select the **Income**, **Instructor Fee**, and **Profit/Loss** check boxes. Compare your screen with **Figure 2**.

   Subtotals will be displayed for each instructor and will include the Income, Instructor Fees, and Profit/Loss columns.

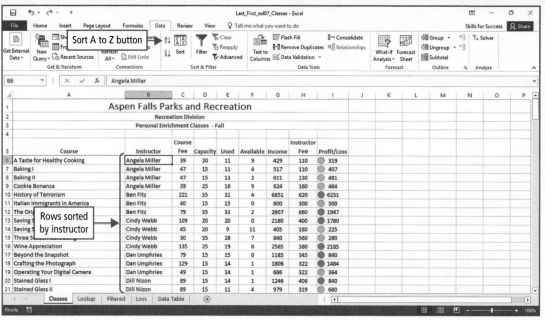

Figure 1   Excel 2016, Windows 10, Microsoft Corporation

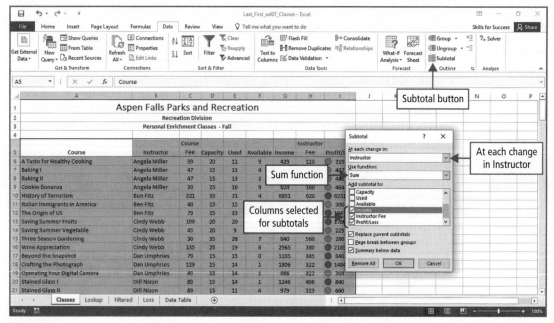

 ■ **Continue to the next page to complete the skill**

Figure 2   Excel 2016, Windows 10, Microsoft Corporation

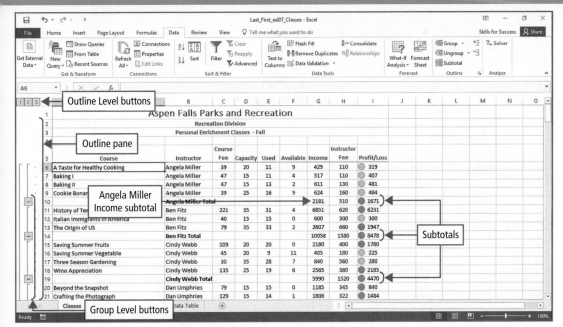

Excel 2016, Windows 10, Microsoft Corporation

Figure 3

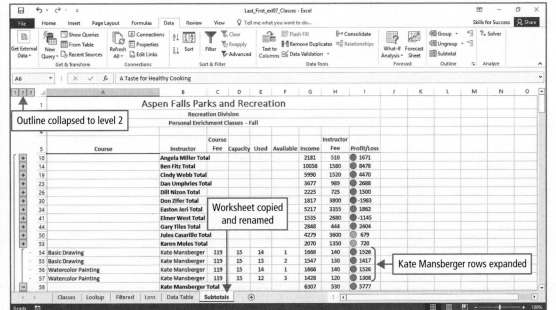

Excel 2016, Windows 10, Microsoft Corporation

Figure 4

4. Click **OK**, and then compare your screen with **Figure 3**.

The result may take several seconds to complete. The table is organized as an outline with three levels, and the Outline pane is displayed. For each instructor, the specified columns display subtotals. For example, the *Income* for Angela Miller's four classes, as shown in cell G10, is *2181*.

5. In the **Outline** pane, click **Outline Level 2** to display just the totals for each instructor.

Obj 2.3.2 C

6. In the **Outline** pane, to the left of row **58**, click the **Expand** button + to display all of the rows for Kate Mansberger.

In this manner, details for individual subtotals can be expanded or collapsed.

7. Right-click the **Classes** worksheet tab, and then in the shortcut menu that displays, click **Move or Copy**. In the **Move or Copy** dialog box, under **Before sheet**, click **(move to end)**. Select the **Create a copy** check box, and then click **OK**.

8. Right-click the **Classes (2)** worksheet tab, and then click **Rename**. Type Subtotals press Enter, and then compare your screen with **Figure 4**.

9. Click the **Classes** worksheet tab, and then on the **Data tab**, in the **Outline group**, click the **Ungroup arrow**. In the list, select **Clear Outline**.

10. Click cell **A6**, and then on the **Data tab**, in the **Sort & Filter group**, click the **Sort A to Z** button.

11. Save the file.

■ **You have completed Skill 4 of 10**

 **WATCH** SKILL 7.5

▶ Tracing the precedents or dependents of a given cell helps you evaluate worksheet formulas and is useful when trying to determine the cause of an error.

▶ A *precedent* is any cell value that is referred to in a formula or a function. A *dependent* is any cell value that depends on the value in a given cell.

MOS
Obj 3.5.3 E

1. On the **Classes** worksheet, click cell **G6**. On the formula bar, change the formula to =A6*E6 Press Enter .

   The #VALUE! error value indicates that the formula contains the wrong type of data. The error displays in cells G6 and I6 because cell A6 contains a text value. Excel cannot perform mathematical calculations when one of the values being multiplied is formatted as text.

MOS
Obj 3.5.1 E

2. Click cell **G6**. Click the **Formulas tab**, and then in the **Formula Auditing group**, click the **Trace Precedents** button, and then click the **Trace Dependents** button. Compare your screen with **Figure 1**.

   The precedent is indicated by a blue line with blue dots indicating the cells used in the formula. The dependents are indicated by red lines.

MOS
Obj 3.5.4 E

3. In the **Formula Auditing group**, click the **Evaluate Formula** button. In the **Evaluate Formula** dialog box, click **Step In**. Compare your screen with **Figure 2**.

   The Evaluate Formula dialog box is used to evaluate each part of a formula in a step-by-step process. The underlying formula in cell G6 displays, and cell A6 is highlighted to indicate that it is the cell being evaluated in this step.

■ **Continue to the next page to complete the skill**

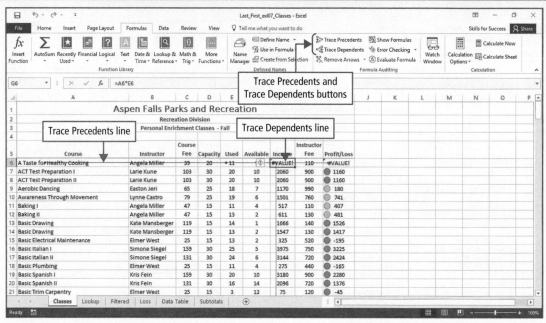

Figure 1

Excel 2016, Windows 10, Microsoft Corporation

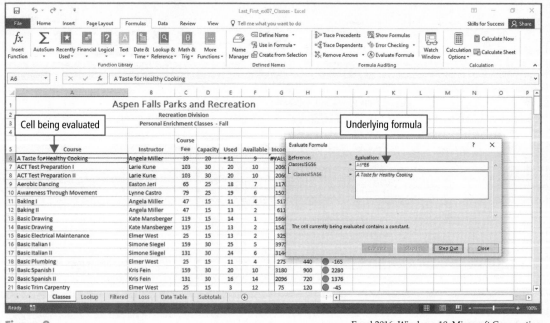

Figure 2

Excel 2016, Windows 10, Microsoft Corporation

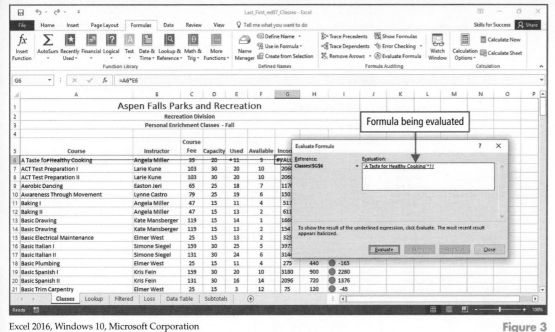

Excel 2016, Windows 10, Microsoft Corporation

Figure 3

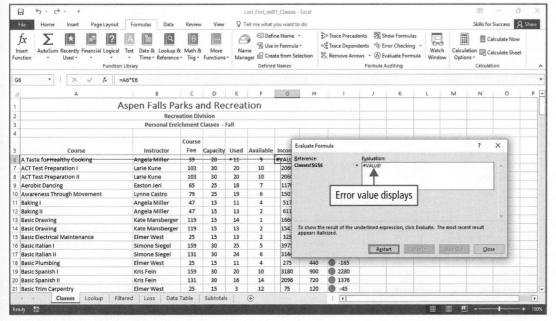

Excel 2016, Windows 10, Microsoft Corporation

Figure 4

4. Notice that cell **A6** contains a text value, *A Taste for Healthy Cooking*, and then click the **Step Out** button. Click **Step In**, notice that cell **E6** contains a numeric value, *11*, and then click **Step Out**. Compare your screen with Figure 3.

The Evaluation box indicates the steps evaluated to this point by displaying actual values and underlining each part of the formula that has been evaluated. Here *"A Taste for Healthy Cooking"*11* has been evaluated. In this manner, each step in a formula can be analyzed.

5. Click the **Evaluate** button, and then compare your screen with Figure 4.

The Evaluation box displays an error value in place of the information that was previously displayed. The error value helps you locate the exact cell causing the error value.

6. If necessary, drag the **Evaluate Formula** dialog box down so that both trace lines display.

7. Using the techniques previously practiced, create a full-screen snip. **Save** 🖫 the snip in your chapter folder as Last_First_exl07_Snip1 and then **Close** ✕ the **Snipping Tool** window.

8. In the **Evaluate Formula** dialog box, click **Close**. In the **Formula Auditing group**, click the **Remove Arrows** button to remove the trace lines.

9. In cell **G6**, change the formula back to =C6*E6 and then press Enter. Click cell **A1**.

10. Save 🖫 the file.

■ **You have completed Skill 5 of 10**

▶ The ***Watch Window*** displays cells and the formulas in cells that are not visible on the screen.

▶ The Watch Window does not change when you scroll in the worksheet, and you can move or dock it as needed.

Obj 3.5.2 E

1. On the **Classes** worksheet, click cell **H12**. On the **Formulas tab**, in the **Formula Auditing group**, click the **Watch Window** button.

2. In the **Watch Window**, click **Add Watch**. If needed, move the **Add Watch** dialog box to view both windows. Compare your screen with Figure 1.

3. In the **Add Watch** dialog box, verify that the value =*Classes!$H$12* displays, and then click **Add**.

4. Click cell **I7**. In the **Watch Window**, click **Add Watch**, and then in the **Add Watch** dialog box, click **Add**. If necessary, resize the **Watch Window** to display all of the VLOOKUP function. Compare your screen with Figure 2.

    The underlying formulas for the two cells are added to the Watch Window. In this manner, multiple cells can be added to the Watch Window.

5. Display the **Lookup** worksheet. Move the **Watch Window** so that the upper left corner is in cell **E3**. In the **Watch Window**, notice that the **Value** column for cell **H12** displays *130*.

■ **Continue to the next page to complete the skill** ▶

Figure 1   Excel 2016, Windows 10, Microsoft Corporation

Figure 2   Excel 2016, Windows 10, Microsoft Corporation

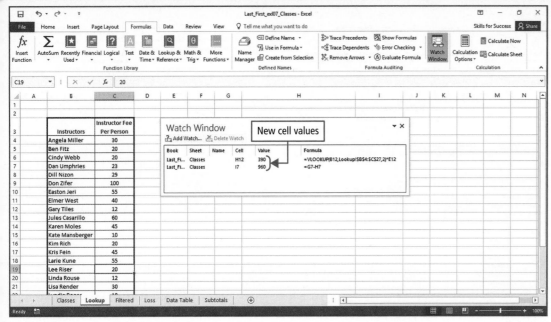

Excel 2016, Windows 10, Microsoft Corporation

Figure 3

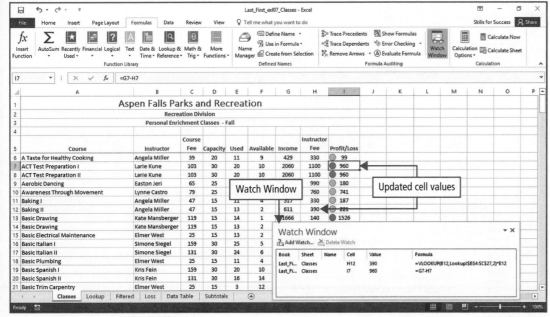

Excel 2016, Windows 10, Microsoft Corporation

Figure 4

6. Click cell **C4**, and then type 30 In the **Watch Window**, watch the **Value** for cell **H12**, and then press Enter. Notice the value changes from *130* to *390*.

   The Watch Window is used to view changes in cells that are not currently displayed in the worksheet.

7. Click cell **C18**, and then replace the existing value with 55 Press Enter. Notice that the **Value** of cell **I7** on the **Watch Window** changes from *1160* to *960*. Compare your screen with **Figure 3**.

8. Display the **Classes** worksheet. Verify that the value in cell **H12** is *390* and that the value in cell **I7** is *960*, and then compare your screen with **Figure 4**. If necessary, move the **Watch Window** as shown in the figure.

9. Using the techniques previously practiced, create a full-screen snip. **Save** 🖫 the snip in your chapter folder as Last_First_exl07_Snip2 **Close** ☒ the **Snipping Tool** window.

10. **Close** ☒ the **Watch Window**, and then click cell **A1**.

11. **Save** 🖫 the file.

■ **You have completed Skill 6 of 10**

▶ In Excel, a ***data table*** is a range of cells set up to show how changing one or two values in a formula will affect the formula's result.

▶ Data tables are used to perform what-if analyses and can contain one or two variables. A ***one-variable data table*** changes one value in a formula using input from either a row or a column.

1. Display the **Data Table** worksheet, and then click cell **B9**. Type =G6 and then press Enter.

2. In cell **B10**, type 3 and then press Enter. In cell **B11**, type 4.5% Press Enter. In cell **B12**, type 1200 Press Enter, and then compare your screen with **Figure 1**.

> These values reflect an investment earning 4.5 percent interest per year. The initial investment is the class profit of $44,770, and monthly payments of $1,200 will be added for three years.

3. With cell **B13** selected, on the **Formulas tab**, in the **Function Library group**, click the **Financial** button. If necessary, scroll down, and then click **FV**.

4. In the **Function Arguments** dialog box, in the **Rate** box, type B11/12 In the **Nper** box, type B10*12 In the **Pmt** box, type -B12 In the **Pv** box, type -B9 and then compare your screen with **Figure 2**.

> The result of the future value function indicates that the initial investment will grow to $97,387.28 if the investment earns 4.5 percent and monthly payments of $1,200 are made. Recall that both the initial amount invested and the payment amount should be negative values because the money is an outflow—money being paid out to the investment.

■ **Continue to the next page to complete the skill**

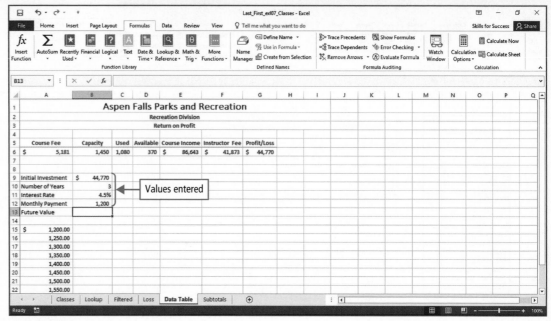

Figure 1

Excel 2016, Windows 10, Microsoft Corporation

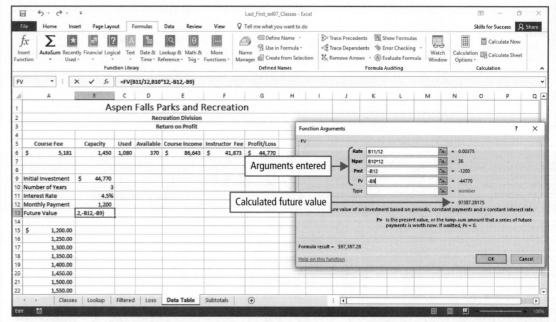

Figure 2

Excel 2016, Windows 10, Microsoft Corporation

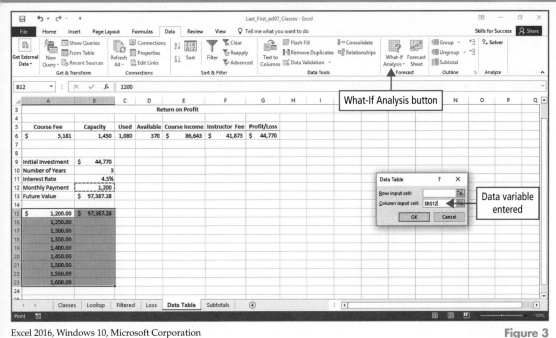

Excel 2016, Windows 10, Microsoft Corporation

Figure 3

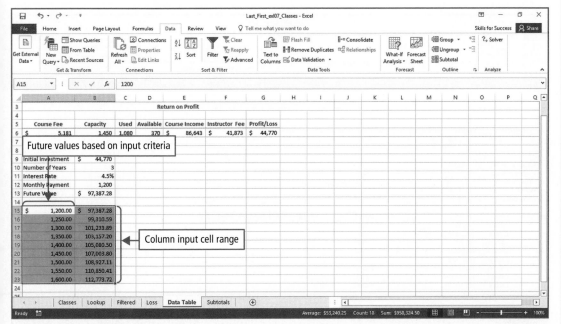

Excel 2016, Windows 10, Microsoft Corporation

Figure 4

5. Click **OK**. Click cell **B15**, type =B13 and then press Enter .

A data table must be built from an underlying formula. Here, the results of the future value formula in cell B13 will be the data table's underlying function.

6. Select the range **A15:B23**. Click the **Data tab**. In the **Forecast group**, click the **What-If Analysis** button, and then click **Data Table**.

7. In the **Data Table** dialog box, click the **Column input cell** box, and then click cell **B12**. If necessary, press F4 to change to an absolute cell reference. Compare your screen with **Figure 3**.

The Monthly Payment value in cell B12 represents the variable that will be changed using the values in the first column of the data table.

8. Click **OK**, and then compare your screen with **Figure 4**.

For each row in this data table, the payment value used in the FV function (B12) was changed to the corresponding value in column A. For example, in cell B17, the future value of the investment with a payment of *$1,300* would be *$101,233.89*.

9. Save 🖫 the file.

■ **You have completed Skill 7 of 10**

▶ A **_two-variable data table_** changes one value in a formula using two inputs—one from a column and one from a row.

▶ Two-variable data tables display the results across a range of cells.

1. On the **Data Table** worksheet, click cell **E15**. Type =B13 and then press Enter.

   Cell E15 will be the underlying formula for a two-variable data table.

2. In cell **E16**, type 1.0% and then press Enter. In cell **E17**, type 1.5% and then press Enter.

3. Select the range **E16:E17**, and then click the **Home tab**. In the **Number group**, click the **Decrease Decimal** button one time. Select the range **E16:E23**. On the **Home tab**, in the **Editing group**, click the **Fill arrow**, and then click **Series**. In the **Series** dialog box, in the **Stop value** box, type 4.5 and then click **OK**. Compare your screen with **Figure 1**.

   In the range E16:E23, the values will be the different interest rates used as the column input in a data table.

4. Click cell **F15**, type 1 and then press Tab. In cell **G15**, type 2 and then press Tab. Select the range **F15:J15**. In the **Editing group**, click the **Fill arrow**, and then click **Series**. In the **Series** dialog box, in the **Stop value** box, type 5 and then click **OK**. Compare your screen with **Figure 2**.

   The range F15:J15 will display the number of years used as the row input in the data table.

■ Continue to the next page to complete the skill ➤

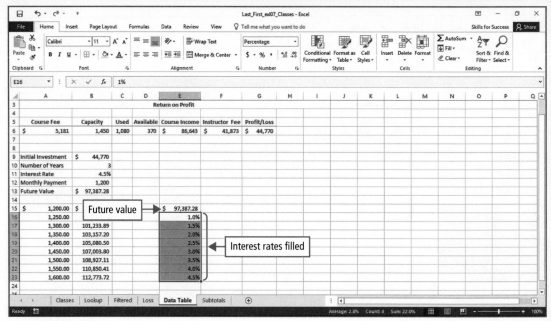

Figure 1

Excel 2016, Windows 10, Microsoft Corporation

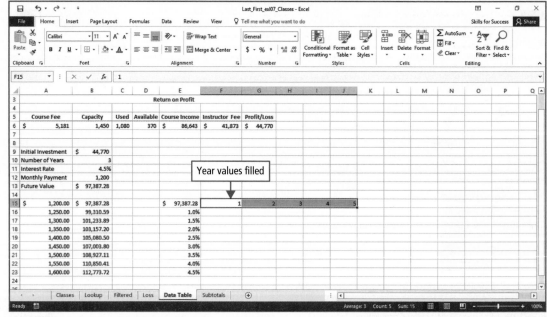

Figure 2

Excel 2016, Windows 10, Microsoft Corporation

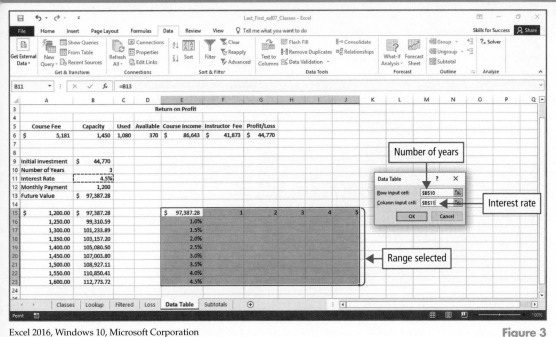

Excel 2016, Windows 10, Microsoft Corporation

Figure 3

5. Select the range **E15:J23**. Click the **Data tab**. In the **Forecast group**, click **What-If Analysis**, and then click **Data Table**.

6. In the **Data Table** dialog box, with the insertion point in the **Row input cell** box, click cell **B10**—the number of years the investment payments will be made. Press F4 if necessary to change to an absolute cell reference. Press Tab.

7. With the insertion point in the **Column input cell** box, click cell **B11**—the interest rate earned by the investment. Press F4 if necessary to change to an absolute cell reference. Compare your screen with Figure 3.

    In this data table, the Row input cell is equal to the number of years, and the Column input cell is equal to the interest rate.

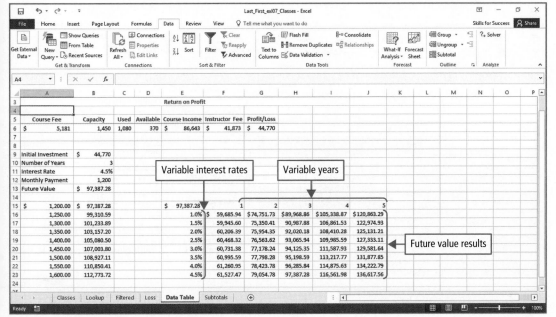

Excel 2016, Windows 10, Microsoft Corporation

Figure 4

8. Click **OK**. AutoFit columns as necessary. Click cell **A4**, and then compare your screen with Figure 4.

    A data table displays the results of its underlying function using two different variables. Here, the future value of the investment is calculated using the different interest rates in column E and the different years in row 15. For example, the future value of the investment after five years at 4.0 percent interest is $134,222.79.

9. **Save** 🖫 the file.

■ **You have completed Skill 8 of 10**

▶ A **table style** is a collection of table formatting options that can be applied to a range with a single click.

▶ Quick styles are displayed in a gallery with a small sample image of the style called a **thumbnail**.

1. Display the **Loss** worksheet. If necessary, AutoFit columns as needed. Select the range **A5:I19**. Click the **Home tab**. In the **Styles group**, click **Format as Table**, and then in the gallery, click **New Table Style**.

2. In the **New Table Style** dialog box, in the **Name** box, type Classes Compare your screen with **Figure 1**.

   You use the New Table Styles dialog box to create custom table styles that you name and format yourself.

3. In the **New Table Style** dialog box, under **Table Element**, verify that **Whole Table** is selected, and then click the **Format** button.

4. In the **Format Cells** dialog box, click the **Border tab**. Under **Line**, in the **Style** box, click the next to last style in the right column—solid thick line. Click the **Color arrow**, and then under **Theme colors**, click the fourth color in the first row—**Blue-Gray, Text 2**. Under **Presets**, click **Outline**. Compare your screen with **Figure 2**.

■ Continue to the next page to complete the skill
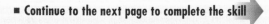

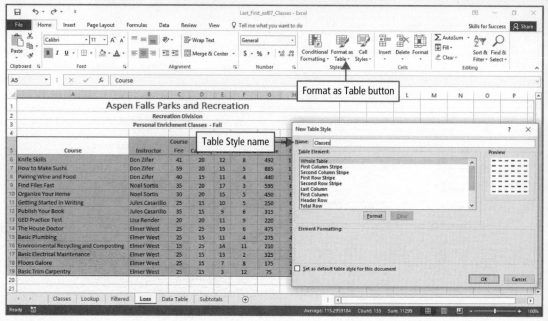

Figure 1   Excel 2016, Windows 10, Microsoft Corporation

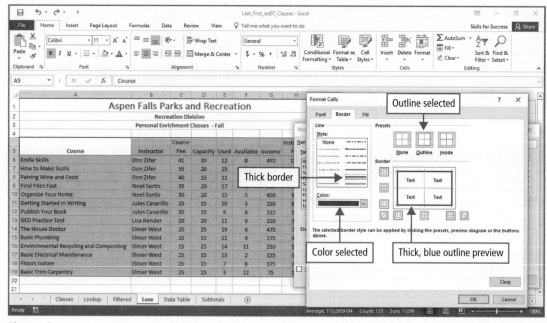

Figure 2   Excel 2016, Windows 10, Microsoft Corporation

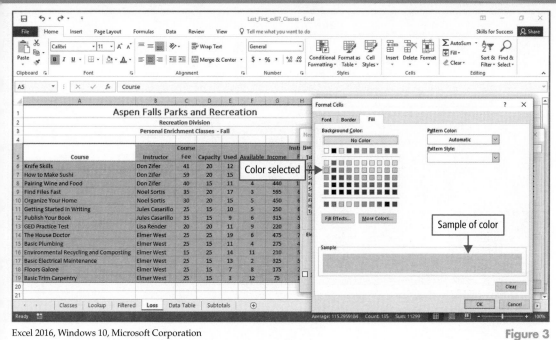

Excel 2016, Windows 10, Microsoft Corporation

Figure 3

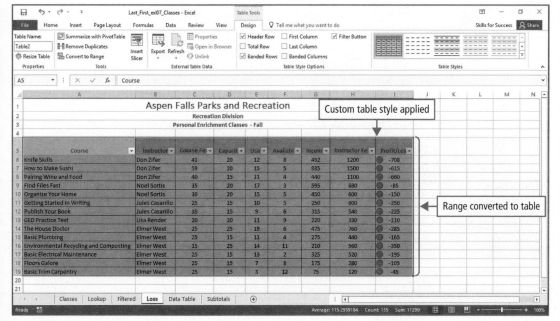

Excel 2016, Windows 10, Microsoft Corporation

Figure 4

5. In the **Style** box, click the last style in the left column—thin solid line, and then under **Presets**, click **Inside**.

6. Click the **Fill tab**. Under **Background Color**, click the first color in the third row. Compare your screen with **Figure 3**, and then click **OK**.

7. In the **New Table Style** dialog box, under **Table Element**, click **Header Row**, and then click the **Format** button. Obj 3.2.2 C

8. In the **Format Cells** dialog box, on the **Fill tab**, under **Background Color**, click the first color in the fourth row, and then click **OK**.

9. In the **New Table Style** dialog box, review the formatting under the **Preview** heading, and then click **OK**.

10. With the range **A5:I19** still selected, in the **Styles group**, click **Format as Table**. In the **Table Styles** gallery, under **Custom**, point to the thumbnail to display the name in the ScreenTip—*Classes*. Click the **Classes** thumbnail to apply the style. Obj 3.2.1 C

11. In the **Format As Table** dialog box, verify that the **Where is the data for your table** box displays *=$A$5:$I$19*. Verify the **My table has headers** check box is selected, and then click **OK**. Click cell **A1**, and then compare your screen with **Figure 4**.

    The custom table style is applied to the specified range, and the range is converted into an Excel table. Darker shading has been applied to the header row.

12. **Save** 💾 the file.

- **You have completed Skill 9 of 10**

▶ By default, Excel names tables when they are created, but you can rename a table to make it more meaningful.

▶ A **name** in Excel is a word that represents a cell, a range of cells, or a table that can be used as a reference.

1. Display the **Classes** worksheet, and then click cell **B6**. Click the **Data tab**, and then in the **Sort & Filter group**, click **Sort A to Z** [↓].

2. Select and copy the range **A1:I19**.

3. Click the **New Sheet** button ⊕. If necessary, click cell **A1**. Using the **Paste arrow,** paste the data using **Keep Source Column Widths (W)** 📋. Compare your screen with **Figure 1**.

4. Right-click the **Sheet1** tab, click **Rename**, and then type Range Press Enter.

5. On the **Home tab**, in the **Styles group**, click **Format as Table**. In the **Table Styles** gallery, under **Custom**, point to the thumbnail to display the name in the ScreenTip—*Classes*. Click the **Classes** thumbnail to apply the style.

6. In the **Format As Table** dialog box, in the **Where is the data for your table** box, select the range **A5:I19**, and then click the **My table has headers** check box.

7. Click **OK**, and then compare your screen with **Figure 2**.

    The range is formatted as an Excel table with filter and sort buttons in the header row.

■ Continue to the next page to complete the skill ▶

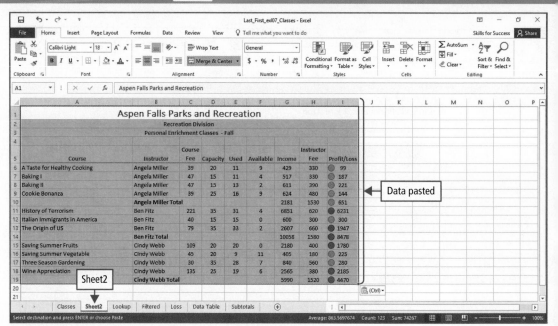

Figure 1

Excel 2016, Windows 10, Microsoft Corporation

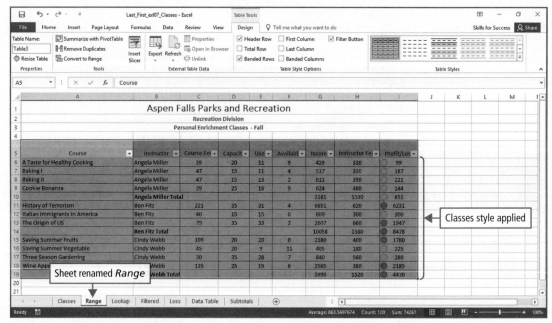

Figure 2

Excel 2016, Windows 10, Microsoft Corporation

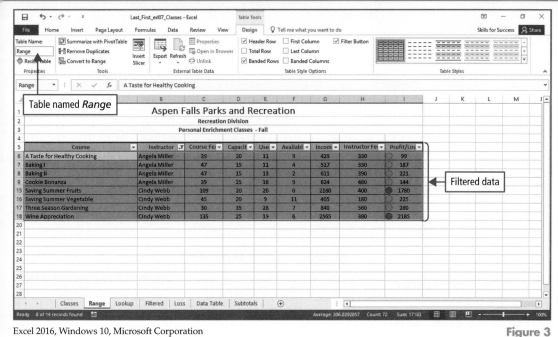

Excel 2016, Windows 10, Microsoft Corporation

Figure 3

8. On the **Table Tools Design tab**, in the **Properties group**, replace the **Table Name** *Table2* with *Range*

MOS
Obj 3.6.3 E

9. In cell **B5**, click the **Filter arrow**. In the **Filter** gallery, clear the **(Select All)** check box, and then select the **Angela Miller** and **Cindy Webb** check boxes. Click **OK**. Compare your screen with **Figure 3**.

The table name can be used in formulas or to select the table.

10. On the **Table Tools Design tab**, in the **Tools group**, click **Convert to Range**. Read the message that displays, and then click **Yes**. Click cell **A1**, and then compare your screen with **Figure 4**.

MOS
Obj 3.1.2 C

Recall that when a table is converted to a range, filters are removed; however, the formatting of the table remains.

11. Select the **Classes** worksheet tab, and then click cell **A1**.

12. **Save** 🖫 the file, and then **Close** ☒ Excel. Submit the files as directed by your instructor.

✔ **DONE!** You have completed Skill 10 of 10 and the workbook is complete!

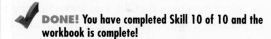

Excel 2016, Windows 10, Microsoft Corporation

Figure 4

More Skills 11

Insert Names into Formulas

To complete this project, you will need the following file:

- exl07_MS11Rentals

You will save your file as:

- Last_First_exl07_MS11Rentals

▶ Names used in formulas and functions clarify the meaning of formulas and assist in navigating large worksheets.

▶ The Name Manager can be used to create, edit, and organize the names.

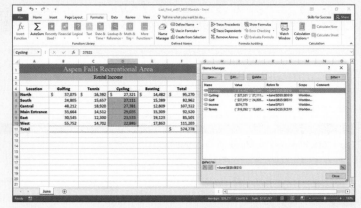

Figure 1   Excel 2016, Windows 10, Microsoft Corporation

1. Start **Excel 2016**, and then open the student data file **exl07_MS11Rentals**. Save the file in your chapter folder as Last_First_exl07_MS11Rentals

Obj 3.6.1 E

2. Click cell **F11**, and then to the left of the formula bar, click in the **Name Box** to select the current value, *F11*.

3. In the **Name Box**, type Income Press [Enter].

> Income has been assigned to the cell F11. A name should begin with a letter, an underscore, or a backslash, and spaces are not allowed.

Obj 3.6.2 E

4. Select the range **C4:C10**, and then click the **Formulas tab**. In the **Defined Names group**, click **Create from Selection**.

5. In the **Create Names from Selection** dialog box, verify that only the **Top row** check box is selected, and then click **OK**.

> The range C5:C10 has been named Tennis, which is the column label of the selected range.

6. Select the range **D5:D10**. In the **Defined Names group**, click the **Define Name arrow**, and then click **Define Name**.

7. In the **New Name** dialog box, verify *Cycling* appears in the **Name** box, and then click **OK**.

8. In the **Defined Names group**, click the **Name Manager button** to display the names in the workbook. Notice *Boating* and *Golf* were previously assigned, and *Income* only **Refers to** a cell. Compare your screen to Figure 1.

Obj 3.6.4 E

9. In the **Name Manager** dialog box, click **Golf**, and then click the **Edit** button. In the **Edit Name** dialog box, in the **Name** box, type Golfing Click **OK**, and then click **Close**.

MOS
Obj 1.1.4 E

10. Click cell **B11**, type =SUM(Golfing) and then press [Tab].

11. In cell **C11**, type =SUM(Te In the displayed **Formula AutoComplete** list, double-click **Tennis** to enter the name in the function, and then press [Tab].

12. In cell **D11**, on the **Formulas tab**, in the **Function Library group**, click the **AutoSum** button, and then press [Tab].

> When a name is available, AutoSum will insert that name as the cell reference. Here, =SUM(Cycling).

13. Use any technique previously practiced to enter a function in **E11** using *Boating* as the name reference.

14. Save 🖫 the file, and then **Close** ☒ Excel. Submit the file as directed by your instructor.

■ **You have completed More Skills 11**

More Skills 12

Use Goal Seek

To complete this project, you will need the following file:

- exl07_MS12Loans

You will save your file as:

- Last_First_exl07_MS12Loans

▶ *Goal Seek* is a what-if analysis tool that finds a specific value for a cell by adjusting the value of another cell.

▶ With Goal Seek, you can work backward from the desired outcome to find the input necessary to achieve your goal.

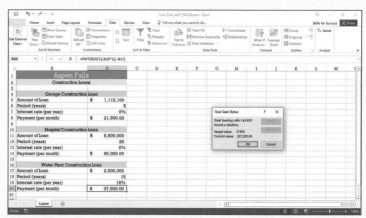

Excel 2016, Windows 10, Microsoft Corporation **Figure 1**

1. Start **Excel 2016**, and then open the student data file **exl07_MS12Loans**. Save the file in your chapter folder as Last_First_exl07_MS12Loans

2. Click cell **B8**. On the formula bar, view the *PMT* function. Click the **Data tab**. In the **Forecast group**, click the **What-If Analysis** button, and then click **Goal Seek**. In the **Goal Seek** dialog box, in the **Set cell** box, verify *B8* displays.   **MOS** Obj 3.4.3 E

3. In the **Goal Seek** dialog box, press ⌨Tab. In the **To value** box, type the payment goal of 21500 and then press ⌨Tab. In the **By changing cell** box, type B5 which is the amount of the loan.

   Goal Seek will determine how much money the city can borrow—the loan amount in cell B5—to stay within its budget of $21,500 per month. The period and interest rate in this scenario will remain unchanged.

4. In the **Goal Seek** dialog box, click **OK** to display the **Goal Seek Status** dialog box. Read the proposed solution, and then click **OK**.

   The calculations indicate that to achieve a monthly payment of $21,500, the city can borrow $1,112,100.

5. Click cell **B14**.

   The City Manager wants to know how much the life of the loan will be extended if monthly payments are reduced to $50,000.

6. Click the **What-If Analysis** button, and then click **Goal Seek**. In the **Set cell** box, confirm that *B14* displays, and then press ⌨Tab. In the **To value** box,

type the payment goal 50000 and then press ⌨Tab. In the **By changing cell** box, type B12 which is the number of years. Click **OK** two times. Apply the **Comma [0]** format to cell **B12**.

   The calculations indicate that if monthly payments of $50,000 are made, the period of the loan will be approximately 25 years—an increase from 20 years.

7. Click cell **B20**.

   For the water plant construction loan, the City Manager wants to know what interest rate would be needed so that monthly payments will be $37,500.

8. Using the techniques previously practiced, use **Goal Seek** to calculate a $37,500 monthly payment by changing the interest rate. Click **OK** to display the **Goal Seek Status** dialog box. Compare your screen with **Figure 1**. Click **OK**.

9. **Save** 🖫 the file, and then **Close** ⊠ Excel. Submit the file as directed by your instructor.

■ **You have completed More Skills 12**

More Skills 13

Use MATCH and INDEX Functions: Part 1

To complete this project, you will need the following file:

- exl07_MS13Supplies

You will save your file as:

- Last_First_exl07_MS13Supplies

▶ The **MATCH *function*** searches for a specific item in a range and returns the relative position of the item.

▶ Use this lookup function when you are looking for the position of an item in a range instead of the item itself.

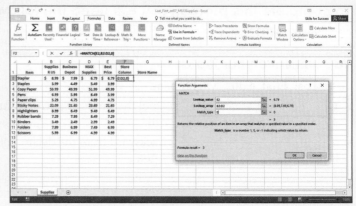

Figure 1   Excel 2016, Windows 10, Microsoft Corporation

1. Start **Excel 2016**, and then open the student data file **exl07_MS13Supplies**. Save the file in your chapter folder as Last_First_exl07_MS13Supplies

2. Click cell **F2**, and then click the **Formulas tab**. In the **Function Library group**, click the **Lookup & Reference** button, and then click **MATCH**.

3. In the **Function Arguments** dialog box, click in the **Lookup_value** box, and then click cell **E2**. Press Tab.

   This is the value to be looked up.

4. With the cursor in the **Lookup_array** box, click the range **B2:D2**, and then press Tab.

   This is the range Excel will search for the Lookup_value.

5. With the cursor in the **Match_type** box, type 0 and then compare your screen with **Figure 1**.

   Match_type is either 1, 0, or −1, indicating which value to return. Type 1 or no value, with the values in the array argument sorted in ascending order, will find the largest value that is less than or equal to the Lookup_value. Type 0 finds the first value that is exactly equal to the Lookup_value. Type −1, with the values in the array argument sorted in descending order, will find the smallest value that is greater than or equal to the Lookup_value.

6. Click **OK**. **AutoFill** the function in **F2** down through **F12**. Compare your screen with **Figure 2**.

   The result indicates the column in the Lookup_array where the *Best Price* for each item is located.

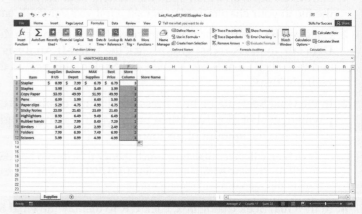

Figure 2   Excel 2016, Windows 10, Microsoft Corporation

7. Save 🖫 the file. Keep the file open if you are required to complete More Skills 14. Otherwise, **Close** ☒ Excel, and submit the file as directed by your instructor.

- **You have completed More Skills 13**

More Skills 14

Use MATCH and INDEX Functions: Part 2

To complete this project, you will need the following file:

- exl07_MS14Supplies

You will save your file as:

- Last_First_exl07_MS14Supplies

▶ An **INDEX *function reference*** is used to return the reference of a cell at the intersection of a specific row and column.

▶ An **INDEX *function array*** is used to return a value of a component in a table or an array.

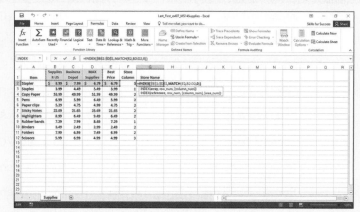

Excel 2016, Windows 10, Microsoft Corporation **Figure 1**

1. If you have **Last_First_exl07_MS13Supplies** open, save the file in your chapter folder as Last_First_exl07_MS14Supplies and then skip to step 2. Otherwise, start **Excel 2016**, and then open the student data file **exl07_MS14Supplies**. Save the file in your chapter folder as Last_First_exl07_MS14Supplies

2. Click cell **G2**, and then click the **Formulas tab**. In the **Function Library group**, click the **Lookup & Reference** button, and then click **INDEX**. Obj 3.2.4 E

3. In the **Select Arguments** dialog box, verify **array,row,num,column_num** is selected, and then click **OK**.

   Selecting the array will verify the value in the cell is returned instead of the reference to the cell.

4. In the **Function Arguments** dialog box, with the cursor in the **Array** box, drag to select the range **B1:D1**. Press **F4** to apply the absolute cell reference to copy the formula to other cells.

   This is the range where the value will be identified.

5. Press **Tab**. In the **Row_num** box, type MATCH(E2,B2:D2,0) and then click **OK**.

6. Double-click cell **G2** to display the formula and function arguments. Compare your screen to **Figure 1**. Press **Enter**.

   The MATCH function is used as a nested function to replace the row and column numbers because the column was identified by using the MATCH function in column F.

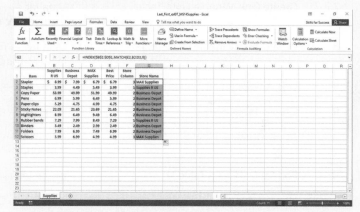

Excel 2016, Windows 10, Microsoft Corporation **Figure 2**

7. **AutoFill** the function in cell **G2** down through cell **G12**. Compare your screen with **Figure 2**.

   The *Store Name* values where the *Best Price* for the item can be found are displayed.

8. **Save** the file, and then **Close** Excel. Submit the file as directed by your instructor.

■ **You have completed More Skills 14**

Chapter Summary

Skills Number	Task	Step	Icon
1	Import text file	Data tab → Get External Data group → From Text → Select file	
2	Apply Advanced AutoFilter	Data tab → Sort & Filter group → Filter	▼
3	Sort Data Using Conditional Formatting	Home tab → Styles group → Conditional Formatting	
3	Sort Data	Data tab → Sort & Filter group → Sort	
4	Sort Data A to Z	Data tab → Sort & Filter group → Sort A to Z	↕
4	Subtotal Data	Data tab → Outline group → Subtotal → Select field to sort by	
5	Trace Precedents	Formulas tab → Formula Auditing group → Trace Precedents	
5	Trace Dependents	Formulas tab → Formula Auditing group → Trace Dependents	
6	Evaluate Formulas	Formulas tab → Formula Auditing group → Watch Window → Add Watch	
7	Create One-Variable Data Table	Data tab → Forecast group → What-If Analysis → Data Table → Enter input row or column address	
8	Create Two-Variable Data Table	Data tab → Forecast group → What-If Analysis → Data Table → Enter input row and column address	
8	Use Advanced Fill Series	Home tab → Editing group → Fill → Series	
9	Create Table Style	Home tab → Styles group → Format as Table → New Table Style	
9	Apply Custom Table Style	Home tab → Styles group → Format as Table → Custom → Click thumbnail	
9	Format Data as a Table	Home tab → Styles group → Format as Table	
10	Name Table	Table Tools Design tab → Properties group → Table Name	
10	Convert Tables to Range	Table Tools Design tab → Tools group → Convert to Range	
MS11	Create Name from Selection	Formulas tab → Defined Names group → Create from Selection	
MS11	Manage Names	Formulas tab → Defined Names group → Name Manager	
MS12	Use Goal Seek	Data tab → Forecast group → What-If Analysis → Goal Seek	
MS13	USE MATCH function	Formulas tab → Lookup & Reference group → MATCH	
MS14	Use INDEX function	Formulas tab → Lookup & Reference group → INDEX	

Project Summary Chart

Project	Project Type	Project Location
Skills Review	Review	In Book & MIL (MyITLab* Grader)
Skills Assessment 1	Review	In Book & MIL (MyITLab* Grader)
Skills Assessment 2	Review	Book
My Skills	Problem Solving	Book
Visual Skills Check	Problem Solving	Book
Skills Challenge 1	Critical Thinking	Book
Skills Challenge 2	Critical Thinking	Book
More Skills Assessment	Review	In Book & MIL (MyITLab* Grader)
Collaborating with Google	Critical Thinking	Book

MOS Objectives Covered (Quiz in MyITLab*)

1.1.4 C Copy and move a worksheet	3.2.4 E Look up data by using the INDEX function
1.1.2 C Import data from a delimited text file	3.4.3 E Perform what-if analysis by using Goal Seek and Scenario Manager
2.3.2 C Outline data	3.4.5 E Calculate data by using financial functions
2.3.3 C Insert subtotals	3.5.1 E Trace precedence and dependence
3.1.2 C Convert a table to a cell range	3.5.2 E Monitor cells and formulas by using the Watch Window
3.2.1 C Apply styles to tables	3.5.3 E Validate formulas by using error checking rules
3.2.2 C Configure table style options	3.5.4 E Evaluate formulas
3.3.2 C Sort data by multiple columns	3.6.1 E Name cells
1.1.4 E Reference data by using structured references	3.6.2 E Name data ranges
2.1.2 E Populate cell by using advanced Fill Series options	3.6.3 E Name tables
3.2.3 E Look up data by using the MATCH function	3.6.4 E Manage named ranges and objects

Key Terms

Online Help Skills

1. Start **Excel 2016**, and then in the upper right corner of the start page, click the **Help** button ? .

2. In the **Excel Help 2016** window **Search** box, type data tables and then press Enter .

3. In the search results, click **Calculate multiple results by using a data table**. **Maximize** the Excel 2016 Help window.

4. Read the article's introduction, and then below **In this article**, click **Data table basics**. Compare your screen with **Figure 1**.

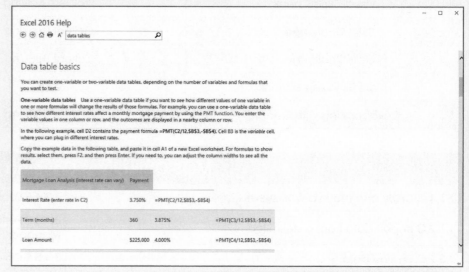

Figure 1   Excel 2016, Windows 10, Microsoft Corporation

5. Read the section to answer the following: How many different what-if analysis tools are available in Excel? Which what-if analysis tool should you use if you want to analyze more than two variables?

Matching  MyITLab®

Match each term in the second column with its correct definition in the first column by writing the letter of the term on the blank line in front of the correct definition.

___ **1.** A file that stores only text characters, not formatting or tables.

___ **2.** A logical operator that returns true if either of the criteria is true.

___ **3.** A tool that displays summary statistics for grouped data in an outline format.

___ **4.** An error value indicating that the wrong type of data is being used in the formula.

___ **5.** A process that analyzes a function by stepping into and out of each part of the function.

___ **6.** A window that provides information about selected cells when those cells are not currently displayed on the screen.

___ **7.** A range of calculations based on a single underlying formula that uses rows and/or columns as inputs.

___ **8.** The Data Table command can be found by clicking this button.

___ **9.** A data table type that takes input from a row and input from a column.

___ **10.** Table styles that you create and name display in the gallery under this category.

A #VALUE

B Custom

C Data table

D Evaluate Formula

E Or

F Subtotal

G Text file

H Two-variable

I Watch Window

J What-If Analysis

Multiple Choice

Choose the correct answer.

1. The type of file in which the data in each field is separated by a comma, a space, or a tab stop.
   A. Delimited
   B. Plain
   C. Comma-separated

2. This command displays only rows that meet a specified condition.
   A. Arranger
   B. Sorter
   C. Filter

3. When you use Subtotals, details can be expanded or collapsed using this.
   A. Outline Level
   B. Filter
   C. Group

4. This is a name for a cell value that is referred to by a function in another cell.
   A. Dependent
   B. Precedent
   C. Variable

5. This type of cell's value depends on the value in a given cell.
   A. Dependent
   B. Precedent
   C. Variable

6. This type of data table is created using input from either a row or a column.
   A. One-variable
   B. Two-variable
   C. Complex-variable

7. This is a collection of formatting options that can be applied with a single click.
   A. Style template
   B. Quick style
   C. Table style

8. This is a small sample image of a style.
   A. Thumbnail
   B. Live preview
   C. Icon

9. Select this option to remove filters from a table while keeping the table formatting.
   A. Sort
   B. Convert to Range
   C. Format as Table

10. This is created by default when a table is created.
    A. Table range
    B. Table size
    C. Table name

Topics for Discussion

1. What kind of information do you think a small business or organization would have in a text file or a database that would need to be imported into a spreadsheet?

2. For what purposes would you use the filter and sort tools when you work with spreadsheets?

Skills Review

To complete this project, you will need the following files:

- exl07_SRConcessions (Excel)
- exl07_SRText (Text)

You will save your files as:

- Last_First_exl07_SRConcessions
- Last_First_exl07_SRSnip1
- Last_First_exl07_SRSnip2
- Last_First_exl07_SRSnip3

1. Start **Excel 2016**, and then open the student data file **exl07_SRConcessions**. Save the file in your chapter folder as Last_First_exl07_SRConcessions

2. On the **Order** worksheet, click cell **A6**. Click the **Data tab**, click the **Get External Data** button, and then click **From Text**. In the **Import Text File** dialog box, locate **exl07_SRText**, and then click **Import**. In the **Text Import Wizard - Step 1 of 3**, click **Finish**, and then in the **Import Data** dialog box, click **OK**. AutoFit columns C:D, and then compare your screen with **Figure 1**.

3. Click cell **B6**. On the **Data tab**, in the **Sort & Filter group**, click **Sort A to Z**.

4. Click cell **E7**, and then click the **Formulas tab**. In the **Formula Auditing group**, click **Trace Precedents**, and then click **Trace Dependents**. Click **Evaluate Formula**. In the **Evaluate Formula** dialog box, click **Evaluate**, and then click **Step In**. Click **Step Out**, and then click **Evaluate**.

5. Create a full-screen snip. **Save** it in your chapter folder as Last_First_exl07_SRSnip1 Close the Snipping Tool window. Compare your screen with **Figure 2**.

6. In the **Evaluate Formula** dialog box, click **Close**. On the **Formulas tab**, in the **Formula Auditing group**, click **Remove Arrows**. Verify cell **E7** is selected, type =C7-D7 and then press Enter.

7. Click cell **E22**. In the **Formula Auditing group**, click the **Watch Window** button. In the **Watch Window**, click **Add Watch**, and then in the **Add Watch** dialog box, click **Add**. Click cell **E9**, click **Add Watch**, and then click **Add**. Click cell **D9**, type 22 and then press Enter. Create a full-screen snip, and then **Save** it in your chapter folder as Last_First_exl07_SRSnip2 Close the Snipping Tool window, and then close the **Watch Window**.

■ **Continue to the next page to complete this Skills Review**

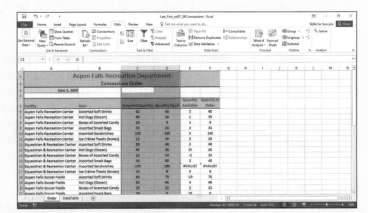

Excel 2016, Windows 10, Microsoft Corporation

Figure 1

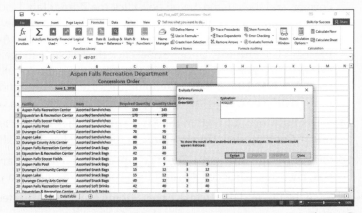

Excel 2016, Windows 10, Microsoft Corporation

Figure 2

8. Click the **Data tab**. In the **Sort & Filter** group, click **Filter**. Click the cell **B5 filter arrow**, point to **Text Filters**, and then click **Contains**. In the dialog box, in the first row, click the second box **arrow**, and then click **Assorted Snack Bags**. Click the **Or** option button. Under **Or**, click the first box **arrow**, scroll down, and then click **contains**. Click the second box **arrow**, and then click **Hot Dogs (Dozen)**. Click **OK**.

9. In the **Sort & Filter group**, click **Sort**. In the dialog box, under **Column**, click the **Sort by arrow**, and then click **Quantity to Order**. Under **Order**, click **Largest to Smallest**, and then click **OK**. Compare your screen with **Figure 3**.

10. Create a full-screen snip, and then **Save** it in your chapter folder as Last_First_exl07_SRSnip3 Close the Snipping Tool window.

11. In the **Sort & Filter group**, click **Filter**. Click cell **B6**, and then click **Sort A to Z**. In the **Outline group**, click **Subtotal**. In the dialog box, under **At each change in**, click the **arrow**, and then select **Item**. Click **OK**. Click **Outline Level 2**.

12. Display the **DataTable** worksheet, and then select the range **A15:B21**. In the **Forecast group**, click **What-If Analysis**, and then click **Data Table**. In the **Data Table** dialog box, click in the **Column input cell** box, and then click cell **D13**. Click **OK**. Select the range **D16:D21**. On the **Home tab**, in the **Editing group**, click **Fill**, and then click **Series**. In the **Stop value** box, type 6.5 and then click **OK**. Select the range **E15:H15**, and then repeat the techniques previously practiced using the **Stop value** of 4 Select the range **D15:H21**. Click the **Data tab**. In the **Forecast group**, click **What-If Analysis**, and then click **Data Table**. In the **Row input cell** box, click cell **D12**. In the **Column input cell** box, click cell **D13**. Click **OK**. AutoFit columns **F:H**.

13. Click the **Home tab**. In the **Styles group**, click **Format as Table**, and then click **New Table Style**. In the dialog box, in the **Name** box, type Concessions Click **Format**, and then in the dialog box, click the **Border tab**. Under **Style**, verify the last style in the left column is selected. Click the **Color arrow**, and then under **Theme colors**, click the last color in the first row—**Brown, Accent 6**. Under **Presets**, click **Outline**. Under **Style**, click the last style in the left column. Under **Presets**, click **Inside**. Click the **Fill tab**. Click the last color in the second row, and then click **OK**. Under **Table Element**, click **Header Row**, and then click **Format**. In the dialog box, click the first color in the third row. Click **OK** two times.

14. Select the range **A4:D11**. In the **Styles group**, click **Format as Table**, and then under **Custom**, click **Concessions**. In the **Format as Table** dialog box, click **OK**.

15. On the **Design tab**, in the **Tools group**, click **Convert to Range**. In the message box, click **Yes**. Click cell **A1**, and then compare your screen with **Figure 4**.

16. **Save** the file, and then **Close** Excel. Submit the files as directed by your instructor.

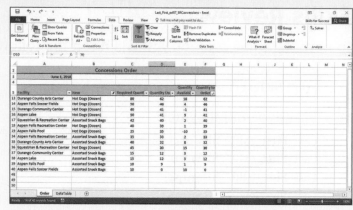

Figure 3   Excel 2016, Windows 10, Microsoft Corporation

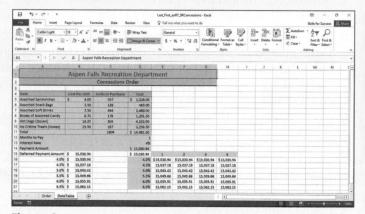

Figure 4   Excel 2016, Windows 10, Microsoft Corporation

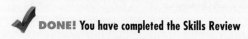

DONE! You have completed the Skills Review

Skills Assessment 1

To complete this project, you will need the following files:

- exl07_SA1Investments (Excel)
- exl07_SA1Text (Text)

You will save your files as:

- Last_First_exl07_SA1Investments
- Last_First_exl07_SA1Snip1
- Last_First_exl07_SA1Snip2
- Last_First_exl07_SA1Snip3

1. Start **Excel 2016**, and then open the student data file **exl07_SA1Investments**. Save the file in your chapter folder as Last_First_exl07_SA1Investments

2. Click cell **A5**, and then using all the wizard defaults, import the data in the delimited text file **exl07_SA1Text**. AutoFit columns **A:E**.

3. In the range **A5:E17**, sort the **Interest Rate** by **Cell Icon**, and then set the **Order** so that the **Green Circle** icon is **On Top**.

4. Filter the range **A4:E17** so that only the rows where the **Account Type** for **Money Market** displays. For the range, add a **Number Filter** so that the interest rate is less than 2.75%

5. Create a full-screen snip, and then **Save** it in your chapter folder as Last_ First_ exl07_SA1Snip1 Close the Snipping Tool window.

6. Remove all filters, and then sort the range **A5:E17** in ascending order by **Facility**. Add subtotals to provide a sum for the **Balance** column at each change in **Facility**. AutoFit column **C**.

7. For cell **E5**, display the **Trace Precedents** line. Use the **Evaluate Formula** dialog box to step through the process. Click **Step In** and **Step Out** one time each, and then click **Evaluate**. Move the **Evaluate Formula** dialog box so that the **Precedent** line displays. Create a full-screen snip, and then **Save** it in your chapter folder as Last_ First_exl07_SA1Snip2 Close the Snipping Tool window. Close the **Evaluate Formula** dialog box. Click **Remove Arrows**.

8. Add cell **E13** to the **Watch Window**. Click cell **D13**, type 4.75 and then press ⎋Tab⎋. Create a full-screen snip, and then **Save** it in your chapter folder as Last_First_ exl07_SA1Snip3 Close the Snipping Tool window. **Close** the **Watch Window**.

Aspen Falls Parks and Recreation
Capital Improvement Investments

Account Type	Facility	Balance	Interest Rate	Future Value
Stock Fund	Arts Center	$15,000.00 ●	4.28%	$22,797.82
Money Market	Arts Center	$8,700.00 ◆	1.05%	$9,657.89
	Arts Center Total	$23,700.00		
Stock Fund	Golf	$11,525.00 △	2.79%	$15,168.35
Money Market	Golf	$54,832.00 ◆	2.15%	$67,829.37
	Golf Total	$66,357.00		
Stock Fund	Parks	$18,550.00 ●	4.28%	$28,193.30
Stock Fund	Parks	$45,529.00 △	2.35%	$57,405.62
Money Market	Parks	$878,546.00 ●	4.75%	$1,397,348.79
	Parks Total	$942,625.00		
Money Market	Pool	$7,500.00 △	2.75%	$9,837.38
Savings	Pool	$68,000.00 △	2.79%	$89,496.55
	Pool Total	$75,500.00		
Savings	Recreation Center	$6,391.00 ●	3.95%	$9,414.86
Savings	Recreation Center	$14,500.00 ◆	1.55%	$16,910.92
Money Market	Recreation Center	$19,000.00 △	2.33%	$23,909.54
	Recreation Center Total	$39,891.00		
Savings	Tennis	$105,250.00 ◆	2.18%	$130,517.45
	Tennis Total	$105,250.00		
	Grand Total	$1,253,323.00		

Excel 2016, Windows 10, Microsoft Corporation

Figure 1

9. Select the range **A4:E23**, and then create a new table style. **Name** the style Investments For the **Whole Table**, apply the **Outline** and **Inside** borders using the last line style in the left column. For the line color, apply the eighth color in the first row—**Green Accent 4**. On the **Fill tab**, click the first color in the third row. Close all open dialog boxes, and then apply the new table style to the range. Click **Yes** on the message box. Convert the table to a normal range. AutoFit the columns. Click cell **A1**. Print Preview the worksheet, and then compare your screen with Figure 1.

10. **Save** the file, and then **Close** Excel. Submit the files as directed by your instructor.

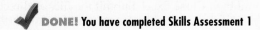

DONE! You have completed Skills Assessment 1

Skills Assessment 2

To complete this project, you will need the following file:

- exl07_SA2Endowment

You will save your files as:

- Last_First_exl07_SA2Endowment
- Last_First_exl07_SA2Snip

---

1. Start **Excel 2016**, and then open then student data file **exl07_SA2Endowment**. Save the file in your chapter folder as Last_First_exl07_SA2Endowment

2. In cell **A8** of the **Endowment** worksheet, insert the **FV** function. Type B5/12 for the **Rate**, B6*12 for the **Nper**, and -B4 for the **Pv**.

3. In the range **A9:A19**, fill the **Series** using **Stop value** 6.0 In the range **B8:G8**, fill the **Series** using **Stop value** 6 For the range **A8:G19**, create a two-variable data table that uses the term for the row input and the interest rate for the column input. AutoFit columns as needed.

4. Display the **Rental** worksheet. Create a new table style with the name Rental For the **Inside** border for the **Whole Table**, apply the last line style in the left column, and the color **Green, Accent 6**. Use the same color and the next-to-last line in the right column for the **Outline** border. On the **Fill tab**, apply the third color in the first row, and then for the table's **Header Row**, on the **Fill tab**, assign the last color in the second row.

5. Select the range **A4:F11**, and then apply the **Rental** custom table style.

6. For the range **A4:F11**, apply a custom **Number Filter** so that only the rows where the **Income** value **is greater than or equal to** 250000 and **is less than or equal to** 500000 display. Name the table Endowment

7. Create a full-screen snip. **Save** the file in your chapter folder as Last_First_exl07_SA2Snip Close the Snipping Tool window.

8. Remove all filters. Convert the table **A4:F11** to a range.

9. On the **Table** worksheet, in cell **C5**, sort the data **A to Z**. Use the **Subtotal** command to sum the **Net** column for each change in **Rate**. Collapse the subtotals to level 2. Print Preview the workbook, and then compare your worksheets with **Figures 1**, **2**, and **3**.

10. **Save** the file, and then **Close** Excel. Submit the files as directed by your instructor.

Aspen Falls Parks and Recreation
Arts Endowment

Amount of Bonds	$129,726
Interest Rate	3.50%
Term	6

$159,991.21	1	2	3	4	5	6
1.00% $	131,029.22	$ 132,345.54	$ 133,675.07	$ 135,017.97	$ 136,374.35	$ 137,744.37
1.50%	131,685.32	133,674.24	135,693.20	137,742.65	139,823.05	141,934.88
2.00%	132,344.44	135,015.72	137,740.93	140,521.14	143,357.47	146,251.05
2.50%	133,006.57	136,370.10	139,818.69	143,354.49	146,979.70	150,696.59
3.00%	133,671.74	137,737.49	141,926.91	146,243.75	150,691.90	155,275.34
3.50%	134,339.96	139,118.02	144,066.03	149,190.02	154,496.25	159,991.21
4.00%	135,011.24	140,511.80	146,236.47	152,194.37	158,395.00	164,848.26
4.50%	135,685.59	141,918.96	148,438.69	155,257.94	162,390.46	169,850.65
5.00%	136,363.03	143,339.62	150,673.15	158,381.87	166,484.99	175,002.68
5.50%	137,043.57	144,773.90	152,940.29	161,567.32	170,680.99	180,308.74
6.00%	137,727.22	146,221.93	155,240.58	164,815.48	174,980.93	185,773.38

Last_First_exl07_SA2Endowment

Figure 1   Excel 2016, Windows 10, Microsoft Corporation

Aspen Falls Parks and Recreation
Property Rental

Property	Rental Fees	Rate	Income	Expenses	Net
Aspen Falls Recreation Center	$ 956,098	0.321	$ 306,907	$ 234,784	$ 72,123
Equestrian and Recreation Center	654,786	0.364	238,342	182,332	56,010
Aspen Falls Pool	345,780	0.238	82,296	62,956	19,339
Durango Community Center	1,345,657	0.312	419,845	321,181	98,664
Aspen Falls Soccer Fields	355,700	0.275	97,818	74,830	22,987
Aspen Lake	235,000	0.312	73,320	56,090	17,230
Durango County Arts Center	1,654,800	0.275	455,070	348,129	106,941

Last_First_exl07_SA2Endowment

Figure 2   Excel 2016, Windows 10, Microsoft Corporation

Aspen Falls Parks and Recreation
Electic Usage

Property	Amount	Rate	Income	Expenses	Net
		38% Total			826,025
		45% Total			1,440,262
		Grand Total			2,266,287

Last_First_exl07_SA2Endowment

Figure 3   Excel 2016, Windows 10, Microsoft Corporation

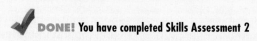

DONE! You have completed Skills Assessment 2

First Last
3rd Quarter Budget

Months	July	August	September	Total
Net Income	$ 2,234.56	$ 2,456.34	$ 2,356.62	$ 7,047.52
Expenses:				
Rent/Mortgage	500.00	500.00	500.00	1,500.00
Car Gas	180.00	165.00	170.00	515.00
Car Payment	225.25	225.25	225.25	675.75
Car Insurance	124.67	124.67	124.67	374.01
Utility Cell Phone	69.76	69.76	69.76	209.28
Utility Internet	49.00	49.00	49.00	147.00
Utility Electricity	92.23	87.43	74.18	253.84
Utility Cable	39.00	39.00	39.00	117.00
Food	400.00	350.00	375.00	1,125.00
Clothing	-	137.89	64.94	202.83
Entertainment	65.00	53.00	48.00	166.00
Savings	489.65	655.34	616.82	1,761.81
Total Expenses	$ 1,744.91	$ 1,801.00	$ 1,739.80	$ 5,285.71

Last_First_exl07_MYBudget

Excel 2016, Windows 10, Microsoft Corporation   **Figure 1**

First Last
Savings Future Value

Savings Investment	$1,761.81
Number of years	3
Interest Rate	1.05%
Monthly payment	100.00
Future Value	$5,473.84
$100.00	$ 5,473.84
$125.00	$ 6,387.76
$150.00	$ 7,301.68
$175.00	$ 8,215.60
$200.00	$ 9,129.52
$225.00	$ 10,043.44
$250.00	$ 10,957.35
$275.00	$ 11,871.27
$300.00	$ 12,785.19
$325.00	$ 13,699.11
$350.00	$ 14,613.03
$375.00	$ 15,526.95
$400.00	$ 16,440.87

Last_First_exl07_MYBudget

Excel 2016, Windows 10, Microsoft Corporation   **Figure 2**

My Skills

To complete this project, you will need the following file:

- exl07_MYBudget

You will save your file as:

- Last_First_exl07_MYBudget

1. Start **Excel 2016**, and then open the student data file **exl07_MYBudget**. Save the file in your chapter folder as Last_First_exl07_MYBudget

2. In the first cell of the **Budget** worksheet, replace *Student Name* with your First and Last names.

3. Enter your **Net Income** (income after taxes) for **July**, **August**, and **September**.

4. Enter your expense data for **July**, **August**, and **September** for all expenses. If you do not have these expenses, use the Internet to search for the data and enter estimated data for the area in which you live. Enter 0 in any cells for which your expenses are zero.

5. Using the techniques practiced in this chapter, create a table style using the name Budget with the following formatting: thick line **Blue-Gray, Text 2**, **Outline** border, thin line **Blue, Accent 1 Inside** border, fill color first row, third color. Add a **Header Row** using fill color second row, third color.

6. Apply the **Budget** table style to the range **A4:E19**, and then click cell **A1**. Print

Preview the worksheet, and then compare your screen with **Figure 1**.

7. On the **Savings tab**, replace *Student Name* with your First and Last names.

8. In cell **B5**, type the current interest rate for your savings account. If you don't have one, use the Internet to search for a rate.

9. In cell **B7**, use the **FV** function to create the result using B5/12 for the **Rate**, B4*12 for **Nper**, -B6 for **Pmt**, and -B3 for **Pv**.

10. Create a **What-if Analysis** one-variable data table for the range **A8:B20** using **B6** as the **Column input**. AutoFit columns as needed.

11. Click cell **A1**. Print Preview the worksheet, and then compare your screen with Figure 2.

12. **Save** the file, and then **Close** Excel. Submit the file as directed by your instructor.

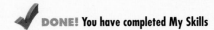 **DONE! You have completed My Skills**

Visual Skills Check

To complete this project, you will need the following files:

- exl07_VSEquipment (Excel)
- exl07_VSText (Text)

You will save your file as:

- Last_First_exl07_VSEquipment

Start **Excel 2016**, and then open the student data file **exl07_VSEquipment**. Save the file in your chapter folder as Last_First_exl07_VSEquipment In cell **A4**, import the data from **exl07_VSText**, accepting all wizard defaults. Create a custom table style named Equipment with borders and shading similar to the table shown in **Figure 1**. If necessary, remove all external data ranges. Apply the table style to the range, and then name the table Equipment Convert the table to a range. Sort the Facility column from A to Z. Use the **Subtotal** tool to organize and summarize the data as shown in **Figure 1**.

Save the file, and then **Close** Excel. Submit the file as directed by your instructor.

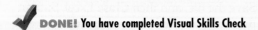 **DONE!** You have completed Visual Skills Check

Aspen Falls Parks and Recreation
Athletic Equipment Inventory

Facility	Facility ID	Description	Quantity
Aspen Lake	17	Long Rafts	32
Aspen Lake	17	Horseshoe Sets	4
Aspen Lake Total			36
Aspen Pool	21	Water Volleyball nets	2
Aspen Pool	21	Ring Rafts	10
Aspen Pool	21	Water Volleyballs	6
Aspen Pool Total			18
Recreation Center	7	Indoor Soccer Goals 6'6" x 12'W	6
Recreation Center	7	Adidas Soccer Balls	16
Recreation Center	7	Basketballs	12
Recreation Center	7	Tennis Racquets	22
Recreation Center	7	Softballs	10
Recreation Center	7	Wooden Bats	16
Recreation Center	7	Pool Tables	4
Recreation Center Total			86
Soccer Fields	3	Adidas Soccer Balls	20
Soccer Fields	3	Soccer Goals 8'H x 24'W	4
Soccer Fields	3	Soccer Goals 6'6"H x 18'6"W	4
Soccer Fields Total			28
Grand Total			168

Figure 1

Excel 2016, Windows 10, Microsoft Corporation

Skills Challenge 1

To complete this project, you will need the following file:

- exl07_SC1Claims

You will save your file as:

- Last_First_exl07_SC1Claims

Aspen Falls tracks employee health care claims on a yearly basis in an effort to reduce costs and promote employee well-being. Start **Excel 2016**, and then open the student data file **exl07_SC1Claims**. Save the file in your chapter folder as Last_First_exl07_SC1Claims Format the range **A4:F106** as a table, using skills practiced in the chapter to create a new table style with the name Claims Apply the following: a thick Dark Blue outline border and thin inside border using the same color. Apply the following fill color: first row, third color. For the Header Row, apply the fill color in the second row, third color.

Remove all external data ranges. Using the trace and evaluation tools, locate and fix the three errors in the table. Sort the table in ascending order by Code. Name the table Claims Convert the table to a range to retain the formatting. Subtotal both the Fee and Co-Pay 15% columns by Code. Collapse the subtotals to Level 2. Save the file with the filter applied. **Close** Excel, and then submit the file as directed by your instructor.

 DONE! You have completed Skills Challenge 1

Skills Challenge 2

To complete this project, you will need the following file:

- exl07_SC2Triathalon

You will save your file as:

- Last_First_exl07_SC2Triathalon

Aspen Falls tracks racers in its annual Women's Triathlon in an effort to provide the results to racing magazines. Start **Excel 2016**, and then open the student data file **exl07_SC2Triathalon**. Save the file in your chapter folder as Last_First_exl07_SC2Triathalon Sort the Total Time in ascending order. Copy the range **A1:H21** and paste it into a new worksheet, keeping the column widths. Name the new sheet Top 20 Apply the following to the Top 20 worksheet: a Subtotal at each change in

Bracket by Total Time, and the Level 2 Outline, which will show the Total Time by Bracket. Sort the Bracket column in ascending order. Save the file with the filter applied. **Close** Excel, and then submit the file as directed by your instructor.

 DONE! You have completed Skills Challenge 2

More Skills Assessment

MyITLab®
Grader

To complete this project, you will need the following file:

- exl07_MSAPressure

You will save your file as:

- Last_First_exl07_MSAPressure

1. Start **Excel 2016**. Open the file **exl07_MSAPressure**, and then save the file in your chapter folder as Last_First_exl07_MSAPressure

2. Select the range **A5:A24**. Use one of the **Defined Names** options, and then name the range Actual

3. Select the range **B5:B24**. Use one of the **Defined Names** options, and then name the range Effective

4. In cell **G5**, insert the **AVG** function to calculate the average and use the name *Actual* in the function. Repeat this technique to enter the **AVG** in cell **G7** for the *Effective* pressure.

5. On the **Loan** worksheet, in cell **B5**, use the **Goal Seek** tool to change the payment to 7500 by changing cell **B4**. Close the **Goal Seek Status** dialog box.

6. In cell **E5**, enter the **MATCH** lookup function to compare the *Effective* value in **B5** to the *Lower* and *Upper* limits in C5:D5 The function should return **match_type** 1 AutoFill the function in **E5** down through **E24**.

7. In cell **F5** enter the **INDEX** function that will return either the value **Lower** or **Upper** nesting the **MATCH** function in column **F**. Ensure the absolute cell reference is applied to the limit array. AutoFill the function in **F5** down through **F24**.

8. Print Preview the worksheet, and then compare your screen with Figure 1.

9. **Save** the file, and then **Close** Excel. Submit the file as directed by your instructor.

DONE! You have completed the More Skills Assessment

Aspen Falls Public Works
Down Station Water Flow Pressure

| Pressure | | Limit | | | | Average |
Actual	Effective	Lower	Upper	Match	Limit	Actual
50.14632083	50	50	80	1	Lower	80.93
65.75295841	75	50	80	1	Lower	Effective
103.4881601	75	50	80	1	Lower	73.75
71.33995233	65	50	80	1	Lower	
89.42815868	75	50	80	1	Lower	
62.28549117	75	50	80	1	Lower	
54.74312184	65	50	80	1	Lower	
63.01944309	75	50	80	1	Lower	
82.39797684	80	50	80	2	Upper	
62.09239442	65	50	80	1	Lower	
82.22902999	80	50	80	2	Upper	
72.91958561	65	50	80	1	Lower	
101.2778886	80	50	80	2	Upper	
94.67332211	80	50	80	2	Upper	
129.2104518	80	50	80	2	Upper	
95.39194563	80	50	80	2	Upper	
73.18687941	75	50	80	1	Lower	
80.83710894	80	50	80	2	Upper	
104.4547511	75	50	80	1	Lower	
79.76808599	80	50	80	2	Upper	

Last_First_exl07__MSAPressure

Figure 1   Excel 2016, Windows 10, Microsoft Corporation

Collaborating with Google

To complete this project, you will need a Google account (refer to the Common Features chapter) and the following file:

- exl07_GPStudents

You will save your file as:

- Last_First_exl07_GPSnip

1. Open the **Google Chrome** web browser. Log into your Google account, and then click the **Apps** button.

2. Click **Drive** to open Google Drive.

3. Click the **New** button, and then click **File upload**. Navigate to the student data files, and then open **exl07_GPStudents**.

4. Double-click the **exl07_GPStudents** in **Google Drive**, and then click **Open** to view the workbook in **Google Sheets**.

5. Click cell **A1**, click **Filter views**, and then click **Create new filter view**.

6. Click the cell **D1 filter arrow**, and then click **Filter by condition**. Click **None** in the next box, and then select **Text is exactly**. In the **Value or formula** box, type Central and then click **OK**.

7. Click the cell **B1 filter arrow**, and then click **Sort A→Z**.

8. Click **Filter 1** in the **Name** box, replace the text with Dorr Dr and then press Enter.

9. Click the cell **B1 filter arrow**, click to uncheck **Dagel**, **Pearl**, and **Teare**, and then click **OK**.

10. Click the cell **C1 filter arrow**, and then click **Filter by condition**. Click **None** in the next box, and then select **Text contains**. In the **Value or formula** box, type Dorr and then click **OK**. Compare your screen with Figure 1.

11. Use the Windows Snipping Tool to take a full-screen Snip, and then save the file to your chapter folder as Last_First_exl07_GPSnip

12. Close all windows, and then submit the file as directed by your instructor.

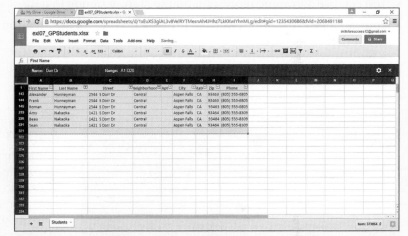

Figure 1

✔ **DONE! You have completed Collaborating with Google**

CHAPTER 8

Manage and Present Data Visually

▶ Excel functions can be used to edit data imported from other files.

▶ You can use legends to help users understand charted data.

▶ You can use a graphic representation to signify trends in data.

▶ You can insert text into shapes to provide additional information about data in a chart.

▶ You can combine data from multiple worksheets into one worksheet.

▶ Excel provides preformatted charts that can be edited to fit your needs.

▶ Excel workbooks can be shared through email or by storing on a secure, web-based application.

Minerva Studio/Fotolia

Aspen Falls City Hall

In this chapter, you will support Janet Neal, Finance Director of Aspen Falls. You will assist her with editing an existing workbook using text functions, chart tools, and Excel templates to manipulate employee expense data, and then save workbooks in different formats to share via email and web-based services. This workbook will assist Janet with evaluating employee expenses for upper management through charts to predict possible future expenses and trends and to compare employees' expenses.

Businesses and organizations often use Excel workbooks to manipulate data downloaded from other types of application programs. When data is imported into an Excel workbook, it can be edited to repair the data or to create new data. The data can then be represented using different chart views and elements.

In this project, you will open files from other application programs, and use text functions to edit data to create employee passwords and to delete extra spaces entered incorrectly. You will edit and create charts incorporating legends, trendlines, data ranges, data labels, and alternate data views. Additionally, you will create dual axis charts to compare data and create chart templates. You will edit an Excel template to create an employee expense report template and combine data from other worksheets into a worksheet within the workbook. Finally, you will save the workbook as different file types in order to share with others through email, the Internet, and OneDrive.

Time to complete all 10 skills — 60 to 90 minutes

Outcome

Using the skills in this chapter, you will be able to edit data using text functions and display data visually using charts and chart elements.

Objectives

8.1 Construct imported data using text functions

8.2 Evaluate data using charts and chart elements

8.3 Understand file type versions and sharing files

Student data files needed for this chapter:

exl08_Expenses (Excel)
exl08_Employee (Excel)
exl08_CityHall (Access)

You will save your files as:

Last_First_exl08_Expenses
Last_First_exl08_Pdf
Last_First_exl08_Snip
Last_First_exl08_Txt
Last_First_exl08_Xml
Last_First_exl08_Xls

SKILLS

MyITLab®
Skills 1–10 Training

Skill 1 Import and TRIM Data from Non-native Files

Skill 2 Use LEFT, RIGHT, and MID Functions

Skill 3 Add Legends and Data Series to Charts

Skill 4 Enhance Charts with Trendlines and Text Boxes

Skill 5 Modify Excel Worksheet Templates

Skill 6 Consolidate Worksheet Data

Skill 7 Construct Dual Axis Charts

Skill 8 Create and Edit Custom Chart Templates

Skill 9 Edit and Save Excel File Type Versions

Skill 10 Send Workbook Files via Email and OneDrive

MORE SKILLS

Skill 11 Modify Charts and Graph Parameters

Skill 12 Manage Workbook Versions

Skill 13 Serialize Numbers Using Functions

Skill 14 Modify the Excel Ribbon

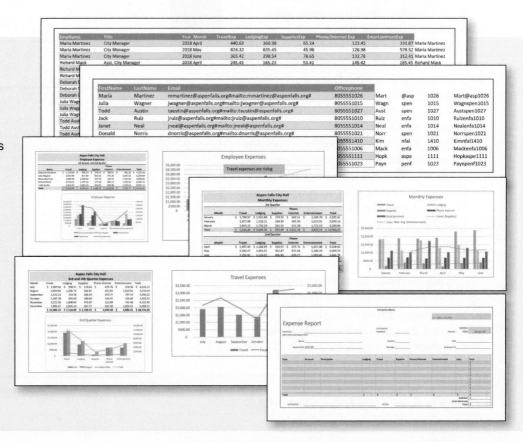

▶ In Excel, you can open *non-native files*—formats that are not current Excel 2016 files—including previous versions, text files, and data tables.

▶ When text data is imported or copied into Excel, extra spaces can sometimes be included with the data.

▶ The *TRIM function* is a text function used to remove all spaces from a text string except for single spaces between words.

1. Start **Excel 2016**, and then open the student data file **exl08_Expenses**. Click the **File tab**, and then click **Save As**. Click the **Browse** button, and then navigate to the location where you are saving your files. Click **New folder**, type Excel Chapter 8 and then press Enter two times. Save the file as Last_First_ exl08_Expenses and then press Enter. If necessary, enable the content.

2. If necessary, select the **Data** worksheet, and then click cell **A1**. Click the **File tab**, and then click **Open**. Navigate to the student data files for this chapter. At the bottom of the **Open** dialog box, click the file extension drop down arrow, and then select **All Files**. Select **exl08_CityHall**, and then compare your screen with **Figure 1**. **Open** the file.

3. In the **Microsoft Excel Security Notice** dialog box, read the information, and then click **Enable**.

   When you link a file to an external file, Excel recognizes potential security issues.

4. In the **Select Table** dialog box, click to select the **2nd Qtr Expenses** table. Compare your screen with **Figure 2**, and then click **OK**.

■ **Continue to the next page to complete the skill**

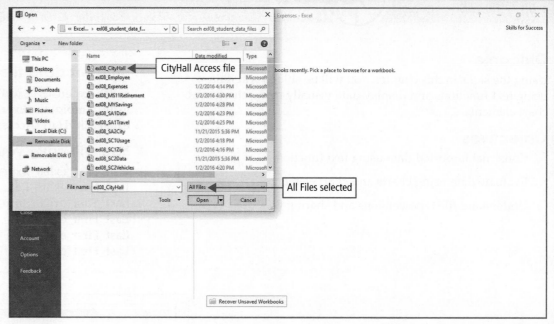

Figure 1

Excel 2016, Windows 10, Microsoft Corporation

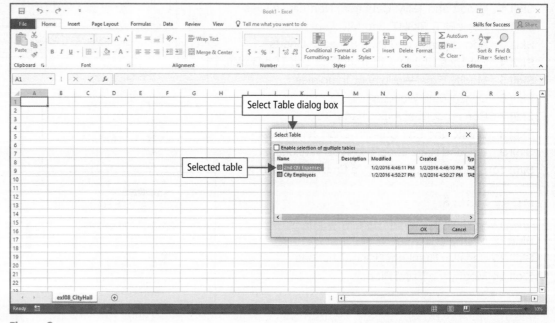

Figure 2

Excel 2016, Windows 10, Microsoft Corporation

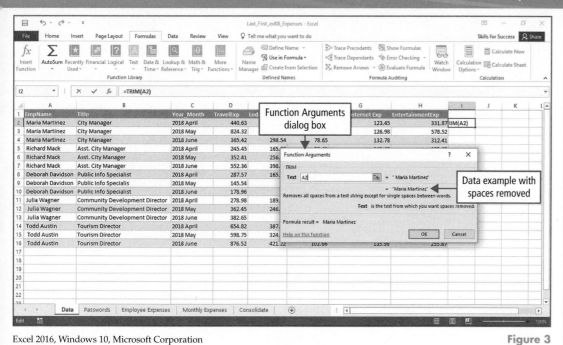

Excel 2016, Windows 10, Microsoft Corporation

Figure 3

Excel 2016, Windows 10, Microsoft Corporation

Figure 4

5. In the **Import Data** dialog box, verify that the **Existing worksheet** is selected and the box displays =$A$1, and then click **OK**.

6. Select and then copy the range **B1:I16**. On the taskbar, click **Excel** ☒, and then navigate to the Last_First_exl08_Expenses window. In the **Data** worksheet, verify cell **A1** is selected. Use techniques previously practiced to paste the range using 📋—**Keep Source Column Widths (W)**.

7. Close the **Book1** Excel file without saving. In the **Microsoft Excel** dialog box, read the information, and then click **No**.

8. On the **Data** worksheet, click cell **I2**. Click the **Formulas tab**. In the **Function Library group**, click the **Text** button, and then click **TRIM**.

9. In the **Function Arguments** dialog box, in the **Text** box, type A2 Compare your screen with **Figure 3**, and then click **OK**.

Maria Martinez is the data that was evaluated. The spaces before the name were removed.

10. With **I2** selected, AutoFill down through cell **I16**. Compare your screen with **Figure 4**.

The data in column A has extra spaces before it; the data in column I does not.

11. Copy the range **I2:I16**, and then click cell **A2**. Use the techniques previously practiced to paste the range using 📋—**Values (V)**. Press Esc .

You are replacing the data that has extra spaces. Paste Values pastes the values, not the functions.

12. **Save** 💾 the file.

■ **You have completed Skill 1 of 10**

► When text data is imported or copied into an Excel spreadsheet, characters from these cells can be extracted to create new data.

► The **LEFT function** returns a specified number of characters starting from the left side of the data.

► The **RIGHT function** returns a specified number of characters starting from the right side of the data.

► The **MID function** returns a specified number of characters starting from a specified position in the data.

1. Click the **Passwords** worksheet tab. Click cell **A1**, and then on the **File tab**, click **Open**. Navigate to the student data files for this chapter. At the bottom of the **Open** dialog box, verify **All Files** is selected, and then **Open** the file **exl08_CityHall**.

2. In the **Microsoft Excel Security Notice** dialog box, click **Enable**.

3. In the **Select Table** dialog box, click the **City Employees** table. Compare your screen with **Figure 1**, and then click **OK**.

4. In the **Import Data** dialog box, verify that the **Existing worksheet** option button is selected and that the box displays the text =$A$1, and then click **OK**.

5. Select and then copy the range **B1:E11**. On the taskbar, click **Excel** 🔣, and then navigate to the Last_First_exl08_ Expenses window. In the **Passwords** worksheet, use the techniques previously practiced to paste the range using 🔘—**Keep Source Column Widths (W)**. Compare your screen with **Figure 2**.

■ Continue to the next page to complete the skill

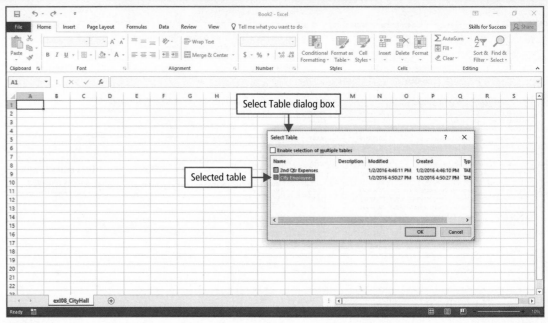

Figure 1   Excel 2016, Windows 10, Microsoft Corporation

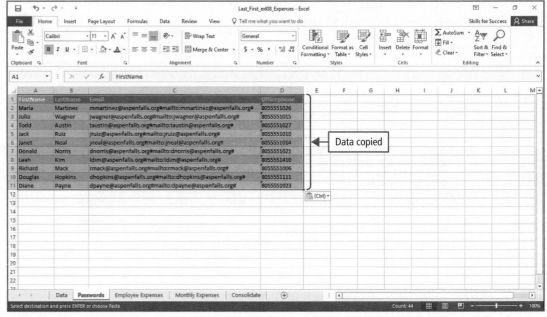

Figure 2   Excel 2016, Windows 10, Microsoft Corporation

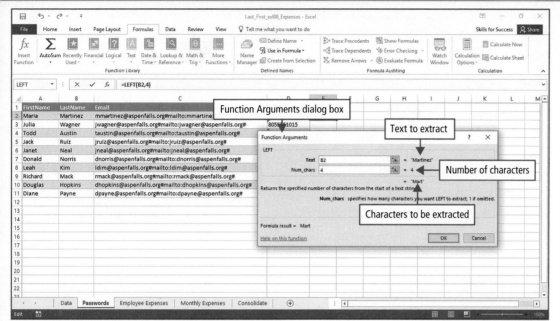

Excel 2016, Windows 10, Microsoft Corporation

Figure 3

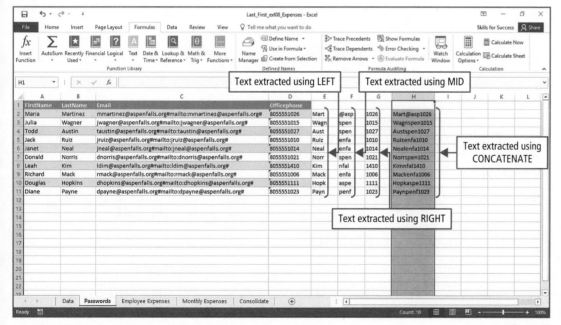

Excel 2016, Windows 10, Microsoft Corporation

Figure 4

6. Click cell **E2**, and then click the **Formulas tab**. In the **Function Library group**, click the **Text** button, and then click **LEFT**.

7. In the **Function Arguments** dialog box, in the **Text** box, type B2 and then press [Tab]. In the **Num_chars** box, type 4 Compare your screen with **Figure 3**, and then click **OK**.

8. Click cell **F2**. In the **Function Library group**, click the **Text** button, and then click **MID**.

9. In the **Function Arguments** dialog box, in the **Text** box, type C2 and then press [Tab]. In the **Start_num** box, type 10 and then press [Tab]. In the **Num_chars** box, type 4 Click **OK**.

10. Click cell **G2**. In the **Function Library group**, click the **Text** button, and then click **RIGHT**.

11. In the **Function Arguments** dialog box, in the **Text** box, type D2 and then press [Tab]. In the **Num_chars** box, type 4 and then click **OK**.

12. Click cell **H2**. In the **Function Library group**, click the **Text** button, and then click **CONCATENATE**.

13. In the **Function Arguments** dialog box, in the **Text1** box, type E2 and then press [Tab]. In the **Text2** box, type F2 press [Tab], and then in the **Text3** box, type G2 Click **OK**.

14. Select the range **E2:H2**, and then AutoFill down through cell **H11**. AutoFit column **H**, and then compare your screen with **Figure 4**.

> New passwords have been created for all the employees.

15. Close the **Book2** Excel file without saving.

16. **Save** 🖫 the file.

■ **You have completed Skill 2 of 10**

► Recall that a legend is a box that identifies the patterns or colors that are assigned to the data series or categories in a chart.

► Recall that data series are data points that are related to one another in a chart.

► One or more data series can be plotted in charts; however, pie charts have only one data series.

1. Click the **Employee Expenses** worksheet tab. Select the **Employee Expenses** chart. Click the **Chart Tools Design tab**, in the **Chart Layouts group**, click the **Add Chart Element** button. In the list, point to **Legend**, and then point to **Bottom**. Compare your screen with **Figure 1**, and then click **Bottom**.

   The legend is inserted at the bottom of the chart.

2. With the chart still selected, in the **Data group**, click the **Select Data** button. In the **Select Data Source** dialog box, click the **Collapse Dialog** button.

3. Select the range **B4:F9**, click the **Expand Dialog** button, and then click **OK**.

   The chart has two new data series, Phone Internet and Entertainment.

4. With the chart still selected, in the **Data group**, click the **Select Data** button. In the **Select Data Source** dialog box, note the **Horizontal (Category) Axis Labels**, and then compare your screen with **Figure 2**. If necessary, move the dialog box to view the chart.

   The horizontal axis labels are currently represented by 1, 2, 3, 4, and 5.

5. Under **Horizontal (Category) Axis Labels**, click the **Edit** button. Select the range **A5:A9**, and then click **OK** two times.

■ Continue to the next page to complete the skill

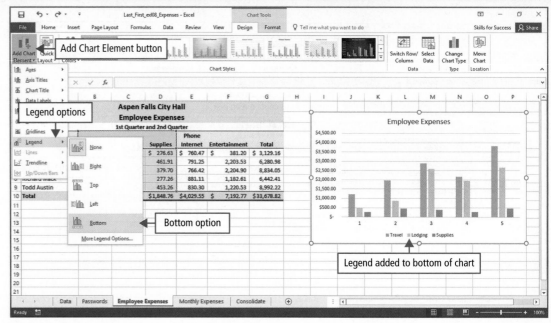

Figure 1

Excel 2016, Windows 10, Microsoft Corporation

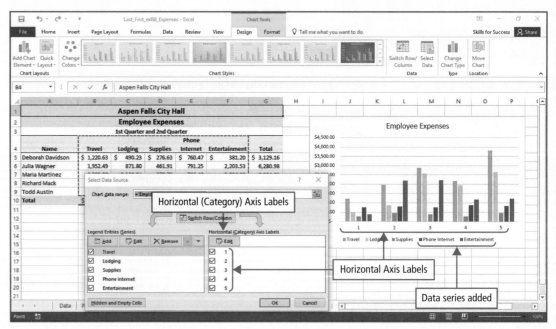

Figure 2

Excel 2016, Windows 10, Microsoft Corporation

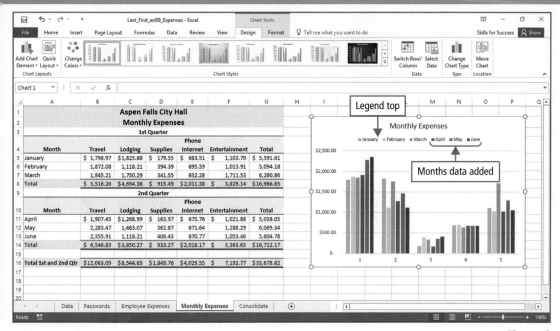

Excel 2016, Windows 10, Microsoft Corporation

Figure 3

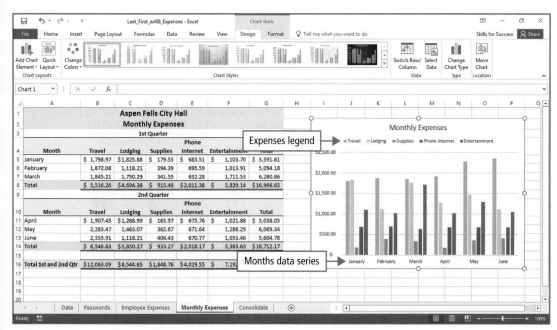

Excel 2016, Windows 10, Microsoft Corporation

Figure 4

6. Click the **Monthly Expenses** worksheet tab, and then select the **Monthly Expenses** chart. On the **Chart Tools Design tab**, in the **Chart Layouts group**, click the **Add Chart Element** button. In the list, point to **Legend**, and then click **Top**.

7. With the chart still selected, in the **Data group**, click the **Select Data** button. In the **Select Data Source** dialog box, click the **Collapse Dialog** button, and then press and hold the Ctrl key. Select the range **A11:F13**, and then release the Ctrl key. Click the **Expand Dialog** button. Click **OK**. Compare your screen with Figure 3.

The series data for April, May, and June is added to the chart.

8. In the **Data group**, click the **Select Data** button. In the **Select Data Source** dialog box, under **Horizontal (Category) Axis Labels**, click the **Edit** button.

9. Select the range **B4:F4**, and then in the **Axis Labels** dialog box, click **OK** two times.

10. In the **Data group**, click the **Switch/Row Column** button. Compare your screen with Figure 4.

Obj 5.1.3 C

The data labels are switched: the horizontal axis is now the months and the expense labels are in the legend. The chart now shows the expenditures categorized by month instead of by expense.

11. Save the file.

▪ **You have completed Skill 3 of 10**

▶ When data is graphed, the data can forecast expenses for the next quarter or the next year, and can project expected results for a data series.

▶ A *trendline* is a graphic representation of trends in a data series. It is used for problem prediction.

▶ Recall that a text box is a rectangular object on a worksheet or chart in which you can type text. It can be added to a chart to provide additional information.

1. Click the **Employee Expenses** worksheet tab, and then click the **Employee Expenses** chart. On the **Chart Tools Design tab**, in the **Chart Layouts group**, click the **Add Chart Element** button. In the list, point to **Trendline**, and then compare your screen with **Figure 1**.

The Trendline gallery displays the types of trendlines. Select trendlines based on how the data appears to be graphed. Some types of trendlines are *Linear*—data points follow nearly a straight line, *Exponential*—data points create a symmetric arc, *Linear Forecast*—data points follow a straight line with a two-period forecast, and *Moving Average*—data points follow a smooth curve to show data fluctuations.

2. Click **Linear Forecast**. In the **Add Trendline** dialog box, verify **Travel** is selected, and then click **OK**. Compare your screen with **Figure 2**.

The trendline is added to the chart and shows a straight line going up based on the increase in travel expenses. The trendline also is added to the legend.

■ **Continue to the next page to complete the skill**

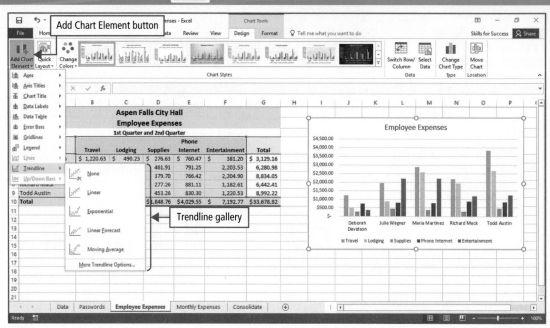

Figure 1

Excel 2016, Windows 10, Microsoft Corporation

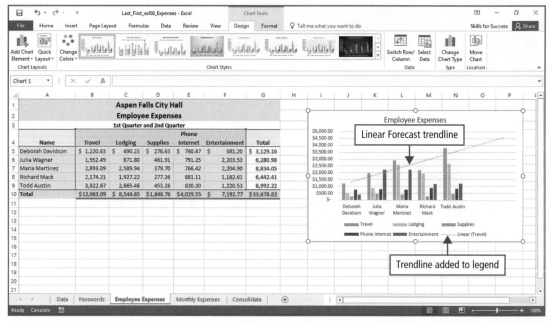

Figure 2

Excel 2016, Windows 10, Microsoft Corporation

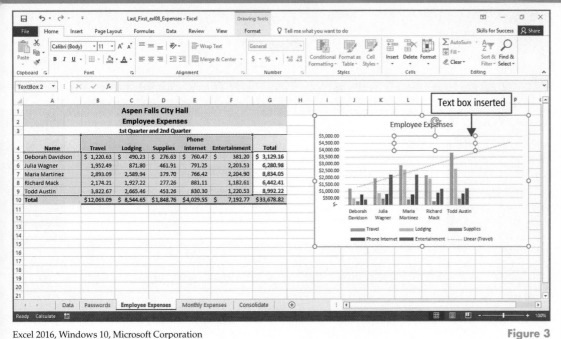

Excel 2016, Windows 10, Microsoft Corporation

Figure 3

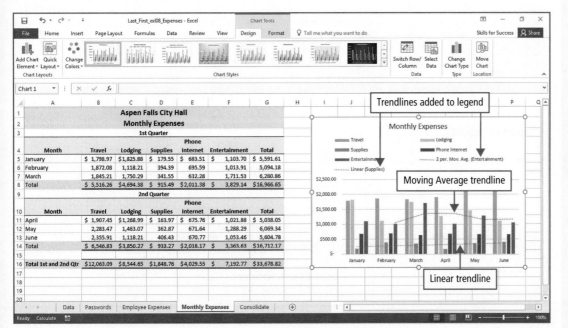

Excel 2016, Windows 10, Microsoft Corporation

Figure 4

3. With the chart still selected, click the **Chart Tools Format tab**, and then in the **Insert Shapes group**, click **Text Box** .

MOS
Obj 5.3.1 C

4. Place the cursor in the chart on the *$5,000* line, where it intersects with the left side of column **L**. Drag the cursor to the right edge of column **N**, and then down to *$4,000*. Compare your screen with **Figure 3**.

5. With the text box selected, type Travel expenses are rising Click the **Drawing Tools Format tab**, in the **Shape Styles group**, click the **Shape Fill arrow**, and then click the eighth color in the top row—**Gold, Accent 4**. Select the text in the text box, and then in the **WordArt Styles group**, click the first style—**Fill - Black, Text 1, Shadow**.

6. Click the **Monthly Expenses** worksheet tab, and then click the **Monthly Expenses** chart. Click the **Chart Tools Design tab**. In the **Chart Layouts group**, click the **Add Chart Element** button. In the list, point to **Trendline**, and then click **Moving Average**. In the **Add Trendline** dialog box, click **Entertainment**, and then click **OK**.

   The trendline is added to the chart and shows a fluctuation in Entertainment expenses from month to month.

7. In the **Chart Layouts group**, click the **Add Chart Element** button. In the list, point to **Trendline**, and then click **Linear**. In the **Add Trendline** dialog box, click **Supplies**, and then click **OK**. Compare your screen with **Figure 4**.

   The trendline is added to the chart and shows a nearly straight line. Supplies costs are similar month to month.

8. **Save** the file.

■ **You have completed Skill 4 of 10**

▶ Recall that a template is a prebuilt workbook used as a pattern for creating new workbooks.

▶ To save time or standardize, templates can be edited to meet an organization's specifications.

1. Click the **File tab**, and then click **New**.

   The categories for available Excel templates are shown.

2. In the **New** window, type Expense report in the **Search** box, and then press Enter. Select the second template titled **Expense report**. Compare your screen with **Figure 1**, and then click **Create**.

3. Right-click the **Expense Report** worksheet tab. Use techniques previously practiced to move the worksheet to the end of the book **Last_First_exl08_Expenses**, and then click **OK**.

4. In the **Last_First_exl08_Expenses** file, verify the **Expense Report** worksheet is selected. Click the **View tab**, and then in the **Workbook Views group**, click **Normal**.

5. Click cell **J4**. Click in the **formula bar**, delete the text **PAY** and the space after it, and then press Tab. In cell **K4**, replace the existing text with MONTH YEAR and then press Tab.

6. In cell **L4**, click the **Home tab**, and then in the **Number group**, click the **Number Format Dialog Box Launcher** 🔲. In the **Format Cells** dialog box, under **Category**, verify **Date** is selected. Under **Type**, scroll down, and then click **March-12**. Click **OK**, and then compare your screen with **Figure 2**.

■ **Continue to the next page to complete the skill**

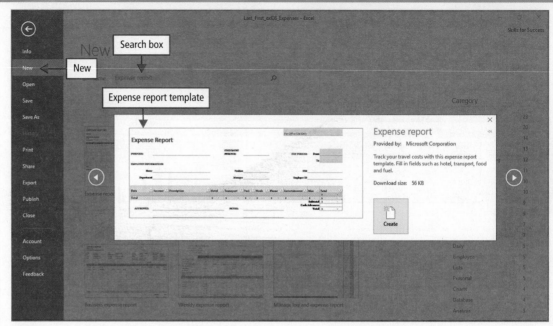

Figure 1   Excel 2016, Windows 10, Microsoft Corporation

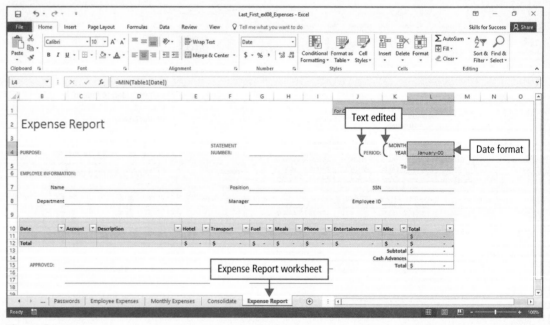

Figure 2   Excel 2016, Windows 10, Microsoft Corporation

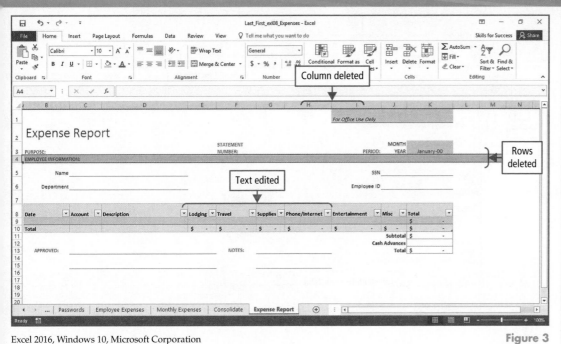

Excel 2016, Windows 10, Microsoft Corporation

Figure 3

7. Click cell **E10**. Replace the existing text with Lodging and then press [Tab]. In cell **F10**, replace the existing text with Travel and then press [Tab]. In cell **G10**, replace the existing text with Supplies and then press [Tab]. AutoFit column **G**. Click cell **I10**. Replace the existing text with Phone/Internet and then press [Tab]. AutoFit column **I**.

8. Select column **H**. In the **Cells group**, click the **Delete** button to delete the column. Select row **3**. In the **Cells group**, click the **Delete** button to delete the row, and then AutoFit row **2**. Select row **4**. In the **Cells group**, click the **Delete** button to delete the row. Compare your screen with Figure 3. Obj 3.1.3 C

9. Select row **10** through row **18**. In the **Cells group**, click the **Insert** button to insert eight additional rows, and then click in one of the newly created rows.

10. Click the **Table Tools Design tab**. In the **Tools group,** click **Convert to Range**, and then click **Yes** to convert to a normal range. Obj 3.1.2 C

11. Select the range **B9:B18**. In the **Number group**, click the **Number Format Dialog Box Launcher** [⌐]. Under **Category**, verify **Date** is selected, and then under **Type**, click **3/14/12**. Click **OK**.

12. Select row **24**. In the **Cells group**, click the **Delete** button to delete the signature lines in the row.

13. Click cell **C6**, and then type City Hall Compare your screen with Figure 4. Press [Enter].

14. **Save** [💾] the file.

■ **You have completed Skill 5 of 10**

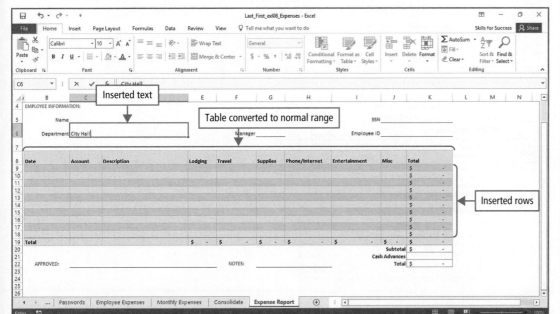

Excel 2016, Windows 10, Microsoft Corporation

Figure 4

▶ Data can be combined into one worksheet using worksheets in the same workbook or other workbooks.

▶ The **Consolidate** command is used to summarize and report results from separate worksheets.

▶ You can consolidate worksheet data by position or by category.

MOS
Obj 3.4.2 E

1. Click the **File tab**, and then click **Open**. Navigate to the student data files for this chapter, and then open **exl08_Employee**.

2. In the taskbar, click **Excel** , and then click the **Last_First_exl08_Expenses** window. Click the **Consolidate** worksheet tab, and then click cell **A3**.

3. Click the **Data tab**, and then in the **Data Tools group**, click the **Consolidate** button. Compare your screen with **Figure 1**.

4. In the **Consolidate** dialog box, verify that **Sum** is selected as the **Function**. For the **Reference**, click the **Collapse Dialog** button . On the **Taskbar**, select the **exl08_Employee** file, and then in the **3rd Qtr** worksheet, select the range **A3:F6**.

5. In the **Consolidate** dialog box, click the **Expand Dialog** button .

6. In the **Consolidate** dialog box, click **Add**. Compare your screen with **Figure 2**.

■ Continue to the next page to complete the skill

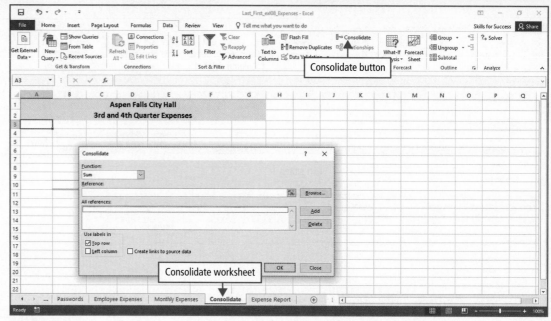

Figure 1

Excel 2016, Windows 10, Microsoft Corporation

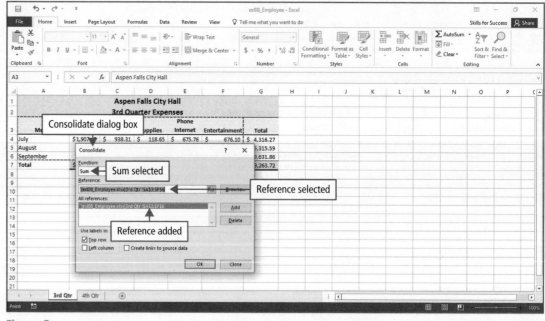

Figure 2

Excel 2016, Windows 10, Microsoft Corporation

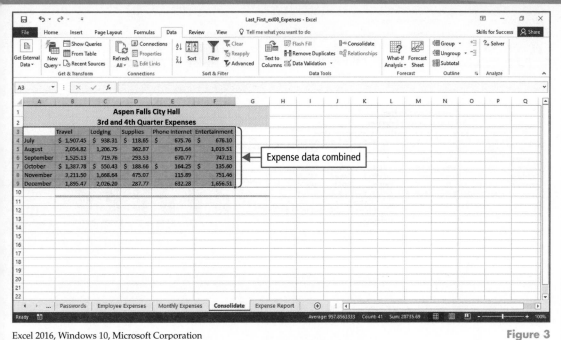

Expense data combined

Excel 2016, Windows 10, Microsoft Corporation

Figure 3

7. Click the **Collapse Dialog** button. In the **Taskbar**, select the **exl08_Employee** file, and then in the **4th Qtr** worksheet, if necessary, select the range **A3:F6**. In the **Consolidate - Reference** dialog box, click the **Expand Dialog** button.

8. In the **Consolidate** dialog box, click **Add**. Under **Use Labels in**, verify that the **Top row** and **Left column** check boxes are selected. Click **OK** to close the **Consolidate** dialog box.

> Checking the top row and left column check boxes ensures that the labels will be included in the consolidation.

9. Close the **exl08_Employee** file without saving. Compare your screen with **Figure 3**.

> The Consolidate worksheet appears with the combined data from the 3rd Qtr and 4th Qtr worksheets.

10. Click cell **A3**, type Month and then press Enter.

11. Select the range **B5:F9**, and then use techniques previously practiced to apply the **Comma Style** number format.

12. Select the range **B10:F10**, and then use techniques previously practiced to apply **AutoSum** ∑ AutoSum.

13. Click cell **G3**, type Total and then press Enter. Select the range **G4:G10**, and then use techniques previously practiced to apply **AutoSum** ∑ AutoSum. Compare your screen with **Figure 4**.

14. **Save** the file.

■ **You have completed Skill 6 of 10**

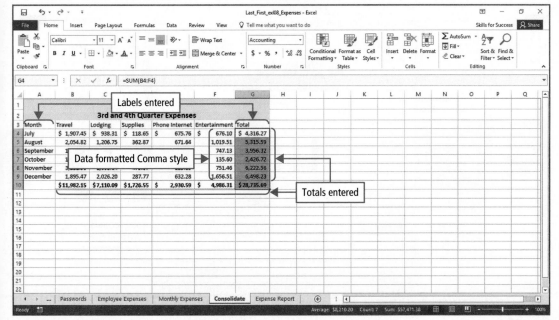

Labels entered

Data formatted Comma style

Totals entered

Excel 2016, Windows 10, Microsoft Corporation

Figure 4

▶ Values in a 2-D chart can vary widely from data series to data series or have mixed types of data.

▶ In a *dual axis chart*, one or more data series is plotted on a secondary vertical axis.

▶ The secondary vertical axis reflects the value series.

1. In the **Consolidate** worksheet, select the range **A3:B9**, press and hold the Ctrl key, and then select **G3:G9**. Release Ctrl. Click the **Insert tab**. In the **Charts group**, click **Insert Column or Bar Chart** ▮▾, and then under **2-D Column**, select the first option in the first row—**Clustered Column**.

2. Drag the chart so that the top left corner is positioned in cell **I2**. Compare your screen with **Figure 1**.

3. In the chart, click the **Chart Title**. Replace the text with Travel Expenses

4. In the chart, click the **Total** data series.

   In the chart, the data series columns for Total should be selected.

5. On the **Chart Tools Design tab**, in the **Type group**, click the **Change Chart Type** button. In the **Change Chart Type** dialog box, click the second option at the top—**Clustered Column - Line on Secondary Axis**.

6. Under **Choose the chart type and axis for your data series**, verify that the check box under **Secondary Axis** for **Total** is selected. Compare your screen with **Figure 2**, and then click **OK**.

   The secondary axis is added showing the travel data and how it compares to the Total Expenses.

■ **Continue to the next page to complete the skill** ▶

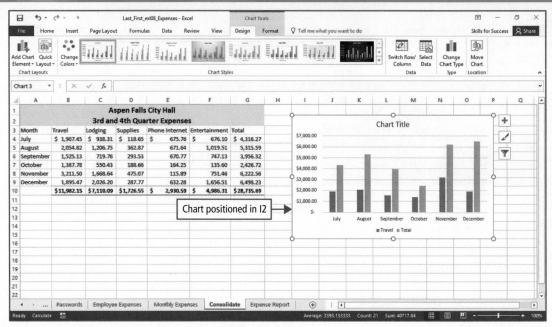

Figure 1

Excel 2016, Windows 10, Microsoft Corporation

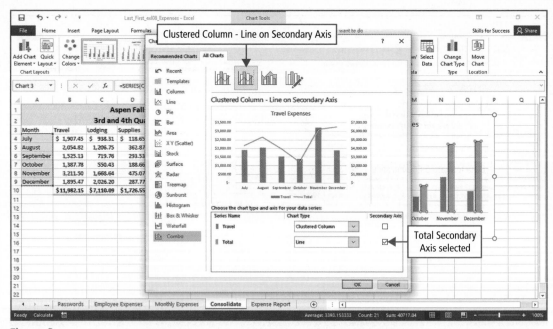

Figure 2

Excel 2016, Windows 10, Microsoft Corporation

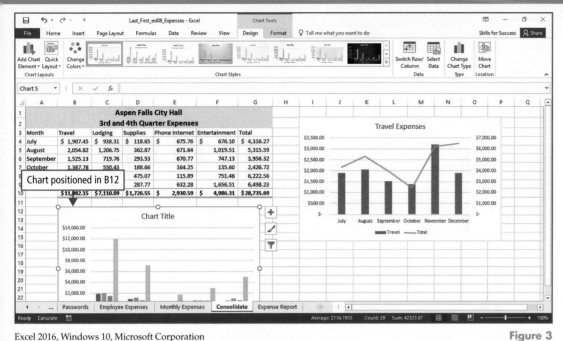

Excel 2016, Windows 10, Microsoft Corporation

Figure 3

Excel 2016, Windows 10, Microsoft Corporation

Figure 4

7. Select the range **A3:F6**, press and hold the `Ctrl` key, and then select **A10:F10**. Release `Ctrl`. Click the **Insert tab**. In the **Charts group**, click **Insert Column or Bar Chart** `ılı ▾`, and then under **2-D Column**, select the first option in the first row—**Clustered Column**.

8. Drag the chart's top left corner to cell **B12**. Compare your screen with **Figure 3**.

   The chart compares the 3rd Qtr expenses with the total expenses for the 3rd Qtr and 4th Qtr.

9. In the chart, click **Chart Title**. Replace the text with 3rd Quarter Expenses

10. On the **Chart Tools Design tab**, in the **Data group**, click **Select Data**. In the **Select Data Source** dialog box under **Legend Entries (Series)**, click **<blank series>**, and then click **Edit**. In the **Edit Series** dialog box, in the **Series name** text box, replace the existing text with Total and then click **OK** two times.

11. In the chart, select the **Total** data series.

12. In the **Type group**, click the **Change Chart Type** button. In the **Change Chart Type** dialog box, click the second option at the top—**Clustered Column - Line on Secondary Axis**.

13. Under **Choose the chart type and axis for your data series**, verify that all have the **Clustered Column** selected as the **Chart Type** except for **September** and **Total**. Under **Secondary Axis**, verify that only **September** and **Total** are selected, and then click **OK**. Compare your screen with **Figure 4**.

   An additional secondary axis shows the comparison of September data related to the Total Expenses.

14. **Save** 🖫 the file.

▪ **You have completed Skill 7 of 10**

▶ To save time formatting charts, you can reuse a chart that you created and save the chart as a template.

▶ A ***chart template*** is a custom chart type that you can apply like any other chart type.

1. In the **Consolidate** worksheet, right-click on the **3rd Quarter Expenses** chart. In the shortcut menu, click **Save as Template**.

2. In the **Save Chart Template** dialog box, replace the **File name** with Dual Axis Chart Verify the **Save as type** is **Chart Template Files**. Compare your screen with **Figure 1**, and then click **Save**.

   The chart template will be saved as a .crtx file.

3. Click the **Employee Expenses** worksheet. Right-click on the **Employee Expenses** chart. In the shortcut menu, click **Save as Template**.

4. In the **Save Chart Template** dialog box, replace the **File name** with Trendline Chart Verify the **Save as type** is **Chart Template Files**. Compare your screen with **Figure 2**, and then click **Save**.

   In the Save Chart Template dialog box, the Dual Axis Chart appears as a saved template.

5. In the **Employee Expenses** worksheet, select the range **A4:F9**.

6. Click the **Insert tab**. In the **Charts group**, click the **See All Charts Dialog Box Launcher**, and then click the **All Charts tab**.

■ Continue to the next page to complete the skill ▶

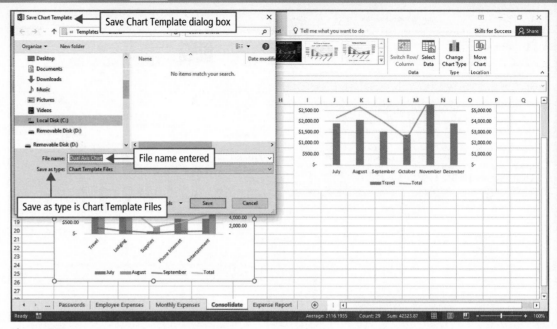

Figure 1

Excel 2016, Windows 10, Microsoft Corporation

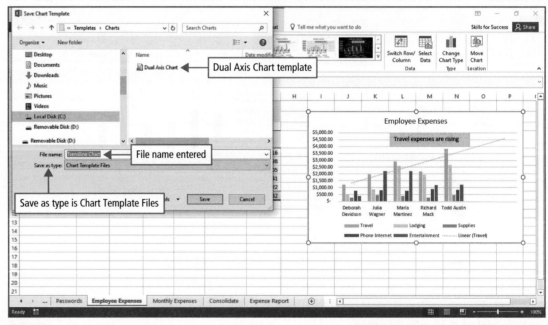

Figure 2

Excel 2016, Windows 10, Microsoft Corporation

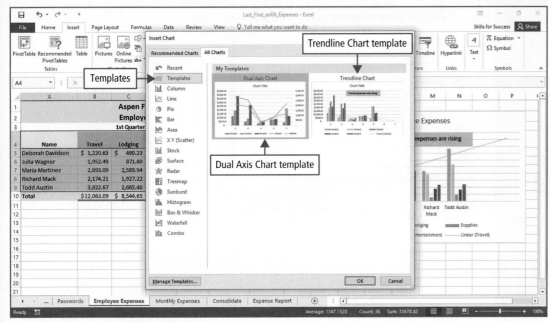

Excel 2016, Windows 10, Microsoft Corporation

Figure 3

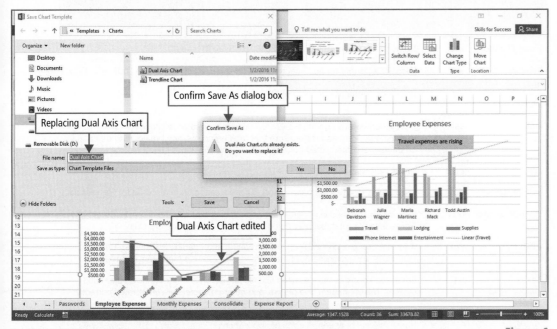

Excel 2016, Windows 10, Microsoft Corporation

Figure 4

7. In the list, click **Templates**, and then compare your screen with **Figure 3**.

The two chart templates you previously saved should appear in this dialog box.

8. In the **Insert Chart** dialog box, click the first option—**Dual Axis Chart**, and then click **OK**.

9. Drag the chart so that the top left corner is positioned in cell **B12**.

10. Click the **Chart Title**. Replace the text with Employee Expenses

11. On the **Chart Tools Design tab**, in the **Type group**, click the **Change Chart Type** button. In the **Change Chart Type** dialog box, under **Choose the chart type and axis for your data series**, verify that each data series has the **Clustered Column** selected as the **Chart Type** except for **Maria Martinez**. Under **Secondary Axis**, verify that only the **Maria Martinez** check box is selected, and then click **OK**.

12. Verify the chart is selected, and then in the **Chart Styles group**, click the **Change Colors** button. In the gallery, under **Colorful**, select the third option—**Color 3**. MOS Obj 5.2.3 C

13. Right-click the chart, and then in the shortcut menu, click **Save as Template**. MOS Obj 4.1.3 E

14. In the **Save Chart Template** dialog box, click **Dual Axis Chart**. Verify the **Save as type** is **Chart Template Files**, and then click **Save**. Compare your screen with **Figure 4**.

15. In the **Confirm Save As** dialog box, read the message, and then click **Yes**.

Because you are replacing the previous template with a new version, confirmation is requested.

16. Save 🖫 the file.

■ **You have completed Skill 8 of 10**

▶ Software is updated to improve the software and meet the needs of the user market.

▶ A *software version* is the software release or format.

▶ A *file type*—the standard way that information is encoded for storage in a computer file—is designated for each software version.

1. Click the **Data** worksheet tab. Click the **File tab**, and then click **Save As**. In the **Save As** dialog box, navigate to your chapter folder. Name the file Last_First_ exl08_Xls and then in the **Save As type** box, click the **arrow**.

2. In the menu, point to the fourth option— **Excel 97-2003 Workbook**. Compare your screen with **Figure 1**, and then click **Save**.

   The list contains several file types. This file type can be opened by any user with a previous version of Excel; however, with newer versions of Excel, additional formatting and tools may make it difficult to transfer exact data and formatting into previous versions. There are several other file type versions compatible with Excel to save the integrity of your data. Common Excel file types are summarized in the table in **Figure 2**.

3. In the **Microsoft Excel - Compatibility Checker** dialog box, read the message, uncheck the **Check compatibility when saving this workbook** checkbox, and then click **Continue**.

■ **Continue to the next page to complete the skill**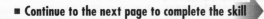

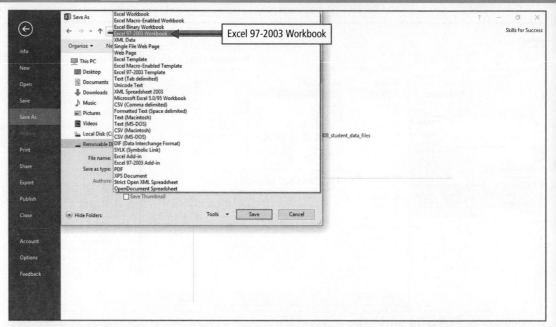

Figure 1   Excel 2016, Windows 10, Microsoft Corporation

Common Excel File Type Versions		
Format	**Extension**	**Description**
Excel Workbook	.xlsx	Default XML file format for Excel 2016, 2013, 2010, and 2007.
Template	.xltx	Default file format for an Excel template for 2016, 2013, 2010, and 2007.
Excel 97-2003 Workbook	.xls	Binary file format for Excel 97-2003.
CSV	.csv	Saves workbook as comma-delimited text file for use on another Windows operating system, and makes sure that tab characters, line breaks, and other characters are interpreted correctly. Saves only the active sheet.
DIF	.dif	Saves only the active sheet.
DBF.3/BDF.4	.dbf	Users can open dBase formats in Excel, but users can't save an Excel file to dBase format.
OpenDocument	.ods	Files can be opened in spreadsheet applications that use the OpenDocument Spreadsheet format, such as Google Docs and OpenOffice.org Calc.
PDF	.pdf	A format that preserves document formatting and enables file sharing. When the PDF file is viewed online or printed, it keeps the format that users intended.
Text	.txt	Saves workbook as tab-delimited text file for use on another Windows operating system. Tab characters, line breaks, and other characters are interpreted correctly.
XML	.xml	A file format that transports and stores data. The most common tool for data transmissions between all sorts of applications.

Figure 2

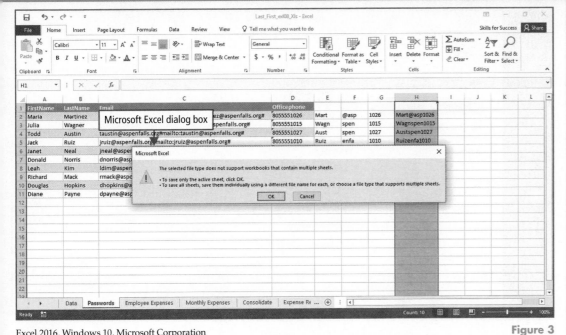

Excel 2016, Windows 10, Microsoft Corporation

Figure 3

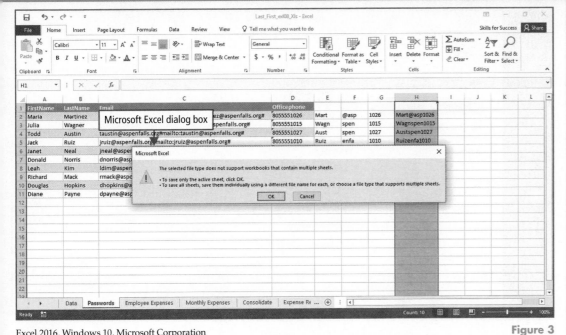

Excel 2016, Windows 10, Microsoft Corporation

Figure 4

4. Click the **Passwords** worksheet tab. On the **File tab**, click **Save As**, and then navigate to your chapter folder. Name the file Last_First_exl08_Txt and then in the **Save As type** box, click the **arrow**. In the list, select the eleventh option—**Text (Tab delimited)**—and then click **Save**.

5. In the **Microsoft Excel** dialog box, read the message, and then compare your screen with **Figure 3**. Click **OK**, click **Yes**, and then close the file without saving the changes.

   Text (Tab delimited) will save only the current worksheet in a file format that separates the data columns with tab characters.

6. Open the **Last_First_exl08_Expenses** file. Click the **Consolidate** worksheet tab. On the **File tab**, click **Save As**, and in the **Save As** dialog box, navigate to your chapter folder. Name the file Last_First_exl08_Pdf and then in the **Save As type** box, click the **arrow**. In the list, select the fourth option from the bottom—**PDF**. Accept the default settings, and then click **Save**. If the file opens in PDF view, close the PDF to go back to the **Last_First_exl08_Expenses** file.

7. On the **File tab**, click **Save As**, and then in the **Save As** dialog box, navigate to your chapter folder. Name the file Last_First_exl08_Xml and then in the **Save As type** box, click the **arrow**. In the list, select the second option from the bottom—**Strict Open XML Spreadsheet**—and then compare your screen with **Figure 4**. Click **Save**.

8. **Save** 🖫 and then **Close** ✕ all open files.

■ **You have completed Skill 9 of 10**

► If your organization uses Outlook, you can share workbooks through the E-mail command in Excel.

► When workbooks are shared, multiple users can simultaneously edit the file; however, changes will need to be merged.

► Recall that OneDrive is a free storage space on the cloud that is created when you create a Microsoft account.

► Files can be uploaded directly to OneDrive through the Share button in Excel.

1. Open the **Last_First_exl08_Expenses** file. In the upper right corner of the Excel window, click **Share**. In the **Share** pane, click **Save to Cloud**. Compare your screen with **Figure 1**.

   This option allows you to save your file to OneDrive and then share it with others.

2. In the **Save As** window, double-click the first option—**OneDrive - Personal**. If you do not see *OneDrive - Personal*, you may need to log into your Microsoft account.

   When you installed your Office 2016 software, you were instructed to register for OneDrive or enter your account information.

3. In the **Save As** dialog box, click **New folder**. Name the folder Excel Chapter 8 click **Open** two times, and then click **Save**. Compare your screen with **Figure 2**.

   When you invite people to see the file, you need to share it to OneDrive first in order for them to access it from the web.

4. Read the message, close the **Share** pane, and then click **Share**. In the **Invite people** box, type janet.neal@aspenfalls.org

■ Continue to the next page to complete the skill

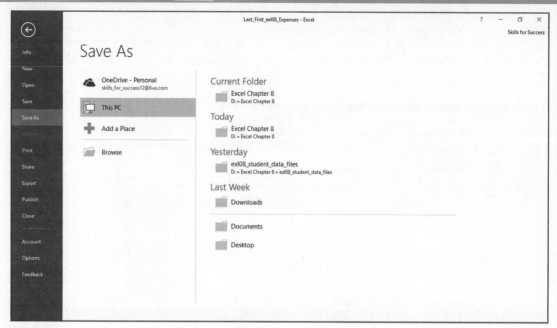

Figure 1

Excel 2016, Windows 10, Microsoft Corporation

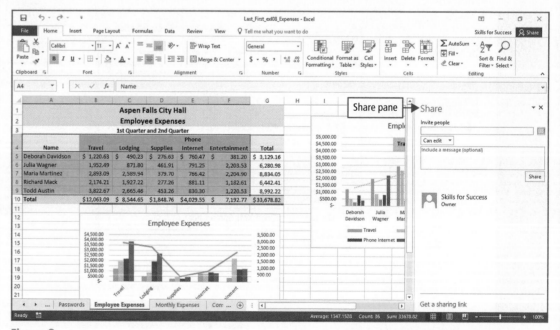

Figure 2

Excel 2016, Windows 10, Microsoft Corporation

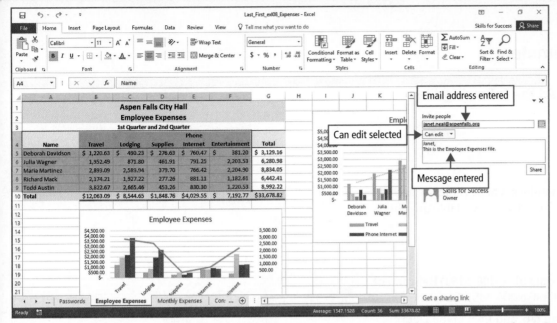

Excel 2016, Windows 10, Microsoft Corporation

Figure 3

5. Verify *Can edit* is selected. In the next box, type Janet, press Enter, and then type This is the Employee Expenses file. Compare your screen with **Figure 3**.

6. Click **Share**. Create a full-screen snip. **Save** 🖫 the snip in your OneDrive chapter folder as Last_First_exl08_Snip and then **Close** ✕ the Snipping Tool.

7. If necessary, in the **Sharing Information** dialog box, read the message, and then click the link, **Click here for the additional authentication step**. You may not need to authenticate if you have previously completed this step; if so, skip to step 9.

The authentication process is a security precaution to verify the identity of the person sharing the file.

8. In the login screen, enter your username and password for OneDrive. In the **Help us fight junk email** window, read the message, and then enter the characters. In the **Thanks for Solving the Puzzle** window, click **Close**, and then click **Proceed**.

In the Share window, under Shared with, there will be an icon with your username and picture (if you have uploaded a picture).

9. Click the **File tab**, and then click **Share**. In the **Share** window, click **Email**, and note the options available for sharing by email. The options are explained in the table in **Figure 4**.

An account with Outlook is needed to send files using this method.

10. Return to the workbook view.

11. **Save** 🖫 the file, and then **Close** ✕ Excel. Submit the files as directed by your instructor.

Sent as Format	Description
Attachment	Excel file is attached to an Outlook email and anyone can edit.
Link	File can be edited by multiple users at the same time and everyone can view the changes.
PDF	File is created as a PDF file and attached to Outlook email. Layout, formatting, and images can't be easily edited.
XPS	File is created as an XPS file and attached to Outlook email. Layout, formatting, and images can't be easily edited.
Internet Fax	Fax service provider is required, but fax machine is not required.

Figure 4

 DONE! You have completed Skill 10 of 10 and your workbook is complete!

More Skills

Modify Charts and Graph Parameters

To complete this project, you will need the following file:

- exl08_MS11Retirement

You will save your file as:

- Last_First_exl08_MS11Retirement

▶ Charts can contain multiple *parameters*—quantities whose value is selected for particular circumstances and in relation to which other variable quantities may be expressed.

---

1. Start **Excel 2016**, and then open the student data file **exl08_MS11Retirement**. Save the file in your chapter folder as Last_First_exl08_MS11Retirement

 2. Select the chart. Click the **Chart Tools Design tab**, and then in the **Data group**, click the **Switch Row/Column** button

Obj 5.1.3 C

    The row labels are now identified in the legend, and the value is the horizontal axis.

3. In the **Type group**, click the **Change Chart Type** button. In the **Change Chart Type** dialog box, on the **All Charts tab**, click **Combo**.

4. Click the second thumbnail, **Clustered Column - Line on Secondary Axis**. Under **Choose the chart type and axis for your data series**, ensure the **Chart Type** for all of the council members is set to **Clustered Column** and the **Secondary Axis** is not checked.

Figure 1   Excel 2016, Windows 10, Microsoft Corporation

5. Scroll down and edit the **Chart Type** for *Total Future Value*, *Total High FV*, and *Average High FV* to the Line chart type, first column, second row—**Stacked Line with Markers**—and verify **Secondary Axis** is checked. Compare your screen with **Figure 1**, and then click **OK**.

Obj 4.1.2 E

    The chart now shows the Totals and Average in relation to the future value.

6. **Save** 🖫 the file, and then **Close** ☒ Excel. Submit the file as directed by your instructor.

- **You have completed More Skills 11**

More Skills 12
Manage Workbook Versions

To complete this project, you will need the following file:

- exl08_MS12Enrollments

You will save your files as:

- Last_First_exl08_MS12Enrollments
- Last_First_exl08_MS12Options
- Last_First_exl08_MS12AutoSave

▶ **AutoRecover** is a feature that saves copies of all open Excel files at user-definable fixed intervals.

▶ Files can be recovered if Excel closes unexpectedly, like during a power outage.

---

1. Start **Excel 2016**, and then open the student data file **exl08_MS12Enrollments**.

2. Click the **File tab**, and then in Backstage view, click **Options**.

3. In the **Excel Options** dialog box, click **Save**. On the **Save Page**, in the **Save AutoRecover information every minutes** box, replace the *10* with 2

4. Verify that *Keep the last autosaved version if I close without saving* check box is selected. Use the **Snipping Tool** to create a full-screen snip, and then save the file in your chapter folder as Last_First_exl08_MS12Options **Close** the Snipping Tool. Click **OK** to update the options.

5. In the header row, click the filter arrow for **Course Fee**. Click **Select All**, and then select **25**. Click **OK**.

6. Click any cell in the table, and then click the **Table Tools Design tab**. In the **Tools group**, click **Convert to Range**, and then click **Yes**.

7. Press Ctrl + Alt + Delete, and then select **Task Manager**. In the **Task Manager** window, select **Microsoft Excel**, and then click **End Task**. **Close** the **Task Manager** window.

8. Start **Excel 2016**, and then open the student data file exl08_MS12Enrollments. Compare your screen with **Figure 1**.

   The Document Recovery pane provides a list of the available recovered files.

9. Use the **Snipping Tool** to create a full-screen snip, and then save the file in your chapter folder as Last_First_exl08_MS12AutoSave **Close** the Snipping Tool.

Excel 2016, Windows 10, Microsoft Corporation

Figure 1

10. Point to the file listed in the **Available Files**, click the arrow for the recovered file, and then click **Save As**. Save the file in your chapter folder as Last_First_exl08_MS12Enrollments

11. **Close** ☒ Excel. Submit the files as directed by your instructor.

■ **You have completed More Skills 12**

More Skills 13

Serialize Numbers Using Functions

To complete this project, you will need the following file:

- exl08_MS13Timesheet

You will save your file as:

- Last_First_exl08_MS13Timesheet

▶ A *serial number* shows the position of an item in a series.

▶ The *WEEKDAY function* converts a serial number to a day of the week.

▶ The *WORKDAY function* returns the serial number of the date before or after a specified number of workdays.

---

1. Start **Excel 2016**, and then open the student data file **exl08_MS13Timesheet**. Save the file in your chapter folder as Last_First_exl08_MS13Timesheet

2. In cell **B3**, replace *Student Name* with your First and Last names.

3. Click cell **B21**, and then click the **Formulas tab**. In the **Function Library group**, click the **Date & Time** button, and then click **WORKDAY**.

4. In the **Function Arguments** dialog box, click in the **Start_date** box, and then click cell **B6**. Press Tab. With the cursor in the **Days** box, type 30 and then press Tab. With the cursor in the **Holidays** box, click cell **B6**. Click **OK**.

   The function will return the date 30 working days after the start date, excluding holidays and weekends.

5. Click cell **C6**. In the **Function Library group**, click the **Date & Time** button, and then click **WEEKDAY**. In the **Function Arguments** dialog box, click in the **Serial_number** box, and then click cell **B6**. Click **OK**. AutoFill the function down through **C19**.

   The default value representing the day of the week is entered.

6. Click cell **A6**, and then type =CHOOSE(WEEKDAY(B6), "Sun", "Mon", "Tue", "Wed", "Thu", "Fri", "Sat") Press Enter. AutoFill the formula down through **A19**, and then compare your screen with Figure 1.

   The days of the week that correspond with the dates are entered. The ***CHOOSE*** *function* is a lookup function that returns a value or action from a list of values based on an index number.

Figure 1   Excel 2016, Windows 10, Microsoft Corporation

7. **Save** the file, and then **Close** Excel. Submit the file as directed by your instructor.

- **You have completed More Skills 13**

More Skills
Modify the Excel Ribbon

To complete this project, you will need the following file:

- exl08_MS14Time

You will save your files as:

- Last_First_exl08_MS14Time
- Last_First_exl08_MS14Ribbon

▶ Recall that the Ribbon contains commands so that you can quickly find the tools you need.

▶ You can create a custom tab, which can be divided into groups.

---

1. Open the student data file **exl08_MS14Time**. Save the file in your chapter folder as Last_First_exl08_MS14Time

2. In cell **B3**, replace *Student Name* with your First and Last names.

3. Click the **File tab**, and then click **Options**. In the **Excel Options** list, click **Customize Ribbon**.

   Two panes display. In the left pane are the commands available to add to the ribbon. In the right pane are tabs and groups already added to the ribbon.

4. At the bottom of the right pane, create a **New Tab**. Under **Main Tabs**, click **New Tab (Custom)**. Click **Rename**, and then type your First and Last names. Click **OK**. Click and drag the new tab up before **Home**.

5. Click **New Group** (Custom), and then **Rename** Functions, and then select **Functions (Custom)**.

6. In the left pane, click the **Popular Commands arrow**, and then select **Main tabs**. Click ⊞ next to **Formulas**. Click ⊞ **Function library.** Click ⊞ Text, and then click **Add**.

7. In the list, select **Date & Time**, and then click **Add**. Click **OK**.

8. Click the tab with your **First** and **Last** names, and then compare your screen with Figure 1.

9. Use the **Snipping Tool** to create a full-screen snip, and then save the file in your chapter folder as Last_First_exl08_MS14Ribbon

10. Click the **File tab**, click **Options**, and then click **Customize Ribbon**. At the bottom of the right pane, click the **Reset arrow**, click **Reset all**

MOS
Obj 1.1.6 E

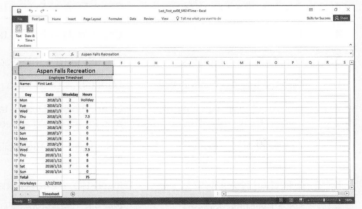

Excel 2016, Windows 10, Microsoft Corporation   **Figure 1**

customization, and then click **Yes**. Click **OK** to close the Options window. Notice the tab is removed from the ribbon.

11. **Save** 💾 the file, and then **Close** ✕ Excel. Submit the files as directed by your instructor.

■ **You have completed More Skills 14**

Chapter Summary

Skills Number	Task	Step	Icon
1	Import non-native files	File tab → Open → All files → Select file → Enable	
1	TRIM data	Formulas tab → Function Library group → Text → TRIM → Text	
2	Extract data from LEFT	Formulas tab → Function Library group → Text → LEFT → Text → Characters	
2	Extract data from RIGHT	Formulas tab → Function Library group → Text → RIGHT → Text → Characters	
2	Extract data from MID	Formulas tab → Function Library group → Text → MID → Text → Characters	
3	Add legend to chart	Chart Tools → Design tab → Chart Layouts group → Add Chart Element → Legend → Position	
3	Add data series to charts	Chart Tools → Design tab → Data group → Select Data → Chart data range	
3	Add data series labels to charts	Chart Tools → Design tab → Data group → Select Data → Edit	
3	Switch axis data	Chart Tools → Design tab → Data group → Switch Row/Column	
4	Add trendline to charts	Chart Tools → Design tab → Chart Layouts group → Add Chart Element → Trendline → Type	
4	Insert text box	Chart Tools → Format tab → Insert Shapes group → Text box	abl
5	Modify Excel templates	File tab → New → Select template → Create	
6	Consolidate worksheet data	Data tab → Data Tools group → Consolidate → Function → Reference → Add	
7	Construct dual axis charts	Chart Tools → Design tab → Type group → Change Chart Type → Choose the chart type and axis for your data series	
8	Create chart templates	Select chart → Right click → Save as Template → File name → Save as type: Chart Template Files	
8	Edit chart templates	Insert tab → See All Charts dialog box launcher → All Charts tab → Templates → Type	
9	Save Excel file versions	File tab → Save As → Navigate to Place → Save as type	
10	Save Excel file to OneDrive	File tab → Share → Save to Cloud → OneDrive → Browse → Save	
10	Share Excel file OneDrive	File tab → Share → Enter Email → Share	
10	Share Excel file Email	File tab → Share → Email → Choose Email Option	
MS12	Change AutoSave	File tab → Options → Save	
MS13	Insert WORKDAY	Formulas tab → Function Library group → Date & Time	
MS13	Insert WEEKDAY	Formulas tab → Function Library group → Date & Time	
MS14	Customize the Ribbon	File tab → Options → Customize Ribbon	

Project Summary Chart

Project	Project Type	Project Location
Skills Review	Review	In Book & MIL MyITLab Grader
Skills Assessment 1	Review	In Book & MIL MyITLab Grader
Skills Assessment 2	Review	Book
My Skills	Problem Solving	Book
Visual Skills Check	Problem Solving	Book
Skills Challenge 1	Critical Thinking	Book
Skills Challenge 2	Critical Thinking	Book
More Skills Assessment	Review	In Book & MIL MyITLab Grader
Collaborating with Google	Critical Thinking	Book

MOS Objectives Covered (Quiz in MyITLab)

3.1.2 C Convert a table to a cell range	5.3.1 C Insert text boxes and shapes
3.1.3 C Add or remove table rows and columns	1.1.6 E Display hidden ribbon tabs
4.3.1 C Format text by using RIGHT, LEFT, and MID functions	1.2.5 E Manage workbook versions
5.1.1 C Create a new chart	3.3.2 E Serialize numbers by using date and time functions
5.1.2 C Add additional data series	3.4.2 E Consolidate data
5.1.3 C Switch between rows and columns in source data	4.1.1 E Add trendlines to charts
5.2.2 C Add and modify chart elements	4.1.2 E Create dual-axis charts
5.2.3 C Apply chart layouts and styles	4.1.3 E Save a chart as a template

Key Terms

Online Help Skills

1. Start **Excel 2016**. In the upper right corner of the start page, click the **Help** button ⟨?⟩.

2. In the **Excel 2016 Help** window Search box, type Excel charts and then press ⟨Enter⟩.

3. In the search results, scroll down, click **Next**, and then click **Create a combo chart with a secondary axis**. **Maximize** the Excel 2016 Help window.

4. Read the article's introduction, and then compare your screen with **Figure 1**.

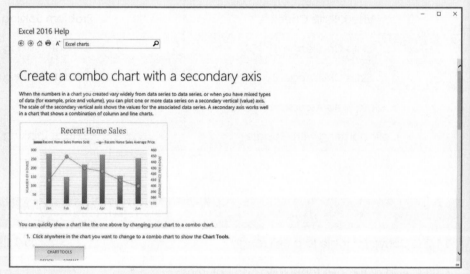

Figure 1　　　　　　　　　　　　　　Excel 2016, Windows 10, Microsoft Corporation

5. Read the section to answer the following questions: What are the advantages of using a combo chart? What types of combo charts are available?

Matching

Match each term in the second column with its correct definition in the first column by writing the letter of the term on the blank line in front of the correct definition.

___ **1.** Formats that are not current Excel versions but can be opened in the current version.

___ **2.** A text function used to remove spaces from a text string, except for a single space between words.

___ **3.** A text function used to return a specified number of characters starting from a specified point in the data.

___ **4.** Helps users to interpret or understand charted data.

___ **5.** Related data points that are plotted in a chart.

___ **6.** A graphic representation of trends in a data series.

___ **7.** A rectangular object that can be inserted into a worksheet or chart to accommodate text.

___ **8.** Data points that create a symmetric arc.

___ **9.** A software release or format.

___ **10.** A storage space on the cloud used to store and share files.

A Data series

B Exponential trendline

C Legend

D MID function

E Non-native files

F OneDrive

G Software version

H Text box

I Trendline

J TRIM function

Multiple Choice

Choose the correct answer.

1. Returns a specified number of characters from the left side of data.
   - A. LEFT function
   - B. TRIM function
   - C. RIGHT function

2. Used to return a specified number of characters starting from the right side of the data.
   - A. MID function
   - B. RIGHT function
   - C. TRIM function

3. Data points that follow nearly a straight line.
   - A. Linear trendline
   - B. Moving Average trendline
   - C. Exponential trendline

4. Data points that follow a straight line with a two-period forecast.
   - A. Linear trendline
   - B. Moving Average trendline
   - C. Linear Forecast trendline

5. Data points that follow a smooth curve to show data fluctuations.
   - A. Exponential trendline
   - B. Moving Average trendline
   - C. Linear trendline

6. A workbook with content and formatting that can be used as a model and edited.
   - A. Worksheet template
   - B. Text box
   - C. Trendline

7. Used to summarize and report results from separate worksheets.
   - A. RIGHT function
   - B. Linear trendline
   - C. Consolidate

8. One or more data series plotted on a secondary vertical axis.
   - A. Linear trendline
   - B. Dual axis chart
   - C. Trendline

9. A custom chart type that can be applied like other chart types.
   - A. Chart template
   - B. File type
   - C. Text box

10. A standard way that information is encoded for storage in a computer file.
    - A. File type
    - B. Worksheet template
    - C. Chart template

Topics for Discussion

1. In this chapter, you have seen a workbook in which data from a non-native file has been inserted. Discuss other situations in which this may be useful to organizations.

2. In this chapter, you used trendlines to predict or show data trends. For what other types of data would trendlines be useful to predict data trends?

Skills Review

MyITLab®
Grader

To complete this project, you will need the following files:

- exl08_SRElectricity (Excel)
- exl08_SRData (Access)

You will save your file as:

- Last_First_exl08_SRElectricity

---

1. Start **Excel 2016**, and then open the student data file **exl08_SRElectricity**. If necessary, enable content, and then click **Continue**. Save the file in your chapter folder as Last_First_exl08_SRElectricity

2. In the **Data** worksheet, verify cell **A1** is selected. Click the **File tab**, and then click **Open**. Navigate to the student data files, change the option to **All Files**, and then open the file **exl08_SRData**. In the Security Warning, click **Enable**. In the **Select Table** dialog box, select the **Residents** table, and then click **OK** two times.

3. Select and then copy the range **B1:G25**. Paste the range into the **Last_First_exl08_SRElectricity** file in the **Data** worksheet using **Paste Options—Keep Source Column Widths (W)**. Close the **Book1** Excel file without saving. Click **No**, to delete it from the Clipboard. Compare your screen with **Figure 1**.

4. Click cell **G2**, and then click the **Formulas tab**. In the **Function Library group**, click the **Text** button, and then click **TRIM**. In the **Function Arguments** dialog box, in the **Text** box, type A2 and then click **OK**. AutoFill the data down through cell **G25**. Copy the range **G2:G25**. Click cell **A2**. Using **Paste Options**, under **Paste Values**, click the first button—**Values (V)**.

5. Click cell **I2**. Click the **Formulas tab**. In the **Function Library group**, click the **Text** button, and then click **LEFT**. In the **Function Arguments** dialog box, in the **Text** box, type A2 and then press Tab. In the **Num_chars** box, type 4 and then click **OK**. AutoFill the data down through cell **I25**.

6. Click cell **J2**, and then using the techniques previously practiced, use **RIGHT**, **Text** F2 and **Num_chars** 4 to enter the data. AutoFill the data down through cell **J25**. Compare your screen with **Figure 2**.

■ Continue to the next page to complete this Skills Review

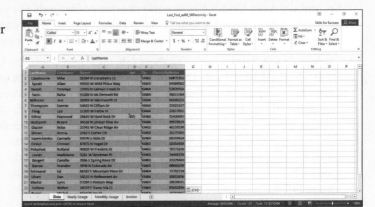

Excel 2016, Windows 10, Microsoft Corporation   Figure 1

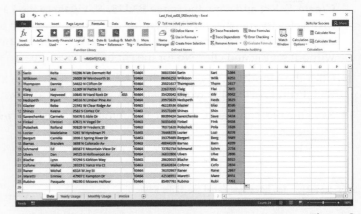

Excel 2016, Windows 10, Microsoft Corporation   Figure 2

7. Click cell **K2**. In the **Function Library group**, click the **Text** button, and then click **CONCATENATE**.

8. In the **Function Arguments** dialog box, in the **Text1** box, type I2 press Tab , and then in the **Text2** box, type J2 Click **OK**. AutoFill the data down through cell **K25**, and then AutoFit column **K**.

9. Click the **Yearly Usage** worksheet tab, and then select the **Yearly Usage** chart. Click the **Chart Tools Design tab**. In the **Chart Layouts group**, click **Add Chart Element**. In the list, point to **Legend**, and then click **Bottom**.

10. Select the **Yearly Fees** chart. In the **Type group**, click **Change Chart Type**. On the **All Charts tab**, click **Combo**, and then select **Clustered Column - Line on Secondary Axis**. Under **Choose the chart type and axis for your data series**, verify the **Chart Type** for **Total Fees** is **Line** and the **Secondary Axi**s box is selected, and then click **OK**. Compare your screen with **Figure 3**.

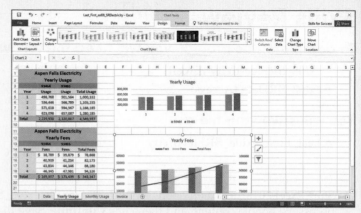

Figure 3   Excel 2016, Windows 10, Microsoft Corporation

11. Click the **Monthly Usage** worksheet tab, and then select the **Monthly Usage** chart. On the **Chart Tools Design tab**, in the **Chart Layouts group**, click **Add Chart Element**, point to **Trendline**, and then click **Linear Forecast**. In the **Add Trendline** dialog box, click **Year 1**, and then click **OK**. Click the **Chart Tools Format tab**, and then in the **Insert Shapes group**, click **Text Box**. Place the cursor in the chart in the top right corner at the border of columns **E** and **F**, and then drag over to the right edge of the chart and down to the $150,000 line. In the text box, type Usage increased in Year 2 In the **Shape Styles group**, click the **Shape Fill arrow**. Under **Theme Colors**, click the tenth color in the first row—**Green, Accent 6**. On the **Home tab**, in the **Alignment group**, click **Center**. Change the text font size to **10**.

12. Click the **File tab**, click **New**, and then in the search box, type invoice and press Enter . In the **New** window, scroll down and select **Invoice tracker**. Click **Create**. Select and copy the range **B3:I18**. Navigate to the **Last_First_exl08_SRElectricity** file, display the **Invoice** worksheet, and then in cell **A1**, paste the range using **Keep Source Column Widths (W)**. Close the **Invoice Tracker1** file without saving and click **No** for the clipboard message.

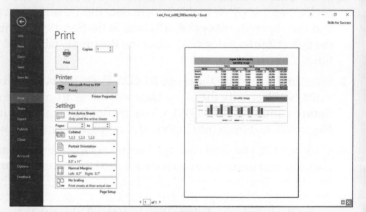

Figure 4   Excel 2016, Windows 10, Microsoft Corporation

13. Click the **Monthly Usage** worksheet tab. Click cell **A1**. Click the **File tab**, and then **Print Preview** the worksheet. Compare your screen with **Figure 4**.

14. Save the file, and then **Close** Excel. Submit the file as directed by your instructor.

✔ **DONE! You have completed the Skills Review**

Skills Assessment 1

MyITLab®
Grader

To complete this project, you will need the following files:

- exl08_SA1Travel
- exl08_SA1Data

You will save your files as:

- Last_First_exl08_SA1Travel
- Last_First_exl08_SA1Pdf
- Last_First_exl08_SA1Snip

---

1. Start **Excel 2016**, and then open the student data file **exl08_SA1Travel**. Save the file in your chapter folder as Last_First_exl08_SA1Travel

2. In the **Travel Year1** worksheet, add a legend to the chart, and position it at the top of the chart. Edit the legend to include **Budgeted**, **Actual**, and **Difference** as the **Legend Entries (Series)**. Edit the **Horizontal (Category) Axis Labels** to include the range **A4:A15**.

3. Change the chart type to **Clustered Column - Line on Secondary Axis**. Ensure the **Difference** is the secondary axis **Line**. Click cell **A1**.

4. Display the **Travel Year2** worksheet. In cell **A3**, consolidate the data from the range **A1:D13** from the **Mileage** worksheet and **A1:D13** from the **Lodging** worksheet in the **exl08_SA1Data** file. Ensure the labels are selected as the **Top row** and **Left column**. AutoFit columns as needed and close **exl08_SA1Data** without saving changes.

5. Select the range **A3:D15**, and then create a **Column chart** using the **Trendline Chart** template located in **My Templates**. (This template was created in Skill 8.) Position the top left edge of the chart in cell **F3**. Change the chart title to Travel Expenses

6. Remove the **Linear** trendline and replace it with a **Moving Average** trendline for **Budgeted**, and then change the chart colors to **Color 4** and the style to **Style 8**. Replace the text in the text box with Travel expenses peak in July and August Resize the textbox so all the text fits on one line.

7. **Save** the chart as a new template with the name Moving Average Chart Click cell **A1**.

8. **Save** the worksheet as a PDF file with the name Last_First_exl08_SA1Pdf

9. **Save** the file to the chapter folder in **OneDrive**, and then share it with janet.neal@aspenfalls.org In the message box, type Janet press ⌷Enter⌷, and then type I am sharing the completed Travel Expenses workbook. Press ⌷Enter⌷, and then type your First and Last names. Allow the user to edit the file. Take a

full-screen snip using the Windows Snipping Tool, and then save the file as Last_First_exl08_SA1Snip **Share** the file. Print Preview your workbook, and then compare your screen with **Figure 1** and **Figure 2**.

10. **Save** the file, and then **Close** Excel. Submit the files as directed by your instructor.

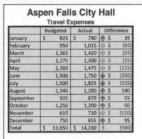

Figure 1

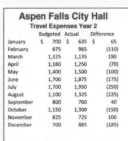

Figure 2

 DONE! You have completed Skills Assessment 1

Skills Assessment 2

To complete this project, you will need the following files:

- exl08_SA2Vehicles (Excel)
- exl08_SA2City (Access)

You will save your file as:

- Last_First_exl08_SA2Vehicles

---

1. Start **Excel 2016**, and then open the student data file **exl08_SA2Vehicles**. Save the file in your chapter folder as Last_First_exl08_SA2Vehicles

2. Open the **exl08_SA2City** file, and then import the data from the **Employees** table. Select and copy the range **B1:D23**, and then paste the range using **Keep Source Column Widths (W)** into cell **A1** of the **Codes** worksheet in the **Last_First_exl08_SA2Vehicles** file. Close the **Book1** file without saving.

3. In cell **D2**, use the **LEFT** function to extract the first two characters from the employee's **First Name**. In cell **E2**, use the **LEFT** function to extract the first four characters from the employee's **Last Name**. In cell **F2**, use the **RIGHT** function to extract the last four characters from the employee's **Social Security Number**.

4. In cell **G2**, use the **CONCATENATE** function to create a code combining **D2**, **E2**, and **F2**. AutoFill **D2:G2** down through row **G23**. AutoFit column **G**. Click cell **A1**.

5. Click the **Vehicles** worksheet tab. Select the range **A3:C10**. On the **All Charts, Combo** tab, create a **Column chart** using the **Clustered Column - Line on Secondary Axis**. **Vehicle Quantity** should be graphed as the secondary axis line chart. Position the top left edge of the chart in cell **E2**. Change the chart title to Vehicle Inventory

6. Move the legend to the **Top**, and then save the chart as a new template as Dual Axis Line Chart

7. Create a new Excel worksheet based on the **Travel expense calculator** template. Move the worksheet to the end of the **Last_First_exl08_SA2Vehicles** file. Replace the title in **A1** with Aspen Falls Expense Log

8. **Save** the file to the chapter folder. **Print Preview** the workbook, and then compare your screen with Figures 1, 2, and 3.

9. **Close** Excel. Submit the file as directed by your instructor.

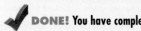
DONE! You have completed Skills Assessment 2

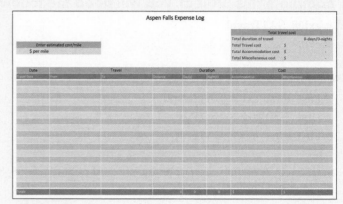

Figure 1

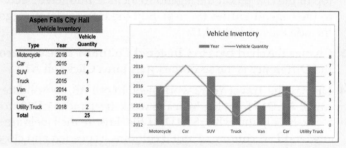

Figure 2

Last Name	First Name	Social Security Number				
Martinez	Maria	123-08-7898	Ma	Mart	7898	MaMart7898
Austin	Todd	987-09-5670	To	Aust	5670	ToAust5670
Ruiz	Jack	234-89-5687	Ja	Ruiz	5687	JaRuiz5687
Norris	Donald	564-09-7868	Do	Norr	7868	DoNorr7868
Neal	Janet	154-45-6787	Ja	Neal	6787	JaNeal6787
Kim	Leah	123-43-7095	Le	Kim	7095	LeKim7095
Cheung	Duncan	450-09-6745	Du	Cheu	6745	DuCheu6745
Cipic	Tad	432-34-0912	Ta	Cipc	0912	TaCipc0912
Shreffler	Natacha	908-78-9034	Na	Shre	9034	NaShre9034
Wagner	Julia	142-90-8903	Ju	Wagn	8903	JuWagn8903
Pettinelli	Amado	321-54-8978	Am	Pett	8978	AmPett8978
Mack	Richard	342-76-9023	Ri	Mack	9023	RiMack9023
Brewer	Rachel	908-56-3210	Ra	Brew	3210	RaBrew3210
Hopkins	Douglas	453-04-5463	Do	Hopk	5463	DoHopk5463
Payne	Diane	412-65-7843	Di	Payn	7843	DiPayn7843
Davidson	Deborah	607-32-9032	De	Davi	9032	DeDavi9032
Shore	Cyril	227-34-2103	Cy	Shor	2103	CyShor2103
Story	Cathy	546-21-9034	Ca	Stor	9034	CaStor9034
Perkins	Thelma	560-98-2309	Th	Perk	2309	ThPerk2309
Mccoy	Ann	429-23-2048	An	Mcco	2048	AnMcco2048
Stone	Evelyn	321-43-8950	Ev	Ston	8950	EvSton8950
Garner	Eugene	345-20-2056	Eu	Garn	2056	EuGarn2056

Figure 3

My Skills

To complete this project, you will need the following file:

- exl08_MYSavings

You will save your file as:

- Last_First_exl08_MYSavings

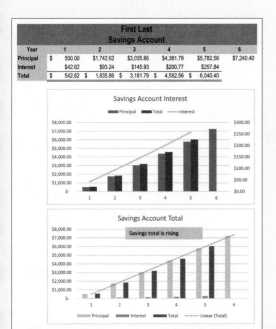

First Last
Savings Account

Year	1	2	3	4	5	6
Principal	$ 500.00	$1,742.62	$3,035.86	$4,381.79	$5,782.56	$7,240.40
Interest	$42.62	$93.24	$145.93	$200.77	$257.84	
Total	$ 542.62	$ 1,835.86	$ 3,181.79	$ 4,582.56	$ 6,040.40	

Last_First_exl08_MYSavings

Figure 1

1. Start **Excel 2016**, and then open the student data file **exl08_MYSavings**. Save the file in your chapter folder as Last_First_exl08_MYSavings

2. In the first cell of the **Savings** worksheet, replace *Student Name* with your First and Last names.

3. Select the range **A3:G6**, and then insert a **Dual Axis Column** chart using the **Dual Axis Chart** template that was created in Skill 8.

4. Move the chart to the top left corner in cell **B8**.

5. Replace the title with the name Savings Account Interest Move the legend to the **Top**.

6. Remove the **Year** from the **Legend Entries**.

7. Change the color of the chart to **Color 4**.

8. Select the range **A3:G6**, and then insert a **Column** chart using the **Trendline Chart** template that was created in Skill 8.

9. Move the chart to the top left corner in cell **B23**.

10. Replace the title with the name Savings Account Total

11. Remove the **Year** from the **Legend Entries**.

12. Add a **Linear** trendline based on the **Total**, and then replace the text in the text box with Savings total is rising

13. Click cell **A1**. **Print Preview** the worksheet, and then compare your screen with **Figure 1**.

14. **Save** the file, and then **Close** Excel. Submit the file as directed by your instructor.

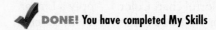 DONE! You have completed My Skills

Visual Skills Check

To complete this project, you will need the following files:

- Blank Excel workbook
- exl08_VSFair (Access)

You will save your file as:

- Last_First_exl08_VSFair

Start **Excel 2016**, and then open a blank workbook. Save the file in your chapter folder as Last_First_exl08_VSFair To create the worksheet shown in **Figure 1**, copy the data from the Revenue table located in the student data file—**exl08_VSFair**. Copy all of the data in the table except for the RevID data, and then paste the data, keeping column widths, into the range A1:F6 of the **Last_First_exl08_VSFair** worksheet. Close the **Book1** file without saving.

Convert table to range. Add labels, formatting, and AutoSums as shown in **Figure 1**. Center headings. Use Accounting and Comma formats with 2 decimal places. Ensure that all data is visible. Insert a dual axis chart, Clustered Column - Line on Secondary Axis, with bottom legend, as shown in **Figure 1**. Move chart to B9 and use Colorful chart Color 4. Apply a Linear trendline for Wednesday data and edit the chart title. **Save** the file, and then **Close** Excel. Submit the file as directed by your instructor.

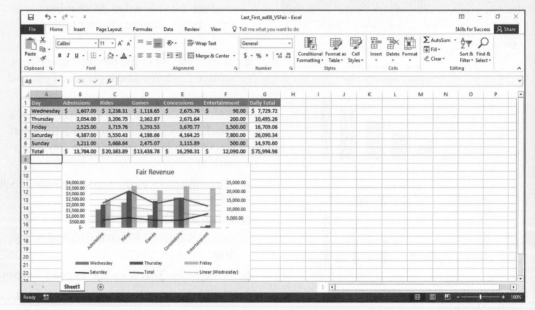

Figure 1

Excel 2016, Windows 10, Microsoft Corporation

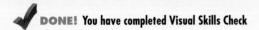

DONE! You have completed Visual Skills Check

Skills Challenge 1

To complete this project, you will need the following files:

- exl08_SC1Usage
- exl08_SC1Zip

You will save your file as:

- Last_First_exl08_SC1Usage

Aspen Falls Public Works tracks electricity usage and fees on a yearly basis in an effort to predict monthly trends. Start **Excel 2016**, and then open the student data file **exl08_SC1Usage**. Save the file in your chapter folder as Last_First_exl08_SC1Usage Open the student data file **exl08_SC1Zip**. In cell A11 of the **Last_First_exl08_SC1Usage** file, import the data from the **exl08_SC1Zip** file, using the skills practiced in the chapter. Consolidate the data from the 93464 and 93465 worksheets

into the Year1-Year2 worksheet. The data from the worksheets should be added and include the month labels in the left column. Close the **exl08_SC1Zip** file without saving. Save the file, and then Close Excel. Submit the file as directed by your instructor.

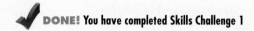 **DONE! You have completed Skills Challenge 1**

Skills Challenge 2

To complete this project, you will need the following files:

- Blank Excel workbook
- exl08_SC2Data (Access)

You will save your file as:

- Last_First_exl08_SC2Courses

Aspen Falls city employees have the benefit of being able to complete business courses at the local community college. If they earn a C or better in a business class, they can submit the tuition for reimbursement. Use the data file provided to search the business classes available. Start **Excel 2016**. Using the All Files option, open the student data file **exl08_SC2Data**, and move the data to a new worksheet before Sheet1 in the open Excel file. Save the file in your chapter folder as Last_First_exl08_SC2Courses Convert the data to a normal range. Trim the extra spaces from the Major ID data, and then replace the data with the trimmed data. In the next column, create the beginning of the course identification using the first

four letters of the Major data. In the next column, create the middle of the course identification using the last three letters of the Major ID. In the next column, create the end of the course identification using the three numbers in the middle of Course Number. To create the Course ID, concatenate columns F through H. Verify that all of the column widths fit the data. Save the file, and then close Excel. Submit the file as directed by your instructor.

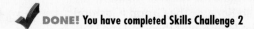 **DONE! You have completed Skills Challenge 2**

More Skills Assessment

MyITLab®
Grader

To complete this project, you will need the following file:

- exl08_MSAStocks

You will save your files as:

- Last_First_exl08_MSARecovered
- Last_First_exl08_MSASnip

---

1. Start **Excel 2016**. Open the student data file **exl08_MSAStocks**, and then save the file in your chapter folder as Last_First_exl08_MSAStocks

2. On the **Stocks** worksheet, change the chart type to **Clustered Column - Line on Secondary Axis**.

3. Verify the **Chart Type** for all of the stocks is set to **Clustered Column** and the **Secondary Axis** is not checked.

4. Edit the **Chart Type** for *Total Future Value*, *Total High FV*, and *Average High FV* to the Line chart type—**Stacked Line with Markers**—and verify **Secondary Axis** is checked. Compare your screen with **Figure 1**.

5. Revise the **Excel Options** to *Save AutoRecover information every minutes* box, replace the *10* with *1* and *Keep the last autosaved version if I close without saving* is selected.

6. On the **Updates** worksheet, insert a function in cell **C4** to calculate the serial number for the day of the week using the date as the serial number. AutoFill the function down through **C17**.

7. On the **Updates** worksheet, insert a function in cell **B19** to return the date *20* workdays after *12/20/2018*, considering the holidays in **D4:D5**.

8. Use the **Task Manager** to end task for **Microsoft Excel**. Open the Last_First_exl08_MSAStocks file, and then in the available recovered files, select the arrow for the file that was saved most recently.

9. Revise the **Excel Options** to customize the Ribbon. Create a custom tab with the name *My Tab* Rename the **Group (Custom)** as *Functions* Move the tab, before **Home**, and then add the **Date & Time** button to the **Functions (Custom) group**.

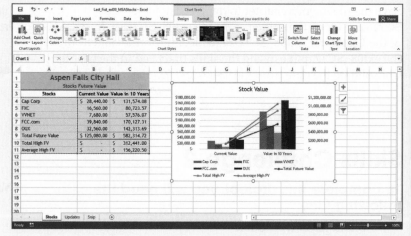

Figure 1
Excel 2016, Windows 10, Microsoft Corporation

10. With **My Tab** selected, use the **Snipping Tool** to take a full-screen snip, and then save the file as Last_First_exl08_MSASnip

11. On the **Snip** worksheet, insert the Last_First_exl08_MSASnip file, and then save the recovered file in your chapter folder as Last_First_exl08_MSARecovered

12. **Close** the **Last_First_exl08_MSAStocks** file without saving. Submit the files as directed by your instructor.

 **DONE! You have completed the More Skills Assessment**

Collaborating with Google

To complete this project, you will need a Google account (refer to the Common Features chapter) and the following file:

- exl08_GPCourses

You will save your file as:

- Last_First_exl08_GPCourses

1. Open the Google Chrome web browser. Log into your Google account, and then click the **Apps** ▦ button.

2. Click **Drive** to open Google Drive.

3. Click the **New** button, and then click **File upload**. Navigate to the student data files, and then open **exl08_GPCourses**.

4. Double-click **exl08_GPCourses** in **Google Drive**, and then click **Open** to view the workbook in **Google Sheets**.

5. Click cell **H5**, type =LEFT(click cell **C5**, and then type ,4) Press Tab .

6. In cell **I5**, type =RIGHT(Click cell **F5**, and then type ,2) Press Tab .

7. In cell **J5**, type =CONCATENATE(Click cell **H5**, and then type, Click cell **I5**, and then type) Press Tab .

8. AutoFill the range **H5:J5** down through row **66**.

9. Copy the range **J5:J66**. Click cell **B5**, and then click **Edit**. In the list, point to **Paste Special**, and then select **Paste values only**.

10. Click the **Registered** worksheet tab. Select the range **A3:C21**, and then click **Insert Chart** 📊. In the **Chart Editor**, select the second thumbnail in the first row, and then click the **Chart types tab**. Under **Line**, select the third thumbnail in the first row, **Combo**.

11. Click the **Customization tab** and then. In the **Title** box, replace the text with Fall Registration Under **Legend**, click the **Right arrow**, and then select **Top**. Click **Insert**.

12. Move the chart to position the top left corner in **E2**. Click **Insert**, click **Drawing**, and then click 🄣. Drag in the window to create a text box 16 blocks wide and two blocks tall. In the text box, type Year 2 enrollment increased Click 🖉, and then select **red**—second row, second column. Click **Save & Close**. Move the text box to position the bottom of the text box even with the **100** line, and

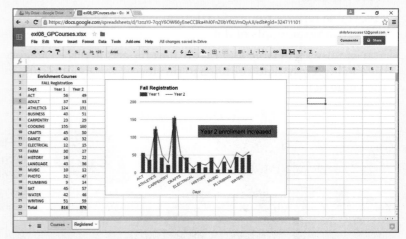

© 2016 Google Inc. All rights reserved. Google and the Google Logo are registered trademarks of Google Inc.; Excel 2016, Windows 10, Microsoft Corporation

Figure 1

the left edge even with the left border of column J. Compare your screen with **Figure 1**.

13. Click **File**, point to **Download as**, and then click **Microsoft Excel (.xlsx)**. Save the file in your chapter folder as Last_First_exl08_GPCourses

14. Close all windows, and then submit the file as directed by your instructor.

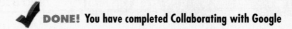

DONE! You have completed Collaborating with Google

CHAPTER 9

Link and Analyze Data in PivotTables and PivotCharts

- ▶ You can import and relate large amounts of data from multiple file sources, rapidly perform information analysis, and easily share insights.
- ▶ PivotTable reports are used to dynamically summarize and analyze large amounts of data.
- ▶ You can use PivotTable and PivotChart reports to place category data in both rows and columns to produce a variety of results in the value fields.

- ▶ Using PivotTable reports, you can perform various calculations on data to provide different types of results in the value fields.
- ▶ PivotChart reports graphically display the results that are calculated in PivotTable reports.
- ▶ You can filter PivotTable reports and PivotChart reports to show only the data that meets criteria you specify.
- ▶ You can use functions to return data in PivotTable reports.

Rawpixel.com/Fotolia

Aspen Falls City Hall

In this chapter, you will support Cyril Shore, Planning Council Director. The Planning Council examines and uses demographic data to plan for new services, communities, and schools. The council analyzes data on housing tenure, transportation, and salaries to determine if there is a need for such things as additional rental and ownership communities, public transportation and sidewalk access, and educators in the public school system.

You can use Excel to connect to data sources from relational databases, multidimensional sources, and text files. Once the connection is established, the data in Excel updates automatically without reconnecting to the data source. In Excel, imported data can be analyzed using database tools, statistical queries, and visualization tools that summarize the data across multiple categories.

In this project, you will create a new workbook by connecting data sources from Access and Excel files. You will apply filters to demographic data from Aspen Falls to analyze average income, household size, housing tenure, and commuting methods. Similarly, you will calculate and filter government salaries to summarize education salary information. You will also create charts and use other data visualization tools to assist with presenting the data.

Outcome

Using the skills in this chapter, you will be able to analyze large volumes of data using advanced data models and tools.

Objectives

9.1 Understand how to link to databases

9.2 Manipulate data using PivotTables and PivotCharts

9.3 Analyze data using PivotTable and PivotChart reports

Student data files needed for this chapter:

Blank Excel Workbook

exl09_Census (Access)

exl09_Employment (Excel)

You will save your file as:

Last_First_exl09_Census

SKILLS

Skills 1–10 Training

At the end of this chapter, you will be able to:

Skill 1 Get and Transform Data

Skill 2 Create PivotTable Reports

Skill 3 Change PivotTable Report Views

Skill 4 Change Calculation Types and Format PivotTable Reports

Skill 5 Create PivotTable Report Calculated Fields

Skill 6 Group and Filter PivotTable Reports

Skill 7 Use Slicers to Filter PivotTable Reports

Skill 8 Create PivotChart Reports

Skill 9 Format PivotChart Reports

Skill 10 Summarize Tables Using GETPIVOTDATA

MORE SKILLS

Skill 11 Use Power Pivot to Link Data to Access Databases

Skill 12 Create PivotChart Reports Using Power View

Skill 13 Add CUBE Functions Using Power Pivot

Skill 14 Use the Inquire Add-In

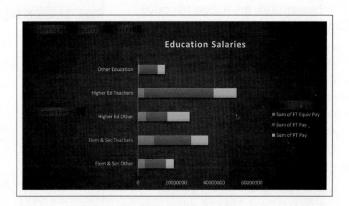

▶ To connect, combine, and refine data from multiple sources, you can use **New Query**.

▶ **Transforming** is modifying data from data sources to meet your needs; the process of applying transformations is known as **shaping data**.

▶ Workbooks can contain only one **data model**—a collection of tables with relationships.

1. Start **Excel 2016**, and then open a blank workbook. Click the **Data tab**. In the **Get & Transform group**, click the **New Query** button, point to **From Database**, and then compare your screen with **Figure 1**. Your choices may be different. Click **From Microsoft Access Database**.

2. Navigate to the student data files for this chapter, click the Access file **exl09_ Census**, and then click **Import**.

   It may take a few minutes to establish the connection.

3. In the **Navigator** window, click the **Demographics** table. Compare your screen with **Figure 2**.

   When the table is selected, a preview of its data is shown in the right pane.

4. In the **Navigator** window, click **Edit**.

   The *Load* option will import the data directly into Excel. The *Edit* option launches the Query Editor.

5. In the **Query Editor** window, if necessary, use the bottom scroll bar to scroll to the right. Click **Census Date** to select the field.

■ **Continue to the next page to complete the skill** ▶

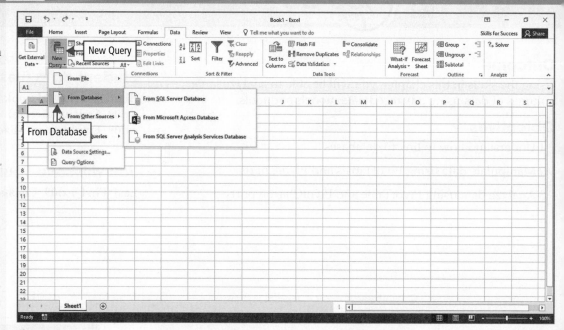

Figure 1

Excel 2016, Windows 10, Microsoft Corporation

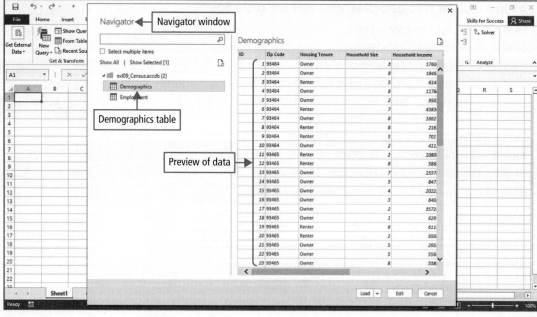

Figure 2

Excel 2016, Windows 10, Microsoft Corporation

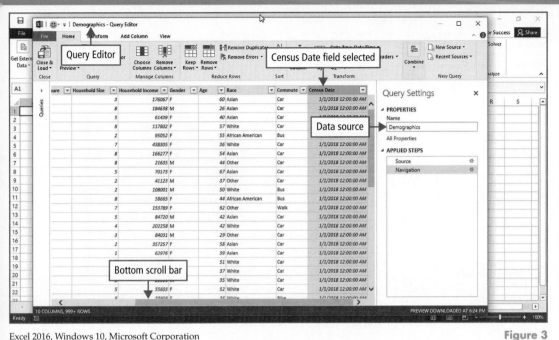

Excel 2016, Windows 10, Microsoft Corporation

Figure 3

Compare your screen with **Figure 3**. Using the Query Editor, you can edit the data source, remove columns, merge data, or change data types. The Query Editor tracks each transformation you apply to the data.

6. On the **Home tab**, in the **Manage Columns group**, click the **Remove Columns** arrow, and then click **Remove Columns**. Notice *Removed Columns* now appears under **APPLIED STEPS** in the **Query Settings** pane.

   The original data source will not change when transforming the data.

7. On the **Home tab**, in the **Close group**, click the **Close & Load** button to import the data into the workbook.

   The data is formatted as an Excel table and the table name is Demographics. In the Workbook Query pane, the Demographics query is created. Each query you create for this workbook will be recorded in this pane.

8. Click the **Data tab**. In the **Get & Transform group**, click the **New Query** button, point to **From File**, and then click **From Workbook**. Navigate to the student data files for this chapter, click **exl09_Employment**, and then click **Import**. Click the **Employment** worksheet, and then click **Load**. Compare your screen with **Figure 4**.

   MOS
   Obj 3.4.1 E

   MOS
   Obj 1.1.3 E

9. Click the **Query Tools Query tab**, and then review the tools related to the query.

   The query can be edited, loaded, reused, and combined with other queries.

10. Click the **File tab**, and then in the list, click **Save As**. Navigate to the location where you are saving your files. Click **New folder**, type Excel Chapter 9 and then press Enter two times. Name the file Last_First_exl09_Census and then click **Save**. **Close** the **Workbook Queries** pane.

Excel 2016, Windows 10, Microsoft Corporation

Figure 4

- **You have completed Skill 1 of 10**

▶ **WATCH** SKILL 9.2

▸ A **PivotTable report** is an interactive way to summarize, explore, and analyze data.

▸ PivotTable reports group, filter, and sort large amounts of data so that you can quickly create different views of the same data.

Obj 4.2.1 E

1. Rename the **Sheet2** worksheet tab as Demographics Rename the **Sheet3** worksheet tab as Employment

2. Click the **Demographics** worksheet tab, and then click the **Table Tools Design tab**. In the **Tools group**, click the **Summarize with PivotTable** button.

3. In the **Create PivotTable** dialog box, verify *Demographics* is selected as the table or range.

   The table stores demographic data **records**—collections of related data that displays in a single row in a database table—from a survey of 1,000 Aspen Falls citizens.

4. Under **Choose where you want the PivotTable report to be placed**, select **Existing Worksheet**. Click the **Collapse dialog** button, click the **Sheet1** worksheet tab, and then click cell **A1**. Click the **Expand dialog** button. Verify **Add this data to the Data Model** is selected, and then compare your screen with Figure 1. Click **OK**.

   A PivotTable report can be placed in a new worksheet or an existing worksheet.

5. In the **PivotTable Fields** pane, click **ALL**. Compare your screen with Figure 2.

   The Demographics and Employment tables are included in the PivotTable Fields pane.

■ **Continue to the next page to complete the skill**

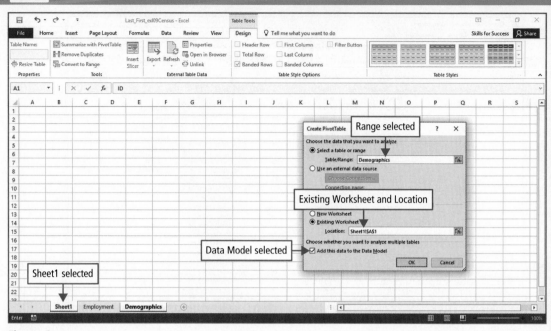

Figure 1

Excel 2016, Windows 10, Microsoft Corporation

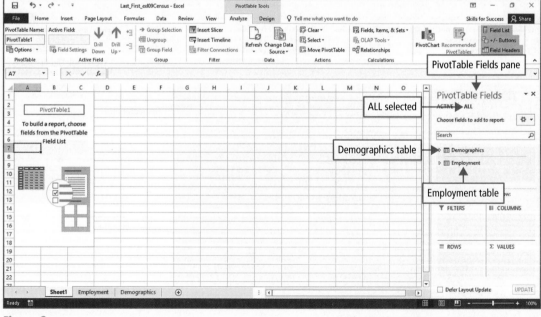

Figure 2

Excel 2016, Windows 10, Microsoft Corporation

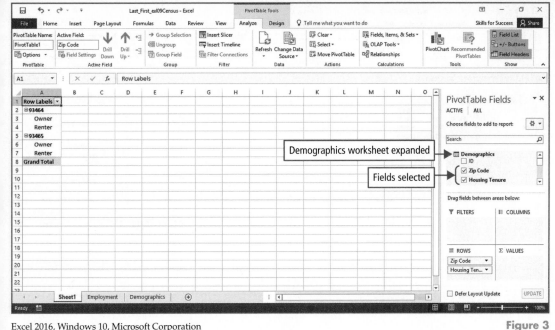

Excel 2016, Windows 10, Microsoft Corporation

Figure 3

6. In the **PivotTable Fields** pane, under **Choose fields to add to report**, expand ▷ **Demographics**, and then select the **Zip Code** and **Housing Tenure** check boxes. Compare your screen with **Figure 3**.

MOS
Obj 4.2.2 E

> In a database, *fields*—categories of data—are organized into columns. In a PivotTable report, fields can be organized in either rows or columns. *Row labels* are the fields used to categorize the data by rows. In this PivotTable report, the *Zip Code* field displays in rows and will group the data in the PivotTable report.

7. In the **PivotTable Fields** pane, under **Choose fields to add to report**, in the **Demographics** area, select the **ID** check box.

> The *Sum of ID* values are *PivotTable values*—the fields for which summary statistics are calculated.

8. Under **Drag fields between areas below**, in the **ROWS** box, click the **Housing Tenure arrow**, and then compare your screen with **Figure 4**.

> The list of field options is displayed.

9. Click cell **C1**, and then rename the **Sheet1** worksheet tab as Housing Tenure

> If you select a cell that is not a cell in the PivotTable, the PivotTable fields pane is hidden.

10. **Save** 🖫 the file.

■ **You have completed Skill 2 of 10**

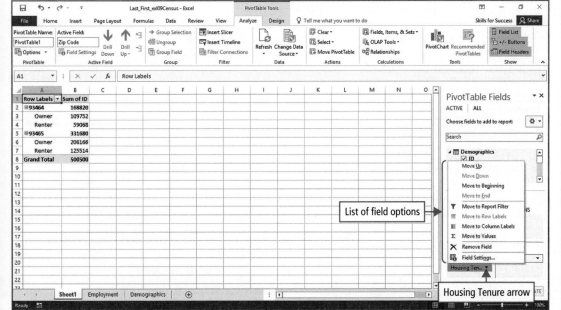

Excel 2016, Windows 10, Microsoft Corporation

Figure 4

▶ You can quickly change how data is presented in PivotTable reports.

▶ The PivotTable Fields pane is used to change fields from rows to columns, to add or remove fields, and to change the fields used to calculate values.

1. Click cell **A3** to select the PivotTable report, and display the PivotTable Fields pane.

   You can also display PivotTable Fields by clicking the Field List button on the Analyze tab, in the Show group.

MOS
Obj 4.2.2 E

2. In the **PivotTable Fields** pane, in the **ROWS** box, click the **Housing Tenure arrow**, and then click **Move to Column Labels** to move the *Housing Tenure* values to the columns in the worksheet. Compare your screen with **Figure 1**.

3. In the **VALUES** box, click the **Sum of ID arrow**, and then click **Value Field Settings**. In the **Value Field Settings** dialog box, under **Summarize value field by**, click **Count**, and then click **OK**.

   The values in the worksheet are changed to the number of owners and renters for each postal code and the grand total for each.

4. Click cell **A2**, replace the text with Zip Code and then press Enter. Click cell **B1**, replace the text with Housing Tenure and then press Enter.

5. In the **PivotTable Fields** pane, under **Choose fields to add to report**, select **Gender**. Compare your screen with **Figure 2**.

   The Gender field is added to the Rows section of the PivotTable Fields pane. The data displayed is the number of households within each postal code, grouped by gender.

■ Continue to the next page to complete the skill ▶

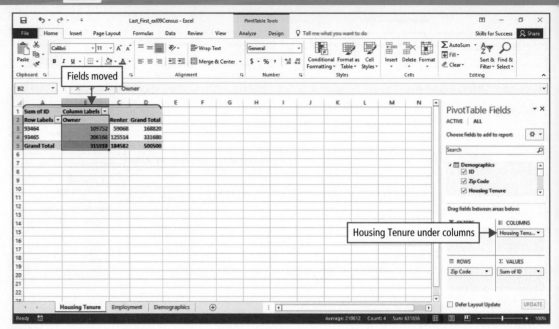

Figure 1

Excel 2016, Windows 10, Microsoft Corporation

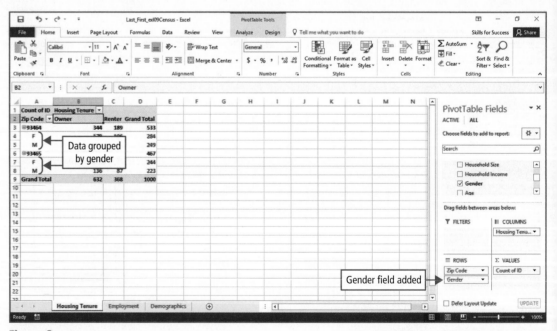

Figure 2

Excel 2016, Windows 10, Microsoft Corporation

6. In the **PivotTable Fields** pane, under **Drag fields between areas below**, click and then drag **Gender** from the **ROWS** box to the **COLUMNS** box.

> The PivotTable report now shows the number of households headed by each gender for each housing tenure.

7. In the **PivotTable Fields** pane, under **Choose fields to add to report**, click and then drag the **Commute** field into the **ROWS** box under *Zip Code*. Compare your screen with **Figure 3**.

> Within each Zip Code and Housing Tenure, the PivotTable displays how many individuals own or rent their homes, how many households are headed by males or females, and how each household commutes to work. In this manner, PivotTable reports can change how data is summarized.

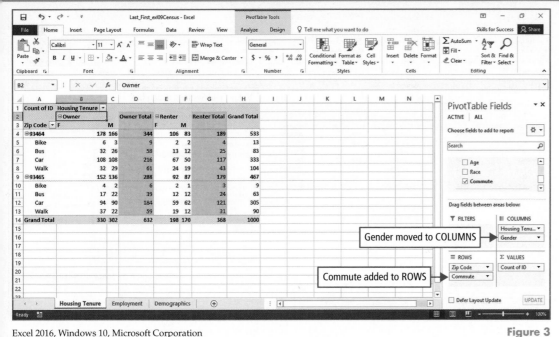

Excel 2016, Windows 10, Microsoft Corporation

Figure 3

8. In the **PivotTable Fields** pane, click and drag the **Gender** field from the **COLUMNS** box into the **ROWS** box.

9. Click and drag the **Commute** field from the **ROWS** box into the **COLUMNS** box.

10. In the **COLUMNS** box, click the **Housing Tenure arrow**, and then select **Remove Field**. Compare your screen with **Figure 4**.

> This chart shows the method by which each household within a particular postal code commutes to work. It also shows the total males and females who are designated as the head of households within each zip code.

11. In the **PivotTable Fields** pane, under **Choose fields to add to report**, select the **Housing Tenure** and **Household Income** check boxes, and then clear the **Commute** check box.

12. **Save** the file.

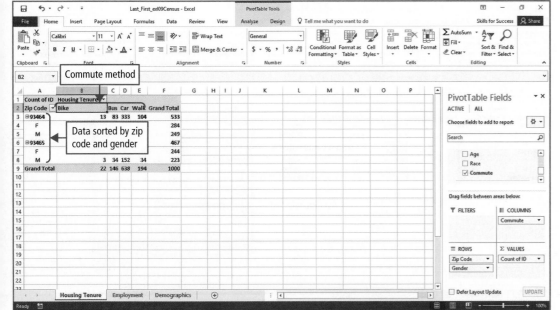

Excel 2016, Windows 10, Microsoft Corporation

Figure 4

■ **You have completed Skill 3 of 10**

- ▶ By default, PivotTable reports summarize fields by calculating a total for each group. Other summary statistics, including count, average, minimum, or maximum, can also be calculated.

- ▶ PivotTable reports are formatted by applying PivotTable styles.

1. In the **PivotTable Fields** pane, drag **Housing Tenure** from the **ROWS** box to the **COLUMNS** box. Position the field above the **Values** field.

2. Click cell **C3**, and then click the **PivotTable Tools Analyze tab**. In the **Active Field group**, click **Field Settings**, and then compare your screen with **Figure 1**.

3. In the **Value Field Settings** dialog box, under **Summarize value field by**, click **Average**, and then click the **Number Format** button.

4. In the **Format Cells** dialog box, under **Category**, click **Accounting**. In the **Decimal places** box, click the spin down arrow to change the value to **0**, and then click **OK**.

5. In the **Value Field Settings** dialog box, in the **Custom Name** box, replace the existing text with Average Income Compare your screen with **Figure 2**, and then click **OK**.

   In this manner, you can customize value fields to calculate different summary statistics and display different number formats.

6. In the **PivotTable Fields** pane, in the **VALUES** box, click the **Count of ID arrow**, and then click **Remove Field**.

7. Click cell **A3**, and then click the **PivotTable Tools Design tab**. In the **Layout group**, click the **Blank Rows** button, and then click **Insert Blank Line after Each Item**.

■ **Continue to the next page to complete the skill**

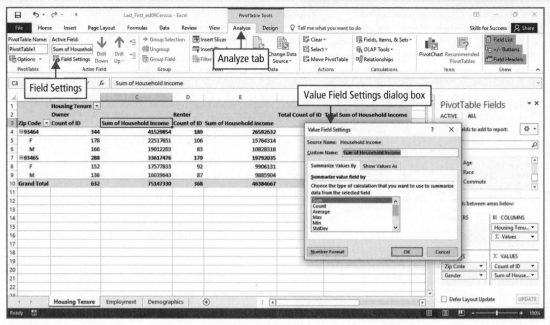

Figure 1

Excel 2016, Windows 10, Microsoft Corporation

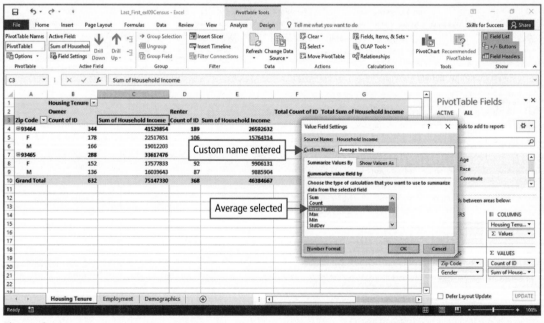

Figure 2

Excel 2016, Windows 10, Microsoft Corporation

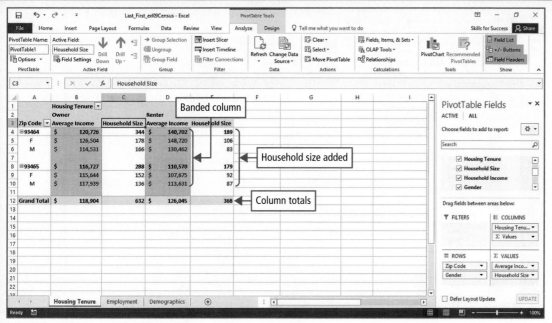

Excel 2016, Windows 10, Microsoft Corporation

Figure 3

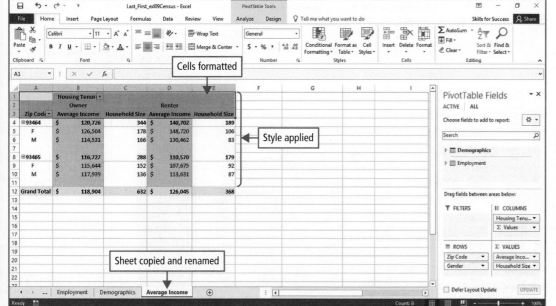

Excel 2016, Windows 10, Microsoft Corporation

Figure 4

8. In the **PivotTable Style Options group**, select the **Banded Columns** check box. MOS Obj 4.2.7 E

   Banded columns visually separate the data, making the information easier to read.

9. In the **Layout group**, click the **Grand Totals** button, and then click **On for Columns Only**.

10. In the **PivotTable Fields** pane, under **Choose fields to add to report**, select the **Household Size** check box.

11. Click cell **C3**, and then click the **PivotTable Tools Analyze tab**. In the **Active Field group**, click **Field Settings**, click **Count**, and then change the custom name to Household Size Click **OK**, and then compare your screen with **Figure 3**.

    This pivot shows the average household income for each zip code area, arranged by household size. It further compares the average income based on the gender of the head of the household.

12. Click the **PivotTable Tools Design tab**. In the **PivotTable Styles group**, click the **More** button . In the gallery, under **Light**, click the style in the third row, sixth column—**Pivot Style Light 19**. MOS Obj 4.2.7 E

13. Select the range **A1:E3**. Click the **Home tab**, and then in the **Alignment group**, click **Center** ≡.

14. Right-click the **Housing Tenure** worksheet tab, and then click **Move or Copy**. In the **Move or Copy** dialog box, under **Before sheet**, select **(move to end)**, select the **Create a copy** check box, and then click **OK**. MOS Obj 1.1.4 C

15. Rename the **Housing Tenure (2)** worksheet tab as Average Income and then compare your screen with **Figure 4**.

16. **Save** the file.

■ **You have completed Skill 4 of 10**

▶ A ***calculated field*** is a data field whose values are derived from formulas that you create. PivotTable fields can be included in these formulas.

▶ A calculated column needs to be created in the PowerPivot window before it can be added to a PivotTable in a worksheet. Calculated columns work much like the formulas and functions in normal Excel cells.

1. Click the **Demographics** tab, and then click the **Query Tools Query tab**. In the **Edit group**, click the **Edit** button. In the **Query Editor**, click the **Add Column tab**, and then in the **General group**, click the **Add Custom Column** button.

2. In the **New column name** box, replace *Custom* with Per Capita Income In the **Custom column formula** box, with the insertion point after the equal sign, in the **Available columns** pane, double-click the **Household Income** field name. Type a slash (/). In the **Available columns** pane, double-click the **Household Size** field name. Compare your screen with **Figure 1**, and then click **OK**.

3. Click the **Home tab**, and then in the **Close group**, click the **Close & Load** button. Select the **Per Capita Income** field. Compare your screen with **Figure 2**.

The formula divides Household Income by Household Size to determine the per capita income of each household.

4. Click the **Housing Tenure** worksheet tab. Click the **PivotTable Tools Analyze tab**, and then in the **Data group**, click the **Refresh** button. In the **PivotTable Fields** pane, if necessary, expand ▷ **Demographics**, scroll down, and then select **Per Capita Income**.

■ **Continue to the next page to complete the skill** ▶

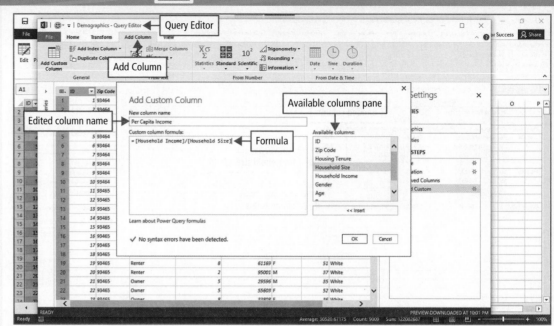

Figure 1

Excel 2016, Windows 10, Microsoft Corporation

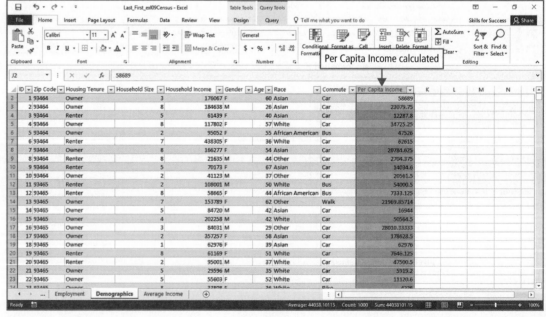

Figure 2

Excel 2016, Windows 10, Microsoft Corporation

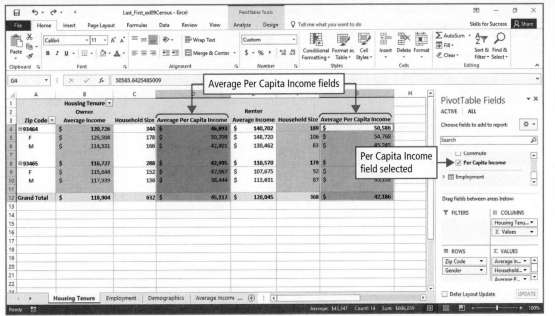

Excel 2016, Windows 10, Microsoft Corporation

Figure 3

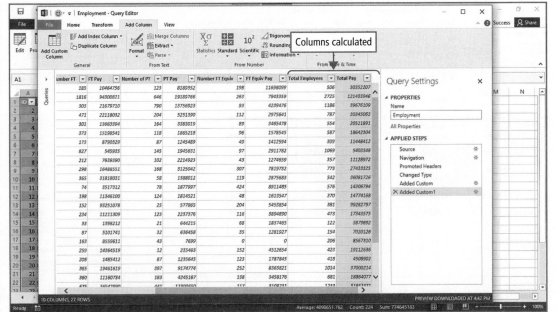

Excel 2016, Windows 10, Microsoft Corporation

Figure 4

5. Click cell **D3**. On the **PivotTable Analyze tab**, in the **Active Field group**, click the **Field Settings** button.

6. In the **Value Field Settings** dialog box, click **Average**. In the **Custom Name** box, replace the text with Average Per Capita Income and then click **OK**. Apply the **Accounting Format**, 0 decimal places to the ranges **D4:D12** and **G4:G12**. Compare your screen with **Figure 3**. Obj 4.2.7 E

7. Right-click the **Housing Tenure** worksheet tab, and then click **Move or Copy**. Using techniques previously practiced, move a copy of the worksheet to the end of the workbook

8. Rename the **Housing Tenure (2)** worksheet as Per Capita Income

9. Click the **Employment** worksheet tab, and then click the **Query Tools Query tab**. In the **Edit group**, click the **Edit** button. In the **Query Editor**, click the **Add Column tab**, and then in the **General group**, click the **Add Custom Column** button.

10. Replace **Custom** with Total Employees With the insertion point after the equal sign, in the **Available columns** pane, double-click **Number FT**, and then type a plus sign (+). Double-click **Number of PT**, type a plus sign (+), and then double-click **Number FT Equiv**. Click **OK**. Obj 4.2.6 E

11. Repeat the techniques previously practiced to create a calculated field named Total Pay that adds **FT Pay**, **PT Pay**, and **FT Equiv Pay** field names. Compare your screen with **Figure 4**.

12. Click the **Home tab**, and then in the **Close group**, click the **Close & Load** button.

13. Save 💾 the file.

■ **You have completed Skill 5 of 10**

▶ PivotTable report groups can be collapsed or expanded to show or hide the details for each group.

▶ Recall that *filtering* displays only the data that satisfies conditions you specify. In a PivotTable report, AutoFilter can filter data by rows or by columns.

1. Click the **Housing Tenure** worksheet tab. Click the **PivotTable Tools Analyze tab**, and then in the **Data group**, click the **Refresh** button.

MOS
Obj 4.2.4 E

2. Click cell **A4**, and then in the **Show group**, verify that the **Field List** button is selected. In the **PivotTable Fields** pane, under **Choose fields to add to report**, expand **Demographics**, clear the **Household Size** and **Gender** check boxes, and then select the **Race** check box.

3. In cell **A4**, click the **Collapse** button – to collapse the row, and then in cell **A6**, click the **Collapse** button – .

A minus symbol – indicates that a group can be collapsed. A plus symbol + indicates that a group can be expanded.

4. Right-click cell **A4**. From the shortcut menu, point to **Expand/Collapse**, and then click **Expand**.

The rows are expanded to show the full details for the category.

5. With cell **A4** still selected, click the **Collapse** button – , to collapse the row again. Compare your screen with **Figure 1**.

6. With cell **A4** still selected, click the **Expand** button + to expand the details for the 93464 Zip Code category. Compare your screen with **Figure 2**.

■ **Continue to the next page to complete the skill** ➤

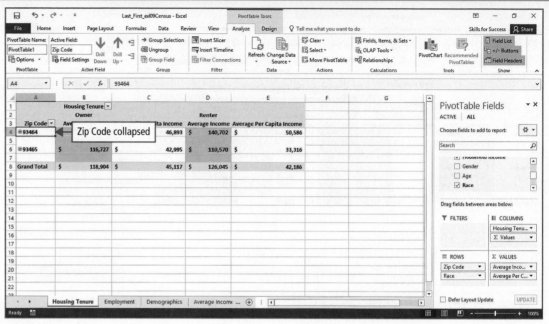

Figure 1

Excel 2016, Windows 10, Microsoft Corporation

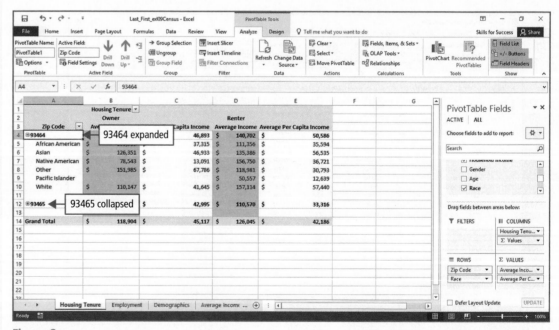

Figure 2

Excel 2016, Windows 10, Microsoft Corporation

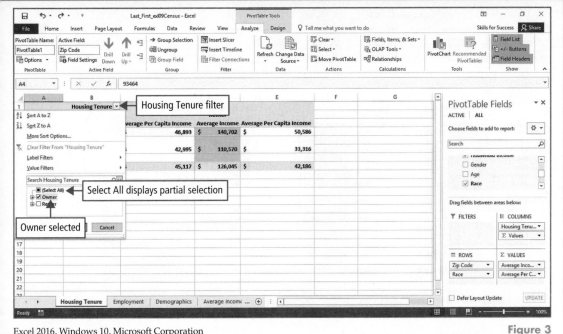

Excel 2016, Windows 10, Microsoft Corporation

Figure 3

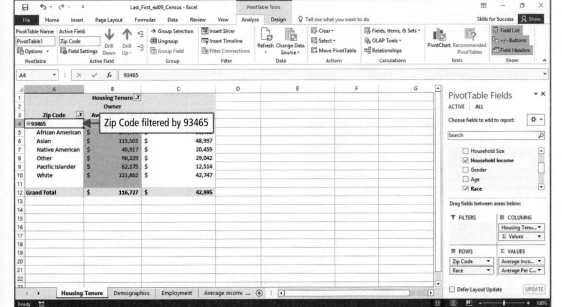

Excel 2016, Windows 10, Microsoft Corporation

Figure 4

7. Click cell **B1**, and then click the **Housing Tenure filter arrow** ⊡. In the list, clear the **Select All** check box, and then select **Owner**. Compare your screen with Figure 3, and then click **OK**.

   The filter displays only the column where the race is by owner.

8. Click cell **A3**, and then click the **Zip Code filter arrow** ⊡. In the list, clear the **Select All** check box, select the **93465** check box, and then click **OK**. In cell **A4**, click the **Expand** button ⊞, and then compare your screen with **Figure 4**.

   The filter is applied to the PivotTable rows so that only the summary data for the selected Zip Code displays.

9. Right-click the **Housing Tenure** worksheet tab, and then click **Move or Copy**. In the **Move or Copy** dialog box, under **Before sheet**, click **(move to end)**. Select the **Create a copy** check box, and then click **OK**.

 MOS Obj 1.1.4 C

10. Rename the new worksheet Filtered Race

11. Click the **Housing Tenure** worksheet tab. Click the **Zip Code filter arrow** ▼, select the **Select All** check box, and then click **OK**.

12. Click the **Housing Tenure Owner filter arrow** ▼, select the **Select All** check box, and then click **OK**.

13. On the **PivotTable Tools Analyze tab**, in the **Show group**, click **Field List** to close the **PivotTable Fields** pane.

14. **Save** 🖫 the file.

■ **You have completed Skill 6 of 10**

- A **slicer** is a tool that is used to filter data in PivotTable views.
- Slicers filter data based on distinct values in columns.

Obj 4.2.3 E

1. On the **Housing Tenure** worksheet, verify cell **A4** is selected. On the **PivotTable Tools Analyze tab**, in the **Filter group**, click the **Insert Slicer** button.

2. In the **Insert Slicers** dialog box, select the **Commute** and **Gender** check boxes, and then click **OK**.

   Two slicers are created. One filters the data based on gender; the other filters the data based on the commute method.

3. Click the **Gender** slicer, and then drag the slicer so that the upper left corner is positioned in the left corner of cell **G1**. Click and then drag the **Commute** slicer so that the upper left corner is positioned in the left corner of cell **G15**. Compare your screen with **Figure 1**.

4. In the **Gender** slicer, select the **M** slice.

   The data in the PivotTable report is now filtered to show only the results when the commuter is a male.

5. In the **Commute** slicer, select **Bus**, and then compare your screen with **Figure 2**.

   The data in the PivotTable report is filtered so that only the information related to male commuters who take the bus to work is displayed. For this Slicer Style, each selected slice has a single blue bar and the slices that are not selected have a white background. This is true for each Light Style; depending on the color selected, the bars will change color. For the Dark Styles, the slices not selected will be gray.

■ **Continue to the next page to complete the skill**

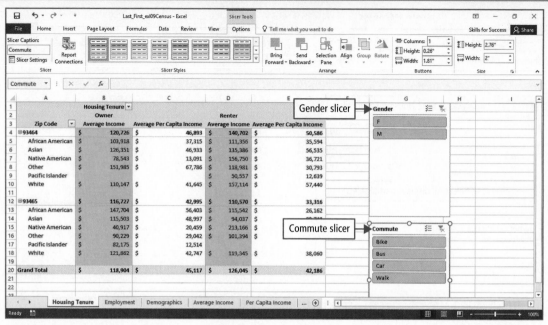

Figure 1

Excel 2016, Windows 10, Microsoft Corporation

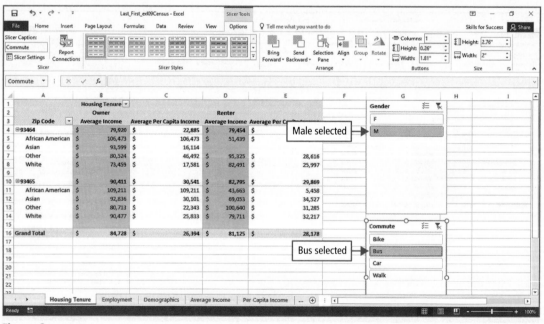

Figure 2

Excel 2016, Windows 10, Microsoft Corporation

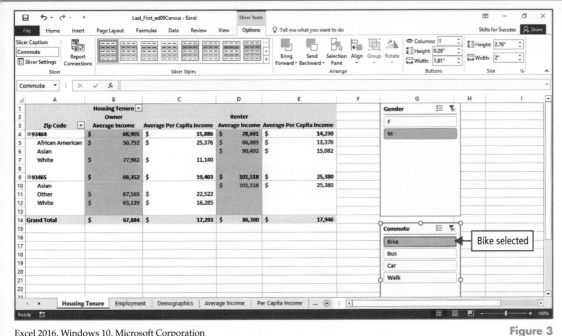

Excel 2016, Windows 10, Microsoft Corporation

Figure 3

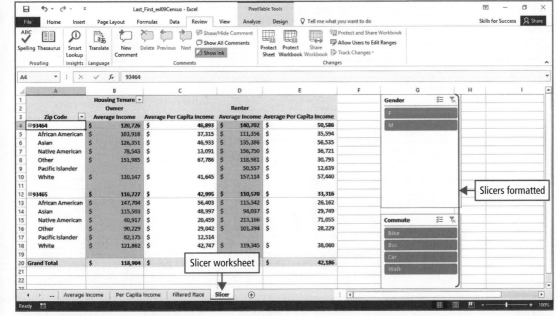

Excel 2016, Windows 10, Microsoft Corporation

Figure 4

6. In the **Commute** slicer, click **Bike**. The PivotTable report now displays only male commuters who ride a bike to work. Compare your screen with Figure 3.

7. If necessary, click the **Commute** slicer to select the slicer. Press Ctrl, and then click the **Gender** slicer. Release Ctrl. On the **Slicer Tools Options tab**, in the **Slicer Styles group**, click **More**, and then under **Dark**, click **Slicer Style Dark 6**.

8. Right-click the **Housing Tenure** worksheet tab, and then click **Move or Copy**. Using techniques previously practiced, move a copy of the worksheet to the end of the workbook, and then rename the new worksheet Slicer

9. In the **Gender** slicer, click **Clear Filter**. The values in the cells change. In the **Commute** slicer, click **Clear Filter**. Compare your screen with Figure 4.

10. Click the **Housing Tenure** worksheet tab. Right-click the **Gender** slicer title bar, and then click **Remove Gender**. Right-click in the **Commute** slicer title bar, and then click **Remove Commute**.

11. **Save** the file.

■ **You have completed Skill 7 of 10**

▶ A *PivotChart* is a dynamic visual representation of data. For example, you can assign any field to the value axis or category axis and then apply filters.

▶ The data source for a PivotChart can be an external file, such as a table in a database file.

1. Click the **Demographics** worksheet tab, click any cell in the table, and then click the **Insert tab**. In the **Charts group**, click the **PivotChart** button.

2. In the **Create PivotChart** dialog box, verify the **Table/Range** is **Demographics**. Select the **New Worksheet** option, and then check the option to **Add this data to the Data Model**. Compare your screen with **Figure 1**, and then click **OK**.

   A PivotChart is created.

3. Rename the sheet tab as Filtered Chart

4. On the **PivotChart Tools Analyze tab**, in the **Show/Hide group**, verify the **Field List** button is selected. In the **PivotChart Fields** pane, under **Choose fields to add to report**, select the **ID**, **Zip Code**, and **Commute** check boxes.

5. In the **PivotChart Fields** pane, under **Drag fields between areas below**, in the **VALUES** box, select the **Sum of ID arrow**. Click **Value Field Settings**. In the **Value Field Settings** dialog box, click **Count**, and then click **OK**. Compare your screen with **Figure 2**.

6. With the **PivotChart** selected, in the **PivotChart Fields** pane, under **Drag fields between areas below**, click **Zip Code**, and then drag it from the **AXIS (CATEGORIES)** box into the **FILTERS** box.

■ Continue to the next page to complete the skill

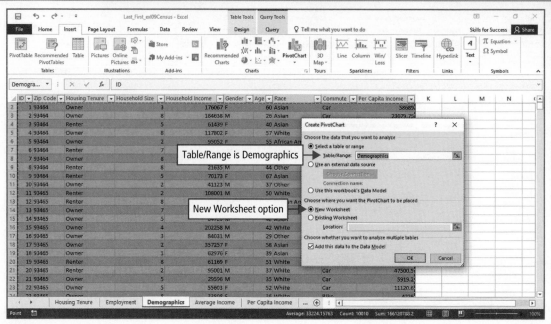

Figure 1

Excel 2016, Windows 10, Microsoft Corporation

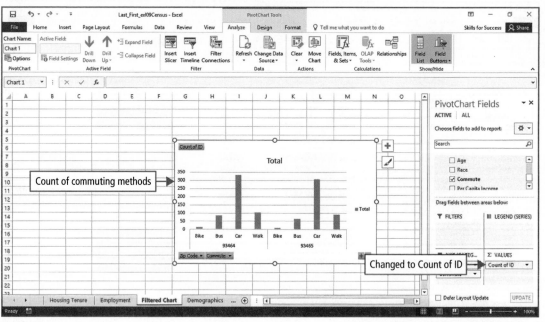

Figure 2

Excel 2016, Windows 10, Microsoft Corporation

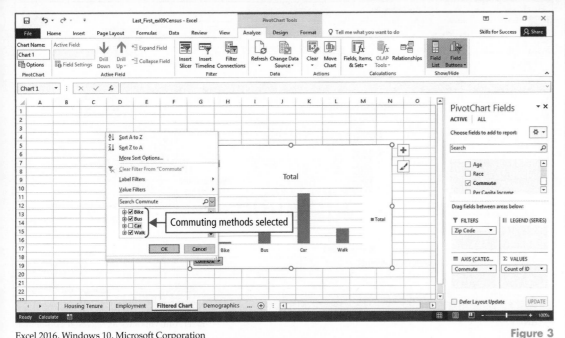

Excel 2016, Windows 10, Microsoft Corporation

Figure 3

Excel 2016, Windows 10, Microsoft Corporation

Figure 4

7. In the **PivotChart**, click the **Commute filter arrow** ⏷, and then in the list, clear the **Select All** check box. Select the **Bike**, **Bus**, and **Walk** check boxes. Compare your screen with **Figure 3**, and then click **OK**.

   The chart displays the number of people who commute by riding a bus or bike or walking, filtered by their zip code.

8. With the **PivotChart** selected, in the **PivotChart Fields** pane, under **Choose fields to add to report**, drag **Housing Tenure** into the **LEGEND (SERIES)** box.

   When you know what type of field you need, you can drag it directly into the desired box, and it will be automatically selected in the PivotChart Fields.

9. Click the **PivotChart Tools Design tab**. In the **Chart Layouts group**, click the **Add Chart Element** button, point to **Chart Title**, and then click **Above Chart**. Replace the title with Commuters

10. In the **Type group**, click the **Change Chart Type** button. In the **Change Chart Type** dialog box, click **Bar**, and then click **OK**. In the **Chart Styles group**, click **Style 3**.

11. Move the **PivotChart** to position the upper left corner in cell **B2**. Click and drag the lower right corner sizing handle down to the right corner of cell **K20**. Compare your screen with **Figure 4**.

12. **Save** 🖫 the file.

MOS
Obj 4.3.3 E

■ **You have completed Skill 8 of 10**

▶ PivotCharts can be formatted using Chart Styles and Layouts.

MOS
Obj 4.3.1 E

1. Click the **Employment** worksheet tab, click any cell in the table, and then click the **Insert tab**. In the **Charts group**, click the **PivotChart** button.

2. In the **Create PivotChart** dialog box, verify the **Table/Range** is **Employment**. Select the **New Worksheet** option, check the option **Add this data to the Data Model**, and then click **OK**.

3. Rename the sheet tab as Employment Chart

MOS
Obj 4.3.2 E

4. In the **PivotChart Fields** pane, select the **Government Function**, **FT Pay**, **PT Pay**, and **FT Equiv Pay** check boxes. In the **Values** box, drag the **Sum of FT Equiv Pay** above **Sum of FT Pay** and **Sum of PT Pay**. Compare your screen with **Figure 1**.

5. If necessary, select the PivotChart. Click the **PivotChart Tools Design tab**, and in the **Type group**, click the **Charge Chart Type** button. In the **Change Chart Type** dialog box, select **Bar**, and then click the second thumbnail **Stacked Bar**. Click **OK**.

MOS
Obj 4.3.4 E

6. In the chart, click the **Government Function filter arrow** ▾. Clear the **Select All** check box, and then select the following check boxes: **Elem & Sec Other**, **Elem & Sec Teachers**, **Higher Ed Other**, **Higher Ed Teachers**, and **Other Education**. Click **OK**, and then compare your screen with **Figure 2**.

Here, you have the ability to filter the chart based on employment functions.

▪ **Continue to the next page to complete the skill** ▶

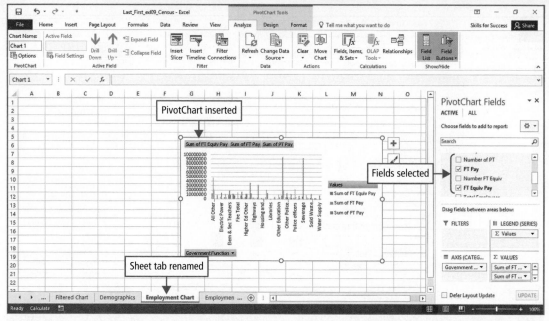

Figure 1

Excel 2016, Windows 10, Microsoft Corporation

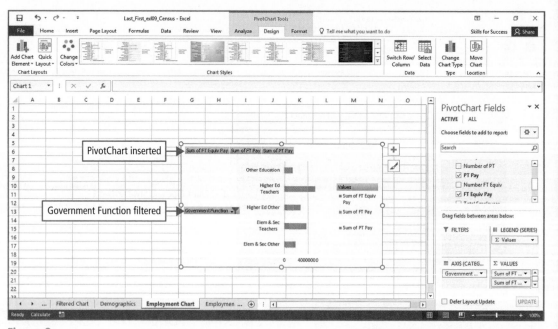

Figure 2

Excel 2016, Windows 10, Microsoft Corporation

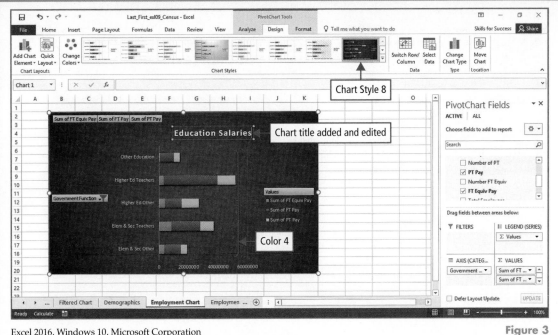

Excel 2016, Windows 10, Microsoft Corporation

Figure 3

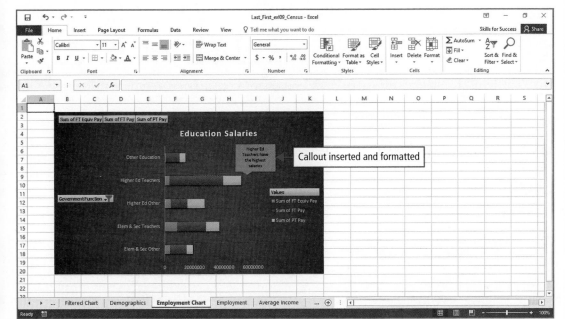

Excel 2016, Windows 10, Microsoft Corporation

Figure 4

7. Move the **PivotChart** to position the upper left corner in cell **B2**. Click and drag the lower right corner sizing handle down to the right corner of cell **K20**.

8. On the **PivotChart Tools Design tab**, in the **Chart Styles group**, click **Style 8**. In the **Chart Styles group**, click the **Change Colors** button, and then select **Color 4**.
   Obj 4.3.3 E

9. In the **Chart Layouts group**, click the **Add Chart Element** button, point to **Chart Title**, and then click **Above Chart**. Replace the title with Education Salaries and then compare your screen with **Figure 3**.

10. Click the **PivotChart Tools Format tab**, and in the **Insert Shapes group**, click **More**. Under **Callouts**, select the first option—**Rectangular Callout**. In the chart, click under the *l* in the title *Salaries*, to position the shape below the title and just above the longest bar in the chart. On the **Drawing Tools Format tab**, in the **Shape Styles group**, click the **Shape Fill arrow**. Under **Theme Colors**, select the last option in the first row—**Green, Accent 6**.
    Obj 5.3.1 C

11. In the callout, type Higher Ed Teachers have the highest salaries

12. Select the text, change the **Font Size** to **8**, and **Font Color** to **Automatic**. **Center** the text in the Callout. Click cell **A1**, and then compare your screen with **Figure 4**.

13. **Save** the file.

■ **You have completed Skill 9 of 10**

 **WATCH** SKILL 9.10

► The **GETPIVOTDATA** *function* returns data stored in a PivotTable report.

► You can use this function to retrieve summary data from a PivotTable report.

1. At the bottom of the Excel window, insert a **New Sheet**. Move the sheet before the **Housing Tenure** worksheet. Rename the worksheet tab Pivot Summary

2. In cell **A1**, type City of Aspen Falls **Merge & Center** the text in **A1:C1**. Increase the **Font Size** to **14**.

3. In cell **A2**, type Census Summary **Merge & Center** the text in **A2:C2**.

4. In cell **A4**, type 93464 In cell **B4**, type Owner In cell **C4**, type Renter **Center** the text in the range **A4:C4**.

5. In cell **A5**, type Average In cell **A6**, enter Income In cell **A7**, type Per Capita Income In cell **A8**, type Household Size **Increase Indent** for the range **A6:A8**. AutoSize column **A**. Compare your screen with **Figure 1**.

6. In cell **A9**, type 93465 and **Center** the text. Select and copy the range **A5:A8**, and then paste the data to the range **A10:A13**.

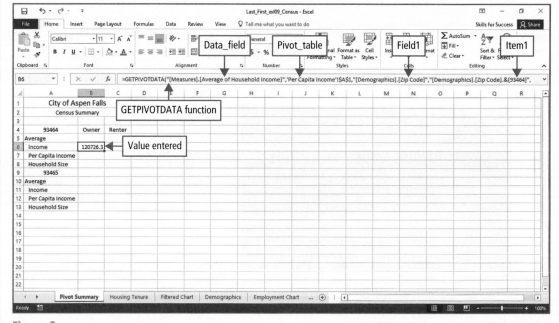

MOS
Obj 4.2.5 E

7. Click cell **B6**, and then type the equal sign (=). At the bottom of the Excel window, right-click **Next Page** ▶, and then double-click **Per Capita Income** to open the worksheet.

8. In the **Per Capita Income** worksheet, click cell **B4**, and then press Ctrl + Enter. Compare your screen with **Figure 2**.

The function arguments include the **data_field**—values you want to retrieve from the PivotTable—the pivot_table, or reference to a range of cells within a PivotTable, and fields and item names. Up to 126 optional pairs of rows and column headers and individual categories can be included.

■ **Continue to the next page to complete the skill**

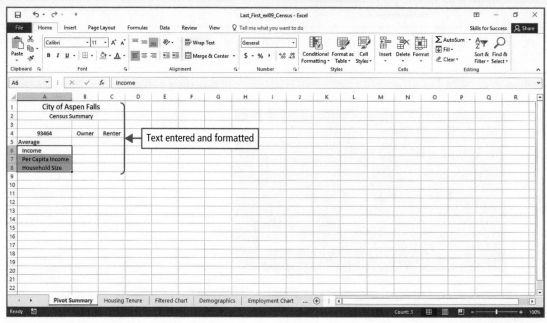

Figure 1

Excel 2016, Windows 10, Microsoft Corporation

Figure 2

Excel 2016, Windows 10, Microsoft Corporation

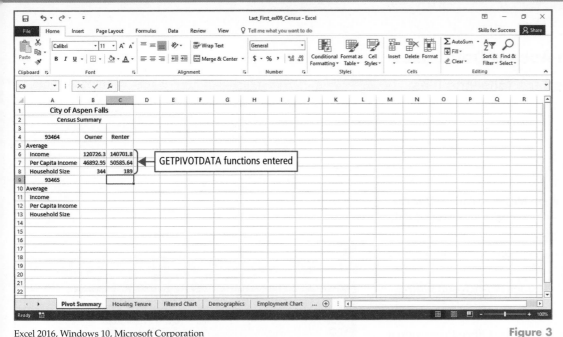

Excel 2016, Windows 10, Microsoft Corporation

Figure 3

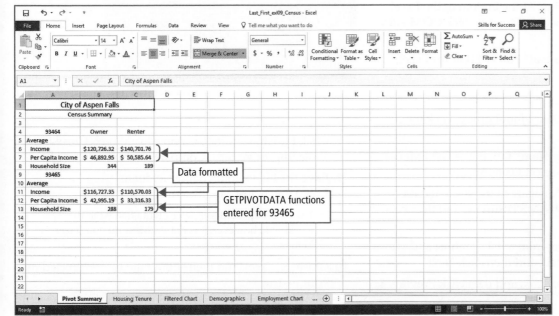

Excel 2016, Windows 10, Microsoft Corporation

Figure 4

9. Click cell **C6**, and then type the equal sign (=). At the bottom of the Excel window, right-click **Next Page** ▶, and then double-click **Per Capita Income** to open the worksheet. In the **Per Capita Income** worksheet, click cell **E4**, and then press Ctrl + Enter.

10. Click cell **B7**. Using the techniques previously practiced, enter the remaining values from the **Per Capital Income** worksheet for zip code **93464**. In cell **B7**, refer to cell **D4**; in cell **C7**, refer to cell **G4**; in cell **B8**, refer to cell **C4**; and in cell **C8**, refer to cell **F4**. In the **Pivot Summary** worksheet, click cell **C9**. Compare your screen with **Figure 3**.

11. Click cell **B11**, and then type the equal sign (=). At the bottom of the Excel window, right-click **Next Page** ▶, and then double-click **Per Capita Income** to open the worksheet. In the **Per Capita Income** worksheet, click cell **B8**, and then press Enter.

12. Click cell **C11**. Using the techniques previously practiced, enter the remaining values from the **Per Capital Income** worksheet for zip code **93465**. In cell **C11**, refer to cell **E8**; in cell **B12**, refer to cell **D8**; in cell **C12**, refer to cell **G8**; in cell **B13**, refer to cell **C8**; and in cell **C13**, refer to cell **F8**.

13. Apply the **Accounting Number Format** to the ranges **B6:C7** and **B11:C12**. Click cell **A1**, and then compare your screen with **Figure 4**.

14. **Save** 🖫 the file, and then **Close** ✕ Excel. Submit the file as directed by your instructor.

✓ **DONE! You have completed Skill 10 of 10 and your workbook is complete!**

More Skills 11

Use Power Pivot to Link Data to Access Databases

To complete this project, you will need the following files:

- Blank Excel Workbook
- exl09_MS11Survey (Access)

You will save your file as:

- Last_First_exl09_MS11Survey

▶ To analyze large volumes of data from various sources, you can use **Power Pivot**—an Office Professional Plus Excel add-in—to perform powerful data analysis and to create sophisticated data models.

▶ An Excel **add-in** is a file that adds functionality to Excel, usually in the form of new functions.

▶ Some add-ins are available only with specific versions of Microsoft Office.

1. This assignment can be completed only if you have the Office Professional Plus version. Start **Excel 2016**, and then open a blank workbook. Click the **File tab**, click **Options**, and then click **Add-ins**. At the bottom of the **Excel Options** dialog box, click the **Manage arrow**. From the list, click **COM Add-ins**, and then click the **Go** button.

2. In the **COM Add-ins** dialog box, select **Microsoft Power Pivot for Excel**, and then click **OK**.

   The PowerPivot tab is added to the Ribbon.

3. Click the **Power Pivot tab**, and then in the **Data Model group**, click the **Manage** button.

4. In the **Power Pivot for Excel** window, on the **Home tab**, in the **Get External Data group**, click **From Database**, and then select **From Access**.

5. In the **Table Import Wizard**, click **Browse**. Navigate to the student data files for this chapter, click the Access file **exl09_MS11Survey**, and then click **Open**. Click **Next**.

6. In the **Table Import Wizard**, verify the **Select from a list of tables and views to choose the data to import** option is selected, and then click **Next**.

7. In the wizard, select the **Demographics** check box, and then click **Preview & Filter**. Click **OK**.

   In Preview Selected Table, you can select columns to import. The data can also be filtered using the drop-down arrows.

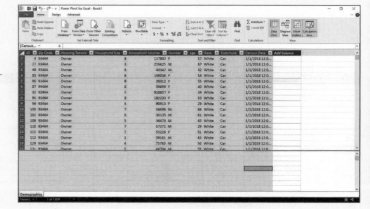

Figure 1   Excel 2016, Windows 10, Microsoft Corporation

8. Click **Finish**, wait for the import, and then **Close** the Table Import Wizard. Compare your screen to **Figure 1**.

9. **Save** the file in your chapter folder as Last_First_exl09_MS11Survey

   The data imported to Power Pivot is saved in the workbook; however, it is not visible until you select Manage.

10. **Close** ☒ Excel, and then submit the file as directed by your instructor.

- **You have completed More Skills 11**

More Skills (12)

Create PivotChart Reports Using Power View

To complete this project, you will need the following file:

- exl09_MS12Demographics

You will save your file as:

- Last_First_exl09_MS12Demographics

► You can interact with data in Excel using **Power View**—an interactive data exploration, visualization, and presentation add-in that encourages ad-hoc reporting.

► You can modify the internal data model without leaving the Power View sheet.

---

1. This assignment can be completed only if you have the Office Professional Plus version. Start **Excel 2016**, and then open the student data file **exl09_MS12Demographics**. Save the file in your chapter folder as Last_First_exl09_MS12Demographics If necessary, enable the content.

2. Click the **File tab**, click **Options**, and then click **Customize Ribbon**. In the right pane, under **Customize the Ribbon**, click the **Insert tab**, and then click **New Group**. Right-click **New Group (Custom)**, rename the group Reports and then click **OK**.

3. With the **Reports (Custom)** selected, in the left pane, under **Choose commands from**, click the arrow, and then select **Commands Not in the Ribbon**. Scroll down, and then select **Insert a Power View Report**. Click **Add**, and then click **OK**. **MOS** Obj 1.1.6 E

4. Click the **Insert tab**, and then in the **Reports group**, click the **Power View** button. In the **Power View Fields** pane, expand **Demographics**. Select the **Commute, Household Income**, and **Zip Code** check boxes. **MOS** Obj 4.3.2 E

5. On the **DESIGN tab**, in the **Tiles group**, click the **Tiles** button. Verify the chart is selected, click the **Tile Type** button, and then click **Tile Flow**. **MOS** Obj 4.3.3 E

6. Point to the lower right corner of the chart, and when the [⤢] arrow appears, drag down and to the right about 1 inch to resize the chart until **Walk** is viewable in the chart.

7. On the **Power View tab**, in the **Themes group**, click the **Themes** button. Click the first option in the second column—**Theme2**. Click **Background**, and then click the first option in the third column—**Dark2 Solid**.

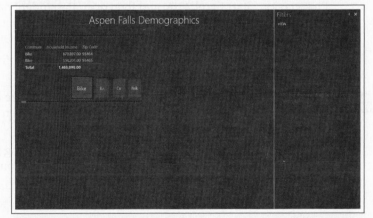

Excel 2016, Windows 10, Microsoft Corporation   **Figure 1**

8. Replace the title text with Aspen Falls Demographics **Print Preview** the worksheet, and then compare your screen with **Figure 1**.

9. **Save** [💾] the file, and then **Close** [✕] Excel. Submit the file as directed by your instructor.

■ **You have completed More Skills 12**

More Skills (13)

Add CUBE Functions Using Power Pivot

To complete this project, you will need the following file:

- exl09_MS13Water

You will save your file as:

- Last_First_exl09_MS13Water

▶ A **CUBE function** is a function that connects to and manipulates data in an **online analytical processing (OLAP) cube**, which extends a two-dimensional worksheet to three or more dimensions, where each dimension is a separate category.

▶ OLAP is a computer-based technique for analyzing business data.

---

1. This assignment can be completed only if you have the Office Professional Plus version. Start **Excel 2016**, and then open the student data file **exl09_MS13Water**. Save the file in your chapter folder as Last_First_exl09_MS13Water If necessary, enable the content.

2. If the Power Pivot tab is not displayed, install the Power Pivot add-in using the instructions in More Skills 11.

3. Click cell **A4**, and then click the **PivotTable Tools Analyze tab**. In the **Calculations group**, click the **OLAP Tools arrow**, and then click **Convert to Formulas**.

4. Click the **Formulas tab**, and then in the **Formula Auditing group**, click **Show Formulas**. AutoFit columns **A:B** to view the functions. **Print Preview** the worksheet, and then compare your screen with **Figure 1**.

   The underlying formulas in a PivotTable use cube functions to access a data cube.

The **CUBEMEMBER function** defines the categories and how the data should be aggregated. Here, the CUBEMEMBER function in B4 specifies that the average Rate should be measured.

The **CUBEVALUE function** defines the specific values derived from the cross-tabulation of the categories. Here, each CUBEVALUE function determines the actual average and total for each category as determined by the CUBEMEMBER function at the beginning of each row and column.

Because the PivotTable was converted into an OLAP cube, the original data connection to the Access database is no longer used. Instead, the local connection—*ThisWorkbookDataModel*—is referred to in the cube function arguments.

5. **Save** the file. **Close** Excel, and submit the file as directed by your instructor.

■ **You have completed More Skills 13**

Aspen Falls Utilities
Water Usage Analysis

Row Labels		
=CUBEMEMBER("ThisWorkbookDataModel","[Residents].[Zip].&[93463]")	=CUBEMEMBER("ThisWorkbookDataModel","[Measures].[Average of Rate]")	=CUBEMEMBER("ThisWorkbc
=CUBEMEMBER("ThisWorkbookDataModel",("[Residents].[Zip].&[93463]","[Water Bills].[Billing Date (Year)].&[2018]"))	=CUBEVALUE("ThisWorkbookDataModel",$A5,B$4)	=CUBEVALUE("ThisWorkbook
=CUBEMEMBER("ThisWorkbookDataModel",("[Residents].[Zip].&[93463]","[Water Bills].[Billing Date (Year)].&[2019]"))	=CUBEVALUE("ThisWorkbookDataModel",$A6,B$4)	=CUBEVALUE("ThisWorkbook
=CUBEMEMBER("ThisWorkbookDataModel","[Residents].[Zip].&[93464]")	=CUBEVALUE("ThisWorkbookDataModel",$A7,B$4)	=CUBEVALUE("ThisWorkbook
=CUBEMEMBER("ThisWorkbookDataModel",("[Residents].[Zip].&[93464]","[Water Bills].[Billing Date (Year)].&[2018]"))	=CUBEVALUE("ThisWorkbookDataModel",$A8,B$4)	=CUBEVALUE("ThisWorkbook
=CUBEMEMBER("ThisWorkbookDataModel",("[Residents].[Zip].&[93464]","[Water Bills].[Billing Date (Year)].&[2019]"))	=CUBEVALUE("ThisWorkbookDataModel",$A9,B$4)	=CUBEVALUE("ThisWorkbook
=CUBEMEMBER("ThisWorkbookDataModel",("[Residents].[Zip].&[93464]","[Water Bills].[Billing Date (Year)].&[2019]"))	=CUBEVALUE("ThisWorkbookDataModel",$A10,B$4)	=CUBEVALUE("ThisWorkbook
=CUBEMEMBER("ThisWorkbookDataModel","[Residents].[Zip].[All]","Grand Total")	=CUBEVALUE("ThisWorkbookDataModel",$A11,B$4)	=CUBEVALUE("ThisWorkbook

Last_First_exl09_MS13Water

Figure 1

Excel 2016, Windows 10, Microsoft Corporation

More Skills (14)

Use the Inquire Add-In

To complete this project, you will need the following files:

- exl09_MS14Expenses
- exl09_MS14Compare

You will save your files as:

- Last_First_exl09_MS14Expenses
- Last_First_exl09_MS14Snip

▶ An *Inquire add-in* assists with analyzing and reviewing workbooks to understand their design function and data dependencies, and uncover a variety of problems including formula errors or inconsistencies, hidden information, broken links, and others.

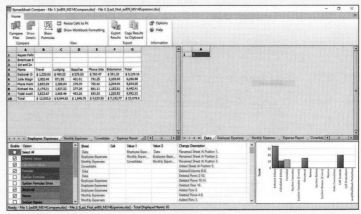

Excel 2016, Windows 10, Microsoft Corporation   **Figure 1**

1. This assignment can be completed only if you have the Office Professional Plus version. Start **Excel 2016**, open the student data file **exl09_MS14Expenses**, and then save the file in your chapter folder as Last_First_exl09_MS14Expenses

2. If the Inquire add-in is already installed, skip to step 4; otherwise, on the **File tab**, click **Options**, and then click **Add-Ins**. At the bottom of the **Excel Options** dialog box, click the **Manage arrow**. From the list, select **COM Add-ins**, and then click the **Go** button.

3. In the **COM Add-Ins** dialog box, select **Inquire**, and then click **OK** to add the **Inquire tab** to the ribbon.

4. Click the **Inquire tab**, and then in the **Report group**, click the **Workbook Analysis** button.

   The report may take a few seconds to several minutes to appear, depending on the size and complexity of the workbook. The report shows five visible sheets and 35 All formulas.

5. In the **Items** area, under **Workbook**, check **Visible sheets**, and then in the **Workbook Analysis Report** dialog box, click **Refresh** in the lower right corner.

6. Close the **Workbook Analysis** dialog box. In the **Diagram group**, click the **Worksheet Relationship** button.

7. In the **Worksheet Relationship Diagram** dialog box, read the information, and then close the dialog box. In the **Miscellaneous group**, click the **Clean Excess Cell Formatting** button. Click **OK**, and then click **Yes** in the message that appears.

   Cleaning removes cells from worksheets that are beyond the last cell that isn't blank.

8. Open the student data file **exl09_MS14Compare**. In the taskbar, select the **Last_First_exl09_MS14Expenses** workbook to make it the active window.

9. In the **Compare group**, click the **Compare Files** button. In the **Select Files to Compare** dialog box, verify **Compare** is exl09_MS14Compare, and **To** is **Last_First_exl09_MS14Expenses**. Click **Compare**. Compare your screen with **Figure 1**.

   Compare Files is used to display the differences between cells in two workbooks. The results are color coded by the type of content—values, formulas, named ranges, and formats.

10. Use the **Snipping Tool** to take a **Full-screen** snip, and then save the file in your chapter folder as Last_First_exl09_MS14Snip **Close** the Snipping Tool.

11. **Close** ☒ the **Spreadsheet Compare** dialog box. **Save** 🖫 the file. **Close** ☒ exl09_MS14Compare without saving, and then submit the files as directed by your instructor.

■ **You have completed More Skills 14**

The following table summarizes the **SKILLS AND PROCEDURES** covered in this chapter.

Skills Number	Task	Step	Icon
1	Get and transform data	Data tab → Get & Transform Data group → New Query button	
2	Create PivotTable	Table Tools Design tab → Summarize with Pivot Table button	⊡
3	Add fields to PivotTable	PivotTable Fields Pane → Expand worksheet → Select Fields	
3	Change PivotTable view	Drag fields between areas below → Select field arrow → Select where to move or click and drag the field to the view	
4	Change calculation types	Analyze tab → Active Fields group → Field settings → Function	
4	Edit PivotTable layout	Design tab → Layout group	
4	Edit PivotTable style	Design tab → PivotTable Styles group → More	
5	Create calculated field	Query Tools Query tab → Edit button → Add Column tab → Add Custom Column button	
6	Show Field List	Analyze tab → Show group → Field List	
6	Group PivotTable reports	Click Expand/Collapse button	+ −
6	Filter PivotTable reports	Click Filter arrow → AutoFilter List → Select option	
7	Insert slicer	Analyze tab → Filter group → Insert Slicer → Select Field(s) → In Slicer click option	
8	Create PivotChart from external data source	Insert tab → Charts group → PivotChart arrow → Pivot Chart → Use an external data source → Choose Communication → Select file	
9	Create PivotChart from PivotTable reports	Select PivotTable → Analyze tab → Tools group → PivotChart → Select chart type	
9	Format PivotChart reports	Select PivotChart Report → Format tab	
10	Use GETPIVOTDATA function	Type = → Click cell → Press Ctrl + Enter	
MS11	Insert add-ins	File tab → Options → Add-ins → Manage → COM Add-ins	
MS11	Link data to Access	PowerPivot tab → Data Model group → Manage → Get External Data → From Database → Select Database Type → Browse → Select file	
MS12	Use Power View	Insert tab → Reports Group → Power View button	
MS13	Insert CUBE functions	PivotTable Tools Analyze tab → Calculations group → OLAP Tools → Convert to Formulas	
MS14	Use Inquire add-in	Inquire tab → Report group → Workbook Analysis button	

Project Summary Chart

Project	Project Type	Project Location
Skills Review	Review	In Book & MIL MyITLab® Grader
Skills Assessment 1	Review	In Book & MIL MyITLab® Grader
Skills Assessment 2	Review	Book
My Skills	Problem Solving	Book
Visual Skills Check	Problem Solving	Book
Skills Challenge 1	Critical Thinking	Book
Skills Challenge 2	Critical Thinking	Book
More Skills Assessment	Review	In Book & MIL MyITLab® Grader
Collaborating with Google	Critical Thinking	Book

MOS Objectives Covered (Quiz in MyITLab®)

1.1.4 C Copy and move a worksheet	4.2.4 E Group PivotTable data
5.3.1 C Insert text boxes and shapes	4.2.5 E Reference data in a PivotTable by using the GETPIVOTDATA function
1.1.3 E Reference data in another workbook	4.2.6 E Add calculated fields
1.1.6 E Display hidden Ribbon tabs	4.2.7 E Format data
3.4.1 E Import, transform, combine, display, and connect to data	4.3.1 E Create PivotCharts
3.4.4 E Use cube functions to get data out of the Excel data model	4.3.2 E Manipulate options in existing PivotCharts
4.2.1 E Create PivotTables	4.3.3 E Apply styles to PivotCharts
4.2.2 E Modify field selections and options	4.3.4 E Drill down into PivotChart details
4.2.3 E Create Slicers	

Key Terms

Online Help Skills

1. Start **Excel 2016**, and then in the upper right corner of the start page, click the **Help** button 「 ? 」.

2. In the **Excel Help 2016** window **Search** box, type power view and then press 「Enter」.

3. In the search results, click **Power View - Overview and Learning**. **Maximize** the Excel 2016 Help window.

4. Read the article's introduction, and then below **Power View visualization types**, click **Charts and other visualizations in Power View**. Compare your screen with **Figure 1**.

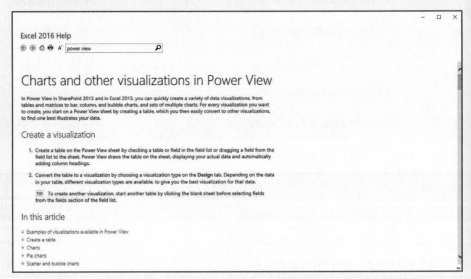

Figure 1   Excel 2016, Windows 10, Microsoft Corporation

5. Read the section to answer the following: What should you start with if you want to create a chart or visualization in Power View? When you convert a table to a visualization, how do you know what charts and visualizations are available to use for that table?

Matching

Match each term in the second column with its correct definition in the first column by writing the letter of the term on the blank line in front of the correct definition.

___ **1.** A tool to connect and combine data from multiple sources.

___ **2.** An interactive way to summarize, explore, and analyze data.

___ **3.** Categories of data organized into columns.

___ **4.** Located in the first column of a PivotTable report, these fields are used to categorize the rows.

___ **5.** Located along the top row of a PivotTable report, these fields are used to categorize the columns.

___ **6.** A new column or row whose values are derived from formulas that you create.

___ **7.** The technique used to display only the data that satisfies conditions you specify.

___ **8.** Indicates that a group can be collapsed.

___ **9.** A dynamic, visual representation of data.

___ **10.** An external data set used to create a PivotTable or PivotChart report, such as a table.

A Calculated field

B Column labels

C Data source

D Fields

E Filtering

F Minus symbol

G New Query

H PivotChart

I PivotTable report

J Row labels

Multiple Choice (MyITLab®)

Choose the correct answer.

1. Modifying data from data sources.
   A. Filtering
   B. Slicer
   C. Transforming

2. A collection of tables within relationships.
   A. Data models
   B. Records
   C. Columns

3. Data can be imported into Excel from this source.
   A. Access database
   B. Word document
   C. PowerPoint presentation

4. Collections of related data that display in a single row in a database table.
   A. Tables
   B. Records
   C. Fields

5. Fields for which summary statistics are calculated.
   A. Tables
   B. Data model
   C. PivotTable values

6. Calculated fields work much like these items.
   A. Formulas
   B. Solutions
   C. Values

7. You can click this to expand a collapsed group.
   A. Minus symbol
   B. Plus symbol
   C. Collapse All button

8. A tool used to filter data in PivotTable views.
   A. Minus symbol
   B. Expand All button
   C. Slicer

9. Values retrieved from the PivotTable report.
   A. Data_field
   B. Records
   C. Values

10. Reference to the range of cells within a PivotTable.
    A. Item
    B. Pivot_table
    C. Field

Topics for Discussion

1. What are the advantages and disadvantages of using PivotTable or PivotChart reports to find meaning from large sets of data?

2. PivotTable and PivotChart reports are designed to be fluid—constantly changing as you work with the data. What problems might this cause, and what techniques could be used to avoid them?

Skills Review

MyITLab®
Grader

To complete this project, you will need the following files:

- Blank Excel workbook
- exl09_SRElectricity (Access)

You will save your file as:

- Last_First_exl09_SRPower

---

1. Start **Excel 2016**, open a blank workbook, and then save it in your chapter folder as Last_First_exl09_SRPower

2. Click the **Data tab**. In the **Get & Transform group**, click the **New Query** button, point to **From Database**, and click **From Microsoft Access Database**. Navigate to the student data files for this chapter, click **exl09_SRElectricity**, and click **Import**.

3. In the **Navigator** window, click to select the **Select multiple items** check box. Select the **Billing Cycles** and **Residents** check boxes. Compare your screen with **Figure 1**. Click **Load**.

4. Click the **Insert tab**. In the **Tables group**, click the **PivotTable** button. Verify **Use this workbook's Data Model** and **Existing Worksheet** are selected and the **Location** box displays *Sheet1!$A$1*, and then click **OK**. If necessary, close the Workbook Queries pane. In the **PivotTables Fields** pane, expand **Billing Cycles**, and select **Electricity Usage**. Expand **Residents**, and select the **Street** and **Zip** check boxes. If necessary, read the message, and click **Auto-Detect**.

5. In the **ROWS** box, drag **Zip** above the **Street** field.

6. On the **PivotTable Tools Analyze tab**, in the **Active Field group**, click **Field Settings**. In the **Value Field Settings** dialog box, under **Summarize value field by**, click **Average**. In the **Custom Name** box, replace the text with Average Usage

7. Click **Number Format**. In the **Format Cells** dialog box, under **Category**, click **Number**, and click **OK** two times.

8. In cell **A2**, click the **Collapse** button. In cell **A3**, click the **Collapse** button. Compare your screen with **Figure 2**.

9. Click the **Data tab**. In the **Get & Transform group**, click the **Show Queries** button. In the **Workbook Queries** pane, double-click **Billing Cycles**. In **Query Editor**, click the **Add Column tab**, and in the **General group**, click the **Add Custom Column** button.

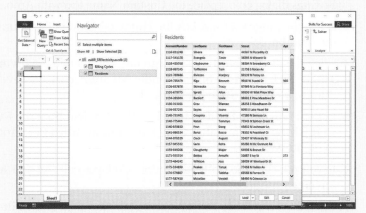
Excel 2016, Windows 10, Microsoft Corporation   **Figure 1**

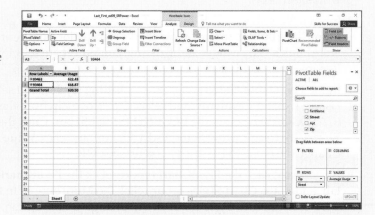
Excel 2016, Windows 10, Microsoft Corporation   **Figure 2**

■ Continue to the next page to complete this Skills Review ▶

10. In the **New column name** box, replace *Custom* with Amount Billed Place the insertion point after the equal sign in the **Custom column formula** box. In the **Available columns** pane, double-click the **Rate** field. Type an asterisk (*). In the **Available columns** pane, double-click the **Electricity Usage** field, and then click **OK**.

11. Click the **Home tab**, and then in the **Close group**, click the **Close & Load** button. If necessary, click **Refresh All**. Close the **Workbook Queries** pane.

12. In the **PivotTables Fields** pane, expand **Billing Cycles**, and then drag **Amount Billed** into the **VALUES** box. Click cell **C1**. Click the **PivotTable Tools Analyze tab**, and then in the **Active Field group**, click **Field Settings**. In the **Value Field Settings** dialog box, replace the **Custom Name** text with Amount Billed Click **OK**.

13. Select the range **C2:C4**. Click the **Home tab**, and in the **Number group**, apply the **Number** format.

14. Click the **PivotTable Tools Design tab**, and then in the **PivotTable Styles group**, click the **More** button. Under **Medium**, click the seventh style, in the third row—**Pivot Style Medium 21**.

15. In the **PivotTable Fields** pane, drag the **Zip** field from the **ROWS** box into the **COLUMNS** box, and then drag the **Amount Billed** field from the **VALUES** box to the **ROWS** box.

16. In cell **A3**, click the **Collapse** button. Collapse cells **A4** and **A5**. Compare your screen with Figure 3.

17. Click the **PivotTable Tools Analyze tab**, and then in the **Filter group**, click **Insert Slicer**. Under **Residents**, select **Zip**, and then click **OK**. Drag the slicer so the upper left corner is positioned in cell **F2**. Select the **93463** slice. Rename the worksheet Slicer

18. Insert a **New sheet**. Click the **Insert tab**, and in the **Charts group**, click the **PivotChart** button. In the **Create PivotChart** dialog box, verify **Use this workbook's Data Model** and **Existing Worksheet** are selected, and click **OK**. Rename the sheet Usage Chart

19. In the **PivotTable Fields** pane, expand **Billing Cycles**, and select **Electricity Usage**. Expand **Residents**, and select **Zip**. Move **Zip** from the **AXIS (CATEGORY)** box into the **LEGEND (SERIES)** box. Click the **Sum of Electricity Usage arrow** in the **VALUES** box, and click **Value Field Settings**. Change the name to Electricity Usage Click **OK**.

20. If necessary, click the **PivotChart report**. Click the **PivotChart Tools Design tab**, and in the **Chart Styles group**, click the **More** button. In the second row, third column, click **Style 11**. Click the **Change Colors** button, and click **Color 4**.

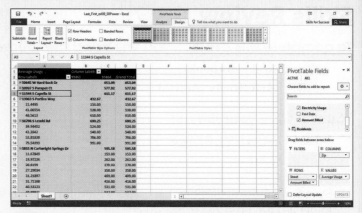

Figure 3　　　　　　　Excel 2016, Windows 10, Microsoft Corporation

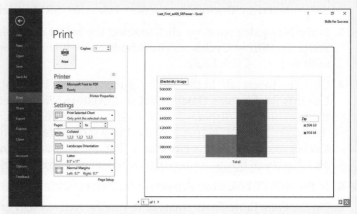

Figure 4　　　　　　　Excel 2016, Windows 10, Microsoft Corporation

21. Click the **File tab**, click **Print**, and then compare your screen with Figure 4.

22. Save the file, and then **Close** Excel. Submit the file as directed by your instructor.

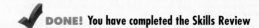 **DONE!** You have completed the Skills Review

Skills Assessment 1

MyITLab®
Grader

To complete this project, you will need the following files:

- Blank Excel workbook
- exl09_SA1Suppliers

You will save your file as:

- Last_First_exl09_SA1Suppliers

---

1. Start **Excel 2016**, open a blank workbook, and then save the file in your chapter folder as Last_First_exl09_SA1Suppliers Create a **New Query** to import the Access table from **exl09_SA1Suppliers**.

2. **Load** the data, and rename **Sheet2** as Suppliers Using the **Suppliers** data, insert a PivotTable report into **Sheet1** cell **A1**. Rename **Sheet1** as PivotTable

3. For the PivotTable, add **Supplier** as a column label, and **Date** and **Invoice** as row labels. In the **ROWS** box, position **Date** above **Invoice**. Add **Amount** as a value field that calculates sums formatted as **Accounting** with 2 decimal places displayed.

4. Edit the layout of the data by inserting a blank line after each item. Change the PivotTable style to the sixth style in the first row under **Medium—Pivot Style Medium 6**. In cell **A1**, type Invoice Amount and then in cell **A2**, type Suppliers

5. Select and collapse each of the date fields to show only the totals for each month. Compare your screen with **Figure 1**.

6. Copy the **PivotTable** worksheet, and then move it to the end of the workbook. Rename the worksheet Slicer Move **Supplier** to the **Rows** box above **Date**, and then remove the blank line after each item.

7. Use a Slicer to display the **Supplier** showing the data for **Falls Catering**. Align the **Slicer** with the top left corner in cell **D2**. Apply the second style under **Dark—Slicer Style Dark 2**. Select the PivotTable to view the **PivotTable Fields** pane. Compare your screen with **Figure 2**.

8. Click the **Suppliers** worksheet. Insert a **PivotChart** into a new worksheet. Rename the worksheet PivotChart and then move the worksheet to the end. Move **Supplier** to **LEGEND (SERIES)**, **Date** to **AXIS (CATEGORY)**, and **Amount** to **VALUES**.

9. Filter the **Date** in the chart to show only invoices for June through September.

10. Change the chart style to **Style 8**. Resize the chart to cells **B2:N19**. Add a title above the chart with the name Supplier Costs Compare your screen with **Figure 3**.

11. **Save** the file, and then **Close** Excel. Submit the file as directed by your instructor.

Excel 2016, Windows 10, Microsoft Corporation   **Figure 1**

Excel 2016, Windows 10, Microsoft Corporation   **Figure 2**

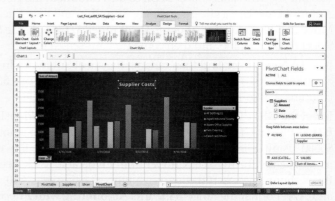

Excel 2016, Windows 10, Microsoft Corporation   **Figure 3**

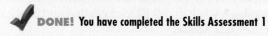

DONE! You have completed the Skills Assessment 1

Skills Assessment 2

To complete this project, you will need the following files:

- Blank Excel workbook
- exl09_SA2Purchases

You will save your file as:

- Last_First_exl09_SA2Purchases

---

1. Start **Excel 2016**, open a blank workbook, and then save the file in your chapter folder as Last_First_exl09_SA2Purchases

2. Create a **New Query**, and then import the Excel **Purchases** worksheet from the Excel **exl09_SA2Purchases** student data file. **Load** the Purchases data, and rename **Sheet2** as Purchases

3. Insert a PivotTable report into **Sheet1** cell **A1** using **Purchases** as the data range. Rename the worksheet PivotTable Filter by **Supplier**. In the **ROWS** box, add **Invoice Number**, and then add **Description**. Add **Amount** to VALUES. In cell **A3**, type Invoices and then in cell **B3**, type Amount Change the PivotTable style to **Pivot Style Medium 7**.

4. Open the **Query Editor**, and then add a custom column named Discount that multiplies the **Amount** field by .02 Add another custom column named Amount Due that subtracts the **Discount** from the **Amount**. Load the new fields, and on the **Purchases** worksheet, format both fields as **Accounting** with **2** decimal places. On the PivotTable worksheet, click **Refresh**. Close the **Workbook Queries** pane. Compare your screen with **Figure 1**.

5. Copy the PivotTable worksheet, and then move it to the end of the workbook. Rename the worksheet Slicer Replace the **Amount** in the values field with **Amount Due**. Use a **slicer** to display **Supplier**, and then filter **Falls Paper Depot**. Move the upper left corner of the **slicer** to cell **D2**. Apply the **Slicer Style Dark 6**. Select the PivotTable, and then compare your screen with **Figure 2**.

6. Insert a **New sheet**, and then rename the sheet Summary In cell **A1**, type Supplier Invoices > $5000 In cell **A3**, type Invoice # In cell **B3**, type Total Resize columns **A:B** to 11.

7. Insert the **GETPIVOTDATA** function in cell **B4**, using PivotTable worksheet cell **B31** as the data_field. Repeat this technique to insert the amounts greater than $5000, using cells **B40**, **B50**, **B59**, **B65**, **B72**, and **B79**. Use the cell reference formula in **A4** to enter the Invoice Number from PivotTable worksheet cell **A31**. Repeat this technique to insert the Invoice Numbers using cells **A40**, **A50**, **A59**, **A65**, **A72**, and **A79**. Format the range **B4:B10** as **Accounting** with **2** decimal places.

8. On the **Summary** worksheet, insert a PivotChart using the range **A3:B10** in the existing worksheet. Click in cell **F5** for Location and check the option to **Add this data to the Data Model**.

Figure 1   Excel 2016, Windows 10, Microsoft Corporation

Figure 2   Excel 2016, Windows 10, Microsoft Corporation

Figure 3   Excel 2016, Windows 10, Microsoft Corporation

9. Set **Invoice #** as the **AXIS (CATEGORY)** and **Total** as the **VALUES**. Apply **Chart Style 4**, and then revise the title of the chart to Supplier Invoices > $5000

10. Compare your screen with **Figure 3**.

11. **Save** the file, and then **Close** Excel. Submit the file as directed by your instructor.

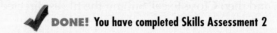 **DONE! You have completed Skills Assessment 2**

My Skills

To complete this project, you will need the following files:

- Blank Excel workbook
- exl09_MYSalvage

You will save your file as:

- Last_First_exl09_MYSalvage

Excel 2016, Windows 10, Microsoft Corporation   **Figure 1**

Figure 2

1. Start **Excel 2016**, and then open a blank workbook. Save the file in your chapter folder as Last_First_exl09_MYSalvage Create a **New Query** and import the **Salvage** worksheet from **exl09_MYSalvage**. In the **Query Editor**, add a custom column that calculates the Net Weight subtracting the **Tare** from **Gross**.

2. Add a custom column that calculates the Total Amount multiplying the **Price per Unit** by the **Net Weight**. **Load** the worksheet. Rename the worksheet Salvage Format **Total Amount** data as **Currency** with **2** decimal places. Compare your screen with **Figure 1**.

3. Create a **PivotChart** in **Sheet1** cell **A1**, using **Salvage** as the range and data model, and then rename the sheet Salvage Chart

4. In the chart, add the **Date** to the **LEGEND (SERIES)**, **Description** to the **AXIS (CATEGORIES)**, and **Total Amount** to the **VALUES** fields. Format as a **Clustered Column Chart**. Filter the **Date** to show **April 12, 2018 to April 17, 2018**.

5. Add a chart title to the top and replace the chart title with Salvage Totals

6. Resize the chart to **B2:N19**. Move the legend to the bottom of the chart. Apply Chart **Style 8**.

7. Click the **File tab**, click **Print**, and then compare your screen with **Figure 2**.

8. **Save** the file, and then **Close** Excel. Submit the file as directed by your instructor.

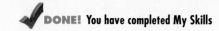

DONE! You have completed My Skills

Visual Skills Check

To complete this project, you will need the following files:

- Blank Excel workbook
- exl09_VSGarden

You will save your file as:

- Last_First_exl09_VSGarden

Start **Excel 2016**, and then open a blank workbook. Save the file in your chapter folder as Last_First_exl09_VSGarden Create a New Query, import and load the Inventory worksheet from **exl09_VSGarden**. Use the imported data to create the PivotChart and PivotTable shown in **Figure 1**. Use the following directions as a guide. In Query Editor, create a custom column using the name Inventory Value calculated by multiplying the Cost Each by the Quantity in Stock. Apply appropriate PivotChart Fields. Apply the Pivot Style Medium 3 table style. Apply 100% Stacked Bar, and Chart Style 9. Rename the worksheets PivotReports and Inventory Save the file, and then close Excel. Submit the file as directed by your instructor.

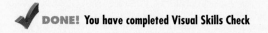 **DONE!** You have completed Visual Skills Check

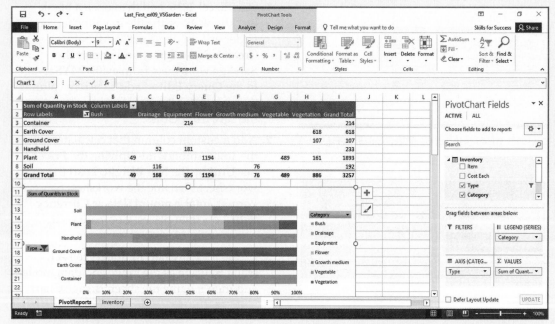

Figure 1

Excel 2016, Windows 10, Microsoft Corporation

Skills Challenge 1

To complete this project, you will need the following files:

- Blank Excel workbook
- exl09_SC1Works

You will save your file as:

- Last_First_exl09_SC1Works

The Aspen Falls Public Works department provides water to the city. In an effort to meet the needs of the city, the department monitors water usage by postal code and month to ensure sufficient water is available. Each household's water usage for the months April, May, and June 2018 is recorded in **exl09_SC1Works**. Start **Excel 2016**, and then open a blank workbook. Save the file in your chapter folder as Last_First_exl09_SC1Works Use New Query to import and load the Excel data source **exl09_SC1Works**, **Water Data** worksheet. Create and format PivotTable and PivotChart reports in the Sheet1 worksheet using the skills practiced in the chapter. Ensure the first row of data is used in the columns and import the table

Water Data. Add fields to the chart and table that will provide information based on the average water usage by postal code for the months of April, May, and June. Apply an appropriate chart style to the chart and table style to the table. Enter an appropriate title for the chart and move the legend to the bottom of the chart. Rename the data worksheet Water Usage and the Sheet1 to PivotChart Save the file, and then Close Excel. Submit the file as directed by your instructor.

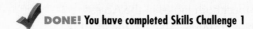 **DONE!** You have completed Skills Challenge 1

Skills Challenge 2

To complete this project, you will need the following files:

- Blank Excel workbook
- exl09_SC2Concessions

You will save your file as:

- Last_First_exl09_SC2Concessions

The Aspen Falls Parks and Recreation Department purchases products for the concessions located in its parks. To determine the associated costs, it analyzes the amount of yearly purchases. The concessions purchases are recorded in **exl09_SC2Concessions**. Start **Excel 2016**, and then open a blank workbook. Save the file in your chapter folder as Last_First_exl09_SC2Concessions Use New Query to import and load the Catering table in the Access data source **exl09_SC2Concessions**. Add a custom column that will provide the Total Cost for each order date and format the Cost Per Unit and Total Cost fields. Rename the Sheet2 worksheet

Concessions Copy the Concessions worksheet as a new worksheet at the end of the workbook. Rename the worksheet Vendors Insert a slicer on the Vendors worksheet that filters Vendor data for Falls Catering. Apply an appropriate slicer style. Rename Sheet1 as PivotChart and insert a PivotChart using the Catering data model on the Concessions worksheet. Apply the Pie chart type Style 3, and enter an appropriate title. Rename the Sum of Total Cost field to Overall Cost Save the file, and then Close Excel. Submit the file as directed by your instructor.

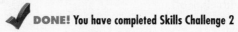 **DONE!** You have completed Skills Challenge 2

More Skills Assessment

MyITLab®
Grader

To complete this project, you will need the following files:

- exl09_MSAPopulation (Access)
- exl09_MSACompare (Excel)

You will save your files as:

- Last_First_exl09_MSAPopulation (Excel)
- Last_First_exl09_MSASnip (JPG)

---

1. This assignment can be completed only if you have the Office Professional Plus version. Start **Excel 2016**, and then open a blank workbook. If necessary, install the **COM Add-ins** for **Inquire**, **Power Pivot**, and **Power View**, using the techniques previously practiced in More Skills 11–14.

2. Use **Power Pivot for Excel** to connect both tables in the Access file **exl09_MSAPopulation** to the workbook. Save the file in your chapter folder as Last_First_exl09_MSAPopulation

3. Insert a **Power View** Pie Chart using data from the **Demographics** worksheet fields **Commute**, **Household Income**, and **Race**.

4. Move the legend to the bottom of the chart. Resize the chart to fill the window, and then replace the title with Aspen Falls Commuter Income Apply **Theme8**. Compare your screen with Figure 1.

5. On the **Sheet1** worksheet, create a PivotTable using data from the data model worksheet fields **Government Function**, **Number of FT**, **Number of PT**, and **Number of FT Equiv**.

6. Use the OLAP tools to convert the PivotTable data to CUBE formulas, and then show the formulas. Rename the worksheet CUBE

7. Use Inquire to perform a workbook analysis report, and then analyze the visible sheets in the workbook.

8. Compare the student data file **exl09_MSACompare** to **Last_First_exl09_MSAPopulation**.

9. Use the **Windows Snipping Tool** to take a full-screen Snip, and then save the file to your chapter folder as Last_First_exl09_MSASnip Close the Snipping Tool window, and then close the compare results window. Compare your screen with Figure 2.

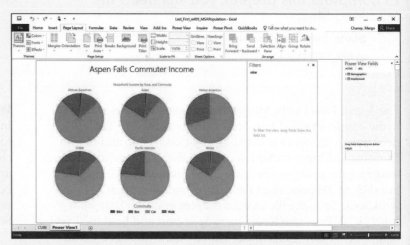

Figure 1   Excel 2016, Windows 10, Microsoft Corporation

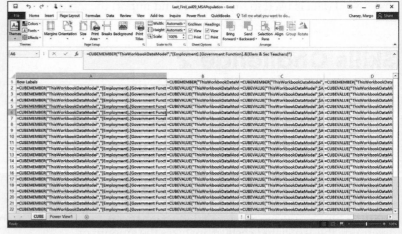

Figure 2   Excel 2016, Windows 10, Microsoft Corporation

10. **Save** the file, and then **Close** Excel and all open windows. Submit the file as directed by your instructor.

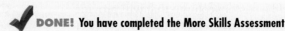 **DONE! You have completed the More Skills Assessment**

Collaborating with Google

To complete this project, you will need a Google account (refer to the Common Features chapter) and the following file:

- exl09_GPHousing

You will save your file as:

- Last_First_exl09_GPSnip

---

1. Open the **Google Chrome** web browser. Log into your Google account, and then click the **Apps** button.

2. Click **Drive** to open Google Drive.

3. Click the **New** button, and then click **File upload**. Navigate to the student data files, and then open **exl09_GPHousing**.

4. Double-click **exl09_GPHousing** in **Google Drive**, and then click **Open** to view the workbook in **Google Sheets**.

5. Click **Data**, and then click **PivotTable**. In the **Report Editor** pane, click **Add field** for **Rows**, and then select **Household Size**.

6. In the **Report Editor** pane, click **Add field** for **Columns**, and then select **Zip Code**.

7. In the **Report Editor** pane, click **Add field** for **Values**. Select **Household Income**, click the **Summarize by arrow**, and then click **AVERAGE**. Select the range **B2:D10**, and then click **Format as currency** [$].

8. Select the range **B1:C9**. In the lower right corner of the window, click **Explore**. Point to the left edge of the chart next to the zip codes title to view the chart tools, and then click **Insert chart**.

9. Close the **Explore** pane, and then close the **Report Editor**. Move the chart into the range **E1: I19**.

10. With the chart selected, in the top right corner of the chart, click the **Edit chart arrow** ▼.

11. Click **Advanced edit**. In the **Chart Editor**, replace the title text with Average Household Income and then click [Tab]. Click the **Legend arrow**, and then click **Top**.

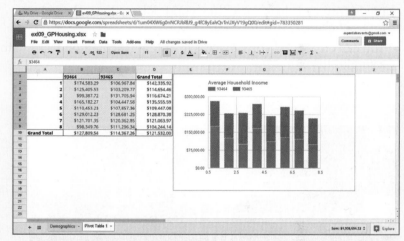

Figure 1

12. Click the **Recommendations tab**, click the second thumbnail in the first row, and then click **Update**. Compare your screen with **Figure 1**.

13. Use the **Windows Snipping Tool** to take a full-screen Snip, and then save the file to your chapter folder as Last_First_exl09_GPSnip

14. Close all windows, and then submit the file as directed by your instructor.

DONE! You have completed Collaborating with Google

CHAPTER 10

Secure and Share Workbooks

- ► You can personalize your version of Excel to identify a workbook's author.
- ► When you collaborate with others to build a workbook, each team member can add comments and you can track each change made. You can also protect the workbook so that only certain types of changes are allowed.
- ► You can create and copy macros to automate common tasks with a single click.

- ► When sharing a workbook, you can track each member's changes so that you can accept or reject those changes later.
- ► You can write validation rules so that only certain types of data can be entered, and you can protect the workbook so that only the cells you specify can be changed.

Mario Beauregard / Fotolia

Aspen Falls City Hall

In this chapter, you will review and revise a workbook for Evelyn Stone, the Aspen Falls Human Resources Director. Payroll is a function of the Human Resources department, and the workbook contains the Fire Department employees' payroll data. It is essential that it is verified for accuracy to ensure payroll is calculated correctly and that promotions are timely.

When several employees collaborate on files, the ability to enter comments, approve modifications, and protect certain cells from being modified assists organizations with communication and helps prevent inaccuracies in the data.

In this project you will edit an existing workbook and create a final version to be posted as a Web Page. To begin, you will change the author of the workbook, review comments in the workbook, and then create new comments. You will create procedures to provide guidance to other editors of the workbook, and you will accept and reject changes. To restrict certain cells from being edited you will protect cells from being modified and then create a series of steps that can be performed at the click of a button in order to save time editing worksheets.

Time to complete all 10 skills — 60 to 90 minutes

Introduction

Outcome

Using the skills in this chapter, you will be able to use collaboration tools to manage and edit workbooks and write and record macros.

Objectives

10.1 Evaluate and apply reviewers' comments.

10.2 Demonstrate how to save files as HTML.

10.3 Construct Visual Basic code to create macros.

Student data files needed for this chapter:

exl10_FireDept

exl10_Macro

You will save your files as:

Last_First_exl10_FireDept

Last_First_exl10_Changes

Last_First_exl10_Snip

Last_First_exl10_Web

Last_First_exl10_Embed

Last_First_exl10_Macro1

Last_First_exl10_Macro2

SKILLS

Skills 1–10 Training

At the end of this chapter, you will be able to:

Skill 1 Modify Excel Options and Work with Comments

Skill 2 Validate Data with Data Entry Rules

Skill 3 Track Changes

Skill 4 Accept and Reject Tracked Changes

Skill 5 Merge Changes

Skill 6 Save Workbooks as Web Pages and Embed Data in Web Pages

Skill 7 Unlock Cells and Protect Worksheets

Skill 8 Enable and Copy Macros Between Workbooks

Skill 9 Record Macros

Skill 10 Write Macros Using VBA

MORE SKILLS

Skill 11 Insert Form Controls

Skill 12 Add Macro Buttons to the Quick Access Toolbar

Skill 13 Prepare Workbooks for Internationalization

Skill 14 Assign Macros to Command Buttons

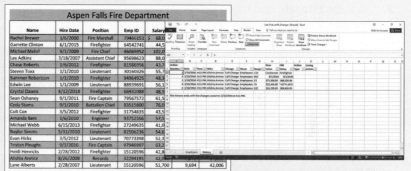

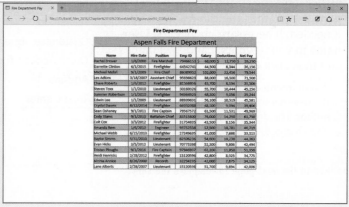

Edge 2016/Excel 2016, Windows 10, Microsoft Corporation

▶ A reviewer *comment* is descriptive text that you can add to cells without modifying the data in the worksheet.

▶ When collaborating on a project, reviewers can use comments to make suggestions.

▶ You can personalize your copy of Excel by changing the settings in the Excel Options dialog box.

1. Start **Excel 2016**, and then open the student data file **exl10_FireDept**. Click the **File tab**, and then click **Save As**. Click the **Browse** button, and then navigate to the location where you are saving your files. Click **New folder**, type Excel Chapter 10 and then press Enter two times. Save the file as Last_First_exl10_FireDept and then press Enter . If necessary, enable the content.

2. Click the **File tab**, and then click **Options**. Compare your screen with Figure 1.

The left side of the Excel Options dialog box displays option tabs. By default, the General tab is selected. The option tabs are summarized in the table shown in Figure 2.

3. In the **Excel Options** dialog box, under **Personalize your copy of Microsoft Office**, note the current value in the **User name** box so that you can restore it later, if needed. If necessary, change the **User name** to your own First and Last names, and then click **OK**.

As comments are added to the worksheet, the user name identifies the comments' author. The document property Author is also changed.

■ **Continue to the next page to complete the skill**

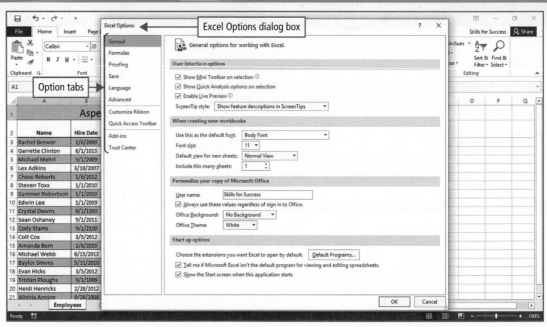

Figure 1

Excel 2016, Windows 10, Microsoft Corporation

Excel Options Window	
Section	**Purpose**
General	Provides access to the most commonly used settings.
Formulas	Provides options for how formulas are calculated and how errors are checked.
Proofing	Provides options for how spelling and grammar are checked.
Save	Provides options for how workbooks are saved.
Language	Provides options for setting Office Language Preferences.
Advanced	Provides access to thirteen subcategories of options.
Customize ribbon	Provides a way to customize the ribbon.
Quick Access Toolba	Provides a way to customize the Quick Access Toolbar
Add-ins	Provides a way to manage Excel Add-ins.
Trust Center	Provides a way to manage privacy and security.

Figure 2

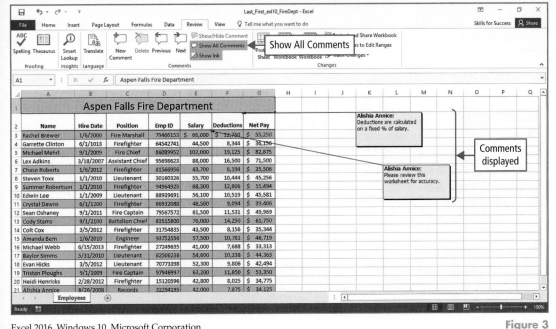

Excel 2016, Windows 10, Microsoft Corporation

Figure 3

Excel 2016, Windows 10, Microsoft Corporation

Figure 4

4. Point to cell **F2** so that the comment from Alishia Annice displays.

   Cells with comments display a ***comment indicator***—a small red triangle in the upper right corner of a cell.

5. Click the **Review tab**, and then in the **Comments group**, click **Show All Comments**. Compare your screen with Figure 3.

   Showing all comments allows you to read all of the comments at one time.

6. Click cell **B13**. In the **Comments group**, click **New Comment**. In the comment box, type Is this date entered correctly?

7. With the comment attached to cell **B13** still selected, point to the comment box border, and then with the ⌖ pointer, drag to the right to position the upper left corner of the comment box in cell **I13**.

8. Click cell **E9**, and then click **New Comment**. In the comment box, type Is this the correct salary? It seems high for a Firefighter.

9. With the comment attached to cell **E9** still selected, point to the comment box border, and then with the ⌖ pointer, drag to the right to position the upper left corner of the comment box in cell **I8**.

10. Click cell **C22**, and then click **New Comment**. In the comment box, type Promote Lane to Lieutenant? Repeat techniques previously practiced to position the comment to cell **I21**. Click cell **A2**. Compare your screen with Figure 4.

11. In the **Comments group**, click **Show All Comments** to hide the comments from view.

12. **Save** 🖫 the file.

■ **You have completed Skill 1 of 10**

▶ A *data validation rule* places a restriction on the types of data that can be entered into cells.

1. Select the range **B3:B22**. Click the **Data tab**, and then in the **Data Tools group**, click the **Data Validation** button.

2. If necessary, move the dialog box to view the data in column B. In the **Data Validation** dialog box, on the **Settings tab**, click the **Allow arrow**, and then click **Date**. Click the **Data arrow**, and then click **greater than**. In the **Start date** box, type 1/1/1985 Compare your screen with **Figure 1**.

3. In the **Data Validation** dialog box, click the **Input Message tab**, and then in the **Title** box, type Hire Date In the **Input message** box, type Hire date cannot be before 1985

> An *input message* is a data validation message that informs the data entry operator about the types of data that can be entered into the cell.

4. Click the **Error Alert tab**. If necessary, select the **Show error alert after invalid data is entered** check box to enable it. In the **Title** box, type Invalid Hire Date In the **Error message** box, type The hire date must be after 1/1/1985 Click **OK**, and then click cell **A1**.

> An *error alert* is a data validation message that informs the data entry operator that invalid data has been entered into the cell.

5. In the **Data Tools group**, click the **Data Validation arrow**, and then click **Circle Invalid Data**. Compare your screen with **Figure 2**.

> When a data rule has been applied to a cell, Excel indicates invalid data by circling the cell whose value does not match the rule.

■ **Continue to the next page to complete the skill** ▶

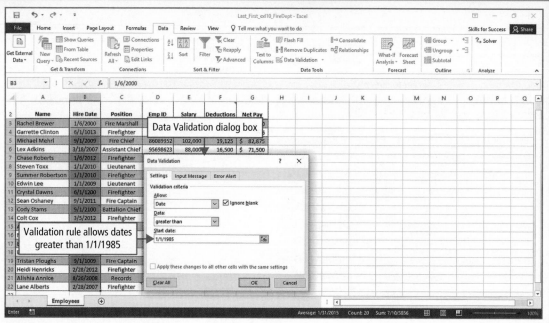

Figure 1

Excel 2016, Windows 10, Microsoft Corporation

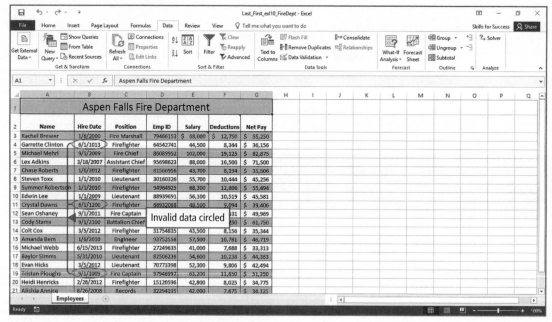

Figure 2

Excel 2016, Windows 10, Microsoft Corporation

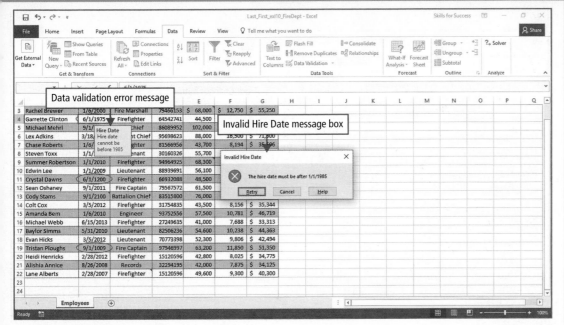

Excel 2016, Windows 10, Microsoft Corporation

Figure 3

Error Message Styles	
Type	**Purpose**
Stop	Prevents users from entering invalid data in a cell. This message has two options: Retry or Cancel.
Warning	Warns users that the data entered is invalid, without preventing them from entering it. When a Warning message appears, users can click Yes to accept the invalid entry, No to edit the invalid entry, or Cancel to remove the invalid entry.
Information	Informs users that the data entered is invalid, without preventing them from entering it. This type of error alert is the most flexible. When an Information alert message appears, users can click OK to accept the invalid value or Cancel to reject it.

Figure 4

6. Click cell **B4**, and then verify that the input message displays.

7. Select the range **E3:E22**, and then click the **Data Validation** button. In the **Data Validation** dialog box, click the **Settings tab**. Click the **Allow arrow**, and then click **Decimal**. With the **Data** box set to **between**, in the **Minimum** box, type 25000.00 In the **Maximum** box, type 110000.00

   This validation rule specifies that decimal numbers between the minimum and the maximum should be entered.

8. In the **Data Validation** dialog box, click the **Error Alert tab**. Click the **Style arrow**, and then click **Warning**. In the **Title** box, type Salary Alert In the **Error message** box, type Salary should be at least $25,000 and no more than $110,000 Click **OK**.

9. Click cell **B4**. Type 6/1/1975 and then press Enter. Compare your screen with **Figure 3**.

   The Invalid Hire Date message box displays because the date entered is before 1985.

10. Click **Retry**, type 6/1/2015 and then press Enter. Click cell **B11**, type 8/12/2014 Click cell **B19**, type 9/1/2016

11. Click cell **E9**. Type 483000 and then press Enter.

    When the Error style is set to *Warning*, you are given the option to proceed when the data is invalid. The three error message styles are summarized in the table shown in **Figure 4**.

12. Read the **Salary Alert** error message, and then click **No**. In cell **E9**, type 48300 and then press Enter.

13. Save 🖫 the file.

■ **You have completed Skill 2 of 10**

▶ When you are collaborating with others, you can see each reviewer's changes by enabling *change tracking*—a feature that tracks all the changes made to a workbook.

1. Click cell **A1**. Click the **Review tab**. In the **Changes group**, click the **Track Changes** button, and then click **Highlight Changes**. Compare your screen with **Figure 1**.

> To track changes, the workbook must be a *shared workbook*—a workbook in which multiple users on a network can make changes at the same time.

2. In the **Highlight Changes** dialog box, select the **Track changes while editing. This also shares your workbook.** Check box to track changes and share the workbook. Select the **Who** check box. Compare your screen with **Figure 2**, and then click **OK**. In the warning box that displays, click **OK**.

> The Excel title bar displays the text *[Shared]* to indicate that the workbook is currently being shared with others.

3. Click the **File tab**, and then click **Save As**. Click **Browse**, and then save the file in your chapter folder as Last_First_exl10_Changes

4. Click the **File tab**, and then click **Options**. In the **Excel Options** dialog box, change the **User name** to Alishia Annice and then click **OK**.

> You will now be editing the workbook as Alishia Annice.

■ Continue to the next page to complete the skill

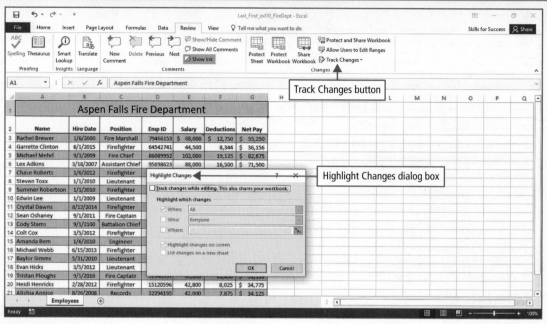

Figure 1

Excel 2016, Windows 10, Microsoft Corporation

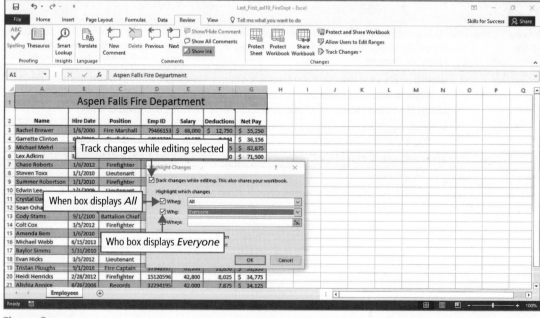

Figure 2

Excel 2016, Windows 10, Microsoft Corporation

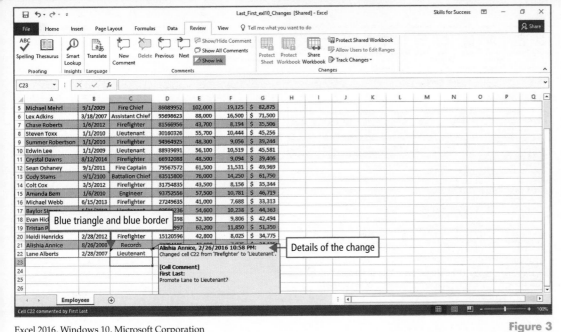

Excel 2016, Windows 10, Microsoft Corporation

Figure 3

5. Click cell **C22**. Type Lieutenant and then press Enter .

6. Scroll down to show row **26**. Point to cell **C22** to display the comment box, as shown in **Figure 3**.

   When a change is tracked, a blue line appears around the changed cell, and a blue triangle appears in the upper left corner of the cell. The row and column heading for also turns red. When you point to the cell, details about that change display such as the date and time of the change and the original values.

7. Click cell **B13**. Type 9/1/2010 and then press Enter . Continue in this manner to make the following changes:

Cell **E3**	71000
Cell **F5**	22456
Cell **E22**	51700

8. Select the range **G4:G22**. Click the **Home** tab. In the **Number group**, click **Comma Style** , and then click **Decrease Decimal** two times. Click cell **A2**, and then compare your screen with **Figure 4**.

   Notice that there are no blue lines around the range G4:G22. Only changes that affect the cell data are tracked. Formatting changes applied to ranges are not tracked.

9. **Save** the file.

- **You have completed Skill 3 of 10**

Excel 2016, Windows 10, Microsoft Corporation

Figure 4

▶ Excel maintains a record of tracked changes in the *change history*—a log that records each data change, who made the change, and when the data was changed.

▶ When changes are tracked, you can choose to accept or reject each change.

1. Click the **Review tab**. In the **Changes group**, click the **Track Changes** button, and then click **Highlight Changes**. In the **Highlight Changes** dialog box, select the **List changes on a new sheet** check box, and then compare your screen with **Figure 1**.

2. Click **OK**, and then compare your screen with **Figure 2**.

   A temporary worksheet—*History*—is added to the workbook. The History worksheet displays the entire change history. All of the changes made by Alishia Annice are listed; your dates and times will be different.

3. With the **History** worksheet tab displayed, use the techniques previously practiced and the Snipping Tool to create a full-screen snip. **Save** 🖫 the snip in your chapter folder as Last_First_exl10_Snip **Close** ✕ the **Snipping Tool** window.

   The History worksheet is dynamic and will not automatically display when the worksheet is opened again. Your date and time will be different.

4. **Save** 🖫 the file.

   Notice that the History worksheet no longer displays.

▪ **Continue to the next page to complete the skill**

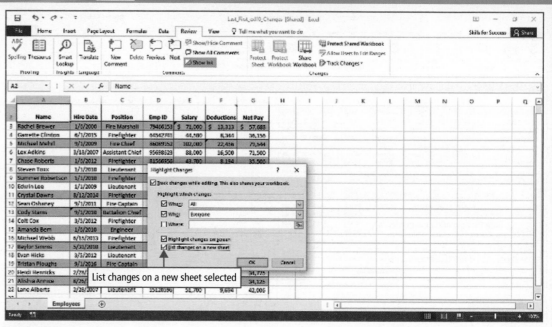

Figure 1

Excel 2016, Windows 10, Microsoft Corporation

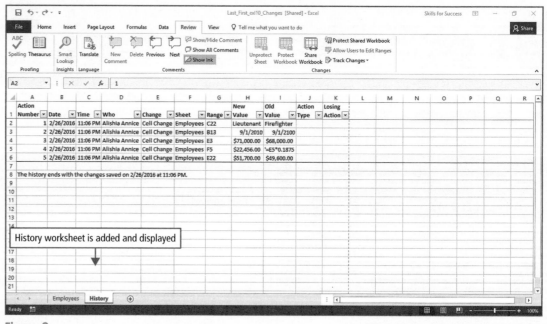

Figure 2

Excel 2016, Windows 10, Microsoft Corporation

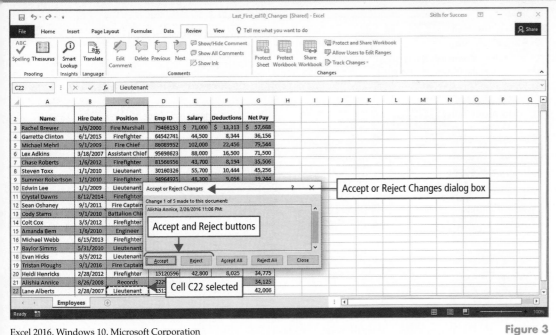

Excel 2016, Windows 10, Microsoft Corporation

Figure 3

5. On the **Review tab**, in the **Changes group**, click the **Track Changes** button, and then click **Accept/Reject Changes**.

6. In the **Select Changes to Accept or Reject** dialog box, verify that the **When** box displays *Not yet reviewed*, and then click **OK**. Compare your screen with **Figure 3**.

   The Accept or Reject Changes dialog box selects changed cells one at a time so that you can accept or reject each change. Cell C22 is selected, and the details of the change display in the dialog box. Your date and time will be different.

7. In the dialog box, click **Accept** to change the value in cell **C22**. Read the change details for change 2 of 5—cell **B13**—and then click **Accept** to change and override the original value.

8. Read the change details for change 3 of 5—cell **E3**—and then click **Reject** to revert to the original value.

9. Click **Accept All** to accept all the remaining changes. Compare your screen with **Figure 4**.

10. Save 🖫, and then **Close** ✕ the file.

■ **You have completed Skill 4 of 10**

Excel 2016, Windows 10, Microsoft Corporation

Figure 4

▶ ***Compare and merge*** is a process that combines the changes from multiple copies of a workbook into a single copy.

▶ To use compare and merge, the Compare and Merge button must be added to the Quick Access Toolbar.

1. Open the file **Last_First_exl10_FireDept**. Using the techniques previously practiced, open the **Excel Options** dialog box, and then change the **User name** to your First and Last names.

2. In the left pane of the **Excel Options** dialog box, click **Quick Access Toolbar**.

3. Under **Customize the Quick Access Toolbar**, click the **Customize Quick Access Toolbar arrow**, and then click **For Last_First_exl10_FireDept.xlsx**.

4. Click the **Choose commands from arrow**, and then click **Commands Not in the Ribbon**.

5. Scroll down the list, click **Compare and Merge Workbooks**, and then click **Add** to add it to the Customize Quick Access Toolbar list. Compare your screen with Figure 1.

6. Click **OK** to close the **Excel Options** dialog box, and then compare your screen with Figure 2.

    In this manner, you can add buttons to the Quick Access Toolbar.

7. On the **Quick Access Toolbar**, click the **Compare and Merge Workbooks** button. Read the message that displays, and then click **OK**.

■ **Continue to the next page to complete the skill**

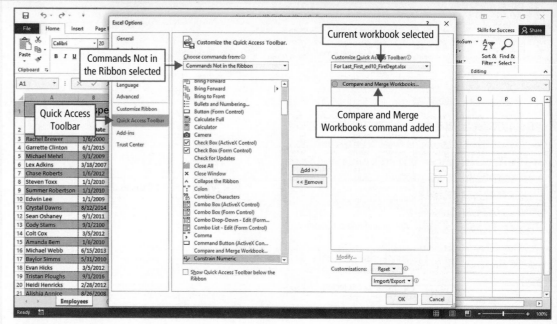

Figure 1

Excel 2016, Windows 10, Microsoft Corporation

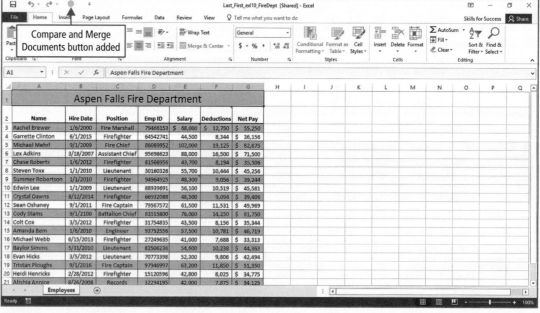

Figure 2

Excel 2016, Windows 10, Microsoft Corporation

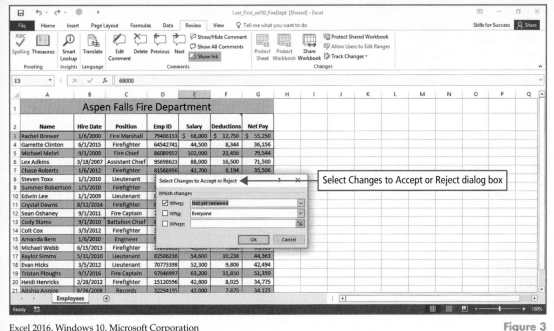

Excel 2016, Windows 10, Microsoft Corporation

Figure 3

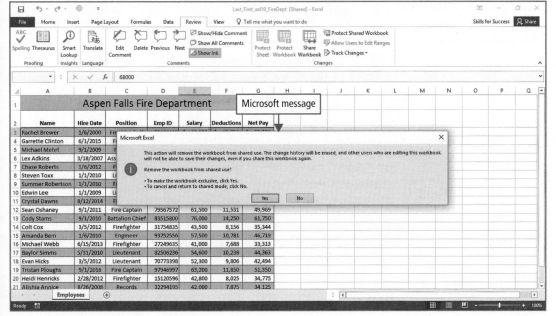

Excel 2016, Windows 10, Microsoft Corporation

Figure 4

8. In the **Select Files to Merge Into Current Workbook** dialog box, open your chapter folder, click **Last_First_exl10_Changes**, and then click **OK**.

9. Click cell **E3**. Click the **Review tab**. In the **Changes group**, click the **Track Changes** button, and then click **Accept/Reject Changes**. Compare your screen with Figure 3.

10. Verify that the **When** box reads *Not yet reviewed*. Select the **Who** check box, and then verify that the **Who** box reads *Everyone*.

11. Click **OK**. Review the information in the **Accept or Reject Changes** dialog box, and then click **Accept**.

   You are now reviewing the changes made by Alishia Annice.

12. In the **Accept or Reject Changes** dialog box, click **Accept All**.

13. In the **Changes group**, click the **Track Changes** button, and then click **Highlight Changes**. In the **Highlight Changes** dialog box, click to clear the **Track changes while editing** check box, and then click **OK**. Compare your screen with Figure 4.

14. Read the message, and then click **Yes**

15. Save 🖫 the file.

■ **You have completed Skill 5 of 10**

▶ *Hypertext Markup Language* (HTML) is used to markup text files so that they can be viewed on the Internet.

▶ HTML text files are typically given an *.htm* or *.html* file extension so that they can be viewed in a web browser.

MOS
Obj 1.5.2 C

1. Click the **File tab**, click **Save As**, click **Browse**, and then navigate to your chapter folder. In the **Save As** dialog box, click the **Save as type arrow**, and then click the seventh file type—**Web Page**.

2. In the **Save As** dialog box, click in the **File name** box, and then type Last_First_exl10_Web Click the **Change Title** button.

3. In the **Enter Text** dialog box, under **Page title**, type Fire Department Pay Compare your screen with **Figure 1**, and then click **OK**.

4. In the **Save As** dialog box, click **Publish**.

5. In the **Publish as Web Page** dialog box, click the **Choose arrow**, and then click **Range of cells**. In the second **Choose** box, type A1:G22 Under **Publish as**, if necessary, select the **Open published web page in browser** check box.

6. Click **Publish**. If the message **How do you want to open this type of file (.htm)?** is displayed, select **Microsoft Edge**. Click **OK**, and then compare your screen with **Figure 2**.

   The title displays in the top of the page and in the page's tab.

7. **Close** ✕ the web browser.

8. In **Backstage view**, click the **Share** tab, and then click **Save to Cloud**.

   You should already have a Microsoft account.

■ **Continue to the next page to complete the skill**

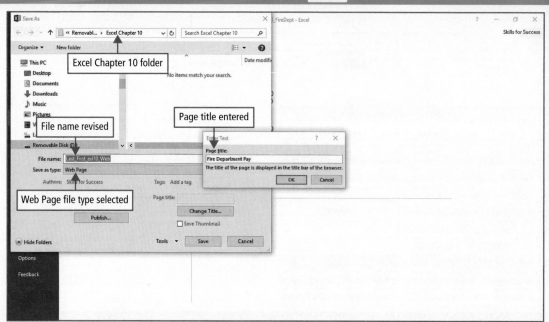

Figure 1

Excel 2016, Windows 10, Microsoft Corporation

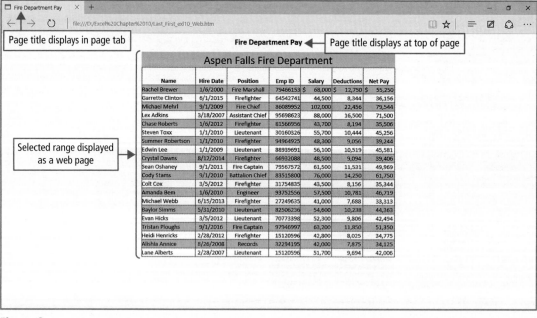

Figure 2

Edge 2016, Windows 10, Microsoft Corporation

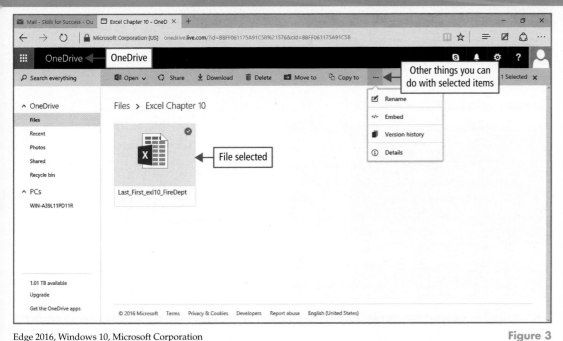

Edge 2016, Windows 10, Microsoft Corporation

Figure 3

9. Double-click **OneDrive - Personal**. Create a new folder named Excel Chapter 10 Click **Open** two times, and then click **Save**.

10. Launch **Microsoft Edge**. In the address bar, type www.onedrive.com Log onto your account, and then open **OneDrive**. Click the **Excel Chapter 10** folder. Point, and then click the circle upper right corner of the **Last_First_exl10_FireDept** file.

11. On the toolbar, to the right of *Copy to*, click ⋯ . Compare your screen with Figure 3.

12. Click **Embed**. Click **Generate** to generate the HTML code for the file.

13. In **Edge**, open a **New tab**, and then type www.blog.com Click **Sign up**. If you already have an account, log in, and then skip to step 14. Enter the information to create a new account, and then verify *Gimme a blog* is selected. Click **Next**.

14. Enter **Blog Title** Excel Chapter 10 Click **Create Blog**. Verify your account, and then **Log In**.

15. On the toolbar, click **Add New**. Enter the title Fire Department Payroll Click the **Excel Chapter 10 - OneDrive** tab. In the right pane, right-click the code in the box, and then **Copy** the code. Click the **Add New Post tab**. In the **Add New Post** window, click the **HTML tab**. Right-click in the window, and then click **Paste**. In the **Publish** pane, in **Visibility**, click **Edit**, select **Private**, and then click **OK**. Click **Preview**. Scroll down, view the embedded worksheet, and then compare your screen with Figure 4.

16. Use the Snipping Tool to create a full-screen snip. Save the file as Last_First_exl10_Embed **Close** the Snipping Tool and all browser windows.

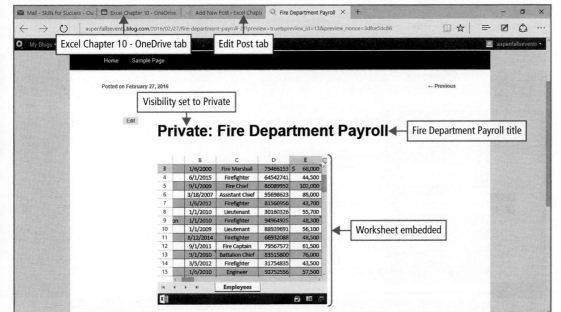

Edge 2016, Windows 10, Microsoft Corporation

Figure 4

■ **You have completed Skill 6 of 10**

▶ **Protect Sheet** prevents unauthorized users from making changes to the worksheet.

▶ To allow revisions to parts of a protected workbook, you must first unlock the cells you want to change.

1. In the **Last_First_exl10_FireDept** file, select the range **A3:E22**. Click the **Home tab**, and then in the **Cells group**, click the **Format** button. In the list, verify that **Lock Cell** is toggled on, as indicated by the light green color around the icon. Compare your screen with **Figure 1**.

 All cells are locked by default, but the lock is not enforced until worksheet protection is enabled.

2. In the list, click **Protect Sheet**.

3. In the **Protect Sheet** dialog box, in the **Password to unprotect sheet** box, type Success16!

4. Under **Allow all users of this worksheet to**, verify **Select locked cells** and **Select unlocked cells** are selected, and then select the **Format cells** check box. Compare your screen with **Figure 2**, and then click **OK**.

 When protecting workbooks, use a **strong password**—a password that contains a combination of uppercase and lowercase letters, numbers, and symbols. In this exercise, the selected protection options will allow individuals to select cells and format cells. No changes to formulas or cell data will be allowed.

5. In the **Confirm Password** dialog box, type Success16! and then click **OK** to confirm the password.

■ **Continue to the next page to complete the skill**

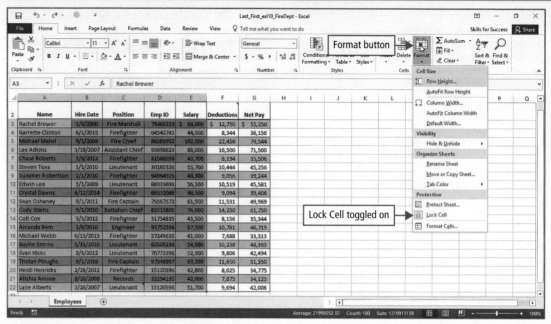

Figure 1

Excel 2016, Windows 10, Microsoft Corporation

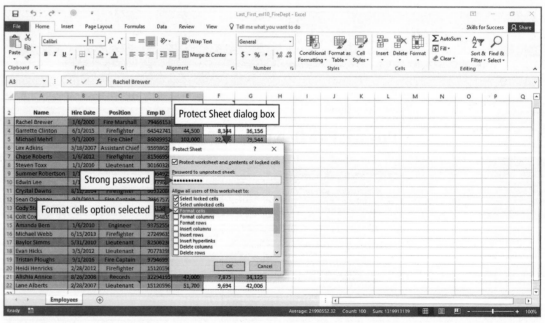

Figure 2

Excel 2016, Windows 10, Microsoft Corporation

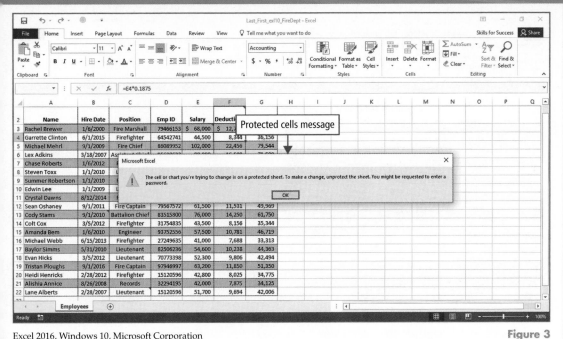

Excel 2016, Windows 10, Microsoft Corporation

Figure 3

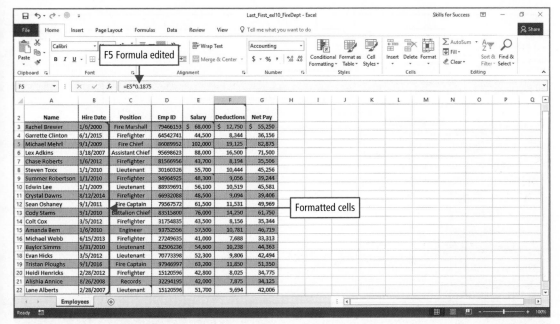

Excel 2016, Windows 10, Microsoft Corporation

Figure 4

6. Click cell **F4**. Attempt to type 8232 and then compare your screen with **Figure 3**.

> The message informs you that the cell is protected and cannot be changed until protection is removed.

7. Click **OK** to close the message. On the **Home tab**, in the **Cells group**, click the **Format** button, and then click **Unprotect Sheet**. In the **Unprotect Sheet** dialog box, in the **Password** box, type Success16! and then click **OK**.

8. Select the range **F3:F22**. In the **Cells group**, click the **Format** button, and then click **Lock Cell** to toggle off the lock of the selected range.

9. Select the range **A3:G22**. Use the techniques previously practiced to toggle on protection for the range using the password Success16!

10. Click cell **E4**, and then attempt to change the value. Read the message, and then click **OK**.

11. Click cell **F5**. In the **formula bar**, select the existing text, and then type =E5*0.1875 Press Enter to change the formula.

> When a cell's lock is toggled off, you can make changes to the cell when protection is on.

12. Select the range **B3:B22**, and then in the **Alignment group**, click the **Align Left** button ≣. Click cell **F5**, and then compare your screen with **Figure 4**.

> Because formatting changes were allowed in the Protect Sheet dialog box, the formatting change was accepted.

13. Save 💾 the file.

■ **You have completed Skill 7 of 10**

 **WATCH** SKILL 10.8

▶ A **macro** is a stored set of instructions that automates common tasks.

▶ If you have created a macro in a workbook, it can be copied to another workbook to save time.

▶ The Developer tab has tools for working with forms, macros, and XML documents that do not contain macros.

MOS
Obj 1.5.2 C

1. Click the **File tab**, click **Save As**, and then click **Browse**. Navigate to your chapter folder, and then in the **Save As** dialog box, click the **Save as type arrow**. In the list, click the second choice, **Excel Macro-Enabled Workbook**. In the **File name** box, type Last_First_exl10_Macro1 and then click **Save**.

MOS
Obj 1.1.6 E

2. If the **Developer tab** is not enabled on the ribbon, complete the following steps; otherwise skip to step 3. Click the **File tab**, and then click **Options**. In the **Excel Options** dialog box, click **Customize Ribbon**. In the right pane, under **Main Tabs**, select the **Developer** check box, and then click **OK**.

3. Click the **Developer tab**, and then compare your screen with **Figure 1**.

The Developer tab displays four groups—Code, Add-ins, Controls, and XML.

MOS
Obj 1.1.5 E

4. In the **Code group**, click **Macro Security**. In the **Trust Center** dialog box, under **Macro Settings**, select **Enable all macros (not recommended; potentially dangerous code can run)**, and then compare your screen with **Figure 2**. Click **OK**.

■ Continue to the next page to complete the skill

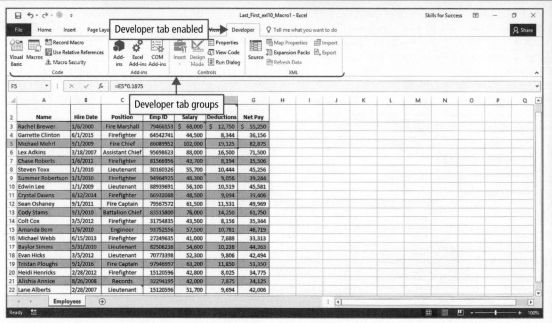

Figure 1

Excel 2016, Windows 10, Microsoft Corporation

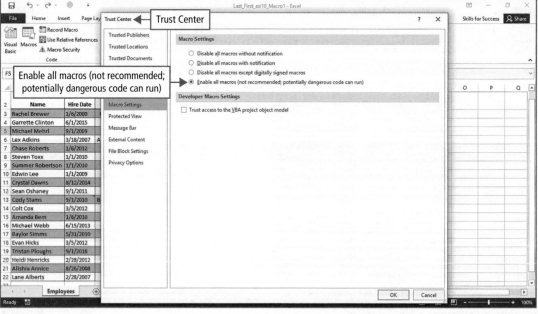

Figure 2

Excel 2016, Windows 10, Microsoft Corporation

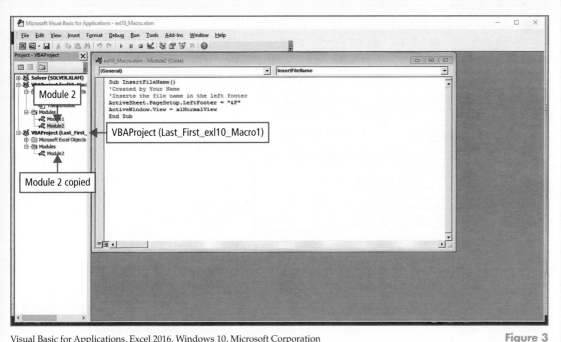

Visual Basic for Applications, Excel 2016, Windows 10, Microsoft Corporation

Figure 3

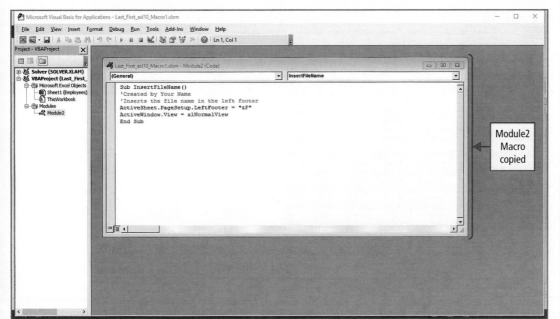

Visual Basic for Applications, Excel 2016, Windows 10, Microsoft Corporation

Figure 4

5. Open the student data file **exl10_Macro**. Click **Enable Content**. In the **exl10_ Macro** file, click the **Developer tab**, and then in the **Code group**, click the **Visual Basic** button. Click the **View** menu, and then on the list, click **Project Explorer**.

> *Visual Basic for Applications (VBA)* is a high-level programming language that can be used to write and modify macros.

6. In the **Project - VBA Project** task pane, under **VBAProject (exl10_Macro)**, click **Module 2**, and then drag down to **VBAProject (Last_First_exl10_Macro1)**. Drop the **Module2** on the workbook. Under **VBAProject (Last_First_exl10_ Macro1)**, click ⊞ to expand **Modules**, and then compare your screen with **Figure 3**.

> VBA code is stored and typed in the VBA Editor in *modules*.

7. Close the **Microsoft Visual Basic for Applications** window, and then close the **exl10_Macro** file without saving.

8. In the **Last_First_exl10_Macro1** file, on the **Developer tab**, in the **Code group**, click the **Visual Basic** button. In the **Project - VBAProject** task pane, double-click **Module2** to open the window. Compare your screen with **Figure 4**.

9. Close the **Microsoft Visual Basic for Applications** window.

10. Save 🖫 the file, and then **Close** ✕ Excel.

■ **You have completed Skill 8 of 10**

▶ The macro recorder creates a macro by recording the steps you perform in a routine activity. The recorded steps are then performed whenever the macro is run.

1. Open the file **Last_First_exl10_FireDept**. Click the **File tab**, click **Save As**, and then click **Browse**. Navigate to your chapter folder, and then in the **Save As** dialog box, click the **Save as type arrow**. In the list, click the second choice, **Excel Macro-Enabled Workbook**. In the **File name** box, type Last_First_exl10_Macro2 and then click **Save**.

2. Click the **File tab**, and then click **Options**. In the **Excel Options** dialog box, click **Customize Ribbon**. Under **Customize the Ribbon**, if necessary, select the **Developer** check box, and then click **OK**.

3. Click cell **A1**. Click the **Developer tab**, and then in the **Code group**, click **Record Macro**.

4. In the **Record Macro** dialog box, in the **Macro name** box, type InsertInfo In the **Shortcut key** box, type m In the **Description** box, type Inserts the name and date in cells A23:A24 Compare your screen with **Figure 1**, and then click **OK**.

5. Click cell **A23**. Click the **Home tab**, and then in the **Cells group**, click the **Format** button. Click **Unprotect sheet**. Enter the password Success16! and then click **OK** to unprotect the worksheet.

6. In cell **A23**, type your First and Last names, and then press Enter . In cell **A24**, type =NOW() and then press Enter . Compare your screen with **Figure 2**. Your date and time will be different.

■ **Continue to the next page to complete the skill**

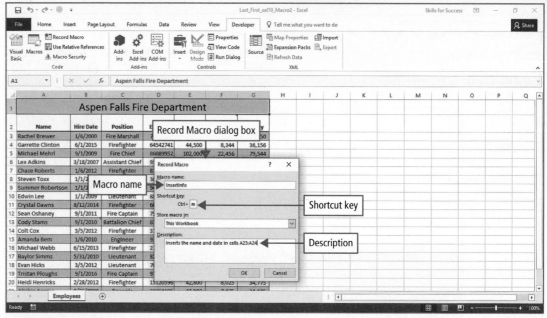

Figure 1

Excel 2016, Windows 10, Microsoft Corporation

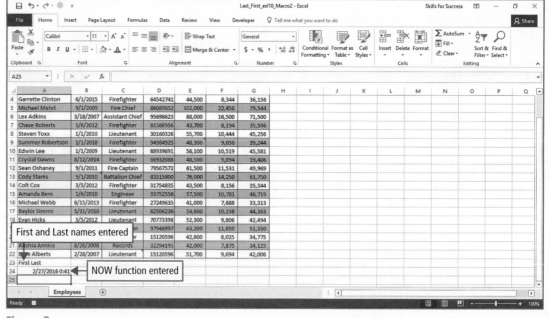

Figure 2

Excel 2016, Windows 10, Microsoft Corporation

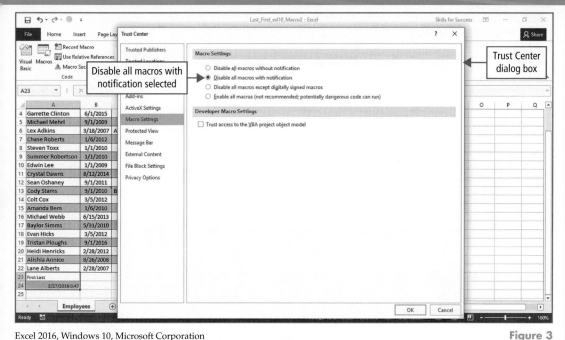

Disable all macros with notification selected

Trust Center dialog box

Excel 2016, Windows 10, Microsoft Corporation

Figure 3

Name and date inserted using macro

Excel 2016, Windows 10, Microsoft Corporation

Figure 4

7. Select the range **A23:A24**, and then in the **Font group**, change the font size to 8. Click the **Font Color arrow**, and then under **Standard Colors**, click **Dark Blue**.

8. Click the **Developer tab**, and then in the **Code group**, click **Stop Recording**.

9. In the **Code group**, click **Macro Security**. In the **Trust Center** dialog box, verify the **Disable all macros with notification** option is selected. Compare your screen with **Figure 3**, and then click **OK**.

> The security setting will not allow a macro to execute without asking your permission to do so. Because macros are sometimes used to spread *malware*—software that is designed to harm a computer—you should enable only macros that are from trusted sources.

10. Delete rows **23:24**. Click cell **A1**, and then click **Save** 🖫. If necessary, read the message, click **Yes**, and then **Close** the workbook.

11. Navigate to the chapter folder, and then open the file **Last_First_exl10_Macro2**. In the **Message Bar**, click **Enable Content**.

> When you open a workbook with a macro, the Security bar informs you when the workbook contains a macro. You can then choose to enable or disable the macro.

12. Click the **Developer tab**, and in the **Code group**, click **Macros**. In the **Macro** dialog box, select **InsertInfo**, and then click **Run**. Compare your screen with **Figure 4**.

13. Delete rows **23:24**, and then click cell **A1**. Press Ctrl + M to verify that the macro runs when the assigned shortcut key is pressed. Click **Save** 🖫. If necessary, read the message, and then click **Yes**.

■ **You have completed Skill 9 of 10**

▶ VBA macros are entered and edited in the Visual Basic Editor (VBE).

1. Click cell **A1**. On the **Developer tab**, in the **Code group**, click **Visual Basic**.

2. In the **Visual Basic Editor**, click the **Insert** menu, and then click **Module**. Compare your screen with **Figure 1**.

   The **Code window**—the window in which VBA code is written—for Module2 displays.

3. In the **Code** window, type the following sub and comments. Be sure the last two lines begin with a single quotation mark, as shown:

   Sub InsertFileName()

   'Created by First Last

   'Inserts the file name in the footer

   A **sub** is a group of instructions that is a subset of a program. After you press [Enter] to go to the next line, *End Sub* will display and remain at the end of the code. In VBA, all subs end with *End Sub*. Each line will have different colors associated with it. The *InsertFileName* sub has two **programming comments**—statements that document what the code does—which display in green.

4. After the last comment, press [Enter], and then type the following statements:

   ActiveSheet.PageSetup.LeftFooter = "&F"

   ActiveWindow.View = xlNormalView

5. Compare your screen with **Figure 2**.

   The sub has two comments and two **programming statements**, which are instructions. The two statements insert the file name in the left footer and then return the spreadsheet to Normal view.

■ **Continue to the next page to complete the skill** ➤

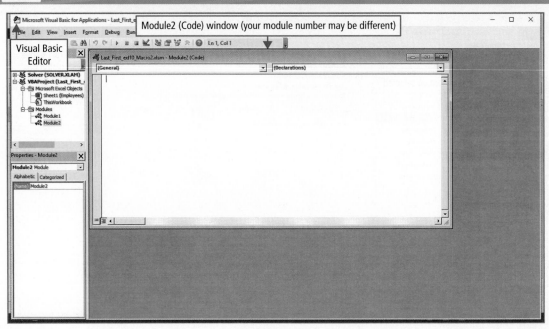

Figure 1   Visual Basic for Applications, Excel 2016, Windows 10, Microsoft Corporation

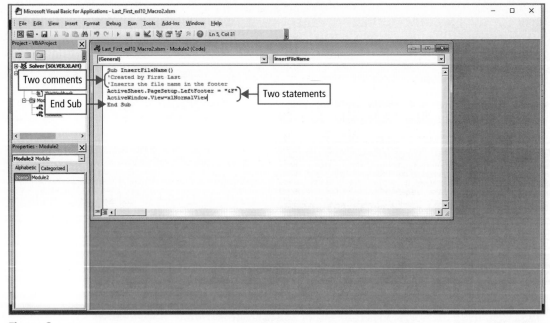

Figure 2   Visual Basic for Applications, Excel 2016, Windows 10, Microsoft Corporation

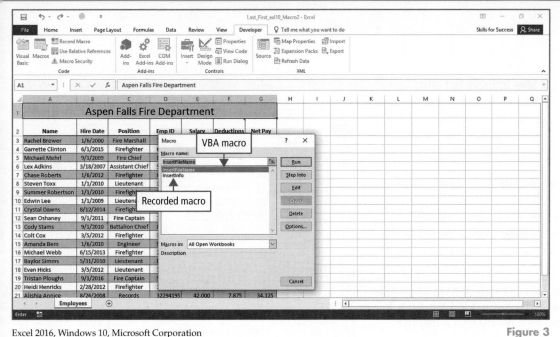

Excel 2016, Windows 10, Microsoft Corporation

Figure 3

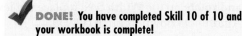

Excel 2016, Windows 10, Microsoft Corporation

Figure 4

6. From the **File** menu, click **Close and Return to Microsoft Excel**.

7. On the **Developer tab**, in the **Code group**, click **Macros**. Compare your screen with **Figure 3**.

> The Macro dialog box displays two macros, the recorded macro and the VBA macro.

8. In the **Macro** dialog box, verify **InsertFileName** is selected, and then click **Run**.

9. If an error message displays, click the **Debug** button, and then on the **VBE Standard** toolbar, click the **Reset** button. In the **Code** window, carefully check your typing, and then return to Excel.

10. Click the **File tab**, click **Print**, and then compare your screen with **Figure 4**.

> The VBA macro inserted the file name in the footer.

11. In **Backstage view**, click **Options**. Click **Customize Ribbon**, and then in the **Customize the Ribbon** area, clear the **Developer** check box. In the left pane, click **General**, and then if necessary, restore the Excel user name to the value you noted in Skill 1. Click **OK**.

12. Click cell **A1**. Click the **File tab**, click **Protect Workbook**, and then click **Encrypt with Password**. In the **Encrypt Document** dialog box, type Success16! two times, and then click **Save**.

> Obj 1.2.6 E

13. **Close** ☒ Excel, and then submit the files as directed by your instructor.

✓ **DONE!** You have completed Skill 10 of 10 and your workbook is complete!

More Skills 11

Insert Form Controls

To complete this project, you will need the following file:

- exl10_MS11Volunteers

You will save your file as:

- Last_First_exl10_MS11Volunteers

▶ A **form control** is an object such as a button or check box that is added to a worksheet.

▶ A **legacy object** is compatible with earlier versions of a program. Newer versions of Excel support both form controls and **ActiveX controls**—objects such as check boxes and buttons that provide interactive options or run macros.

---

1. Start **Excel 2016**, and then open the student data file **exl10_MS11Volunteers**. Save the file in your chapter folder as an **Excel Macro-Enabled Workbook**, with the name Last_First_exl10_MS11Volunteers If necessary, enable the content.

2. If necessary, use the techniques previously practiced to show the **Developer tab**.

Obj 2.3.5 E

3. Click the **Developer tab**, and then in the **Controls group**, click the **Insert** button. Under **Form Controls**, point to the third control in the first row—**Check Box (Form Control)**.

   A **check box** is a control that allows a user to select one or more values in a group of choices.

4. Click the **Check Box (Form Control)**, and then click cell **D5**. With the control selected, press the arrow keys as needed to align the top left corner of the control's border with the top left corner of cell **D5**.

5. Right-click the control, and then click **Edit Text**. Press Delete until all of the text is deleted. Type Yes Right-click the control, and then click **Format Control**. In the **Format Control** dialog box, click the **Size tab**. Under **Size and rotate**, in the **Width** box, replace the text with .45 and then click **OK**. Autofill **D5** down through cell **D9**.

6. In the **Controls group**, click the **Insert** button. Under **Form Controls**, click the first control—**Button (Form Control)**.

7. Click cell **A12** to insert the button. In the **Assign Macro** dialog box, select **File_Name_Date**. Click **OK**.

   A **button** is a control that typically starts a macro when it is clicked.

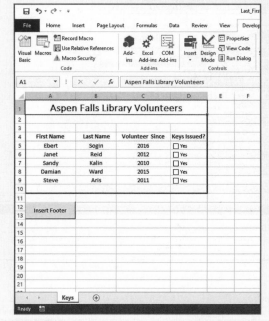

Figure 1

Excel 2016, Windows 10,
Microsoft Corporation

8. Use the sizing handles to resize the button in the range **A12:B13**. Right-click the control, click **Edit Text**, and then replace the existing text with Insert Footer

9. Click cell **C12**. If necessary, in the **Controls group**, click **Design Mode** to toggle off.

10. Click the button to run the macro. **Print Preview** the worksheet to view the file name and date in the footer. Click the **Back** button to return to the **Keys** worksheet. Compare your screen with **Figure 1**.

11. **Save** the file, and then **Close** Excel. Submit the file as directed by your instructor.

■ **You have completed More Skills 11**

More Skills 12

Add Macro Buttons to the Quick Access Toolbar

To complete this project, you will need the following file:

- exl10_MS12Library

You will save your files as:

- Last_First_exl10_MS12Library
- Last_First_exl10_MS12Snip

▸ A macro can be run from a button added to the Quick Access Toolbar.

---

1. Start **Excel 2016**, and then open the student data file **exl10_MS12Library**. Save the file as an **Excel Macro-Enabled Workbook** in your chapter folder as Last_First_exl10_MS12Library If necessary, enable the content.

2. If necessary, use the techniques previously practiced to show the **Developer tab**.

3. Click the **Developer tab**, and then in the **Code group**, click **Macro Security**.

4. In the **Trust Center** dialog box, verify that the **Disable all macros with notification** option is selected, and then click **OK**.

5. Click the **File tab**, and then click **Options**. In the **Excel Options** dialog box, in the left pane, click **Quick Access Toolbar**.

6. Under **Customize the Quick Access Toolbar**, click the **Customize Quick Access Toolbar arrow**, and then select **For Last_First_exl10_MS12Library.xlsm**.
Obj 1.4.3 C

7. Click the **Choose commands from arrow**, and then click **Macros**.

    The worksheet's macro—*File_Name_Date*—displays in the left pane.

8. In the left pane, click **File_Name_Date**, and then click the **Add** button.

9. Click **OK** to close the **Excel Options** dialog box.

10. On the **Quick Access Toolbar**, click the **File_Name_Date** button.

11. Click the **File tab**, and then click **Print**. Compare your screen with **Figure 1**.

12. Click the **back arrow**, and then use the Snipping Tool to create a full-screen snip. **Save** the snip in your chapter folder as Last_First_exl10_MS12Snip **Close** the Snipping Tool window.

13. Click **Options**. In the **Excel Options** dialog box, in the left pane, click **Customize Ribbon**. Click the **Reset arrow** and then click **Reset all customizations**. Read the message, and then click **Yes**. Click **OK**.

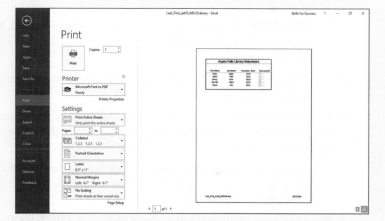

Excel 2016, Windows 10, Microsoft Corporation   **Figure 1**

14. Click the **Review tab**, and then in the **Changes group**, click **Protect and Share Workbook**. In the **Protect Shared Workbook** dialog box, select the **Sharing with track changes** check box, and then in the **Password (optional)** box, type Success16! Click **OK**, type the password again, and then click **OK**. Read the next two messages, and then click **OK** for both.
Obj 1.2.1 E

15. **Save** 🖫 the file, and then **Close** ☒ Excel. Submit the files as directed by your instructor.

- **You have completed More Skills 12**

More Skills ⑬

Prepare Workbooks for Internationalization

To complete this project, you will need the following file:

- exl10_MS13Fares

You will save your file as:

- Last_First_exl10_MS13Fares

▸ Excel provides internationalization features you can use to create workbooks. These features should be determined based on the intended audience for the workbook.

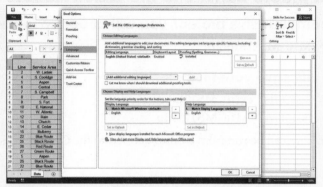

Figure 1   Excel 2016, Windows 10, Microsoft Corporation

1. Start **Excel 2016**, and then open the student data file **exl10_MS13Fares**. Save the file in your chapter folder as Last_First_exl10_MS13Fares If necessary, enable the content.

2. Click the **File tab**. In Backstage view, click **Options**, and then click **Language**. Compare your screen with **Figure 1**.

3. In the **Excel Options** dialog box, under **Choose Editing Languages**, click the **[Add additional editing languages] arrow**. Scroll down the list, click **Spanish (Mexico)**, and then click **Add**. Click **OK**.

   Enabling another language allows you to add additional keyboards. Once the keyboard is added, you will be able to view the Language Bar to switch between keyboards and languages.

4. Read the message that displays, and then click **OK**. **Save** the file, and then **Close** Excel. Navigate to your chapter folder, and then open the file **Last_First_exl10_MS13Fares**.

MOS
Obj 2.4.1 E

5. Click cell **B37**. On the **Home tab**, in the **Number group**, click the **Number Dialog Box Launcher**. In the **Format Cells** dialog box, click the **Locale (location) arrow**. Scroll down the list, click **Spanish (Mexico)**, and then in the **Type** box, select **miercoles, 14 de marzo de 2012**. Click **OK**.

6. AutoFit column **B**. Notice the date format has been edited to the Spanish (Mexico) format.

MOS
Obj 2.4.2 E

7. Select the range **F2:F35**. Click the **Custom Number Format arrow**, and then click **More Number Formats**. Under **Category**, click **Accounting,** and then click the **Symbol arrow**. Scroll down to view **Spanish (Mexico)**. Notice that

Figure 2   Excel 2016, Windows 10, Microsoft Corporation

it is the same sign as the current format. Scroll up, select **Russian**, and then click **OK**. AutoFit column **F**, and then if necessary, scroll down to view cell **B37**. Compare your screen with **Figure 2**.

8. **Save** 🖫 the file, and then **Close** ☒ Excel. Submit the file as directed by your instructor.

- **You have completed More Skills 13**

More Skills (14)

Assign Macros to Command Buttons

To complete this project, you will need the following file:

- exl10_MS14Members

You will save your file as:

- Last_First_exl10_MS14Members

▸ A **command button** is a control that runs a VBA macro.
▸ A macro can be run from a button added to the ribbon.

---

1. Start **Excel 2016**, and then open the student data file **exl10_MS14Members**. Save the file as an **Excel Macro-Enabled Workbook** in your chapter folder as Last_First_exl10_MS14Members If necessary, enable the content.

2. If necessary, use the techniques previously practiced to show the **Developer tab** on the ribbon.

3. Click the **Developer tab**, and then in the **Code group**, click **Macro Security**.

4. In the **Trust Center** dialog box, verify that the **Disable all macros with notification** option is selected, and then click **OK**.

5. On the **Developer tab**, in the **Controls group**, click the **Insert** button. Under **ActiveX Controls**, click the first control—**Command Button (ActiveX Control)**.

6. Click cell **A13**. Use the sizing handles to resize the button in the range **A13:B14**.

7. With the command button selected, in the **Controls group**, click **View Code**. Click the arrow next to **General**, and then select **CommandButton1**. Verify **Click** is selected in the adjacent box.

8. In the Visual Basic Editor, expand **Modules**, and double-click **Module2**. In the **Last_First_exl10_MS14Members.xlsm-Module2 (Code)** window, select the code beginning with the first blank line under **Sub Insert_heading()** down through the last line before *End Sub*.

9. Click the **Edit** menu, and then click **Copy**. Click the **Last_First_exl10_MS14Members.xlsm-Sheet1 (Code)** window. Click in the blank line after **Private Sub**, right-click, and then click **Paste**.

    The code will insert three blank lines at the top of the worksheet, enter and merge and center two lines of text, change the text to dark blue, and insert a dark red line at the bottom of row 2.

Excel 2016, Windows 10, Microsoft Corporation   **Figure 1**

10. Close the **Last_First_exl10_MS14Members.xlsm-Module2 (Code)** window. Click the **File** menu, and then click **Close and return to Microsoft Excel**.

11. In the **Controls group**, click the **Design Mode** button to toggle off. Click **CommandButton1** to run the macro. Click cell **F1**. Compare your screen with **Figure 1**.

12. If necessary, use the techniques previously practiced to remove the **Developer tab** from the ribbon.

13. **Save** the file, and then **Close** Excel. Submit the file as directed by your instructor.

■ **You have completed More Skills 14**

Skills Number	Task	Step	Icon
1	Personalize Microsoft Office	File tab → Options → Personalize your copy of Microsoft Office	
1	Add comments	Review tab → Comments group → New Comment button	
1	Delete comments	Review tab → Comments group → Delete button	
1	Show all comments	Review tab → Comments group → Show All Comments button	
2	Validate data criteria	Data tab → Data Tools group → Data Validation button → Data Validation dialog box → Settings tab	
2	Create validate data message	Data tab → Data Tools group → Data Validation button → Data Validation dialog box → Input Message tab	
2	Create validate data error alert	Data tab → Data Tools group → Data Validation button → Data Validation dialog box → Error Alert tab	
2	Circle invalid data	Data tab → Data Tools group → Data Validation arrow → Circle Invalid Data	
2	Clear validation circles	Data tab → Data Tools group → Data Validation arrow → Clear Validation Circles	
3	Track changes	Review tab → Changes group → Track Changes button → Highlight Changes → Track changes while editing.	
4	Accept/reject changes	Review tab → Changes group → Track Changes button → Accept/Reject Changes	
5	Merge changes	Quick Access toolbar → Compare and Merge Workbooks button → Select workbooks	
6	Save workbook as Webpage	File tab → Save As → Save as type → Webpage → Publish	
6	Embed data in Webpage	Share → Select file → Embed → Copy code → Paste code in Webpage	
7	Lock/unlock cells	Home tab → Cells group → Format arrow → Lock Cell	
7	Protect/unprotect worksheets	Home tab → Cells group → Format arrow → Protect Sheet	
8	Enable macro	Developer tab → Code group → Macro Security button → Macro Settings	
8	Copy macro	Developer tab → Code group → Visual Basic button → View tab → Drag code	
9	Create macro	Developer tab → Code group → Record Macro button → Macro dialog box	
9	End macro	Developer tab → Code group → Stop Recording button	
9	Run macro	Developer tab → Code group → Macros button → Select Macro name → Run	
10	Create VBA macro	Developer tab → Code group → Visual Basic button → Insert tab → Module	
11	Insert form controls	Developer tab → Controls group → Design Mode button → Insert button	
12	Add macro to Quick Access toolbar	File tab → Options → Quick Access Toolbar → Customize → Add	
13	Add internationalization	File tab → Options → Language → Add additional editing languages	
13	Format internationalization	Home tab → Number group → Number Dialog Box Launcher → Locale	
14	Assign macro to command button	Developer tab → Controls group → Design Mode button → Insert button → View code → General → Select code	

Project Summary Chart

Project	Project Type	Project Location
Skills Review	Review	In Book & MIL MyITLab® Grader
Skills Assessment 1	Review	In Book & MIL MyITLab® Grader
Skills Assessment 2	Review	Book
My Skills	Problem Solving	Book
Visual Skills Check	Problem Solving	Book
Skills Challenge 1	Critical Thinking	Book
Skills Challenge 2	Critical Thinking	Book
More Skills Assessment	Review	In Book & MIL MyITLab® Grader
Collaborating with Google	Critical Thinking	Book

MOS Objectives Covered (Quiz in MyITLab®)

1.4.3 C Customize the Quick Access Toolbar	1.2.4 E Protect workbook structure
1.4.6 C Modify document properties	1.2.6 E Encrypt a workbook with a password
1.5.2 C Save workbooks in alternative file formats	2.1.3 E Configure data validation
1.1.2 E Copy macros between workbooks	2.3.4 E Create and modify simple macros
1.1.5 E Enable macros in a workbook	2.3.5 E Insert and configure form controls
1.1.6 E Display hidden Ribbon tabs	2.4.1 E Display data in multiple international formats
1.2.1 E Restrict editing	2.4.2 E Apply international currency formats
1.2.2 E Protect a worksheet	3.31 E Reference the date and time by using the NOW and TODAY functions

Key Terms

Online Help Skills

1. Start **Excel 2016**. In the upper right corner of the start page, click the **Help** button ? .

2. In the **Excel 2016 Help** window **Search** box, type track changes and then press Enter .

3. In the search results, click **Track changes in a shared workbook in Excel 2016 for**.

4. Read the article's introduction, and then in the **In this article** section, click **Changes that Excel does not track or highlight**. Compare your screen with **Figure 1**.

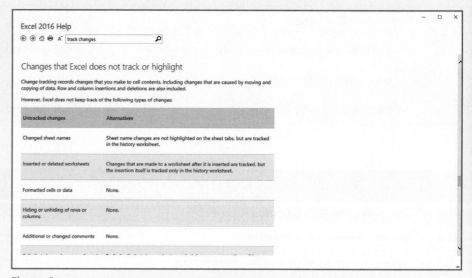

Figure 1

5. Read the section and answer the following: What are three changes that Excel does not track? What are three features of Excel that cannot be used when you share a workbook?

Matching

Match each term in the second column with its correct definition in the first column by writing the letter of the term on the blank line in front of the correct definition.

___ **1.** Descriptive text added to cells that does not modify the data in the worksheet.

___ **2.** A rule that restricts the type of data that can be entered into a cell.

___ **3.** A box that displays when data is entered in a cell that specifies what types of data can be entered into the cell.

___ **4.** A feature that tracks any modifications that are made to the data in a worksheet.

___ **5.** The log that records tracked changes.

___ **6.** A language used to write Webpages.

___ **7.** Used to project a workbook or worksheet from editing.

___ **8.** A group of stored instructions that perform with a single click.

___ **9.** Software that is designed to harm a computer.

___ **10.** A high-level programming language that can be used to write and modify macros.

A Change history

B Track Changes

C Comment

D Data Validation

E HTML

F Input Message

G Macro

H Malware

I Strong password

J Visual Basic for Applications

Multiple Choice

Choose the correct answer.

1. To assign tracked changes and comments to individual reviewers, Excel uses this file property.
   A. User name
   B. File owner
   C. File creator

2. A red triangle in the upper right or left corner of a cell.
   A. Input message
   B. Document Inspector
   C. Comment indicator

3. A data validation message that informs the data entry operator that invalid data has been entered into the cell.
   A. Error Alert
   B. Input message
   C. Comments

4. This term refers to a workbook in which multiple users on a network can make changes at the same time.
   A. Common
   B. Shared
   C. Master

5. What uses a combination of uppercase and lowercase letters, numbers, and symbols to protect a workbook?
   A. User name
   B. Password
   C. Malware

6. Prevents unauthorized users from modifying the worksheet.
   A. Document Inspector
   B. Protect Sheet
   C. Data Validation

7. VBA code is written in this window.
   A. VBE
   B. Module
   C. Code

8. The instructions that are a subset of a program.
   A. VBE
   B. Programming statements
   C. Sub

9. These lines in the programming code document what the code does.
   A. Programming comments
   B. File notes
   C. Instructions

10. These statements are instructions stored in a subroutine.
    A. Informational
    B. Comment
    C. Programming

Topics for Discussion

1. What types of common tasks might a business worker want to automate by recording those tasks' steps in a macro?

2. In a worksheet that you plan to give to others to use, what types of cells should be locked and what types should be unlocked?

Skills Review

To complete this project, you will need the following file:

- exl10_SRTransit

You will save your files as:

- Last_First_exl10_SRTransit
- Last_First_exl10_SRChanges
- Last_First_exl10_SRWeb
- Last_First_exl10_SRMacro

---

1. Start **Excel 2016**, and then open the student data file **exl10_SRTransit**. Save the file in your chapter folder as Last_First_exl10_SRTransit

2. Click the **File tab**, and then click **Options**. Note the **User name**. If necessary, in the **User name** box, type your First and Last names. Click **OK**.

3. Click cell **E13**. Click the **Review tab**, click **New Comment**, and then type This seems too high. Click cell **A1**, and then toggle on then off the **Show All Comments** button.

4. Select the range **C6:C22**. Click the **Data tab**, and then click **Data Validation**. In the **Data Validation** dialog box, on the **Settings tab**, click the **Allow arrow**, and then click **Decimal**. In the **Minimum** box, type 1000 In the **Maximum** box, type 5000

5. Click the **Error Alert tab**, and then in the **Title** box, type Transit Fare In the **Error message** box, type Invalid Fare and then click **OK**. Click the **Data Validation arrow**, and then click **Circle Invalid Data**. Compare your screen with **Figure 1**.

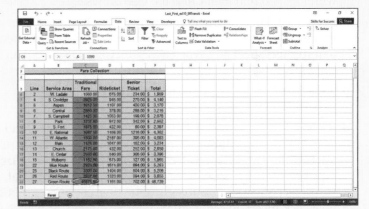

Figure 1

6. Click the **Review tab**, and then click **Track Changes**. Click **Highlight Changes**, and then select the **Track changes while editing** check box. Click **OK** two times. **Save** the file in your chapter folder as Last_First_exl10_SRChanges

7. Click the **File tab**, and then click **Options**. Change the **User name** to Ann McCoy and then click **OK**. Change cell **C22** to 4875.50 and then change cell **E13** to 216.00

8. Click the **Review tab**, and then click **Track Changes**. Click **Accept/Reject Changes**. Click **OK** two times. Click **Accept All**. **Save** and then **Close** the file.

9. Open **Last_First_exl10_SRTransit**. Click the **File tab**, and then click **Options**. Change the user name to your First and Last names. In the left pane, click **Quick Access Toolbar**. Click the **Customize Quick Access Toolbar arrow**, and then click **Last_First_exl10_SRTransit.xlsx**. Compare your screen with **Figure 2**.

10. Click the **Choose commands from arrow**, and then click **Commands Not in the Ribbon**. Click **Compare and Merge Workbooks**, click **Add**, and then click **OK**.

Figure 2

▪ Continue to the next page to complete this Skills Review

11. On the **Quick Access Toolbar**, click **Compare and Merge Workbooks**, and then click **OK**. Click **Last_First_exl10_SRChanges**, and then click **OK**. Click the **Review tab**, click **Track Changes**, and then click **Accept/Reject Changes**. Click **OK**, and then click **Accept All**.

12. Click **Track Changes**. Click **Highlight Changes**. Clear the **Track changes while editing** check box, click **OK**, and then click **Yes**. **Save** the file.

13. Click cell **A1**. Click **Save As**, navigate to your chapter folder, and then in the **File name** box, type Last_First_exl10_SRWeb Click the **Save as type arrow**, and then click **Web Page**. Click **Change Title**, and then in the **Page title** box, type Transit Fares and then click **OK**. Click **Publish** two times. Compare your screen with **Figure 3**, and then **Close** the web browser.

14. In the **Last_First_exl10_SRTransit** file, click **Back**, and then click the **Home tab**. In the **Cells group**, click **Format**, and then click **Protect Sheet**. In the **Password to unprotect sheet** box, type Success16! Click **OK**, and then type Success16! Click **OK**.

15. **Save** the file as an **Excel Macro-Enabled Workbook** in your chapter folder as Last_First_exl10_SRMacro

16. If necessary, show the Developer tab. Click the **File tab**, and then click **Options**. Click **Customize Ribbon**. Select the **Developer** check box. Click **OK**. Click the **Developer tab**, and then click **Record Macro**. In the **Macro name** box, type InsertInfo Click **OK**. Click the **Home tab**, click **Format**, and then click **Unprotect Sheet**. Type Success16! and then click **OK**. Right-click row **1**, and then click **Insert**. In cell **A1**, type your First and Last names. Click cell **A2**. Click the **Developer tab**, and then in the **Code group**, click **Stop Recording**.

17. On the **Developer tab**, click **Visual Basic**. If necessary, in the **VBE** window, click the **Insert** menu, and then click **Module**. In the **Code** window, type the following, and then compare your screen with **Figure 4**:

```
Sub InsertFileName()
'Created by First Last
'Inserts the file name in the left footer
ActiveSheet.PageSetup.LeftFooter = "&F"
ActiveWindow.View = xlNormalView
```

18. Click **File**, and then click **Close and Return to Microsoft Excel**. Click **Macros**, click **InsertFileName**, and then click **Run**.

19. If necessary, restore the Excel user name, and then hide the **Developer tab**.

20. **Save** the file, and then **Close** Excel. Submit the files as directed by your instructor.

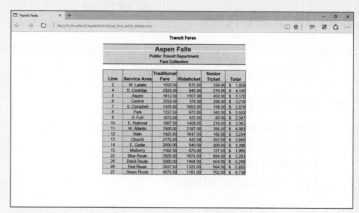

Figure 3　　　　　　　　　　　　　　Edge 2016, Windows 10, Microsoft Corporation

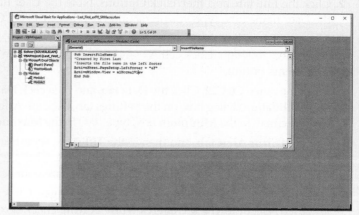

Figure 4　　　　　Visual Basic for Applications, Excel 2016, Windows 10, Microsoft Corporation

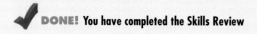

DONE! You have completed the Skills Review

Skills Assessment 1

To complete this project, you will need the following file:

- exl10_SA1Bonds

You will save your files as:

- Last_First_exl10_SA1Bonds
- Last_First_exl10_SA1Changes
- Last_First_exl10_SA1Web
- Last_First_exl10_SA1Macro

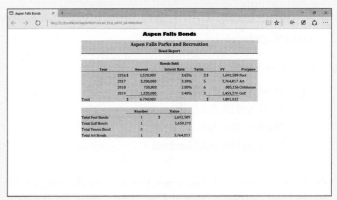

Edge 2016, Windows 10, Microsoft Corporation **Figure 1**

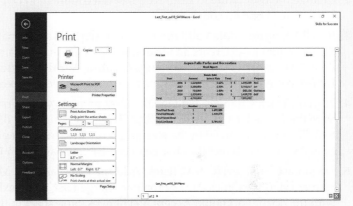

Excel 2016, Windows 10, Microsoft Corporation **Figure 2**

1. Start **Excel 2016**, and then open the student data file **exl10_SA1Bonds**. Save the file in your chapter folder as Last_First_exl10_SA1Bonds Change the user name to Cyril Shore

2. In cell **C7**, insert the following comment: Can bond be resold? If necessary, hide all of the comments.

3. In the range **C6:C9**, write a data validation rule that requires a decimal value that is less than or equal to .04 Create an input message titled Interest Rate that displays The interest rate should not exceed 4.00% Create a **Warning Style** error alert with the title Excessive Rate and the message Interest rate is too high!

4. Turn on **Track Changes**. Save the file as Last_First_exl10_SA1Changes Change the **User name** to your First and Last names. Change cell **C7** to 3.3% Change cell **F8** to Clubhouse

5. Accept all changes. **Save** and then **Close** the file.

6. Open **Last_First_exl10_SA1Bonds**. Add the **Compare and Merge Workbooks** command to the **Quick Access Toolbar**. Merge **Last_First_exl10_Changes** with the open document. Accept all changes. Stop sharing the workbook.

7. Publish the entire workbook as an HTML Webpage file named Last_First_exl10_SA1Web Title the page Aspen Falls Bonds Compare your screen with **Figure 1**. **Close** the browser.

8. Save the **Last_First_exl10_SA1Bonds** file in your chapter folder as an **Excel Macro-Enabled Workbook** named Last_First_exl10_SA1Macro

9. If necessary, add the **Developer tab**. Record a macro named FileInfo While recording, complete the following three tasks, and then stop recording: in the right header section, add the **Sheet Name**; in the left header section, type your First and Last names; click cell **A1**. Return to **Normal view**.

10. Delete the header text, and then run the macro to verify that it runs correctly.

11. Use the **Visual Basic Editor** to create a macro, using the code from Skill 10 as your guide, to type a VBA statement that inserts the file name in the left footer. **Close** the **Visual Basic Editor**, and then run the macro.

12. **Print Preview** the worksheet, and then compare your screen with **Figure 2**.

13. If necessary, restore the Excel user name and hide the **Developer tab**.

14. **Save** the file, and then **Close** Excel. Submit the files as directed by your instructor.

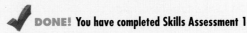 **DONE! You have completed Skills Assessment 1**

Skills Assessment 2

To complete this project, you will need the following file:

- exl10_SA2Truck

You will save your files as:

- Last_First_exl10_SA2Truck
- Last_First_exl10_SA2Changes
- Last_First_exl10_SA2Macro
- Last_First_exl10_SA2Embed

---

1. Start **Excel 2016**, and then open the student data file **exl10_SA2Truck**. Save the file in your chapter folder as Last_First_exl10_SA2Truck

2. Change the user name to Leah Kim Insert a comment in cell **B6**: Can we get a better rate? Hide all comments.

3. In cell **E4**, write a data validation rule that requires a decimal value that is less than or equal to 48 Create an input message Fire Truck Loan that displays Loan term cannot exceed 48 months Create a **Warning Style** error alert titled Excessive Term with the message Truck term should not exceed 48 months

4. Turn on **Track Changes**. Change the **User name** to your First and Last names. Save the file as Last_First_exl10_SA2Changes Change cell **B5** to 215,000 cell **B6** to 3.75 and cell **E4** to 60 In the warning box, click **Yes**. **Accept** the changes in cells **B5** and **B6**. **Reject** the change in cell **E4**. **Save** and then **Close** the file.

5. Open **Last_First_exl10_SA2Truck**. Add the **Compare and Merge Workbooks** command to the Quick Access Toolbar. Merge **Last_First_exl10_SA2Changes** with the open workbook. **Accept** all changes. Stop sharing the workbook.

6. **Share** the file to the **Excel Chapter 10** OneDrive folder. **Launch Edge**, and then in OneDrive generate the embedding code. Create a new post at www.blog.com titled Amortization Copy and paste the code, and then **Publish** and **Preview the Changes**. Scroll down, and then use the scroll bars to scroll to view **A1:C12**. Compare your screen to **Figure 1**. Use the **Snipping Tool** to create a full-screen snip. **Save** the file as Last_First_exl10_SA2Embed Close all web browser windows.

7. In the **Last_First_exl10_SA2Truck** file, unlock the range **A6:E6**, and then protect the worksheet using Success16! **Save** the file, and then save the file as an **Excel Macro-Enabled Workbook** named Last_First_exl10_SA2Macro Activate and then click the **Developer tab**. Open the **Visual Basic Editor**. Insert a new module, and type the following:

```
Sub AddFooter ()
'Created by First Last
'Add the file name to the left footer
```

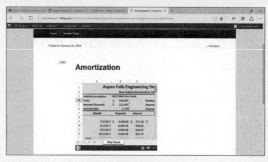

Figure 1   Edge 2016, Windows 10, Microsoft Corporation

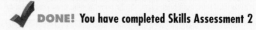

Figure 2

8. Use the code from Skill 10, step 4 as your guide to type VBA statements that insert the file name in the left footer. **Close** the Visual Basic Editor. Run the macro.

9. If necessary, restore the Excel user name and hide the Developer tab. Preview the worksheet. Compare your screen with **Figure 2**.

10. **Save** the file, and then **Close** Excel. Submit the files as directed by your instructor.

✔ **DONE! You have completed Skills Assessment 2**

My Skills

To complete this project, you will need the following file:

- exl10_MYRecycle

You will save your file as:

- Last_First_exl10_MYMacro

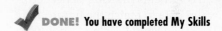

Aspen Falls Recycling					
Transaction #	Date	Description	Price per Unit	Gross	Tare
1353716	4/12/2018	#1 Steel Unprepared	0.105	18700	13860
1353716	4/12/2018	#2 Copper	2.65	69	0
1353716	4/12/2018	#2 Insulated Copper	0.95	11	0
1353716	4/12/2018	#3 Ins. Copper Wire	0.5	8	0
1353716	4/12/2018	304 Stainless Steel	0.53	188	0
1353716	4/17/2018	305 Stainless Steel	0.53	13860	12760
1353716	4/17/2018	Aluminum Radiators	0.43	48	0
1353716	4/17/2018	Aluminum/Copper Radiators	1.45	76	0
1353716	4/17/2018	Electric Motors	0.26	15	0
1353716	4/17/2018	Radiators	1.91	102	0
1353929	4/22/2018	#1 Steel Unprepared	0.105	15860	13480
1353929	4/22/2018	Unclean Motor Block	0.1	13480	10320
1355641	4/22/2018	#1 Steel Unprepared	0.11	18920	12740
1355641	4/22/2018	#2 Copper	2.58	2	0
1355641	4/22/2018	Batteries	0.27	88	0

Last_First_exl10_MYMacro

Figure 1

1. Start **Excel 2016**, and then open the student data file **exl10_MYRecycle**. Save the file in your chapter folder as a macro-enabled workbook with the name Last_First_exl10_MYMacro

2. Record a macro named RecycleHeader and assign the shortcut key as s

3. Select rows **1:2**, and then insert two blank rows. In cell **A1**, enter Aspen Falls Recycling

4. Change the font size to 14 and the font color to **Dark Red**, and then **Merge** and **Center A1:F1**.

5. **Stop Recording** the macro, and then delete rows **1:2**. **Run** the macro by pressing [Ctrl] + [S].

6. Create a macro in the **Visual Basic Editor** that will enter the file name in the left footer using the comments and statements below:

   Sub InsertFileName ()
   'Created by First Last
   'Inserts the file name in the left footer
   ActiveSheet.PageSetup.LeftFooter="&F"
   ActiveWindow.View=xlNormalView

7. **Run** the macro. Preview the worksheet, and then compare your screen with **Figure 1**.

8. **Save** the file, and then **Close** Excel. Submit the file as directed by your instructor.

DONE! You have completed My Skills

Visual Skills Check

To complete this project, you will need the following file:

- exl10_VSDisputes

You will save your files as:

- Last_First_exl10_VSDisputes
- Last_First_exl10_VSSnip

Start **Excel 2016**, and then open the student data file **exl10_VSDisputes**. Save the file in your chapter folder as Last_First_exl10_VSDisputes If necessary, change the **User name** for the workbook to your First and Last names. Apply comments and the validation rules necessary to mark the circled invalid data as shown in **Figure 1**. For the **Usage** data, the Usage should not be greater than 50,000. Create an information error alert using the title Usage with the message: Usage over 50,000 may be incorrect For the **Late Fees** data, create an **Input Message** as shown and apply the settings as appropriate to the message for Late Fees over $200. Show all comments (moving as needed), circle the invalid data to match the figure, and then select the range **F4:F14**. Using techniques previously practiced, create a full-screen snip. **Save** the snip in your chapter folder as Last_First_exl10_VSSnip **Close** the **Snipping Tool** window. **Save** the file, and then **Close** Excel. Submit the files as directed by your instructor.

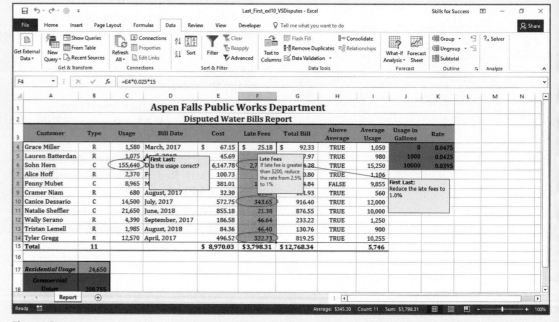

Figure 1

Excel 2016, Windows 10, Microsoft Corporation

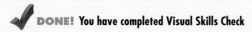 **DONE!** You have completed Visual Skills Check

Skills Challenge 1

To complete this project, you will need the following file:

- exl10_SC1Classes

You will save your files as:

- Last_First_exl10_SC1Web
- Last_First_exl10_SC1Embed
- Last_First_exl10_SC1Classes

Start **Excel 2016**, and then open the student data file **exl10_SC1Classes**. Save the file in your chapter folder as a **Web page** with the name Last_First_exl10_SC1Web If necessary, enable the content. Change the title of the page to Enrichment Classes **Publish** the workbook. **Close** the browser. **Save** the file to the **OneDrive Excel Chapter 10** folder as Last_First_exlSC1Classes Generate the code for the worksheet, and then embed the code into a blog using www.blog.com. Enter the title Enrichment

Classes Preview the blog, scroll down, and then create a full-screen snip. **Save** the file as Last_First_exl10_SC1Embed **Close** all browser windows. **Close** Excel. Submit the files as directed by your instructor.

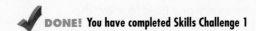 **DONE! You have completed Skills Challenge 1**

Skills Challenge 2

To complete this project, you will need the following file:

- exl10_SC2Budget

You will save your files as:

- Last_First_exl10_SC2Budget
- Last_First_exl10_SC2Snip

Start **Excel 2016**, and then open the student data file **exl10_SC2Budget**. **Save** the file in your chapter folder as Last_First_exl10_SC2Budget Using the skills you have practiced in this chapter, verify the user name is your first and last names. Review the displayed comments, and then turn on **Track Changes** to track the changes while you are editing the worksheet. Turn the comments off to see the cells. Using the comments as your guide, edit the cells. Accept all changes,

and then create the list of changes as a new sheet. Create a full-screen snip of the **History** sheet, and then save it as Last_First_exl10_SC2Snip **Close** the Snipping Tool. **Save** the file, and then **Close** Excel. Submit the files as directed by your instructor.

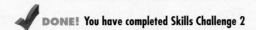 **DONE! You have completed Skills Challenge 2**

More Skills Assessment

To complete this project, you will need the following file:

- exl10_MSAKeys

You will save your files as:

- Last_First_exl10_MSAKeys
- Last_First_exl10_MSASnip

---

1. Start **Excel 2016**. Open the file **exl10_MSAKeys**, and then save the file in your chapter folder as a **Macro-Enabled Workbook**, Last_First_exl10_MSAKeys

2. If necessary, use the techniques previously practiced to show the **Developer tab**.

3. If necessary, toggle on the **Design Mode**, and then insert a **check box** form control in cell **E2**. Resize the control to align the top left corner of the control in the top left corner of **E2**.

4. Edit the control text, and then replace with Yes Change the width of the control to 0.5 Autofill **E2** down through **E15**.

5. Insert an **ActiveX Command Button** in the range **A18:B19**, and then rename the button Internationalization

6. Insert a form control **Button** in the range **D18:E19**, and then rename the button Heading

7. Create a macro named Heading that inserts two blank lines in rows 1:2, inserts the text Aspen Falls New Employees in **A1**, merges and centers the text in **A1:E1**, changes the font size to **14** and color to **Dark Teal, Text2**, and makes the text **Bold**.

8. Delete rows **A1:A2**. Assign the **Heading** macro to the **Heading** control button. Run the macro.

9. Create a macro named Internationalization that changes the range **D4:D17** to **French (France)** using **Type 14 mars 2012**, and the range **C4:C17** to currency **Symbol French (Mali)**. AutoFit the columns in the macro. Undo the macro changes. Copy the Internationalization macro code to the command button window. Click the button to run the macro.

10. Add the **Heading** and **Internationalization** macros to the **Quick Access Toolbar**. Compare your screen with **Figure 1**.

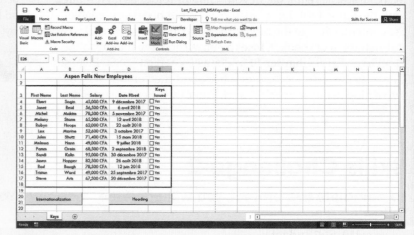

Figure 1   Excel 2016, Windows 10, Microsoft Corporation

11. Use the **Snipping Tool** to create a full-screen snip, and then save the file as Last_First_exl10_MSASnip

12. **Save** the file, and then **Close** Excel. Submit the files as directed by your instructor.

DONE! You have completed the More Skills Assessment

Collaborating with Google

To complete this project, you will need a Google account (refer to the Common Features chapter) and the following file:

- exl10_GPParks

You will save your files as:

- Last_First_exl10_GPSnip
- Last_First_exl10_GPParks

---

1. Open the **Google Chrome** web browser. Log into your Google account, and then click the **Apps** button ⊞.

2. Click **Drive** 🔺 to open Google Drive.

3. Click the **New** button, and then click **File upload**. Navigate to the student data files, and then open **exl10_GPParks**.

4. Double-click **exl10_GPParks** in **Google Drive**, and then click **Open** to view the workbook in **Google Sheets**.

5. Click cell **C6**, click **Insert**, and then click **Comment**. In the comment box, type Is this rate correct? and then click **Comment**.

6. Click cell **F9**, right-click, and then click **Insert comment**. In the comment box, type Revise cell to Pool and then click **Comment**.

7. Select the range **B6:B9**, click **Data**, and then click **Validation**. In the **Data validation** box, click the **Criteria arrow**, and then select **Number**. Click the **between arrow**, and then select **greater than**. In the last box, type 500000

8. Verify **Show warning** is selected, and then select the **Show help** check box. Click **Save**. Click cell **B6** to view the warning.

9. Click **Data**, and then click **protected sheets and ranges**. In the pane, click **Add a Sheet or range**, and then click **Set permissions**. Verify **Restrict who can edit this range** is selected and that **Only you** is displayed. Click **Done**.

10. At the bottom of the worksheet, point to the **2** in the **Bonds** worksheet tab to view the comments entered. Compare your screen with Figure 1.

11. Use the **Snipping Tool** to take a full-screen snip, and then save the file to your chapter folder as Last_First_exl10_GPSnip

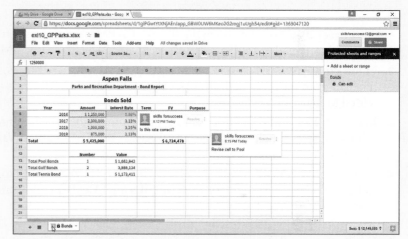

Figure 1

12. Click **File**, point to **Download as**, and then click Microsoft Excel (.xlsx). Open the downloaded file, and then save the file in your chapter folder as Last_First_exl10_GPParks Notice the Excel file has comments in cells C6 and F9, and data validation was created in B6:B9.

13. **Close** all windows, and then submit the file as directed by your instructor.

 **DONE!** You have completed Collaborating with Google

CAPSTONE PROJECT

To complete this project, you will need the following files:

exl_CAPMarket (Excel)
exl_CAPProducts (Text)
exl_CAPData (Access)
exl_CAPSales (Excel)

MyITLab®
Grader

You will save your files as:

Last_First_exl_CAPMarket
Last_First_exl_CAPWeb
Last_First_exl_CAPMacro

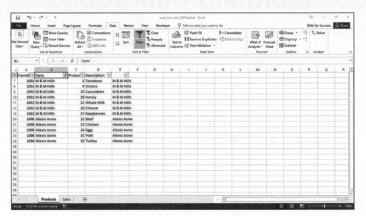

Figure 1 Excel 2016, Windows 10, Microsoft Corporation

1. Start **Excel 2016**, and then open the file **exl_CAPMarket**. **Save** the file in a new folder named Excel Capstone Projects as Last_First_exl_CAPMarket

2. In the **Products** worksheet, in cell **A1**, using all the wizard defaults, import the data from the delimited text file, **exl_CAPProducts**. Verify data is not added to the Data Model.

3. In cell **E2**, **TRIM** the data from cell **B2**, and AutoFill the function through cell **E47**. Copy the selected text to cell **B2** using the **Paste Values**, **Values (V)** option. AutoFit columns **B** and **D**.

4. Sort the range **A1:E47**, smallest to largest by **FarmID**. Apply a custom filter to **Farm** to display the data for **M & M Hills** and **Alexis Acres**. Compare your screen with **Figure 1**.

5. On the **Sales** worksheet, in cell **B3**, use the custom number format -yyyy-Use the **Format Painter** to copy the format to **C3**. **Save** the file.

6. Open the **exl_CAPSales** file, and then switch to the **Last_First_exl_CAPMarket** window.

7. **Consolidate** the data from the **June**, **July**, and **August** worksheets in the **exl_CAPSales** workbook to **A4** in the **Sales** worksheet. Use **Sum** as the **Function** and A4:B23 as the range for each worksheet. Include the **Farm** labels in **Left Column**.

8. In cell **D4**, insert an **AND** function, entering **Logical1** $B$4>$C$4 and **Logical2** B4>C4 AutoFill the function through **D23**.

9. In cell **D24**, insert a **SUMIF** function, entering **Range** D4:D23 **Criteria** TRUE and **Sum_Range** B4:B23

10. In the **Sales** worksheet, add a **Legend** to the **Bottom** of the **Farm Sales** chart. Edit the **Series value** using the range B4:B23. Edit the **Horizontal Axis Labels** to include the range A4:A23. Apply **Color 1** and **Chart Style 8**. Compare your screen with **Figure 2**.

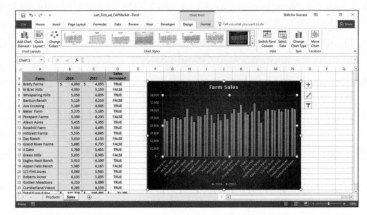

Figure 2 Excel 2016, Windows 10, Microsoft Corporation

11. Using **New Query**, import the **Farm Sales Week1** table from the **exl_CAPData** Access file.

12. In **New Query**, add three custom columns: one named Total Sales/lb that multiplies the **Cost/lb** field by **QtySold**, one named Total Sales/piece that multiplies the **Cost/piece** field by **QtySold**, and one named Total Sales that adds the **Total Sales/piece** and **Total Sales/lb** fields.

■ **Continue to the next page to complete the project**

Excel 2016, Windows 10, Microsoft Corporation

Figure 3

Excel 2016, Windows 10, Microsoft Corporation

Figure 4

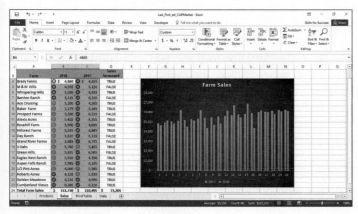

Excel 2016, Windows 10, Microsoft Corporation

Figure 5

13. Load the **Farm Sales Week1** data into a **New Worksheet**, and then rename the worksheet Data In a **New Worksheet**, create a PivotTable and rename the sheet as PivotTable Delete rows **1:2**. **Save** the file.

14. For the PivotTable, add **Farm** and **Description** as the row labels, and **Cost/lb** and **Cost/piece** as values. In cell **A1**, replace **Row Labels** with Farms In cell **B1**, replace **Sum of Cost/lb** with Cost/Pound In cell **C1**, replace **Sum of Cost/piece** with Cost/Piece Compare your screen with **Figure 3**.

15. **Save** the file as Last_First_exl_CAPWeb and publish the worksheet as a **Web Page** with the title Farmer's Market Verify the **Item to Publish** is set to **Selection: Sheet**.

16. On the **PivotTable** sheet, remove the **Cost/lb** and **Cost/piece** fields, and then add **QtySold** and **Total Sales** as values. In cell **B1**, replace **Sum of QtySold** with Quantity Sold and then in cell **C1**, replace **Sum of Total Sales** with Total Farm Sales Collapse all of the **Farms** except for **Alexis Acres** and **M & M Hills**.

17. Use a **Slicer** to display **Description**. Move the upper left corner of the **Slicer** to cell **E2**, and then drag the lower right corner through **G24**. Show the value **Cheese**, and then apply the **Slicer Style Dark 5** style. If necessary, expand the **Farms**. Compare your screen with **Figure 4**. Click cell **A1**.

18. Change the user name of the workbook to your First and Last names. In the **Sales** worksheet, insert a comment in cells **B7**, **B15**, and **B17** that reads Please recheck sales total

19. Apply the conditional formatting **Indicators** set 3 **Symbols (Circled)** to the range **B4:C23**. Compare your screen with **Figure 5**. Click cell **A1**, and then **Save** the file.

20. If necessary, show the **Developer tab**. In the **Products** worksheet, record a **Macro** using the name InsertInfo and shortcut key i that will insert your first and last names in cell **B50** and =NOW() in cell **B51**. To the same cells, apply font size **10**, font color **Standard Color Green**, and **Bold**. Stop the recording. **Save** the file as a **Macro-Enabled Workbook** as Last_First_exl_CAPMacro Close the file.

21. Open the **Last_First_exl_CAPMarket** file. Protect each worksheet in the workbook using the password Success16!

22. If necessary, restore the Excel user name, and hide the **Developer tab**. **Save** the file, and then **Close** Excel. Submit the files as directed by your instructor.

 DONE! You have completed the Excel Capstone Project

Using Excel Online to Create a Flyer

- ▶ Recall that Excel Online can be used to create, edit, and format basic worksheets using a web browser. Excel 2016 does not have to be installed on your computer to use Excel Online.

- ▶ Recall that OneDrive is a free cloud-based service from Microsoft that allows you to save your work to the cloud from an Internet-enabled computer and then work on the file from any other computer that is connected to the Internet.

- ▶ Using Excel Online and OneDrive, you can easily collaborate with colleagues or a team on workbooks. You have full control over who accesses your workbooks and what they can do with them.

- ▶ Excel Online provides a minimal number of features. If you need a feature that is not available, you can open your workbook in Microsoft Excel, make the changes you need, and save the workbook on your OneDrive.

© Yvan Reistserof/Fotolia

Aspen Falls Volunteer Fire Department

In this project, you will create a worksheet for Jim Holt, Fire Chief of the Aspen Falls Volunteer Fire Department (AFVFD). The AFVFD recently sponsored a rummage sale to raise funds for the purchase of new lifesaving equipment. The department exceeded its goal, raising $10,000. The worksheet you will create will compare the recent fund-raiser results with the results of fund-raisers held over the past five years to determine which type of fund-raiser is most effective.

Anyone with a Microsoft OneDrive account can use Excel Online to create or open Excel workbooks from any Internet-connected computer or device. In addition to basic text and numbers, you can add formatting and styles to text and cells. You can create these workbooks on your OneDrive, and then open the files in Excel 2016 to access the features not available in Excel Online. In Excel Online, workbooks are edited in *Editing view* and viewed to see how they will print in *Reading view*.

In this project, you will use Excel Online to create a workbook with formatted and styled text, basic formulas, charts, and tables. You will open the workbook in Excel 2016 to add formatting to the charts, import data, and save the file back to your OneDrive.

Outcome

Using the skills in this chapter, you will be able to create new workbooks, use charts and chart elements to represent data visually, filter data in tables, and share workbooks to the cloud.

Objectives

1 Generate workbooks in Excel Online

2 Apply formatting to workbooks in Excel Online

3 Analyze data using charts and tables

4 Manipulate workbooks in Excel Online and desktop Excel

Student data files needed for this project:

New Blank Excel Online Workbook
exl_OPVolunteers

You will save your file as:

Last_First_exl_OPRummage

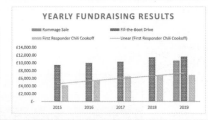

SKILLS

At the end of this project, you will be able to use Excel Online to:

▶ Create new Excel workbooks in OneDrive
▶ Type text in Editing view
▶ Format text for internationalization
▶ Switch to desktop Excel to complete editing
▶ Create and format charts
▶ Import data using New Query
▶ Filter and sort data in Excel tables
▶ Save and open workbooks to OneDrive
▶ Create new sheets and copy and paste data
▶ View workbook in Reading view
▶ Enter comments in worksheet cells
▶ Share workbooks using OneDrive

1. Start **Edge**, navigate to OneDrive .com and then log on to your Microsoft account. If you do not have an account, follow the links and directions on the page to create one.

2. After logging in, navigate as needed to display the OneDrive page, and then click the **Apps** button. Compare your screen with **Figure 1**.

   Due to the volatile nature of web pages, the formatting and layout of some pages in OneDrive may appear different than the figures in this book. If the OneDrive web page has changed, you will need to adjust the steps in the assignment to complete the actions specified.

3. Select the **Excel** thumbnail, and then click **New blank workbook**. Click **Book** in the title bar, type Last_First_exl_ OPRummage and then press Enter to save the workbook.

4. If necessary, click cell **A1**. Type Aspen Falls Volunteer Fire Department Fund-Raising Click cell **A2**, and then type 2015 - 2019 Press Enter.

5. Click cell **B4**. Type 2015 and then press Tab. Type 2016 Select the range **B4:C4**, and then use fill handle to Autofill the years through cell **F4**.

6. Click cell **A5**. Type Rummage Sale and then press Enter. In cell **A6**, type Fill-the-Boot Drive and then press Enter. In cell **A7**, type First Responder Chili Cookoff and then press Enter.

7. Widen column **A** until the column is wide enough to contain *First Responder Chili Cookoff*. Compare your screen with **Figure 2**.

■ **Continue to the next page to complete the project**

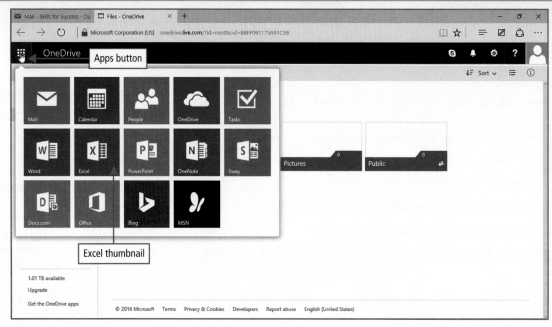

Figure 1

Edge/OneDrive 2016, Windows 10, Microsoft Corporation

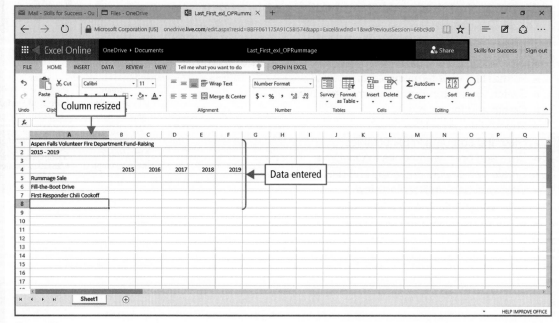

Figure 2

Excel 2016, Windows 10, Microsoft Corporation

8. Type the following data into your worksheet:

	2015	2016	2017	2018	2019
Rummage Sale	0	0	0	0	10612
Fill-the-Boot Drive	9458	9981	10258	11437	0
First Responder Chili Cookoff	4219	5406	6524	6857	0

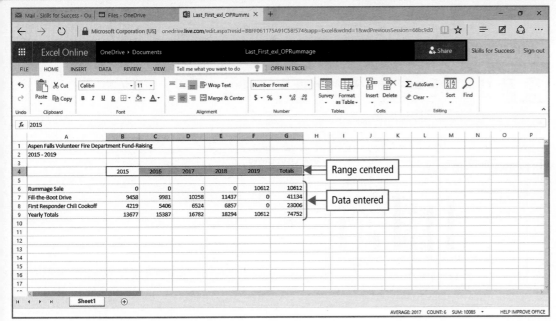

Excel 2016, Windows 10, Microsoft Corporation

Figure 3

9. Click cell **A5**. On the **HOME tab**, in the **Cells group**, click the **Insert button arrow**, and then click **Insert Rows**.

10. In cell **A9**, type Yearly Totals and then press Tab. Select the range **B9:F9**, and then in the **Editing group**, click **AutoSum**.

11. In cell **G4**, type Totals and then press Enter. Select the range **G6:G9**, and then in the **Editing group**, click **AutoSum**.

12. Select the range **B4:G4**, and then in the **Alignment group**, click the **Center** button. Compare your screen with **Figure 3**.

13. Select the range **B6:G6**. In the **Number group**, click the **Accounting Format arrow**, and then click **English (United Kingdom)**. Select the range **B9:G9**, and then use the techniques previously practiced to format the cells as **English (United Kingdom)**. Select the range **B7:G8**, and then in the **Number group**, click **Comma Style**.

14. Click cell **A1**, and then in the **Font group**, change the font to **Arial Black.** Change the font size to **16**. Select the range **A1:G1**, and then in the **Alignment group**, click **Merge & Center**.

15. Select the range **A2:G2**, and then click **Merge & Center**. Change the font to **Arial Black**. Change the font size to **14**. Compare your screen with **Figure 4**.

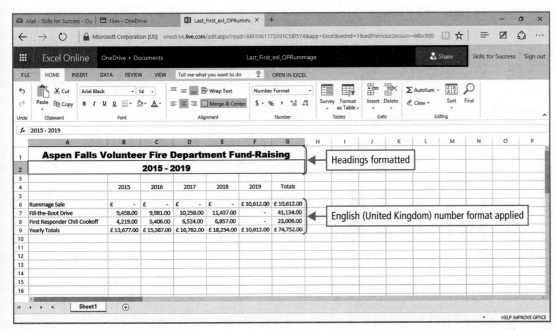

Excel 2016, Windows 10, Microsoft Corporation

Figure 4

■ **Continue to the next page to complete the project**

16. Select the range **A4:F8**. Click the **INSERT tab**, and then in the **Charts group**, click the **Column** button. Click the first thumbnail, **Clustered Column**. Move the chart until the top right corner is in the top right of cell **E11**.

17. On the **Chart Tools Chart tab**, in the **Labels group**, click **Chart Title**. Select **Above Chart**, and then in the **Edit Title** dialog box, type Yearly Fundraising Results and then click **OK**.

18. In cell **F7**, enter 11619 In cell **F8**, enter 6924 Scroll down, and then view the updated chart. Compare your screen with **Figure 5**.

The chart automatically updates with the new values.

19. On the **Chart Tools Chart tab**, in the **Data group**, click **Switch Row/Column**. In the **Labels group**, click the **Legend** button, and then click **Show Legend at Top**.

20. To add formatting that is not available in Excel Online, click **OPEN IN EXCEL**. Read the message, and then click **Yes**. If necessary, enter your OneDrive log in information.

21. Select the chart. Click the **Chart Tools Design tab**. In the **Chart Styles group**, click **Change Colors**, and then click **Color 4**. Click **Style 3**.

22. In the **Chart Layouts group**, click **Add Chart Element**, point to **Trendline**, and then click **Linear**. In the **Add Trendline** dialog box, select **First Responder Chili Cookoff**, and then click **OK**. Compare your screen with **Figure 6**.

23. Select cells **B9:G9**. On the **HOME tab**, in the **Styles group**, click the **Cell Styles arrow**, and then click the **Total** style. AutoFit columns **B:G**.

▪ **Continue to the next page to complete the project** ➤

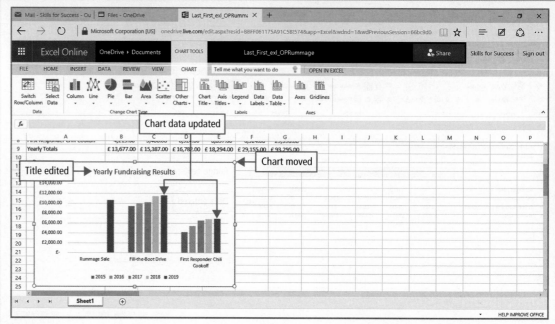

Figure 5

Excel 2016, Windows 10, Microsoft Corporation

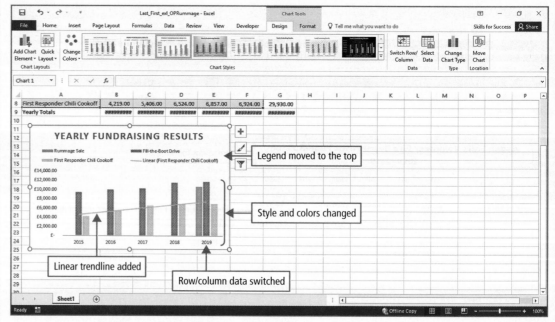

Figure 6

Excel 2016, Windows 10, Microsoft Corporation

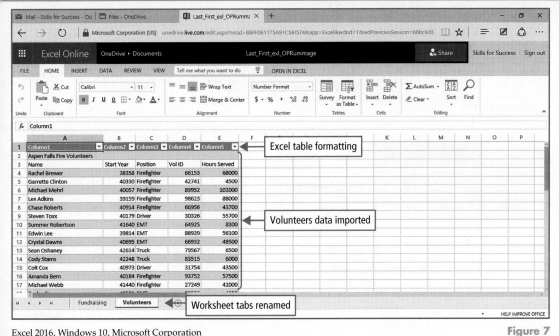

Excel 2016, Windows 10, Microsoft Corporation

Figure 7

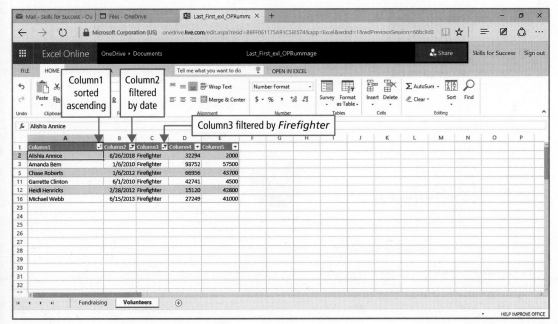

Excel 2016, Windows 10, Microsoft Corporation

Figure 8

24. Click the **Data tab**, and then in the **Get & Transform group**, click **New Query**. In the list, point to **From File**, and then click **From Workbook**. Navigate to the student data files for this project, click to open **exl_OPVolunteers**, and then **Import** the file. Select the **Volunteers** worksheet, and then **Load** the data as a new sheet in the **Last_First_exl_OPRummage** workbook. Rename *Sheet1* as Fundraising and then rename *Sheet2* as Volunteers **Save**, and then **Close** the file.

25. In OneDrive, click **Continue editing in Excel Online**, and then compare your screen with Figure 7.

> Data in the Volunteers worksheet is formatted as an Excel table.

26. In the **Volunteers** worksheet, select the range **B4:B23**. On the **HOME tab**, in the **Number group**, click the **Number Format arrow**. In the list, click **Short Date**. Click row **2**, and then in the **Cells group**, click the **Delete** button.

27. Click the **Column1 filter arrow**, and then click **Sort Ascending**.

28. Click the **Column2 filter arrow**, point to **Date Filters**, and then click **Custom Filter**. In the **Custom Filter** box, click the **equals arrow**, and then click **is between**. In the first box, type 1/1/2010 and then in the second box, type 12/31/2019 Click **OK**.

29. Click the **Column3 filter arrow**, click **Filter**, click the **Select All** check box to deselect, and then select the **Firefighter** check box. Click **OK**. Compare your screen with Figure 8.

30. On the **HOME tab**, in the **Cells group**, click the **Insert arrow**, and then click **Insert Sheet**. Rename the *Sheet1* worksheet tab as Firefighters

■ **Continue to the next page to complete the project**

31. Click the **Volunteers** worksheet tab, and then select the range **A2:E16**. **Copy** the range, click the **Firefighters** worksheet tab, click cell **A2**, and then **Paste** the data. AutoFit columns **A:C**.

32. Click the **Volunteers** worksheet tab, and then press [Esc]. Click the **Column3** filter, and then click **Clear Filter from 'Column3'**. Repeat this technique to clear the filter from **Column2**. Scroll down to row **17**, and then select the range **A17:E17**. **Cut** the range, and then paste it in row **1** of the **Firefighters** worksheet. With the range still selected, in the **Alignment group**, click **Wrap Text**, and then **Center**. In the **Font group**, click **Bold**. Compare your screen with **Figure 9**.

33. Click the **Volunteers** worksheet tab. Click to select row **17**, and then on the **Home tab**, in the **Cells group**, click the **Delete** button. Select the range **A2:E17**, and then click **Copy**. In the **Cells group**, click the **Insert button arrow**, and then click **Insert Sheet**. In *Sheet1*, click cell **A2**. In the **Clipboard group**, click the **Paste arrow**, and then click **Paste Values**.

34. Select columns **B:D**. In the **Cells group**, click the **Delete arrow**, and then click **Delete Columns**. AutoFit column **A**. In cell **A1**, type Volunteers and then in cell **B1**, type Hours Served **Wrap Text** in **B1**, and then rename *Sheet1* worksheet as Hours

35. Select the range **A1:B17**. Click the **Insert tab**. In the **Charts group**, click **Pie**, and then click the **2-D Pie** thumbnail. Compare your screen with **Figure 10**.

■ **Continue to the next page to complete the project**

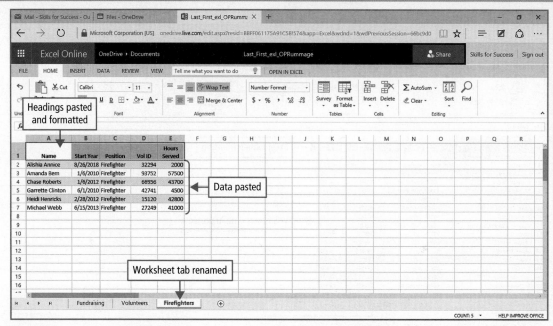

Figure 9

Excel 2016, Windows 10, Microsoft Corporation

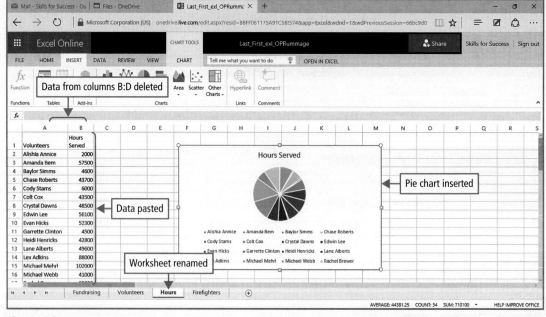

Figure 10

Excel 2016, Windows 10, Microsoft Corporation

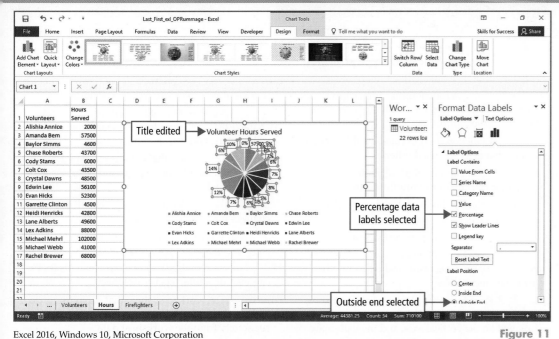

Excel 2016, Windows 10, Microsoft Corporation

Figure 11

36. Move and resize the chart in the range **D2:L16**.

37. In the **Labels group**, click the **Chart Title button**, and then click **Edit Chart Title**. In the **Edit Title** box, replace the text with Volunteer Hours Served and then click **OK**.

38. To add formatting that is not available in Excel Online, click **OPEN IN EXCEL**. Read the message, and then click **Yes**.

39. Select the chart. Click the **Chart Tools Design tab**, and then in the **Chart Layouts group**, click the **Add Chart Element** button. Point to **Data Labels**, and then select **More Data Label options**. In the **Format Data Labels** pane, click to deselect the **Value** check box, and then click to select **Percentage** to see only chart percentage values. Click **Outside End**. Compare your screen with **Figure 11**.

40. Save, and then **Close** the file. In OneDrive, click **Continue editing in Excel Online**.

41. Click the **Fundraising** worksheet tab. Click cell **A2**. Click the **REVIEW tab**, and then in the **Comments group**, click **New Comment**. In the **Comments** pane, in the **New Comment** box, type Volunteers are planning a Crab Feast for 2020. Click **Post**. Compare your screen with **Figure 12**.

42. Click the **Firefighters** worksheet tab, and then click cell **E3**. In the **Comments** pane, click **New Comment**. In the **New Comment** box, type Firefighter has the highest hours served, will be recognized at the Banquet. Click **Post**.

43. Share the file using the email your instructor provides. Click **OPEN IN EXCEL**, click **Yes**, and then **Save** the file in your **Excel Chapter Projects** folder. **Close** Excel and all browser windows. Submit the file as directed by your instructor.

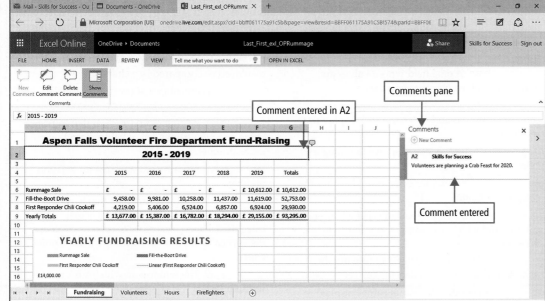

Excel 2016, Windows 10, Microsoft Corporation

Figure 12

✔ **DONE! You have completed the Excel Online Project**

Glossary

Absolute cell reference A cell reference address that remains the same when it is copied or filled to other cells. To make a cell reference absolute, insert a dollar sign ($) before the row and column references.

Accessibility Technologies that adapt the display for nonvisual users.

Accessibilty Checker Finds potential accessibility issues and creates a report.

Active cell The cell outlined in green in which data is entered when you begin typing.

ActiveX control Object such as a check box or button that provides interactive options or runs macros.

Add-in A file that adds functionality to Excel, usually in the form of new functions.

Alternative (Alt) text Text used in documents and web pages to provide a text description of an object.

Amortization table Tracks loan payments over the life of a loan.

AND A function that evaluates two or more conditions. When all conditions are true, the displayed value is TRUE.

Area chart A chart type that emphasizes the magnitude of change over time.

Argument The values that a function uses to perform operations or calculations.

Arithmetic operator A symbol that specifies a mathematical operation such as addition or subtraction.

Array A collection of data typically arranged in multiple columns and rows. Most workbooks arrange data in arrays.

Array formula A formula that can perform calculations across multiple items in an array. For example, you can use an array formula to calculate the sum of the values in one column multiplied by the values in another column.

AutoFit A command that automatically changes the column width to accommodate the longest entry.

AutoRecover A feature that saves copies of all open Excel files at user-definable fixed intervals.

AVERAGE function A function that adds a group of values and then divides the result by the number of values in the group.

AVERAGEIF A function used to calculate the average for cells that meet specified criteria.

AVERAGEIFS A function used to calculate the average for cells that meet multiple criteria.

Axis A line bordering the chart plot area used as a frame of reference for measurement.

Background color Shading assigned to a cell.

Backstage view A collection of pages on the File tab used to open, save, print, and perform other file management tasks.

Bar chart A chart type that illustrates comparisons among individual items. The categories are displayed on the vertical axis, and the values are displayed on the horizontal axis.

Button A control that typically starts a macro when it is clicked.

Calculated column A column in an Excel table that uses a single formula that adjusts for each row.

Calculated field A data field whose values are derived from formulas that you create.

Calculation The process that Excel uses to compute formulas and functions and display the results.

Category axis The axis that displays the category labels.

Category label Nonnumeric text that identifies the categories of data.

Cell A box formed by the intersection of a row and column into which text, objects, and data can be inserted.

Cell address The column letter and row number that identify a cell; also called the cell reference.

Cell border Decorative lines that can be applied to worksheet cells and that are added to differentiate, emphasize, or group cells.

Cell fill color Shading assigned to a cell.

Cell reference The column letter and row number that identify a cell; also called a cell address.

Cell style A prebuilt set of formatting characteristics, such as font, font size, font color, cell borders, and cell shading.

Change history A log that records each data change, who made the change, and when the data was changed.

Change tracking A feature that tracks all the changes made to a workbook.

Chart A graphic representation of data used to show comparisons, patterns, and trends.

Chart layout A prebuilt set of chart elements that can include a title, legend, or labels.

Chart sheet A workbook sheet that contains only a chart and is useful when you want to view a chart separately from the worksheet data.

Chart style A prebuilt chart format that applies an overall visual look to a chart by modifying its graphic effects, colors, and backgrounds.

Chart template A custom chart type that you can apply like any other chart type.

Chart type A specific design of how data is displayed or compared in a chart.

Check box A control that allows a user to select one or more values in a group of choices.

CHOOSE function A lookup function that returns a value or action from a list of values based on an index number.

Clipboard A temporary storage area for text and graphics.

Clustered bar chart A chart type that is useful when you want to compare values across categories; bar charts organize categories along the vertical axis and values along the horizontal axis.

Code window The window in which VBA code is written.

Column chart A chart type useful for illustrating comparisons among related numbers.

Column heading The letter that displays at the top of a column.

Command button A control that runs a VBA macro.

Comma-separated values Text that uses commas to separate each column of text.

Comment Descriptive text that you can add to cells without modifying the data in the worksheet.

Comment indicator A small red triangle in the upper right corner of a cell.

Compare and merge A process that combines the changes from multiple copies of a workbook into a single copy.

Comparison operator Compares two values and returns either TRUE or FALSE.

CONCATENATE A text function used to join the text from two or more cells into one cell.

Conditional formatting A format, such as cell shading or font color, that is applied to cells when a specified condition is true.

Consolidate A command used to summarize and report results from separate worksheets.

Content Underlying formulas and data in a cell.

Contextual tab A tab that displays on the Ribbon only when a related object such as a graphic or chart is selected.

Copy A command that places a copy of the selected text or object in the Office Clipboard.

COUNT function A function that counts the number of cells that contain numbers.

COUNTA A function used to count the number of cells containing specified values.

COUNTIF A function used to count the number of cells in the range that meet a specified condition.

Criteria The conditions specified in the logical test.

CUBE function A function that connects to and manipulates data in an OLAP cube.

CUBEMEMBER function Defines the categories and how the data should be aggregated.

CUBEVALUE function Defines the specific values derived from the cross-tabulation of the categories.

Data bar A format that provides a visual cue about the value of a cell relative to other cells in a range.

Data marker A column, a bar, an area, a dot, a pie slice, or another symbol that represents a single data point.

Data model A collection of tables with relationships.

Data point A chart value that originates in an Excel worksheet cell.

Data series In a chart, data points that are related to one another.

Data table A range of cells that is set up to show how changing one or two values in a formula will affect the formula's result.

Data validation rule Places a restriction on the types of data that can be entered into cells.

Data_field The values that you want to retrieve from the PivotTable report.

Default printer The printer that is automatically selected when you do not choose a different printer.

Delimited text file A file in which the data in each column is separated by an identifying character such as a comma, a space, or a tab stop.

Delimiter The character used to separate columns of text in a data table.

Dependent Any cell value that depends on the value in a given cell.

Detail sheet A worksheet with cells referred to by summary sheet formulas.

Displayed value Data displayed in a cell.

Document properties Details about a file that describe or identify the file, such as the title, author name, and keywords.

Double-click To click the left mouse button two times quickly without moving the mouse.

Double-tap To tap the screen in the same place two times quickly.

Drag To press and hold the left mouse button while moving the mouse.

Drag and drop A method of moving objects in which you point to the selection and drag it to a new location.

Dual axis chart One or more data series is plotted on a secondary vertical axis.

Edit To insert, delete, or replace text in an Office document, workbook, or presentation.

Editing view A view that opens the workbook in a browser and allows you to edit the workbook. If the workbook is shared, you will see the other editors' names in the top of the window and changes will be updated immediately.

Embedded chart A chart that is placed on the worksheet containing the data.

Error alert A data validation message that informs the data entry operator that invalid data has been entered into the cell.

Error indicator A green triangle that indicates a possible error in a formula.

Error value A message that displays whenever a formula or function cannot perform its calculations.

Excel add-in A tool that adds features and commands to Excel, extending Excel's capabilities as if the tool were part of Excel.

Excel table A series of rows and columns that contain related data that have been formatted as a table.

Exponential trendline Data points create a symmetric arc.

Fields Categories of data organized into columns.

File type A standard way that information is encoded for storage in a computer file. It is designated for each type of software.

Fill handle The small green square in the lower right corner of the selection.

Filter A command to display only the rows of a table that meet specified criteria. Filtering temporarily hides rows that do not meet the criteria.

Filtering Displays only the data that satisfies conditions you specify.

Flash Fill Recognizes a pattern in data and automatically enters the rest of the data.

Font A set of characters with the same design and shape.

Form control Object such as a button or check box that is added to a worksheet.

Format To change the appearance of the text—for example, changing the text color to red.

Format Painter A tool used to copy formatting from one place to another.

Formatting The process of specifying the appearance of cells or the overall layout of a worksheet.

Formula An equation that performs mathematical calculations on number values in the worksheet.

Formula AutoComplete A feature that suggests values as you type a function.

Formula bar A bar below the Ribbon that displays the value contained in the active cell and is used to enter or edit values or formulas.

Freeze Panes A command used to keep rows or columns visible when scrolling in a worksheet. The frozen rows and columns become separate panes.

Function A prewritten Excel formula that takes a value or values, performs an operation, and returns a value or values.

Future value (FV) The value at the end of a period of time.

Gallery A visual display of selections from which you can choose.

General format The default number format. It does not display commas or trailing zeros to the right of a decimal point.

GETPIVOTDATA function Returns data stored in a PivotTable report.

Goal Seek A what-if analysis tool that finds a specific value for a cell by adjusting the value of another cell.

Gridlines The lines that run horizontally and vertically across a worksheet and intersect to create cells.

HLOOKUP A function that looks for a value in the top row of a table or array of values and returns the value in the same column from a row you specify.

Hyperlink Text or a graphic that you click to go to a file, a location in a file, a web page on the World Wide Web, or a web page on an organization's intranet.

Hypertext Markup Language (HTML) Used to mark up text files so that they can be viewed on the Internet.

Icon sets Classify a range of data into three to five categories and display small graphics in each cell depending on that cell's value.

IF function A logical function that checks whether criteria are met, and then returns one value when the condition is TRUE and another value when the condition is FALSE.

INDEX function array A function used return a value of a component in a table or an array.

INDEX function reference A function used to return the reference of a cell at the intersection of a specific row and column.

Input message A data validation message that informs the data entry operator about the types of data that can be entered into the cell.

Inquire add-in Assists with analyzing and reviewing workbooks to understand their design function and data dependencies, and uncover a variety of problems including formula errors or inconsistencies, hidden information, and broken links.

Insertion point A flashing vertical line that indicates where text will be inserted when you start typing.

Interest The charge for borrowing money; generally a percentage of the amount borrowed.

Keyboard shortcut A combination of keys that performs a command.

Label Text data in a cell that identifies a number value.

LEFT function A text function used to return a specified number of characters starting from the left side of the data.

Legacy object Object that is compatible with earlier versions of a program.

Legend A box that identifies the patterns or colors that are assigned to the data series or categories in the chart.

Line chart A chart type that illustrates trends over time, with time displayed along the x-axis and the data point values connected by a line.

Linear Forecast trendline Data points follow a straight line with a two-period forecast.

Linear trendline Data points follow nearly a straight line.

Live Preview A feature that displays what the results of a formatting change will be if you select it.

Logical function A function used to test whether a condition is true or false.

Logical test Any value or expression that can be evaluated as TRUE or FALSE.

Lookup function A function used to find values stored in a lookup table.

Lookup table Data organized into rows and columns in such a way that values can be easily retrieved.

LOWER function A text function used to convert a text string to all lowercase letters.

Macro A stored set of instructions that automates common tasks.

Malware Software that is designed to harm a computer.

MATCH function A function that searches for a specific item in a range and returns the relative position of the item.

Match_type Either 1, 0, or –1, indicating which value to return.

MAX function A function that returns the largest value in a range of cells.

Metadata Information that describes the data in an Excel file.

Microsoft account Personal account that you use to access your files, settings, and online services from devices connected to the Internet.

MID function A text function used to return a specified number of characters starting from a specified position in the data.

MIN function A function that returns the smallest value in a range of cells.

Mini toolbar A toolbar with common formatting commands that displays near selected text.

Module The element where VBA code is typed and stored.

Moving Average trendline Data points follow a smooth curve to show data fluctuations.

Name In Excel, a word that represents a cell, a range of cells, or a table that can be used as a reference.

Name Box An area that displays the active cell reference.

Nested function A function placed inside another function.

New Query A tool to connect, combine, and refine data from multiple sources.

Non-native file A file format that is not a current Excel 2016 file, including previous versions, text files, and data tables.

Normal view A view that maximizes the number of cells visible on the screen.

NOW function A function that returns the serial number of the current date and time.

Nper The total number of payments for the loan.

Number format A specific way that Excel displays numbers.

Number value Numeric data in a cell.

Office Add-in A plugin that adds extra features or custom commands to Office programs.

Office Clipboard A temporary storage area that holds text or an object that has been cut or copied.

One-variable data table Changes one value in a formula using input from either a row or a column.

Online analytical processing (OLAP) cube Extends a two-dimensional spreadsheet into three or more dimensions, where each dimension is a separate category.

Operator precedence A set of mathematical rules for performing calculations within a formula.

OR A function that evaluates two or more conditions. If one condition is true, the displayed value is TRUE.

Or A logical operator that evaluates two conditions.

Organization chart A chart that graphically represents the hierarchy of relationships between individuals and groups within an organization.

Page Layout view A view used to adjust how a worksheet will look when it is printed.

Parameter A quantity whose value is selected for particular circumstances and in relation to which other variable quantities may be expressed.

Paste A command that inserts a copy of the text or object from the Office Clipboard.

Paste area The target destination for data that has been cut or copied.

Pie chart A chart type that displays the relationship of parts to a whole.

PivotChart A dynamic visual representation of data.

PivotTable report An interactive way to summarize, explore, and analyze data.

PivotTable values Fields for which summary statistics are calculated.

Placeholder A reserved, formatted space into which you enter your own text or object. If no text is entered, the placeholder text will not print.

PMT function A function that calculates the payment for a loan based on constant payments and a constant interest rate.

Power Pivot An Office Professional Plus Excel add-in used to perform powerful data analysis and to create sophisticated data models.

Power View An interactive data exploration, visualization, and presentation experience that encourages intuitive ad-hoc reporting.

Precedent Any cell value that is referred to in a formula or a function.

Present value (Pv) The initial amount of the loan, and the total amount that a series of future payments is worth today.

Principal The initial amount of the loan, and the total amount that a series of future payments is worth today. Also called the present value (Pv) of a loan.

Programming comments Statements that document what the code does.

Programming statements Instructions stored in a subroutine.

PROPER A function that converts text to title case—the first letter of each word is capitalized.

Protect Sheet Prevents unauthorized users from making changes to the worksheet.

Protected View A view applied to files downloaded from the Internet that allows you to decide if the content is safe before working with the file.

Quick Access Toolbar A small toolbar that contains buttons for commonly used commands such as Save and Undo.

RAM The computer's temporary memory.

Range Two or more cells in a worksheet that are adjacent.

Range finder An Excel feature that outlines all of the cells referenced in a formula. It is useful for verifying which cells are used in a formula and for editing formulas.

Rate The percentage that is paid for the use of the borrowed money.

Reading view A view that opens the workbook in the browser to view the workbook as it will print.

Records A collection of related data that displays in a single row in a database table.

Relative cell reference Refers to cells based on their position in relation to (relative to) the cell that contains the formula.

Replace A feature that finds and then replaces a character or string of characters in a worksheet or in a selected range.

Report A database object that presents tables or query results in a way that is optimized for onscreen viewing or printing.

RGB values Colors constructed from combinations of red, green, and blue.

Ribbon Contains commands placed in groups that are organized by tabs so that you can quickly find the tools you need.

RIGHT function A text function used to return a specified number of characters starting from the right side of the data.

Row heading The number that displays at the left of a row.

Row labels Fields used to categorize the data by rows.

Scenario A set of values that Excel can save and automatically substitute in cells.

Screen clipping A picture of a portion of the computer screen that can be inserted into a worksheet.

Screen shot An image of the computer screen.

Serial number A number showing the position of an item in a series.

Series A group of numbers, text, dates, or time periods that come one after another in succession. For example, the months January, February, March.

Shape An object such as a line, arrow, rectangle, circle, square, or callout.

Shaping data The process of applying transformations.

Shared workbook A workbook in which multiple users on a network can make changes at the same time.

Slicer A tool that is used to filter data in PivotTable views.

Slide (PowerPoint) An individual page in a presentation that can contain text, pictures, or other objects.

SmartArt graphic A visual representation of information used to effectively communicate ideas.

Software version A software release or format.

Solver A what-if analysis tool used to find solutions to complex problems. It looks for solutions to achieve a desired goal.

Sparkline A chart contained in a single cell that is used to show data trends.

Special character Characters, such as degree symbol and trademark symbol, that are not found on the standard keyboard, but are included on a shorter list of frequently used symbols on the Special Characters tab.

Split window A command that divides the window into separate panes so that each pane can be scrolled separately.

Spreadsheet The primary document that you use in Excel to store and work with data, also called a worksheet.

Statistical function A predefined formula that describes a collection of data; for example, averages, maximums, and minimums.

String Any sequence of letters and numbers. It is designated by quotation marks.

Strong password A password that contains a combination of uppercase and lowercase letters, numbers, and symbols.

Style A group of formatting choices that can be applied in a single step.

Sub A group of instructions that is a subset of a program.

SUM An Excel function that adds all the numbers in a range of cells.

SUMIF A function that adds the cells in a range that meet a specified criterion.

SUMIFS A function that adds the cells in a range that meet multiple criteria.

Summary sheet A worksheet that displays and summarizes totals from other worksheets.

Symbol A character such as font symbol or a bullet character that is not found on a common keyboard.

Tab scrolling buttons The buttons to the left of the worksheet tabs used to display worksheet tabs that are not in view.

Table style A collection of table formatting options that can be applied to a range with a single click.

Template Prebuilt workbook used as a pattern for creating new workbooks.

Text Box Rectangular object on a worksheet or chart in which you type text.

Text file A file that stores only text characters, not formatting or tables.

Text format A format that treats the cell value as text even when the cell contains numbers.

Text value Character data in a cell that usually labels number values.

Text wrap A format that displays text on multiple lines within a cell.

The Cloud An Internet technology used to store files and to work with programs that are stored in a central location.

Theme A prebuilt set of unified formatting choices including colors and fonts.

3-D Short for three-dimensional.

Three-dimensional Refers to an image that appears to have all three spatial dimensions—length, width, and depth.

Thumbnail A small sample image of a style located in the gallery.

TODAY function A function that returns the serial number of the current date.

Total row A row that displays as the last row in an Excel table and provides summary functions in drop-down lists for each column.

Transforming Modifying data from data sources to meet your needs.

TRANSPOSE function A lookup function used to convert a vertical range of cells to a horizontal range, or vice versa.

Trendline A graphic representation of trends in a data series. It is used for problem prediction.

TRIM function A text function used to remove all spaces from a text string except for single spaces between words.

Truncated Cut off.

Two-variable data table Changes one value in a formula using two inputs—one from a column and one from a row.

Underlying formula The formula as displayed in the formula bar.

Underlying value Data displayed in the formula bar.

UPPER function A text function used to convert a text string to all uppercase letters.

Value Data in a cell.

Value axis The axis that displays the worksheet's numeric data.

Visual Basic for Applications (VBA) A high-level programming language that can be used to write and modify macros.

VLOOKUP A function that finds values in a table where categories are organized by columns.

Volatile The result of a function will not remain as entered, but will be updated each time the workbook is opened.

Watch Window Displays cells and the formulas in cells that are not visible on the screen.

Watermark A graphic inserted into a workbook background. Watermarks are typically inserted into the header.

WEEKDAY function A function that converts a serial number to a day of the week.

What-if analysis A set of tools that change the values in cells to show how those changes affect the outcome of other formulas on the worksheet.

Word wrap Words at the right margin automatically move to the beginning of the next line if they do not fit.

Workbook A file that you can use to organize various kinds of related information.

WORKDAY function A function that returns the serial number of the date before or after a specified number of workdays.

Worksheet The primary document that you use in Excel to store and work with data, also called a spreadsheet.

Worksheet tab The labels along the lower border of the workbook window that identify each worksheet.

X-axis The horizontal axis of a chart.

Y-axis The vertical axis of a chart.

Appendix

Microsoft Office Specialist Excel 2016				C = CORE
Chapter	MOS Obj #	Objective	Skills Heading	Page
1		Create and Manage Worksheets and Workbooks		
	1.1 C	Create Worksheets and Workbooks		
Ch1	1.1.1 C	Create a Workbook	Create and Save Workbooks	40
Online/Ch5/Ch7	1.1.2 C	Import Data From a Delimited Text File	Convert Comma-Separated Text into Columns/Import Data from Text Files	228/288
Ch3	1.1.3 C	Add a Worksheet to an Existing Workbook	Insert, Hide, Delete, and Move Worksheets	134
Ch4/Ch7/Ch9	1.1.4 C	Copy and Move a Worksheet	Freeze and Unfreeze Panes/Create and Sort Excel Tables/Sort Data and Use the Subtotal Tool to Summarize Data/Change Calculation Types and Format PivotTable Reports/Group and Filter PivotTable Reports	173/175/295/379
	1.2 C	Navigate in Worksheets and Workbooks		
Ch4	1.2.1 C	Search for Data within a Workbook	Use Find and Replace	170
Ch1/Ch4	1.2.2 C	Navigate to a Named Cell, Range, or Workbook Element	Enter Data and Merge and Center Titles/Set Print Areas/Use Text and Lookup Functions	43/60/183
Ch3	1.2.3 C	Insert and Remove Hyperlinks	Create and Edit Hyperlinks	143
	1.3 C	Format Worksheets and Workbooks		
Ch3	1.3.1 C	Change Worksheet Tab Color	Organize Worksheet Tabs	121
Ch1/Ch3	1.3.2 C	Rename a Worksheet	Insert Footers and Adjust Page Settings/Organize Worksheet Tabs	56/120
Ch3	1.3.3 C	Change Worksheet Order	Insert, Hide, Delete, and Move Worksheets	135
Ch1/Ch2/Ch5	1.3.4 C	Modify Page Setup	Insert Footers and Adjust Page Settings/Display Formulas and Print Worksheets/Update Charts and Insert WordArt/Customize, Save, and Apply Themes	57/58/97/223

Chapter	MOS Obj #	Objective	Skills Heading	Page
Online/Ch5	1.3.5 C	Insert and Delete Columns or Rows	Insert and Delete Rows, Columns, and Cells	216
Ch3	1.3.6 C	Change Workbook Themes	Organize Worksheet Tabs	121
Ch1	1.3.7 C	Adjust Row Height and Column Width	Adjust Column Widths and Apply Cell Styles	48
Ch1/Ch3	1.3.8 C	Insert Headers and Footers	Insert Footers and Adjust Page Settings/Create Clustered Bar Charts	56/139
	1.4 C	**Customize Options and Views for Worksheets and Workbooks**		
Ch3	1.4.1 C	Hide or Unhide Worksheets	Insert, Hide, Delete, and Move Worksheets	134, 135
Ch4	1.4.2 C	Hide or Unhide Columns and Rows	Convert Tables to Ranges and Adjust Worksheet Print Settings	179
Ch3/Ch10	1.4.3 C	Customize the Quick Access Toolbar	Modify the Quick Access Toolbar/Merge Changes/Add Macro Buttons to the Quick Access Toolbar	142/416/429
Ch1/Ch5	1.4.4 C	Change Workbook Views	Insert Footers and Adjust Page Settings/Display Formulas and Print Worksheets/Add Watermarks and Modify Background Colors	57/59/224
Ch4	1.4.5 C	Change Window Views	Freeze and Unfreeze Panes/Customize Workbook Views	172/182
Ch1/Ch10	1.4.6 C	Modify Document Properties	Insert Footers and Adjust Page Settings/Manage Document Properties/Modify Excel Options and Work with Comments	56/63/408
Online/Ch5/Ch8	1.4.7 C	Change Magnification by Using Zoom Tools	Apply Icon Sets as Conditional Formatting/Customize, Save, and Apply Themes	213/223
Ch1/Ch3	1.4.8 C	Display Formulas	Display Formulas and Print Worksheets/Enter and Format Dates	58/122

Chapter	MOS Obj #	Objective	Skills Heading	Page
	1.5 C	**Configure Worksheets and Workbooks for Distribution**		
Ch1	1.5.1 C	Set a Print Area	Display Formulas and Print Worksheets/ Set Print Areas	60
Ch1/ Ch10	1.5.2 C	Save Workbooks in Alternative File Formats	Create Templates and Workbooks from Templates/Save Workbooks as Web Pages and Embed Data in Web Pages/Enable and Copy Macros Between Workbooks	62/418/ 422
Ch2	1.5.3 C	Print All or Part of a Workbook	Display Formulas and Print Worksheets/ Preview and Print Multiple Worksheets	99
Ch1/Ch2/ Ch3/Ch4	1.5.4 C	Set Print Scaling	Display Formulas and Print Worksheets/ Set Print Areas/Preview and Print Multiple Worksheets/Create Summary Worksheets/ Convert Tables to Ranges and Adjust Worksheet Print Settings	59/98/ 137/178
Ch4	1.5.5 C	Display Repeating Row and Column Titles on Multipage Worksheets	Convert Tables to Ranges and Adjust Worksheet Print Settings	178
Online/ Ch5	1.5.6 C	Inspect a Workbook for Hidden Properties or Personal Information	Inspect Document Properties to Remove Personal Information	229
Ch2	1.5.7 C	Inspect a Workbook for Accessibility Issues	Validate Workbooks for Accessibility	100
Ch2	1.5.8 C	Inspect a Workbook for Compatibility Issues	Validate Workbooks for Accessibility	100
2		**Manage Data Cells and Ranges**		
	2.1 C	**Insert Data in Cells and Ranges**		
Ch4	2.1.1 C	Replace Data	Move Functions, Add Borders, and Rotate Text/	164
Ch1/Ch3	2.1.2 C	Cut, Copy, or Paste Data	Construct Multiplication and Division Formulas/Insert, Hide, Delete, and Move Worksheets	47/135
Ch3/Ch6	2.1.3 C	Paste Data by Using Special Paste Options	Move Cell Contents and Use Paste Options/ Use Paste Options to Change Underlying Values	126/251

Chapter	MOS Obj #	Objective	Skills Heading	Page
Ch1	2.1.4 C	Fill Cells by Using Autofill	AutoFill Formulas and Data/Fill Data with Flash Fill/Create Templates and Workbooks from Templates	52, 53/61/62
Online/ Ch5	2.1.5 C	Insert and Delete Cells	Insert and Delete Rows, Columns, and Cells	217
	2.2 C	**Format Cells and Ranges**		
Ch1/Ch3	2.2.1 C	Merge Cells	Enter Data and Merge and Center Titles	43/417
Ch2/Ch4	2.2.2 C	Modify Cell Alignment and Indentation	Align and Wrap Text/Move Functions, Add Borders, and Rotate Text	81/165
Online/ Ch5	2.2.3 C	Format Cells by Using Format Painter	Format Cells Using Format Painter	210
Ch2	2.2.4 C	Wrap Text within Cells	Align and Wrap Text	81
Ch1/Ch2	2.2.5 C	Apply Number Formats	Format, Edit, and Check Spelling/Format Numbers	54/84
Ch1/Ch2/ Ch4	2.2.6 C	Apply Cell Formats	Adjust Column Widths and Apply Cell Styles/Format Numbers/Move Functions, Add Borders, and Rotate Text	49/85/ 165
Ch1/Ch2/ Ch5	2.2.7 C	Apply Cell Styles	Adjust Column Widths and Apply Cell Styles/Format, Edit, and Check Spelling/ Format Numbers/Create and Apply Custom Cell Styles	49, 54, 55/85/ 220
	2.3 C	**Summarize And Organize Data**		
Ch4	2.3.1 C	Insert Sparklines	Insert Sparklines	168
Online/ Ch7	2.3.2 C	Outline Data	Sort Data and Use the Subtotal Tool to Summarize Data	295
Online/ Ch7	2.3.3 C	Insert Subtotals	Sort Data and Use the Subtotal Tool to Summarize Data	294
Ch4/Ch5	2.3.4 C	Apply Conditional Formatting	Apply Conditional Formatting/Apply Icon Sets as Conditional Formatting	166, 167/212

Chapter	MOS Obj #	Objective	Skills Heading	Page
3		**Create Tables**		
	3.1 C	**Create and Manage Tables**		
Ch4	3.1.1 C	Create an Excel Table from a Cell Range	Create and Sort Excel Tables	174
Ch4/Ch7/ Ch8	3.1.2 C	Convert a Table to a Cell Range	Convert Tables to Ranges and Adjust Worksheet Print Settings/Name Tables and Convert Tables to a Range/Modify Excel Worksheet Templates	178/307/ 337
Ch4/Ch8	3.1.3 C	Add or Remove Table Rows and Columns	Add and Remove Table Columns and Rows/Modify Excel Worksheet Templates	180/337
	3.2 C	**Manage Table Styles and Options**		
Ch4/Ch7	3.2.1 C	Apply Styles to Tables	Create and Sort Excel Tables/Generate Custom Table Styles	174/305
Ch7	3.2.2 C	Configure Table Style Options	Generate Custom Table Styles	305
Ch4	3.2.3 C	Insert Total Rows	Filter Excel Tables	176
	3.3 C	**Filter and Sort a Table**		
Ch4	3.3.1 C	Filter Records	Filter Excel Tables	176, 177
Ch4/Ch7	3.3.2 C	Sort Data by Multiple Columns	Filter Excel Tables/Sort Data Using Conditional Formatting	176/293
Ch4	3.3.3 C	Change Sort Order	Create and Sort Excel Tables	175
Online/ Ch5	3.3.4 C	Remove Duplicate Records	Remove Duplicate Records	230
4		**Perform Operations with Formulas and Functions**		
	4.1 C	**Summarize Data by Using Functions**		
Ch1/Ch2/ Ch3	4.1.1 C	Insert References	AutoFill Formulas and Data/Apply Absolute Cell References/Create Summary Worksheets	52/83/136

Chapter	MOS Obj #	Objective	Skills Heading	Page
Ch1	4.1.2 C	Perform Calculations by Using the SUM Function	Insert the SUM Function	50
Ch2	4.1.3 C	Perform Calculations by Using MIN and MAX Functions	Insert the MIN and MAX Functions	88
Ch4/Ch6	4.1.4 C	Perform Calculations by Using the COUNT Function	Insert the TODAY, NOW, and COUNT Functions/Use COUNTA and COUNTIF Functions	161/256
Ch2	4.1.5 C	Perform Calculations by Using the AVERAGE Function	Insert the AVERAGE Function	86
	4.2 C	**Perform Conditional Operations by Using Functions**		
Ch4/Ch6	4.2.1 C	Perform Logical Operations by Using the IF Function	Insert the IF Function/Use Lookup and Nested Functions	162/268
Online/Ch6	4.2.2 C	Perform Logical Operations by Using the SUMIF Function	Calculate Conditional Sums	264
Online/Ch6	4.2.3 C	Perform Logical Operations by Using the AVERAGEIF Function	Calculate Conditional Averages	266
Online/Ch6	4.2.4 C	Perform Statistical Operations by Using the COUNTIF Function	Use COUNTA and COUNTIF Functions	256
	4.3 C	**Format and Modify Text by Using Functions**		
Online/Ch8	4.3.1 C	Format Text by Using RIGHT, LEFT, and MID Functions	Use LEFT, RIGHT, and MID Functions	331
Ch4/Ch6	4.3.2 C	Format Text by Using UPPER, LOWER, and PROPER Functions	Use Text and Lookup Functions/Modify Text Using Text Functions	183/249
Online/Ch6	4.3.3 C	Format Text by Using the CONCATENATE Function	Modify Text Using Text Functions	248

Appendix

Chapter	MOS Obj #	Objective	Skills Heading	Page
5		**Create Charts and Objects**		
	5.1 C	**Create Charts**		
Ch2/Ch3/Ch8	5.1.1 C	Create a New Chart	Create Column Charts/Create and Format Pie Charts/Change Chart Types/Create Line Charts/Create Clustered Bar Charts/Construct Dual Axis Charts	90/94/101/103/138/340
Online/Ch8	5.1.2 C	Add Additional Data Series	Add Legends and Data Series to Charts	332
Ch3/Ch8	5.1.3 C	Switch Between Rows and Columns in Source Data	Create Clustered Bar Charts/Add Legends and Data Series to Charts/Modify Charts and Graph Parameters	138/333/348
Ch2	5.1.4 C	Analyze Data by Using Quick Analysis	Apply Absolute Cell References/Create Column Charts	82/90
	5.2 C	**Format Charts**		
Ch2	5.2.1 C	Resize Charts	Create Column Charts/Change Chart Types	91/101
Ch2/Ch3/Ch8	5.2.2 C	Add and Modify Chart Elements	Format Column Charts/Create and Format Pie Charts/Create Line Charts/Create Clustered Bar Charts/Add Legends and Data Series to Charts	92/95/103/139/332
Ch2/Ch3/Ch8	5.2.3 C	Apply Chart Layouts and Styles	Format Column Charts/Create and Format Pie Charts/Change Chart Types/Create Line Charts/Create Clustered Bar Charts/Create and Edit Custom Chart Templates	92/95/101/103/138/343
Ch2/Ch3	5.2.4 C	Move Charts to a Chart Sheet	Create and Format Pie Charts/Create Line Charts/Create Clustered Bar Charts	94/103/138
	5.3 C	**Insert and Format Objects**		
Online/Ch5/Ch8/Ch9	5.3.1 C	Insert Text Boxes and Shapes	Insert Shapes and Text Boxes/Enhance Charts with Trendlines and Text Boxes/Format PivotChart Reports	231/335/385

Chapter	MOS Obj #	Objective	Skills Heading	Page
Ch3/Ch5	5.3.2 C	Insert Images	Create and Insert Screen Shots/Add Watermarks and Modify Background Colors	141/224
Ch3	5.3.3 C	Modify Object Properties	Create SmartArt Organization Charts	140
Ch2	5.3.4 C	Add Alternative Text to Objects for Accessibility	Validate Workbooks for Accessibility	100

Microsoft Office Specialist Expert Excel 2016				
Chapter	MOS Obj #	Objective	Skills Heading	Page
5		Manage Workbook Options and Settings		
	1.1 E	Manage Workbooks		
Ch1	1.1.1 E	Save a workbook as a template	Create Templates and Workbooks from Templates	62
Ch10	1.1.2 E	Copy macros between workbooks	Enable and Copy Macros Between Workbooks	422
Ch9	1.1.3 E	Reference data in another workbook	Get and Transform Data/Use the Inquire Add-In	369/391
Ch7	1.1.4 E	Reference data by using structured references	Insert Names into Formulas	308
Ch10	1.1.5 E	Enable macros in a workbook	Enable and Copy Macros Between Workbooks	422
Ch8/Ch9	1.1.6 E	Display hidden ribbon tabs	Modify the Excel Ribbon/Create PivotChart Reports Using Power View	351/389
	1.2 E	Manage Workbook Review		
Ch10	1.2.1 E	Restrict editing	Add Macro Buttons to the Quick Access Toolbar	429
Ch10	1.2.2 E	Protect a worksheet		420
Ch6	1.2.3 E	Configure formula calculation options	Update Calculations Manually	270
Online	1.2.4 E	Protect workbook structure		

Chapter	MOS Obj #	Objective	Skills Heading	Page
Ch8	1.2.5 E	Manage workbook versions	Manage Workbook Versions	349
Ch10	1.2.6 E	Encrypt a workbook with a password	Unlock Cells and Protect Worksheets/ Write Macros Using VBA	420/427
2		**Apply Custom Data Formats and Layouts**		
	2.1 E	**Apply Custom Data Formats and Validation**		
Ch5	2.1.1 E	Create custom number formats	Insert Symbols and Create Custom Number Formats	209
Ch7	2.1.2 E	Populate cells by using advanced Fill Series options	Create Two-Variable Data Tables	302
Ch10	2.1.3 E	Configure data validation	Validate Data with Data Entry Rules	410
	2.2 E	**Apply Advanced Conditional Formatting and Filtering**		
Ch5	2.2.1 E	Create custom conditional formatting rules	Apply Icon Sets as Conditional Formatting	212
Ch5	2.2.2 E	Create conditional formatting rules that use formulas	Insert Formulas into Conditional Formatting Rules	214
Ch5	2.2.3 E	Manage conditional formatting rules	Insert Formulas into Conditional Formatting Rules	215
	2.3 E	**Create and Modify Custom Workbook Elements**		
Ch5	2.3.1 E	Create custom color formats	Add Watermarks and Modify Background Colors	225
Ch5	2.3.2 E	Create and modify cell styles	Create and Apply Custom Cell Styles	220
Ch5	2.3.3 E	Create and modify custom themes	Customize, Save, and Apply Themes	222
Ch10	2.3.4 E	Create and modify simple macros	Record Macros	424
Ch10	2.3.5 E	Insert and configure form controls	Insert Form Controls	428
	2.4 E	**Prepare a Workbook for Internationalization**		
Ch10	2.4.1 E	Display data in multiple international formats	Prepare Workbooks for Internationalization	430

Chapter	MOS Obj #	Objective	Skills Heading	Page
Ch10	2.4.2 E	Apply International currency formats	Prepare Workbooks for Internationalization	430
Ch5	2.4.3 E	Manage multiple options for +Body and +heading fonts	Customize, Save, and Apply Themes	222
3		**Create Advanced Formulas**		
	3.1 E	**Apply Functions in Formulas**		
Ch6	3.1.1 E	Perform logical operations by using AND, OR, and NOT functions	Edit Conditions in Logical Functions/Use Lookup and Nested Functions	255/268
Ch6	3.1.2 E	Perform logical operations by using nested functions	Modify Text Using Text Functions/Use Lookup and Nested Functions	249/268
Ch6	3.1.3 E	Perform logical operations by using SUMIFS, AVERAGEIFS, and COUNTIFS functions	Calculate Conditional Sums/Calculate Conditional Averages	264/267
	3.2 E	**Look Up Data by Using Functions**		
Ch6	3.2.1 E	Look up data by using the VLOOKUP function	Look Up Data Using Lookup Functions	252
Ch6	3.2.2 E	Look up data by using the HLOOKUP function	Use Lookup and Nested Functions	268
Ch7	3.2.3 E	Look up data by using the MATCH function	Use MATCH and INDEX Functions: Part 1	310
Ch7	3.2.4 E	Look up data by using the INDEX function	Use MATCH and INDEX Functions: Part 2	311
	3.3 E	**Apply Advanced Date and Time Functions**		
Ch4/Ch10	3.3.1 E	Reference the date and time by using the NOW and TODAY functions	Insert the TODAY, NOW, and COUNT Functions/Record Macros	160/424
Ch8	3.3.2 E	Serialize numbers by using date and time functions	Serialize Numbers Using Functions	350
	3.4 E	**Perform Data Analysis and Business Intelligence**		
Ch9	3.4.1 E	Import, transform, combine, display, and connect to data	Get and Transform Data	368, 369

Chapter	MOS Obj #	Objective	Skills Heading	Page
Ch6/Ch8	3.4.2 E	Consolidate data	Create Amortization Tables/Consolidate Worksheet Data	338
Ch6/Ch7	3.4.3 E	Perform what-if analysis by using Goal Seek and Scenario Manager	Perform What-If Analyses Using Scenario Manager/Use Solver/Use Goal Seek	258/269/309
Ch9	3.4.4 E	Use CUBE functions to get data out of the Excel data model	Add CUBE Functions Using Power Pivot	390
Ch4/Ch6/Ch7	3.4.5 E	Calculate data by using financial functions	Perform What-If Analyses Using Scenario Manager/Estimate Future Value/Create One-Variable Data Tables	260/271/300
	3.5 E	**Troubleshoot Formulas**		
Ch7	3.5.1 E	Trace precedence and dependence	Trace and Evaluate Formulas	296
Ch7	3.5.2 E	Monitor cells and formulas by using the Watch Window	Audit Formulas Using Cell Watch	298
Ch6/Ch7	3.5.3 E	Validate formulas by using error checking rules	Use Paste Options to Change Underlying Values/Trace and Evaluate Formulas	250/296
Ch7	3.5.4 E	Evaluate formulas	Trace and Evaluate Formulas	296
	3.6 E	**Define Named Ranges and Objects**		
Ch7	3.6.1 E	Name cells	Insert Names into Formulas	308
Ch7	3.6.2 E	Name data ranges	Insert Names into Formulas	308
Ch2/Ch7	3.6.3 E	Name tables	Validate Workbooks for Accessibility/Name Tables and Convert Tables to a Range	100/307
Ch7	3.6.4 E	Manage named ranges and objects	Insert Names into Formulas	308
4		**Create Advanced Charts and Tables**		
	4.1 E	**Create Advanced Charts**		
Ch8	4.1.1 E	Add trendlines to charts	Enhance Charts with Trendlines and Text Boxes	334
Ch8	4.1.2 E	Create dual-axis charts	Construct Dual Axis Charts/Modify Charts and Graph Parameters	340/348

Chapter	MOS Obj #	Objective	Skills Heading	Page
Ch8	4.1.3 E	Save a chart as a template	Create and Edit Custom Chart Templates	342, 343
	4.2 E	**Create and Manage PivotTables**		
Ch9	4.2.1 E	Perform PivotTables	Create PivotTable Reports	370
Ch9	4.2.2 E	Modify field selections and options	Create PivotTable Reports/Change PivotTable Report Views	371/372
Ch9	4.2.3 E	Create slicers	Use Slicers to Filter PivotTable Reports	380
Ch9	4.2.4 E	Group PivotTable data	Group and Filter PivotTable Reports	378
Ch9	4.2.5 E	Reference data in a PivotTable by using the GETPIVOTDATA function	Summarize Tables Using GETPIVOTDATA	386
Ch9	4.2.6 E	Add calculated fields	Create PivotTable Report Calculated Fields	376, 377
Ch9	4.2.7 E	Format data	Change Calculation Types and Format PivotTable Reports/Create PivotTable Report Calculated Fields	375/377
	4.3 E	**Create and Manage Pivot Charts**		
Ch9	4.3.1 E	Create Pivot Charts	Create PivotChart Reports/Format PivotChart Reports	382/384
Ch9	4.3.2 E	Manipulate options in existing Pivot Charts	Create PivotChart Reports/Format PivotChart Reports/Create PivotChart Reports Using Power View	382/384/389
Ch9	4.3.3 E	Apply styles to Pivot Charts	Create PivotChart Reports/Format PivotChart Reports/Create PivotChart Reports Using Power View	383/384/389
Ch9	4.3.4 E	Drill down into Pivot Chart details	Create PivotChart Reports/Format PivotChart Reports	382/384

Index